Philip Morant (*History and Antiquities of Essex,* 2nd ed., Chelmsford, 1816, II, 538) wrote that in the mid-eighteenth century there was still visible, painted on a window in Harrison's rectory at Radwinter, "these capital letters, W. H.—Near them the sun in his glory; within it a hare couchant, argent: around the hare, in a circle, IN SOLE POSUIT TABERNACULUM SUUM: in the sun hath he set his tabernacle. Being this mean rebus, *Hare in Sun,* to denote *Harrison.*" The sketch of the rebus (*frontispiece*) occurs in one of Harrison's books preserved at Londonderry (Benedictus Aretius, *Problemata theologica,* Lausanne, 1573, shelf mark C-i-j-4).

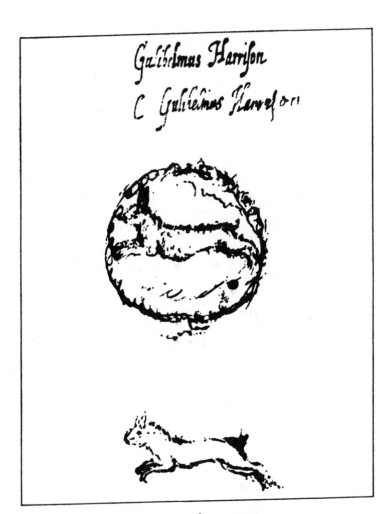

HARRISON'S REBUS

THE DESCRIPTION
OF ENGLAND
The Classic Contemporary Account
of Tudor Social Life

BY

WILLIAM HARRISON

EDITED BY
GEORGES EDELEN

A JOINT PUBLICATION OF
THE FOLGER SHAKESPEARE LIBRARY
WASHINGTON, D.C.
AND
DOVER PUBLICATIONS, INC.
NEW YORK

Bibliographical Note

This Dover edition, first published in 1994, is an unabridged republication of the edition published for The Folger Shakespeare Library by the Cornell University Press, Ithaca, New York, in 1968 as part of the series, *Folger Documents of Tudor and Stuart Civilization*. The editor has added a new Preface to this edition. The Dover edition is published by special arrangement with The Folger Shakespeare Library, 201 East Capitol Street, S.E., Washington, D.C., 20003.

Library of Congress Cataloging-in-Publication Data

Harrison, William, 1535–1593.
   The description of England: the classic contemporary account of Tudor social life / by William Harrison; edited by Georges Edelen.
       p.   cm.
   Originally published: Ithaca, N.Y.: Published for the Folger Shakespeare Library by Cornell University Press, [1968], in series: Folger documents of Tudor and Stuart civilization.
   Includes bibliographical references (p.) and index.
   ISBN 0-486-28275-9 (pbk.)
   1. England—Description and travel—Early works to 1800.   2. Shakespeare, William, 1564-1616—Contemporary England.   3. England—Social life and customs—16th century.   I. Edelen, Georges.   II. Title.
DA610.H3   1994
942.05—dc20   94-31219
                                                         CIP

Manufactured in the United States of America
Dover Publications, Inc., 31 East 2nd Street, Mineola, N.Y. 11501

PREFACE

HARRISON's *Descriptions* have been reprinted four times. The only complete version is that which appears in the first volume of the 1807–1808 reprinting of Holinshed's *Chronicles*. The 1587 text is there reproduced intact, faithfully and readably, but without editing of any kind. The standard edition has been that undertaken by Frederick J. Furnivall for the New Shakspere Society under the title, *Harrison's Description of England in Shakspere's Youth* (4 parts; London, 1877–1908). Furnivall reprints, with reasonable accuracy, the entire *Description of England*, four complete chapters as well as briefer selections from *The Description of Britain*, and a few excerpts from Harrison's Chronology. This edition also contains a great deal of useful material from other sources on Elizabethan social history, but the *Descriptions* are fitfully and quixotically annotated. Furnivall's edition will remain of great value for some purposes, since it preserves the original spelling and is printed so as to indicate conveniently the changes and additions made by Harrison in 1587; for this reason I have included on pages 463–464 a list of substantive corrections to Furnivall's text. Lothrop Withington's edition in the Camelot Series (London, [?1889]), which is derived from Furnivall's, is the first to modernize Harrison's spelling; the text is inaccurate, arbitrarily rearranged, and radically excerpted, nineteen of the chapters printed by Furnivall being omitted, as well as sections in most others. The surprisingly lengthy version in the Harvard Classics, comprising almost half of Volume XXXV, is reprinted from Withington's text, with further deletions.

The present edition is based on a collation of Furnivall's text with three copies of the 1587 folio. *The Description of England* is reprinted complete, except for four lengthy and readily detachable historical digressions: the catalogue of bishops and deans of London, Harrison's version of the ceremony accompanying ordeal by fire, Canute's forest laws, and the Antonine Itinerary (occurring at pages 64, 169, 262, and 406). I follow Furnivall's lead in omitting the historical and topographical chapters of *The Description of Britain*, whose inclusion would have extended this edition to twice its present length and cost. Three complete chapters of Harrison's first book and parts of three others are here reprinted, and briefer excerpts have been incorporated into the notes. Unlike Furnivall, I have included from *The Description of Britain* all of the chapter on "Languages Spoken in This Island," while omitting Harrison's account of the Roman roads and the chapter on English marvels. Excerpts from the chapters on weights and measures are here reprinted for the first time since 1577. My ideal of selection throughout was to include what is relevant to the series on social and intellectual history in which this edition appears, while avoiding omissions that would falsify Harrison's own range of interests.

In accordance with the principles of the series, I have modernized Harrison's spelling. Anyone who has undertaken a similar task will know the nettling choices between inconsistency and absurdity that modernizing entails. In general I have tried to change only variant spellings, while preserving archaic forms, but the lines are not easily drawn. In some cases, where several versions of the same word appear (such as *account, accompt, murder, murther, statutes, estatutes, wax, wex*), I have regularized to the modern form; on the other hand, I distinguish, as Harrison does not, between *travel* and *travail, divers* and *diverse*. Personal and geographical names are either modernized (English personal names, with some misgivings, to the versions used by the *Dictionary of National Biography*) or, where Harrison's form is significantly different, glossed. Punctuation, capitalization, and the handling of abbreviations have also been modernized and some further paragraphing added; no attempt of course has been made to improve Harrison's sentence structure. Quotations in foreign languages have not been tampered with. I have silently corrected obvious printer's errors and, rarely, I have preferred a clearly superior 1577 reading. Sidenotes have been included (as footnotes, signed "*H.*") only when they add substantially to the text.

Harrison's *Descriptions* have a breadth of appeal that has inspired fuller notes than a more specialized text would be given; obsolete and unusual words are accordingly glossed, proper names are identified, and translations are supplied for passages in other languages. To prevent the multiplication of footnotes, glosses of sufficient brevity have been included in the text between square brackets. Editorial matter handled in this way is doubtless distracting, but no more so, I am convinced, than footnote numbers, with their invitation to bob. I have also been concerned to indicate, where I could, Harrison's sources, particularly in contemporary English and Continental works, and the manner in which he uses them. At some points I have unhappily failed in the search, but I believe sufficient evidence is here given, for the first time, to permit some firm distinctions between what is original and what borrowed, as well as to suggest how the *Descriptions* were constructed. I have usually succeeded in resisting the temptation to supply purely illustrative notes or to guess at the identities of contemporaries to whom Harrison makes oblique references.

I owe scholarly and other debts of many kinds to Professors Bernard M. Wagner and Franklin B. Williams, Jr., of Georgetown University, and Herschel C. Baker and the late Hyder E. Rollins (who first directed my studies toward Harrison) of Harvard University. Among friends and colleagues who have generously answered queries or assisted in other ways are Mr. F. G. Emmison and Professors Craig R. Thompson, George B. Parks, Clarence H. Miller, Jack B. Oruch, Rudolf Gottfried, Gerald Strauss, James W. Halporn, Mark Musa, Ernest Bernhardt-Kabisch, Frederick P. Hard, Alfred David, and Mary Elizabeth David. Agnes M. McAulay, Librarian of Magee University College in Londonderry, secured for me the photograph of Harrison's rebus reproduced as the frontispiece. The staffs of the Lilly Library at Indiana University, the Houghton Library at Harvard, and the Folger Shakespeare Library in Washington (particularly Miss Dorothy E. Mason) have been unfailingly helpful. Part of my research was financed by a Folger Library Fellowship. I am especially grateful to the late Virginia A. LaMar, Executive Secretary of the Folger, whose unflagging patience and editorial acuity spared me some egregious blunders. Finally, my wife's assistance in proofreading and indexing has been invaluable.

GEORGES EDELEN

Indiana University
February 1, 1968

PREFACE TO THE DOVER EDITION

I AM pleased, on the occasion of this reissue, to have the opportunity to correct or modify several readings in the first edition.

On page 280, note 15, "Derbyshire" is not in error. Since Leland sometimes uses "shire" as equivalent to "hundred," by Derbyshire here he means the hundred of (West) Derby in Lancashire, now a suburb of Liverpool. On page 349, note 5, "sives" should be defined as seaves (or sieves), a northern-dialect term for the common rush, *Juncus conglomeratus* and *J. effusus*. For these corrections I am indebted to Mr. W. B. Yapp of the University of Birmingham.

My comments on Harrison's unpublished "Chronology" on pages xviii and 3 need to be updated. Dr. Glyn J. R. Parry, of Victoria University, Wellington, New Zealand, has since discovered in the library of Trinity College, Dublin (MS 165), an early, much-revised draft of that work: see his valuable study based partly on the MS, *A Protestant Vision: William Harrison and the Reformation of Elizabethan England* (Cambridge University Press, 1987). In 1992 the later version of the "Chronology," seen and excerpted by Furnivall, finally resurfaced after a century out of sight. Now in the British Library (Add. MS 70984), its entries for the years 1485–1593 have been transcribed by Dr. Parry for forthcoming publication by the Camden Society.

GEORGES EDELEN

Indiana University
April 15, 1994

x

CONTENTS

INTRODUCTION

IN HIS *Description of Britain* and *Description of England*,[1] written to provide the introductory books to Holinshed's *Chronicles*, William Harrison intended no less than a total portrait of Elizabethan England, of the land and the people. His subject was his society: how his contemporaries traveled and worked, ate and drank, clothed and sheltered themselves, how they were educated and protected, organized and governed; his setting was the land itself, its islands and streams, cities and villages, woods, parks, marshes, springs, its climate and resources; his bias was antiquarian, keeping him in quest for roots, precedents, and points of origin. The resulting work, given an author of Elizabethan ambition and energy, was inevitably sprawling and untidy, but Harrison's sharpness of vision and vigor of style combined to produce a classic of social description. No other work of the age gives so compendious and readable an account of life in Shakespeare's England, and no similar book has been so deeply quarried by later writers on the period.

The genre represented by Harrison's amalgam of social, topographical, and antiquarian description—if anything so ebulliently

---

[1] Harrison's treatise is divided into three books. In the first (1577) edition the entire work was titled *An Historical Description of the Island of Britain*. In the second (1587) edition Harrison reordered some chapters and reserved that title for the first book alone, while calling the second and third books together (although only in the running title) *The Description of England*. Harrison seems to have intended the following rough outline: the first book was to include the topographical and historical chapters, as well as any topics concerning "the general estate of the whole island" (*Des. Brit.*, 1587, p. 128), that is, including Scotland; the second and third books were to concentrate on England and Wales, the second covering social organization, the third, physical resources. The distinctions are not firmly followed, and miscellaneous chapters appear at the end of each book.

discursive can properly be termed a genre—has obvious roots in such classical writers as Pausanias, Strabo, and Tacitus and a family resemblance to the rich Continental outpouring of Renaissance cosmography, as practiced by Enea Silvio Piccolomini, Sebastian Franck, Sebastian Münster, Abraham Ortelius, and many lesser figures.[2] The similarity between Harrison's *Descriptions* and the Continental cosmographies is, however, better seen as a parallel response to corresponding impulses than as evidence of direct influence. The tradition that principally shaped Harrison's work was a native one, developed by the English monastic chroniclers.

This native tradition begins in the sixth century with Gildas, who opens his history with a brief passage on the site and size of the island of Britain; he mentions the Thames and the Severn, notes the existence of twenty-eight cities and numerous castles, and closes with a few vague and ornate phrases extolling the richness of the soil and the beauty of British streams and lakes. From these slight origins the genre in England arises, and the lineal descent of Harrison's massive work from Gildas' few sentences can be traced through the chronicles. Bede, for example, in his *Ecclesiastical History*, borrowing from Orosius, Pliny, and Solinus, as well as from Gildas, expands the descriptive opening to include more circumstantial praise of British pastures and vines, wildfowl, fishes, pearls and jet, salt springs and hot baths, and mines of copper, iron, lead, and silver; he also mentions the five languages spoken in Britain and the earliest invaders of the land. The prefatory description in the eighth-century history by Nennius is little longer, but he does initiate into the tradition the names of the twenty-eight cities and of the islands of Wight, Man, and Orkney, as well as the legend of the founding of Britain by Brut.

In the twelfth-century chronicle by Henry of Huntingdon the tendency of the descriptive opening to enlarge by accretion is well illustrated. Virtually all of Bede's chapter is absorbed by Henry, so uncritically that he repeats Bede's list of the languages spoken in the island without mentioning the introduction of Norman French, although he does comment on the extinction of the language of the Picts. From Nennius, Henry takes the Brut

---

[2] For an account of this Continental work see Gerald Strauss, *Sixteenth-Century Germany: Its Topography and Topographers* (Madison, 1959).

legend and the ancient names of the cities, adding their later equivalents. Henry's own contributions include lists of shires and bishoprics, and accounts of the five invasions, the Saxon heptarchy, English marvels, and the Roman roads.

The medieval descriptive tradition is seen at its fullest in the immensely popular, fourteenth-century *Polychronicon* of Ranulf Higden. Higden's entire first book is an exercise in descriptive geography, a "map of the world." Twenty-two chapters are devoted to Britain. All the subjects handled by Henry of Huntingdon are here: the site and dimensions of Britain, her natural resources, marvels, adjacent islands, ancient highways, rivers, cities, shires, bishoprics, languages, ethnology, and Saxon kingdoms, as well as some additional topics: the ancient names applied to Britain, the geographical divisions of the island and the source of their names, laws and legal language, and the manners of the people. The briefest glance at the chapter headings in Higden and Harrison makes clear the relationship between them: Harrison found in the *Polychronicon* the basic structure for his *Descriptions*. Every chapter in Higden's account of England has at least one corresponding chapter in Harrison's work, typically of similar title and content, although greatly expanded in detail, and there are very few topics treated in the *Descriptions* which are not at least seminally present in the *Polychronicon*.

Higden's first book in fact defines the genre. The description preceding a chronicle should not only range freely over the factual details of physical and political geography, but also include eponymous legends, a panegyric to the natural resources of England, such antiquarian concerns as the locations of the Roman roads and the names of ancient cities, a history of the language, accounts of ecclesiastical polity, of marvels of varying degrees of respectability, and of legal organization and terminology, as well as a commentary on the morals and manners of the writer's contemporaries. Harrison varied the proportions considerably, but the ingredients had been prescribed by Higden and his predecessors.

To the modern reader the mixture, in whatever proportions, is apt to seem indigestible, and no doubt some of the topics owed their introduction into the formula solely to the private interests of one of the more popular chroniclers, or to the accidental availability in his library of certain sources. For the chroniclers, as Harrison comments about royal prerogative, "a thing once done is well done and to be done oftentimes" (pp. 24–25). Yet bearing in mind the purposes and biases of the authors, one can detect some rationale in the scope of the genre. The descriptions were normally written by chroniclers, for whom later distinctions between myth, history, and antiquarianism were at best hazy, and whose bent was incurably encyclopedic. The topographical details and the lists of cities, shires, bishoprics, and the heptarchy represented, at a time when no maps worthy of the name were available, the historian's natural impulse to sketch the stage on which his events occurred. The paeans to British resources remind us that the love of the English for their demiparadise was no Tudor invention. Finally, the descriptions were often the work of clergymen of homiletic persuasion, quick to judge and eager to reform the morals of their contemporaries.

In essential ways William Harrison was a late survival of the type of the monastic chronicler. He, too, was a clergyman of deep moral commitments, and if he passed most of his life as the rector of a rural parish rather than in a monastery, that difference served only to sharpen both his knowledge and his criticism of secular ways. His lifelong avocation was historical study, over which he must have labored with monastic stamina, for, like Higden, he succeeded in completing a great chronicle, or "Chronology," covering, in annalistic form, the history of the world from the Creation to his own time.[3] When he was persuaded to undertake the *Descriptions* to precede Holinshed's *History of England*, he approached the task, with the model of Higden before him, in the perspective of a chronicler, freely admitting that the commissioned work represented the "crumbs" that "fell out" from his labors on his Chronology (p. 5). Thus, just as Holinshed's history was essentially a chronicle in the medieval tradition, Harrison's contribution fitted comfortably within the ancient formulas of the chroniclers' prefatory descriptions.

Nor did Harrison have any sense of reviving a moribund tradition when he modeled himself on Higden, whose description of England, in the Trevisa translation, had been separately printed

---

[3] Harrison's Chronology was never printed. It survived in MS, at least until the end of the nineteenth century, in the Diocesan Library at Londonderry. Furnivall saw it and printed brief extracts in his edition of Harrison (I, v, xlvii–lx). I cannot uncover its present location.

by both Caxton (1480) and Wynkyn de Worde (1498). The descriptive tradition had certainly showed no signs of atrophying in the sixteenth century. Even the Italian Polydore Vergil begins his *Anglicae historiae* (1534) in a manner that recalls Higden, with accounts of British shires, bishoprics, rivers, islands, natural resources, and manners. Similar, although much briefer, descriptions preface the chronicles of Grafton and Stow. Harrison himself provided Holinshed with a *Description of Scotland* by translating the opening section of John Bellenden's Scottish version (1536) of Hector Boece's Latin history of Scotland (1527), a description that foreshadows Harrison's own by its much greater emphasis on topographical detail. In short, when Harrison boasts of being "the first that . . . hath taken upon him so particularly to describe this Isle of Britain" (p. 7), the force of his claim falls entirely on his greater particularization.

Nonetheless, Harrison should not be robbed of his right to the title of innovator; quantitative differences of sufficient magnitude can surely become qualitative. Between the brevity of the medieval chroniclers in handling many of the descriptive topics and Harrison's heroic dilations there is a gulf great enough to warrant seeing the *Descriptions* as a new departure. Higden, for example, devotes one brief chapter to English resources in the nature of soil, waters, animal life, mines, and quarries; Harrison takes seventeen chapters to cover the same ground. Where the earlier writers had been content to mention the islands of Wight, Man, and Orkney, Harrison devotes a lengthy chapter to an imaginary voyage around Great Britain, in the course of which he names over three hundred offshore islands, describing many in detail and regretting only his inability to fulfill his intention "at the first to have written at large of the number, situation, names, quantities, towns, villages, castles, mountains, fresh waters, plashes, or lakes, salt waters, and other commodities of the aforesaid isles" (*Des. Brit.*, 1587, p. 45). In a similar way Harrison expands the chroniclers' terse descriptions of the Thames, Severn, and Humber to sixty-three folio pages, in which he attempts to trace the courses, by naming the parishes through which they flow, of all the rivers, streams, and rills in England and Wales. Some five thousand villages are thus named and located, and although Harrison is aware of the "imperfection and rudeness" of his labors, he again claims to his patron that he is an innovator:

"The ice, My Lord, is broken, and from henceforth it will be more easy for such as shall come after to wade through with the rest" (*Des. Brit.*, 1587, p. 45). Despite the lack of alphabetical ordering, Harrison had, in fact, produced the first English gazetteer.

To the conventional topics of the monastic chroniclers, then, Harrison brought new standards of thoroughness and detail, standards so much more exacting that they produced a work as novel as it was traditional. In England these radically changed standards of topographical study were largely the work of John Leland. Armed with Henry VIII's commission to undertake antiquarian research, Leland had traveled tirelessly around England for six years, making a vast if jumbled collection of geographical and historical notes. Although he died, after a period of insanity, in 1552, before he had been able to organize the fruits of his research, he left his notes as a mine and a challenge for his successors. The description of England could no longer be written as formulaic borrowings. Now the material had to be comprehensive, detailed, and gathered in the field. Harrison felt Leland's challenge strongly enough to apologize, in a way that would have been incomprehensible to a monastic chronicler, for not having "by mine own travel and eyesight viewed such things as I do here entreat of" (p. 6).

For those areas on which Harrison was not himself an authority, he attempted to meet Leland's standards in various ways, most directly by absorbing quantities of Leland's notes into his own work. The greatest part of this explicit and grateful borrowing occurs in the topographical chapters of *The Description of Britain*. Often Leland's details are supplemented or corrected from other primary sources, notably from Christopher Saxton's new county maps (p. 219, n. 47) and from local descriptions solicited by Harrison from acquaintances (p. 5, n. 6). Excerpts from Leland also occur at many points in *The Description of England;* most of the English details in the chapters on archaeology, metals, and quarries, for example, derive from Leland. Some topics, such as the descriptions of Bath and of saltmaking at Droitwich (pp. 287–291, 375–378), clearly owe their inclusion to the availability of Leland's eyewitness reports. Other subjects seem to have been expanded because dependable sources came to hand. Harrison kept dogs himself, including a pet mastiff that tried to prevent him from spanking his children, but the appearance of a whole chapter on the subject stems from the contemporary translation by Abraham Fleming of John Caius' treatise on English dogs (p. 339, n. 2). Harrison's access to the Brooke family papers provides many details about the Order of the Garter (p. 106, n. 26). An entire chapter on Parliament is added in the 1587 edition, after the appearance of Sir Thomas Smith's *De republica Anglorum* (1583; p. 149, n. 1). Thomas Harman's *Caveat or Warning for Common Cursitors* (1566) supplies the cant names of the rogues in the chapter on the poor (p. 184, n. 8), and most of the facts about legal punishments come from a printed collection of current statutes (p. 188, n. 2). From the almanacs, by way of John Stow, come the lists of law terms, fairs, and itineraries (pp. 176, n. 28; 392, n. 1; 399, n. 5).

The quantity of Harrison's borrowings and his modest disclaimers of authority must not be allowed to conceal the extent to which his particulars, often in those areas of greatest value to social historians, are his own. Much of the material on social classes, food, clothing, housing and furnishings, and fairs and markets, for example, comes from Harrison's immediate experience or, at least, from his "conference with divers, either at the table or secretly alone" (p. 5). His own career at the universities, as a pastor and as the presiding official of an ecclesiastical court, his travels, the occupations and foibles of his parishioners, all supply him with a store of details and anecdotes. His hobbies, gardening and numismatics, and his scholarly interests, in weights and measures and in chronological computations, become the foundation of separate chapters. Certainly the *Descriptions* are far more than the work of a diligent anthologist.

But whether drawing from Leland, from other manuscript and printed sources, from his own experience, or from the memories of "old men yet dwelling in the village where I remain" (p. 200), Harrison is eager to portray his land as particularly as he can, and it is precisely this radical change in sense of detail that distinguishes his work from that of the medieval chroniclers. Such a passion for the circumstantial was very much a part of the Renaissance psyche; everywhere, in Continental as well as English scholarship, the demand had appeared for a vastly more detailed account of secular and nationalistic subjects. Leland did not so much establish as symbolize the new standards. Harrison found at hand the sources he needed because he was part of the movement which hoped to delineate every aspect, however minute, of the English scene.

Thus, Harrison's *Descriptions*, like so much else in his age, can best be understood as a point of convergence between the traditional and the novel. Although he was working in a genre whose range of subject had been defined by the medieval chroniclers, he brought to his task the standards of detail established by Renaissance scholars: panoramic range, exhaustive detail. Such a convergence was bound to strain the capabilities of any single man. No wonder that Harrison, attempting to bestraddle these mutually hostile impulses, sometimes was thrown into ungainly postures. Specialization was the only practical solution. Already the Holinshed group had divided, for separate treatment, the prefatory description from the chronicle history. But a description of such scope, even by itself, was an improbable undertaking for one man. Harrison was the only writer in England who succeeded in bringing one to print. Leland had gone mad in the attempt, and Harrison's successors, Camden and the county historians, imposed more discreet boundaries upon themselves.

There are other, less integral ways in which the *Descriptions* reflect the age that produced them. Religious controversy inevitably left a mark, especially since much contemporary historical scholarship was devoted to finding in the past precedents and justifications for the Elizabethan Church. Harrison, with some enthusiasm, parrots the anti-Roman formulas like "servile yoke of popish tyranny" or "rakehells of the clergy and puddles of all ungodliness" (pp. 222, 21), and he makes the standard attack upon monasteries as "dens of spiritual robbers" (*Des. Brit.*, 1587, p. 26). More substantially, he is betrayed into lengthy digressions, quoting papal letters that offend his Erastian instincts (pp. 17–19, 35) and developing instances of episcopal aggressiveness, such as Anselm's answer to William Rufus or Thomas Lisle's struggle with Lady Wake (pp. 16–17, 52–55). Like Shakespeare, he is seduced into the unhappy attempt to recast King John as a protoreformer (p. 21). Historical evidence to support his antipapistry is, for Harrison, a golden apple. Fortunately, most of these lapses are limited to the two chapters on the church which open *The Description of England*.

More pervasive through the *Descriptions* is that peculiarly

Renaissance form of pedantry that thought no treatise complete until the author, under the guise of finding origins and parallels, had paraded his classical learning. However liberal and invigorating humanism may have been to the finest spirits of the time, in the hands of lesser men it presented a constant temptation to irrelevancy and display. Harrison happily plays the game. In his chapter on the English navy he makes the bemusing assertion that "it shall not be amiss, therefore, to begin at the navy of Xerxes," even while admitting that "the discourse hereof maketh little to the description of our present navy in England" (p. 240). But having found in Budé an impressive discussion of the forms and sizes of ancient vessels, he cannot resist incorporating it. His chapter on English food contains many references to classical customs, and a lengthy description of the Roman calendar is worked into the chapter on "Our Account of Time"; the discussion of "The Building and Furniture of Our Houses" is somehow made to end with a glossary of Roman rates of interest (pp. 141–144, 385–388, 203). Very few parts of the *Descriptions* are entirely free from this classical veneer. Actually, Harrison's familiarity with the classics seems to have been slight; most of his references are borrowed from such humanistic sources as Francesco Patrizi, Guillaume Budé, Alexander ab Alexandro, and Jean Bodin. A more powerful and original genius than Harrison's might have risen above the petty vices of the time. Harrison succumbed, but we value him none the less for that. His preeminent virtue is precisely to be so bound to his age, in manner as well as matter.

In still another way Harrison's *Descriptions* show a clear change of emphasis from their medieval counterparts. Like all his fellow historians, Harrison believed that pragmatic values were inherent in his work. The old monastic sense of history as demonstrating the workings of God's providence and inculcating valuable moral lessons continued, if not so strongly, but there was also in the sixteenth-century antiquaries and chroniclers a somewhat obscure faith that their investigations had relevance to less exalted aspects of daily life. Precisely what this relevance was to the ordinary reader was left undefined and probably was undefinable, but it became an article of faith that the history, antiquities, and topography of his country were of immediate, "profitable" concern to every Englishman. Such a faith explains the appearance of conveniently pocket-sized "summaries" of English chronicle history by John Stow, to which in various editions were added useful calendars and tables of the law terms, fairs, itineraries, and the Oxford and Cambridge colleges. Stow's manual was successful enough to be reprinted eleven times between 1566 and 1604. A similarly odd amalgam of history and almanac was Richard Grafton's 1572 edition of his chronicle, which, in addition to the tables supplied by Stow, included lists of members of Parliament, wards and parishes in London, instructions for determining the times of ebb and flow at London Bridge, and the like.

In part this belief in the pragmatic value of historical studies must have derived from the involvement in them of clergymen, for whom the authority of the past was a prime tool in religious controversy. For heralds and lawyers, too, the establishment of origins, precedents, and successions was an essential part of their working life, and it was around this group, men of substance and position, that the Society of Antiquaries formed at about the time the second edition of Holinshed appeared.[4] Certainly the antiquary of Elizabethan days was far from the comic figure he was to become in the next century, when John Earle in his *Microcosmography* (1633) describes him as one who "loves all things (as Dutchmen do cheese) the better for being moldy and worm-eaten."

There is no evidence that Harrison had any direct associations with the Society of Antiquaries, but he pursued a parallel path in his conviction that he was setting forth "profitable things" (p. 7) in his *Descriptions*. His diction is often revealing, as when he decides to omit lists of the bishops of every see because "it would have extended this treatise to an unprofitable length" and brought "small benefit . . . unto the commodity of the readers" (pp. 63–64). Similarly he regrets that part of his roll of seaports has been stolen, "whose knowledge I am right sure would have been profitable, and for the which I hoped to have reaped great thanks at the hands of such seafaring men as should have had use hereof" (p. 428, n. 8). Since it is difficult to see what usefulness a mere catalogue of ports could have had, Harrison's assertion suggests the intensity of his conviction that his treatise would touch at

[4] Joan Evans, *A History of the Society of Antiquaries* (Oxford, 1956), pp. 1–12; T. D. Kendrick, *British Antiquity* (London, 1950), p. 114.

many points the lives of his "timefellows." Actually, this faith tended to be self-justifying. Convinced that his work as a whole is profitable, Harrison sees nothing incongruous about including a great deal of baldly useful material. Not only does he follow the lead of Stow and Grafton by printing lists of the law terms, fairs, journeys, colleges, and members of Parliament, but he also gives quantities of homely advice on the making of brawn and the brewing of beer (pp. 313–314, 137–139), on outwitting alewives who adulterate their wares, and on calculating to a penny the profits derivable from an acre planted in saffron (pp. 139, 351). He propounds schemes to improve the state of the roads, to fill benefices more effectively, and to hamper grain speculators (pp. 444, 75, 252–253). He worries about the lack of a standard measure, and he calls the attention of the government, on the eve of the Armada, to the dangerously unprotected state of the East Anglian coast (pp. 251–252, 222–223). There is nothing abstracted or unworldly about the tone of Harrison's *Descriptions;* they are intended not only to reflect but to contribute to the mainstream of Elizabethan life.

Last among the broader qualities that identify the *Descriptions* as a product of sixteenth-century England is the ingenuous patriotism they display. Panegyrics to English resources find a place in the descriptive tradition from Gildas on, but in the earlier chroniclers these advantages are cited only as evidence of God's bounty. Harrison's praise of his country tends to have a competitive edge. England is not merely blessed by God, she is clearly the divine favorite; no other nation can match her resources. English domestic animals far surmount "the like in other countries"; "there is no country that may (as I take it) compare with ours in number, excellency, and diversity of dogs"; "the saffron of England . . . is the most excellent of all other"; "no nation can have more excellent and greater diversity of stuff for building than we may have in England" (pp. 305, 339, 348, 359). Girolamo Cardan's suggestion that English waters "are hurtful to our sheep" brings the indignant rejoinder, "there is no parcel of the main wherein a man shall generally find more fine and wholesome water than in England" (p. 310). English physicians are "men of no less learning no doubt than the best of foreign countries"; the beauty of English women "commonly exceedeth the fairest of those of the main, their comeliness of person and good proportion of limbs most of theirs that come over unto us from beyond the seas" (Harrison's wife was Flemish); even the English climate must be defended as "no less pure, wholesome, and commodious than is that of other countries," although in a passage notably awkward in style and argument (pp. 381, 449, 429).

This national pride was a part of the sharpened perceptions of national identity that developed as a common denominator throughout the countries of Europe in the sixteenth century. National boundaries were being more firmly drawn, psychically as well as politically. Most of the thrust for the great work of the age in topographical and historical studies of individual countries came from this nascent self-consciousness. Harrison's *Descriptions* would scarcely have been possible without it. His work was essentially a celebration of the new England, recently cut off from many of her Continental associations, pursuing now her independent way. He was writing for his countrymen, sharing their excitement in the discovery of whatever was distinctively British. As a result, his work, like Holinshed's, had the power to arouse deep responses. John Lyly incorporated passages from the *Descriptions* into *Euphues and His England* (1580), and Edmund Spenser, almost incredibly, saw in Harrison's jejune catalogue of rivers the stuff of poetry.[5]

The intense national pride that characterized the Elizabethans thus appears in the *Descriptions* in several lights. Patriotism supplied most of the impetus for Harrison's enthusiastic expansion of the traditional topics; from this perspective there is scarcely a sentence in the work that is not imbued with his love for his country. But where the patriotic sentiments surface, they are apt

---

[5] Lyly, *Works*, ed. R. Warwick Bond (Oxford, 1902), II, 191–196. In a letter to Gabriel Harvey (1580), Spenser speaks of a projected *Epithalamion Thamesis*, in which he will "describe all the rivers throughout England which came to this wedding and their right names and right passage, etc. A work, believe me, of much labor, wherein notwithstanding Master Holinshed [i.e., Harrison] hath much furthered and advantaged me, who therein hath bestowed singular pains in searching out their first heads and sources, and also in tracing and dogging out all their course till they fall into the sea" (*The Prose Works*, ed. Rudolf B. Gottfried, Variorum Ed., Baltimore, 1949, p. 17). This poem, if actually composed, has not survived, but fossils of it may be imbedded in the passages describing the wedding of the Thames and the Medway in *The Faerie Queene* (IV, xi).

to have a touchy, adolescent tone, to protest a little too vociferously. England is a relative newcomer to the center of the European stage; her propagandists must elbow and jostle others aside to assert her rights. If Harrison writes in English, as an Englishman, for his compatriots, he is nonetheless conscious of being heard by a foreign audience;[6] if he joins his fellows in celebrating their dear, dear land, he simultaneously challenges all others to doubt English pre-eminence. "It was not said of old time without great reason that all countries have need of Britain and Britain itself of none"; Harrison cites the proverb twice in eight pages (pp. 357, 365).

Spurts of xenophobia appear. If it must be admitted that foreigners often surpass the English "in pregnancy of wit, nimbleness of limbs, and politic inventions, . . . these gifts of theirs do often degenerate into mere subtlety, instability, unfaithfulness, and cruelty" (p. 446). Frenchmen "color craftiness, subtle practices, doubleness, and hollow behavior with a cloak of policy, amity, and wisdom" (p. 447). Italy, "by reason of the wickedness of such as dwell therein . . . may be called the sink and drain of hell" (p. 433). Like Roger Ascham, Harrison deplores the "sending of noblemen's and mean gentlemen's sons into Italy, from whence they bring home nothing but mere atheism, infidelity, vicious conversation, and ambitious and proud behavior, whereby it cometh to pass that they return far worse men than they went out" (p. 114). Harrison has, in fact, some of Ascham's roast-beef syndrome. He cites with approval Sir Thomas Smith's judgment that even "our condemned persons do go so cheerfully to their deaths, for our nation is free, stout, haughty, prodigal of life and blood" (p. 187). Again like Ascham, he regrets the disuse of the English longbow: "The Frenchmen and rutters, deriding our new archery in respect of their corselets, will not let in open skirmish, if any leisure serve, to turn up their tails and cry, 'Shoot, English!' and all because our strong shooting is decayed and laid in bed. But if some of our Englishmen now lived that served King Edward the Third in his wars with France, the

---

[6] On occasion explicitly, as when he notes, "I do not see any great difference used in the observation of time and her parts between our own and any other foreign nation, wherefore I shall not need to stand long on this matter" (p. 379).

breech of such a varlet should have been nailed to his bum with one arrow and another feathered in his bowels before he should have turned about to see who shot the first" (p. 234).

Chauvinism also misled the Elizabethan antiquaries into a mass abandonment of their critical faculties when they came to write of British prehistory. All were intent upon providing England with a past as ancient and imposing as that claimed for any other country. Harrison joins the effort; he spends much space in the early chapters of *The Description of Britain* elaborating John Bale's theory that England was originally settled by a grandson of Noah named Samothes (p. 163, n. 1). The myth was too far-fetched to survive long, but in Elizabeth's reign it was widely accepted as fulfilling a deeply felt need. Harrison uses a revealing phrase in support of the argument that the name Britain derives from Brut, who supposedly led a band of Trojan settlers there: other origins of the name have been advanced, but "the antiquity of our history carrieth me withal unto the former judgments" (*Des. Brit.*, 1587, p. 4). For Harrison, as for his fellow historians, the antiquity of British history is a premise rather than a conclusion of his studies.

Harrison shared, in fact, virtually every premise, prejudice, and passion of his generation, in part because his own life mirrored the mid-sixteenth-century English experience.[7] He was born in 1535, three months before More went to the scaffold. In the later, less radical years of Henry VIII's reign he attended St. Paul's School, founded by Dean Colet and still embodying some of the older, more conservative humanism of the More circle. During the reign of Edward VI he was a student at Westminster School, under the headmastership of the reformer Alexander Nowell. His college at Oxford was Christ Church, which became a center of the Marian reaction, and Harrison accordingly converted to Roman Catholicism. He returned to the English Church before Mary's death, apparently not without personal danger. His own experience with the treacherous eddies of religious change no doubt contributed to his total sympathy with Elizabeth's highly pragmatic attempts to achieve religious stability. First among the reforms he hopes to see effected in England

---

[7] For a fuller discussion of Harrison's biography see my article, "William Harrison (1535-1593)," *Studies in the Renaissance*, IX (1962), 256-272.

he places "the want of discipline in the church" (p. 281), and he stifles latent sympathy with the Puritan attacks upon the episcopacy for fear lest there be no agreement upon the "form of discipline and government of the church succedent" (p. 98). Harrison is capable of moral idealism about his vocation, but the practical questions of religious organization are what principally attract him. It is striking how often his discussions of the church resolve into questions of money.

While enthusiastically supporting Elizabeth's efforts to bring her subjects "within a limited compass of uniformity" (p. 98) by a religious settlement that would not break too sharply with the past, Harrison rejoices in his consciousness of deep and crucial changes. His opening chapter in *The Description of England*, revealingly entitled "Of the Ancient and Present Estate of the Church of England," is built around the contrast between the medieval, Roman modes and those of the reformed, English Church. As an apologist Harrison emphasizes the improvements; the services "in our vulgar tongue, that each one present may hear and understand" (p. 34; Harrison could remember the first time he had heard the litany in English, when he was a schoolboy at St. Paul's), the stripped and whitewashed churches, and the more learned and zealous ministry represented for him necessary reforms.

Public change is of course a constant of human existence, but the rate of change is not. In some ages transitions in religious, social, and economic life are so slow, even, and predictable as to be almost imperceptibly absorbed by those affected. At other times the gradient becomes much steeper; not only specific developments but the dominance of change forces itself upon the consciousness. With this heightened realization of transience comes the impulse to describe, to come to terms with the novel by verbal ordering, to weigh against the past, to record the potentially unstable. There is little reason to describe for a native audience modes of living which have continued the same for generations and promise to remain equally constant. The medieval chroniclers accordingly slighted the details of daily life in their descriptions; for much the same reason, no doubt, Harrison has almost nothing to say of English sports and pastimes. In most aspects of their life, however, the Elizabethans were conscious of radical transformations, if not by modern hectic standards, certainly by contrast with the stability of the Middle Ages. Mutability was one of the great themes of Elizabethan poetry.

Economic life was as much a focus of change as the religious. The *Descriptions* reflect at many points the effects the spread of the new wealth was having on English life. Actually Harrison had very limited insight into the developments that were transforming the countryside, as the older, self-sufficient community economy gave way to larger, more specialized farms that could supply distant urban demand. Harrison's Essex was commercialized by its proximity to the great London market; middlemen and shippers were necessary to its thriving economy. Harrison's perspective, however, remains obstinately that of the village consumer, grumbling about rising prices. His ideal in commerce is the local market, where, "as it cometh to pass that no buyer shall make any great journey in the purveyance of his necessities, so no occupier shall have occasion to travel far off with his commodities" (p. 246). He complains that the realm is "pestered with purveyors, who take up eggs, butter, cheese, pigs, capons, hens, chickens, hogs, bacon, etc., in one market . . . and suffer their wives to sell the same in another or to poulterers of London." Since buttermen "come to men's houses for their butter faster than they can make it, it is almost incredible to see how the price of butter is augmented," from 18*d.* the gallon to 3*s.* 4*d.* or even 5*s.* (p. 251). Similarly, the more efficient and larger farms that are being created appear to Harrison only in terms of the inevitable dislocations involved. Many are reduced to poverty and begging by the "covetous man," who, "espying a further commodity in their commons, holds, and tenures, doth find such means as thereby to wipe many out of their occupyings and turn the same unto his private gains" (pp. 181–182). Through the "encroaching and joining of house to house and laying land to land, . . . the inhabitants of many places of our country are devoured and eaten up and their houses either altogether pulled down or suffered to decay by little and little" (p. 216). Harrison can express only amazement that although landlords rack their tenants, so that " £4 of old rent be improved to £40, £50, or £100, yet will the farmer . . . think his gains very small toward the end of his term if he have not six or seven years' rent lying by him, therewith to purchase a new lease" (p. 202).

If Harrison's grasp of the causes of economic prosperity is slight, he records, often with satisfaction, the visible results. Great houses are everywhere being built, "so magnificent and stately as the basest house of a baron doth often match in our days with some honors of princes in old time" (p. 199). Costly furnishings are found not only in these noble houses; they have "descended yet lower, even unto the inferior artificers and many farmers," who have "learned also to garnish their cupboards with plate, their joint beds with tapestry and silk hangings, and their tables with carpets and fine napery, whereby the wealth of our country (God be praised therefor and give us grace to employ it well) doth infinitely appear" (p. 200). Table glass is greatly valued; wooden platters have been exchanged for pewter, wooden spoons for silver (pp. 128, 201). Stoves and chimneys are multiplying; fancy foods are being imported (pp. 201, 126). In the *Descriptions* the great economic movements of the age are crystallized into domestic detail.

Harrison is also aware of developments in the social sphere as a result of the increase and redistribution of wealth. These less dramatic changes principally involve greater social mobility. New money can buy a patent of gentility from the heralds, who "of custom pretend antiquity and service and many gay things"; the practice hurts no one, Harrison observes, except perhaps the recipient, who will "now and then bear a bigger sail than his boat is able to sustain" (p. 114). Merchants "often change estate with gentlemen, as gentlemen do with them, by a mutual conversion of the one into the other" (p. 115). Yeomen sometimes accumulate great wealth; their sons attend the university and become gentlemen (p. 118). On the other hand, to Harrison's dismay, some noblemen take an active interest in their estates and "themselves become graziers, butchers, tanners, sheepmasters, woodmen, . . . thereby to enrich themselves and bring all the wealth of the country into their own hands" (p. 204).

Not for centuries could a man have seen so many changes in a single lifetime, and this awareness of transformations in religious, economic, and social life is one of the factors shaping Harrison's work. For all his antiquarian interests, he is at least equally fascinated by the new England he sees emerging about him; he recognizes and celebrates its novelty because he can remember the very different England of his boyhood. The near as well as the distant past gives him his perspective on the present.

Harrison was fortunate in having other multiple perspectives available to him. The range of his social experience gave him a vantage ground beside which his failure to travel broadly was a minor disability. He was born and bred in London, apparently in the prosperous mercantile class. He attended two of the finest schools in England and took degrees at both Oxford and Cambridge. Most of his adult life, however, was spent in a small rural parish, where his conscientiousness and broad sympathies, as well as a system of tithing in produce, involved him in the concerns of the agricultural classes. As the presiding official of an archdeacon's court he was even more deeply immersed in country ways. Yet at the same time his position as Lord Cobham's household chaplain gave him a window on life in higher places, including, at least by the time of his second edition, the court.

The advantage of this broad experience, top to bottom, town and country, can be seen, for example, in Harrison's chapter on the food and diet of the English. He begins with an account of the lavish tables of the nobility, with their great "number of dishes and change of meat," prepared by "musical-headed Frenchmen," served in silver vessels, the wine and beer in Venice glass (pp. 126–128). A note on the more moderate ways of gentlemen and merchants dining at home includes by contrast a menu of one of the great guild feasts of the merchants (pp. 128–129). Harrison then moves easily and authoritatively to the normal diet of artificers and husbandmen and to country feasts, "each one bringing such a dish or so many with him as his wife and he do consult upon," where, if the poorer people "happen to stumble upon a piece of venison and a cup of wine or very strong beer or ale, . . . they think their cheer so great and themselves to have fared so well as the Lord Mayor of London," and where, to Harrison's regret, "their talk is now and then such as savoreth of scurrility and ribaldry, a thing naturally incident to carters and clowns" (pp. 131–132). The country folk, too, are liable to "surfeiting and drunkenness," although their pastor is understanding: "It may be that divers of them, living at home with hard and pinching diet, small drink, and some of them having scarce enough of that, are soonest overtaken when they come unto such banquets" (p. 132). No doubt from his own experience, too, comes the contrast of generous country hospitality with that of London; in the city "a cup of wine or beer, with a napkin to wipe their lips and an 'You are heartily welcome,' is thought to be great entertainment" (pp. 132–133).

The voice of the country rector is, however, that principally heard in the *Descriptions*. Harrison's style, as well as his bias, owes far more to his years of sermonizing in an Essex village than to his cosmopolitan background and academic career. Although he admires Abraham Fleming's ornate English enough to appropriate swatches of it (p. 342, n. 11), and he is himself capable, in attacking excesses in clothing, of a file of rhetorical exclamations (p. 146), his normal mode is far more homely. In the inkhorn controversy he characteristically takes the side of the purists, protesting against writers who "stain" English "by fond affectation of foreign and strange words" (p. 416), which is at best unnecessary, since "there is no one speech under the sun spoken in our time that hath or can have more variety of words, copy [copiousness] of phrases, or figures and flowers of eloquence" (p. 414). Harrison explicitly shuns the eloquence, insisting that he "never made any choice of style or words, . . . thinking it sufficient truly and plainly to set forth such things as I minded to entreat of" (p. 6). The potential of Elizabethan English for variety and copiousness, however, is demonstrated on every page of the *Descriptions*. Despite occasional protestations that he "covets to be brief," Harrison has all the stigmata of the fluent speaker: the introductory formulas ("It is a world to see . . ."; "I might here take occasion to speak of . . ."; "It is no marvel therefore that . . ."); the tautological doublings ("greatest and most," "shun and avoid," "laws and statutes," "committed and done"); the unabashed rambles ("But to my purpose, from whence I have now digressed"; "but whither am I slipped?" . . . ; "but then should I swerve yet further from my purpose, whereunto I now return"); the confiding tone ("Bear with me, gentle reader, I beseech thee"; "give me leave, gentle reader, to . . ."). The haste of the printer, Harrison insists, meant that he "could seldom with any deliberation peruse or almost with any judgment deliberate exactly upon such notes as were to be inserted." Since most of the book "was no sooner penned than printed" (p. 6, n. 7), his style was necessarily indeliberate, the serviceable, facile, even chatty English that came naturally to the gregarious rector.

Yet for all his cheerful volubility, Harrison has the Elizabethan gift for vivid language. A Scottish historian celebrates a minor victory over the English like "an hen that for laying of one egg will make a great cackling" (*Des. Brit.*, 1587, p. 118). The clergy are heavily taxed, "as if the Church were now become the ass whereon every marketman is to ride and cast his wallet" (p. 31). Widows remarry unwisely, but "Eve will be Eve, though Adam would say nay" (p. 38). Harlots are punished by "doing of open penance in sheets, in churches and marketsteads," but "what great smart is it to be turned out of an hot sheet into a cold?" (p. 189). Harrison delights in the slang of the tavern: pot knights drink "mad-dog, father-whoreson, angels'-food, dragons'-milk," until they are "cupshotten"; "maltbugs lug at this liquor, even as pigs should lie in a row," and "hale at huffcap till they be red as cocks and little wiser than their combs" (p. 247). C. S. Lewis' suggestion that much of what "now pleases us flows, no doubt, less from his own talent than from the common language of the age"[8] is surely true, but Harrison's prime gift remained his ability not merely to describe but to embody the modes of his age.

Holinshed's *Chronicles* were popular enough to require a second edition within ten years. Harrison accordingly set about a thorough revision of his *Descriptions*. He dropped the four brief chapters on weights and measures (p. 453, n. 1), added six completely new chapters, and rearranged others. Scarcely a paragraph escaped verbal tinkering, and a great deal of new material was inserted at more or less appropriate places, making the *Descriptions* almost a third again as long. The changes did not affect the basic character of the work; rather they served to magnify traits already present in 1577. Many of the less happy digressions into historical and classical lore, such as the lengthy accounts of Earl Godwin and of ancient navies (pp. 12–16, 239–241), were added in 1587, but so were many of the most sprightly and frequently-quoted passages, such as Harrison's complaints about the cheating in awarding college fellowships, about the manipulating of juries, the state of the roads, and the venality of London lawyers (pp. 71, 91, 443–444, 173–174), his defense of the English episcopacy, his attacks on monopolies and on travel in Italy (pp. 98, 257, 114–115), the accounts of English inns, of fashions in beards, and of brewing beer in the Harrison household

[8] *English Literature in the Sixteenth Century* (Oxford, 1954), p. 304.

(pp. 397–399, 146–147, 137–138), his worries about imminent invasion, his expositions of the ruses of horse thieves and highwaymen, his entire chapter on gardens (pp. 222–223, 308, 238–239, 263–271). These important additions added immeasurably to the value of the work, and doubtless we have lost much through the failure of a half-expected third edition [9] to materialize.

William Harrison's *Descriptions* are, above all, a deliberate survey of a nation on the threshold of a golden age, a spirited portrait of the mid-Elizabethan land and society, drawn with honesty and skill sufficient to validate Harrison's claim to have had "an especial eye unto the truth of things" (p. 6). Yet Harrison draws an equally telling self-portrait, all the more truthful because indeliberate. If he is not a man of any obvious genius, if often enough he can be disorganized and shallow and inconsistent, his very flaws become a source of strength. Too limited to rise above his age, he mirrors it almost perfectly. He not only describes the Elizabethan scene, he thinks and speaks as an ordinary Elizabethan. In Harrison we come exceptionally close to that elusive aspect in the study of the past, what the common people thought about common things.

[9] "If it shall please God that I may live to have the filing of these rude pamphlets yet once again, and somewhat more leisure to peruse them than at this time is granted" (*Des. Brit.,* 1587, p. 100).

THE DESCRIPTION
OF ENGLAND

To the Right Honorable, and his singular good lord and master, Sir William Brooke, Knight, Lord Warden of the Cinque Ports, and Baron of Cobham,[1] all increase of the fear and knowledge of God, firm obedience toward his prince, infallible love to the commonwealth, and commendable renown here in this world, and in the world to come life everlasting.

HAVING had just occasion, Right Honorable, to remain in London during the time of Trinity term last past,[2] and being earnestly required of divers my friends to set down some brief discourse of parcel of those things which I had observed in the reading of such manifold antiquities as I had perused toward the furniture of a Chronology, which I have yet[3] in hand, I was at the first very loath to yield to their desires: first, for that I thought myself unable, for want of skill and judgment, so suddenly and with so hasty speed to take such a charge upon me; secondly, because the dealing therein might prove an hindrance and impeachment unto

[1] *Sir William Brooke* (1527–1597): 10th Baron Cobham, Knight of the Garter, 1585, Privy Councilor, 1586, Lord Chamberlain, 1596. In addition to his estate at Cobham in Kent, which he rebuilt extensively, he maintained a town house in Blackfriars. In 1559 Harrison was presented by Cobham to the rectory of Radwinter in northwest Essex, the parish which was to be his permanent home; he also served as Cobham's chaplain. Writing to Robert Cecil in the year of Harrison's death, Cobham describes him as "one who of long time hath served me."

[2] That is, June 22–July 11, 1576.

[3] In 1587 Harrison changed "had then" to "have yet" and added the adjective "earnest" later in the sentence. He had apparently been severely criticized for his avocation. In *The Description of Scotland* (1577, p. 21) he announces that he will close with one more item and then "give over not only to write more at this present but forever hereafter of any historical matters, sith I see that this honest kind of recreation is denied me and all time spent about the same in these days utterly condemned as vain and savoring of negligence and heathenish impiety." His resolution was not kept: the entries in his Chronology continue until 1593, the year of his death. On the Chronology, see my introduction, p. xviii.

mine own treatise; and finally, for that I had given over all earnest study of histories, as judging the time spent about the same to be an hindrance unto my more necessary dealings in that vocation and function whereunto I am called in the ministry. But when they were so importunate with me that no reasonable excuse could serve to put by this travail, I condescended at the length unto their irksome suit, promising that I would spend such void time as I had to spare, whilst I should be enforced to tarry in the city, upon some thing or other that should satisfy their request and stand in lieu of a description of my country. For their parts also they assured me of such helps as they could purchase, and thus with hope of good, although no gay success, I went in hand withal, then almost as one leaning altogether unto memory, sith my books and I were parted by forty miles in sunder. In this order also I spent a part of Michaelmas and Hilary terms ensuing,[4] being enforced thereto, I say, by other businesses which compelled me to keep in the city and absent myself from my charge, though in the mean season I had some repair unto my poor library, but not so great as the dignity of the matter required, and yet far greater than the printers' haste would suffer.

One help, and none of the smallest that I obtained herein, was by such commentaries as Leland had sometime collected of the state of Britain, books utterly mangled, defaced with wet and weather, and finally, unperfect through want of sundry volumes;[5]

[4] That is, October 9–November 28, 1576, and January 23–February 12, 1577. Although the first edition of Holinshed was not licensed in the Stationers' Register until July 1, 1578, it is described in the Acts of the Privy Council on December 5, 1577, as "lately printed." The mention of the law terms, coupled with Harrison's remark later in the dedication, "how other affairs troubled me in the writing hereof, many know," suggests that he was in legal difficulties. His forthright opinion of lawyers in Book I, chapter ix, seems to have empirical force.

[5] *John Leland* (?1505–1552): the first of the great Tudor antiquarians. His *Itinerary*, or *Commentaries* (first printed in the eighteenth century), is comprised of topographical and historical notes gathered during his six years' travel about England. Harrison makes clear that he had Leland's original MSS, now in the Bodleian; he had borrowed them from John Stow (*Survey of London*, ed. C. L. Kingsford, Oxford, 1908, I, 349). In *The Description of Britain* (1587, p. 63) he complains further of their condition: "So moth-eaten, moldy, and rotten are those books of Leland which I have, and, beside that, his annotations are such and so confounded, as no man can (in a manner) pick out any sense from them by a leaf together. Wherefore I suppose that he dispersed and made his notes intricate of set purpose, or else he was loath that any man should easily come to that knowledge by reading which he, with his great charge and no less travail, attained unto by experience."

secondly, I gat some knowledge of things by letters and pamphlets from sundry places and shires of England, but so discordant now and then amongst themselves, especially in the names and courses of rivers and situation of towns, that I had oft greater trouble to reconcile them one with another than orderly to pen the whole discourse of such points as they contained;[6] the third aid did grow by conference with divers, either at the table or secretly alone, wherein I marked in what things the talkers did agree and wherein they impugned each other, choosing in the end the former and rejecting the latter, as one desirous to set forth the truth absolutely, or such things indeed as were most likely to be true. The last comfort arose by mine own reading of such writers as have heretofore made mention of the condition of our country, in speaking whereof, if I should make account of the success and extraordinary coming by sundry treatises not supposed to be extant, I should but seem to pronounce more than may well be said with modesty and say farther of myself than this treatise can bear witness of. Howbeit, I refer not this success wholly unto my purpose about this *Description,* but rather give notice thereof to come to pass in the penning of my Chronology whose crumbs, as it were, fell out very well in the framing of this pamphlet.

In the process therefore of this book, if Your Honor regard the substance of that which is here declared, I must needs confess that it is none of mine own; but if Your Lordship have consideration of the barbarous composition showed herein, that I may boldly claim and challenge for mine own, sith there is no man of any so slender skill that will defraud me of that reproach which is due unto me for the mere negligence, disorder, and evil disposition of matter comprehended in the same. Certes I protest

[6] For topographical detail Harrison, remembering perhaps the example of Sebastian Münster, depended heavily on requests for local information sent to friends around England. *The Description of Britain* is studded with such references as: "a friend of mine, prosecuting the rest of this description, reporteth thereof as followeth"; "the next I exhibit as it was given unto me by one that hath taken pains (as he saith) to search out and view the same but very lately to speak of"; "having another note delivered me thereof from a friend, I will yield so far unto his gratification that I will remember his travail here and set down also what he hath written thereof" (1587, pp. 48, 85, 101). As a source this method proved disappointing. Equally frequent are Harrison's complaints that "mine informations are not so fully set down as the promises of some on the one side and mine expectation on the other did extend unto," or "the description thereof be not so exactly delivered me as I looked for" (1587, pp. 29, 99).

before God and Your Honor that I never made any choice of style or words, neither regarded to handle this treatise in such precise order and method as many other would have done, thinking it sufficient truly and plainly to set forth such things as I minded to entreat of, rather than with vain affectation of eloquence to paint out a rotten sepulcher, a thing neither commendable in a writer nor profitable to the reader. How other affairs troubled me in the writing hereof, many know, and peradventure the slackness showed herein can better testify; but howsoever it be done, and whatsoever I have done, I have had an especial eye unto the truth of things, and for the rest, I hope that this foul frizzled treatise of mine will prove a spur to others better learned, more skillful in chorography, and of greater judgment in choice of matter to handle the selfsame argument, if in my lifetime I do not peruse it again.[7] It is possible also that Your Honor will mislike hereof, for that I have not by mine own travel and eyesight viewed such things as I do here entreat of. Indeed I must needs confess that until now of late, except it were from the parish where I dwell unto Your Honor in Kent, or out of London, where I was born, unto Oxford and Cambridge, where I have been brought up, I never traveled forty miles forthright and at one journey in all my life; nevertheless, in my report of these things I use their authorities who either have performed in their persons or left in writing upon sufficient ground (as I said before) whatsoever is wanting in mine.

It may be in like sort that Your Honor will take offense at my rash and rechless behavior used in the composition of this volume, and much more that being scambled [scraped] up after this manner, I dare presume to make tender of the protection thereof unto Your Lordship's hands. But when I consider the singular affec-

---

[7] This clause was substituted in 1587 for the following passage: "As for the faults escaped herein, as there are divers, I must needs confess, both in the penning and printing, so I have to crave pardon of Your Honor and of all the learned readers. For such was my shortness of time allowed in the writing and so great the speed made in the printing that I could seldom with any deliberation peruse or almost with any judgment deliberate exactly upon such notes as were to be inserted. Sometimes indeed their leisure gave me liberty, but that I applied in following my vocation; many times their expedition abridged my perusal; and by this latter it came to pass that most of this book was no sooner penned than printed, neither well conceived before it came to writing. But it is now too late to excuse the manner of doing."

tion that Your Honor doth bear to those that in any wise will travail to set forth such profitable things as lie hidden, and thereunto do weigh on mine own behalf my bounden duty and grateful mind to such a one as hath so many and sundry ways benefited me, that otherwise can make no recompense, I cannot but cut off all such occasion of doubt and thereupon exhibit it, such as it is and so penned as it is, unto Your Lordship's tuition, unto whom if it may seem in any wise acceptable, I have my whole desire.

And as I am the first that (notwithstanding the great repugnancy to be seen among our writers) hath taken upon him so particularly to describe this Isle of Britain, so I hope the learned and godly will bear withal and reform with charity where I do tread amiss. As for the curious [captious], and such as can rather evil-favoredly espy than skillfully correct an error, and sooner carp at another man's doings than publish anything of their own (keeping themselves close, with an obscure admiration of learning and knowledge among the common sort), I force [care] not what they say hereof; for whether it do please or displease them, all is one to me, sith I refer my whole travail in the gratification of Your Honor and such as are of experience to consider of my travail and the large scope of things purposed in this treatise, of whom my service in this behalf may be taken in good part; that I will repute for my full recompense and large guerdon of my labors.

The Almighty God preserve Your Lordship in continual health, wealth, and prosperity, with my good Lady, your wife, Your Honor's children (whom God hath endued with a singular towardness unto all virtue and learning), and the rest of your reformed family, unto whom I wish farther increase of His Holy Spirit, understanding of His Word, augmentation of honor, and continuance of zeal to follow His commandments.

> Your Lordship's humble servant
> and household chaplain, W. H.

BOOK II

The Description of England

CHAPTER I

Of the Ancient and Present Estate
of the Church of England

THERE are now two provinces only in England, of which the first and greatest is subject to the see of Canterbury, comprehending a part of Loegria, whole Cambria,[1] and also Ireland, which in time past were several and brought into one by the archbishop of the said see and assistance of the Pope, who, in respect of meed, did yield unto the ambitious desires of sundry Archbishops of Canterbury, as I have elsewhere declared. The second province is under the see of York; and, of these, either hath her archbishop resident commonly within her own limits, who hath not only the chief dealing in matters appertaining to the hierarchy and jurisdiction of the church but also great authority in civil affairs touching the government of the commonwealth, so far forth as their commissions and several circuits do extend.

In old time there were three archbishops and so many provinces in this isle, of which one kept at London, another at York, and the third at Caerleon-upon-Usk. But as that of London was translated to Canterbury by Augustine, and that of York remaineth (notwithstanding that the greatest part of his jurisdiction is now bereft him and given to the Scottish archbishop), so that of Caerleon is utterly extinguished and the government of the country united to that of Canterbury in spiritual cases, after it was once before removed to St. David's in Wales by David, successor to Dubricius and uncle to King Arthur, in the 519 of grace,[2] to the end that he and his clerks might be further off from

[1] *Loegria* (Welsh *Lloegr*): the eponymous Celtic name for England, so called, Harrison explains (*Des. Brit.*, 1587, p. 116), from the legendary King Locrine (or Logris), oldest son of Brut, who inherited that part of his father's kingdom. To Camber, the second son, was left Wales, or Cambria.

[2] Most of these details about the early Welsh "archbishoprics" derive from Geoffrey of Monmouth, IX, xv, and XI, iii. As a native Londoner, Harrison harps upon Augustine's "translation" of his see to Canterbury.

the cruelty of the Saxons, where it remained till the time of the Bastard [William the Conqueror] and for a season after, before it was annexed unto the see of Canterbury.

The Archbishop of Canterbury is commonly called Primate of All England, and, in the coronations of the kings of this land and all other times wherein it shall please the prince to wear and put on his crown, his office is to set it upon their heads. They bear also the name of their high chaplains continually, although not a few of them have presumed (in time past) to be their equals and void of subjection unto them. That this is true it may easily appear by their own acts yet kept in record, beside their epistles and answers written or in print, wherein they have sought not only to match but also to mate them with great rigor and more than open tyranny. Our adversaries will peradventure deny this absolutely, as they do many other things apparent, though not without shameless impudency, or at the leastwise defend it as just and not swerving from common equity, because they imagine every archbishop to be the king's equal in his own province. But how well their doing herein agreeth with the saying of Peter and examples of the primitive church, it may easily appear. Some examples also of their demeanor (I mean in the time of popery) I will not let to remember, lest they should say I speak of malice and without all ground of likelihood.

Of their practices with mean persons I speak not, neither will I begin at Dunstan, the author of all their pride and presumption here in England.[3] But forsomuch as the dealing of Robert the Norman against Earl Godwin is a rare history and deserveth to be remembered, I will touch it in this place, protesting to deal withal in more faithful manner than it hath heretofore been delivered unto us by the Norman writers, or French-English, who (of set purpose) have so defaced Earl Godwin that, were it not for the testimony of one or two mere Englishmen living in those days, it should be impossible for me (or any other) at this present to declare the truth of that matter according to her circumstances.[4] Mark therefore what I say. For the truth is that such

[3] *St. Dunstan:* Archbishop of Canterbury in 960–988; he earned Harrison's ire as a reviver of monasticism, a supposed persecutor of the married clergy, and a powerful voice in secular affairs.

[4] Harrison had already given, in chapter iv of his *Description of Britain,* a circumstantial account of this power struggle in 1051–1052 between Godwin, Earl of Wessex and leader of the Saxon nobles, and Robert of

Normans as came in with Emma in the time of Ethelred and Canute and the Confessor [5] did fall by sundry means into such favor with those princes that the gentlemen did grow to bear great rule in the court and their clerks to be possessors of the best benefices in the land. Hereupon therefore one Robert, a jolly, ambitious priest, gat first to be Bishop of London and after the death of Eadsige to be Archbishop of Canterbury by the gift of King Edward, leaving his former see to William, his countryman. Ulf, also a Norman, was preferred to Lincoln and other to other places as the King did think convenient.

These Norman clerks and their friends being thus exalted, it was not long ere they began to mock, abuse, and despise the English, and so much the more as they daily saw themselves to increase in favor with King Edward, who also called divers of them to be of his secret council, which did not a little incense the hearts of the English against them. A fray also was made at Dover between the servants of Earl Godwin and the French, whose masters came over to see and salute the King (whereof I have spoken in my Chronology), which so inflamed the minds of the French clergy and courtiers against the English nobility that each part sought for opportunity of revenge, which ere long took hold between them. For the said Robert, being called to be Archbishop of Canterbury, was no sooner in possession of his see than he began to quarrel with Earl Godwin (the King's father-in-law by the marriage of his daughter), who also was ready to acquit his demeanor with like malice, and so the mischief begun. Hereupon therefore the Archbishop charged the Earl with the murder of Aelfred, the King's brother, whom not he but Harold, the son of Canute, and the Danes had cruelly made away.

Jumièges, the Norman Archbishop of Canterbury. No doubt he was attracted to the story by the happy triumph of the native Saxons over the pesky French and of the secular nobility over a political archbishop. His pro-Saxon account, which he frequently paraphrases here, was a MS "in the hands of John Stow my very [true] friend" (*Des. Brit.*, 1587, p. 7), the *Vita Aedwardi* written for Edith, widow of Edward and daughter of Godwin (now B.M., Harl. MS 526, edited as *The Life of King Edward* by Frank Barlow, Oxford, 1962).

[5] *Emma* (d. 1052): daughter of Richard I, Duke of Normandy; she married the English King Ethelred (r. 979–1013), by whom her sons were Edward the Confessor (1042–1066) and the Aelfred whose murder in 1036 was an issue in the Godwin affair. After Ethelred's death she married Canute (1016–1035). With Emma, Norman influence in England began.

For Aelfred and his brother coming into the land with five-and-twenty sail upon the death of Canute and being landed, the Normans that arrived with them giving out how they came to recover their right, to wit, the crown of England, and thereunto the unskillful [ingenuous] young gentlemen showing themselves to like of the rumor that was spread in this behalf, the report of their demeanor was quickly brought to Harold, who caused a company forthwith of Danes privily to lay wait for them as they rode toward Guildford, where Aelfred was slain and whence Edward with much difficulty escaped to his ships and so returned into Normandy.

But to proceed. This affirmation of the Archbishop, being greatly soothed out with his crafty utterance (for he was learned), confirmed by his French friends (for they had all conspired against the Earl), and thereunto the King being desirous to revenge the death of his brother, bred such a grudge in his mind against Godwin that he banished him and his sons clean out of the land. He sent also his wife, the Earl's daughter, prisoner to Wilton, with one only maiden attending upon her, where she lay almost a year before she was released. In the mean season the rest of the peers, as Siward, Earl of Northumberland, surnamed *"Digera"* or *"Fortis,"* Leofric, Earl of Chester, and other went to the King before the departure of Godwin, endeavoring to persuade him unto the revocation of his sentence and desiring that his cause might be heard and discussed by order of law. But the King, incensed by the Archbishop and his Normans, would not hear on that side, saying plainly and swearing by St. John the Evangelist (for that was his common oath) that Earl Godwin should not have his peace till he restored his brother Aelfred alive again unto his presence. With which answer the peers departed in choler from the court and Godwin toward the coast.

Coming also unto the shore, and ready to take shipping, he kneeled down in presence of his conduct (to wit, at Bosham, in the month of September, from whence he intended to sail into Flanders unto Baldwin, the Earl) and there prayed openly before them all that if ever he attempted anything against the King's person of England or his royal estate, that he might never come safe unto his cousin nor see his country any more but perish in this voyage. And herewith he went aboard the ship that was provided for him, and so from the coast into the open sea. But see what followed. He was not yet gone a mileway from the land before he saw the shore full of armed soldiers, sent after by the Archbishop and his friends to kill him ere he should depart and go out of the country, which yet more incensed the hearts of the English against them.

Being come also to Flanders, he caused the Earl, the French king, and other of his friends, among whom also the Emperor was one, to write unto the King in his behalf; but all in vain, for nothing could be obtained from him of which the Normans had no liking, whereupon the Earl and his sons changed their minds, obtained aid, and invaded the land in sundry places. Finally joining their powers, they came by the Thames into Southwark near London, where they lodged and looked for the King to encounter with them in the field. The King, seeing what was done, commanded the Londoners not to aid nor victual them. But the citizens made answer how the quarrel of Godwin was the cause of the whole realm, which he had in manner given over unto the spoil of the French; and thereupon they not only victualed them abundantly but also received the Earl and his chief friends into the city, where they lodged them at their ease till the King's power was ready to join with them in battle.

Great resort also was made unto them from all places of the realm, so that the Earl's army was wonderfully increased and the day and place chosen wherein the battle should be fought. But when the armies met, the King's side began, some to flee to the Earl, other to lay down their weapons, and not a few to run away outright, the rest telling him plainly that they would never fight against their own countrymen to maintain Frenchmen's quarrels. The Normans also, seeing the sequel, fled away so fast as they might gallop, leaving the King in the field to shift for himself as he best might, whilst they did save themselves elsewhere.

In the mean season the Earl's power would have set upon the King, either to his slaughter or apprehension; but he stayed them, saying after this manner, "The King is my son, as you all know, and it is not for a father to deal so hardly with his child, neither a subject with his sovereign; it is not he that hath hurt or done me this injury but the proud Normans that are about him; wherefore, to gain a kingdom I will do him no violence." And therewithal, casting aside his battle-ax, he ran to the King, that stood altogether amazed, and, falling at his feet, he craved his peace, accused the Archbishop, required that his cause might be heard in open assembly of his peers and finally determined as truth and equity should deserve.

The King (after he had paused a pretty while), seeing his old father-in-law to lie groveling at his feet and conceiving with himself that his suit was not unreasonable, seeing also his children and the rest of the greatest barons of the land to kneel before him and make the like request, he lifted up the Earl by the hand, bade him be of good comfort, pardoned all that was past, and friendly having kissed him and his sons upon the cheeks, he led them to his palace, called home the Queen, and summoned all his lords unto a council.

Wherein it is much to read how many bills were presented against the Bishop and his Normans, some containing matter of rape, other of robbery, extortion, murder, manslaughter, high treason, adultery, and not a few of battery. Wherewith the King (as a man now awaked out of sleep) was so offended that, upon consultation had of these things, he banished all the Normans out of the land, only three or four excepted, whom he retained for sundry necessary causes, albeit they came never more so near him afterward as to be of his privy council.

After this also the Earl lived almost two years, and then, falling into an apoplexy as he sat with the King at the table, he was taken up and carried into the King's bedchamber, where (after a few days) he made an end of his life. And thus much of our first broil raised by the clergy and practice of the Archbishop. I would entreat of all the like examples of tyranny practiced by the prelates of this see against their lords and sovereigns, but then I should rather write an history than a description of this island.

Wherefore I refer you to those reports of Anselm and Becket sufficiently penned by other, the which Anselm also, making a show as if he had been very unwilling to be placed in the see of Canterbury, gave this answer to the letters of such his friends as did make request unto him to take the charge upon him:

Secularia negotia nescio, quia scire nolo, eorum namque occupationes horreo, liberum affectans animum. Voluntati sacrarum intendo scripturarum, vos dissonantiam facitis, verendumque est ne aratrum sanctae ecclesiae, quod in Anglia duo boves validi et pari fortitudine, ad bonum certantes, id est rex et archiepiscopus, debeant trahere, nunc ove vetula cum tauro indomito jugata, distorqueatur a recto. Ego ovis vetula, qui si quietus essem, verbi Dei lacte, et operimento lanae, aliquibus possem fortassis non ingratus esse, sed si me cum hoc tauro conjungitis, videbitis pro disparilitate trahentium, aratrum non recte procedere, etc.

Which is in English thus:

Of secular affairs I have no skill because I will not know them, for I even abhor the troubles that rise about them, as one that desireth to have his mind at liberty. I apply my whole endeavor to the rule of the Scriptures; you lead me to the contrary. And it is to be feared lest the plow of Holy Church, which two strong oxen of equal force and both like earnest to contend unto that which is good (that is, the King and the Archbishop) ought to draw, should thereby now swerve from the right furrow by matching of an old sheep with a wild, untamed bull. I am that old sheep, who, if I might be quiet, could peradventure show myself not altogether ungrateful to some by feeding them with the milk of the Word of God and covering them with wool; but if you match me with this bull you shall see that through want of equality in draft the plow will not go to right, etc.,[6]

as followeth in the process of his letters. The said Thomas Becket was so proud that he wrote to King Henry the Second as to his lord, to his king, and to his son, offering him his counsel, his reverence, and due correction, etc.[7] Others in like sort have protested that they ought [owed] nothing to the kings of this land but their counsel only, reserving all obedience unto the see of Rome.[8]

And as the old cock of Canterbury did crow in this behalf, so the young cockerels of other sees did imitate his demeanor, as may be seen by this one example also in King Stephen's time, worthy to be remembered; unto whom the Bishop of London would not so much as swear to be true subject, wherein also he was maintained by the Pope, as appeareth by these letters:

Eugenius episcopus, servus servorum Dei, dilecto in Christo filio Stephano illustri regi Anglorum salutem et apostolicam benedictionem. Ad haec superna providentia in ecclesia pontifices ordinavit, ut Christ-

[6] *St. Anselm:* Archbishop of Canterbury in 1093–1109; he was in fact physically forced to accept the crozier. His description of William Rufus as "a wild, untamed bull" is accurate.

[7] The full Latin text of this famous letter, dated 1166, is given in *Materials for the History of Thomas Becket,* ed. James Craigie Robertson, Rolls Ser., LXVII, Vol. V (1881), 278–282.

[8] The 1577 edition adds, "whereby we may easily see the pride and ambition of the clergy in the blind time of ignorance."

ianus populus ab eis pascua vitae reciperet, et tam principes seculares, quam inferioris conditionis homines, ipsis pontificibus, tanquam Christi vicariis, reverentiam exhiberent. Venerabilis siquidem frater noster Robertus London episcopus, tanquam vir sapiens et honestus, et relligionis amator, a nobilitate tua benigne tractandus est, et pro collata a Deo prudentia propensius honorandus. Quia ergo, sicut in veritate comperimus cum animae suae salute, ac suae ordinis periculo, fidelitate quae ab eo requiritur astringi non potest: volumus, et ex paterno tibi affectu consulimus, quatenus praedictum fratrem nostrum super hoc nullatenus inquietes, immo pro beati Petri et nostra reverentia, eum in amorem et gratiam tuam recipias. Cum autem illud juramentum praestare non possit, sufficiat discretioni tuae, ut simplici et veraci verbo promittat, quod laesionem tibi vel terrae tuae non inferat: Vale. Dat. Meldis 6. cal. Julii.[9]

Thus we see that kings were to rule no further than it pleased the Pope to like of, neither to challenge more obedience of their subjects than stood also with their good will and pleasure. He wrote in like sort unto Queen Maud [10] about the same matter, making her Samson's calf (the better to bring his purpose to pass), as appeareth by the same letter here ensuing:

Solomone attestante, didicimus quod mulier sapiens aedificat domum; insipiens autem constructam destruet manibus. Gaudemus pro te, et devotionis studium in Domino collaudamus; quoniam sicut relligio-

---

[9] "Bishop Eugenius, servant of the servants of God, to his beloved son in Christ, Stephen, illustrious King of the English, greetings and apostolic benediction. Heavenly providence has ordained bishops in the church in order that Christian people might receive from them the food of life and that secular princes, so well as men of inferior condition, might show reverence to these bishops as vicars of Christ. Hence our venerable brother, Robert, Bishop of London, as a wise and honorable man and a lover of religion, must be treated kindly by Your Highness and be readily respected for the prudence bestowed on him by God. Because, as we have in truth learned, he cannot in good conscience, even at the risk of his office, be bound by the oath which is required of him, we will and advise, in paternal love for you, that you disturb our said brother no further about this matter but rather that you receive him into your love and favor in reverence for St. Peter and for us. Since he cannot swear that oath, let it suffice in your discretion that he give a simple and straightforward promise that he will commit no injury against you or your land. Given at Meaux, 6 calends July [June 26, 1147]." Robert de Sigillo was preferred to the bishopric of London by the Empress Matilda in 1141. Later he refused the oath of allegiance to the King, pleading pre-engagement to Stephen's rival, a position in which he is here supported by Pope Eugenius III (1145-1153).

[10] Matilda of Boulogne, Stephen's Queen, not the Empress Matilda, or Maud.

sorum relatione accepimus, timorem Dei prae oculis habens, operibus
pietatis intendis, et personas ecclesiasticas et diligis et honoras. Ut ergo
de bono in melius (inspirante Domino) proficere valeas, nobilitatem
tuam in Domino rogamus, et rogando monemus, et exhortamur in
Domino, quatenus bonis initiis exitus meliores injungas, et venerabilem
fratrem nostrum Robertum London episcopum, pro illius reverentia,
qui cum olim dives esset, pro nobis pauper fieri voluit, attentius diligas,
et honores. Apud virum tuum, et dilectum filium nostrum, Stephanum,
insignem regem Anglorum efficere studeas, ut monitis, hortatu, et con-
silio tuo, ipsum in benignitatem et dilectionem suam suscipiat, et pro
beati Petri, et nostra reverentia propensius habeat commendatum. Et
quia sicut (veritate teste) attendimus eum sine salute, et sui ordinis
periculo, praefato filio nostro astringi non posse; volumus, et paterno
sibi et tibi affectu consulimus, ut vobis sufficiat, veraci et simplici verbo
promissionem ab eo suscipere, quod laesionem vel detrimentum ei, vel
terrae suae non inferat. Dat. ut supra.[11]

Is it not strange that a peevish order of religion (devised by
man) should break the express law of God, who commandeth
all men to honor and obey their kings and princes, in whom some
part of the power of God is manifest and laid open unto us? And
even unto this end the Cardinal of Ostia also wrote to the canons
of Paul's, after this manner, covertly encouraging them to stand
to their election of the said Robert, who was no more willing to
give over his new bishopric than they careful to offend the King,

---

[11] "We know, from the testimony of Solomon, that the wise woman builds
her house but the foolish one plucks down the structure with her hands
[Prov. 14:1]. We rejoice in you, and we extol the zeal of your devotion
to the Lord, because we have heard from the account of religious people
that you, having the fear of God before your eyes, exert yourself in pious
works and esteem and honor ecclesiastical persons. In order that you may
be able, therefore, with the Lord's inspiration, to progress from good to
better, we request Your Highness in the Lord, and, requesting, we ad-
monish and exhort you in the Lord, to go on from such good beginnings
to even nobler achievements and to esteem and honor more carefully our
venerable brother, Robert, Bishop of London, out of respect for him, who
was formerly wealthy and was willing to become poor for our sake. You
should strive by your admonitions, exhortation, and advice to induce your
husband and our beloved son, Stephen, the distinguished King of the English,
to receive him into his favor and love and to value him all the more highly
out of reverence for St. Peter and for us. And because we consider, in
truth, that he cannot without peril to his salvation and position take the
oath to our said son, we will and advise, in paternal love for him and you,
that it suffice you to take from him a straightforward and simple promise
that he will commit no injury or harm to him or to his land. Given as
above."

but rather imagined which way to keep it still, mauger his displeasure, and yet not to swear obedience unto him, for all that he should be able to do or perform unto the contrary.

Humilis Dei gratia Hostiensis episcopus, Londinensis ecclesiae canonicis spiritum consilii in Domino. Sicut rationi contraria prorsus est abjicienda petitio, ita in hiis, quae juste desiderantur, effectum negare omnino non convenit. Sane nuper accepimus, quod Londinensis ecclesia, diu proprio destituta pastore, communi voto, et pari assensu cleri et populi, venerabilem filium nostrum[12] Robertum, eiusdem ecclesiae archidiaconum, in pastorem et episcopum animarum suarum susceperit et elegerit. Novimus quidem eum esse personam, quam sapientia de super ei attributa, et honestas conversationis, et morum reverentia plurimum commendabilem reddidit. Inde est quod fraternitati vestrae mandando consulimus, ut proposito vestro bono (quod ut credimus ex Deo est) et ut ex literis domini papae cognoscetis, non tepide, non lente debitum finem imponatis: ne tam nobilis ecclesia, sub occasione huiusmodi, spiritualium, quod absit, et temporalium detrimentum patiatur. Ipsius namque industria credimus, quod antiqua relligio, et forma disciplinae, et gravitas habitus, in ecclesia vestra reparari: et si quae fuerint ipsius contentiones, ex pastoris absentia, Dei gratia cooperante, et eodem praesente, poterint reformari. Dat. etc.[13]

Hereby you see how King Stephen was dealt withal. And albeit the Archbishop of Canterbury is not openly to be touched

---

[12] *"Forsitan naturalem."*—H. That is, "perhaps his natural son."

[13] "[Alberic], by the grace of God humbly the Bishop of Ostia, to the canons of the London church, the spirit of counsel in the Lord. Just as a suit which is contrary to reason must be utterly rejected, so it is not at all fitting to forbid the execution of those things which are justly desired. Indeed we have learned lately that the church of London, deprived for a long time of her pastor, by common desire as well as by agreement of both clergy and laity chose and elected our venerable son, Robert, archdeacon of this same church, as bishop and pastor of their souls. Furthermore we know him to be a person whose wisdom, given him from above, and integrity of behavior and gravity of conduct have entitled him to the highest praise. Hence it is that we urge and enjoin your brotherhood to bring to a suitable conclusion, without any reluctance or delay, the fine plan of which you are aware from the letters of our lord, the Pope (which we believe derives from God), lest so noble a church suffer through such an occasion either spiritual (God forbid!) or temporal harm. We are convinced that through his energy the ancient religion and form of discipline and sobriety of manner can be restored in your church; and if it has been troubled by any disputes through the absence of your pastor, they can be resolved, with the help of God's grace, when he is present." *Alberic:* Cardinal-Bishop of Ostia in 1138–1147; he had been papal legate in England in 1138.

herewith, yet it is not to be doubted but he was a doer in it, so far as might tend to the maintenance of the right and prerogative of Holy Church. And even no less unquietness had another of our princes with John [for Thomas] of Arundel, who fled to Rome for fear of his head and caused the Pope to write an ambitious and contumelious letter unto his sovereign about his restitution. But when (by the King's letters yet extant and beginning thus: *Thomas proditionis non expers nostrae regiae majestati insidias fabricavit*) the Pope understood the bottom of the matter, he was contented that Thomas should be deprived and another archbishop chosen in his stead.[14]

Neither did this pride stay at archbishops and bishops but descended lower, even to the rakehells of the clergy and puddles of all ungodliness. For beside the injury received of their superiors, how was King John dealt withal by the vile Cistercians at Lincoln in the second of his reign? Certes when he had (upon just occasion) conceived some grudge against them for their ambitious demeanor, and, upon denial to pay such sums of money as were allotted unto them, he had caused seizure to be made of such horses, swine, neat, and other things of theirs as were maintained in his forests, they denounced him as fast amongst themselves with bell, book, and candle to be accursed and excommunicated. Thereunto they so handled the matter with the Pope and their friends that the King was fain to yield to their good graces, insomuch that a meeting for pacification was appointed between them at Lincoln by means of the present [attending] Archbishop of Canterbury, who went oft between him and the Cistercian commissioners before the matter could be finished. In the end the King himself came also unto the said commissioners as they sat in their chapter house and there with tears fell down at their feet, craving pardon for his trespasses against them and heartily requiring that they would (from thenceforth) commend him and his realm in their prayers unto the protection of the Almighty and receive him into their fraternity, promising moreover full satisfaction of their damages sustained and to build an house of their order in whatsoever place

---

[14] *Thomas Arundel:* consecrated Archbishop of Canterbury in 1396, impeached by the House of Commons and banished in 1397. Richard II's letter to Boniface IX, beginning, "Thomas with great treason has concocted a plot against the majesty of our crown," was printed by Matthew Parker, *De antiquitate Britannicae ecclesiae* (1572), p. 305.

of England it should please them to assign. And this he confirmed
by charter, bearing date the seven-and-twentieth of November
after the Scottish king was returned into Scotland and departed
from the King.[15] Whereby (and by other the like, as between
John Stratford and Edward the Third, etc.) a man may easily
conceive how proud the clergymen have been in former times,
as wholly presuming upon the primacy of their Pope. More matter could I allege of these and the like broils, not to be found
among our common historiographers; howbeit, reserving the
same unto places more convenient, I will cease to speak of them
at this time and go forward with such other things as my purpose
is to speak of.

At the first therefore there was like and equal authority in both
our archbishops; but as he of Canterbury hath long since obtained the prerogative above York (although, I say, not without
great trouble, suit, some bloodshed, and contention), so the Archbishop of York is nevertheless written Primate of England, as
one contenting himself with a piece of a title at the least, when
all could not be gotten. And as he of Canterbury crowneth the
King, so this of York doth the like to the Queen, whose perpetual
chaplain he is and hath been from time to time since the determination of this controversy, as writers do report. The first also
hath under his jurisdiction to the number of one-and-twenty
inferior bishops; the other hath only four, by reason that the
churches of Scotland are now removed from his obedience unto
an archbishop of their own, whereby the greatness and circuit
of the jurisdiction of York is not a little diminished.[16] In like sort,
each of these seven-and-twenty sees have their cathedral
churches, wherein the deans (a calling not known in England
before the Conquest) do bear the chief rule, being men especially chosen to that vocation both for their learning and godli-

---

[15] William the Lion (r. 1165–1214) performed his homage to John at
Lincoln in 1200. Hubert Walter, Archbishop of Canterbury (1193–1205),
acted as mediator in this quarrel between the Cistercians of York and the
King, in reparation for which John founded Beaulieu Abbey. Harrison
found these details and a copy of the charter in Ralph of Coggeshall's
Chronicon Anglicanum (ed. Joseph C. Stevenson, Rolls Ser., LXVI, 1875,
107–110).

[16] In 1472 St. Andrews was raised to metropolitan rank, ending York's
shadowy claims to primacy over Scotland.

ness, so near as can be possible.[17] These cathedral churches have in like manner other dignities and canonries still remaining unto them, as heretofore under the popish regiment. Howbeit, those that are chosen to the same are no idle and unprofitable persons (as in times past they have been, when most of these livings were either furnished with strangers, especially out of Italy, boys, or such idiots as had least skill of all in discharging of those functions whereunto they were called, by virtue of these stipends) but such as by preaching and teaching can and do learnedly set forth the glory of God and further the overthrow of Antichrist to the uttermost of their powers.

These churches are called cathedral because the bishops dwell or lie near unto the same, as bound to keep continual residence within their jurisdictions, for the better oversight and governance of the same, the word being derived *a cathedra*, that is to say, a chair or seat where he resteth and for the most part abideth. At the first there was but one church in every jurisdiction, whereinto no man entered to pray but with some oblation or other toward the maintenance of the pastor. For as it was reputed an infamy to pass by any of them without visitation, so it was a no less reproach to appear empty before the Lord. And for this occasion also they were builded very huge and great, for otherwise they were not capable of such multitudes as came daily unto them to hear the Word and receive the sacraments.

But as the number of Christians increased, so first monasteries, then finally parish churches were builded in every jurisdiction; from whence I take our deanery churches to have their original (now called mother churches and their incumbents archpriests), the rest being added since the Conquest, either by the lords of every town or zealous men loath to travel far and willing to have some ease by building them near-hand. Unto these deanery churches also the clergy in old time of the same deanery were

[17] This sentence and the next are drawn, practically verbatim, from the brief account "how the Church of England is administered and governed" appended to the second, 1564, edition of John Jewel's *Apology of the Church of England* (sigs. Q8r–R2r), translated by Lady Ann Bacon (ed. J. E. Booty, 1963, pp. 139–141). Harrison works other phrases from this account into his description of cathedral sermons on p. 24 and of the functions of archdeacons on p. 25. Since the 1564 edition of the *Apology* was printed by Reginald Wolfe, it is possible that Harrison was the original author of the appendix; see p. 404, n. 9.

appointed to repair at sundry seasons, there to receive wholesome ordinances and to consult upon the necessary affairs of the whole jurisdiction, if necessity so required; and some image hereof is yet to be seen in the north parts. But as the number of churches increased, so the repair of the faithful unto the cathedrals did diminish, whereby they now become, especially in their nether parts, rather markets and shops for merchandise than solemn places of prayer, whereunto they were first erected. Moreover, in the said cathedral churches upon Sundays and festival days the canons do make certain ordinary sermons by course, whereunto great numbers of all estates do orderly resort; and upon the working days, thrice in the week, one of the said canons, or some other in his stead, doth read and expound some piece of Holy Scripture, whereunto the people do very reverently repair.

The bishops themselves in like sort are not idle in their callings, for being now exempt from court and council, which is one (and a no small) piece of their felicity (although Richard, Archbishop of Canterbury, thought otherwise, as yet appeareth by his letters to Pope Alexander, *Epistola 44, Petri Blesensis,* where he saith, because the clergy of his time were somewhat narrowly looked unto, *Supra dorsum ecclesiae fabricant peccatores, etc.*),[18] they so apply their minds to the setting forth of the Word that there are very few of them which do not every Sunday or oftener resort to some place or other within their jurisdictions, where they expound the Scriptures with much gravity and skill, and yet not without the great misliking and contempt of such as hate the Word. Of their manifold translations from one see to another I will say nothing, which is not now done [so much] for the benefit of the flock as the preferment of the party favored and advantage unto the prince, a matter in time past much doubted of, to wit, whether a bishop or pastor might be translated from one see to another, and left undecided, till prescription by royal authority made it good. For among princes a thing

---

[18] "Sinful men build upon the back of the church, [and the effrontery of the layman savagely and intolerably crushes the cleric, unless bishops are members of the household and councils of the king]," Richard of Dover (Archbishop in 1174–1184) to Pope Alexander III (1159–1181). *Petrus Blesensis:* Peter of Blois (fl. 1170–1205), a French scholar who entered the employ of Henry II and became Richard's secretary. The full text of the letter is given in *Epistolae Alexandri III,* ed. J.-P. Migne, *Patrologia Latina,* CC (1855), cols. 1459–1461.

once done is well done and to be done oftentimes, though no warrant be to be found therefor.

They have under them also their archdeacons, some one, divers two, and many four or mo, as their circuits are in quantity, which archdeacons are termed in law "the bishop's eyes"; and these (beside their ordinary courts, which are holden within so many or more of their several deaneries by themselves or their officials once in a month at the least)[19] do keep yearly two visitations or synods (as the bishop doth in every third year, wherein he confirmeth some children, though most care but a little for that ceremony), in which they make diligent inquisition and search, as well for the doctrine and behavior of the ministers as the orderly dealing of the parishioners in resorting to their parish churches and conformity unto religion. They punish also with great severity all such trespassers, either in person or by the purse (where permutation of penance is thought more grievous to the offender), as are presented unto them; or if the cause be of the more weight, as in cases of heresy, pertinacity, contempt, and suchlike, they refer them either to the bishop of the diocese or his chancellor, or else to sundry grave persons set in authority by virtue of an high commission directed unto them from the prince to that end, who in very courteous manner do see the offenders gently reformed, or else severely punished if necessity so enforce.[20]

Beside this, in many of our archdeaconries we have an exercise lately begun, which for the most part is called a prophecy or conference and erected only for the examination or trial of the diligence of the clergy in their study of Holy Scriptures. Howbeit, such is the thirsty desire of the people in these days to hear

[19] Harrison was himself an "official," that is, a judge of the Archdeacon of Colchester's court. The records of his court are preserved in the act books, now in the Essex Records Office at Chelmsford. In the year July, 1569–July, 1570, he convened his court twenty-four times, in his own parish of Radwinter, at the neighboring market town of Saffron Walden, and at Colchester, Kelvedon, and Witham. From 1570 to 1576 he presided only at the sessions in Walden. The archidiaconal courts handled such business as charges of imperfect morals against the villagers, local tax cases, and testamentary affairs. For further details of Harrison's judicial experience see my article in *Studies in the Renaissance*, IX (1962), 265–268.

[20] On September 11, 1578, the Privy Council ordered Harrison and John Lawson, Vicar of Walden, to confer with one "Rooke Grene, gentleman," of Little Sampford near Radwinter, "to bring him to conformity in religion." Grene remained pertinacious and was confined to Colchester Castle.

the Word of God that they also have, as it were, with zealous violence intruded themselves among them (but as hearers only) to come by more knowledge through their presence at the same. Herein also (for the most part) two of the younger sort of ministers do expound, each after other, some piece of the Scriptures ordinarily appointed unto them in their courses (wherein they orderly go through with some one of the Evangelists or of the Epistles, as it pleaseth the whole assembly to choose at the first in every of these conferences); and when they have spent an hour or a little more between them, then cometh one of the better-learned sort, who, being a graduate for the most part or known to be a preacher sufficiently authorized and of a sound judgment, supplieth the room of a moderator, making first a brief rehearsal of their discourses and then adding what him thinketh good of his own knowledge, whereby two hours are thus commonly spent at this most profitable meeting. When all is done, if the first speakers have showed any piece of diligence, they are commended for their travail and encouraged to go forward. If they have been found to be slack or not sound in delivery of their doctrine, their negligence and error is openly reproved before all their brethren, who go aside of purpose from the laity, after the exercise ended, to judge of these matters and consult of the next speakers and quantity of the text to be handled in that place. The laity never speak, of course (except some vain and busy head will now and then intrude themselves with offense), but are only hearers; and as it is used in some places weekly, in other once in fourteen days, in divers monthly, and elsewhere twice in a year, so is it a notable spur unto all the ministers thereby to apply their books, which otherwise (as in times past) would give themselves to hawking, hunting, tables [backgammon], cards, dice, tippling at the alehouse, shooting of matches, and other like vanities, nothing commendable in such as should be godly and zealous stewards of the good gifts of God, faithful distributors of His Word unto the people, and diligent pastors according to their calling.

But alas! as Satan, the author of all mischief, hath in sundry manners heretofore hindered the erection and maintenance of many good things, so in this he hath stirred up adversaries of late unto this most profitable exercise, who, not regarding the commodity that riseth thereby, so well to the hearers as speakers, but either stumbling (I cannot tell how) at words and terms, or at the leastwise not liking to hear of the reprehension of vice, or peradventure taking a misliking at the slender demeanors of such negligent ministers as now and then in their courses do occupy the rooms, have either by their own practice, their sinister information, or suggestions made upon surmises unto other procured the suppression of these conferences, condemning them as hurtful, pernicious, and daily breeders of no small hurt and inconvenience. But hereof let God be judge, unto whom the cause belongeth.[21]

Our elders, or ministers, and deacons (for subdeacons and the other inferior orders sometime used in the popish church we have not) are made according to a certain form of consecration, concluded upon in the time of King Edward the Sixth by the clergy of England and soon after confirmed by the three estates of the realm in the High Court of Parliament. And out of the first sort, that is to say, of such as are called to the ministry (without respect whether they be married or not), are bishops, deans, archdeacons, and such as have the higher places in the hierarchy of the Church elected; and these also, as all the rest, at the first coming unto any spiritual promotion, do yield unto the prince the entire tax of that their living for one whole year, if it amount in value unto £10 and upwards, and this under the name and title of first fruits.

With us also it is permitted that a sufficient man may (by dispensation from the prince) hold two livings, not distant either from other above thirty miles; whereby it cometh to pass that as Her Majesty doth reap some commodity by the faculty [dispensation], so the unition of two in one man doth bring oftentimes more benefit to one of them in a month (I mean for doctrine) than they have had before peradventure in many years.

Many exclaim against such faculties, as if there were mo good preachers that want maintenance than livings to maintain them. Indeed, when a living is void there are so many suitors for it that a man would think the report to be true and most certain; but when it cometh to the trial, who are sufficient and who not, who are staid men in conversation, judgment, and learning, of

---

[21] This paragraph was added in 1587. The prophecies, which flourished in Essex in the 1570's, had powerful lay and episcopal support as a means of improving the quality of the clergy; it was Elizabeth herself who determinedly suppressed them as seminaries of Puritanism.

that great number you shall hardly find one or two such as they ought to be, and yet none more earnest to make suit, to promise largely, bear a better show, or find fault with the state of things than they. Nevertheless, I do not think that their exclamations, if they were wisely handled, are altogether grounded upon rumors or ambitious minds, if you respect the state of the thing itself and not the necessity growing through want of able men to furnish out all the cures in England, which both our universities are never able to perform. For if you observe what numbers of preachers Cambridge and Oxford do yearly send forth, and how many new compositions are made in the Court of First Fruits by the deaths of the last incumbents, you shall soon see a difference. Wherefore if in country towns and cities, yea, even in London itself, four or five of the little churches were brought into one, the inconvenience would in great part be redressed and amended.[22]

And to say truth, one most commonly of these small livings is of so little value that it is not able to maintain a mean scholar, much less a learned man, as not being above £10, £12, £16, £17, £20, or £30 at the most toward their charges, which now (more than beforetime) do go out of the same. I say more than before because every small trifle, nobleman's request, or courtesy craved by the bishop doth impose and command a twentieth part, a threescore part, or twopence in the pound, etc., out of our livings, which hitherto hath not been usually granted but by consent of a synod, wherein things were decided according to equity and the poorer sort considered of, which now are equally burdened.

We pay also the tenths of our livings to the prince yearly, according to such valuation of each of them as hath been lately made, which nevertheless in time past were not annual but voluntary and paid at request of King or Pope. Hereupon also hangeth a pleasant story, though done of late years, to wit, 1452, at which time the clergy, seeing the continual losses that the King of

---

[22] This defense of pluralism was added in 1587, by which time Harrison had benefited considerably by the practice. In addition to his home parish of Radwinter he held the rectory of St. Olave's, Silver Street, London, 1567–1571, the vicarage of Wimbish, a parish adjoining Radwinter, 1571–1581, and the rectory of St. Thomas the Apostle, the parish in London where he had been born, 1583–1587. His London parishes were appreciably farther from Radwinter than the thirty miles technically permitted for pluralities.

England sustained in France, upon some motion of relief made, granted in an open convocation to give him two tenths toward the recovery of Bordeaux, which His Grace very thankfully received.[23] It fortuned also at the same time that Vincent Clement, the Pope's factor, was here in England, who, hearing what the clergy had done, came into the convocation house also in great haste and less speed, where in a solemn oration he earnestly required them to be no less favorable to their spiritual father, the Pope, and mother, the see of Rome, than they had showed themselves unto his vassal and inferior, meaning their sovereign lord in temporal jurisdiction, etc. In delivering also the cause of his suit, he showed how grievously the Pope was disturbed by cutthroats, varlets, and harlots, which do now so abound in Rome that His Holiness is in daily danger to be made away amongst them. To be short, when this fine tale was told, one of the company stood up and said unto him, "My Lord, we have heard your request, and, as we think, it deserveth little consideration and less ear; for how would you have us to contribute to his aid in suppression of such as he, and such as you are, do continual uphold? It is not unknown in this house what rule is kept in Rome."

"I grant," quoth Vincent, "that there wanteth just reformation of many things in that city, which would have been made sooner, but now it is too late; nevertheless, I beseech you to write unto His Holiness with request that he would leave and abandon that Babylon, which is but a sink of mischief, and keep his court elsewhere in place of better fame. And this he shall be the better able also to perform if by your liberality extended towards him, unto whom you are most bound, he be encouraged thereto." Many other words passed to and fro amongst them; howbeit, in the end Vincent overcame not but was dismissed without any penny obtained.

But to return to our tenths, a payment first as devised by the Pope and afterward taken up as by the prescription of the King, whereunto we may join also our first fruits,[24] which is one whole year's commodity of our living, due at our entrance into the same (the tenths abated) unto the prince's coffers, and paid commonly

---

[23] Apparently the convocation at St. Paul's, February 7–March 15, 1453.

[24] Payments to Rome of first fruits, or annates, and tenths of the annual income from benefices were suppressed in 1531 and appropriated to the crown in 1534.

in two years. For the receipt also of these two payments an especial office or court is erected, which beareth name of First Fruits and Tenths, whereunto if the party to be preferred do not make his dutiful repair by an appointed time after possession taken, there to compound for the payment of his said fruits, he incurreth the danger of a great penalty, limited by a certain statute provided in that behalf, against such as do intrude into the ecclesiastical function and refuse to pay the accustomed duties belonging to the same.

They pay likewise subsidies [25] with the temporalty, but in such sort that if these pay after 4s. for land, the clergy contribute commonly after 6s. of the pound, so that of a benefice of £20 by the year the incumbent thinketh himself well acquitted if, all ordinary payments being discharged, he may reserve £13 6s. 8d. towards his own sustentation and maintenance of his family.[26] Seldom also are they without the compass of a subsidy, for if they be one year clear from this payment, a thing not often seen of late years, they are like in the next to hear of another grant; so that I say again, they are seldom without the limit of a subsidy. Herein also they somewhat find themselves grieved, that the laity may at every taxation help themselves, and so they do through consideration had of their decay and hindrance, and yet their impoverishment cannot but touch also the parson or vicar, unto whom such liberty is denied, as is daily to be seen in their accounts and tithings.

Some of them also, after the marriages of their children, will have their proportions qualified, or by friendship get themselves quite out of the book. But what stand I upon these things, who have rather to complain of the injury offered by some of our neighbors of the laity, which daily endeavor to bring us also within the compass of their fifteens or taxes for their own ease, whereas the tax of the whole realm, which is commonly greater in the champaign than woodland soil, amounteth only to £37,930 9½d., [which] is a burden easy enough to be borne upon so many shoulders, without the help of the clergy, whose tenths and subsidies make up commonly a double if not treble sum unto

---

[25] *Subsidies:* extraordinary taxes granted by Parliament to the crown.

[26] Harrison's rectory at Radwinter was valued for first fruits at £21 12s. 1d. In 1577 he also held the vicarage of Wimbish, which was worth an additional £8.

their aforesaid payments. Sometimes also we are threatened with a *melius inquirendum* [sharper investigation], as if our livings were not racked high enough already. But if a man should seek out where all those church lands were which in time past did contribute unto the old sum required or to be made up, no doubt no small number of the laity of all states should be contributors also with us, the prince not defrauded of her expectation and right. We are also charged with armor and munitions from £30 upwards,[27] a thing more needful than divers other charges imposed upon us are convenient; by which and other burdens our case groweth to be more heavy by a great deal (notwithstanding our immunity from temporal services) than that of the laity and, for aught that I see, not likely to be diminished, as if the Church were now become the ass whereon every marketman is to ride and cast his wallet.

The other payments due unto the archbishop and bishop at their several visitations (of which the first is double to the latter), and such also as the archdeacon receiveth at his synods, etc., remain still as they did without any alteration; only this, I think, be added within memory of man, that at the coming of every prince his appointed officers do commonly visit the whole realm under the form of an ecclesiastical inquisition, in which the clergy do usually pay double fees, as unto the archbishop. Hereby, then, and by those already remembered, it is found that the Church of England is no less commodious to the prince's coffers than the state of the laity, if it do not far exceed the same, since their payments are certain, continual, and seldom abated; howsoever, they [the laity] gather up their own duties with grudging, murmuring, suit, and slanderous speeches of the payers, or have their [the clergy's] livings otherwise hardly valued unto the uttermost farthing or shrewdly canceled by the covetousness of the patrons,[28] of whom

[27] That is, clergymen holding benefices valued at £30 or more were required to "provide, have, and maintain armor, and other provision requisite, according to such proportion and rate as the temporalty are bound and charged" (*The Correspondence of Matthew Parker*, ed. John Bruce and T. T. Perowne, Parker Soc., XXXIII, 1853, 346). See p. 217.

[28] "The very cause why weavers, peddlers, and glovers have been made ministers, for the learned refuse such matches, so that if the bishops in times past had not made such [learned men pastors] by oversight and friendship, I wot not how such men should have done with their advowsons, as for [since] a glover or a tailor will be glad of an augmentation of £8 or £10 by the year, and well contented that his patron shall have all the rest, so he may be sure of this pension."—*H.*, 1577 only.

some do bestow advowsons [patronage] of benefices upon their bakers, butlers, cooks, good archers, falconers, and horsekeepers, instead of other recompense for their long and faithful service, which they employ afterward unto their most advantage.

Certes here they resemble the Pope very much, for as he sendeth out his idols, so do they their parasites, pages, chamberlains, stewards, grooms, and lackeys; and yet these be the men that first exclaim of the insufficiency of the ministers, as hoping thereby in due time to get also their glebes and grounds into their hands. In times past bishoprics went almost after the same manner under the lay princes, and then under the Pope, so that he which helped a clerk unto a see was sure to have a present or purse fine, if not an annual pension, besides that which went to the Pope's coffers, and was thought to be very good merchandise. Hereof one example may be touched, as of a thing done in my younger days whilst Queen Mary bare the sway and governed in this land. After the death of Stephen Gardiner the see of Winchester was void for a season, during which time Cardinal Pole made seizure upon the revenues and commodities of the same, pretending authority thereunto, *sede vacante*, by virtue of his place. With this act of his the Bishop of Lincoln (called White) took such displeasure that he stepped in like a mate, with full purpose (as he said) to keep that see from ruin. He wrote also to Paulus, the fourth Pope [of that name], requiring that he might be preferred thereunto, promising, so as he might be *compos voti* [in possession of his desire], to pay to the Pope's coffers £1,600 yearly during his natural life and for one year after. But the Pope, nothing liking of his motion and yet desirous to reap a further benefit, first showed himself to stomach his simoniacal practice very grievously, considering the dangerousness of the time and present estate of the Church of England, which hung as yet in balance, ready to yield any way saving forthright,[29] as he alleged in his letters. By which reply he so terrified the poor Bishop that he was driven unto another issue, I mean, to recover the Pope's good will with a further sum than stood with his ease to part withal. In the end, when the Pope had gotten this fleece, a new device was found and means made to and by the prince that White might be Bishop of Winchester, which at the last he obtained but in such wise as that the Pope

[29] *Forthright:* proceeding in a straight course, predictably.

and his nearest friends did lose but a little by it.[30] I could, if need were, set down a report of divers other the like practices, but this shall suffice instead of all the rest, lest in reprehending of vice I might show myself to be a teacher of ungodliness or to scatter more ungracious seed in lewd ground already choked with wickedness.

To proceed therefore with the rest, I think it good also to remember that the names usually given unto such as feed the flock remain in like sort as in times past, so that these words, parson, vicar, curate, and such are not yet abolished more than the canon law itself, which is daily pleaded as I have said elsewhere, although the statutes of the realm have greatly infringed the large scope and brought the exercise of the same into some narrower limits.

There is nothing read in our churches but the canonical Scriptures, whereby it cometh to pass that the Psalter is said over once in thirty days, the New Testament four times, and the Old Testament once in the year. And hereunto if the curate be adjudged by the bishop or his deputies sufficiently instructed in the Holy Scriptures, and therewithal able to teach, he permitteth him to make some exposition or exhortation in his parish unto amendment of life.[31] And forsomuch as our churches and universities have been so spoiled in time of error as there cannot yet be had such number of able pastors as may suffice for every parish to have one, there are (beside four sermons appointed by public order in the year) certain sermons or homilies (devised by sundry learned men, confirmed for sound doctrine by consent of the divines and public authority of the prince) and those appointed to be read by the curates of mean understanding (which homilies do comprehend the principal parts of Christian doctrine, as of original sin, of justification by faith, of charity, and suchlike) upon the Sabbath days unto the congregation.[32] And after a certain number of Psalms read, which are limited according to the days

[30] John White was translated to Winchester in 1556, after costly and protracted negotiations with Rome. According to Parker (*De antiquitate*, p. 418) he had to pay Cardinal Pole £1000 a year from the income of the see.

[31] Harrison is described as a "preacher" in the Acts of the Privy Council (August 22, 1578).

[32] To this point in the paragraph Harrison borrows freely from the appendix to Jewel's *Apology* (ed. Booty, pp. 140–141; see n. 17).

of the month, for Morning and Evening Prayer we have two lessons, whereof the first is taken out of the Old Testament, the second out of the New; and of these latter, that in the morning is out of the Gospels, the other in the afternoon out of some one of the Epistles. After Morning Prayer also we have the Litany and Suffrages, an invocation in mine opinion not devised without the great assistance of the spirit of God, although many curious, mind-sick persons utterly condemn it as superstitious and savoring of conjuration and sorcery.

This being done, we proceed unto the Communion, if any communicants be to receive the Eucharist; if not, we read the Decalogue, Epistle, and Gospel, with the Nicene Creed (of some in derision called the "dry communion"), and then proceed unto an homily or sermon, which hath a Psalm before and after it, and finally unto the baptism of such infants as on every Sabbath day (if occasion so require) are brought unto the churches; and thus is the forenoon bestowed. In the afternoon likewise we meet again, and after the Psalms and lessons ended we have commonly a sermon or at the leastwise our youth catechized by the space of an hour. And thus do we spend the Sabbath day in good and godly exercises, all done in our vulgar tongue, that each one present may hear and understand the same, which also in cathedral and collegiate churches is so ordered that the Psalms only are sung by note, the rest being read (as in common parish churches) by the minister with a loud voice, saving that in the administration of the Communion the choir singeth the answers, the Creed, and sundry other things appointed, but in so plain, I say, and distinct manner that each one present may understand what they sing, every word having but one note, though the whole harmony consist of many parts, and those very cunningly set by the skillful in that science.

Certes this translation of the service of the church into the vulgar tongue hath not a little offended the Pope almost in every age, as a thing very often attempted by divers princes but never generally obtained, for fear lest the consenting thereunto might breed the overthrow (as it would indeed) of all his religion and hierarchy; nevertheless, in some places where the kings and princes dwelled not under his nose, it was performed mauger his resistance. Vratislav, Duke of Bohemia, would long since have done the like also in his kingdom; but not daring to venture so far without the consent of the Pope, he wrote unto him thereof and received his answer inhibitory unto all his proceeding in the same:

Gregorius Septimus, Vratislao Bohemorum duci, etc. Quia nobilitas tua postulat, quod secundum Sclavonicam linguam apud vos divinum celebrari annueremus officium, scias nos huic petitioni tuae nequaquam posse favere, ex hoc nempe se volventibus liquet, non immerito sacram scripturam optimo Deo placuisse quibusdam locis esse occultam; ne si ad liquidum cunctis pateret, forte vilesceret, et subjaceret despectui, aut prave intellecta a mediocribus in errorem induceret. Neque enim ad excusationem juvat, quod quidam viri hoc, quod simplex populus quaerit patienter tulerunt, seu incorrectum dimiserunt: cum primitiva ecclesia multa dissimulaverit, quae a sanctis patribus postmodum, firmata christianitate et religione crescente, subtili examinatione correcta sunt: unde id ne fiat, quod a vestris imprudenter exposcitur, authoritate beati Petri inhibemus; teque ad honorem optimi Dei huic vanae temeritati viribus totis resistere praecipimus, etc. Datum Romae, etc.[33]

I would set down two or three more of the like instruments passed from that see unto the like end, but this shall suffice, being less common than the other, which are to be had more plentifully.

As for our churches themselves, bells and times of Morning and Evening Prayer remain as in times past, saving that all images, shrines, tabernacles, rood lofts, and monuments of idolatry are removed, taken down, and defaced; only the stories in glass windows excepted, which, for want of sufficient store of new

[33] "Gregory VII to Vratislav, Duke of the Bohemians. Concerning Your Highness' request that we permit the divine service to be celebrated among you in the Slavonic language, know that we absolutely cannot favor this your petition, for this reason: it is clear to thoughtful men that it has quite rightly pleased Almighty God to have sacred Scripture obscure in certain places, lest it be perhaps debased and brought into contempt if it should be openly exposed to all, or lest, wrongly understood by common men, it should lead them into error. Nor can any justification be found in the fact that certain men tolerated this practice patiently or let it go uncorrected because simple people seek it, for the primitive church overlooked many things which afterwards were corrected by the subtle investigations of the holy fathers, as Christianity became strong and religion spread. Thus what you imprudently request must not be. We forbid it by the authority of St. Peter, and we enjoin you to honor Almighty God by resisting this vain rashness with all your might. Given at Rome [January 2, 1080]." This letter, of which Harrison quotes about a quarter, is preserved in the register of Gregory's correspondence (VII, 11). For the full text see *Epistolae Gregorii VII*, ed. Migne, *Patrologia Latina*, CXLVIII (1853), cols. 554–555.

stuff and by reason of extreme charge that should grow by the alteration of the same into white panes throughout the realm, are not altogether abolished in most places at once but by little and little suffered to decay, that white glass may be provided and set up in their rooms. Finally, whereas there was wont to be a great partition between the choir and the body of the church, now it is either very small or none at all and, to say the truth, altogether needless, sith the minister saith his service commonly in the body of the church with his face toward the people, in a little tabernacle of wainscot provided for the purpose; by which means the ignorant do not only learn divers of the Psalms and usual prayers by heart, but also such as can read do pray together with him, so that the whole congregation at one instant pour out their petitions unto the living God for the whole estate of His church in most earnest and fervent manner.

Our holy and festival days are very well reduced also unto a less number; for whereas (not long since) we had under the Pope fourscore-and-fifteen called festival, and thirty *profesti* [feasts not kept as holy days], beside the Sundays, they are all brought unto seven-and-twenty; and with them the superfluous numbers of idle wakes, guilds, fraternities, church-ales, help-ales, and soul-ales, called also dirge-ales, with the heathenish rioting at bride-ales,[34] are well diminished and laid aside. And no great matter were it if the feasts of all our apostles, evangelists, and martyrs, with that of All Saints', were brought to the holy days that follow upon Christmas, Easter, and Whitsuntide, and those of the Virgin Mary with the rest utterly removed from the calendars as neither necessary nor commendable in a reformed church.

The apparel in like sort of our clergymen is comely, and in truth more decent than ever it was in the popish church before the universities bound their graduates unto a stable attire, afterward usurped also even by the blind Sir Johns [ignorant priests]. For if you peruse well my Chronology ensuing, you shall find

---

[34] The suffix "-ale" indicates a rustic feast at which ale was freely imbibed, as at weddings (bride-ales) and funerals (soul-ales, or dirge-ales). At church-ales, usually held on feast days, the proceeds from selling the ale went to the church. Help-ales were celebrations of rural work completed with the help of neighbors. Guilds and fraternities here seem to mean parish organizations, originally religious or economic in purpose, but surviving largely as instruments for conviviality.

that they went either in diverse colors like players, or in garments of light hue, as yellow, red, green, etc., with their shoes piked [with a long peak at the toes], their hair crisped, their girdles armed with silver, their shoes, spurs, bridles, etc., buckled with like metal, their apparel (for the most part) of silk and richly furred, their caps laced and buttoned with gold; so that to meet a priest in those days was to behold a peacock that spreadeth his tail when he danceth before the hen; which now, I say, is well reformed.

Touching hospitality, there was never any greater used in England, sith by reason that marriage is permitted to him that will choose that kind of life, their meat and drink is more orderly and frugally dressed, their furniture of household more convenient and better looked unto, and the poor oftener fed generally than heretofore they have been, when only a few bishops and double- or treble-beneficed men did make good cheer at Christmas only, or otherwise kept great houses for the entertainment of the rich, which did often see and visit them. It is thought much, peradventure, that some bishops, etc., in our time do come short of the ancient gluttony and prodigality of their predecessors; but to such as do consider of the curtailing of their livings, or excessive prices whereunto things are grown, and how their course is limited by law and estate looked into on every side, the cause of their so doing is well enough perceived. This also offendeth many, that they should after their deaths leave their substances to their wives and children; whereas they consider not that in old time such as had no lemans nor bastards (very few were there, God wot, of this sort) did leave their goods and possessions to their brethren and kinfolks, whereby (as I can show by good record) many houses of gentility have grown and been erected. If in any age some one of them did found a college, almshouse, or school, if you look unto these our times you shall see no fewer deeds of charity done, nor better grounded upon the right stub of piety, than before. If you say that their wives be fond [foolish], after the decease of their husbands, and bestow themselves not so advisedly as their calling requireth (which God knoweth these curious surveyors make small account of in truth, further than thereby to gather matter of reprehension), I beseech you then to look into all states of the laity and tell me whether some duchesses, countesses, barons' or knights' wives do not fully so

often offend in the like as they? For Eve will be Eve, though
Adam would say nay.

Not a few also find fault with our threadbare gowns, as if not
our patrons but our wives were causes of our woe. But if it were
known to all that I know to have been performed of late in
Essex—where a minister taking a benefice (of less than £20 in
the Queen's books, so far as I remember) was enforced to pay to
his patron twenty quarters of oats, ten quarters of wheat, and
sixteen yearly of barley, which he called "hawk's meat," and
another let the like in farm to his patron for £10 by the year,
which is well worth forty at the least—the cause of our threadbare gowns would easily appear, for such patrons do scrape the
wool from our cloaks.[35] Wherefore I may well say that such a
threadbare minister is either an ill man, or hath an ill patron, or
both; and when such cooks and cobbling shifters shall be removed
and weeded out of the ministry, I doubt not but our patrons will
prove better men and be reformed whether they will or not, or
else the single-minded bishops shall see the living bestowed upon
such as do deserve it. When the Pragmatic Sanction took place
first in France,[36] it was supposed that these enormities should
utterly have ceased; but when the elections of bishops came once
into the hands of the canons and spiritual men, it grew to be far
worse. For they, also, within a while waxing covetous, by their
own experience learned aforehand, raised the markets and sought
after new gains by the gifts of the greatest livings in that country,
wherein (as Machiavelli writeth) are 18 archbishoprics, 146
bishoprics, 740 abbeys, 11 universities, 1,000,700 steeples (if his
report be sound).[37]

Some are of the opinion that if sufficient men in every town
might be sent for from the universities, this mischief would soon
be remedied, but I am clean of another mind. For when I consider whereunto the gifts of fellowships in some places are grown,
the profit that ariseth at sundry elections of scholars out of grammar schools to the posers [examiners], schoolmasters, and pre-

[35] In *The Description of Britain* (1587, p. 104) Harrison mentions South
Runcton in Norfolk, "which at one time might have been my living if I
would have given Sir Thomas Rugband money enough."

[36] An edict issued in 1438 by Charles VII, limiting papal presentations to
ecclesiastical positions.

[37] In "An Account of the Affairs of France," Machiavelli actually lists
the bishoprics as thirty-six in number.

ferrers of them to our universities,[38] the gifts of a great number of almshouses builded for the maimed and impotent soldiers by princes and good men heretofore moved with a pitiful consideration of the poor distressed, how rewards, pensions, and annuities also do reign in other cases, whereby the giver is brought sometimes into extreme misery, and that not so much as the room of a common soldier is not obtained oftentimes without a "What will you give me?" I am brought into such a mistrust of the sequel of this device that I dare pronounce (almost for certain) that if Homer were now alive, it should be said to him:

> *Tuque licet venias musis comitatus Homere,*
> *Si nihil attuleris, ibis Homere foras.*[39]

More I could say, and more I would say of these and other things, were it not that in mine own judgment I have said enough already for the advertisement of such as be wise. Nevertheless, before I finish this chapter I will add a word or two (so briefly as I can) of the old estate of cathedral churches, which I have collected together here and there among the writers and whereby it shall easily be seen what they were and how near the government of ours do in these days approach unto them; for that there is an irreconcilable odds between them and those of the papists, I hope there is no learned man indeed but will acknowledge and yield unto it.

We find therefore in the time of the primitive church that there was in every see or jurisdiction one school at the least whereinto such as were catechists in Christian religion did resort. And hereof, as we may find great testimony for Alexandria, Antioch, Rome, and Jerusalem, so no small notice is left of the like in the inferior sort, if the names of such as taught in them be called to mind and the histories well read which make report of the same. These schools were under the jurisdiction of the bishops, and from thence did they and the rest of the elders choose out such as were the ripest scholars and willing to serve in the ministry, whom they placed also in their cathedral churches, there not only to be further instructed in the knowledge of the Word, but also to inure them to the delivery of the same unto the people in sound

[38] "Pretty packing!"—*H*. See p. 71.
[39] "Though you come accompanied by all the Muses, Homer, if you bring nothing, off you go!" (Ovid, *Ars amatoria*, II, 279–280).

manner, to minister the sacraments, to visit the sick and brethren imprisoned, and to perform such other duties as then belonged to their charges. The bishop himself and elders of the church were also hearers and examiners of their doctrine, and, being in process of time found meet workmen for the Lord's harvest, they were forthwith sent abroad (after imposition of hands and prayer generally made for their good proceeding) to some place or other then destitute of her pastor and other taken from the school also placed in their rooms. What number of such clerks belonged now and then to some one see the Chronology following shall easily declare; and, in like sort, what officers, widows, and other persons were daily maintained in those seasons by the offerings and oblations of the faithful it is incredible to be reported, if we compare the same with the decays and ablations [removals] seen and practiced at this present. But what is that in all the world which avarice and negligence will not corrupt and impair?

And as this is a pattern of the estate of the cathedral churches in those times, so I wish that the like order of government might once again be restored unto the same, which may be done with ease, sith the schools are already builded in every diocese, the universities [are] places of their preferment unto further knowledge, and the cathedral churches great enough to receive so many as shall come from thence to be instructed unto doctrine. But one hindrance of this is already, and more and more to be looked for (beside the plucking and snatching commonly seen from such houses and the Church), and that is the general contempt of the ministry and small consideration of their former pains taken, whereby less and less hope of competent maintenance by preaching the Word is likely to ensue. Wherefore the greatest part of the more excellent wits choose rather to employ their studies unto physic and the laws, utterly giving over the study of the Scriptures, for fear lest they should in time not get their bread by the same. By this means also the stalls in their choirs would be better filled, which now (for the most part) are empty, and prebends should be prebends indeed,[40] there to live till they

---

[40] Harrison has in mind the ultimate derivation of the word from L. *prae*, "before," and *habere*, "to hold." Curiously, this attack on prebendaries was added in 1587 (compare the praise accorded them in 1577, pp. 22–23), although Harrison had himself recently become a canon of St. George's Chapel at Windsor, by letters patent from the Queen dated April 23, 1586.

were preferred to some ecclesiastical function, and then other men chosen to succeed them in their rooms, whereas now prebends are but superfluous additaments unto former excesses and perpetual commodities unto the owners, which beforetime were but temporal (as I have said before). But as I have good leisure to wish for these things, so it shall be a longer time before it will be brought to pass. Nevertheless, as I will pray for a reformation in this behalf, so will I here conclude this my discourse of the estate of our churches and go in hand with the limits and bounds of our several sees, in such order as they shall come unto my present remembrance.

CHAPTER II

Of the Number of Bishoprics and Their Several Circuits

HAVING already spoken generally of the state of our Church, now will I touch the sees severally, saying so much of each of them as shall be convenient for the time, and not only out of the ancient, but also the later writers, and somewhat of mine own experience, beginning first with the see of Canterbury as the most notable, whose archbishop is the primate of all this land for ecclesiastical jurisdiction and most accounted of commonly, because he is nearer to the prince and ready at every call.

The jurisdiction of Canterbury, therefore, erected first by Augustine the monk [1] in the time of Ethelbert, King of Kent, if

---

Perhaps he was unhappy at the abuses he found current in the chapter at Windsor. In 1590 Sir Christopher Hatton wrote to the dean and canons there, complaining of the neglect of their other benefices and suggesting that they clean their own house, lest he be forced to issue "such other necessary ordinances as shall not peradventure be so well to your liking" (*Visitation Articles*, ed. W. H. Frere, 1910, III, 248–250).

[1] The epithet is contemptuous. Augustine is the villain in Harrison's reading of British ecclesiastical history: "This Augustine, after his arrival, converted the Saxons indeed from paganism, but, as the proverb saith, bringing them out of God's blessing into the warm sun, he also imbued them with no less hurtful superstition than they did know before; for beside the only name of Christ and external contempt of their pristinate idolatry,

you have respect to her provincial regiment, extendeth itself over all the south and west parts of this island, and Ireland, as I have noted in the chapter precedent, and few shires there are wherein the Archbishop hath not some peculiars.[2] But if you regard the same only that was and is proper unto his see from the beginning, it reacheth but over one parcel of Kent, which Rudborne calleth Cantwarland,[3] the jurisdiction of Rochester including the rest; so that in this one county the greatest archbishopric and the least bishopric of all are linked in together. That of Canterbury hath under it one archdeaconry, who hath jurisdiction over 11 deaneries or 161 [261?] parish churches; and in the popish time, instead of the £3,093 18s. ¾d. which it now payeth unto Her Majesty under the name of first fruits, there went out of this see to Rome at every alienation 10,000 ducats or florins, beside 5,000 that the new elect did usually pay for his pall,[4] each ducat being then worth an English crown or thereabout, as I have been informed.[5]

The see of Rochester is also included within the limits of Kent, being erected by Augustine in the 604 of grace and reign of Ceolric[6] over the West Saxons. The bishop of this see hath one archdeacon, under whose government in causes ecclesiastical are

---

he taught them nothing at all but rather (I say) made an exchange from gross to subtle treachery, from open to secret idolatry, and from the name of pagans to the brave title of Christians, thinking this sufficient for their soul's health and the establishment of his monachism, of which kind of profession the Holy Scriptures of God can in no wise like or allow. But what cared he? sith he got the great fish for which he did cast his hook, and so great was the fish that he caught indeed that within the space of 1,000 years and less it devoured the fourth part and more of the best soil of the island, which was wholly bestowed upon his monks and other religious broods that were hatched since his time" (*Des. Brit.*, 1587, p. 27).

[2] *Peculiars:* parishes subject to an ecclesiastical jurisdiction other than that in which they are located.

[3] *Thomas Rudborne* (fl. 1460): monastic chronicler of St. Swithin's, Winchester. Harrison's reference is borrowed from Leland, *Collectanea* (ed. Thomas Hearne, Oxford, 1715, I, 405). In *The Description of Britain* Harrison mentions this compilation of Leland's, "which I have had, written with his own hand" (1587, p. 117).

[4] *Pall:* a woolen vestment conferred on archbishops by the Pope as a symbol and necessary preliminary of their primacy.

[5] The silver ducat was worth about 4s. 6d., the gold florin about 6s. Harrison's figures for the current values of the sees derive from the *Valor Ecclesiasticus*, an official valuation of ecclesiastical revenue made in 1535 and used as the basis for the collection of taxes by the Court of First Fruits and Tenths.

[6] Actually Ceolwulf, who succeeded his brother Ceol, or Ceolric, in 597.

3 deaneries or 132 parish churches; so that hereby it is to be gathered that there are 393 parish churches in Kent, over which the said two archdeacons have especial cure and charge. He was wont to pay also unto the court of Rome at his admission to that see 1,300 ducats or florins, as I read, which was an hard valuation, considering the smallness of circuit belonging to his see. Howbeit, in my time it is so far from ease by diminution that it is raised to 1,432 crowns, etc., or, as we resolve them into our pounds, £358 3s. 6¾d., a reckoning a great deal more precisely made than any bishop of that see doth take any great delight in. He was cross-bearer in times past unto the Archbishop of Canterbury. And there are and have been few sees in England which at one time or other have not fetched their bishops for the most part from this see; for as it is of itself but a small thing indeed, so it is commonly a preparative to an higher place. But of all that ever possessed it, Thomas Kemp had the best luck, who, being but a poor man's son of Wye (unto which town he was a great bene-factor), grew first to be doctor of both laws, then of divinity, and afterward, being promoted to this see, he was translated from thence to Chichester, thirdly to London, next of all to York, and finally, after seven-and-twenty years, to Canterbury, where he became also cardinal-deacon, and then [cardinal-]priest in the court of Rome, according to this verse, *Bis primas, ter praeses, bis cardine functus.*[7] Certes I note this man because he bare some favor to the furtherance of the gospel, and to that end he either builded or repaired the pulpit in Paul's churchyard and took order for the continual maintenance of a sermon there upon the Sabbath, which doth continue unto my time as a place from whence the soundest doctrine is always to be looked for, and for such strangers to resort unto as have no habitation in any parish within the city where it standeth.[8]

The see of London was erected at the first by Lucius, who

---

[7] "Twice he acted as primate, three times as bishop, twice as cardinal." In reality this was John Kemp (?1380–1454), who, in addition to his spec-tacular career in the English hierarchy, was made Cardinal-Priest of St. Balbina in 1439 and Cardinal-Bishop of St. Rufina in 1452. All of Harrison's information here comes from Leland, *Itinerary* (ed. Lucy Toulmin Smith, 5 vols., London, 1906–1910, reprinted Carbondale, Ill., 1964, IV, 37–38).

[8] The benefactor of the famous Paul's Cross sermons preached in London every Sunday was Thomas Kemp, Bishop of London (1450–1489), John's nephew.

made it, of an archflamen and temple of Jupiter, an archbishop's see and temple unto the living God,[9] and so it continued until Augustine translated the title thereof to Canterbury. The names of the Archbishops of London are these: Theon, Elvan, Cadoc, Owen, Conan, Palladius, Stephan, Iltutus *restitutus, anno* 350, Theodromus, Theodredus, Hilarius, Fastidius, *anno* 420, Guittelinus, Vodinus, slain by the Saxons, and Theonus Junior.[10] But for their just order of succession, as yet I am not resolved; nevertheless, the first bishop there was ordained by Augustine the monk in the year of Christ 604, in the time of Ceolric, after he had removed his see further off into Kent, I wot not upon what secret occasion if not the speedy hearing of news from Rome and readiness to flee out of the land if any trouble should betide him. For jurisdiction it includeth Essex, Middlesex, and part of Hertfordshire, which is neither more nor less in quantity than the ancient kingdom of the East Angles before it was united to the West Saxons. The cathedral church belonging to this see was first begun by Ethelbert of Kent, *Indic.* I., 598 of Inuber,[11] as I find, whilst he held that part of the said kingdom under his government. Afterward, when the Danes had sundry times defaced it, it was repaired and made up with hard stone, but in the end it was taken down and wholly re-edified by Maurice, bishop of that see and sometimes chaplain to the Bastard, Henry the First allowing him stone and stuff from Baynard's Castle near unto Ludgate, then ruinous, for the furtherance of his works. Howbeit, the mold of the choir was not stately enough in the eyes of some of his successors; wherefore, in the year of grace 1256, it was taken down and brought into another form, and called the "New Work," at which time also the bodies of divers kings and bishops were taken up and bestowed in the walls, to the end their memories should be of longer continuance.

The jurisdiction of this see also, under the bishop, is committed

---

[9] *Lucius:* a mythical British king, supposedly converted about 170; Geoffrey of Monmouth credits him with establishing the see of London (IV, xix).

[10] Stow gives a similar list, citing Jocelyn of Furness' lost "Book of Bishops" (*Survey of London,* ed. Kingsford, II, 125-126). Harrison repeats his catalogue at the end of the chapter, with Guittelinus omitted and *restitutus* promoted from a participle to a bishop, "who lived 350 of grace."

[11] The indiction, a method of dating much used by papal and imperial notaries, counted from 312 in cycles of fifteen years. The year 598 began a new cycle and was thus *indictione prima. Inuber:* unidentified, perhaps a garble.

to four archdeacons, to wit, of London, Essex, Middlesex, and Colchester, who have amongst them to the number of 363 parish churches or thereabouts, beside the peculiars belonging to the archbishop and chapter of that house; and at every alienation the bishop payeth for his own part £1,119 8*s.* 4*d.* (but in old time 3,000 florins), which divers suppose to be more than (as it now standeth) the bishop is able to make of it. Of the archdeaconry of St. Albans, added thereunto by King Henry the Eighth (whereby the bishop hath five eyes), I speak not, for although it be under the Bishop of London for visitations and synods, yet is it otherwise reputed as member of the see of Lincoln and therefore worthily called an exempt; it hath also 25 parishes, of which 4 are in Buckingham, the rest in Hertfordshire.

The first beginning of the see of Chichester was in the Isle of Seals, or Selsey, and from thence translated to Chichester in the time of William the Bastard and general removing of sees from small villages unto the greater towns. It containeth Sussex only under her jurisdiction, wherein are 16 deaneries and 551 parish churches; it paid at every alienation to the see of Rome 333 ducats; and after Eadbert, the first bishop, one Cella succeeded, after whom the pontifical chair (not then worth £677 by the year, as now it is) was void by many years. It was erected in Selsey also, 711, by the decree of a synod holden in Sussex, which borrowed it from the jurisdiction of Winchester, whereof before it was reputed a parcel. Of all the bishops that have been in this see, Thomas [John] Kemp always excepted, I read not of any one that hath been of more estimation than William Rede, sometime fellow of Merton College in Oxford, Doctor of Divinity, and the most profound astronomer that lived in his time, as appeareth by his collection which sometime I did possess;[12] his image is yet in the library there and many instruments of astronomy reserved in that house (a college erected sometime by Walter Merton, Bishop of Rochester and Lord Chancellor of England); he builded also the castle of Amberley from the very foundation, as Edward Scory, or Story, his successor, did the new cross in the market place of Chichester.

The Bishop of Winchester was sometime called Bishop of the

---

[12] That is, borrow? *William Rede:* Bishop of Chichester in 1368–1385; he built the library of Merton College and bequeathed it many of his scientific MSS.

West Saxons and of Dorchester, which town was given to Birinus and his successors by Cynegils and Oswald of the Northumbers,[13] in whose time it was erected by Birinus and his fellows. In my time it hath jurisdiction only over Hampshire, Surrey, Jersey, Guernsey, and the Wight, containing 8 deaneries, 276 parish churches, and beside all this he is perpetual prelate to the honorable Order of the Garter, devised by Edward the Third; he paid in old time to Rome 12,000 ducats or florins, but now his first fruits are £2,491 9s. 8½d. Canterbury was said to be the higher rack, but Winchester hath borne the name to be the better manger. There are also which make Lucius to be the first founder of an house of prayer in Winchester, as Cynegils did build the second and Cenwalh, his son, the third; but you shall see the truth hereof in the Chronology ensuing. And hereunto, if the old catalogue of the bishops of this see be well considered of, and the acts of the greatest part of them indifferently weighed as they are to be read in our histories, you shall find the most egregious hypocrites, the stoutest warriors, the cruelest tyrants, the richest money-mongers and politic counselors in temporal affairs to have, I wot not by what secret working of the divine providence, been placed here in Winchester since the foundation of that see,[14] which was erected by Birinus, 639 (whom Pope Honorius sent hither out of Italy), and first planted at Dorchester in the time of Cynegils, then translated to Winchester, where it doth yet continue.

Salisbury was made the chief see of Sherborne by Bishop Hermann (predecessor to Osmund), who brought it from Sherborne to that city; it hath now Berkshire, Wiltshire, and Dorsetshire under her jurisdiction. For after the death of Heddi,[15] which was 704, Winchester was divided in two, so that only Hampshire and Surrey were left unto it and Wilton [Wiltshire], Dorset, Berkshire, Somerset, Devon, and Cornwall assigned unto Sherborne, till other order was taken. Bishop Aldhelm did first sit in that bishopric (704, as I said) and placed his chair at Sherborne

[13] St. Oswald, King of Northumbria (633–641) was suzerain of Cynegils, King of the West Saxons (611–643), who was baptized in 635 by Birinus, Bishop of Dorchester (634–?650).

[14] Harrison is remembering such politically-minded incumbents as John de Stratford (1323–1333; see p. 22), William of Wykeham (1367–1404), Henry Beaufort (1404–1447), and, of course, Thomas Wolsey (1529–1530).

[15] *Heddi*: Bishop of Winchester (676–?705).

upon the said division. And as many learned bishops did succeed him in that room, before and after it was removed to Sarum, so there was never a more noble ornament to that see than Bishop Jewel,[16] of whose great learning and judgment the world itself beareth witness, notwithstanding that the papists prefer St. Osmund (as they call him) because he builded the minster there and made the portass [breviary] called *Ordinale ecclesiastici officii,* which old priests were wont to use.[17] The bishops also of this see were sometimes called Bishops of Sonning, of their old mansion house near unto Reading (as it should seem), and, among those that lived before the said Jewel, one Roger builded the castle of the Vies in the time of Henry the First, taken in those days for the strongest hold in England, as unto whose gate there were regals and gripes for six or seven portcullises.[18] Finally, this see paid unto Rome 4,000 florins but unto Her Majesty in my time £1,367 12s. 8d., as I did find of late.

Exeter hath Devonshire and Cornwall, sometime two several bishoprics but in the end brought into one of Cornwall, and from thence to Exeter in the time of the Bastard or soon after. It began upon this occasion, *anno gratiae* 905, in a provincial council holden by the elder Edward and Plegmund, Archbishop of Canterbury, among the Gewissas, wherein it was found that the see of Winchester had not only been without her pastor by the space of seven years, but also that her jurisdiction was far greater than two men were able well to govern; therefore from the former two, to wit, Winchester and Sherborne, three other were taken, whereby that see was now divided into five parts, the latter three being Wells, Crediton, and Cornwall; this of Cornwall having her see then at St. Patroks, not far from North Wales, upon the River Helmouth,[19] he of Devon holding his

[16]*John Jewel:* Bishop of Salisbury (1560–1571); see p. 416.

[17] The Sarum use, most influential of the diocesan ritual orders.

[18] *Regals:* grooves; *gripes:* devices to secure portcullises. This was Devizes Castle, built by Roger le Poer, Bishop of Salisbury in 1107–1139. The details are from Leland, *Itinerary* (V, 82).

[19] *St. Patroks:* Bodmin, from St. Petrock's Church there. The odd geographical placement is simply Harrison's translation of Matthew Westminster's *apud Sanctum Petrocum juxta Walenses aquilonales super flumen Heilmuthe* (*Flores Historiarum,* under A.D. 905). Most of Harrison's details about Saxon bishops seem to be drawn from this composite chronicle (ed. John Stow, 1567, 1570), which is little more than a transcription of Matthew Paris to 1066. Harrison's copy of the *Flores Historiarum* is extant in the diocesan library at Londonderry.

jurisdiction in Devonshire, Crediton, or Cridioc, and the Bishop of Wells being allowed Dorset- and Berkshires for his part, to govern and look unto according to his charge. Finally, these two of Devon and Cornwall being united, the valuation thereof was taxed by the see of Rome at 6,000 ducats or florins, which were truly paid at every alienation, but very hardly (as I guess), sith that in my time, wherein all things are racked to the very uttermost, I find that it is little worth above £500 by the year, because her tenths are but £50.

Bath, whose see was sometime at Wells before John, the bishop there, annexed the church of Bath unto it, which was 1094, hath Somersetshire only, and the valuation thereof in the court of Rome was 430 florins; but in Her Majesty's books I find it £533 and about one odd shilling, which declareth a precise examination of the estate of that see. Of the erection of this bishopric mentioned in the discourse of Exeter, I find the former assertion confirmed by another author and in somewhat more large manner, which I will also remember, only because it pleaseth me somewhat better than the words before alleged out of the former writer. This bishopric (saith he) was erected 905, in a council holden among the Gewissas, whereat King Edward of the West Saxons and Plegmund, Archbishop of Canterbury, were present. For that part of the country had been seven years without any pastoral cure. And therefore in this council it was agreed that for the two bishoprics (whereof one was at Winchester, another at Sherborne) there should be five ordained, whereby the people there might be the better instructed. By this means Frithustan was placed at Winchester and Ethelme at Sherborne, both of them being then void. Sherborne also sustained the subdivision, so that Werstane was made Bishop of Cridioc, or Devonshire (whose see was at Crediton), Herstan of Cornwall, and Eadulfe of Wells, unto whom Berkshire and Dorsetshire were appointed.[20] But now you see what alteration is made, by consideration of the limits of their present jurisdictions.

Worcester, sometime called *episcopatus Wicciorum* (that is, the bishopric of the Wiccies or Hwiccas) hath Worcester- and part of Warwickshires. And before the bishopric of Gloucester was taken out of the same, it paid to the Pope 2,000 ducats of gold

[20] This version of the creation of the new sees is in Matthew Westminster, under 905. The details are somewhat garbled in the chronicle.

at every change of prelate; but now the valuation thereof is £1,049 7¾d. (except my remembrance do deceive me). This see was begun either in, or not long before, the time of Offa, King of the East Angles, and Bosel was the first bishop there; after whom succeeded Oftfor, then Egwine, who went in pilgrimage to Rome with Coenred of Mercia and the said Offa, and there gat a monastery (which he builded in Worcester) confirmed by Constantine, the Pope. In this see was one of Your Lordship's ancestors sometime bishop, whose name was Cobham, and doctor both of divinity and of the canon law, who, during the time of his pontificality there, builded the vault of the north side of the body of the church and there lieth buried in the same (as I have been informed). Certes this man was once elected and should have been Archbishop of Canterbury in the room of Reginald, that died 1313, under Edward the Second; but the Pope frustrated his election, fearing lest he would have showed himself more affectionate towards his prince than to his court of Rome; wherefore he gave Canterbury to the Bishop of Worcester then being. And furthermore, lest he should seem altogether to reject the said Thomas and displease the King, he gave him in the end the bishopric of Worcester, whereinto he entered 1317, *Martii* 31, being Thursday (as appeareth by the register of that house),[21] after long plea holden for the aforesaid see of Canterbury in the court of Rome, wherein most money did oftenest prevail. This is also notable of that see, that five Italians succeeded each other in the same, by the Pope's provision: as Egidius, Sylvester, Egidius his nephew (for nephews might say in those days, "Father, shall I call you uncle?" and uncles also, "Son, I must call thee nephew"), Julius de' Medici, afterward Pope Clement, and Hieronymus de Nugutiis;[22] men very likely, no doubt, to benefit the common people by their doctrine. Some of these, being at the first but poor men in Rome and yet able by selling all they had to make a round sum against a rainy day, came first into favor with the Pope, then into familiarity, finally into orders, and

[21] Thomas Cobham held the see of Worcester in 1317–1327. Robert (not Reginald) de Winchelsea, Archbishop of Canterbury in 1294–1313, was succeeded by Walter Reynolds, translated from Worcester in 1313.

[22] Giovanni Gigli (1497–1498), his nephew, Silvestro Gigli (1498–1521; Harrison here seems to have misread an entry "Sylvester Egidius" as two men), Giulio de' Medici (1521–1522, Pope Clement VII, 1523–1534), and Geronimo Ghinucci (1522–1534).

from thence into the best livings of the church, far off where their parentage could not easily be heard of nor made known unto their neighbors.

Gloucester hath Gloucestershire only, wherein are 9 deaneries and to the number of 294 parish churches, as I find by good record. But it never paid anything to Rome—because it was erected by King Henry the Eighth, after he had abolished the usurped authority of the Pope—except in Queen Mary's, if any such thing were demanded, as I doubt not but it was; yet is it worth yearly £315 7s. 3d., as the book of first fruits declareth.

Hereford hath Herefordshire and part of Shropshire, and it paid to Rome at every alienation 1,800 ducats at the least; but in my time it payeth unto Her Majesty's coffers £768 10s. 10¾d. In this see there was a bishop sometime called John Breton, upon whom the King then reigning, by likelihood for want of competent maintenance, bestowed the keeping of his wardrobe, which he held long time with great honor, as his register saith. A wonderful preferment, that bishops should be preferred from the pulpit to the custody of wardrobes! But such was the time. Nevertheless, his honorable custody of that charge is more solemnly remembered than any good sermon that ever he made,[23] which function peradventure he committed to his suffragan, sith bishops in those days had so much business in the court that they could not attend to doctrine and exhortation.

Lichfield, whereunto Coventry was added in the time of Henry the First, at the earnest suit of Robert [de Limesey], bishop of that see, hath Staffordshire, Derbyshire, part of Shropshire, and the rest of Warwickshire that is void of subjection to the see of Worcestershire. It was erected in the time of Peada, King of the South Mercians, which lay on this side the Trent, and therein one Dinas [Diuma] was installed about the year of grace 656, after whom Kellach [Ceollach], then Tunher [Trumhere], an Englishman, succeeded, this latter being well learned and consecrated by the Scots. In the time of the Bastard, I wot not upon what occasion, one Peter, bishop of this see, translated his chair to Chester and there held it for a season, whereby it came to pass that the Bishops of Lichfield were for a while called Bishops of

---

[23] Breton was Bishop of Hereford in 1269–1275; he is described by Leland as *custos Garderobe domini regis*, from an inscription in the nave of his cathedral (*Itinerary*, V, 183).

Chester. But Robert, his successor, not liking of this precedent, removed his chair from Chester to Coventry and there held it whilst he lived, whereby the original division of the bishopric of Lichfield into Lichfield, Chester, and Coventry doth easily appear, although in my time Lichfield and Coventry be united and Chester remaineth a bishopric by itself. It paid the Pope at every alienation 1,733 florins, or (as some old books have) 3,000, a good round sum, but not without a just punishment, as one saith, sith that *anno* 765, Aldulf, bishop there under Offa, King of Mercia, would by his help have bereaved the Archbishop of Canterbury of his pall, and so did indeed under Pope Adrian, holding the same until things were reduced unto their ancient form.[24] Before the time also of Bishop Langton the prebends of this see lay here and there abroad in the city, where the vicars also had an house, of which this honest bishop misliked not a little for sundry causes; wherefore he began their close and bestowed so much in building the same and paving the streets that his hungry kinsmen did not a little grudge at his expenses, thinking that his empty coffers would never make them gentlemen, for which preferment the friends of most bishops gaped earnestly in those days. King John was the greatest benefactor unto this see, next unto Offa; and it is called Lichfield, *quasi mortuorum campus*, [that is, the field of corpses], because of the great slaughter of Christians made there (as some write) under Diocletian.[25] Howbeit, in my time the valuation thereof is £703 5s. 2¾d., a sum very narrowly cast by that auditor which took it first in hand.

Oxford hath Oxfordshire only, a very young jurisdiction erected by King Henry the Eighth and where in the time of Queen Mary one Goldwell was bishop, who (as I remember) was a Jesuit, dwelling in Rome and more conversant (as the constant fame went) in the black art than skillful in the Scriptures, and yet he was of great countenance amongst the Roman monarchs. It is said that, observing the canons of his order, he regarded not the temporalities of that see; but I have heard since that he wist well enough what became of those commodities, for by one mean and other he found the sweetness of £354 16s. 3½d. yearly

[24] Actually it was Higbert, predecessor to Aldulf, who received the pall at Lichfield in 787, but Harrison is here following Matthew Westminster (under 765–766).
[25] Leland, *Itinerary* (II, 159).

growing to him, which was even enough (if not too much) for the maintenance of a friar toward the drawing-out of circles, characters, and lineaments of imagery, wherein he was passing skillful, as the fame then went in Rome and not unheard of in Oxford.[26]

Ely hath Cambridgeshire and the Isle of Ely. It was erected, 1109, by Henry the First, being before a rich and wealthy abbey. One Hervey also was made bishop there, as I have found in a register belonging sometime to that house, being translated from Bangor. Finally, it paid to the Pope at every alienation 7,000 ducats, as the registers there do testify at large. Albeit that in my time I find a note of £2,134 16s. 3¾d., whose dime, joined to those of all the bishoprics in England, do yield yearly to Her Majesty's coffers £23,370 16s. 3¾d.,[27] whereby also the huge sums of money going out of this land to the court of Rome doth in some measure appear. Ethelwold, afterward Bishop of Winchester, builded the first monastery of Ely upon the ruins of a nunnery then in the King's hands; howbeit, the same house, whereof he himself was abbot, was ere long destroyed by enemies and he, in lieu of his old preferment, rewarded by King Edgar with the aforesaid bishopric, from whence with more than lion-like boldness he expelled the secular priests and stored with monks provided from Abingdon near Oxford, by the help of Edgar and Dunstan, then metropolitan of England.[28]

There was sometime a grievous contention between Thomas Lisle, bishop of this see, and the King of England, about the year of grace 1355, which I will here deliver out of an old record, because the matter is so partially penned by some of the brethren of that house in favor of the Bishop, and for that I was also abused with the same in the entrance thereof at the first into my Chronology. The Black Prince favoring one Robert Stretton, his chap-

---

[26] *Thomas Goldwell* (d. 1585): a member of the Theatine Order, Bishop of St. Asaph in 1555. He was translated to Oxford in 1558, but Mary's death prevented his consecration. Fleeing to the Continent in 1559, he remained active in plans to reclaim England for Rome. As the last survivor of the Marian episcopacy, he was the object of much scurrilous propaganda.

[27] This figure seems to represent an approximate total for first fruits; the annual payment of tenths would in fact have been one-tenth of Harrison's total.

[28] *St. Ethelwold* (d. 984): Abbot of Abingdon, not Ely. As Bishop of Winchester he rebuilt the monasteries at Ely and Peterborough, which had been ruined by Danish attacks.

lain, a man unlearned and not worthy the name of a clerk, the matter went on so far that, what for love and somewhat else of a canon of Lichfield, he was chosen bishop of that see. Hereupon the Pope, understanding what he was by his nuncio here in England, stayed his consecration by his letters for a time and in the mean season committed his examination to the Archbishop of Canterbury and the Bishop of Rochester, who felt and dealt so favorably with him in golden reasoning that his worthiness was commended to the Pope's Holiness, and to Rome he goeth. Being come to Rome, the Pope himself apposed [examined] him and after secret conference utterly disableth his election till he had proved by substantial argument and of great weight before him also that he was not so lightly to be rejected. Which kind of reasoning so well pleased His Holiness that, *ex mera plenitudine potestatis* [solely from the fullness of his power], he was made capable of the benefice and so returned into England;[29] when he came home, this bishop [i.e., Thomas Lisle], being in the King's presence, told him how he had done he wist not what in preferring so unmeet a man unto so high a calling. With which speech the King was so offended that he commanded him out of hand to avoid out of his presence. In like sort the Lady Wake, then Duchess of Lancaster, standing by and hearing the King, her cousin, to gather up the Bishop so roundly, and thereto [having] an old grudge against him for some other matter, doth presently pick a quarrel against him about certain lands then in his possession, which he defended and in the end obtained against her by plea and course of law; ere long also a fire happened in a part of her house, for which she accused the Bishop and in the end, by verdict of twelve men, found that he was privy unto the fact of his men in the said fact, wherefore he was condemned in £900 damages, which he paid, every penny.

Nevertheless, being sore grieved that she had (as he said) wrested out such a verdict against him and therein packed up a quest [jury] at her own choice, he taketh his horse, goeth to the court, and there complaineth to the King of his great injury received at her hands. But in the delivery of his tale his speech was so blockish and terms so evil-favoredly (though maliciously)

[29] *Robert de Stretton* (d. 1385): although virtually illiterate, he was, at royal insistence over the protests of both the Pope and the English hierarchy, finally consecrated Bishop of Lichfield and Coventry in 1359.

placed that the King took yet more offense with him than before, insomuch that he led him with him into the Parliament House, for then was that court holden, and there before the lords accused him of no small misdemeanor toward his person by his rude and threatening speeches. But the Bishop eagerly denieth the King's objections, which he still avoucheth upon his honor and in the end confirmeth his allegations by witness; whereupon he is banished from the King's presence during his natural life by verdict of that house. In the meantime the Duchess hearing what was done, she beginneth anew to be dealing with him, and in a brabbling fray between their servants one of her men was slain, for which he was called before the magistrate as chief accessory unto the fact. But he, fearing the sequel of his third cause by his success had in the two first, hideth himself, after he had sold all his movables and committed the money unto his trusty friends. And being found guilty by the inquest, the King seizeth upon his possessions and calleth up the Bishop to answer unto the trespass. To be short, upon safe-conduct the Bishop cometh to the King's presence, where he denieth that he was accessory to the fact, either before, at, or after the deed committed, and thereupon craveth to be tried by his peers. But this petition was in vain, for sentence passeth against him also by the King's own mouth. Whereupon he craveth help of the Archbishop of Canterbury and privileges of the church, hoping by such means to be solemnly rescued. But they, fearing the King's displeasure, who bare small favor to the clergy of his time, gave over to use any such means but rather willed him to submit himself unto the King's mercy, which he refused, standing upon his innocency from the first unto the last. Finally, growing into choler that the malice of a woman should so prevail against him, he writeth to Rome, requiring that his case might be heard there, as a place wherein greater justice (saith he) is to be looked for than to be found in England. Upon the perusal of these his letters also, his accusers were called thither. But, forsomuch as they appeared not at their peremptory times, they were excommunicated. Such of them also as died before their reconciliations were taken out of the churchyards and buried in the fields and dunghills, *unde timor et turba* (saith my note) *in Anglia* [which caused fear and turmoil in England]. For the King inhibited the bringing-in and receipt of all processes, bills, and whatsoever instruments should

come from Rome; such also as adventured, contrary to this prohibition, to bring them in were either dismembered of some
joint or hanged by the necks. Which rage so incensed the Pope
that he wrote in very vehement manner to the King of England,
threatening far greater curses except he did the sooner stay the
fury of the lady, reconcile himself unto the Bishop, and finally,
making him amends for all his losses sustained in these broils.
Long it was ere the King would be brought to peace. Nevertheless, in the end he wrote to Rome about a reconciliation to be had
between them; but ere all things were concluded, God Himself
did end the quarrel by taking away the Bishop. And thus much
out of an old pamphlet, in effect word for word; but I have
somewhat framed the form of the report after the order that
Stephen Birchington doth deliver it, who also hath the same in
manner as I deliver it.[30]

The see of Norwich, called in old time *episcopatus Donnicensis,
Dononiae,* or *Eastanglorum,* was erected at Felstow, or Felixstowe,
where Felix of Burgundy (sometime schoolmaster to Sigebert of
the East Angles, by whose persuasion also the said Sigebert
erected the university at Cambridge), being made Bishop of the
East Angles, first placed his see; afterward it was removed from
thence to Dunwich, and thence to Elmham, *anno* 870, about the
death of Ceolnoth of Canterbury; thirdly, to Theodford, or Thetford; and finally, after the time of the Bastard, to Norwich. For
jurisdiction it containeth in our days Norfolk and Suffolk only,
whereas at the first it included Cambridgeshire also and so much
as lay within the kingdom of the East Angles. It began about the
year 632, under Eorpwald, King of the East Saxons, who bestowed it upon Felix, whom Pope Honorius also confirmed, and
after which he held it by the space of seventeen years. It paid
sometimes at every alienation 5,000 ducats to Rome. But in my
time Her Majesty hath £899 8s. 7¼d., as I have been informed.
In the same jurisdiction also there were once 1,563 parish churches
and 88 religious houses, but in our days I cannot hear of more
churches than 1,200; and yet of these I know one converted into a

[30] *Thomas Lisle:* Bishop of Ely in 1345–1361; *Lady Wake* (d. 1380):
Blanche, daughter of Henry of Lancaster. Most of Harrison's details here
seem to derive from the account in Matthew Parker, *De antiquitate Britannicae ecclesiae* (1572), pp. 270–273. Parker cites as his source a *Catalogus
episcoporum Eliensium* by Stephen Birchington (fl. 1382), a monk of Christ
Church, Canterbury.

barn, whilst the people hear service further off upon a green; their bell also, when I heard a sermon there preached in the green, hanged in an oak for want of a steeple. But now I understand that the oak likewise is gone. There is, nevertheless, a little chapelet hard by on that common, but nothing capable of the multitude of Ashley Town [31] that should come to the same in such wise, if they did repair thither as they ought.

Peterborough, sometimes a notable monastery, hath Northampton- and Rutlandshires under her jurisdiction, a diocese erected also by King Henry the Eighth. It never paid first fruits to the Pope before Queen Mary's days (if it were then delivered, whereof I doubt), because it was not recorded in his ancient register of tenths and fruits, although peradventure the collectors left it not ungathered, I wot not for what purpose; it yieldeth now £450, one penny abated. I have seen and had an ancient terrier of the lands of this monastery, which agreeth very well with the history of Hugo le Blanc, monk of that house. In the charter also of donation annexed to the same, I saw one of Wulfhere, King of Mercia, signed with his own and the marks of Sigheri, King of Sussex, Sebbi of Essex, with the additions of their names; the rest of the witnesses also ensued in this order:

> Ethelred, brother to Wulfhere,
> Cyniburg and Cyneswith, sisters to Wulfhere,
> Deusdedit, Archbishop,
> Ithamar, Bishop of Rochester,
> Wini, Bishop of London,
> Jaruman, Bishop of Mearc [Mercia],
> Wilfrid and Eoppa, priests,
> Saxulf, the abbot. [32]

Then all the earls and ealdermen of England in order; and, after all these, the name of Pope Agatho, who confirmed the instrument at the suit of Wilfrid, Archbishop of York, in a council holden at Rome, 680, of 125 bishops, wherein also these churches were appropriated to the said monastery, to wit, Breding,

---

[31] Ashley-cum-Silverley, on the eastern border of Cambridgeshire, near Newmarket.

[32] *Hugo le Blanc:* Hugh Albus, or Candidus (d. ?1175), Peterborough chronicler; see *The Chronicle of Hugh Candidus*, ed. W. T. Mellows (Peterborough, 1949), p. 13. All of Harrison's citations from Hugh here and elsewhere are drawn from the excerpts made by Leland, *Collectanea* (1715, I, 2-18).

Reping, Cedenac, Swinesheved, Lusgerd, Edelminglond, and Barchaing,[33] whereby we have in part an evident testimony how long the practice of appropriation of benefices hath been used, to the hindrance of the gospel and maintenance of idle monks, an human invention grounded upon hypocrisy.

Bristol hath Dorsetshire, sometime belonging to Salisbury, a see also lately erected by King Henry the Eighth, who took no small care for the Church of Christ and therefore eased a number of ancient sees of some part of their huge and overlarge circuits and bestowed those portions deducted upon such other erections as he had appointed for the better regiment and feeding of the flock; the value thereof is £383 8s. 4d. (as I have been informed).

Lincoln of all other of late times was the greatest; and albeit that out of it were taken the sees of Oxford and Peterborough, yet it still retaineth Lincoln-, Leicester-, Huntingdon-, Bedford-, Buckinghamshires, and the rest of Hertford, so that it extendeth from the Thames unto the Humber, and paid unto the Pope 5,000 ducats (as appeareth by his note) at every alienation. In my time, and by reason of her diminution, it yieldeth a tribute to whom tribute belongeth of the valuation of £899 8s. 7¼d. It began since the Conquest, about the beginning of William Rufus, by one Remigius, who removed his see from Dorchester to Lincoln[34] (not without license well paid for unto the King). And thus much of the bishoprics which lie within Loegria, or England, as it was left unto Locrine. Now it followeth that I proceed with Wales.

Llandaff, or the church of Taff, hath ecclesiastical jurisdiction in Glamorgan-, Monmouth-, Brecknock-, and Radnorshires. And although it paid 700 ducats at every exchange of prelate, yet is it scarcely worth £155 by the year (as I have heard reported). Certes it is a poor bishopric, and (as I have heard) the late incumbent thereof, being called for not long since by the lord president, in open court made answer, "The daff is here, but the land is gone." [35] What he meant by it I cannot well tell, but I hope

---

[33] Hugh's *Chronicle* (p. 20). I have not attempted to modernize these place names, some of which remain unidentified.

[34] "As Matthew Westminster doth report [under 1088]."—*H.*, 1577 only.

[35] *Daff:* a simpleton or coward. The reference is either to Anthony Kitchin, a kind of episcopal Vicar of Bray, who managed to hold the see from 1545 to 1566, plundering it in the process, or to his impoverished successor, Hugh Jones (1567–1574).

that in the seedtime and the free planting of the gospel the meat of the laborer shall not be diminished and withdrawn.

St. David's hath Pembroke- and Carmarthenshires, whose livery or first fruits to the see of Rome was 1,500 ducats at the hardest (as I think). For if record be of any sufficient credit, it is little above the value of £457 1s. 10¼d. in our time, and so it payeth unto Her Majesty's coffers; but in time past I think it was far better. The present Bishop misliketh very much of the cold situation of his cathedral church, and therefore he would gladly pull it down and set it in a warmer place, but it would first be learned what surety he would put in to see it well performed; of the rest I speak not.[36]

Bangor is in North Wales and hath Caernarvon-, Anglesey, and Merionethshires under her jurisdiction. It paid to Rome 126 ducats, which is very much. For of all the bishoprics in England it is now the least for revenues and not worth above £131 16d. to Her Majesty's coffers at every alienation (as appeareth by the tenths, which amount to much less than those of some good benefice, for it yieldeth not yearly above £13 3s. 7½d., as by that Court is manifest).

St. Asaph hath Prestholm[37] and part of Denbigh- and Flint-shires under her jurisdiction in causes ecclesiastical, which being laid together do amount to little more than one good county and therefore, in respect of circuit, the least that is to be found in Wales; nevertheless, it paid to Rome 470 ducats at every alienation. In my time the first fruits of this bishopric came unto £187 11s. 6d., whereby it seemeth to be somewhat better than Llandaff or Bangor last remembered. There is one Howel, a gentleman of Flintshire in the compass of this jurisdiction, who is bound to give an harp of silver yearly to the best harper in Wales; but did any bishop, think you, deserve that in the popish time? Howel or ap Howel in English is all one (as I have heard) and signify so much as Hugo, or Hugh.[38]

[36] This sentence was added in 1587. Marmaduke Middleton was consecrated Bishop of St. David's in 1582 and deprived in 1590 for simony and attachment of episcopal lands.

[37] *Prestholm:* Priestholm, Puffin Island, near Anglesey.

[38] Leland, *Itinerary* (III, 92–93). Harrison seems to pun on "harper" (that is, harpy) in the sense of "a rapacious person," apparently in sardonic reference to the depredations of William Hughes, the contemporary Bishop of St. Asaph (1573–1600), who was also noted for his encouragement of the bards.

Hitherto of the province of Canterbury, for so much thereof as now lieth within the compass of this island. Now it resteth that I proceed with the curtailed archbishopric of York; I say "curtailed," because all Scotland is cut from his jurisdiction and obedience.

The see of York was restored about the year of grace 625, which after the coming of the Saxons lay desolate and neglected; howbeit, at the said time Justus, Archbishop of Canterbury, ordained Paulinus to be first bishop there, in the time of Edwin, King of Northumberland. This Paulinus sat six years ere he was driven from thence, and after whose expulsion that seat was void long time, whereby Lindisfarne grew into credit and so remained until the days of Oswy of Northumberland, who sent Wilfrid the priest over into France, there to be consecrated Archbishop of York; but whilst he tarried overlong in those parts, Oswy, impatient of delay, preferred Ceadda, or Chad, to that room, who held it three years, which being expired, Wilfrid recovered his room and held it as he might until it was severed in two, to wit, York [and] Halgulstad [Hexham], or Lindisfarne, where Eata was placed, at which time also Egfrid was made Bishop of Lincoln, or Lindsey, in that part of Mercia which he had gotten from Wulfhere.[39] Of itself it hath now jurisdiction over Yorkshire, Nottinghamshire (whose shire town—I mean the new part thereof with the bridge—was builded by King Edward the First, surnamed "the Elder," before the Conquest), and the rest of Lancashire only not subject to the see of Chester; and when the Pope bare authority in this realm, it paid unto his see 1,000 ducats, beside 5,000 for the pall of the new elect, which was more than he could well spare of late, considering the curtailing and diminution of his see through the erection of a new metropolitan in Scotland; but in my time it yieldeth £1,609 19*s*. 2*d*. to Her Majesty, whom God long preserve unto us to His glory, her comfort, and our welfares.

Chester-upon-Dee, otherwise called West Chester, hath under her jurisdiction in causes ecclesiastical Cheshire, Derbyshire, the most part of Lancashire (to wit, unto the Ribble), Richmond, and a part of Flint- and Denbighshires in Wales. It was made a

---

[39] Harrison here seems to be misreading Bede (IV, xii), who says that Edhed was ordained Bishop of Lindsey, which King Egfrid had recently won from Wulfhere. He corrects the details on p. 63.

bishopric by King Henry the Eighth, *anno regni* 33, *Julii* 16, and so hath continued since that time, being valued [at] £420 by the year beside odd 20*d*. (a strait [exact] reckoning), as the record declareth.

Durham hath the county of Durham and Northumberland with the Dales only under her jurisdiction, and hereof the bishops have sometimes been earls palatine and ruled the roast under the name of the bishopric and succession of St. Cuthbert. It was a see (in mine opinion) more profitable of late unto Her Majesty's coffers by £221 18*s*. 10¼*d*.,[40] and yet of less countenance than her provincial; nevertheless, the sunshine thereof (as I hear) is now somewhat eclipsed and not likely to recover the light, for this is not a time wherein the church may look to increase in her estate. I hear also that some other flitches have forgone the like collops, but let such matters be scanned by men of more discretion. Capgrave saith how that the first bishop of this see was called Bishop of Lindsey (or Lincoln) and that Ceadda lay in Lichfield of the Mercians, in a mansion house near the church.[41] But this is more worthy to be remembered, that Guthred of the Northumbers and Alfred of the West Saxons bestowed all the land between the Tees and the Tyne now called the bishopric upon St. Cuthbert,[42] beside whatsoever belonged to the see of Hagulstad. Edgar of Scotland also, in the time of the Bastard, gave Coldingham and Berwick, with all their appurtenances, to that house, but whether these donations be extant or no as yet, I cannot tell. Yet I think not but that Leland had a sight of them, from whom I had this ground.[43] But whatsoever this bishopric be now in external and outward appearance, sure it is that it paid in old time 9,000 ducats at every alienation to Rome, as the record expresseth. Aidan, a Scot or Irishman, was the first bishop of this see, who held himself (as did many of his successors) at Colchester [44] and in Lindisfarne Isle, till one came that removed it to Durham. And now judge

[40] That is, tenths, not first fruits.

[41] *John Capgrave* (1393–1464): Augustinian friar at Lynn, hagiographer and chronicler; the citation is to his life of Ceadda in *Nova legenda Anglie* (printed by Wynkyn de Worde, 1516; ed. Carl Horstman, Oxford, 1901, I, 186).

[42] Not in person. The bishopric and St. Cuthbert's body were removed from Lindisfarne to Chester-le-Street near Durham in 883 (Matthew Westminster, under 882).

[43] *Itinerary* (II, 148).

[44] *Colchester*: apparently in error for Chester-le-Street.

you whether the allegation of Capgrave be of any account or not.

Carlisle was erected 1132 by Henry the First, and hereof one Ethelwulf, confessor to Osmund, Bishop of Sarum, was made the first bishop, having Cumberland and Westmorland assigned to his share; of the deaneries and number of parish churches contained in the same as yet I have no knowledge, more than of many other. Howbeit, hereof I am sure, that notwithstanding the present valuation be risen to £531 14s. 11½d., the Pope received out of it but 1,000 florins, albeit that it might have spared much more, as an adversary thereto confessed sometime even before the Pope himself, supposing no less than to have gained by his tale, and so peradventure should have done if his platform had taken place. But as wise men oft espy the practices of flatteries, so the Pope saw to what end this profitable speech was uttered. As touching Carlisle itself, it was sometime sacked by the Danes and eftsoons repaired by William Rufus and planted with a colony of southern men. I suppose that in old time it was called Caerdoill. For in an ancient book which I have seen and yet have, entitled *Liber formularum literarum curiae Romanae, octo capitulorum*, [it appears as] *episcopatus Cardocensis*. And thus much generally of the names and numbers of our bishoprics of England, whose tenths, in old time yearly amounting unto £21,111 12s. 1¾d.[45] of current money in those days, do evidently declare what store of coin was transported out of the land unto the papal uses in that behalf only.

Certes I take this not to be one quarter of his gains gotten by England in those days, for such commodities were raised by his courts holden here, so plentifully gat he by his perquisites, as elections, procurations, appeals, preventions, pluralities, totquots, trialities, tolerations,[46] legitimations, bulls, seals, priests, concubines, eating of flesh and white meats [dairy products], dispensations for marriages, and times of celebration, Peter's pence, and suchlike faculties, that not so little as £1,200,000 [47] went yearly

[45] As earlier (n. 27), Harrison's pursuit of his thesis leads him to confuse first fruits and tenths.

[46] *Procurations:* provisions of necessary entertainment for visiting ecclesiastical superiors, often commuted to money; *preventions:* privileges granted an ecclesiastical superior to assume the rights of an inferior; *totquots:* dispensations to hold as many benefices as a clergyman could get; *trialities:* dispensations to hold three benefices simultaneously; *tolerations:* licenses.

[47] Numbers for Harrison are servants, not masters. Here and elsewhere he adds a cipher for emphasis.

from hence to Rome. And therefore no marvel though he seek much in these days to reduce us to his obedience. But what are the tenths of England (you will say) in comparison of all those of Europe? For notwithstanding that many good bishoprics lately erected be left out of his old books of record, which I also have seen, yet I find nevertheless that the whole sum of them amounted to not above £61,521, as money went two hundred years before my time, of which portion poor St. Peter did never hear of so much as one gray groat. Mark therefore, I pray you, whether England were not fully answerable to a third part of the rest of his tenths over all Europe; and thereupon tell me whether our island was one of the best pair of bellows or not that blew the fire in his kitchen, wherewith to make his pot seethe, beside all other commodities.

Beside all these we have another bishopric yet in England, almost slipped out of my remembrance because it is very obscure, for that the bishop thereof hath not wherewith to maintain his countenance sufficiently, and that is the see of Mona, or Man, sometime named *episcopatus Sodorensis,* whereof one Wimund was ordained the first bishop and John the second in the troublesome time of King Stephen. The gift of this prelacy resteth in the Earls of Derby, who nominate such a one from time to time thereto as to them doth seem convenient. Howbeit, if that see did know and might reap her own commodities and discern them from other men's possessions (for it is supposed that the mother hath devoured the daughter), I doubt not but the state of her bishop would quickly be amended.[48] Having therefore called this latter see after this manner unto mind, I suppose that I have sufficiently discharged my duty concerning the state of our bishoprics and manner how the ecclesiastical jurisdiction of the Church of England is divided among the shires and counties of this realm. Whose bishops, as they have been heretofore of less learning and yet of greater port and doings in the commonwealth than at this present, so are they now for the most part the best learned that are to be found in any country of Europe, sith neither high parentage nor great riches (as in other countries)

[48] The charge is blunter in *The Description of Britain* (1587, p. 38): "Now he that is bishop there is but a bishop's shadow, for albeit he bear the name of Bishop of Man, yet have the Earls of Derby, as it is supposed, the chief profit of his see (saving that they allow him a little somewhat for a flourish)."

but only learning and virtue, commended somewhat by friendship, do bring them to this honor.

I might here have spoken more at large of divers other bishoprics sometime in this part of the island, as of that of Caerleon, tofore overthrown by Ethelfrid in the behalf of Augustine the monk (as Malmesbury saith), where Dubricius governed, which was afterward translated to St. David's and taken for an archbishopric;[49] secondly, of the bishopric of Leicester called *Legerensis*, whose fourth bishop (Unwona) went to Rome with Offa, King of Mercia;[50] thirdly, of Ramsbury, or Wilton, and of Gloucester (of which you shall read in Matthew Westminster, 489), where the bishop was called Eldad; also of Hagulstad, one of the members whereinto the see of York was divided after the expulsion of Wilfrid. For (as I read) when Egfrid, the King, had driven him away, he divided his see into two parts, making Bosa over the Deiranes, that held his see at Hagulstad, or Lindisfarne, and Eata over the Bernicians, who sat at York; and thereto placing Edhed over Lindsey (as is afore noted), whose successors were Ethelwine, Edgar, and Cynebert, notwithstanding that one Saxulf was over Lindsey before Edhed, who was Bishop of the Mercians and Middle England till he was banished from Lindsey and came into those quarters to seek his refuge and succor.[51]

I could likewise entreat of the Bishops of Whithorn, or *Ad Candidam Casam*, an house, with the country wherein it stood, belonging to the province of Northumberland but now a parcel of Scotland; also of the erection of the late see at Westminster by Henry the Eighth. But as the one, so the other is ceased and the lands of this latter either so divided or exchanged for worse tenures that, except a man should see it with his eyes and point out with his finger where every parcel of them is bestowed, but a few men would believe what is become of the same. I might likewise, and with like ease also, have added the successors of the bishops of every see to this discourse of their cathedral churches and places of abode, but it would have extended this treatise to

[49] Harrison here confuses Caerlegion (Chester), destroyed about 614 by Ethelfrid, with the Welsh Caerleon in Monmouthshire. The relevant passage is in William of Malmesbury, *Gesta regum Anglorum*, I, iii.

[50] Matthew Westminster, under 768.

[51] All these details, correcting the error on p. 59, are derived from Bede, IV, xii, but Harrison follows Matthew Westminster (under 678) in reversing the placement of the sees of Bosa and Eata.

an unprofitable length. Nevertheless, I will remember the same of London, my native city, after I have added one word more of the house called *Ad Candidam Casam*, in English, Whithorn, which taketh denomination of the white stone wherewith it was builded, and was seen far off as standing upon an hill to such as did behold it.

[Harrison concludes the chapter with "the names and successions of so many Archbishops and Bishops of London as are extant and to be had, from the faith first received." The catalogue of "Archbishops" is merely a variant form of that already given on p. 44, but included is "Augustine the monk, sent over by Gregory the Great, till he removed his see to Canterbury, to the intent he might the sooner flee if persecution should be raised by the infidels, or hear from or send more speedily unto Rome without any great fear of the interception of his letters." Sixty-seven bishops are enumerated, from Mellitus to John Aylmer. Harrison follows with a list of fifty Deans of St. Paul's, beginning with "Wulmannus, who made a distribution of the Psalms contained in the whole Psalter and appointed the same daily to be read amongst the prebendaries" and "Radulfus de Diceto, whose noble history is yet extant in their library," and closing with Alexander Nowell, "mine old master now living in this present year, 1586, who is none of the least ornaments that have been in that seat" (see p. 76). The chapter ends:]

And thus much of the archbishops, bishops, and deans of that honorable see. I call it honorable because it hath had a succession for the most part of learned and wise men, albeit that otherwise it be the most troublesome seat in England, not only for that it is near unto check, but also the prelates thereof are much troubled with suitors and no less subject to the reproaches of the common sort, whose mouths are always wide open unto reprehension and eyes ready to espy anything that they may reprove and carp at. I would have done so much for every see in England, if I had not had consideration of the greatness of the volume and small benefit rising by the same unto the commodity of the readers; nevertheless, I have reserved them unto the publication of my great Chronology, if (while I live) it happen to come abroad.

CHAPTER III

Of Universities

THERE have been heretofore and at sundry times divers famous universities in this island, and those even in my days not altogether forgotten, as one at Bangor, erected by Lucius, and afterward converted into a monastery, not by Congallus (as some write) but by Pelagius the monk. The second at Caerleon-upon-Usk, near to the place where the river doth fall into the Severn, founded by King Arthur. The third at Thetford, wherein were six hundred students in the time of one Rond, sometime king of that region. The fourth at Stamford, suppressed by Augustine the monk, and likewise other in other places, as Salisbury, Eridon or Cricklade, Lechlade, Reading, and Northampton; albeit that the two last rehearsed were not authorized but only arose to that name by the departure of the students from Oxford in time of civil dissension unto the said towns, where also they continued but for a little season. When that of Salisbury began, I cannot tell; but that it flourished most under Henry the Third and Edward the First I find good testimony by the writers, as also by the discord which fell, 1278, between the chancellor for the scholars there on the one part and William the Archdeacon on the other, whereof you shall see more in the chronology here following.[1]

In my time there are three noble universities in England, to wit, one at Oxford, the second at Cambridge, and the third in London; of which the first two are the most famous, I mean Cambridge and Oxford, for that in them the use of the tongues, philosophy, and the liberal sciences, besides the profound studies of the civil law, physic, and theology, are daily taught and had;

[1] Harrison's source for these details, and for other misinformation later in the chapter concerning the origin of Cambridge, is John Caius, *De antiquitate Cantabrigiensis academiae* (1568, 1574). Perhaps because of his loyalty to both Oxford and Cambridge, Harrison remains comparatively aloof from the notorious fray over their relative antiquity. In *The Description of Britain* (1587, p. 48) he expresses some skepticism on the whole subject, noting that Lechlade is "a town whereunto one piece of an old university is ascribed, which it did never possess, more than Cricklade did the other."

whereas in the latter the laws of the realm are only read and learned, by such as give their minds unto the knowledge of the same. In the first there are not only divers goodly houses builded foursquare, for the most part of hard freestone or brick, with great numbers of lodgings and chambers in the same for students after a sumptuous sort, through the exceeding liberality of kings, queens, bishops, noblemen, and ladies of the land, but also large livings and great revenues bestowed upon them (the like whereof is not to be seen in any other region, as Peter Martyr [2] did oft affirm), to the maintenance only of such convenient numbers of poor men's sons as the several stipends bestowed upon the said houses are able to support.

When these two schools should be first builded and who were their original founders, as yet it is uncertain; nevertheless, as there is great likelihood that Cambridge was begun by one Cantaber, a Spaniard (as I have noted in my Chronology), so Alfred is said to be the first beginner of the university at Oxford, albeit that I cannot warrant the same to be so young, sith I find by good authority that John of Beverley studied in the University Hall at Oxford, which was long before Alfred was either born or gotten. Some are of the opinion that *Cantabrigia* was not so called of Cantaber but Caer Grant, of the finisher of the work, or at the leastwise of the river that runneth by the same, and afterward by the Saxons, Grantchester. Another sort affirm that the river is better written *Canta* than *Granta*, etc., but why then is not the town called *Canta*, *Cantium*, or *Cantodunum*, according to the same? All this is said only (as I think) to deface the memory of Cantaber, who, coming from the Brigantes or out of Biscay, called the said town after his own and the name of the region from whence he came. Neither hath it been a rare thing for the Spaniards heretofore to come first into Ireland and from thence over into England, sith the Chronology shall declare that it hath been often seen, and that out of Britain they have gotten over also into Scythia [Germany], and contrariwise, coasting still through Yorkshire, which of them also was called *Brigantium*, as by good testimony appeareth.

Of these two, that of Oxford (which lieth west and by north from London) [3] standeth most pleasantly, being environed in

[2] *Pietro Martire Vermigli* (1500–1562): reformer, theologian, Regius Professor of Divinity at Oxford in 1548–1553.

manner round about with woods on the hills aloft and goodly rivers in the bottoms and valleys beneath, whose courses would breed no small commodity to that city and country about if such impediments were removed as greatly annoy the same and hinder the carriage which might be made thither also from London. That of Cambridge is distant from London about forty-and-six miles north and by east and standeth very well, saving that it is somewhat near unto the fens, whereby the wholesomeness of the air there is not a little corrupted. It is excellently well served with all kinds of provision, but especially of fresh-water fish and wild fowl, by reason of the river that passeth thereby, and thereto the Isle of Ely, which is so near at hand. Only wood is the chief want to such as study there, wherefore this kind of provision is brought them either from Essex and other places thereabouts, as is also their coal, or otherwise the necessity thereof is supplied with gale (a bastard kind of *myrtus*, as I take it) and sea coal,[4] whereof they have great plenty, led thither by the Grant. Moreover it hath not such store of meadow ground as may suffice for the ordinary expenses of the town and university, wherefore the inhabitants are enforced in like sort to provide their hay from other villages about, which minister the same unto them in very great abundance.

Oxford is supposed to contain in longitude 18 degrees and 28 minutes, and in latitude 51 degrees and 50 minutes, whereas that of Cambridge, standing more northerly, hath 20 degrees and 20 minutes in longitude and thereunto 52 degrees and 15 minutes in latitude, as by exact supputation is easy to be found.[5]

The colleges of Oxford, for curious workmanship and private commodities, are much more stately, magnificent, and commodious than those of Cambridge and thereunto the streets of the town for the most part more large and comely. But for uniformity of building, orderly compaction, and politic regiment, the town of Cambridge, as the newer workmanship,[6] exceedeth that of Oxford (which otherwise is, and hath been, the greater

---

[3] "Oxford fifty miles from London."—*H.*

[4] *Gale:* the sweet gale or bog myrtle, which Leland describes as "sweet in burning" (*Itinerary*, ed. Smith, I, 38); *sea coal:* mineral coal, as distinguished from charcoal.

[5] Harrison's longitudes are based on the Ptolemaic "meridian of Ferro" (Hierro in the Canary Islands, now 18 degrees west longitude), with an error of about 2 degrees.

of the two) by many-a-fold (as I guess), although I know divers that are of the contrary opinion. This also is certain, that whatsoever the difference be in building of the town streets, the townsmen of both are glad when they may match and annoy the students by encroaching upon their liberties, and keep them bare by extreme sale of their wares, whereby many of them become rich for a time but afterward fall again into poverty, because that goods evil-gotten do seldom long endure.

Castles also they have both, and in my judgment [it] is hard to be said whether of them would be the stronger if each were accordingly repaired; howbeit, that of Cambridge is the higher, both for manner of building and situation of ground, sith Oxford Castle standeth low and is not so apparent to our sight. That of Cambridge was builded (as they say) by Gurguintus, sometime King of Britain, but the other by the Lord Robert d'Oilgi, a nobleman which came in with the Conqueror, whose wife Edith, a woman given to no less superstition than credulity, began also the Abbey of Osney near unto the same, upon a fond (but yet a rare) occasion, which we will here remember, though it be beside my purpose, to the end that the reader may see how ready the simple people of that time were to be abused by the practice of the clergy. It happened on a time, as this lady walked about the fields, near unto the aforesaid castle, to recreate herself with certain of her maidens, that a number of pies sat chattering upon the elms which had been planted in the hedgerows, and in fine so troubled her with their noise that she wished them all further off or else herself at home again, and this happened divers times. In the end, being weary of her walk, she demanded of her chaplain the cause wherefore these pies did so molest and vex her. "Oh, madam," saith he, the wiliest pie of all, "these are no pies but souls in purgatory that crave relief." "And is it so, indeed?" quoth she. "Now, depardieu, if old Robert will give me leave, I will do what I can to bring these souls to rest." Hereupon she consulted, craved, wept, and became so importunate with her husband that he joined with her, and they both began that synagogue, 1120, which afterward proved to be a notable den. In that church also lieth this lady buried, with her image, having an heart in her hand, couched upon the same in the habit of a vowess, and yet

⁶ "Cambridge burned not long since."—*H.*

to be seen, except the weather have worn out the memorial.[7]
But to proceed with my purpose.

In each of these universities also is likewise a church dedicated
to the Virgin Mary, wherein once in the year, to wit, in July,
the schools [8] are holden, and in which such as have been called
to any degree in the year precedent do there receive the ac-
complishment of the same in solemn and sumptuous manner. In
Oxford this solemnity is called an Act, but in Cambridge they
use the French word, Commencement; and such resort is made
yearly unto the same from all parts of the land by the friends of
those which do proceed [graduate] that all the town is hardly
able to receive and lodge those guests. When and by whom the
churches aforesaid were builded I have elsewhere made relation.
That of Oxford also was repaired in the time of Edward the
Fourth and Henry the Seventh, when Doctor Fitzjames, a great
helper in that work, was Warden of Merton College; but ere long
after it was finished one tempest in a night so defaced the same
that it left few pinnacles standing about the church and steeple,
which since that time have never been repaired.[9] There were
sometime four-and-twenty parish churches in the town and suburbs, but now there are scarcely sixteen. There have been also
1,200 burgesses, of which 400 dwelled in the suburbs, and so
many students were there in the time of Henry the Third that
he allowed them twenty miles' compass about the town for their
provision of victuals.

The common schools of Cambridge also are far more beautiful
than those of Oxford, only the divinity school at Oxford excepted, which for fine and excellent workmanship cometh next
the mold of the King's Chapel in Cambridge, than the which two,
with the chapel that King Henry the Seventh did build at Westminster, there are not (in mine opinion) made of lime and stone
three more notable piles within the compass of Europe.

In all other things there is so great equality between these two

---

[7] This account of the founding of Osney Priory is Harrison's free
dramatization of the tamer passage in Leland (I, 123–124). Harrison confuses
the Robert d'Oilgi who built the castle at Oxford with his nephew of the
same name, Edith's husband.
[8] *Schools:* an assembly of the schools of a university; misprinted as
"scholers" in 1587.
[9] Leland (V, 231).

universities as no man can imagine how to set down any greater, so that they seem to be the body of one well-ordered commonwealth, only divided by distance of place and not in friendly consent and orders. In speaking therefore of the one, I cannot but describe the other; and in commendation of the first, I cannot but extol the latter; and so much the rather for that they are both so dear unto me as that I cannot readily tell unto whether of them I owe the most good will. Would to God my knowledge were such as that neither of them might have cause to be ashamed of their pupil, or my power so great that I might worthily requite them both for those manifold kindnesses that I have received of them. But to leave these things and proceed with other more convenient for my purpose.

The manner to live in these universities is not as in some other of foreign countries we see daily to happen, where the students are enforced, for want of such houses, to dwell in common inns and taverns, without all order or discipline. But in these our colleges we live in such exact order and under so precise rules of government as that the famous learned man Erasmus of Rotterdam, being here among us fifty years past, did not let to compare the trades in living of students in these two places even with the very rules and orders of the ancient monks, affirming moreover in flat words our orders to be such as not only came near unto but rather far exceeded all the monastical institutions that ever were devised.[10]

In most of our colleges there are also great numbers of students, of which many are found by the revenues of the houses and other by the purveyances and help of their rich friends, whereby in some one college you shall have 200 scholars, in others 150, in divers 140, and in the rest less numbers, as the capacity of the said houses is able to receive; so that at this present, of one sort and other, there are about 3,000 students nourished in them both (as by a late survey it manifestly appeared). They were erected by their founders at the first only for poor men's sons, whose parents were not able to bring them up unto learning, but now they have the least benefit of them, by

[10] Erasmus' opinion is expressed in a letter to Servatius dated July 8, 1514, but the citation and other phrases in the paragraph are borrowed from the appendix, "Touching the universities," to Jewel's *Apology* (ed. Booty, p. 141; see p. 23, n. 17).

reason the rich do so encroach upon them. And so far hath this inconvenience spread itself that it is in my time an hard matter for a poor man's child to come by a fellowship (though he be never so good a scholar and worthy of that room). Such packing also is used at elections that not he which best deserveth, but he that hath most friends, though he be the worst scholar, is always surest to speed, which will turn in the end to the overthrow of learning.[11] That some gentlemen also, whose friends have been in times past benefactors to certain of those houses, do intrude into the disposition of their estates, without all respect of order or statutes devised by the founders, only thereby to place whom they think good (and not without some hope of gain), the case is too-too evident; and their attempt would soon take place if their superiors did not provide to bridle their endeavors. In some grammar schools likewise, which send scholars to these universities, it is lamentable to see what bribery is used; for, ere the scholar can be preferred, such bribage is made that poor men's children are commonly shut out and the richer sort received (who in time past thought it dishonor to live, as it were, upon alms), and yet, being placed, most of them study little other than histories [tales, romances], tables, dice, and trifles, as men that make not the living by their study the end of their purposes, which is a lamentable hearing. Beside this, being for the most part either gentlemen or rich men's sons, they oft bring the universities into much slander. For, standing upon their reputation and liberty, they ruffle and roist it out, exceeding in apparel and haunting riotous company (which draweth them from their books unto another trade). And for excuse, when they are charged with breach of all good order, think it sufficient to say that they be gentlemen, which grieveth many not a little. But to proceed with the rest.

Every one of these colleges have in like manner their professors or readers of the tongues and several sciences, as they call them, which daily trade up the youth there abiding privately in their halls, to the end they may be able afterward (when their turn cometh about, which is after twelve terms) to show them-

---

[11] Harrison's aggrieved tone may be explained by his own failure to attain a place on the foundation of Christ Church. He appears as a commoner on the weekly summary of battels at that college from the beginning of the Christmas term in 1554 until the ninth week of St. John the Baptist in 1557.

selves abroad by going from thence into the common schools and public disputations (as it were, *in aream*),[12] there to try their skills and declare how they have profited since their coming thither.

Moreover in the public schools of both the universities there are found at the prince's charge (and that very largely) five professors and readers, that is to say, of divinity, of the civil law, physic, the Hebrew and the Greek tongues. And for the other lectures, as of philosophy, logic, rhetoric, and the quadrivials—although the latter (I mean arithmetic, music, geometry, and astronomy, and with them all skill in the perspectives [optics]) are now smally regarded in either of them—the universities themselves do allow competent stipends to such as read the same, whereby they are sufficiently provided for touching the maintenance of their estates and no less encouraged to be diligent in their functions.

These professors in like sort have all the rule of disputations and other school exercises which are daily used in common schools severally assigned to each of them; and such of their hearers as by their skill showed in the said disputations are thought to have attained to any convenient ripeness of knowledge, according to the custom of other universities, although not in like order, are permitted solemnly to take their deserved degrees of school in the same science and faculty wherein they have spent their travail. From that time forward also they use such difference in apparel as becometh their callings, tendeth unto gravity, and maketh them known to be called to some countenance.

The first degree is that of the general sophisters, from whence, when they have learned more sufficiently the rules of logic, rhetoric, and obtained thereto competent skill in philosophy and in the mathematicals, they ascend higher unto the estate of Bachelors of Art, after four years of their entrance into their sophistery. From thence also, giving their minds to more perfect knowledge in some or all the other liberal sciences and the tongues, they rise at the last (to wit, after other three or four years) to be called Masters of Art, each of them being at that time reputed for

[12] *In aream:* in the open space of the circus reserved for games; the 1577 edition reads "into the plain battle." This paragraph and the two succeeding ones come almost verbatim from the appendix to Jewel's *Apology* (p. 143).

a doctor in his faculty if he profess but one of the said sciences (beside philosophy), or for his general skill if he be exercised in them all.[13] After this they are permitted to choose what other of the higher studies them liketh to follow, whether it be divinity, law, or physic; so that, being once Masters of Art, the next degree, if they follow physic, is the doctorship belonging to that profession, and likewise in the study of the law, if they bend their minds to the knowledge of the same. But if they mean to go forward with divinity, this is the order used in that profession. First, after they have necessarily proceeded Masters of Art, they preach one sermon to the people in English and another to the university in Latin. They answer all comers, also, in their own persons unto two several questions of divinity in the open schools at one time, for the space of two hours; and afterward reply twice against some other man upon a like number and on two several days in the same place, which being done with commendation, he receiveth the fourth degree, that is, Bachelor of Divinity, but not before he hath been Master of Art by the space of seven years, according to their statutes.[14]

The next and last degree of all is the doctorship, after other three years, for the which he must once again perform all such exercises and acts as are afore remembered;[15] and then is he reputed able to govern and teach others and likewise taken for a doctor. I have read that John of Beverley was the first doctor that ever was in Oxford, as Bede was in Cambridge. But I suppose herein that the word "doctor" is not so strictly to be taken in this report as it is now used, sith every teacher is in Latin called by that name, as also such in the primitive church as kept schools of catechists, wherein they were trained up in the rudiments

[13] Harrison was admitted B.A. at Oxford on December 9, 1557, and commenced as M.A. on July 29, 1560.

[14] Harrison was admitted to Cambridge as a candidate for the B.D. on June 17, 1569. Apparently he was not in residence but commuted from Radwinter. He had considerable difficulty in fulfilling, within the statutory limit of one year, the exercises he describes above, doubtless because he was busy at this period as an official of the archidiaconal court (see p. 25, n. 19). Twice he was forced to petition for postponements of the exercises, which he finally completed in 1571 (*Grace Book* Δ, ed. John Venn, Cambridge, 1910, pp. 225–226, 229, 240, 248).

[15] Harrison once remarked to Gabriel Harvey that "he wanted nothing to be doctor but will, skill, and bear it out" (*Gabriel Harvey's Marginalia*, ed. G. C. Moore Smith, Stratford-upon-Avon, 1913, p. 114).

and principles of religion, either before they were admitted unto baptism or any office in the church.

Thus we see that from our entrance into the university unto the last degree received is commonly eighteen or, peradventure, twenty years, in which time if a student hath not obtained sufficient learning thereby to serve his own turn and benefit his commonwealth, let him never look, by tarrying longer, to come by any more. For after this time and forty years of age the most part of students do commonly give over their wonted diligence and live like drone bees on the fat of colleges, withholding better wits from the possession of their places and yet doing little good in their own vocation and calling. I could rehearse a number (if I listed) of this sort, as well in the one university as the other. But this shall suffice instead of a larger report, that long continuance in those places is either a sign of lack of friends or of learning or of good and upright life, as Bishop Foxe sometime noted, who thought it sacrilege for a man to tarry any longer at Oxford than he had a desire to profit.[16]

A man may (if he will) begin his study with the law or physic (of which this giveth wealth, the other honor) so soon as he cometh to the university, if his knowledge in the tongues and ripeness of judgment serve therefor, which if he do, then his first degree is Bachelor of Law or Physic, and for the same he must perform such acts in his own science as the Bachelors or Doctors of Divinity do for their parts, the only sermons except, which belong not to his calling. Finally, this will I say, that the professors of either of those faculties come to such perfection in both universities as the best students beyond the sea do in their own or elsewhere. One thing only I mislike in them, and that is their usual going into Italy, from whence very few, without special grace, do return good men, whatsoever they pretend of conference or practice, chiefly the physicians, who, under pretense of seeking of foreign simples, do oftentimes learn the framing of such compositions as were better unknown than practiced, as I have heard oft alleged; [17] and therefore it is most true that Doctor Turner said, Italy is not to be seen without a guide, that

---

[16] "This Foxe builded Corpus Christi College in Oxford."—*H*. Richard Foxe was Bishop of Winchester in 1501–1528.

[17] "So much also may be inferred of lawyers."—*H*.

is, without special grace given from God, because of the licentious and corrupt behavior of the people.[18]

There is moreover in every house a master or provost, who hath under him a president and certain censors or deans appointed to look to the behavior and manners of the students there, whom they punish very severely if they make any default, according to the quantity and quality of their trespasses. And these are the usual names of governors in Cambridge. Howbeit, in Oxford the heads of houses are now and then called presidents, in respect of such bishops as are their visitors and founders. In each of these also they have one or mo treasurers, whom they call *bursarios*, or bursars, beside other officers whose charge is to see unto the welfare and maintenance of these houses. Over each university also there is a several chancellor, whose offices are perpetual; howbeit, their substitutes, whom we call vice-chancellors, are changed every year, as are also the proctors, taskers, masters of the streets, and other officers, for the better maintenance of their policy and estate.

And thus much at this time of our two universities, in each of which I have received such degree as they have vouchsafed— rather of their favor than my desert—to yield and bestow upon me, and unto whose students I wish one thing, the execution whereof cannot be prejudicial to any that meaneth well, as I am resolutely persuaded and the case now standeth in these our days. When any benefice, therefore, becometh void, it were good that the patron did signify the vacation thereof to the bishop, and the bishop the act of the patron to one of the universities, with request that the vice-chancellor with his assistants might provide some such able man to succeed in the place as should, by their judgment, be meet to take the charge upon him. Certes if this order were taken, then should the church be provided of good pastors, by whom God should be glorified, the universities better stored, the simoniacal practices of a number of patrons utterly abolished, and the people better trained to live in obedience toward God and their prince, which were an happy estate.

To these two also we may in like sort add the third, which is at

---

[18] *William Turner* (d. 1568): Dean of Wells, religious controversialist, physician, and botanist; he had taken his medical degree in Italy. Harrison refers to him in words that suggest they were personally acquainted (p. 289).

London (serving only for such as study the laws of the realm), where there are sundry famous houses, of which three are called by the name of Inns of the Court, the rest of the Chancery, and all builded beforetime for the furtherance and commodity of such as apply their minds to our common laws. Out of these also come many scholars of great fame, whereof the most part have heretofore been brought up in one of the aforesaid universities and prove such commonly as, in process of time, rise up (only through their profound skill) to great honor in the commonwealth of England. They have also degrees of learning among themselves and rules of discipline, under which they live most civilly in their houses, albeit that the younger sort of them abroad in the streets are scarce able to be bridled by any good order at all. Certes this error was wont also greatly to reign in Cambridge and Oxford between the students and the burgesses, but as it is well left in these two places, so in foreign countries it cannot yet be suppressed.

Besides these universities also there are great number of grammar schools throughout the realm, and those very liberally endued for the better relief of poor scholars, so that there are not many corporate towns now under the Queen's dominion that hath not one grammar school at the least, with a sufficient living for a master and usher appointed to the same.

There are in like manner divers collegiate churches, as Windsor, Winchester, Eton, Westminster (in which I was sometime an unprofitable grammarian under the reverend father, Master Nowell, now Dean of Paul's),[19] and in those a great number of poor scholars daily maintained by the liberality of the founders with meat, books, and apparel, from whence, after they have been well entered in the knowledge of the Latin and Greek tongues and rules of versifying (the trial whereof is made by certain apposers yearly appointed to examine them), they are sent to certain especial houses in each university, where they are received, then trained up in the points of higher knowledge in their private halls till they be adjudged meet to show their faces in the schools, as I have said already. And thus much have I thought

---

[19] *Alexander Nowell:* Headmaster of Westminster School in 1547–1553; as Dean of St. Paul's (1560–1602) he was the patron who presented Harrison to his London parishes (p. 28, n. 22). Harrison had also been a student at St. Paul's in 1545 (Furnivall, I, li).

good to note of our universities, and likewise of colleges in the same, whose names I will also set down here, with those of their founders, to the end the zeal which they bare unto learning may appear and their remembrance never perish from among the wise and learned.[20]

Of the colleges in Cambridge with their founders

Years of the foundations	Colleges	Founders
1546	1. Trinity College	King Henry VIII
1441	2. The King's College	King Henry VI, Edward IV, Henry VII, and Henry VIII
1511	3. St. John's	Lady Margaret, grandmother to Henry VIII
1505	4. Christ's College	King Henry VI and the Lady Margaret aforesaid.
1446	5. The Queens' College	Lady Margaret, wife to King Henry VI
1496	6. Jesus College	John Alcock, Bishop of Ely
1342	7. Benet College [21]	The brethren of a popish guild called *Corporis Christi*
1343	8. Pembroke Hall	Mary de Valence, Countess of Pembroke
1256	9. Peter College	Hugh Balsham, Bishop of Ely
1348 1557	10. Gonville and Caius College	Edmund Gonvile, parson of Terrington, and John Caius, Doctor of Physic
1354	11. Trinity Hall	William Bateman, Bishop of Norwich
1326	12. Clare Hall	Richard Badew, Chancellor of Cambridge
1459	13. Catharine Hall	Robert Wodelarke, Doctor of Divinity

[20] Virtually all Harrison's information regarding founders and foundation dates in the following lists comes from the appendix, entitled "Of the Universities in England," in John Stow's *Summary of English Chronicles* (1575), but the order of listing the colleges and the names of the halls on p. 79 (except for Postminster) are taken from the appendix to Jewel's *Apology* (pp. 141-142).

[21] Corpus Christi College, in Harrison's day often known as St. Benet's or St. Benedict's from the nearby church associated with the founding guild of Corpus Christi.

1519	14. Magdalene College	Edward, Duke of Buckingham, and Thomas, Lord Audley
1585	15. Emmanuel College	Sir Walter Mildmay, etc.

Of colleges in Oxford

Years	*Colleges*	*Founders*
1539	1. Christ Church	King Henry VIII
1459	2. Magdalen College	William Waynflete, first, fellow of Merton College, then, scholar at Winchester, and afterward bishop there.[22]
1375	3. New College	William Wykeham, Bishop of Winchester
1276	4. Merton College	Walter Merton, Bishop of Rochester
1437	5. All Souls College	Henry Chichele, Archbishop of Canterbury
1516	6. Corpus Christi College	Richard Foxe, Bishop of Winchester
1430	7. Lincoln College	Richard Fleming, Bishop of Lincoln
1323	8. Oriel College	Adam Browne [Brome], almoner to Edward II
1340	9. The Queen's College	R. Eglesfield, chaplain to Philippa, Queen of England, wife to Edward III
1263	10. Balliol College	John Baliol, King of Scotland [23]
1557	11. St. John's	Sir Thomas White, Knight
1556	12. Trinity College	Sir Thomas Pope, Knight
1316	13. Exeter College	Walter Stapledon, Bishop of Exeter
1513	14. Brasenose	William Smith, Bishop of Lincoln
873	15. University College	William, Archdeacon of Duresine [Durham]

[22] "He founded also a good part of Eton College and a free school at Wainfleet, where he was born."—*H.*

[23] Harrison follows Stow in confusing the Regent, John de Baliol (d. 1269), the founder of the College, with his son of the same name (1249–1315), King of Scotland.

16. Gloucester College	John Giffard, who made it a cell for thirteen monks
17. St. Mary College [24]	
18. Jesus College, now in hand	Hugh ap Rice [Price], Doctor of the Civil Law.

There are also in Oxford certain hostels, or halls, which may right well be called by the names of colleges if it were not that there is more liberty in them than is to be seen in the other. In mine opinion the livers in these are very like to those that are of Inns in the Chancery; their names also are these, so far as I now remember:

Broadgates	Postminster [Postmasters] Hall
Hart Hall	St. Mary Hall
Magdalen Hall	White Hall
Alburne [St. Alban] Hall	New Inn
Edmund Hall.	

The students also that remain in them are called "hostelers," or halliers. Hereof it came of late to pass that the Right Reverend Father in God, Thomas, late Archbishop of Canterbury, being brought up in such an house at Cambridge, was of the ignorant sort of Londoners called an "hosteler" [hostler], supposing that he had served with some innholder in the stable, and therefore, in despite, divers hanged up bottles [bundles] of hay at his gate when he began to preach the gospel, whereas indeed he was a gentleman born of an ancient house and in the end a faithful witness of Jesus Christ, in whose quarrel he refused not to shed his blood and yield up his life unto the fury of his adversaries.[25]

---

[24] The founder's name for New College. Oriel was also originally St. Mary the Virgin. Both colleges have been listed previously, however.

[25] Thomas Cranmer, Archbishop of Canterbury (1533–1555), was deprived for a time of his fellowship at Jesus College because of his marriage, and he held briefly a position as lecturer at Buckingham Hall, now Magdalene College. The more common form of the story has it that he earned the epithet "hostler" for his frequent visits to the Dolphin Inn at Cambridge, where he had installed his wife (John Foxe, *Acts and Monuments*, ed. Stephen Reed Cattley, VIII, London, 1839, 4–5). Cranmer was burned at Oxford in 1556, while Harrison was in residence at Christ Church. The Londonderry biography states that it was the influence of the Oxford martyrs, Cranmer, Ridley, and Latimer, which recalled Harrison from the "filth of papistry" into which he had "flung himself" at the university.

Besides these, there is mention and record of divers other halls, or hostels, that have been there in times past, as Beef Hall, Mutton Hall, etc., whose ruins yet appear, so that if antiquity be to be judged by the show of ancient buildings, which is very plentiful in Oxford to be seen, it should be an easy matter to conclude that Oxford is the elder university. Therein are also many dwelling houses of stone yet standing that have been halls for students, of very antique workmanship, besides the old walls of sundry other, whose plots have been converted into gardens since colleges were erected.

In London also the houses of students at the common law are these:

Sergeant's Inn	Furnival's Inn
Gray's Inn	Clifford's Inn
The Temple	Clement's Inn
Lincoln's Inn	Lyon's Inn
David's [Thavie's] Inn	Barnard's Inn
Staple's Inn	New Inn.

And thus much in general of our noble universities, whose lands some greedy gripers do gape wide for and of late have (as I hear) propounded sundry reasons whereby they supposed to have prevailed in their purposes. But who are those that have attempted this suit, other than such as either hate learning, piety, and wisdom, or else have spent all their own and know not otherwise than by encroaching upon other men how to maintain themselves? When such a motion was made by some unto King Henry the Eighth, he could answer them in this manner:

Ah, sirrah, I perceive the abbey lands have fleshed you and set your teeth on edge to ask also those colleges. And whereas we had a regard only to pull down sin by defacing the monasteries, you have a desire also to overthrow all goodness by subversion of colleges.[26] I tell you, sirs, that I judge no land in England better bestowed than that which is given to our universities, for by their maintenance our realm shall be well governed when we be dead and rotten. As you love your wel-

---

[26] "Now abbeys be gone, our dingthrifts [spendthrifts] pry after church and college possessions."—*H.*

fares, therefore, follow no more this vein, but content yourselves with that you have already, or else seek honest means whereby to increase your livelods [livelihoods], for I love not learning so ill that I will impair the revenues of any one house by a penny whereby it may be upholden.

In King Edward's days likewise the same suit was once again attempted (as I have heard), but in vain; for, saith the Duke of Somerset,[27] among other speeches tending to that end—who also made answer thereunto in the King's presence by his assignation—

If learning decay, which of wild men maketh civil, of blockish and rash persons, wise and godly counselors, of obstinate rebels, obedient subjects, and of evil men, good and godly Christians, what shall we look for else but barbarism and tumult? For when the lands of colleges be gone, it shall be hard to say whose staff shall stand next the door; for then I doubt not but the state of bishops, rich farmers, merchants, and the nobility shall be assailed by such as live to spend all and think that whatsoever another man hath is more meet for them and to be at their commandment than for the proper owner that hath sweat and labored for it.

In Queen Mary's days the weather was too warm for any such course to be taken in hand; but in the time of our gracious Queen Elizabeth I hear that it was after a sort in talk the third time, but without success, as moved also out of season, and so I hope it shall continue forever. For what comfort should it be for any good man to see his country brought into the estate of the old Goths and Vandals, who made laws against learning and would not suffer any skillful man to come into their council house, by means whereof those people became savage tyrants and merciless hellhounds, till they restored learning again and thereby fell to civility?

---

[27] *Duke of Somerset:* Edward Seymour, Lord Protector (1547–1550) under Edward VI. I can find no source for these speeches, and it seems likely that they are Harrison's re-creation from "conference with divers" (p. 5). He might have learned of Somerset's pronouncement, for example, from Sir Thomas Smith, who was a secretary of state at the time, or from William Turner, who was Somerset's chaplain and physician.

CHAPTER IV

Of the Partition of England into Shires and Counties

IN READING of ancient writers, as Caesar, Tacitus, and others, we find mention of sundry regions to have been sometime in this island, as the Novantae, Selgovae, Damnonii, Gadeni, Otadini, Epidii, Cerones, Carnonacae, Carini, Cornavii, Caledonii, Decantae, Lugi, Smertae, Vacomagi, Venicones, Taexali, or *polii* Devani,[1] Selgovi, Brigantes, Parisi, Ordovices, *alias* Ordoluci, Cornovii, Coritani, Catieuchlani, Simeni, Trinovantes, Demetae, Cangi, Silures, Dobuni, Atrebatii, Cantii, Regni, Belgae, Durotriges, Dumnonii, Girvii, Murotriges, Severiani, Iceni, Tegenes, Cassi, Cenimagni, Segontiaci, Ancalites, Bibroci,[2] and Kentishmen, and suchlike. But sith the several places where most of them lay are not yet very perfectly known unto the learned of these days, I do not mean to pronounce my judgment upon such doubtful cases, lest that in so doing I should but increase conjectures and, leading peradventure the reader from the more probable, entangle his mind in the end with such as are of less value and things nothing so likely to be true as those which other men have remembered and set down before me. Neither will I speak aught of the Roman partitions and limits of their legions, whose number and place of abode, except of the Victorian and Augustan, is to me utterly unknown.

It shall suffice therefore to begin with such a ground as from whence some better certainty of things may be derived, and that is with the estate of our island in the time of Alfred, who first divided England into shires, which before his days and since the coming of the Saxons was limited out by families and hidelands,[3]

---

[1] That is, Devana, the city of the Taexali.

[2] The first thirty-six tribal names, through the Dumnonii, are derived from the second-century *Geography* of Claudius Ptolemaeus, II, iii. The names from the Cassi through the Bibroci occur in Caesar's *Gallic War*, V, xxi.

[3] *Hidelands:* a hideland, or hide, was the amount of land necessary to support a family.

as the Britons did the same in their time, by hundreds of towns, which then were called cantreds, as old records do witness.

Into how many shires the said Alfred did first make this partition of the island, it is not yet found out; howbeit, if my conjecture be anything at all, I suppose that he left not under eight-and-thirty, sith we find by no good author that above fifteen have been added by any of his successors since the time of his decease. This prince, therefore, having made the general partition of his kingdom into shires, or shares, he divided again the same into lathes, as lathes into hundreds, and hundreds into tithings, or denaries,[4] as divers have written and Master Lambarde, following their authorities, hath also given out, saying almost after this manner in his description of Kent: the Danes, saith he, both before and in the time of King Alfred, had flocked by the seacoasts of this island in great numbers, sometimes wasting and spoiling with sword and fire wheresoever they might arrive, and sometime taking great booties with them to their ships, without doing any further hurt or damage to the country. This inconvenience, continuing for many years together, caused our husbandmen to abandon their tillage and gave occasion and hardiness to evil-disposed persons to fall to the like pillage, as practicing to follow the Danes in these their thefts and robberies.[5] And the better to cloak their mischief withal, they feigned themselves to be Danish pirates, and would sometime come aland in one port and sometime in another, driving daily great spoils (as the Danes had done) unto their ships before them. The good King Alfred therefore (who had marvelously travailed in repelling the barbarous Danes), espying this outrage and thinking it no less the part of a politic prince to root out the noisome subject than to hold out the foreign adversary, by the advice of his nobility and the example of Moses (who followed the counsel of Jethro, his father-in-law, to the like effect), divided the whole realm into certain parts or sections, which (of the Saxon word *schyran*, signifying "to cut") he termed shires, or as we yet speak, shares or portions, of which some one hath 40 miles in length (as Essex) and almost so many broad, Hereford 24 in length and 20 in breadth, and Warwick 36 in length, etc.; and some of them also

---

[4] *Lathes:* administrative units, each comprising several hundreds, apparently unique to Kent; *tithings,* or *denaries:* units of ten families.
[5] "Englishmen noisome to their own country."—*H.*

contain 10, 12, 13, 16, 20, or 30 hundreds, more or less, as some hundreds do 16, 20, 30, 40, 50, or 60 towns, out of which the King was always to receive 100 able men to serve him in the wars, or 100 men able to be pledges; and over each of the portions he appointed either an earl or ealderman, or both, to whom he committed the government of the same.

These shires also he brake into lesser parts, whereof some were called "lathes," of the word *gelathian*, which is "to assemble together," other, "hundreds," for that they enjoyed jurisdiction over 100 pledges, and other, "tithings," because there were in each of them to the number of 10 persons, whereof every one from time to time was surety for others' good abearing. He provided also that every man should procure himself to be received into some tithing, to the end that if any were found of so small and base a credit that no man would become pledge or surety for him, he should forthwith be committed to prison, lest otherwise he might happen to do more harm abroad. Hitherto Master Lambarde.[6] By whose words we may gather very much of the state of this island in the time of Alfred, whose institution continued after a sort until the coming of the Normans, who changed the government of the realm in such wise (by bringing in of new officers and offices, after the manner of their countries) that very little of the old regiment remained more than the bare names of some officers (except peradventure in Kent), so that in these days it is hard to set down any great certainty of things as they stood in Alfred's time, more than is remembered and touched at this present.

Some, as it were roaming or roving at the name "lathe," do say that it is derived of a barn, which is called in Old English a "lathe," as they conjecture.[7] From which speech in like sort some derive the word "laystow," [8] as if it should be truly written "lathestow," a place wherein to lay up or lay on things, of whatsoever condition. But hereof as yet I cannot absolutely be

---

[6] *William Lambarde* (1536-1601): county historian and legal writer. Harrison probably knew him through Lord Cobham, who made Lambarde an executor and trustee in his will. Harrison borrows this passage from Lambarde's *Perambulation of Kent* (1576), pp. 20-21. Except for the insertion concerning the size of the counties, he follows Lambarde closely, making only minor stylistic changes.

[7] So Sir Thomas Smith, *De republica Anglorum*, II, xvi. See p. 94, n. 1.

[8] *Laystow*: laystall, a place where refuse and dung are laid.

satisfied, although peradventure some likelihood in their judgments may seem to be therein. Other, upon some further consideration, affirm that they were certain circuits in every county or shire, containing an appointed number of towns, whose inhabitants always assembled, to know and understand of matters touching their portions, into some one appointed place or other within their limits, especially whilst the causes were such as required not the aid or assistance of the whole county. Of these lathes also (as they say) some shires had more, some less, as they were of greatness. And Master Lambarde seemeth to be of the opinion that the leets of our time (wherein these pledges be yet called *franci plegii,* of the word "freeborough")[9] do yield some shadow of that politic institution of Alfred. But sith my skill is so small in these cases that I dare not judge anything at all as of mine own knowledge, I will not set down anything more than I read, lest I should rove at random in our obscure antiquities; and reading no more of lathes, my next talk shall be of hundreds.

The hundred and the wapentake [10] is all one, as I read in some, and by this division not a name appertinent to a set number of towns (for then all hundreds should be of equal quantity) but a limited jurisdiction, within the compass whereof were an hundred persons called pledges (as I said), or ten denaries, or tithings, of men, of which each one was bound for others' good abearing and laudable behavior in the commonwealth of the realm. The chief man likewise of every denary, or tithing, was in those days called a tithingman, in Latin, *decurio,* but now in most places a borsholder or burgholder, as in Kent (where every tithing is moreover named a burgh or borrow), although that in the West Country he be still called a tithingman and his circuit a tithing, as I have heard at large.[11] I read furthermore (and it is partly afore noted) that the said Alfred caused each man of free condition (for the better maintenance of his peace) to be ascribed into some hundred by placing himself in one denary or other, where he might always have such as should swear or say upon

[9] *Perambulation of Kent,* p. 21. *Leets:* manorial courts; *franci plegii:* frankpledge was the system which made every member of a tithing responsible for the good conduct of the others; frankpledges were members of such a tithing; *freeborough:* corrupt for *frithborh,* literally, peace pledge, the OE term for frankpledge.

[10] *Wapentake:* the term applied to a hundred in certain northern counties.

[11] *Perambulation of Kent,* p. 22.

their certain knowledge for his honest behavior and civil conversation, if it should happen at any time that his credit should come in question.

In like sort I gather out of Leland [Lambarde?] and other that if any small matter did fall out worthy to be discussed, the tithingman or borsholder (now officers at the commandment of the high constable, of which every hundred hath one at the least) should decide the same in their leets, whereas the great causes were referred to the hundreds, the greater to the lathes, and the greatest of all to the shire days, where the earls or ealdermen did set themselves and make final ends of the same, according unto justice. For this purpose likewise in every hundred were twelve men chosen of good age and wisdom, and those sworn to give their sentences without respect of person, and in this manner (as they gather) were things handled in those days.

Which way the word wapentake came in use, as yet I cannot tell; howbeit, the signification of the same declareth (as I conceive) that at the chief town the soldiers which were to serve in that hundred did meet, fetch their weapons, and go together from thence to the field or place of service, by an ordinary custom then generally known amongst them.[12] It is supposed also that the word "rape"[13] cometh *a rapiendo,* as it were of catching and snatching, because the tenants of the hundred or wapentakes met upon one or sundry days and made quick dispatch of their lord's harvest at once and in great haste. But whether it be a true imagination or not, as yet I am uncertain, and therefore it lieth not in me to determine anything thereof, wherefore it shall suffice to have touched them in this manner.

In my time there are found to be in England forty shires, and likewise thirteen in Wales, and these latter erected of late years by King Henry the Eighth, who made the Britons, or Welshmen, equal in all respects unto the English and brought to pass that both nations should indifferently be governed by one law, which in times past were ordered by divers, and those far discrepant and disagreeing one from another, as by the several view of the same is yet easy to be discerned. The names of the shires in England are these, whereof the first ten lie between the British

---

[12] Harrison has in mind the derivation of wapentake from "weapon" and "take," a sound etymology.

[13] *Rape:* an administrative unit in Sussex, comprising several hundreds.

sea and the Thames, as Polydore also doth set them down: [14] Kent, Sussex, Surrey, Hampshire, Berkshire, Wiltshire, Dorsetshire, Somerset, Devon, Cornwall. There are moreover on the north side of the Thames and between the same and the river Trent, which passeth through the midst [middle] of England (as Polydore saith), sixteen other shires, whereof six lie toward the east, the rest toward the west, more into the midst of the country: Essex (sometime all forest, save one hundred), Middlesex, Hertfordshire, Suffolk, Norfolk, Cambridgeshire (in which are twelve hundreds), Bedford, Huntingdon (wherein are four hundreds), Buckingham, Oxford, Northampton, Rutland, Leicestershire, Nottinghamshire, Warwick, Lincoln. We have six also that have their place westward towards Wales, whose names ensue: Gloucester, Hereford, Worcester, Shropshire, Stafford, Cheshire. And these are the thirty-two shires which lie by south of the Trent. Beyond the same river we have in like sort other eight, as: Derby, York, Lancashire, Cumberland, Westmorland, Richmond (wherein are five wapentakes, and when it is accounted as parcel of Yorkshire, out of which it is taken, then is it reputed for the whole Riding), Durham, Northumberland. So that in the portion sometime called Loegria there are now forty shires. In Wales furthermore are thirteen, whereof seven are in South Wales: Cardigan, or Cereticon; Penmoroke, or Pembroke; Carmarthen (wherein are nine hundreds, or commots); [15] Glamorgan; Monmouth; Brecknock; Radnor. In North Wales likewise are six, that is to say: Anglesey, Caernarvon, Merioneth, Denbigh, Flint, Montgomery. Which, being added to those of England, yield fifty-and-three shires, or counties, so that under the Queen's Majesty are so many counties, whereby it is easily discerned that her power far exceedeth that of Offa, who of old time was highly honored for that he had so much of Britain under his subjection as afterward contained thirty-nine shires, when the division was made whereof I spake before.

This is moreover to be noted in our division of shires, that they be not always counted or laid together in one parcel,

[14] *Polydore Vergil* (d. ?1555): Italian scholar and historian, long resident in England. His *Anglicae historiae,* undertaken at the request of Henry VII, was first printed in 1534. Harrison follows closely the order and division of the English counties given by Polydore at the beginning of his work.

[15] *Commots:* Welsh administrative units, each comprising two cantreds, or hundreds.

whereof I have great marvel. But sith the occasion hath grown (as I take it) either by privilege or some like occasion, it is better briefly to set down how some of these parts lie than to spend the time in seeking a just cause of this their odd division. First, therefore, I note that in the part of Buckinghamshire between Amersham and Beaconsfield there is a piece of Hertfordshire to be found, environed round about with the county of Buckingham, and yet this patch is not above three miles in length and two in breadth at the very most. In Berkshire, also, between Ruscombe and Wokingham, is a piece of Wiltshire, one mile in breadth and four miles in length, whereof one side lieth on the Loddon River. In the borders of Northamptonshire, directly over against Luffield, a town in Buckinghamshire, I find a parcel of Oxfordshire, not passing two miles in compass.

With Oxfordshire divers do participate, insomuch that a piece of Gloucestershire lieth half in Warwickshire and half in Oxfordshire, not very far from Hornton. Such another patch is there of Gloucestershire, not far from Long Compton but lying in Oxford County, and a piece of Worcestershire directly between it and Gloucestershire. Gloucester hath the third piece upon the north side of the Windrush near Fulbrook, as Berkshire hath one parcel also upon the self side of the same water, in the very edge of Gloucestershire; likewise another in Oxfordshire, not very far from Burford; and the third over against Lechlade, which is parted from the main county of Berkshire by a little strake of Oxfordshire. Who would think that two fragments of Wiltshire were to be seen in Berkshire upon the Loddon and the river that falleth into it? whereof and the like, sith there are very many, I think good to give this brief admonition.[16] For although I have not presently gone through with them all, yet these may suffice to give notice of this thing, whereof most readers (as I persuade myself) are ignorant.

But to proceed with our purpose. Over each of these shires in time of necessity is a several lieutenant chosen under the prince, who, being a nobleman of calling, hath almost regal authority over the same for the time being in many cases which do concern his office; otherwise, it is governed by a sheriff (a word derived of "schire" and "greve," and pronounced as "shire" and "reeve"),

<hr />

[16] Harrison drew all these details directly from Saxton's single map of Oxford, Buckinghamshire, and Berkshire (engraved 1574). See p. 219, n. 47.

whose office is to gather up and bring his accounts into the exchequer, of the profits of his county received, whereof he is or may be called *quaestor comitatus* or *provinciae*. This officer is resident and dwelling somewhere within the same county and called also a viscount, *quasi vicarius comitis* or *procomes*,[17] in respect of the earl (or, as they called him in time past, the ealderman), that beareth his name of the county, although it be seldom seen in England that the earl hath any great store of possessions or aught to do in the shire whereof he taketh his name, more than is allowed to him through his personal resiance, if he happen to dwell and be resident in the same.

In the election also of these magistrates, divers able persons, as well for wealth as wisdom, are named by the commons at a time and place appointed for their choice, whose names being delivered to the prince, he forthwith pricketh some such one of them as he pleaseth to assign unto that office, to whom he committeth the charge of the county, and who hereupon is sheriff of that shire for one whole year, or until a new be chosen. The sheriff also hath his undersheriff, that ruleth and holdeth the shire courts and law days under him, upon sufficient caution unto the high sheriff for his true execution of justice, preservation from impeachment, and yielding of account when he shall be thereunto called. There are likewise under him certain bailiffs, whose office is to serve and return such writs and processes as are directed unto them from the high sheriff; to make seizure of the goods and chattels and arrest the bodies of such as do offend, presenting either their persons unto him, or at the leastwise taking sufficient bond or other assurance of them for their dutiful appearance at an appointed time, when the sheriff by order of law ought to present them to the judges according to his charge. In every hundred also are one or more high constables, according to the quantity thereof, who, receiving the writs and injunctions from the high sheriff under his seal, or from any other officers of the prince, either for the provision of victuals or for other causes, or private purveyance of cates [provisions, delicacies] for the maintenance of the royal family, do forthwith charge the petty con-

---

[17] *Quaestor comitatus* or *provinciae:* treasurer of the county or shire; *quasi vicarius comitis* or *procomes:* that is, the earl's deputy or one acting for the earl. Harrison borrowed the Latin phrases from Smith, *De republica Anglorum*, II, xiv.

stables of every town within their limits with the execution of
the same.

In each county likewise are sundry law days holden at their
appointed seasons, of which some retain the old Saxon name
and are called motelagh, of the words "moot" [18] and "law." They
have also another called the sheriff's tourn, which they hold twice
in their times in every hundred, according to the old order appointed by King Edgar (as King Edward reduced the folkmoot,
ordained by King Arthur to be held yearly on the first of May,
until the first of every month), and in these two latter such small
matters as oft arise amongst the inferior sort of people are heard
and well determined. They have, finally, their quarter sessions,
wherein they are assisted by the justices and gentlemen of the
country, and twice in the year jail delivery,[19] at which time the
judges ride about in their circuits into every several county
(where the nobility and gentlemen with the justices there resiant
associate them) and minister the laws of the realm with great
solemnity and justice. Howbeit, in doing of these things they
retain still the old order of the land in use before the Conquest.
For they commit the full examination of all causes there to be
heard to the consideration of twelve sober, grave, and wise men
chosen out of the same county, and four of them of necessity
out of the hundred where the action lieth or the defendant in-
habiteth (which number they call an inquest), and of these
inquests there are more or less impaneled at every assize, as the
number of cases there to be handled doth crave and require,
albeit that some one inquest hath often diverse matters to consider of. And when they have (to their uttermost power) consulted and debated of such things as they are charged withal,
they return again to the place of justice with their verdict in
writing, according whereunto the judge doth pronounce his sentence, be it for life or death, or any other matter whatsoever is
brought before him. It is also very often seen that such as are
nominated to be of these inquests do, after their charge received,
seldom or never eat or drink until they have agreed upon their
verdict and yielded it up unto the judge of whom they received
the charge; by means whereof sometimes it cometh to pass that

---

[18] *Moot:* a popular assembly, especially one forming a court of judicature.
[19] *Jail delivery:* clearing a jail of prisoners by bringing them to trial at the
assizes.

divers of the inquest have been wellnear famished, or at least taken such a sickness thereby as they have hardly avoided [with difficulty recovered from]. And this cometh by practice, when the one side feareth the sequel and therefore conveyeth some one or more into the jury that will in his behalf never yield unto the rest but of set purpose put them to this trouble.

Certes it is a common practice (if the undersheriff be not the better man) for the craftier or stronger side to procure and pack such a quest as he himself shall like of, whereby he is sure of the issue before the charge be given; and beside this, if the matter do justly proceed against him, it is a world to see now and then how the honest yeomen that have *bona fide* discharged their consciences shall be sued of an attaint [20] and bound to appear at the Star Chamber, with what rigor they shall be carried from place to place, county to county, yea, and sometime in carts, which hath and doth cause a great number of them to abstain from the assizes and yield to pay their issues [exemptions], rather than they would for their good meaning be thus disturbed and dealt withal. Sometimes also they bribe the bailiffs to be kept at home, whereupon poor men, not having in their purses wherewith to bear their costs, are impaneled upon juries, who very often have neither reason nor judgment to perform the charge they come for. Neither was this kind of service at any time half so painful as at this present; for until of late years (that the number of lawyers and attorneys hath so exceedingly increased that some shifts must needs be found and matters sought out whereby they may be set on work) a man should not have heard at one assize of more than two or three *nisi prius*,[21] but very seldom of an attaint, whereas now an hundred and more of the first and one or two of the latter are very often perceived, and some of them for a cause arising of sixpence or twelvepence. Which declareth that men are grown to be far more contentious than they have been in time past, and readier to revenge their quarrels of small importance, whereof the lawyers complain not. But to my purpose, from whence I have now digressed.

[20] *Attaint:* the conviction of a jury for giving a false verdict.
[21] *Nisi prius:* a writ directed to a sheriff commanding him to provide a jury to hear a civil cause from the county which has been commenced in the courts at Westminster, unless before (*nisi prius*) the appointed day it has been heard by the judges of assize; thus the phrase may also mean, more generally, the hearing of any civil cause by the judges of assize.

Beside these officers afore mentioned, there are sundry other in every county, as coroners, whose duty is to inquire of such as come to their death by violence, to attach and present the pleas of the Crown, to make inquiry of treasure found, etc. There are divers also of the best learned of the law, beside sundry gentlemen, where the number of lawyers will not suffice (and whose revenues do amount to above £20 by the year), appointed by especial commission from the prince to look unto the good government of her subjects in the counties where they dwell. And of these the least skillful in the law are of the peace, the other both of the peace and quorum, otherwise called of oyer and determiner,[22] so that the first have authority only to hear, the other to hear and determine such matters as are brought unto their presence. These also do direct their warrants to the keepers of the jails within their limitations for the safekeeping of such offenders as they shall judge worthy to commit unto their custody, there to be kept under ward until the great assizes, to the end their causes may be further examined before the residue of the county; and these officers were first devised about the eighteenth year of Edward the Third, as I have been informed.

They, meeting also and together with the sheriffs, do hold their aforesaid sessions at four times in the year, whereof they are called quarter sessions, and herein they inquire of sundry trespasses and the common annoyances of the King's liege people and divers other things, determining upon them as justice doth require. There are also a third kind of sessions holden by the high constables and bailiffs afore mentioned, called petty sessions, wherein the weights and measures are perused by the clerk of the market for the county, who sitteth with them. At these meetings also victualers and, in like sort, servants, laborers, rogues, and runagates are often reformed for their excesses, although the burning of vagabonds through their ear be referred to the quarter sessions or higher courts of assize, where they are judged either to death, if they be taken the third time and have not since their second apprehension applied themselves to labor, or else to be set perpetually to work in an house erected in every shire for that purpose, of which punishment they stand in greatest fear.

I might here deliver a discourse of sundry rare customs and

---

[22] *Oyer and determiner:* a commission empowering the justices to hear and determine indictments on treasons, felonies, etc.

courts, surnamed baron's,[23] yet maintained and holden in England; but forsomuch as some of the first are beastly and therefore by the lords of the soils now living converted into money, being for the most part devised in the beginning either by malicious or licentious women, in mere contempt and slavish abuse of their tenants, under pretense of some punishment due for their excesses, I pass over to bring them unto light, as also the remembrance of sundry courts-baron likewise holden in strange manner; yet none more absurd and far from law than are kept yearly at King's Hill in Rochford, and therefore may well be called a lawless court, as most are that were devised upon such occasions. This court is kept upon Wednesday ensuing after Michaelmas Day after midnight, so that it is begun and ended before the rising of the sun. When the tenants also are all together in an alehouse, the steward secretly stealeth from them with a lantern under his cloak and goeth to the King's Hill, where, sitting on a molehill, he calleth them with a very soft voice, writing their appearance upon a piece of paper with a coal, having none other light than that which is enclosed in the lantern; so soon as the tenants also do miss the steward, they run to the hill with all their might, and there answer all at once, "Here, here," whereby they escape their amercements, which they should not do if he could have called over his bill of names before they had missed him in the alehouse. And this is the very form of the court devised at the first (as the voice goeth) upon a rebellion made by the tenants of the honor of Raibie [Rayleigh] against their lord, in perpetual memory of their disobedience showed.[24] I could beside this speak also of some other, but sith one hath taken upon him to collect a number of them into a particular treatise, I think it sufficient for me to have said so much of both.

And thus much have I thought good to set down generally of the said counties and their manner of governance, although not in so perfect order as the cause requireth, because that, of all the rest, there is nothing wherewith I am less acquainted than with our temporal regiment, which (to say truth) smally concerneth

[23] *Court-baron:* a manorial court; one form was the customary court, presided over by the steward, which dealt with matters affecting leases and customary obligations to the lord of the manor.

[24] A similar account of this famous "lawless court" of southeastern Essex is given by John Norden, *The Surveyor's Dialogue* (1610), p. 98.

my calling. What else is to be added after the several shires of England, with their ancient limits (as they agreed with the division of the land in the time of Ptolemy and the Romans) and commodities yet extant, I reserve unto that excellent treatise of my friend, W. Camden, who hath travailed therein very far, and whose work, written in Latin, shall in short time (I hope) be published, to the no small benefit of such as will read and peruse the same.[25]

CHAPTER V

Of Degrees of People in the Commonwealth of England [1]

WE IN England divide our people commonly into four sorts, as gentlemen, citizens or burgesses, yeomen, and artificers[2] or laborers. Of gentlemen the first and chief (next the King) be the prince, dukes, marquises, earls, viscounts, and barons, and these are called gentlemen of the greater sort, or (as our common usage of speech is) lords and noblemen; and next unto them be knights, esquires, and, last of all, they that are simply called gentlemen; so that in effect our gentlemen are divided into their conditions, whereof in this chapter I will make particular rehearsal.

[25] This sentence was added in the 1587 edition. *William Camden* (1551-1623): perhaps the greatest of the Elizabethan antiquarians. His monumental *Britannia* was first printed in 1586.

[1] Much of this chapter was borrowed by Sir Thomas Smith for his *De republica Anglorum* (I, xvi-xxiv), as Harrison notes (p. 152). Smith, a native of Saffron Walden near Radwinter, revised this work during the lingering illness that terminated in his death on August 12, 1577. He may have survived long enough to see Holinshed in print, or Harrison may have showed him a draft of the chapter, since he was Chancellor of the Order of the Garter, on which Harrison here discourses at length. Smith often adds to or rephrases Harrison, and Harrison cross-borrows some of the changes in 1587. *De republica* was first printed in 1583.

[2] So 1577; the 1587 edition reads, "yeomen, which are artificers." Harrison seems to have been in some doubt where to classify craftsmen. On p. 117 he distinguishes yeomen from "laborers and the common sort of artificers," noting that they are usually farmers "or at the leastwise artificers," but on p. 118 he seems to rank "all artificers" among the "fourth and last sort."

The title of prince doth peculiarly belong with us to the King's eldest son, who is called Prince of Wales and is the heir apparent to the crown, as in France the King's eldest son hath the title of Dolphin and is named peculiarly *Monsieur.* So that the Prince is so termed of the Latin word *princeps,* sith he is (as I may call him) the chief or principal next the King. The King's younger sons be but gentlemen by birth (till they have received creation or donation from their father of higher estate, as to be either viscounts, earls, or dukes) and called after their names, as Lord Henry or Lord Edward, with the addition of the word "Grace," properly assigned to the King and Prince, and now also by custom conveyed to dukes, archbishops, and (as some say) to marquises and their wives.

The title of duke cometh also of the Latin word *dux, a ducendo* [leading], because of his valor and power over the army, in times past a name of office due to the emperor, consul, or chief governor of the whole army in the Roman wars, but now a name of honor, although perished in England, whose ground will not long bear one duke at once; but if there were many, as in time past, or as there be now earls, I do not think but that they would flourish and prosper well enough.[3]

In old time he only was called marquis *qui habuit terram limitaneam,* a marching [border] province upon the enemy's countries, and thereby bound to keep and defend the frontiers. But that also is changed in common use and reputed for a name of great honor next unto the duke, even over counties and sometimes small cities, as the prince is pleased to bestow it.

The name of earl likewise was among the Romans a name of office, who had *comites sacri palatii, comites aerarii, comites stabuli, comites patrimonii, largitionum, scholarum, commerciorum,* and suchlike.[4] But at the first they were called *comites* which were joined in commission with the proconsul, legate, or

---

[3] The last representative of the ducal order in Elizabeth's reign, the Duke of Norfolk, went to the scaffold in 1572.

[4] In the later empire *comites* were civil administrators who assisted the emperor in the exercise of his peculiar rights (*comites sacri palatii*), managed the treasury (*comites aerarii*) or the emperor's private property (*comites sacri patrimonii*) or his private and public revenues (*comites privatarum* and *sacrarum largitionum*), acted as masters of the horse (*comites stabuli,* whence "constable"), or administered the imperial guard (*comites scholarum*) or trade (*comites commerciorum*).

judges for counsel and aid's sake in each of those several charges. As Cicero (*Epistola ad Quintum fratrem*) remembereth, where he saith: *Atque inter hos quos tibi comites et adjutores negotiorum publicorum dedit ipsa respublica duntaxat finibus his praestabis, quos ante praescripsi, etc.*[5] After this I read also that every president in his charge was called *comes*, but our English Saxons used the word "heretoch"[6] and "earl" for *comes*, and indifferently as I guess, sith the name of duke was not in use before the Conquest. Goropius saith that *comes* and *grave* is all one,[7] to wit, the viscount, called either *procomes* or *vicecomes*, and in time past governed in the county under the earl, but now, without any such service or office, it is also become a name of dignity next after the earl and in degree before the baron. His relief also by the Great Charter is £100, as that of a barony a hundred marks, and of a knight five at the most for every fee.[8]

The baron, whose degree answered to the dignity of a senator in Rome, is such a free lord as hath a lordship or barony, whereof he beareth his name, and hath divers knights or freeholders holding of him, who with him did serve the King in his wars, and held their tenures in *baronia*, that is, for performance of such service. These Bracton (a learned writer of the laws of England in King Henry the Third's time)[9] termeth *barones, quasi robur belli* [that is, the best in war]. The word *baro* indeed is older than that it may easily be found from whence it came, for even in the oldest histories both of the Germans and Frenchmen, written since the Conquest, we read of barons, and those are at this day called among the Germans *liberi vel ingenui* [freemen or free-

[5] "And you will be responsible, at least within the limits I have previously set down, for the associates and assistants in public business whom the state itself has assigned you" (I, i, 3). Quintus Tullius Cicero, the orator's brother, was proconsul in Asia, 61-58 B.C.

[6] *Heretoch:* heretoga, an ealderman, the commander of the militia of a shire.

[7] *Goropius:* Jean Becan (1518-1572), a Flemish doctor, linguist, and antiquary, best known for his defense of German as the language of Eden. The reference here is to his *Origines Antwerpianae* (Antwerp, 1569), p. 148, from which the preceding quotation from Cicero and other details in the paragraph are also derived. *Grave:* in Middle Dutch a title equivalent to count (German, *Graf*).

[8] *Relief:* an inheritance tax, the rate fixed by Article 2 of the Magna Carta.

[9] *Henry de Bracton* (d. 1268): author of a comprehensive treatise on English law, *De legibus et consuetudinibus Angliae* (I, viii), printed by Tottel in 1569.

born], or *Freihers* in the German tongue, as some men do conjecture, or (as one saith) the citizens and burgesses of good towns and cities were called *barones*. Nevertheless, by diligent inquisition it is imagined, if not absolutely found, that the word *baro* and *filius* in the old Scythian or German language are all one, so that the King's children are properly called *barones*, from whom also it was first translated to their kindred and then to the nobility and officers of greatest honor indifferently. That *baro* and *filius* signifieth one thing, it yet remaineth to be seen, although with some corruption; for to this day even the common sort do call their male children "barnes" [bairns] here in England, especially in the North Country, where that word is yet accustomably in use. And it is also grown into a proverb in the South, when any man sustaineth a great hindrance, to say, "I am beggared, and all my barnes." In the Hebrew tongue (as some affirm) it signifieth *filii solis*,[10] and what are the nobility in every kingdom but *filii* or *servi regum?* But this is farfetched, wherefore I conclude that from henceforth the original of the word *baro* shall not be any more to seek; and the first time that ever I read thereof in any English history is in the reign of Canute, who called his nobility and head officers to a council holden at Cirencester by that name, 1030, as I have elsewhere remembered.[11] Howbeit, the word *baro* doth not always signify or is attributed to a nobleman by birth or creation, for now and then it is a title given to one or other with his office, as the chief or high tribune of the Exchequer is of custom called Lord Chief Baron, who is, as it were, the great or principal receiver of accounts next unto the Lord Treasurer, as they [who] are under him are called *tribuni aerarii, et rationales*.[12] Hereunto I may add so much of the word "lord," which is an addition going not seldom and in like sort with sundry offices and to continue so long as he or they do execute the same, and no longer.

Unto this place I also refer our bishops, who are accounted honorable, called lords, and hold the same room in the Parliament House with the barons, albeit, for honor sake, the right hand of

[10] *Filii solis:* sons of the sun. Harrison seems to have in mind the Aramaic *bar*, son.

[11] The *Anglo-Saxon Chronicle* assigns this council to Easter in 1020. Since no other mention of it occurs in the *Descriptions*, Harrison is probably recalling his Chronology.

[12] *Tribuni aerarii, et rationales:* paymasters and accountants of the treasury.

the prince is given unto them, and whose countenances in time
past were much more glorious than at this present it is, because
those lusty prelates sought after earthly estimation and authority
with far more diligence than after the lost sheep of Christ, of
which they had small regard, as men being otherwise occupied
and void of leisure to attend upon the same. Howbeit, in these
days their estate remaineth no less reverend than before, and the
more virtuous they are that be of this calling, the better are
they esteemed with high and low. They retain also the ancient
name (lord) still, although it be not a little impugned by such as
love either to hear of change of all things or can abide no superiors. For notwithstanding it be true that, in respect of function, the office of the eldership is equally distributed between
the bishop and the minister,[13] yet for civil government's sake the
first have more authority given unto them by kings and princes,
to the end that the rest may thereby be with more ease retained
within a limited compass of uniformity than otherwise they
would be, if each one were suffered to walk in his own course.
This also is more to be marveled at, that very many call for an
alteration of their estate, crying to have the word "lord" abolished, their civil authority taken from them, and the present condition of the Church in other things reformed; whereas to say
truly, few of them do agree upon form of discipline and government of the church succedent, wherein they resemble the
Capuans, of whom Livy doth speak, in the slaughter of their
senate.[14] Neither is it possible to frame a whole monarchy after
the pattern of one town or city, or to stir up such an exquisite
face of the church as we imagine or desire, sith our corruption
is such that it will never yield to so great perfection; for that
which is not able to be performed in a private house will much
less be brought to pass in a commonwealth and kingdom, before
such a prince be found as Xenophon describeth, or such an
orator as Tully hath devised. But whither am I digressed from
my discourse of bishops, whose estates do daily decay and suffer
some diminution?

Herein nevertheless their case is grown to be much better than

---

[13] "I Sam., b. 15, I Reg., a. 7."—*H*. For I Sam. 15:30 and I Kings 8:1–3.
[14] The Capuans were persuaded to spare their senators when they discovered the impossibility of agreeing upon less bad replacements (XXIII,
iii).

before, for whereas in times past the clergymen were feared because of their authority and severe government under the prince, now are they beloved generally for their painful diligence daily showed in their functions and callings, except peradventure of some hungry wombs that covet to pluck and snatch at the loose ends of their best commodities; with whom it is (as the report goeth) a common guise, when a man is to be preferred to an ecclesiastical living, what part thereof he will first forgo and part with to their use. Finally, how it standeth with the rest of the clergy for their places of estate, I neither can tell nor greatly care to know. Nevertheless, with what degrees of honor and worship they have been matched in times past Joannes Boemus, in his *De omnium gentium moribus*,[15] and others do express; and this also found beside their reports, that in time past every bishop, abbot, and pelting [paltry] prior were placed before the earls and barons in most statutes, charters, and records made by the prince, as may also appear in the Great Charter and sundry years of Henry the Third, wherein no duke was heard of. But as a number of their odious comparisons and ambitious titles are now decayed and worthily shrunk in the wetting, so giving over in these days to maintain such pompous vanity, they do think it sufficient for them to preach the Word and hold their livings to their sees (so long as they shall be able) from the hands of such as endeavor for their own preferment to fleece and diminish the same.

This furthermore will I add generally in commendation of the clergy of England, that they are for their knowledge reputed in France, Portingale, Spain, Germany, and Polonia to be the most learned divines, although they like not anything at all of their religion, and thereto they are indeed so skillful in the two principal tongues that it is accounted a maim in any one of them not to be exactly seen in the Greek and Hebrew, much more, then, to be utterly ignorant or nothing conversant in them.[16] As for the

---

[15] "*De Asia, cap.* 12."—H. Boemus' treatise was first published in 1520. Harrison has in mind a passage showing the manner in which the early Christians organized themselves on the Roman imperial model: "[Peter] should at Rome be president over the universal church, as the emperor there was ruler of the universal world. . . . In the place of the senators they took the cardinals. To match their kings, which had three dukes at commandment, they devised primates, to whom were subject three archbishops" (trans. William Waterman as *The Fardel of Fashions*, 1555, sig. R3r-v).

[16] "No Greek, no grace."—H.

Latin tongue, it is not wanting in any of the ministry, especially in such as have been made within this twelve or fourteen years, whereas before there was small choice and many cures were left unserved because they had none at all. And to say truth, our adversaries were the only causers hereof. For whilst they made no further account of their priesthood than to construe, sing, read [17] their service and their portass, it came to pass that, upon examination had, few made in Queen Mary's days and the latter end of King Henry were able to do any more, and very hardly so much, so void were they of further skill and so unapt to serve at all.

Dukes, marquises, earls, viscounts, and barons either be created of the prince or come to that honor by being the eldest sons or highest in succession to their parents. For the eldest son of a duke during his father's life is an earl, the eldest son of an earl is a baron, or sometimes a viscount, according as the creation is. The "creation" I call the original donation and condition of the honor given by the prince for good service done by the first ancestor with some advancement, which, with the title of that honor, is always given to him and his heirs males only. The rest of the sons of the nobility by the rigor of the law be but esquires, yet in common speech all dukes' and marquises' sons and earls' eldest sons be called lords, the which name commonly doth agree to none of lower degree than barons, yet by law and use these be not esteemed barons.

The barony, or degree of lords, doth answer to the degree of senators of Rome (as I said), and the title of nobility (as we use to call it in England) to the Roman *patricii*. Also in England no man is commonly created baron except he may dispend of yearly revenues £1,000, or so much as may fully maintain and bear out his countenance and port. But viscounts, earls, marquises, and dukes exceed them according to the proportion of their degree and honor. But though by chance he or his son have less, yet he keepeth this degree; but if the decay be excessive and not able to maintain the honor, as *senatores Romani* were *amoti a senatu* [banished from the senate], so sometimes they are not admitted

---

[17] "*Bene con, bene can, bene le.*"—H. The phrase seems to have the same meaning as the English it glosses; apparently it represents Harrison's satirical reproduction (for *bene construo, bene canto, bene lego*) of the small Latin of the Roman priests.

to the upper house in the Parliament, although they keep the name of lord still, which cannot be taken from them upon any such occasion. The most of these names have descended from the French invention, in whose histories we shall read of them eight hundred years past.

This also is worthy the remembrance, that Otto, the first emperor of that name, endeavoring to restore the decayed estate of Italy unto some part of her pristinate magnificence, did after the French example give *dignitates et praedia* [18] to such knights and soldiers as had served him in the wars, whom he also adorned with the names of dukes, marquises, earls, vavasors or captains, and vavasines.

His *praedia* in like manner were tributes, tolls, portage, bankage, stackage,[19] coinage, profits by salt pits, mills, watercourses (and whatsoever emoluments grew by them), and suchlike. But at that present I read not that the word *baro* was brought into those parts. And as for the vavasors, it was a denomination applied unto all degrees of honor under the first three (which are properly named the king's captains), so that they are called *majores, minores, et minimi valvasores*. This also is to be noted, that the word "captain" hath two relations, either as the possessor thereof hath it from the prince or from some duke, marquis, or earl, for each had captains under them. If from the prince, then are they called *majores valvasores*, if from any of his three peers, then were they *minores valvasores*, but if any of these vavasors do substitute a deputy, those are called *minimi valvasores* and their deputies also *valvasini*, without regard unto which degree the vavasor doth appertain; but the word vavasors is now grown out of use, wherefore it sufficeth to have said thus much of that function.

Knights be not born, neither is any man a knight by succession, no, not the King or prince; but they are made either before

[18] *Dignitates et praedia:* titles and estates. This paragraph and the next are largely translated from the *Historiarum de regno Italiae* (Basel, 1575, p. 287) of Carlo Sigonio, or Sigonius (?1524–1584), Italian humanist and historian.

[19] *Portage, bankage, stackage:* for Sigonio's *portus, ripatica, pedatica. Portus:* properly a tax due on entering a port or the gates of a city; *ripatica:* levies connected with the banks of rivers; *pedatica:* tolls paid for passing through a place. Harrison's "bankage" and "stackage," both of which have found their way into the *NED*, are coinages, the latter seemingly based on an error.

the battle, to encourage them the more to adventure and try their manhood, or after the battle ended, as an advancement for their courage and prowess already showed (and then are they called *milites*), or out of the wars for some great service done, or for the singular virtues which do appear in them (and then are they named *equites aurati*,[20] as common custom intendeth). They are made either by the King himself, or by his commission and royal authority given for the same purpose, or by his lieutenant in the wars. This order seemeth to answer in part to that which the Romans called *equitum Romanorum*. For as *equites Romani* were chosen *ex censu*, that is, according to their substance and riches, so be knights in England most commonly according to their yearly revenues or abundance of riches wherewith to maintain their estates. Yet all that had *equestrem censum* were not chosen to be knights, and no more be all made knights in England that may spend a knight's lands, but they only whom the prince will honor. Sometime divers ancient gentlemen, burgesses, and lawyers are called unto knighthood by the prince and nevertheless refuse to take that state upon them, for which they are of custom punished by a fine that redoundeth unto his coffers and, to say truth, is oftentimes more profitable unto him than otherwise their service should be if they did yield unto knighthood. And this also is a cause wherefore there be many in England able to dispend a knight's living which never come unto that countenance, and by their own consents.

The number of the knights in Rome was also uncertain, and so is it of knights likewise with us, as at the pleasure of the prince. And whereas the *equites Romani* had *equum publicum*[21] of custom bestowed upon them, the knights of England have not so but bear their own charges in that also, as in other kind of furniture, as armory meet for their defense and service. This nevertheless is certain, that whoso may dispend £40 by the year of free land, either at the coronation of the King or marriage of his daughter or time of his dubbing, may be enforced unto the taking of that degree or otherwise pay the revenues of his land

---

[20] *Equites aurati:* knights provided with gold, that is, the gold spurs which were a mark of the rank.

[21] *Equum publicum:* a horse supplied at public expense, together with an allowance for its annual support. This sentence and the next are examples of Harrison's cross-borrowing from Smith (I, xviii).

for one year, which is only £40 by an old proportion, and so for a time be acquitted of that title. We name him knight in English that the French calleth *chevalier* and the Latins *equitem*, or *equestris ordinis virum*. And when any man is made a knight, he, kneeling down, is stricken of the King or his substitute with his sword naked upon the back or shoulder, the prince, etc., saying, *Soyes chevalier au nom de Dieu*. And when he riseth up, the King saith, *Advances, bon chevalier*. This is the manner of dubbing knights at this present, and the term "dubbing" is the old term for that purpose, and not "creation"; howbeit, in our time the word "making" is most in use among the common sort.

At the coronation of a King or Queen there be other knights made with longer and more curious ceremonies, called Knights of the Bath. But howsoever one be dubbed or made knight, his wife is by and by called "Madam" or "Lady" so well as the baron's wife; he himself having added to his name in common appellation this syllable "Sir," which is the title whereby we call our knights in England. His wife also of courtesy so long as she liveth is called "My Lady," although she happen to marry with a gentleman or man of mean calling, albeit that by the common law she hath no such prerogative. If her first husband also be of better birth than her second, though this latter likewise be a knight, yet in that she pretendeth a privilege to lose no honor, through courtesy yielded to her sex she will be named after the most honorable or worshipful of both, which is not seen elsewhere.

The other order of knighthood in England, and the most honorable, is that of the Garter, instituted by King Edward the Third, who—after he had gained many notable victories, taken King John of France and King James of Scotland (and kept them both prisoners in the Tower of London at one time), expelled King Henry of Castile, the bastard, out of his realm, and restored Don Pedro unto it (by the help of the Prince of Wales and Duke of Aquitaine, his eldest son, called the Black Prince)—he then invented this society of honor and made a choice out of his own realm and dominions and throughout all Christendom of the best, most excellent, and renowned persons in all virtues and honor, and adorned them with that title to be knights of his order, giving them a garter garnished with gold and precious stones to wear daily on the left leg only; also a kirtle, gown, cloak, chaperon,[22] collar, and other solemn and magnificent apparel, both of stuff and fashion exquisite and heroical, to wear at high feasts, and as to so high and princely an order appertaineth. Of this company also he and his successors, Kings and Queens of England, be the sovereigns, and the rest by certain statutes and laws amongst themselves be taken as brethren and fellows in that order, to the number of six-and-twenty, as I find in a certain treatise written of the same, an example whereof I have here inserted word for word as it was delivered unto me, beginning after this manner.

I might at this present make a long tractation of the Round Table and estate of the knights thereof, erected sometimes by Arthur, the great monarch of this island; and thereunto entreat of the number of his knights and ceremonies belonging to the order, but I think in so doing that I should rather set down the later inventions of other men than a true description of such ancient actions as were performed indeed. I could furthermore, with more facility, describe the royalty of Charles the Great and his twelve peers, with their solemn rites and usages, but unto this also I have no great devotion, considering the truth hereof is now so stained with errors and fables inserted into the same by the lewd religious sort that, except a man should profess to lie with them for company, there is little sound knowledge to be gathered hereof worthy the remembrance. In like manner divers as well subjects as princes have attempted to restore again a Round Table in this land (as, for example, Roger, Lord Mortimer at Kenilworth),[23] but such were the excessive charges appertaining thereunto (as they did make allowance) and so great molestation daily ensued thereupon, beside the breeding of sundry quarrels among the knights and such as resorted hitherto from foreign countries (as it was first used), that in fine they gave it over and suffered their whole inventions to perish and decay, till Edward the Third devised another order, not so much pestered with multitude of knights as the Round Table, but much more honorable for princely port and countenance, as shall appear hereafter.

The Order of the Garter, therefore, was devised in the time

---

[22] *Kirtle:* a tunic; *chaperon:* a hood.
[23] Roger de Mortimer (d. 1282) celebrated his retirement from martial life with a great "round table" tournament at Kenilworth in 1279.

of King Edward the Third and (as some write) upon this oɗ
The Queen's Majesty then living, being departed from his presence the next way toward her lodging, he, following soon after,
happened to find her garter, which slacked by chance and so fell
from her leg, unespied in the throng by such as attended upon
her. His grooms and gentlemen also passed by it, disdaining to
stoop and take up such a trifle;[24] but he, knowing the owner,
commanded one of them to stay and reach it up to him. "Why,
an like Your Grace," saith a gentleman, "it is but some woman's
garter that hath fallen from her as she followed the Queen's
Majesty." "Whatsoever it be," quoth the King, "take it up and
give it me." So when he had received the garter, he said to such
as stood about him, "You, my masters, do make small account of
this blue garter here," and therewith held it out, "but if God
lend me life for a few months, I will make the proudest of you
all to reverence the like." And even upon this slender occasion
he gave himself to the devising of this order. Certes I have not
read of anything that, having had so simple a beginning, hath
grown in the end to so great honor and estimation.[25] But to proceed. After he had studied awhile about the performance of his
device and had set down such orders as he himself invented concerning the same, he proclaimed a royal feast to be holden at
Windsor, whither all his nobility resorted with their ladies, where
he published his institution and forthwith invested an appointed
number into the aforesaid fellowship, whose names ensue, himself being the sovereign and principal of that company. Next
unto himself also he placed:

Edward, Prince of Wales	*N.*, son of Sir John Beauchamp
Henry, Duke of Lancaster	Sir *N.* de Mohun
N[*omen*], Earl of Warwick	Sir Hugh Courtenay
N., Captain de Bouche	Sir Thomas Holland
N., Earl of Stafford	Sir John Grey
N., Earl of Sarum	Sir Richard Fitzsimon
N., Lord Mortimer	Sir Miles Stapleton
Sir John Lisle	Sir Thomas Wale
Sir Bartholomew Burwash [Burghersh]	

---

[24] "Peradventure but a blue ribbon."—*H.*
[25] This account of the famous incident seems to be Harrison's free para-
phrase and dramatization of a passage in Polydore Vergil. Harrison ignores
Polydore's suggestion that the garter belonged either to the Queen or to
one of Edward's *amicae.*

Sir Hugh Wrottesley	Sir Henry Eme
Sir Nele Lorying	Sir Sanchet Dambricourt
Sir John Chandos	[D'Abrichecourt]
Sir James Audley	Sir Walter Pannell, *alias* Paganell
Sir Otho Holland	[Paveley].

What order of election and what statutes were prescribed unto the elected at this first institution, as yet I cannot exactly understand, neither can I learn what every prince afterward added thereunto before the six-and-thirtieth year of King Henry the Eighth and third of King Edward the Sixth, wherefore of necessity I must resort unto the estate of the said order as it is at this present, which I will set down so briefly as I may. When any man therefore is to be elected (upon a room found void for his admission) into this fellowship, the King directeth his letters unto him, notwithstanding that he beforehand be nominated to the same, to this effect: "Right trusty and well-beloved, we greet you well, ascertaining you that in consideration as well of your approved truth and fidelity as also of your courageous and valiant acts of knighthood, with other your probable merits known by experience in sundry parties and behalfs, we, with the companions of the noble Order of the Garter, assembled at the election holden this day within our manor of N[*omen*], have elected and chosen you amongst other to be one of the companions of the said order, as your deserts do condignly require. Wherefore we will that with convenient diligence upon the sight hereof you repair unto our presence, there to receive such things as to the said order appertaineth. Dated under our signet at our manor of N.," etc. These letters are the exemplification of certain which (as it should seem) were written *an.* 3, *Edwardi sexti*, at Greenwich, *Aprilis* 24, unto the Earl of Huntingdon and the Lord George Cobham, Your Lordship's honorable father, at such time as they were called unto the aforesaid company.[26] I find also these names subscribed unto the same:

> Edward, Duke of Somerset, uncle to the King
> The Marquis of Northampton
> Earl of Arundel, Lord Chamberlain

[26] This reference would suggest that Harrison had access to the Cobham family papers and that his source for many of the details concerning the statutes of the order was the copy customarily presented to newly nominated members.

Earl of Shrewsbury
Lord Russell, Lord Privy Seal
Lord St. John, Lord Great Master
Sir John Gage
Sir Anthony Wingfield
Sir William Paget.

Being elected, preparation is made for his installing at Windsor (the place appointed always for this purpose), whereat it is required that his banner be set up, of two yards and a quarter in length and three-quarters in breadth, besides the fringe. Secondly, his sword, of whatsoever length him seemeth good. Thirdly, his helm, which from the charnel [hinge] upwards ought to be of three inches at the least. Fourthly, the crest, with mantles[27] to the helm belonging, of such convenient stuff and bigness as it shall please him to appoint.

Item, a plate of arms at the back of his stall, and crest with mantles and beasts supportant, to be graven in the metal.

Item, lodging scutcheons of his arms, environed with a Garter, and painted in paper or cloth of buckram, which, when he traveleth by the way, are to be fixed in the common inns where he doth lodge as a testimony of his presence and stays from time to time as he did travel.

Item, two mantles, one to remain in the college at Windsor, the other to use at his pleasure, with the scutcheon of the arms of St. George in the Garter, with laces, tasselets, and knops of blue silk and gold belonging to the same.

Item, a surcoat or gown of red or crimson velvet, with a hood of the same, lined with white sarsenet or damask.

Item, a collar of the Garter of thirty ounces of gold troy weight.

Item, a tablet of St. George, richly garnished with precious stones or otherwise.

Item, a Garter for his (left) leg, having the buckle and pendant garnished with gold.

Item, a book of the statutes of the said order.

Item, a scutcheon of the arms of St. George in the Garter to set upon the mantle. And this furniture is to be provided against his installation.

[27] *Mantles:* mantling, heraldric drapery behind a coat of arms.

When any knight is to be installed, he hath with his former letters a Garter sent unto him, and when he cometh to be installed, he is brought into the chapter house, where incontinently his commission is read before the sovereign, or his deputy, and the assembly present; from hence he is led by two knights of the said order, accompanied with the other of the nobility and officers, toward the chapel, having his mantle borne before him, either by a knight of the order or else the king-at-arms, to whom it secondarily appertaineth to bear it. This mantle shall be delivered unto him for his habit after his oath taken before his stall and not before; which done, he shall return unto the chapter house, where the sovereign, or his deputy, shall deliver him his collar, and so he shall have the full possession of his habit. As for his stall, it is not given according unto the calling and countenance of the receiver, but as the place is that happeneth to be void, so that each one called unto this knighthood (the sovereign and emperors and kings and princes always excepted) shall have the same seat which became void by the death of his predecessor, howsoever it fall out, whereby a knight only oftentimes doth sit before a duke, without any murmuring or grudging at his room, except it please the sovereign once in his life only to make a general alteration of those seats and to set each one according to his degree.

Now as touching the apparel of these knights, it remaineth such as King Edward, the first deviser of this order, left it, that is to say, every year one of the colors, that is to say, scarlet, sanguine in grain,[28] blue, and white. In like sort the King's Grace hath at his pleasure the content of cloth for his gown and hood, lined with white satin or damask, and multitude of Garters with letters of gold.

The Prince hath 5 yards of cloth for his gown and hood, and Garters with letters of gold at his pleasure, beside 5 timber[29] of the finest miniver.

A duke hath 5 yards of woolen cloth, 5 timber of miniver, 120 Garters with title of gold.

A marquis hath 5 yards of woolen cloth, 5 timber of miniver, 110 Garters of silk.

---

[28] *Sanguine in grain:* dyed blood-red.
[29] "A timber containeth forty skins, pelts, or fells."—*H.*

An earl, 5 yards of woolen cloth, 5 timber of miniver, and 100 Garters of silk.

A viscount, 5 yards of woolen cloth, 5 timber of miniver, 90 Garters of silk.

A baron, 5 yards of woolen cloth, 3 timber of miniver gresle,[30] 80 Garters of silk.

A banneret, 5 yards of woolen cloth, 3 timber of miniver, 70 Garters of silk.

A knight, 5 yards of woolen cloth, 3 timber of miniver, 60 Garters of silk.

The Bishop of Winchester, chaplain of the Garter, hath 28 timber of miniver pure,[31] 19 timber gresle, 3½ timber of the best, and 24 yards of woolen cloth.

The chancellor of the order, 5 yards of woolen cloth, 3 timber of miniver pure.

The registrar of the order, 5 yards of woolen cloth, 3 timber of miniver pure. And this order to be holden generally among the knights of this company, which are twenty-six in number, and whose patron in time of superstition was supposed to be St. George, of whom they were also called St. George's knights, as I have heard reported. Would to God they might be called knights of honor or by some other name, for the title of St. George argueth a wrong patron.

Furthermore, at his installation he is solemnly sworn, the manner whereof I have thought good also to annex, in this manner:

You, being chosen to be one of the honorable company of the Order of the Garter, shall promise and swear upon the holy Evangelies [Gospels], by you bodily touched, to be faithful and true to the King's Majesty, and to observe and keep all the points of the statutes of the said order and every article in them contained, the same being agreeable and not repugnant to the King's Highness' other godly proceedings, so far as to you belongeth and appertaineth, as God you help, etc.

And thus much have I thought good to note touching the premises.

As touching the statutes belonging to this order, they are many and therefore not to be touched here. Howbeit, if any

---

[30] *Gresle:* from "gris," a gray fur, usually weasel.
[31] *Miniver pure:* the white fur from the belly of the gray squirrel in winter.

doubt do arise about the interpretation of them, the King, who is the perpetual sovereign of that order, hath to determine and resolve the same. Neither are any chosen thereunto under the degree of a knight and that is not a gentleman of blood and of sound estimation.

And for the better understanding what is meant by a gentleman of blood, he is defined to descend of three descents [generations] of nobleness, that is to say, of name and of arms both by father and mother.

There are also four degrees of reproach which may inhibit from the entrance into this order, of which the first is heresy lawfully proved, the second, high treason, the third is flight from the battle, the fourth, riot and prodigal excess of expenses, whereby he is not likely to hold out and maintain the port of knight of this order according to the dignity thereof. Moreover, touching the wearing of their aforesaid apparel, it is their custom to wear the same when they enter into the Chapel of St. George or be in the chapter house of their order or, finally, do go about anything appertaining to that company. In like sort they wear also their mantles upon the Even of St. George and go with the sovereign or his deputy in the same, in manner of procession from the King's great chamber unto the chapel, or unto the college, and likewise back again unto the aforesaid place, not putting it from them until supper be ended and the avoid [withdrawal] done. The next day they resort unto the chapel also in the like order, and from thence unto dinner, wearing afterward their said apparel unto Evening Prayer and likewise all the suppertime, until the avoid be finished. In the solemnity likewise of these feasts the thirteen canons there and six-and-twenty poor knights have mantles of the order, whereof those for the canons are of murrey with a roundel of the arms of St. George, the other of red, with a scutcheon only of the said arms.[32]

If any knight of this order be absent from this solemnity upon the Even and Day of St. George and be enforced not to be present either through bodily sickness or his absence out of the land, he doth in the church, chapel, or chamber where he is remaining provide an honorable stall for the King's Majesty in

---

[32] *Murrey:* a purplish or blood-red. This passage was written years before Harrison himself became a canon of St. George's. Perhaps his account of the order was instrumental in his preferment to the chapter.

the right hand of the place, with a cloth of state and cushions and scutcheon of the Garter, and therein the arms of the order. Also his own stall, of which side soever it be, distant from the King's or the emperor's in his own place, appointed so nigh as he can, after the manner and situation of his stall at Windsor, there to remain the first Evening Prayer on the Even of St. George, or three of the clock, and likewise the next day during the time of the divine service until the Morning Prayer and the rest of the service be ended; and to wear in the meantime his mantle only, with the George and the lace, without either hood, collar, or surcoat. Or if he be so sick that he do keep his bed, he doth use to have that habit laid upon him during the times of divine service aforesaid.

At the service time also upon the morrow after St. George, two of the chief knights (saving the deputy of the sovereign if he himself be absent) shall offer the King's banner of arms, then other two the sword with the hilts forwards, which being done the first two shall return again and offer the helm and crest, having at each time two heralds-of-arms going before, according to the statutes. The lord deputy or lieutenant unto the King's Grace, for the time being alone, and assisted with one of the chief lords, doth deliver at his offering a piece of gold, and having all the kings-of-arms and heralds going before him, he so proceedeth to the offering. When he hath thus offered for the prince, he returneth with like solemnity unto his stall and next of all goeth again with one herald to offer for himself, whose oblation being made, every knight, according to their stalls with an herald before him, proceedeth to the offering.

What solemnity is used at the burial of any knight of the Garter it is but in vain to declare, wherefore I will show generally what is done at the disgrading of one of these knights, if through any grievous offense he be separated from this company. Whereas otherwise the sign of the order is never taken from him until death do end and finish up his days. Therefore when any such thing is done, promulgation is made thereof after this manner ensuing:

Be it known unto all men that *N. N[omen]*, knight of the most noble Order of the Garter, is found guilty of the abominable and detestable crime of high treason, for he hath most traitorously conspired against our most high and mighty prince, sovereign of the said order, contrary to all right, his duty, and the faithful oath which he hath sworn and taken. For which causes, therefore, he hath deserved to be deposed from this noble order and fellowship of the Garter. For it may not be suffered that such a traitor and disloyal member remain among the faithful knights of renowned stomach and bountiful prowess, or that his arms should be mingled with those of noble chivalry. Wherefore our most excellent prince and supreme of this most honorable order, by the advice and counsel of his colleagues, willeth and commandeth that his arms, which he beforetime hath deserved, shall be from henceforth taken away and thrown down, and he himself clean cut off from the society of this renowned order, and never from this day reputed any more for a member of the same, that all other by his example may hereafter beware how they commit the like trespass or fall into such notorious infamy and rebuke.

This notice being given, there resorteth unto the party to be disgraded certain officers with divers of his late fellows appointed, which take from him his George and other investiture, after a solemn manner.

And hitherto of this most honorable order, hoping that no man will be offended with me in uttering thus much. For sith the noble Order of the Toison d'Or or Golden Fleece, with the ceremonies appertaining unto the creation and investiture of the six-and-thirty knights thereof,[33] and likewise that of St. Michael and his one-and-thirty knights, are discoursed upon at large by the historiographers of their own countries, without reprehension or check, especially by Vincent Lupan (*lib.* I, *De mag. Franc.*, *cap.*, *De equitibus ordinis*),[34] where he calleth them *chevaliers sans reproche*, and thereto addeth that their chain is commonly of two hundred crowns at the least and honor thereof so great that it is not lawful for them to sell, give, or lay the same to mortgage (would to God they might once brook [act consistently with] their name, *sans reproche*, but their general dealing in our time with all men will not suffer some of the best of their own countries to have that opinion of them),[35] I trust I have not given any cause of displeasure briefly to set forth those things

---

[33] The Order of the Golden Fleece was founded in 1430 by Philip the Good, Duke of Burgundy.

[34] *Vincent Lupan:* Vincent de la Loupe, whose *Commentarii de magistratibus et praefecturis Francorum* was published at Paris in 1551.

[35] The Order of St. Michael was established by Louis XI in 1469; Harrison is correct about its murky reputation in his day.

that appertain unto our renowned Order of the Garter, in whose compass is written commonly, *Honi soit qui mal y pense,* which is so much to say as, "Evil come to him that evil thinketh," [36] a very sharp imprecation, and yet such as is not contrary to the Word, which promiseth like measure to the meter as he doth mete to others.

There is yet another order of knights in England called knights bannerets, who are made in the field with the ceremony of cutting away the point of his pennant of arms and making it as it were a banner, so that, being before but a bachelor knight, he is now of an higher degree and allowed to display his arms in a banner, as barons do. Howbeit, these knights are never made but in the wars, the King's standard being unfolded.

Esquire (which we call commonly squire) is a French word and so much in Latin as *scutiger vel armiger* [shield or arms-bearer], and such are all those which bear arms or armories, testimonies of their race from whence they be descended. They were at the first custrels, or bearers of the arms of barons or knights and, thereby being instructed in martial knowledge, had that name for a dignity given to distinguish them from common soldiers, called *gregarii milites,* when they were together in the field.

Gentlemen be those whom their race and blood, or at the least their virtues, do make noble and known. The Latins call them *nobiles et generosos,* as the French do *nobles* or *gentlehommes.* The etymology of the name expoundeth the efficacy of the word, for as *gens* in Latin betokeneth the race and surname, so the Romans had *Cornelios, Sergios, Appios, Curios, Papyrios, Scipiones, Fabios, Aemilios, Julios, Brutos,* etc., of which, who were *agnati,*[37] and therefore kept the name, were also called *gentiles,* gentlemen of that or that house and race.

Moreover, as the King doth dub knights and createth the barons and higher degrees, so gentlemen whose ancestors are not known to come in with William, Duke of Normandy (for of the Saxon races yet remaining we now make none account, much less of the British issue), do take their beginning in England after this manner in our times. Whosoever studieth the laws of the realm,

---

[36] "Some think that this was the answer of the Queen when the King asked what men would think of her, in losing the garter after such a manner."—*H.*

[37] *Agnati:* blood relatives on the father's side.

whoso abideth in the university giving his mind to his book, or professeth physic and the liberal sciences, or, beside his service in the room of a captain in the wars or good counsel given at home, whereby his commonwealth is benefited, can live without manual labor, and thereto is able and will bear the port, charge, and countenance of a gentleman, he shall for money have a coat and arms bestowed upon him by heralds (who in the charter of the same do of custom pretend antiquity and service and many gay things), and thereunto being made so good cheap, be called master, which is the title that men give to esquires and gentlemen, and reputed for a gentleman ever after. Which is so much the less to be disallowed of for that the prince doth lose nothing by it, the gentleman being so much subject to taxes and public payments as is the yeoman or husbandman, which he likewise doth bear the gladlier for the saving of his reputation. Being called also to the wars (for with the government of the commonwealth he meddleth little), whatsoever it cost him, he will both array and arm himself accordingly and show the more manly courage and all the tokens of the person which he representeth. No man hath hurt by it but himself who peradventure will go in wider buskins than his legs will bear or, as our proverb saith, now and then bear a bigger sail than his boat is able to sustain.

Certes the making of new gentlemen bred great strife sometimes amongst the Romans, I mean when those which were *novi homines* were more allowed of for their virtues newly seen and showed than the old smell of ancient race, lately defaced by the cowardice and evil life of their nephews and descendants, could make the other to be. But as envy hath no affinity with justice and equity, so it forceth not what language the malicious do give out against such as are exalted for their wisdoms. This nevertheless is generally to be reprehended in all estates of gentility, and which in short time will turn to the great ruin of our country, and that is the usual sending of noblemen's and mean gentlemen's sons into Italy, from whence they bring home nothing but mere atheism, infidelity, vicious conversation, and ambitious and proud behavior, whereby it cometh to pass that they return far worse men than they went out. A gentleman at this present is newly come out of Italy who went thither an earnest Protestant, but coming home he could say after this manner, "Faith and truth is to be kept where no loss or hindrance of a further purpose is sustained by holding of the same and forgiveness only to be showed when full revenge is made." Another, no less forward than he, at his return from thence could add thus much, "He is a fool that maketh account of any religion, but more fool that will lose any part of his wealth or will come in trouble for constant leaning to any; but if he yield to lose his life for his possession [obsession], he is stark mad and worthy to be taken for most fool of all the rest." This gay booty gat these gentlemen by going into Italy, and hereby a man may see what fruit is afterward to be looked for where such blossoms do appear. "I care not," saith a third, "what you talk to me of God, so as I may have the prince and the laws of the realm on my side." Such men as this last are easily known, for they have learned in Italy to go up and down also in England with pages at their heels finely appareled, whose face and countenance shall be such as showeth the master not to be blind in his choice. But lest I should offend too much, I pass over to say any more of these Italianates and their demeanor, which alas is too open and manifest to the world, and yet not called into question.

Citizens and burgesses have next place to gentlemen, who be those that are free within the cities and are of some likely substance to bear office in the same.[38] But these citizens or burgesses are to serve the commonwealth in their cities and boroughs, or in corporate towns where they dwell. And in the common assembly of the realm, wherein our laws are made (for in the counties they bear but little sway), which assembly is called the High Court of Parliament, the ancient cities appoint four and the boroughs two burgesses to have voices in it and give their consent or dissent unto such things as pass or stay there, in the name of the city or borough for which they are appointed.

In this place also are our merchants to be installed, as amongst the citizens (although they often change estate with gentlemen, as gentlemen do with them, by a mutual conversion of the one into the other), whose number is so increased in these our days that their only maintenance is the cause of the exceeding prices of foreign wares, which otherwise, when every nation was per-

---

[38] In the Londonderry biography Harrison's parents, John and Anne, are described as honorable citizens (*cives perhonestos*) of London.

mitted to bring in her own commodities, were far better cheap and more plentifully to be had.[39] Of the want of our commodities here at home by their great transportation of them into other countries I speak not, sith the matter will easily bewray itself. Certes among the Lacedaemonians it was found out that great numbers of merchants were nothing to the furtherance of the state of the commonwealth, wherefore it is to be wished that the huge heap of them were somewhat restrained, as also of our lawyers; so should the rest live more easily upon their own and few honest chapmen be brought to decay by breaking of the bankrupt. I do not deny but that the navy of the land is in part maintained by their traffic, and so are the high prices of wares kept up, now they have gotten the only sale of things, upon pretense of better furtherance of the commonwealth, into their own hands; whereas in times past, when the strange bottoms were suffered to come in, we had sugar for 4d. the pound that now, at the writing of this treatise, is well worth half-a-crown, raisins or currants for a penny that now are holden at 6d., and sometime at 8d. and 10d. the pound, nutmegs at 2½d. the ounce, ginger at a penny an ounce, prunes at halfpenny farthing, great raisins [40] three pound for a penny, cinnamon at 4d. the ounce, cloves at 2d., and pepper at 12d. and 16d. the pound. Whereby we may see the sequel of things not always but very seldom to be such as is pretended in the beginning.

The wares that they carry out of the realm are for the most part broadcloths and kerseys of all colors, likewise cottons, friezes, rugs, tin, wool, our best beer, baize, bustian, mockadoes tufted and plain, rash, lead, fells, etc.,[41] which, being shipped at sundry ports of our coasts, are borne from thence into all quarters of the world and there either exchanged for other wares or ready money, to the great gain and commodity of our merchants. And whereas in times past their chief trade was into Spain, Portingale, France, Flanders, Dansk [Denmark], Norway, Scotland, and Iceland only, now in these days, as men not contented with these journeys, they have sought out the East and

[39] Harrison has in mind such statutes as 5 Eliz., c. 5, which prohibited the importation of French wines in any but British ships.

[40] *Great raisins:* as distinguished from small raisins, or currants. The prices are included in the 1577 edition.

[41] *Kerseys, friezes, baize, mockadoes, rash:* various woolen fabrics; *bustian:* a cotton fabric.

West Indies and made now and then suspicious [promising] voyages, not only unto the Canaries and New Spain, but likewise into Cathay, Moscovia [Russia], Tartary, and the regions thereabout, from whence (as they say) they bring home great commodities. But alas! I see not by all their travel that the prices of things are any whit abated. Certes this enormity (for so I do account of it) was sufficiently provided for, *an.* 9, Edward III, by a noble statute made in that behalf, but upon what occasion the general execution thereof is stayed or not called on, in good sooth I cannot tell.[42] This only I know, that every function and several vocation striveth with other which of them should have all the water of commodity run into their own cistern.

Yeomen are those which by our law are called *legales homines*, freemen born English, and may dispend of their own free land in yearly revenue to the sum of 40*s*. sterling, or £6 as money goeth in our times. Some are of the opinion, by *cap.* 2, Rich. II, *an.* 20, that they are the same which the Frenchmen call varlets,[43] but, as that phrase is used in my time, it is far unlikely to be so. The truth is that the word is derived from the Saxon term ȝeoman, or *geoman*, which signifieth (as I have read) a settled or staid man, such I mean as, being married and of some years, betaketh himself to stay in the place of his abode for the better maintenance of himself and his family, whereof the single sort have no regard but are likely to be still fleeting, now hither, now thither, which argueth want of stability in determination and resolution of judgment for the execution of things of any importance. This sort of people have a certain pre-eminence and more estimation than laborers and the common sort of artificers, and these commonly live wealthily, keep good houses, and travail to get riches. They are also for the most part farmers to gentlemen (in old time called *pagani, et opponuntur militibus*, and therefore Persius calleth himself *semipaganus*)[44] or at the leastwise artificers; and with grazing, frequenting of markets, and keeping of servants (not idle servants as the gentlemen do, but

[42] The statute of 1335 gave foreign merchants the right to trade freely in England.
[43] According to the statute "no varlets, called yeomen, . . . shall use or bear livery, called livery of company, of any lord within the realm, unless he be menial and familiar or continual officer of his said lord."
[44] *Pagani, et opponuntur militibus*: countrymen, as opposed to soldiers. Persius applies this epithet to himself in the "Prologue" to his *Satires*, l. 6.

such as get both their own and part of their master's living) do come to great wealth, insomuch that many of them are able and do buy the lands of unthrifty gentlemen, and often, setting their sons to the schools, to the universities, and to the Inns of the Court, or otherwise leaving them sufficient lands whereupon they may live without labor, do make them by those means to become gentlemen; these were they that in times past made all France afraid. And albeit they be not called master as gentlemen are, or sir, as to knights appertaineth, but only John and Thomas, etc., yet have they been found to have done very good service; and the Kings of England in foughten battles were wont to remain among them (who were their footmen) as the French kings did amongst their horsemen, the prince thereby showing where his chief strength did consist.

The fourth and last sort of people in England are day laborers, poor husbandmen, and some retailers (which have no free land), copyholders, and all artificers, as tailors, shoemakers, carpenters, brickmakers, masons, etc.[45] As for slaves and bondmen, we have none; nay, such is the privilege of our country by the especial grace of God and bounty of our princes that if any come hither from other realms, so soon as they set foot on land they become so free of condition as their masters, whereby all note of servile bondage is utterly removed from them, wherein we resemble (not the Germans, who had slaves also, though such as in respect of the slaves of other countries might well be reputed free, but) the old Indians and the Taprobanes [Ceylonese], who supposed it a great injury to Nature to make or suffer them to be bond whom she in her wanted course doth product and bring forth free. This fourth and last sort of people, therefore, have neither voice nor authority in the commonwealth, but are to be ruled and not to rule other; yet they are not altogether neglected, for in cities and corporate towns, for default of yeomen, they are fain to make up their inquests of such manner of people. And in villages they are commonly made churchwardens, sidemen, ale-conners,[46] now and then constables, and many times enjoy the name of headboroughs.

---

[45] "*Capite censi* or *proletarii*."—H. *Capite censi* were those assessed according to their ability to labor.

[46] *Sidemen:* sidesmen, assistants to the churchwardens; *aleconners:* inspectors of ale.

Unto this sort also may our great swarms of idle servingmen be referred, of whom there runneth a proverb, "Young serving-men, old beggars," because service is none heritage. These men are profitable to none, for if their condition be well perused, they are enemies to their masters, to their friends, and to themselves; for by them oftentimes their masters are encouraged unto un-lawful exactions of their tenants, their friends brought unto pov-erty by their rents enhanced, and they themselves brought to confusion by their own prodigality and errors, as men that, hav-ing not wherewith of their own to maintain their excesses, do search in highways, budgets [pouches], coffers, mails [bags], and stables which way to supply their wants. How divers of them also, coveting to bear an high sail, do insinuate themselves with young gentlemen and noblemen newly come to their lands, the case is too much apparent, whereby the good natures of the parties are not only a little impaired but also their livelihoods and revenues so wasted and consumed that if at all, yet not in many years, they shall be able to recover themselves. It were very good therefore that the superfluous heaps of them were in part dimin-ished. And sith necessity enforceth to have some, yet let wisdom moderate their numbers; so shall their masters be rid of unneces-sary charge and the commonwealth of many thieves. No nation cherisheth such store of them as we do here in England, in hope of which maintenance many give themselves to idleness that otherwise would be brought to labor and live in order like sub-jects. Of their whoredoms I will not speak anything at all, more than of their swearing, yet is it found that some of them do make the first a chief pillar of their building, consuming not only the goods but also the health and welfare of many honest gentlemen, citizens, wealthy yeomen, etc., by such unlawful dealings. But how far have I waded in this point, or how far may I sail in such a large sea? I will therefore now stay to speak any more of those kind of men.

In returning therefore to my matter, this furthermore among other things I have to say of our husbandmen and artificers, that they were never so excellent in their trades as at this present. But as the workmanship of the latter sort was never more fine and curious to the eye, so was it never less strong and substantial for continuance and benefit of the buyers. Neither is there anything that hurteth the common sort of our artificers more than haste and a barbarous or slavish desire to turn the penny and, by ridding their work, to make speedy utterance of their wares, which enforceth them to bungle up and dispatch many things, they care not how, so they be out of their hands, whereby the buyer is often sore defrauded and findeth to his cost that haste maketh waste, according to the proverb.

Oh, how many trades and handicrafts are now in England whereof the commonwealth hath no need! How many needful commodities have we which are perfected with great cost, etc., and yet may with far more ease and less cost be provided from other countries if we could use the means! I will not speak of iron, glass, and suchlike, which spoil much wood and yet are brought from other countries better cheap than we can make them here at home; I could exemplify also in many other. But to leave these things and proceed with our purpose, and herein (as occasion serveth) generally, by way of conclusion, to speak of the commonwealth of England, I find that it is governed and maintained by three sorts of persons.

1. The prince, monarch, and head governor, which is called the King or (if the crown fall to the woman) the Queen, in whose name and by whose authority all things are administered.

2. The gentlemen, which be divided into two sorts, as the barony, or estate of lords (which containeth barons and all above that degree), and also those that be no lords, as knights, esquires, and simple gentlemen, as I have noted already. Out of these also are the great deputies and high presidents chosen, of which one serveth in Ireland, as another did sometime in Calais, and the captain now at Berwick, as one lord president doth govern in Wales, and the other the north parts of this island, which latter, with certain councilors and judges, were erected by King Henry the Eighth. But forsomuch as I have touched their conditions elsewhere, it shall be enough to have remembered them at this time.

3. The third and last sort is named the yeomanry, of whom and their sequel, the laborers and artificers, I have said somewhat even now. Whereto I add that they be not called masters and gentlemen but goodmen, as Goodman Smith, Goodman Coot, Goodman Cornell, Goodman Mascall, Goodman Cockswet, etc.; and in matters of law these and the like are called thus: Giles Jewd, yeoman, Edward Mountford, yeoman, James Cocke,

yeoman, Harry Butcher, yeoman, etc.; by which addition they are exempt from the vulgar and common sorts. Cato calleth them *aratores et optimos cives rei publicae,* of whom also you may read more in the book *Of Commonwealth,* which Sir Thomas Smith sometime penned of this land.[47]

Of gentlemen also some are by the prince chosen and called to great offices in the commonwealth, of which said offices divers concern the whole realm, some be more private and peculiar to the King's house. And they have their places and degrees, prescribed by an act of Parliament made *an.* 31, *Henrici octavi,* after this manner ensuing.

These four, the Lord Chancellor, the Lord Treasurer (who is *supremus aerarii Anglici quaestor* or *tribunus aerarius maximus*),[48] the Lord President of the Council, and the Lord Privy Seal, being persons of the degree of a baron or above, are in the same act appointed to sit in the Parliament and in all assemblies or council above all dukes not being of the blood royal, *videlicet,* the King's brother, uncle, or nephew.

And these six, the Lord Great Chamberlain of England, the Lord High Constable of England, the Lord Marshal of England, the Lord Admiral of England, the Lord Great Master, or steward of the King's house, and the Lord Chamberlain, by that act are to be placed in all assemblies of council after the Lord Privy Seal, according to their degrees and estates, so that if he be a baron, then he is to sit above all barons, or an earl, above all earls.

And so likewise the King's secretary, being a baron of the Parliament, hath place above all barons, and if he be a man of higher degree, he shall sit and be placed according thereunto.

The rehearsal of the temporal nobility of England
according to the anciency of their creations or
first calling to their degrees, as they are to be
found at this present

---

[47] *Aratores et optimos cives rei publicae:* plowmen and the best citizens of the state. These two sentences were borrowed from Smith, I, xxiii, but for the examples of yeomen's names given in *De republica Anglorum* Harrison substitutes the names of his Radwinter parishioners: for example, a "Thomas Smith, yeoman," was a witness to Harrison's will; Edward Mountford and Giles Jewd were the churchwardens of Radwinter; John Cockswet owned the "house named the Rotherwell" (see p. 424).

[48] *Supremus aerarii Anglici quaestor* or *tribunus aerarius maximus:* chief treasurer of the English Exchequer or principal director of the treasury.

The Marquis of Winchester [49]

The Earl of Arundel	The Earl of Huntingdon
The Earl of Oxford	The Earl of Bath
The Earl of Northumberland	The Earl of Warwick
The Earl of Shrewsbury	The Earl of Southampton
The Earl of Kent	The Earl of Bedford
The Earl of Derby	The Earl of Pembroke
The Earl of Worcester	The Earl of Hertford
The Earl of Rutland	The Earl of Leicester
The Earl of Cumberland	The Earl of Essex
The Earl of Sussex	The Earl of Lincoln
The Viscount Montague	The Viscount Bindon
The Lord of Abergavenny [50]	The Lord Wentworth
The Lord Audley	The Lord Burgh
The Lord Zouche [51]	The Lord Mordaunt
The Lord Berkeley	The Lord Cromwell
The Lord Morley	The Lord Eure
The Lord Dacre of the South	The Lord Wharton
The Lord Cobham [51]	The Lord Rich
The Lord Stafford	The Lord Willoughby
The Lord Grey of Wilton	The Lord Sheffield
The Lord Scrope	The Lord Paget
The Lord Dudley	The Lord Darcy of Chiche
The Lord Latimer	The Lord Howard of Effingham
The Lord Stourton	The Lord North
The Lord Lumley	The Lord Chandos
The Lord Mountjoy	The Lord of Hunsdon
The Lord Ogle	The Lord St. John of Bletso
The Lord Darcy [Dacre?]	The Lord of Buckhurst
of the North	The Lord De La Warr
The Lord Monteagle	The Lord Burghley
The Lord Sandys	The Lord Compton
The Lord Vaux	The Lord Cheney
The Lord Windsor	The Lord Norris.

Bishops in their anciency, as they sat in Parliament in the fifth
of the Queen's Majesty's reign that now is

The Archbishop of Canterbury
The Archbishop of York

---

[49] "No duke in England."—*H.*   [50] "Barons."—*H.*
[51] The 1577 edition included, after the Lords Zouche and Cobham, the
baronies of Strange and Talbot, held by the eldest sons of the Earls of Derby
and Shrewsbury respectively.

London
Durham
Winchester.

The rest had their places in seniority of consecration:

Chichester	Rochester
Llandaff	Bath and Wells
Hereford	Coventry and Lichfield
Ely	Exeter
Worcester	Norwich
Bangor	Peterborough
Lincoln	Carlisle
Salisbury	Chester
St. David's	St. Asaph
	Gloucester.

And this for their placing in the Parliament House. Howbeit, when the Archbishop of Canterbury sitteth in his provincial assembly, he hath on his right hand the Archbishop of York, and next unto him the Bishop of Winchester, on the left hand the Bishop of London; but if it fall out that the Archbishop of Canterbury be not there by the vacation of his see, then the Archbishop of York is to take his place, who admitteth the Bishop of London to his right hand and the prelate of Winchester to his left, the rest sitting always as afore, that is to say, as they are elders by consecration, which I thought good also to note out of an ancient precedent.

CHAPTER VI

Of the Food and Diet of the English

THE situation of our region, lying near unto the north, doth cause the heat of our stomachs to be of somewhat greater force; therefore our bodies do crave a little more ample nourishment than the inhabitants of the hotter regions are accustomed withal, whose digestive force is not altogether so vehement, because their internal heat is not so strong as ours, which is kept in by the coldness of the air that from time to time (especially in winter) doth environ our bodies.

It is no marvel therefore that our tables are oftentimes more plentifully garnished than those of other nations, and this trade hath continued with us even since the very beginning. For before the Romans found out and knew the way unto our country, our predecessors fed largely upon flesh and milk, whereof there was great abundance in this isle, because they applied their chief studies unto pasturage and feeding. After this manner also did our Welsh Britons order themselves in their diet so long as they lived of themselves, but after they became to be united and made equal with the English, they framed their appetites to live after our manner, so that at this day there is very little difference between us in our diets.

In Scotland likewise they have given themselves (of late years to speak of) unto very ample and large diet, wherein, as for some respect Nature doth make them equal with us, so otherwise they far exceed us in overmuch and distemperate gormandize, and so engross their bodies that divers of them do oft become unapt to any other purpose than to spend their times in large tabling and bellycheer. Against this pampering of their carcasses doth Hector Boece in his description of the country very sharply inveigh in the first chapter of that treatise.[1] Henry Wardlaw also, Bishop of St. Andrews, noting their vehement alteration from competent frugality into excessive gluttony to be brought out of England with James the First (who had been long time prisoner there under the fourth and fifth Henries and at his return carried divers English gentlemen into his country with him, whom he very honorably preferred there), doth vehemently exclaim against the same in open Parliament, holden at Perth, 1433, before the three estates, and so bringeth his purpose to pass in the end by force

---

[1] "Some by long sickness and languishing griefs do grow into such deformity only through excessive feeding and greedy abuse of wine that, if you knew them when they were children and young men, you shall hardly remember them when they be old and aged; and that which more is, in comparison of other that live more soberly, you will hardly think them to be born in the isle, but rather suppose them to be changelings and monsters, brought out of other countries to gaze and look upon" (*Des. Scot.*, 1587, p. 8). *The Description of Scotland* that Harrison contributed to Holinshed was largely a translation of John Bellenden's Scottish version (Edinburgh, 1536) of Hector Boece's introductory chapters to his Latin *Scotorum historiae* (Paris, 1527).

of his learned persuasions that a law was presently made there for the restraint of superfluous diet; amongst other things, baked meats (dishes never before this man's days seen in Scotland) were generally so provided for by virtue of this act that it was not lawful for any to eat of the same under the degree of a gentleman, and those only but on high and festival days; but alas it was soon forgotten.[2]

In old time these North Britons did give themselves universally to great abstinence, and in time of wars their soldiers would often feed but once or twice at the most in two or three days (especially if they held themselves in secret or could have no issue out of their bogs and marshes, through the presence of the enemy), and in this distress they used to eat a certain kind of confection, whereof so much as a bean would qualify their hunger above common expectation. In woods, moreover, they lived with herbs and roots, or if these shifts served not through want of such provision at hand, then used they to creep into the water or said moorish [boggy] plots up unto the chins and there remain a long time, only to qualify the heats of their stomachs by violence, which otherwise would have wrought and been ready to oppress them for hunger and want of sustenance.[3] In those days likewise it was taken for a great offense over all to eat either goose, hare, or hen, because of a certain superstitious opinion which they had conceived of those three creatures;[4] howbeit, after that the Romans (I say) had once found an entrance into this island, it was not long ere open shipwreck was made of this religious observation, so that in process of time so well the North and South Britons as the Romans gave over to make such difference in meats as they had done before.

From thenceforth also unto our days, and even in this season wherein we live, there is no restraint of any meat, either for religion's sake or public order, in England, but it is lawful for every man to feed upon whatsoever he is able to purchase, except it be upon those days whereon eating of flesh is especially forbidden by the laws of the realm, which order is taken only to the

---

[2] Bellenden (1536), II, 503–505.

[3] Harrison repeats these details at the end of *The Description of Scotland*, in a brief chapter of his own coinage entitled "The Description of an Ancient Pict" (1587, p. 23), citing as his source "Dion" (Dio Cassius, *Roman History*, LXXVII, xii).

[4] Caesar, *Gallic War*, V, xii.

end our numbers of cattle may be the better increased and that abundance of fish which the sea yieldeth more generally received. Beside this there is great consideration had in making of this law for the preservation of the navy and maintenance of convenient numbers of seafaring men, both which would otherwise greatly decay if some means were not found whereby they might be increased.[5] But howsoever this case standeth, white meats, as milk, butter, and cheese, which were never so dear as in my time and wont to be accounted of as one of the chief stays throughout the island, are now reputed as food appertinent only to the inferior sort, whilst such as are more wealthy do feed upon the flesh of all kinds of cattle accustomed to be eaten, all sorts of fish taken upon our coasts and in our fresh rivers, and such diversity of wild and tame fowls as are either bred in our island or brought over unto us from other countries of the main.

In number of dishes and change of meat, the nobility of England (whose cooks are for the most part musical-headed Frenchmen and strangers) do most exceed, sith there is no day in manner that passeth over their heads wherein they have not only beef, mutton, veal, lamb, kid, pork, cony, capon, pig, or so many of these as the season yieldeth, but also some portion of the red or fallow deer, beside great variety of fish and wild fowl, and thereto sundry other delicates wherein the sweet hand of the seafaring Portingale is not wanting; so that for a man to dine with one of them and to taste of every dish that standeth before him (which few use to do, but each one feedeth upon that meat him best liketh for the time, the beginning of every dish notwithstanding being reserved unto the greatest personage that sitteth at the table, to whom it is drawn up still by the waiters, as order requireth, and from whom it descendeth again even to the lower end, whereby each one may taste thereof) is rather to yield unto a conspiracy with a great deal of meat for the speedy suppression of natural health than the use of a necessary mean to satisfy himself with a competent repast, to sustain his body withal. But as this large feeding is not seen in their guests, no more is it in their own persons, for sith they have daily much resort unto their tables (and many times unlooked for), and thereto retain great

[5] The eating of flesh was forbidden during Lent, on all Fridays and Saturdays, and on certain other days, to the total of 153 in the year. One statute, 5 Eliz., c. 5, specified that the prohibition was "meant politicly for the increase of fishermen and mariners, . . . and not for any superstition to be maintained in the choice of meats."

numbers of servants, it is very requisite and expedient for them to be somewhat plentiful in this behalf.

The chief part likewise of their daily provision is brought in before them (commonly in silver vessel if they be of the degree of barons, bishops, and upwards) and placed on their tables, whereof, when they have taken what it pleaseth them, the rest is reserved and afterward sent down to their servingmen and waiters, who feed thereon in like sort with convenient moderation, their reversion also being bestowed upon the poor, which lie ready at their gates in great numbers to receive the same. This is spoken of the principal tables whereat the nobleman, his lady, and guests are accustomed to sit; beside which they have a certain ordinary allowance daily appointed for their halls, where the chief officers and household servants (for all are not permitted by custom to wait upon their master), and with them such inferior guests do feed as are not of calling to associate the nobleman himself; so that besides those afore mentioned, which are called to the principal table, there are commonly forty or threescore persons fed in those halls, to the great relief of such poor suitors and strangers also as oft be partakers thereof and otherwise like to dine hardly.

As for drink, it is usually filled in pots, goblets, jugs, bowls of silver in noblemen's houses, also in fine Venice glasses of all forms, and for want of these elsewhere, in pots of earth of sundry colors and molds, whereof many are garnished with silver, or at the leastwise in pewter; all which notwithstanding are seldom set on the table, but each one, as necessity urgeth, calleth for a cup of such drink as him listeth to have, so that when he hath tasted of it, he delivered the cup again to some one of the standers-by, who, making it clean by pouring out the drink that remaineth, restoreth it to the cupboard from whence he fetched the same. By this device (a thing brought up at the first by Mnestheus of Athens, in conservation of the honor of Orestes, who had not yet made expiation for the death of his adulterous parents, Aegisthus and Clytemnestra),[6] much idle tippling is furthermore cut off, for if the full pots should continually stand at the elbow or near the trencher, divers would always be dealing

---

[6] *Mnestheus:* an Athenian physician of the fourth century B.C., whose lost works, including a letter *On Hard Drinking*, are often cited by later writers. Harrison seems to have in mind some version of the entertainment of Orestes by Demophon, King of Athens, who would not permit his guest to use the sacred cups until Orestes had been tried for matricide: see Athenaeus, *The Diepnosophists*, X, 437; XI, 483–484.

with them, whereas now they drink seldom, and only when necessity urgeth, and so avoid the note of great drinking or often troubling of the servitors with filling of their bowls. Nevertheless, in the noblemen's halls this order is not used, neither in any man's house commonly under the degree of a knight or esquire of great revenues.

It is a world to see in these our days, wherein gold and silver most aboundeth, how that our gentility, as loathing those metals (because of the plenty), do now generally choose rather the Venice glasses, both for our wine and beer, than any of those metals or stone wherein beforetime we have been accustomed to drink; but such is the nature of man generally that it most coveteth things difficult to be attained; and such is the estimation of this stuff that many become rich only with their new trade unto Murano (a town near to Venice, situate on the Adriatic Sea), from whence the very best are daily to be had, and such as for beauty do wellnear match the crystal or the ancient *murrhina vasa*, whereof now no man hath knowledge.[7] And as this is seen in the gentility, so in the wealthy commonalty the like desire of glass is not neglected, whereby the gain gotten by their purchase is yet much more increased to the benefit of the merchant. The poorest also will have glass if they may, but sith the Venetian is somewhat too dear for them, they content themselves with such as are made at home of fern and burned stone; but in fine all go one way, that is, to shards at the last, so that our great expenses in glasses (beside that they breed much strife toward such as have the charge of them) are worst of all bestowed in mine opinion, because their pieces do turn unto no profit. If the philosophers' stone were once found, and one part hereof mixed with forty of molten glass, it would induce such a metallical toughness thereunto that a fall should nothing hurt it in such manner, yet it might peradventure bunch or batter it; nevertheless, that inconvenience were quickly to be redressed by the hammer.[8] But whither am I slipped?

The gentlemen and merchants keep much about one rate, and

---

[7] *Murrhina vasa:* a mineral substance (jade or fluorspar?) from which cups and bowls were made.

[8] "Ro[ger] Bacon."—*H*. Bacon (?1214–1294), an English philosopher and scientist, was best known in Elizabethan days for his interest in alchemy. The malleability of glass was one supposed benefit to be derived from the discovery of the philosophers' stone.

each of them contenteth himself with four, five, or six dishes when they have but small resort, or peradventure with one or two or three at the most when they have no strangers to accompany them at their tables. And yet their servants have their ordinary diet assigned, beside such as is left at their master's boards and not appointed to be brought thither the second time, which nevertheless is often seen generally in venison, lamb, or some especial dish whereon the merchantman himself liketh to feed when it is cold, or peradventure, for sundry causes incident to the feeder, is better so than if it were warm or hot. To be short, at such time as the merchants do make their ordinary [9] or voluntary feasts, it is a world to see what great provision is made of all manner of delicate meats from every quarter of the country, wherein, beside that they are often comparable herein to the nobility of the land, they will seldom regard anything that the butcher usually killeth, but reject the same as not worthy to come in place. In such cases also geliffes [jellies] of all colors, mixed with a variety in the representation of sundry flowers, herbs, trees, forms of beasts, fish, fowls, and fruits, and thereunto marchpane wrought with no small curiosity, tarts of divers hues and sundry denominations, conserves of old fruits, foreign and homebred, suckets, codiniacs, marmalades, marchpane, sugarbread, gingerbread, florentines,[10] wild fowl, venison of all sorts, and sundry outlandish [foreign] confections, altogether seasoned with sugar (which Pliny calleth *mel ex arundinibus*, a device not common nor greatly used in old time at the table but only in medicine, although it grew in Arabia, India, and Sicily),[11] do generally bear the sway, besides infinite devices of our own not possible for me to remember. Of the potato and such venerous roots [12] as are brought out of Spain, Portingale, and the Indies to furnish up our banquets, I speak not, wherein our mures, of no less force and to be had about Crosby Ravensworth, do now begin to have place.[13]

[9] *Ordinary:* according to the ordinances or rules of the company, as distinguished from voluntary.

[10] *Suckets:* succades, candied fruits; *codiniacs:* quince marmalades; *marchpane:* marzipan; *florentines:* pies or tarts, especially of meat.

[11] *Mel ex arundinibus:* honey from cane; *Natural History,* XII, xvii.

[12] *Potato:* that is, batata or sweet potato; its supposed aphrodisiac qualities are often mentioned (see *Merry Wives of Windsor,* V, v, 20–21). The common potato was not introduced into England until ca. 1596.

[13] *Mures: myrrhis odorata,* sweet cicely, an herb with a fleshy, carrot-like root, formerly used in salads.

But among all these the kind of meat which is obtained with most difficulty and cost is commonly taken for the most delicate, and thereupon each guest will soonest desire to feed. And as all estates do exceed herein, I mean for strangeness and number of costly dishes, so these forget not to use the like excess in wine, insomuch as there is no kind to be had (neither anywhere more store of all sorts than in England, although we have none growing with us but yearly [have] to the proportion of 20,000 or 30,000 tun and upwards, notwithstanding the daily restraints of the same, brought over unto us) whereof at great meetings there is not some store to be had. Neither do I mean this of small [weak] wines only as claret, white, red, French, etc., which amount to about fifty-six sorts, according to the number of regions from whence they come, but also of the thirty kinds of Italian, Grecian, Spanish, Canarian, etc., whereof vernage, cute, piment, raspis, muscatel, rumney, bastard, tyre, osey, caprike, clary, and malmsey [14] are not least of all accounted of, because of their strength and valure. For, as I have said in meat, so the stronger the wine is, the more it is desired; by means whereof in old time the best was called *theologicum*, because it was had from the clergy and religious men, unto whose houses many of the laity would often send for bottles filled with the same, being sure that they would neither drink nor be served of the worst, or such as was anyways mingled or brewed by the vintner; nay, the merchant would have thought that his soul should have gone straightway to the devil if he should have served them with other than the best. Furthermore, when these have had their course which Nature yieldeth, sundry sorts of artificial stuff, as hippocras and wormwood wine,[15] must in like manner succeed in their turns, beside stale ale and strong beer, which nevertheless bear the greatest brunt in drinking and are of so many sorts and ages as it pleaseth the brewer to make them.

The beer that is used at noblemen's tables in their fixed and standing houses is commonly of a year old, or peradventure of two years' tunning or more, but this is not general. It is also

[14] *Cute:* new wine boiled down; *piment:* wine mixed with honey and spices, similar to *clary*. The other names are those of sweet imported wines. Such catalogues are common; a strikingly similar list is given in John Russell's *Book of Nurture* (ca. 1460; ed. from the MS by Frederick J. Furnivall, *Manners and Meals in Olden Times*, EETS, XXXII, 1868, 125).

[15] *Hippocras:* a cordial wine flavored with spices; *wormwood wine:* a cordial prepared, like absinthe, from wormwood.

brewed in March and therefore called March beer; but for the household it is usually not under a month's age, each one coveting to have the same stale as he may, so that it be not sour, and his bread new as is possible, so that it be not hot.

The artificer and husbandman make greatest account of such meat as they may soonest come by and have it quickliest ready, except it be in London when the companies of every trade do meet on their quarter days, at which time they be nothing inferior to the nobility. Their food also consisteth principally in beef and such meat as the butcher selleth, that is to say, mutton, veal, lamb, pork, etc., whereof he [1577: the artificer] findeth great store in the markets adjoining, beside souse, brawn, bacon, fruit, pies of fruit, fowls of sundry sorts, cheese, butter, eggs, etc., as the other wanteth it not at home by his own provision, which is at the best hand and commonly least charge. In feasting also this latter sort (I mean the husbandmen) do exceed after their manner, especially at bride-ales, purifications of women,[16] and such odd meetings, where it is incredible to tell what meat is consumed and spent, each one bringing such a dish or so many with him as his wife and he do consult upon, but always with this considera-tion, that the liefer [dearer] friend shall have the better provision. This also is commonly seen at these banquets, that the goodman of the house is not charged with anything saving bread, drink, sauce, houseroom, and fire. But the artificers in cities and good towns do deal far otherwise; for, albeit that some of them do suffer their jaws to go oft before their claws, and divers of them, by making good cheer, do hinder themselves and other men, yet the wiser sort can handle the matter well enough in these junket-ings, and therefore their frugality deserveth commendation. To conclude, both the artificer and the husbandman are sufficiently liberal and very friendly at their tables; and when they meet they are so merry without malice and plain without inward Italian or French craft and subtlety, that it would do a man good to be in company among them. Herein only are the inferior sort some-what to be blamed, that being thus assembled their talk is now and then such as savoreth of scurrility and ribaldry, a thing naturally incident to carters and clowns, who think themselves not to be merry and welcome if their foolish veins in this behalf be

[16] *Purifications of women:* churchings, the public appearances of women at church to return thanks after childbirth.

never so little restrained. This is moreover to be added in these meetings, that if they happen to stumble upon a piece of venison and a cup of wine or very strong beer or ale (which latter they commonly provide against their appointed days), they think their cheer so great and themselves to have fared so well as the Lord Mayor of London, with whom, when their bellies be full, they will not often stick to make comparison, because that of a subject there is no public officer of any city in Europe that may compare in port and countenance with him during the time of his office.

I might here talk somewhat of the great silence that is used at the tables of the honorable and wiser sort, generally over all the realm (albeit that too much deserveth no commendation, for it belongeth to guests neither to be *muti* nor *loquaces*), likewise of the moderate eating and drinking that is daily seen, and finally of the regard that each one hath to keep himself from the note of surfeiting and drunkenness (for which cause salt meat, except beef, bacon, and pork, are not any whit esteemed, and yet these three may not be much powdered); but as in rehearsal thereof I should commend the nobleman, merchant, and frugal artificer, so I could not clear the meaner sort of husbandmen and country inhabitants of very much babbling (except it be here and there some odd yeoman), with whom he is thought to be the merriest that talketh of most ribaldry, or the wisest man that speaketh fastest among them, and now and then surfeiting and drunkenness, which they rather fall into for want of heed-taking than willfully following or delighting in those errors of set mind and purpose. It may be that divers of them, living at home with hard and pinching diet, small drink, and some of them having scarce enough of that, are soonest overtaken when they come unto such banquets; howbeit, they take it generally as no small disgrace if they happen to be cup-shotten, so that it is a grief unto them, though now sans remedy, sith the thing is done and past. If the friends also of the wealthier sort come to their houses from far, they are commonly so welcome till they depart as upon the first day of their coming, whereas in good towns and cities, as London, etc., men oftentimes complain of little room; and in reward of a fat capon or plenty of beef and mutton largely bestowed upon them in the country, a cup of wine or beer, with a napkin to wipe their lips and an "You are heartily welcome," is thought to be great entertainment; and therefore the old country clerks have framed this saying in that behalf, I mean upon the entertainment of townsmen and Londoners, after the days of their abode in this manner:

> *Primus jucundus, tollerabilis estque secundus,*
> *Tertius est vanus, sed fetet quatriduanus.*[17]

The bread throughout the land is made of such grain as the soil yieldeth; nevertheless, the gentility commonly provide themselves sufficiently of wheat for their own tables, whilst their household and poor neighbors in some shires are enforced to content themselves with rye or barley, yea, and in time of dearth, many with bread made either of beans, peason [peas], or oats, or of all together and some acorns among, of which scourge the poorest do soonest taste, sith they are least able to provide themselves of better. I will not say that this extremity is oft so well to be seen in time of plenty as of dearth, but if I should, I could easily bring my trial. For albeit that there be much more ground eared [cultivated] now almost in every place than hath been of late years, yet such a price of corn continueth in each town and market without any just cause (except it be that landlords do get licenses to carry corn out of the land only to keep up the prices for their own private gains and ruin of the commonwealth) that the artificer and poor laboring man is not able to reach unto it but is driven to content himself with horse corn, I mean, beans, peason, oats, tares, and lentils; and therefore it is a true proverb, and never so well verified as now, that "hunger setteth his first foot into the horse manger." If the world last awhile after this rate, wheat and rye will be no grain for poor men to feed on; and some caterpillars [18] there are that can say so much already.

Of bread made of wheat we have sundry sorts daily brought to the table, whereof the first and most excellent is the manchet, which we commonly call white bread, in Latin *primarius panis*, whereof Budé also speaketh, in his first book, *De asse;* [19] and our

---

[17] "The first is pleasant, and the second tolerable, the third is empty, but the fourth day stinks."

[18] *Caterpillars:* men who prey on society, pillagers, in reference to the landlords above.

[19] *Guillaume Budé* (1468–1540): French humanist, whose *De asse et partibus* (first published in 1514) is a treatise principally on ancient measures. The following citation to Celsus also derives from this source (Lyons, 1551, p. 594).

good workmen deliver commonly such proportion that of the flour of one bushel with another they make forty cast[20] of manchet, of which every loaf weigheth eight ounces into the oven and six ounces out, as I have been informed. The second is the cheat, or wheaten bread, so named because the color thereof resembleth the gray or yellowish wheat, being clean and well dressed, and out of this is the coarsest of the bran (usually called gurgeons or pollard) taken. The raveled is a kind of cheat bread also, but it retaineth more of the gross and less of the pure substance of the wheat; and this [manchet], being more sleightly[21] wrought up, is used in the halls of the nobility and gentry only, whereas the other [cheat bread] either is or should be baked, in cities and good towns, of an appointed size (according to such price as the corn doth bear) and by a statute provided by King John in that behalf.[22] The raveled cheat therefore is generally so made that out of one bushel of meal, after two-and-twenty pounds of bran be sifted and taken from it (whereunto they add the gurgeons that rise from the manchet), they make thirty cast, every loaf weighing eighteen ounces into the oven and sixteen ounces out; and beside this they so handle the matter that to every bushel of meal they add only two-and-twenty or three-and-twenty pound of water, washing also (in some houses) their corn before it go to the mill, whereby their manchet [cheat?] bread is more excellent in color and pleasing to the eye than otherwise it would be. The next sort is named brown bread, of the color, of which we have two sorts, one baked up as it cometh from the mill, so that neither the bran nor the flour are any whit diminished; this Celsus called *autopirus panis* (*lib.* 2) and putteth it in the second place of nourishment. The other hath little or no flour left therein at all; howbeit, he calleth it *panem cibarium*,[23] and it is not only the worst and weakest of all the other sorts but also appointed in old time for servants, slaves, and the inferior kind of people to feed upon. Hereunto likewise, because it is

---

[20] *Cast:* a batch, here apparently a dozen loaves.

[21] *Sleightly:* dexterously, or perhaps "slightly," of less weight.

[22] "The size of bread is very ill kept or not at all looked unto in the country towns and markets."—*H*. Holinshed, under 1202, gives a detailed account of John's proclamation: "When wheat was sold for 6*s.* the quarter, then shall every loaf of fine manchet weigh 41*s.*, and every loaf of cheat shall weigh 24*s.*, etc."

[23] Celsus, *De medicina*, II, xviii.

dry and brickle in the working (for it will hardly be made up handsomely into loaves) some add a portion of rye meal in our time, whereby the rough dryness or dry roughness thereof is somewhat qualified, and then it is named miscelin [maslin], that is, bread made of mingled corn, albeit that divers do sow or mingle wheat and rye of set purpose at the mill, or before it come there, and sell the same at the markets under the aforesaid name.

In champaign countries much rye and barley bread is eaten, but especially where wheat is scant and geason [rare]. As for the difference that is between the summer and winter wheat, most husbandmen know it not, sith they are neither acquainted with summer wheat nor winter barley; yet here and there I find of both sorts, especially in the north and about Kendal, where they call it March wheat, and also of summer rye, but in so small quantities as that I dare not pronounce them to be greatly common among us.

Our drink, whose force and continuance is partly touched already, is made of barley, water, and hops, sodden and mingled together by the industry of our brewers in a certain exact proportion. But before our barley do come unto their hands, it sustaineth great alteration and is converted into malt, the making whereof I will here set down in such order as my skill therein may extend unto (for I am scarce a good maltster), chiefly for that foreign writers have attempted to describe the same and the making of our beer, wherein they have shot so far wide as the quantity of ground was between themselves and their mark. In the meantime bear with me, gentle reader (I beseech thee), that lead thee from the description of the plentiful diet of our country unto the fond report of a servile trade, or rather, from a table delicately furnished into a musty malthouse; but such is now thy hap, wherefore I pray thee be contented.

Our malt is made all the year long in some great towns, but in gentlemen's and yeomen's houses, who commonly make sufficient for their own expenses only, the winter half is thought most meet for that commodity; howbeit, the malt that is made when the willow doth bud is commonly worst of all; nevertheless, each one endeavoreth to make it of the best barley, which is steeped in a cistern, in greater or less quantity, by the space of three days and three nights, until it be thoroughly soaked. This being done, the water is drained from it by little and little till it be quite gone. Afterward they take it out, and, laying it upon the clean floor on a round heap, it resteth so until it be ready to shoot at the root end, which maltsters call "coming." When it beginneth, therefore, to shoot in this manner, they say it is come, and then forthwith they spread it abroad, first thick, and afterward thinner and thinner, upon the said floor (as it cometh), and there it lieth (with turning every day four or five times) by the space of one-and-twenty days at the least, the workman not suffering it in any wise to take any heat, whereby the bud end should spire that bringeth forth the blade, and by which oversight or hurt of the stuff itself the malt would be spoiled and turn small commodity to the brewer. When it hath gone, or been turned, so long upon the floor, they carry it to a kill [kiln] covered with haircloth, where they give it gentle heats (after they have spread it there very thin abroad) till it be dry, and in the meanwhile they turn it often, that it may be uniformly dried. For the more it be dried (yet must it be done with soft fire), the sweeter and better the malt is and the longer it will continue, whereas if it be not "dried down" (as they call it) but slackly handled, it will breed a kind of worm, called a weevil, which groweth in the flour of the corn and in process of time will so eat out itself that nothing shall remain of the grain but even the very rind or husk.

The best malt is tried by the hardness and color, for if it look fresh, with a yellow hue, and thereto will write like a piece of chalk after you have bitten a kernel in sunder in the midst, then you may assure yourself that it is dried down. In some places it is dried at leisure with wood alone, or straw alone, in other with wood and straw together, but, of all, the straw-dried is the most excellent. For the wood-dried malt, when it is brewed, beside that the drink is higher of color, it doth hurt and annoy the head of him that is not used thereto, because of the smoke. Such also as use both indifferently do bark, cleave, and dry their wood in an oven, thereby to remove all moisture that should procure the fume, and this malt is in the second place, and with the same likewise that which is made with dried furze, broom, etc.; whereas if they also be occupied green, they are in manner so prejudicial to the corn as is the moist wood. And thus much of our malts, in brewing whereof some grind the same somewhat grossly, and, in seething well the liquor that shall be put unto it, they add to every nine quarters of malt one of head-corn, which consisteth of sundry grain, as wheat and oats ground. But what have I to do with this matter, or rather so great a quantity, wherewith I am not acquainted? Nevertheless, sith I have taken occasion to speak of brewing, I will exemplify in such a proportion as I am best skilled in, because it is the usual rate for mine own family and once in a month practiced by my wife and her maidservants, who proceed withal after this manner, as she hath oft informed me.

Having therefore ground eight bushels of good malt upon our quern, where the toll is saved,[24] she addeth unto it half a bushel of wheat meal and so much of oats small ground, and so tempereth or mixeth them with the malt that you cannot easily discern the one from the other; otherwise these latter would clunter [clot], fall into lumps, and thereby become unprofitable. The first liquor —which is full eighty gallons, according to the proportion of our furnace—she maketh boiling hot and then poureth it softly into the malt, where it resteth (but without stirring) until her second liquor be almost ready to boil. This done, she letteth her mash run till the malt be left without liquor, or at the leastwise the greatest part of the moisture, which she perceiveth by the stay and soft issue thereof; and by this time her second liquor in the furnace is ready to seethe, which is put also to the malt, as the first wort also again into the furnace, whereunto she addeth two pounds of the best English hops and so letteth them seethe together by the space of two hours in summer or an hour and an half in winter, whereby it getteth an excellent color and continuance without impeachment or any superfluous tartness. But before she putteth her first wort into the furnace or mingleth it with the hops, she taketh out a vesselful, of eight or nine gallons, which she shutteth up close and suffereth no air to come into it till it become yellow, and this she reserveth by itself unto further use, as shall appear hereafter, calling it brackwort or charwort,[25] and as she saith, it addeth also to the color of the drink, whereby it yieldeth not unto amber or fine gold in hue unto the eye. By this time also her second wort is let run; and, the first being taken out of the furnace and placed to cool, she returneth the middle wort unto the furnace, where it is stricken [laded] over,

[24] *Toll:* a portion of the grain claimed by a miller as his compensation.
[25] *Brackwort* or *charwort:* a portion of the wort reserved for another brewing.

or from whence it is taken again when it beginneth to boil and mashed the second time, whilst the third liquor is heated (for there are three liquors), and this last put into the furnace when the second is mashed again. When she hath mashed also the last liquor (and set the second to cool by the first), she letteth it run and then seetheth it again with a pound and an half of new hops, or peradventure two pounds, as she seeth cause by the goodness or baseness of the hops; and when it hath sodden [boiled], in summer two hours and in winter an hour and an half, she striketh it also and reserveth it unto mixture with the rest when time doth serve therefor. Finally, when she setteth her drink together, she addeth to her brackwort or charwort half an ounce of orris and half a quarter of an ounce of bayberries finely powdered, and then, putting the same into her wort, with an handful of wheat flour, she proceedeth in such usual order as common brewing requireth. Some, instead of orris and bays, add so much long pepper only, but in her opinion and my liking it is not so good as the first, and hereof we make three hogsheads of good beer, such (I mean) as is meet for poor men as I am to live withal, whose small maintenance (for what great thing is £40 a year, *computatis computandis* [taking everything into account], able to perform?) may endure no deeper cut, the charges whereof groweth in this manner. I value my malt at 10*s*., my wood at 4*s*. (which I buy), my hops at 20*d*., the spice at 2*d*., servants' wages, 2*s*. 6*d*., with meat and drink, and the wearing of my vessel at 20*d*., so that for my 20*s*. I have tenscore gallons of beer or more, notwithstanding the loss in seething, which some being loath to forgo do not observe the time and therefore speed thereafter in their success, and worthily. The continuance of the drink is always determined after the quantity of the hops, so that, being well hopped, it lasteth longer. For it feedeth upon the hop and holdeth out so long as the force of the same continueth, which being extinguished, the drink must be spent, or else it dieth and becometh of no value.

In this trade also our brewers observe very diligently the nature of the water which they daily occupy, and soil through which it passeth, for all waters are not of like goodness, sith the fattest [26] standing water is always the best; for although the waters that

---

[26] *Fattest:* hardest, fullest of mineral particles.

run by chalk or cledgy [clayey] soils be good, and next unto the Thames water, which is the most excellent, yet the water that standeth in either of these is the best for us that dwell in the country, as whereon the sun lieth longest and fattest fish is bred. But of all other the fenny and moorish is the worst and the clearest spring water next unto it. In this business, therefore, the skillful workman doth redeem the iniquity of that element by changing of his proportions, which trouble in ale (sometime our only, but now taken with many for old and sick men's drink) is never seen nor heard of. Howbeit, as the beer well sodden in the brewing, and stale, is clear and well colored as muscatel or malvasia [malmsey], or rather, yellow as the gold noble, as our potknights call it, so our ale, which is not at all or very little sodden and without hops, is more thick, fulsome, and of no such continuance, which are three notable things to be considered in that liquor. But what for that? Certes I know some aleknights so much addicted thereunto that they will not cease from morrow until even to visit the same, cleansing house after house, till they defile themselves and either fall quite under the board, or else, not daring to stir from their stools, sit still pinking [blinking] with their narrow eyes as half-sleeping till the fume of their adversary be digested, that he may go to it afresh. Such sleights also have the alewives for the utterance of this drink that they will mix it with rosin and salt; but if you heat a knife red-hot and quench it in the ale so near the bottom of the pot as you can put it, you shall see the rosin come forth hanging on the knife. As for the force of salt, it is well known by the effect, for the more the drinker tippleth, the more he may, and so doth he carry off a dry drunken noll to bed with him, except his luck be the better. But to my purpose.

In some places of England there is a kind of drink made of apples which they call cider or pommage, but that of pears is named perry, and both are ground and pressed in presses made for the nonce. Certes these two are very common in Sussex, Kent, Worcester, and other steads where these sorts of fruits do abound; howbeit, they are not their only drink at all times but referred unto the delicate sorts of drink, as metheglin [mead] is in Wales, whereof the Welshmen make no less account (and not without cause, if it be well handled) than the Greeks did of their ambrosia or nectar, which for the pleasantness thereof was supposed to be such as the gods themselves did delight in. There is a kind of swish-swash made also in Essex and divers other places with honeycombs and water, which the homely country wives, putting some pepper and a little other spice among, call mead, very good in mine opinion for such as love to be loose-bodied at large or a little eased of the cough; otherwise it differeth so much from the true metheglin as chalk from cheese.[27] Truly it is nothing else but the washing of the combs, when the honey is wrung out, and one of the best things that I know belonging thereto is that they spend but little labor and less cost in making of the same, and therefore no great loss if it were never occupied. Hitherto of the diet of my countrymen, and somewhat more at large peradventure than many men will like of, wherefore I think good now to finish this tractation, and so will I when I have added a few other things incident unto that which goeth before, whereby the whole process of the same shall fully be delivered and my promise to my friend in this behalf performed.

Heretofore there hath been much more time spent in eating and drinking than commonly is in these days, for whereas of old we had breakfasts in the forenoon, beverages or nuncheons after dinner, and thereto reresuppers [28] generally when it was time to go to rest (a toy brought into England by Hardecanute and a custom whereof Athenaeus also speaketh, *lib*. 1, albeit Hippocrates speak but of twice at the most, *lib*. 2, *De rat. vict. in. feb. ac*.).[29] Now these odd repasts—thanked be God—are very well left, and each one in manner (except here and there some young hungry stomach that cannot fast till dinnertime) contenteth himself with dinner and supper only. The Normans, misliking the gormandize of Canute, ordained after their arrival that no table should be covered above once in the day, which Huntingdon imputeth to their avarice;[30] but in the end, either waxing weary of their own frugality or suffering the cockle of old

---

[27] "Hydromel."—*H*. Pliny attributes these medicinal properties to hydromel, or skinned honey (XXII, 51–52).

[28] *Reresuppers:* late or second suppers.

[29] Athenaeus in *The Deipnosophists* mentions the four meals of the ancients, distinguishing between *hesperisma,* the evening meal, and *deipnon,* supper (I, 11). Hippocrates speaks of those accustomed to two meals a day, as distinguished from those who usually eat but one (*De ratione victus in febribus* [*morbis*] *acutis,* xi).

[30] Henry of Huntingdon, *Chronicle,* under 1040.

custom to overgrow the good corn of their new constitution, they fell to such liberty that in often feeding they surmounted Canute, surnamed "the Hardy." For whereas he covered his table but three or four times in the day, these spread their cloths five or six times, and in such wise as I before rehearsed. They brought in also the custom of long and stately sitting at meat, whereby their feasts resembled those ancient pontifical banquets whereof Macrobius speaketh (*lib.* 3, *cap.* 13) and Pliny (*lib.* 10, *cap.* 10), and which for sumptuousness of fare, long sitting, and curiosity showed in the same exceeded all other men's feasting;[31] which fondness is not yet left with us, notwithstanding that it proveth very beneficial for the physicians, who most abound where most excess and misgovernment of our bodies do appear, although it be a great expense of time and worthy of reprehension. For the nobility, gentlemen, and merchantmen, especially at great meetings, do sit commonly till two or three of the clock at afternoon, so that with many is an hard matter, to rise from the table to go to Evening Prayer and return from thence to come time enough to supper.

For my part, I am persuaded that the purpose of the Normans at the first was to reduce [restore] the ancient Roman order or Danish custom in feeding once in the day and toward the evening, as I have read and noted. And indeed the Romans had such a custom and likewise the Grecians, as may appear by the words of Socrates, who said unto the Athenians, *Oriente sole consilium, occidente convivium est cogitandum,*[32] although a little something was allowed in the morning to young children, which we now call a breakfast. Plato called the Sicilians monsters for that they used to eat twice in the day.[33] Among the Persians only the king dined when the sun was at the highest and shadow of the style [34] at the shortest; the rest (as it is reported) went always but once to meat, when their stomachs craved it, as the Canarians and Indians do in my time (who, if appetite serve, refuse not to go to meat at any hour of the night), and likewise the ancient Caspians.

[31] Both Macrobius (*Saturnalia,* III, xiii) and Pliny (X, xxiii) mention the orator Hortensius as the first Roman who had the peacock killed for the table, on the occasion of his inauguration into the college of priests.

[32] "When the sun is in the east, deliberation should occupy our minds; when it is in the west, feasting."

[33] *Epistles,* VII, 326.

[34] *Style:* the pin or gnomon of a sundial.

Yet Arrianus noteth it as a rare thing (*lib.* 4, *cap.* 16) that the Tyrrhenians had taken up an ill custom to feed twice in a day.[35] Howbeit, at the last they fell generally to allow of suppers toward the setting of the sun in all places, because they would have their whole family to go to meat together, and whereunto they would appoint their guests to come at a certain length of the shadow, to be perceived in their dials. And this is more to be noted of antiquity, that if any man (as Plutarch saith) did feed before that time, he incurred a note of reprehension, as if he had been gluttonous and given unto the belly (8. *Sympos.* 6).[36] Their slaves in like sort were glad when it grew to the tenth foot, for then were they sure soon after to go to meat. In the Scripture we read of many suppers and few dinners, only for that dining was not greatly used in Christ's time but taken as a thing lately sprung up, when pampering of the belly began to take hold, occasioned by idleness and great abundance of riches. It is pretty to note in Juvenal how he taunteth Marius for that he gave himself to drink before the ninth hour of the day; for, thinking three hours to be too little for the filling of his belly, he began commonly at eight, which was an hour too soon.[37] Afterwards, when gormandize increased yet more amongst the Romans and from them was dispersed unto all nations under their subjection, it came to pass that six hours only were appointed to work and consult in, and the other six of the day to feed and drink in, as the verse saith:

> *Sex horae tantum rebus tribuantur agendis,*
> *Vivere post illas, littera zetha monet.*[38]

Whereunto Maximus Planudes (except my memory fail me) addeth this scholy after his manner, saying that from morning

---

[35] I cannot locate this passage in the extant works of Flavius Arrianus, an historian of the second century A.D. In all probability Harrison is relying on secondary sources for most of these details of ancient eating habits.

[36] "In ancient times, dining too early was a source of reproach; they say that *akratisma*, breakfast, is derived from *akrasia*, incontinence."

[37] "That is, at three of the clock at afternoon."—H. Juvenal, *Satires*, I, 49–50.

[38] "Only six hours are assigned to transact business; after these, the letter *zeta* bids us live" (translated from an anonymous epigram in the *Greek Anthology*, X, 43).

unto noon (which is six of the clock, after the unequal account) [39]
each one doth travail about his necessary affairs; that being done,
he betaketh himself to the refreshing of his body, which is noted
and set down by the Greek letters of the dial (wherewith the
Roman horologes were marked, as ours be with their numeral
letters), whereby the time is described; for those which point
7, 8, 9, and 10 are written with ζ, η, θ, ι and being joined yield
$\zeta\eta\theta\iota$ which in English signifieth so much as "live," as if they
should mean, "Eat that thou mayest live." But how Martial
divided his day, and with him the whole troop of the learned and
wiser sort, these verses following do more evidently declare:

> *Prima salutantes, atque altera continent horas [hora],*
> *Exercet raucos tertia causidicos.*
> *In quintam varios extendit Roma labores,*
> *Sexta quies lassis, septima finis erit.*
> *Sufficit in nonam nitidis octava palestris,*
> *Imperat extructos frangere nona thoros.*
> *Hora libellorum decima est Eupheme meorum,*
> *Temperat ambrosias cum tua cura dapes.*
> *Et bonus aethereo laxatur nectare Caesar,*
> *Ingentique tenet pocula parca manu.*
> *Tunc admitte jocos: gressu timet ire licenti,*
> *Ad matutinum nostra Thaleia Jovem.*[40]

Thus we see how the ancient manner of the gentiles was to
feed but once in the day, and that toward night, till gluttony
grew on and altered this good custom. I might here remember
also their manner in pulling off their shoes when they sat down to
meat, whereof Martial saith:

[39] *Unequal account:* reckoning the hour as one-twelfth of daylight and
hence of variable duration through the year (see p. 380). *Maximus Planudes*
(d. 1330): a Byzantine monk, who edited a version of the *Greek Anthology*.
[40] "*Li.* 4, *epig.* 8."—H. "The first and second hours are given over to
suitors at the imperial levee; the third keeps lawyers busy till they are
hoarse; Rome busies herself through the fifth in various labors; the sixth
gives to the tired rest; the seventh will end the work; the eighth to the ninth
suffices for the oiled wrestling; the ninth bids us press down the couches that
have been drawn out. The tenth, Euphemus, is the hour for my lampoons,
when your care provides the ambrosial feast and the noble Caesar is relaxed
with heavenly nectar and holds a frugal cup in his mighty hand. Then
admit my jests: our Thalia fears with unrestrained step to approach Jove in
the morning."

Deposui soleas, affertur protinus ingens
Inter lactucas oxygarmumque liber, etc.[41]

And Tully also remembereth, where he saith, *servum a pedibus ad te misi*,[42] which office grew of the said custom, as *servus ad limina* did of keeping the door, though in most houses both these were commonly one man's office, also *ad pocula*, of attending on the cup. But because the good writers of our time have observed these phrases and suchlike, with their causes and descriptions, in their infinite and several treatises, I shall not need to discourse any farther upon them.

With us the nobility, gentry, and students do ordinarily go to dinner at eleven before noon and to supper at five, or between five and six at afternoon. The merchants dine and sup seldom before twelve at noon and six at night, especially in London. The husbandmen dine also at high noon, as they call it, and sup at seven or eight; but out of the term in our universities the scholars dine at ten. As for the poorest sort, they generally dine and sup when they may, so that to talk of their order of repast it were but a needless matter. I might here take occasion also to set down the variety used by antiquity in their beginnings of their diets, wherein almost every nation had a several fashion, some beginning of custom (as we do in summertime) with salads at supper and some ending with lettuce, some making their entry with eggs and shutting up their tables with mulberries, as we do with fruit and conceits [preserves] of all sorts. Divers (as the old Romans) began with a few crops [heads] of rue, as the Venetians did with the fish called *gobius*, the Belgies with butter or (as we do yet also) with butter and eggs upon fish days. But whereas we commonly begin with the most gross food and end with the most delicate, the Scot, thinking much to leave the best for his menial servants, maketh his entrance at the best, so that he is sure thereby to leave the worst. We use also our wines by degrees, so that the hottest cometh last to the table; but to stand upon such toys would spend much time and turn to small profit, wherefore I will deal with other things more necessary for this turn.

[41] "I have set aside my shoes; immediately a huge volume is brought in with the lettuce and the fish sauce" (*Epigrams*, III, 50).
[42] "I have sent my footman to you" (Cicero, *Letters to Atticus*, VIII, v. 1).

CHAPTER VII

Of Their Apparel and Attire

AN ENGLISHMAN, endeavoring sometime to write of our attire, made sundry platforms [sketches] for his purpose, supposing by some of them to find out one steadfast ground whereon to build the sum of his discourse. But in the end (like an orator long without exercise), when he saw what a difficult piece of work he had taken in hand, he gave over his travail and only drew the picture of a naked man, unto whom he gave a pair of shears in the one hand and a piece of cloth in the other, to the end he should shape his apparel after such fashion as himself liked, sith he could find no kind of garment that could please him any while together; and this he called an Englishman. Certes this writer (otherwise being a lewd popish hypocrite and ungracious priest)[1] showed himself herein not to be altogether void of judgment, sith the fantastical folly of our nation, even from the courtier to the carter, is such that no form of apparel liketh us longer than the first garment is in the wearing, if it continue so long and be not laid aside to receive some other trinket newly devised by the fickle-headed tailors, who covet to have several tricks in cutting, thereby to draw fond customers to more expense of money.

For my part, I can tell better how to inveigh against this enormity than describe any certainty of our attire; sithence [since] such is our mutability that today there is none to the Spanish guise, tomorrow the French toys are most fine and delectable,

---

[1] "Andrew Boorde."—H. Boorde (d. 1549), originally a Carthusian monk, later a traveler and doctor, begins his *Introduction of Knowledge* (1548, ed. Frederick J. Furnivall, EETS, Extra Ser., X, 1870, 111-222) with a chapter on the English. A similar reference to Boorde's jibe occurs in the "Homily against Excess in Apparel," whose rhetoric Harrison echoes elsewhere in the chapter. The explanation for the charge of lewdness against Boorde is found in the *Apology* of John Ponet (Bishop of Winchester, 1551-1553): "Master Doctor Boorde . . . under the color of virginity and of wearing a shirt of hair and hanging his shroud and socking, or burial sheet, at his bed's feet and mortifying his body and straitness of life, kept three whores at once in his chamber at Winchester, to serve not only himself but also to help the virgin priests about in the country" (1555, p. 32).

ere long no such apparel as that which is after the High Almain
[German] fashion, by and by the Turkish manner is generally best
liked of, otherwise the Morisco [Moorish] gowns, the Barbarian
sleeves, the mandilion worn to Collyweston-ward,[2] and the short
French breeches make such a comely vesture that, except it were
a dog in a doublet, you shall not see any so disguised as are my
countrymen of England. And as these fashions are diverse, so
likewise it is a world to see the costliness and the curiosity, the
excess and the vanity, the pomp and the bravery, the change and
the variety, and finally, the fickleness and the folly that is in all
degrees, insomuch that nothing is more constant in England than
inconstancy of attire. Oh, how much cost is bestowed nowadays
upon our bodies and how little upon our souls! How many suits
of apparel hath the one, and how little furniture hath the other!
How long time is asked in decking up of the first, and how little
space left wherein to feed the latter! How curious, how nice also,
are a number of men and women, and how hardly can the tailor
please them in making it fit for their bodies! How many times
must it be sent back again to him that made it! What chafing,
what fretting, what reproachful language doth the poor workman
bear away! And many times when he doth nothing to it at all,
yet when it is brought home again, it is very fit and handsome;
then must we put it on, then must the long seams of our hose be
set by a plumb line, then we puff, then we blow, and finally,
sweat till we drop that our clothes may stand well upon us.

I will say nothing of our heads, which sometimes are polled,
sometimes curled or suffered to grow at length like woman's locks,
many times cut off above or under the ears round, as by a wooden
dish. Neither will I meddle with our variety of beards, of which
some are shaven from the chin like those of Turks, not a few
cut short like to the beard of Marquis Otto, some made round
like a rubbing brush, other with a *pique de vant*[3] (oh, fine fashion!) or now and then suffered to grow long, the barbers being
grown to be so cunning in this behalf as the tailors. And therefore,

---

[2] *Mandilion:* a cape with sleeves; the style of wearing it sideways so that
the sleeves hung in front and behind was known as Collyweston-ward. The
origin of the term has not been explained, but it would seem to be associated
with Elizabeth's manor of Collyweston in Northamptonshire.

[3] *Marquis Otto:* from the French phrase, *barbe faite à la marquisotte,* to
shave all but the mustache, although Harrison seems to intend a type of
close-cropped beard; *pique de vant:* pickedevant, a short Vandyke beard.

if a man have a lean and strait face, a Marquis Otto's cut will make it broad and large; if it be platter-like, a long slender beard will make it seem the narrower; if he be weasel-becked [-beaked], then much hair left on the cheeks will make the owner look big, like a bowdled [ruffled] hen, and so grim as a goose, if Cornelius of Chelmsford[4] say true; many old men do wear no beards at all. Some lusty courtiers also and gentlemen of courage do wear either rings of gold, stones, or pearl in their ears, whereby they imagine the workmanship of God not to be a little amended. But herein they rather disgrace than adorn their persons, as by their niceness in apparel, for which I say most nations do, not unjustly, deride us, as also for that we do seem to imitate all nations round about us, wherein we be like to the *polypus* [octopus] or chameleon; and thereunto bestow most cost upon our arses, and much more than upon all the rest of our bodies, as women do likewise upon their heads and shoulders.

In women also it is most to be lamented that they do now far exceed the lightness of our men (who nevertheless are transformed from the cap even to the very shoe), and such staring attire as in time past was supposed meet for none but light housewives [hussies] only is now become an habit for chaste and sober matrons. What should I say of their doublets with pendant codpieces on the breast, full of jags and cuts, and sleeves of sundry colors? their galligaskins to bear out their bums and make their attire to fit plum-round (as they term it) about them? their farthingales and diversely colored netherstocks[5] of silk, jersey, and suchlike, whereby their bodies are rather deformed than commended? I have met with some of these trulls in London so disguised that it hath passed my skill to discern whether they were men or women.

Thus it is now come to pass that women are become men and men transformed into monsters; and those good gifts which Almighty God hath given unto us to relieve our necessities withal (as a nation turning altogether the grace of God into wantonness, for *Luxuriant animi rebus plerunque secundis*)[6] not otherwise

[4] An Essex barber?

[5] *Codpieces:* bagged appendages, properly a part of male attire; *jags:* slashes in the material to show a different color beneath; *galligaskins:* loose breeches; *plum-round:* perhaps "plumb-round"; *farthingales:* hooped petticoats; *netherstocks:* stockings.

[6] "Desires usually run riot in prosperity" (Ovid, *Ars amatoria*, II, 437).

bestowed than in all excess, as if we wist not otherwise how to consume and waste them. I pray God that in this behalf our sin be not like unto that of Sodom and Gomorrah, whose errors were pride, excess of diet, and abuse of God's benefits abundantly bestowed upon them, beside want of charity toward the poor and certain other points which the prophet shutteth up in silence.[7] Certes the commonwealth cannot be said to flourish where these abuses reign but is rather oppressed by unreasonable exactions made upon rich farmers and of poor tenants, wherewith to maintain the same. Neither was it ever merrier with England than when an Englishman was known abroad by his own cloth and contented himself at home with his fine kersey hosen and a mean slop, his coat, gown, and cloak of brown-blue or puke, with some pretty furniture of velvet or fur, and a doublet of sad tawny [8] or black velvet or other comely silk, without such cuts and garish colors as are worn in these days and never brought in but by the consent of the French, who think themselves the gayest men when they have most diversities of jags and change of colors about them.

Certes of all estates our merchants do least alter their attire and therefore are most to be commended, for albeit that which they wear be very fine and costly, yet in form and color it representeth a great piece of the ancient gravity appertaining to citizens and burgesses, albeit the younger sort of their wives, both in attire and costly housekeeping, cannot tell when and how to make an end, as being women indeed in whom all kind of curiosity is to be found and seen, and in far greater measure than in women of higher calling. I might here name a sort of hues devised for the nonce wherewith to please fantastical heads, as gooseturd green, pease-porridge tawny, popinjay blue, lusty gallant, the-devil-in-the-head (I should say "the hedge"),[9] and suchlike; but I pass them over, thinking it sufficient to have said thus much of apparel generally, when nothing can particularly be spoken of any constancy thereof.

---

[7] "Ezech. 16."—*H.*

[8] *Slop:* wide breeches; *puke:* blue-black; *sad tawny:* dark orange-brown.

[9] *Lusty gallant:* light red; *devil-in-the-hedge:* apparently an off shade of red. The other colors are self-explanatory.

CHAPTER VIII

Of the High Court of Parliament
and Authority of the Same

IN SPEAKING of Parliament law, I have in the chapter precedent [1] said somewhat of this high and most honorable court. Wherefore it shall not need to remember aught here that is there touched; I will only speak of other things, therefore, concerning the state of assembly, whereby the magnificence thereof shall be in some part better known unto such as shall come after us. This house hath the most high and absolute power of the realm, for thereby kings and mighty princes have from time to time been deposed from their thrones, laws either enacted or abrogated, offenders of all sorts punished, and corrupted religion either disannulled or reformed, which commonly is divided into two houses or parts, the higher or upper house consisting of the nobility, including all even unto the baron and bishop, the lower, called the nether house, of knights, squires, gentlemen, and burgesses of the commons, with whom also the inferior members of the clergy are joined, albeit they sit in diverse places, and these have to deal only in matters of religion till it come that they join with the rest in confirmation of all such acts as are to pass in the same. For without the consent of the three estates, that is, of the nobility, clergy, and laity, seldom anything is said to be concluded upon and brought unto the prince for his consent and allowance. To be short, whatsoever the people of Rome did in their *centuriatis* or *tribunitiis comitiis*,[2] the same is and may be done by authority of our Parliament House, which is the head and body of all the realm and the place wherein every particular person is intended

---

[1] Actually the succeeding chapter. Except for the parliamentary list at the end, Harrison added this entire chapter viii to the 1587 edition, borrowing it largely and practically verbatim from Sir Thomas Smith, *De republica Anglorum*, II, i–ii. See pp. 152 and 154.

[2] *Centuriatis* or *tribunitiis comitiis*: the *comitia centuriata* and *comitia tributa* were the legislative assemblies of the whole Roman people. Harrison errs in changing Smith's *tributis* to *tribunitiis*.

to be present, if not by himself, yet by his advocate or attorney. For this cause, also, anything there enacted is not to be misliked but obeyed of all men without contradiction or grudge.

By the space of forty days before this assembly be begun, the prince sendeth his writs unto all his nobility particularly, summoning them to appear at the said court. The like he doth to the sheriff of every county, with commandment to choose two knights within each of their counties to give their advice in the name of the shire; likewise to every city and town, that they may choose their burgesses, which commonly are men best skilled in the state of their city or town, either for the declaration of such benefits as they want or to show which way to reform such enormities as, through the practices of ill members, are practiced and crept in among them; the first being chosen by the gentlemen of the shire, the other by the citizens and burgesses of every city and town, whereby that court is furnished. The first day of the Parliament being come, the lords of the upper house, as well ecclesiastical as temporal, do attend upon the prince, who rideth thither in person, as it were to open the door of their authority; and, being come into the place, after prayers made and causes showed wherefore some not present are enforced to be absent, each man taketh his place according to his degree. The house itself is curiously furnished with tapestry, and, the King being set in his throne, the spiritual lords take up the side of the house which is on the right hand of the prince and the temporal lords the left, I mean so well dukes and earls as viscounts and barons, as I before remembered. In the midst, and a pretty distance from the prince, lie certain sacks stuffed with wool or hair, whereon the judges of the realm, the Master of the Rolls, and secretaries of state do sit. Howbeit, these judges have no voice in the house but only show what their opinion is of such and such matters as come in question among the lords, if they be commanded so to do, as the secretaries are to answer such letters or things passed in the council whereof they have the custody and knowledge. Finally, the consent of this house is given by each man severally, first for himself being present, then severally for so many as he hath letters and proxies directed unto him, saying only, "Content," or "Not content," without any further debating.

Of the number assembled in the lower house I have already made a general report in the chapter precedent, and their particulars shall follow here at hand. These, therefore, being called over by name, do choose a Speaker, who is as it were their mouth, and him they present unto the prince, in whom it is either to refuse or admit him by the Lord Chancellor, who in the prince's name doth answer unto his oration, made at his first entrance and presentation into the house, wherein he declareth the good liking that the King hath conceived of his choice unto that office and function. Being admitted, he maketh five requests unto that honorable assembly: first, that the house may (as in times past) enjoy her former liberties and privileges; secondly, that the congregates may frankly show their minds upon such matters as are to come in question; thirdly, that if any of the lower house do give any cause of offense during the continuance of this assembly, that the same may inflict such punishment upon the party culpable as to the said assembly shall be thought convenient; fourthly, if any doubt should arise among them of the lower house, that he, in their name, might have free access and recourse unto His Majesty and lords of the higher house, to be further instructed and resolved in the same; fifthly and last, he craveth pardon for himself, if in his going to and fro between the houses he forget or mistake anything, requiring that he may return and be better informed in such things as he did fail in without offense; unto which petitions the Lord Chancellor doth answer as appertaineth, and this is done on the first day, or peradventure the second, if it could not be conveniently performed in the first.

Beside the Lord Chancellor there is another in the upper house called the Clerk of the Parliament, whose office is to read the bills. For everything that cometh in consultation in either house is first put in writing in paper, which being read, he that listeth riseth up and speaketh either with it or against it, and so one after another so long as they shall think good; that done, they go to another, and so to the third, etc., the instrument still wholly or in part rased or reformed, as cause moveth for the amendment of the same, if the substance be reputed necessary. In the upper house the Lord Chancellor demandeth if they will have it engrossed, that is to say, put in parchment, which done, it is read the third time; and after debating of the matter to and fro, if the more part do conclude withal, upon the utterance of these words, "Are ye contented that it be enacted or no?" the clerk writeth underneath, *Soit baille aux commons;* and so, when they see time, they send such bills approved to the commons by some of them that sit on the woolsacks, who, coming into the house and demanding license to speak, do use this kind of words or the like to the Speaker, as Sir Thomas Smith doth deliver and set them down, whose only direction I use, and almost word for word, in this chapter, requiting him with the like borrowage as he hath used toward me in his discourse of the sundry degrees of estates in the commonwealth of England, which (as I hope) shall be no discredit to his travail: "Master Speaker, my lords of the upper house have passed amongst them, and think good that there should be enacted by Parliament, such an act and such an act (reading their titles in such sort as he received them); they pray you, therefore, to consider and show your advice upon them." Which done, they go their way, and the door being shut after them, the Speaker declareth what message was sent unto them, and if they be then void of consultation upon any other bill, he presently demandeth what their pleasures are, first of one, then of another, etc., which are solemnly read or their contents briefly showed and then debated upon among them.

The Speaker sitteth in a chair erected somewhat higher than the rest, that he may see and be seen of all men; and before him on a lower seat sitteth his clerk, who readeth such bills as be first propounded in the lower house or sent down from the lords; for in that point each house hath equal authority to propound what they think meet, either for the abrogation of old or making of new laws. All bills be thrice, and on diverse days, read and disputed upon before they come to the question, which is, whether they shall be enacted or not; and in discourse upon them very good order is used in the lower house, wherein he that will speak giveth notice thereof by standing up bareheaded. If many stand up at once (as now and then it happeneth), he speaketh first that was first seen to move out of his place, and telleth his tale unto the Speaker, without rehearsal of his name whose speeches he meaneth to confute, so that with a perpetual oration and not with altercation these discourses are continued. But as the party confuted may not reply on that day, so one man cannot speak twice to one bill in one day, though he would change his opinion, but on the next day he may speak again, and yet but once as afore. No vile, seditious, unreverent, or biting words are used in this assembly, yet if any happen to escape and be uttered, the party is punished according to the censure of the assembly and custom in that behalf. In the afternoon they sit not except upon some urgent occasion, neither hath the Speaker any voice in that house wherewith to move or dissuade the furtherance or stay of any bill, but his office is, upon the reading thereof, briefly to declare the contents. If any bill pass which cometh unto them from the lords, it is thus subscribed, *Les commons ont assentus;* so, if the lords agree upon any bill sent unto them from the commons, it is subscribed after this manner, *Les seigniours ont assentus.* If it be not agreed on after thrice reading, there is conference required and had between the upper and nether houses, by certain appointed for that purpose, upon the points in question, whereupon, if no final agreement by the more part can be obtained, the bill is dashed and rejected, or (as the saying is) clean cast out of the doors.

None of the nether house can give his voice by proxy but in his own person; and, after the bill twice read, then engrossed, and the third time read again and discoursed upon, the Speaker asketh if they will go to the question, whereunto if they agree, he holdeth up the bill and saith, "So many as will have this bill go forward, say, 'Yea' "; hereupon, so many as allow of the thing cry, "Yea," the other, "No," and as the cry is more or less on either side, so is the bill to stay or else go forward. If the number of negative and affirmative voices seem to be equal, so many as allow of the bill go down withal, the rest sit still, and, being told by the poll, the greater part do carry away the matter. If something be allowed and in some part rejected, the bill is put to certain committees to be amended, and then, being brought in again, it is read and passeth or stayeth as the voices yield thereto. This is the order of the passage of our laws, which are not ratified till both houses have agreed unto them and yet not holden for law till the prince have given his assent.

Upon the last day, therefore, of the Parliament or session, the prince cometh in person again into the house, in his robes as at the first. Where, after thanks given to the prince, first in the name of the lords by the Lord Chancellor, then in the name of the commons by the Speaker, for his great care of the welfare of his realm, etc., the Lord Chancellor, in the prince's name, giveth thanks to the lords and commons likewise for their pains, with promise of recompense as opportunity and occasion shall serve therefor. This done, one readeth the title of every act passed in that session, and then it is noted upon them what the prince doth allow of, with these words, *Le roy veult*. If the prince like not of them, it is written upon them, *Le roy advisera*. And so those acts are dashed, as the other from thenceforth are taken and holden for law and all imprinted except such as concern some private persons, which are only exemplified under the seal of the Parliament, as privileges to his use. And this is the sum of the manner after which our Parliaments in England are holden, without which no forfeiture of life, member, or lands of any Englishman, where no law is ordained for the same beforehand, is available or can take place amongst us. And so much in manner out of the third [second] chapter of the second book of *The Commonwealth of England*, written by Sir Thomas Smith; whereunto I will annex a table of the counties, cities, boroughs, and ports which send knights, burgesses, and barons to the Parliament House, and doth ensue as followeth:

The names of counties, cities, boroughs, and ports sending knights, citizens, burgesses, and barons to the Parliament of England

Bedford

Knights	2
The borough of Bedford	2

Buckingham

Knights	2
The borough of Buckingham	2
The borough of Wycombe	2
The borough of Aylesbury	2

Berkshire

Knights	2
The borough of New Windsor	2
The borough of Reading	2
The borough of Wallingford	2
The borough of Abingdon	2

Cornwall

Knights	2

The borough of Launceston, *alias* Newport[a]	2
The borough of Liskeard	2
The borough of Lostwithiel	2
The borough of Dunheved[a]	2
The borough of Truro	2
The borough of Bodmin	2
The borough of Helston	2
The borough of Saltash	2
The borough of Camelford	2
The borough of Portighsham, *alias* Portloe	2
The borough of Grampound	2
The borough of East Looe	2
The borough of Prurie [Penryn?]	2
The borough of Tregony	2
The borough of Trevena, *alias* Bossiney	2
The borough of St. Ives	2
The borough of Fowey	2
The borough of [St.] Germans	2
The borough of Mitchell	2
The borough of St. Mary's [St. Mawes]	2

Cumberland

Knights	2
The city of Carlisle	2

Cambridge

Knights	2
The borough of Cambridge	2

Chester

Knights	2
The city of Chester	2

Derby

Knights	2
The borough of Derby	2

Devon

Knights	2
The city of Exeter	2
The borough of Totnes	2

[a] Launceston and Newport were adjoining towns, each of which returned two M.P.'s. Dunheved was the older name for Launceston.

The borough of Plymouth	2
The borough of Barnstaple	2
The borough of Plympton	2
The borough of Tavistock	2
The borough of Dartmouth, Clifton, and Hardness	2

Dorsetshire

Knights	2
The borough of Poole	2
The borough of Dorchester	2
The borough of Lyme	2
The borough of Melcombe	2
The borough of Weymouth	2
The borough of Bridport	2
The borough of Shaftesbury	2
The borough of Wareham	2

Essex

Knights	2
The borough of Colchester	2
The borough of Maldon	2

Yorkshire

Knights	2
The city of York	2
The borough of Kingston-upon-Hull	2
The borough of Knaresborough	2
The borough of Scarborough	2
The borough of Ripon	2
The borough of Hedon	2
The borough of Boroughbridge	2
The borough of Thirsk	2
The borough of Aldborough	2
The borough of Beverley	2

Gloucestershire

Knights	2
The city of Gloucester	2
The borough of Cirencester	2

Huntingdonshire

Knights	2
The borough of Huntingdon	2

Hertfordshire

Knights	2
The borough of St. Albans	2

Herefordshire

Knights	2
The city of Hereford	2
The borough of Leominster	2

Kent

Knights	2
The city of Canterbury	2
The city of Rochester	2
The borough of Maidstone	2
The borough of Queenborough	2

Lincoln

Knights	2
The city of Lincoln	2
The borough of Boston	2
The borough of Great Grimsby	2
The borough of Stamford	2
The borough of Grantham	2

Leicestershire

Knights	2
The borough of Leicester	2

Lancastershire

Knights	2
The borough of Lancaster	2
The borough of Preston in Andernes [Amounderness]	2
The borough of Liverpool	2
The borough of Newton	2
The borough of Wigan	2
The borough of Clitheroe	2

Middlesex

Knights	2
The city of London	4
The city of Westminster	2

Monmouth

Knights	2
The borough of Monmouth	1

Northampton

Knights	2
The city of Peterborough	2
The borough of Northampton	2
The borough of Brackley	2
The borough of Higham Ferrers	1

Nottingham

Knights	2
The borough of Nottingham	2
The borough of East Retford	2

Norfolk

Knights	2
The city of Norwich	2
The borough of Lynn	2
The borough of Great Yarmouth	2
The borough of Thetford	2
The borough of Castle Rising	2

Northumberland

Knights	2
The borough of Newcastle-upon-Tyne	2
The borough of Morpeth	2
The borough of Berwick	2

Oxford

Knights	2
The city of Oxford	2
The borough of Banbury	2
The borough of Woodstock	2

Rutland

Knights	2

Surrey

Knights	2
The borough of Southwark	2
The borough of Bletchingley	2
The borough of Reigate	2

The borough of Guildford 2
The borough of Gatton 2

Stafford

Knights 2
The city of Lichfield 2
The borough of Stafford 2
The borough of Newcastle under Lyme 2
The borough of Tamworth 2

Salop

Knights 2
The borough of Salop 2
The borough of Brug, *alias* Bridgnorth 2
The borough of Ludlow 2
The borough of Wenlock 2

Southampton

Knights 2
The city of Winton [Winchester] 2
The borough of Southampton 2
The borough of Portsmouth 2
The borough of Petersfield 2
The borough of Stockbridge 2
The borough of Christchurch 2

Suffolk

Knights 2
The borough of Ipswich 2
The borough of Dunwich 2
The borough of Orford 2
The borough of Aldeburgh 2
The borough of Sudbury 2
The borough of Eye 2

Somerset

Knights 2
The city of Bristol 2
The city of Bath 2
The city of Wells 2
The borough of Taunton 2
The borough of Bridgwater 2
The borough of Minehead 2

Sussex

Knights	2
The city of Chichester	2
The borough of Horsham	2
The borough of Midhurst	2
The borough of Lewes	2
The borough of Shoreham	2
The borough of Bramber	2
The borough of Steyning	2
The borough of East Grinstead	2
The borough of Arundel	2

Westmorland

Knights	2
The borough of Appleby	2

Wilton

Knights	2
The city of New Sarum	2
The borough of Wilton	2
The borough of Downton	2
The borough of Hindon	2
The borough of Heytesbury	2
The borough of Westbury	2
The borough of Calne	2
The borough of Devizes	2
The borough of Chippenham	2
The borough of Malmesbury	2
The borough of Cricklade	2
The borough of Bedwyn	2
The borough of Ludgershall	2
The borough of Old Sarum	2
The borough of Wootton Basset	2
The borough of Marlborough	2

Worcester

Knights	2
The city of Worcester	2
The borough of Withee [4]	2

[4] *Withee:* in error for Wich, that is, Droitwich, perhaps through confusion with the Robert Wyth (Wyethe) who was returned by the borough in the Parliaments from 1554 to 1567.

Warwick

Knights	2
The city of Coventry	2
The borough of Warwick	2

Barons of the ports

Hastings	2
Winchelsea	2
Rye	2
Romney	2
Hythe	2
Dover	2
Sandwich	2

Montgomery

Knights	1
The borough of Montgomery	1

Flint

Knights	1
The borough of Flint	1

Denbigh

Knights	1
The borough of Denbigh	1

Merioneth

Knights	1
The borough of Haverfordwest [5]	1

Caernarvon

Knights	1
The borough of Caernarvon	1

Anglesey

Knights	1
The borough of Beaumaris	1

Carmarthen

Knights	1
The borough of New Carmarthen	1

[5] Haverfordwest should be placed in Pembroke.

Pembroke

Knights	1
The borough of Pembroke	1

Cardigan

Knights	1
The borough of Cardigan	1

Brecknock

Knights	1
The borough of Brecknock	1

Radnor

Knights	1
The borough of Radnor	1

Glamorgan

Knights	1
The borough of Cardiff	1

The sum of the foresaid number of the common house, *videlicet*, of

Knights	90
Citizens	46
Burgesses	289
Barons	14
	439

CHAPTER IX

Of the Laws of England since Her First Inhabitation

THAT Samothes, or Dis, gave the first laws to the Celts (whose kingdom he erected about the fifteenth of Nimbrote), the testimony of Berossos is proof sufficient. For he not only affirmeth him to publish the same in the fourth of Ninus but also addeth thereto how there lived none in his days of more excellent wisdom nor politic invention than he, whereof he was named Samothes, as some other do affirm. What his laws were it is now altogether unknown, as most things of this age; but that they were altered again at the coming of Albion no man can absolutely deny, sith new lords use commonly to give new laws, and conquerors abolish such as were in use before them.[1]

The like also may be affirmed of our Brut,[2] notwithstanding that the certain knowledge so well of the one as of the other is perished and nothing worthy memory left of all their doings. Somewhat yet we have of Molmutius,[3] who not only subdued such princes as reigned in this land but also brought the realm to good order, that long before had been torn with civil discord. But where his laws are to be found and which they be from other men's, no man living in these days is able to determine.

[1] Harrison happily accepted the Samothean theory, which provided England with a postdiluvial settlement: "In the diligent perusal of their treatises who have written of the state of this our island, I find that at the first it seemed to be a parcel of the Celtic kingdom, whereof Dis, otherwise called Samothes, one of the sons of Japheth, was the Saturn or original beginner, and of him thenceforth for a long while called Samothea. Afterward, in process of time, when desire of rule began to take hold in the minds of men and each prince endeavored to enlarge his own dominions, Albion, the son of Neptune, . . . hearing of the commodities of the country and plentifulness of soil here, made a voyage over, and finding the thing not only correspondent unto but also far surmounting the report that went of this island, it was not long after ere he invaded the same by force of arms, brought it to his subjection in the twenty-ninth year after his grandfather's [Osiris, son of Ham] decease, and finally changed the name thereof into Albion, whereby the former denomination after Samothes did grow out of mind and fall into utter forgetfulness." According to Harrison's calculations, Samothes, the grandson of Noah, settled England "in the 1910 after the creation of Adam"; the Samothean dynasty reigned for 335 years until the invasion of Albion, who was killed by Hercules in the seventh year of his reign (*Des. Brit.*, 1587, pp. 3–5). The originator of this elaborate fantasy was the indefatigable John Bale (1495–1563) in his *Illustrium majoris Britanniae scriptorum summarium* (Ipswich, 1548). Bale, in turn, relied on hints in a MS supposedly detailing the repopulation of the world after the Flood; actually a forgery, it was attributed to Berossos the Chaldean (ca. 300 B.C.) and edited by Annius of Viterbo in 1498. In this pseudo-Berossos, Nimbrote was the founder of Babylon and Ninus, husband of Semiramis, the founder of Nineveh. The Samothean concoction had a vigorous but brief life. Although accepted by Leland, Caius, Lambarde, and Holinshed, it was doubted by Stow, ignored by Camden, and lost ground rapidly in the seventeenth century. See T. D. Kendrick, *British Antiquity* (London, 1950), pp. 69–76.

[2] *Brut:* Brutus, according to Geoffrey of Monmouth (I, xvi-xvii) Aeneas' great-grandson, who led a colony of Trojans to Britain and built New Troy, or Trinovantum (London).

[3] *Molmutius:* Dunwallo Molmutius, a legendary Cornish king, who achieved hegemony over Britain and founded the dynasty which replaced that of Brut (Geoffrey, II, xvii).

Certes there was never prince in Britain of whom his subjects conceived better hope in the beginning than of Bladud, and yet I read of none that made so ridiculous an end;[4] in like sort there hath not reigned any monarch in this isle whose ways were more feared at the first than those of Dunwallo [Molmutius] (King Henry the Fifth excepted), and yet in the end he proved such a prince as after his death there was in manner no subject that did not lament his funerals. And this only for his policy in governance, severe administration of justice, and provident framing of his laws and constitutions for the government of his subjects. His people, also, coveting to continue his name unto posterity, entitled those his ordinances according to their maker, calling them by the name of "The Laws of Molmutius," which endured in execution among the Britons so long as our homelings had the dominion of this isle. Afterward, when the comeling Saxons had once obtained the superiority of the kingdom, the majesty of those laws fell for a time into such decay that although *non penitus cecidit, tamen potuit cecidisse videri*, as Leland saith;[5] and the decrees themselves had utterly perished indeed at the very first brunt had they not been preserved in Wales, where they remained amongst the relics of the Britons, and not only until the coming of the Normans but even until the time of Edward the First, who, obtaining the sovereignty of that portion, endeavored very earnestly to extinguish those of Molmutius and to establish his own.

But as the Saxons at their first arrival did what they could to abolish the British laws, so in process of time they yielded a little to relent and not so much to abhor and mislike of the laws of Molmutius as to receive and embrace the same, especially at such time as the said Saxon princes entered into amity with the British nobility and after that began to join in matrimony with the British ladies, as the British barons did with the Saxon frows [women], both by an especial statute and decree whereof in another treatise

---

[4] *Bladud:* the father of Lear and founder of Bath; noted as a craftsman, he attempted to fashion wings for himself and came to earth, fatally, on the temple of Apollo in London (Geoffrey, II, x).

[5] The Molmutine code "did not perish completely, yet it gave the appearance of having perished" (Leland, *Commentarii de scriptoribus Britannicis*, ed. Anthony Hall, Oxford, 1709, I, 12). Harrison apparently had access to the MS (now in the Bodleian) of this biographical dictionary. Most of his discussion here of the laws of Molmutius and Martia is freely translated from Leland's Latin (see p. 166); Leland, in turn, derived it from Geoffrey of Monmouth.

I have made mention at large.[6] Hereof also it came to pass in the end that they were contented to make a choice and insert no small numbers of them into their own volumes, as may be gathered by those of Ethelbert, "the Great" surnamed, King of Kent, Ine and Alfred, Kings of the West Saxons, and divers other yet extant to be seen.[7] Such also was the lateward estimation of them that when any of the Saxon princes went about to make new ordinances they caused those of Molmutius (which Gildas sometime translated into Latin)[8] to be first expounded unto them; and in this perusal, if they found any there already framed that might serve their turns, they forthwith revived the same and annexed them to their own.

But in this dealing the diligence of Alfred is most of all to be commended, who not only chose out the best but gathered together all such whatsoever the said Molmutius had made; and then, to the end they should lie no more in corners as forlorn books and unknown to the learned of his kingdom, he caused them to be turned into the Saxon tongue, wherein they continued long after his decease.

As for the Normans, who for a season neither regarded the British nor cared for the Saxon statutes, they also at the first utterly misliked of them; till at the last, when they had well weighed that one kind of regiment is not convenient for all peoples and that no stranger, being in a foreign country newly brought under obedience, could make such equal ordinances as he might thereby govern his new commonwealth without some care and trouble, they fell in with such a desire to see by what rule the state of the land was governed in time of the Saxons that, having perused the same, they not only commended their manner of regiment but

[6] "For had not King Edward, surnamed 'the Saint' in his time, after grievous wars made upon them ['the natural homelings or Britons'], 1063, . . . permitted the remnant of their women to join in marriage with the Englishmen (when the most part of their husbands and male children were slain with the sword), it could not have been otherwise chosen but their whole race must needs have sustained the uttermost confusion and thereby the memory of the Britons utterly have perished among us" (*Des. Brit.*, 1587, pp. 7–8).

[7] The laws of Alfred, to which were appended those of Ine, had been printed in 1568 by William Lambarde, *Archaionomia, sive de priscis Anglorum legibus.*

[8] *Gildas:* British historian of the sixth century. The notion that he translated the Molmutine laws seems to be based on a misreading of Geoffrey (II, xvii).

also admitted a great part of their laws (now current under the name of "St. Edward's Laws" and used as principles and grounds),[9] whereby they not only qualified the rigor of their own and mitigated their almost intolerable burden of servitude, which they had lately laid upon the shoulders of the English, but also left us a great number of the old Molmutian laws, whereof the most part are in use to this day, as I said, albeit that we know not certainly how to distinguish them from others that are in strength amongst us.

After Dunwallo the next lawgiver was Martia, whom Leland surnameth Proba; and after him John Bale also, who in his *Centuries* doth justly confess himself to have been holpen by the said Leland, as I myself do likewise for many things contained in this treatise.[10] She was wife unto Guithelin, King of the Britons;[11] and, being made protectrix of the realm after her husband's decease, in the nonage of her son, and seeing many things daily to grow up among her people worthy reformation, she devised sundry, and those very politic, laws for the governance of her kingdom, which her subjects, when she was dead and gone, did name "The Martian [Mercian] Statutes." Who turned them into Latin, as yet I do not read; howbeit (as I said before of the laws of Molmutius, so) the same Alfred caused those of this excellently well-learned lady (whom divers commend also for her great knowledge in the Greek tongue) to be turned into his own language;[12] whereupon it came to pass that they were daily executed among his subjects, afterward allowed of (among the rest) by the Normans, and finally remain in use in these our days, notwithstanding that we cannot dissever them also very readily from the other.

The seventh alteration of laws was practiced by the Saxons; for I overpass the use of the civil ordinances used in Rome, finally brought hither by the Romans and yet in perfect notice

[9] The laws attributed to Edward the Confessor seem to be a fabrication of the twelfth century; they were printed by Lambarde.

[10] Bale revised and expanded his earlier work as *Scriptorum illustrium majoris Britanniae . . . catalogus* (Basle [1557–1559]), drawing heavily on Leland's MS. Harrison's well-annotated copy of the Bale volume is extant at Londonderry.

[11] *Guithelin:* supposedly the great-grandson of Dunwallo Molmutius.

[12] This notion, which occurs in Geoffrey (III, xiii), seems to derive from Alfred's statement in the preface to his laws that his code is based partly on the laws of Offa, King of the Mercians.

among the civilians [students of civil law] of our country, though never generally nor fully received by all the several regions of this island. Certes there are great numbers of these latter which yet remain in sound knowledge and are to be read, being comprehended for the most part under the names of the Martian and the Saxon law. Beside these also I read of the Dane-law,[13] so that the people of Middle England were ruled by the first, the West Saxons by the second, as Essex, Norfolk, Suffolk, Cambridgeshire, and part of Hertfordshire were by the third, of all the rest the most inequal and intolerable. And as in these days whatsoever the prince in public assembly commanded upon the necessity of his subjects on his own voluntary authority was counted for law, so none of them had appointed any certain place whereunto his people might repair at fixed times for justice but caused them to resort commonly to their palaces, where in proper person they would often determine their causes and so make shortest work, or else commit the same to the hearing of other and so dispatch them away. Neither had they any house appointed to assemble in for the making of their ordinances, as we have now at Westminster. Wherefore Edmund gave laws at London and Lincoln, Ethelred at Habam, Alfred at Woodstock and Wannetting, Athelstan in Exeter, Grecklade, Faversham, and Thundersley,[14] Canute at Winchester, etc., other in other places, whereof this may suffice.

Among other things also used in the time of the Saxons, it shall not be amiss to set down the form of their ordalian law, which they brought hither with them from beyond the seas out of Scythia and used only in the trial of guilti- and unguiltiness. Certes it contained not an ordinary proceeding by days and terms, as in the civil and common law we see practiced in these days, but a short dispatch and trial of the matter by fire or water, whereof at this present I will deliver the circumstance as I have faithfully translated it out of an ancient volume and conferred with an imprinted copy lately published by Master Lambarde

[13] *Danelaw:* the law imposed by the Danes on that part of northeastern England which they held.

[14] *Habam:* apparently, for *Badam*, Bath; *Wannetting:* Wantage; *Grecklade* (that is, Cricklade) and *Thundersley* (a hamlet in southeastern Essex): Harrison's identifications for the Saxon "Greatanlee" and "Thunresfelde," actually Grateley in Hampshire and Thunderfield in Surrey.

and now extant to be read.[15] Nevertheless, as the Scythians were the first that used this practice, so I read that it was taken up and occupied also in France in process of time, yea, and likewise in Greece, as G. Pachymeres remembereth in the first book of his history (which beginneth with the empire of M. Paleologus), where he noteth his own sight and view in that behalf.[16] But what stand I hereupon?

The ordalian (saith the aforesaid author)[17] was a certain manner of purgation used two ways, whereof the one was by fire, the other by water. In the execution of that which was done by fire, the party accused should go a certain number of paces with an hot iron in his hand, or else barefooted upon certain plowshares, red-hot according to the manner. This iron was sometime of one-pound weight, and then was it called single *ordalium*, sometimes of three and then named treble *ordalium*, and whosoever did bear or tread on the same without hurt of his body, he was adjudged guiltless; otherwise, if his skin were scorched, he was forthwith condemned as guilty of the trespass whereof he was accused, according to the proportion and quantity of the burning.

There were in like sort two kinds of trial by the water, that is to say, either by hot or cold; and in this trial the party thought culpable was either tumbled into some pond or huge vessel of cold water, wherein if he continued for a season without wrestling or struggling for life, he was forthwith acquitted as guiltless of the fact whereof he was accused; but if he began to plunge and labor once for breath immediately upon his falling into that liquor, he was by and by condemned as guilty of the crime. Or else he did thrust his arm up to the shoulder into a lead, copper,[18] or caldron of seething water, from whence if he withdrew the same without any manner of damage, he was discharged of further molestation; otherwise he was taken for a trespasser and punished accordingly. The fiery manner of purgation belonged only to noblemen and -women and such as were freeborn, but the

---

[15] *Archaionomia,* sigs. C2v–C4r.

[16] *George Pachymeres* (1242–?1310): Byzantine historian; *Michael Paleologus:* Eastern Emperor in 1261–1282.

[17] The following two paragraphs are largely translated from Lambarde's Latin.

[18] *Lead, copper:* large vessels.

husbandmen and villeins were tried by water. Whereof, to show the unlearned dealing and blind ignorance of those times, it shall not be impertinent to set forth the whole manner, which continued here in England until the time of King John, who, seeing the manifold subtleties in the same (by sundry sorcerous and artificial practices, whereby the working of the said elements were restrained), did extinguish it altogether as flat lewdness and bobbery [trickery].

[Harrison here includes a lengthy account of the religious ceremony accompanying a trial by ordeal, giving the prayers both in Latin and in his English translation. He follows closely Lambarde's version. The passage ends:]

After this the priest shall sprinkle the iron with holy water, saying: "The blessing of God the Father, the Son, and the Holy Ghost be upon this iron, to the revelation of the just judgment of God." And forthwith let him that is accused bear it by the length of nine foot, and then let his hand be wrapped and sealed up for the space of three days; after this, if any corruption or raw flesh appear where the iron touched it, let him be condemned as guilty; if it be whole and sound, let him give thanks to God.

And thus much of the fiery *ordalia*, whereunto that of the water hath so precise relation that in setting forth of the one I have also described the other, wherefore it shall be but in vain to deal any further withal.

Hitherto also (as I think) sufficiently of such laws as were in use before the Conquest. Now it resteth that I should declare the order of those that have been made and received since the coming of the Normans, referred to the eighth alteration or change of our manner of governance, and thereunto do produce threescore-and-four several courts. But forasmuch as I am no lawyer and therefore have but little skill to proceed in the same accordingly, it shall suffice to set down some general discourse of such as are used in our days and so much as I have gathered by report and common hearsay.

We have therefore in England sundry laws, and first of all the civil, used in the chancery, admiralty, and divers other courts, in some of which the severe rigor of justice is often so mitigated

by conscience[19] that divers things are thereby made easy and
tolerable which otherwise would appear to be mere injury and
extremity.

We have also a great part of the canon law daily practiced
among us, especially in cases of tithes, contracts of matrimony,
and suchlike, as are usually to be seen in the consistories of our
bishops and higher courts of the two archbishops, where the
exercise of the same is very hotly followed. The third sort of
laws that we have are our own, and those always so variable and
subject to alteration and change that oft in one age diverse judgments do pass upon one manner of case, whereby the saying of
the poet,

Tempora mutantur, et nos mutamur in illis,[20]

may very well be applied unto such as, being urged with these
words, "In such a year of the prince this opinion was taken for
sound law," do answer nothing else but that the judgment of our
lawyers is now altered so that they say far otherwise. The regiment that we have, therefore, after our own ordinances depend-
eth upon three laws, to wit, statute law, common law, [and]
customary law and prescription, according to the triple manner
of our trials and judgments, which is by Parliament, verdict of
twelve men at an assize, or wager of battle, of which the last is
little used in our days, as no appeal doth hold in the first and last
rehearsed.[21] But to return to my purpose.

The first is delivered unto us by Parliament, which court,
being for the most part holden at Westminster near London, is
the highest of all other and consisteth of three several sorts of
people, that is to say, the nobility, clergy, and commons of this
realm. And thereto [it] is not summoned but upon urgent occasion when the prince doth see his time, and that by several writs
dated commonly full six weeks before it begin to be holden.
Such laws as are agreed upon in the higher house by the lords
spiritual and temporal, and in the lower house by the commons

---

[19] "The court of chancery is called of common people 'the court of
conscience,' because that the chancellor is not strained by rigor or form of
words of law to judge but *ex aequo* and *bono* and according to conscience" (Sir Thomas Smith, *De republica Anglorum,* II, xi).

[20] "Times change and we change with them." Proverbial.

[21] The last part of this sentence, after "prescription," is based on Smith,
II, v, vii, viii.

and body of the realm (whereof the convocation of the clergy, holden in Paul's or, if occasion so require, in Westminster Church, is a member), there speaking by the mouth of the knights of the shire and burgesses, remain in the end to be confirmed by the prince, who commonly resorteth thither of custom upon the first and last days of this court, there to understand what is done and give his royal consent to such statutes as him liketh of. Coming therefor thither into the higher house and having taken his throne, the Speaker of the Parliament (for one is always appointed to go between the houses as an indifferent mouth for both) readeth openly the matters there determined by the said three estates and then craveth the prince's consent and final confirmation to the same. The King, having heard the sum and principal points of each statute briefly recited unto him, answereth in French with great deliberation unto such as he liketh, *Il nous plaist*, but to the rest, *Il ne plaist*, whereby the latter are made void and frustrate. That also which His Majesty liketh of is hereby authorized, confirmed, and ever after holden for law, except it be repealed in any the like assembly.

The number of the commons assembled in the lower house, beside the clergy, consisteth of ninety knights. For each shire of England hath two gentlemen or knights of greatest wisdom and reputation chosen out of the body of the same for that only purpose, saving that for Wales one only is supposed sufficient in every county, whereby the number afore mentioned is made up. There are likewise 46 citizens, 289 burgesses, and 14 barons, so that the whole assembly of the laity of the lower house consisteth of 439 persons, if the just number be supplied. Of the laws here made likewise, some are penal and restrain the common law, and some again are found to enlarge the same. The one sort of these also are for the most part taken strictly according to the letter, the other more largely and beneficially after their intendment and meaning.

The common law standeth upon sundry maxims or principles and years or terms, which do contain such cases as by great study and solemn argument of the judges, sound practice, confirmed by long experience, fetched even from the course of most ancient laws made far before the Conquest, and thereto the deepest reach and foundations of reason, are ruled and adjudged for law. Certes these cases are otherwise called pleas or action, whereof there are two sorts, the one criminal and the other civil. The means and messengers also to determine those causes are our writs or briefs, whereof there are some original and some judicial.[22] The parties plaintiff and defendant, when they appear, proceed (if the case do so require) by plaint or declaration, bar or answer, replication, rejoinder, and so, by rebut, surrebut to issue and trial, if occasion so fall out, the one side affirmatively, the other negatively, as common experience teacheth. Our trials and recoveries are either by verdict and demurrer, confession, or default, wherein if any negligence or trespass hath been committed, either in process and form or in matter and judgment, the party grieved may have a writ of error to undo the same but not in the same court where the former judgment was given.

Customary law consisteth of certain laudable customs used in some private country, intended first to begin upon good and reasonable considerations, as gavelkind, which is all the male children equally to inherit, and continued to this day in Kent, where it is only to my knowledge retained and nowhere else in England. It was at the first devised by the Romans, as appeareth by Caesar in his *Commentaries,* wherein I find that to break and daunt the force of the rebellious Germans they made a law that all the male children (or females for want of males, which holdeth still in England) should have their father's inheritance equally divided amongst them. By this means also it came to pass that, whereas beforetime for the space of sixty years they had put the Romans to great and manifold troubles, within the space of thirty years after this law made, their power did wax so feeble and such discord fell out amongst themselves that they were not able to maintain wars with the Romans nor raise any just army against them. For as a river running with one stream is swift and more plentiful of water than when it is drained or drawn into many branches, so, the lands and goods of the ancestors being dispersed amongst their issue males, of one strong there were raised sundry weak, whereby the original or general strength to resist the adversary became enfeebled and brought almost to nothing. *Vis unita,* saith the philosopher, *fortior est eadem dispersa,*[23] and one

---

[22] *Judicial writs:* in an action at law, the writs issued subsequent to the original writ, which is the beginning of common-law actions.
[23] "Power united is stronger than the same dispersed." Proverbial.

good purse is better than many evil; and when every man is benefited alike, each one will seek to maintain his private estate and few take care to provide for public welfare.

Boroughkind [borough-English] is where the youngest is preferred before the eldest, which is the custom of many countries of this region; also [as other examples of customary law] the woman to have the third of her husband's possessions, the husband that marrieth an heir to have such lands as move by her during his natural life if he survive her and hath a child by her which hath been heard cry through four walls, etc., of suchlike to be learned elsewhere, and sometimes frequented generally overall.

Prescription is a certain custom which hath continued time out of mind, but it is more particular than customary law, as where only a parish or some private person doth prescribe to have common, or a way in another man's soil, or tithes to be paid after this or that manner, I mean otherwise than the common course and order of the law requireth, whereof let this suffice at this time instead of a larger discourse of our own laws, lest I should seem to enter far into that whereof I have no skill. For what hath the meditation of the law of God to do with any precise knowledge of the law of man, sith they are several trades and incident to diverse persons?

There are also sundry usual courts holden once in every quarter of the year, which we commonly call terms, of the Latin word *terminus*, wherein all controversies are determined that happen within the Queen's dominions. These are commonly holden at London, except upon some great occasion they be transferred to other places. At what times also they are kept, both for spiritual and temporal dealing, the table ensuing shall easily declare. Finally, how well they are followed by suitors the great wealth of lawyers, without any travail of mine, can readily express. For as, after the coming of the Normans, the nobility had the start [competitive advantage], and after them the clergy, so now all the wealth of the land doth flow unto our common lawyers, of whom some one, having practiced little above thirteen or fourteen years, is able to buy a purchase of so many thousand pounds, which argueth that they wax rich apace and will be richer if their clients become not the more wiser and wary hereafter. It is not long since a sergeant-at-the-law (whom

I could name) was arrested upon an extent [24] for £300 or £400, and another standing by did greatly marvel that he could not spare the gains of one term for the satisfaction of that duty. The time hath been that our lawyers did sit in Paul's upon stools against the pillars and walls to get clients, but now some of them will not come from their chambers to the Guildhall in London under £10, or twenty nobles at the least. And one, being demanded why he made so much of his travel, answered that it was but folly for him to go so far when he was assured to get more money by sitting still at home. A friend of mine also had a suit of late of some valure, and to be sure of counsel at his time he gave unto two lawyers (whose names I forbear to deliver) 20s. apiece, telling them of the day and hour wherein his matter should be called upon. To be short, they came not unto the bar at all,[25] whereupon he stayed for that day. On the morrow after, he met them again, increased his former gifts by so much more, and told them of the time, but they once again served him as before. In the end he met them both in the very hall door and, after some timorous reprehension of their uncourteous demeanor toward him, he bestowed either three angels or four more upon each of them, whereupon they promised peremptorily to speak earnestly in his cause. And yet for all this, one of them, having not yet sucked enough, utterly deceived him; the other indeed came in, and, wagging a scroll which he had in his hand before the judge, he spake not above three or four words, almost so soon uttered as a "good morrow," and so went from the bar; and this was all the poor man gat for his money and the care which his counselors did seem to take of his cause, then standing upon the hazard.[26] But enough of these matters, for if I should set down how little law poor men can have for their small fees in these days and the great murmurings that are on all sides uttered against their excessive taking of money (for they can abide no small gain), I should extend this treatise into a far greater volume than is convenient for my purpose. Wherefore it shall suffice to have set down so much of their demeanor, and so much as is even enough to cause them to look with somewhat more conscience into their dealings, except they be dull and senseless.

---

[24] *Extent:* a writ to recover taxes or debts owed the Crown.
[25] "Deceit."—*H.*   [26] "Many of our lawyers stoop not at small fees."—*H.*

This furthermore is to be noted, that albeit the princes heretofore reigning in this land have erected sundry courts, especially
of the chancery at York and Ludlow, for the ease of poor men
dwelling in those parts, yet will the poorest (of all men commonly most contentious) refuse to have his cause heard so near
home but endeavoreth rather, to his utter undoing, to travel up
to London, thinking there soonest to prevail against his adversary, though his case be never so doubtful. But in this toy our
Welshmen do exceed of all that ever I heard, for you shall here
and there have some one odd poor David of them given so much
to contention and strife that without all respect of charges he
will up to London, though he go barelegged by the way and carry
his hosen on his neck (to save their feet from wearing) because
he hath no change. When he cometh there also he will make such
importunate begging of his countrymen, and hard shift otherwise, that he will sometimes carry down six or seven writs with
him in his purse wherewith to molest his neighbor, though the
greatest quarrel be scarcely worth the fee that he hath paid for
any one of them. But enough of this, lest in revealing the superfluous folly of a few brabblers [quarrelers over trifles] in this
behalf, I bring no good will to myself amongst the wisest of that
nation.

Certes it is a lamentable case to see furthermore how a number of poor men are daily abused and utterly undone by sundry
varlets that go about the country as promoters or brokers between
the pettifoggers of the law and the common people, only to
kindle and espy coals of contention whereby the one side may
reap commodity and the other spend and be put to travail. But of
all that ever I knew in Essex, Denis and Mainford excelled, till
John of Ludlow, *alias* Mason, came in place, unto whom in comparison they two were but children;[27] for this last, in less than
three or four years, did bring one man (among many elsewhere
in other places) almost to extreme misery (if beggary be the
uttermost), that before he had the shaving of his beard was
valued at £200 (I speak with the least), and finally feeling that
he had not sufficient wherewith to sustain himself and his family, and also to satisfy that greedy ravener, which still called
upon him for new fees, he went to bed and within four days

---

[27] "Three varlets worthy to be chronicled."—*H.*, 1577 only.

made an end of his woeful life, even with care and pensiveness. After his death, also, he so handled his son that there was never sheep shorn in May so near-clipped of his fleece present as he was of many to come, so that he was compelled to let away his land, because his cattle and stock were consumed and he no longer able to occupy the ground. But hereof let this suffice, and instead of these enormities a table shall follow of the terms, containing their beginnings and endings, as I have borrowed them from my friend, John Stow, whose study is the only storehouse of antiquities in my time and he worthy therefor to be had in reputation and honor.

A man would imagine that the time of the execution of our laws, being little above one quarter or not fully a third part of the year, and the appointment of the same to be holden in one place only, to wit, near London in Westminster, and finally, the great expenses employed upon the same, should be no small cause of the stay and hindrance of the administration of justice in this land; but, as it falleth out, they prove great occasions and the stay of much contention. The reasons of these are soon to be conceived, for as the broken sleeve doth hold the elbow back and pain of travel cause many to sit at home in quiet, so the shortness of time and fear of delay doth drive those oftentimes to like of peace who otherwise would live at strife and quickly be at odds. Some men desirous of gains would have the terms yet made shorter, that more delay might engender longer suit; other would have the houses made larger and more offices erected wherein to minister the laws. But as the times of the terms are rather too short than too long by one return apiece, so, if there were smaller rooms and fouler ways unto them, they would enforce many to make pauses before they did rashly enter into plea. But sith my purpose is not to make an ample discourse of these things, it shall suffice to deliver the times of the holding of our terms, which ensueth after this manner:

A perfect rule to know the beginning and ending of every term, with their returns [28]

Hilary term beginneth the three-and-twentieth day of January (if it be not Sunday, otherwise the next day after) and is finished

---

[28] As Harrison notes above, the remainder of the chapter comes verbatim from the table of the terms prefixed to Stow's *Summary of the Chronicles*

the twelfth of February; it hath four returns:

Octavis Hilarii	Crastino Purific.
Quind. Hilarii	Octavis Purific.

Easter term beginneth seventeen days after Easter, endeth four days after the Ascension Day, and hath five returns:

Quind. Pasch.	Mense Paschae
Tres Paschae	Quinque Paschae
Crast. Ascension	

Trinity term beginneth the Friday after Trinity Sunday and endeth the Wednesday fortnight after, in which time it hath four returns:

Crast. Trinitatis	Quind. Trinitatis
Octavis Trinitatis	Tres Trinitatis

Michaelmas term beginneth the ninth of October (if it be not Sunday) and, ending the eight-and-twentieth of November, it hath eight returns:

Octavis Michael.	Crast. anima.
Quind. Michael.	Crast. Martini
Tres Michael.	Octa. Martini
Mense Michael.	Quind. Martini [29]

Note also that the Exchequer, which is *fiscus* or *aerarium publicum principis* [the state treasury of the prince], openeth eight days before any term begin, except Trinity term, which openeth but four days before.

And thus much for our usual terms as they are kept for the administration of our common laws, whereunto I think good to add the law days accustomably holden in the Arches and Audience of Canterbury, with other ecclesiastical and civil courts through the whole year or for so much time as their execution endureth (which in comparison is scarcely one-half of the time, if it be diligently examined), to the end each one at home, being

---

of England (1575). In 1587 Harrison made minor stylistic changes and added his complaint about the retention of the "popish calendar."

[29] *Returns:* return days, the days appointed for the return of all writs issued since the last return; *octavis:* the eighth day after; *quindena:* the fifteenth day after; *crastino:* the day after; *tres:* three weeks after; *mense:* one month after; *quinque:* five weeks after. The Feast of St. Hilary is January 13; the Purification, February 2; Michaelmas, September 29; *animarum commemoratio* (All Souls' Day), November 2; St. Martin's, November 11; Easter (*Pascha*), Ascension Day, and Trinity Sunday are movable feasts.

called up to answer, may truly know the time of his appearance; being sorry in the mean season that the use of the popish calendar is so much retained in the same and not rather the usual days of the month placed in their rooms, sith most of them are fixed and palter [shift] not their place of standing. Howbeit, some of our infected lawyers will not let them go away so easily, pretending facility and custom of usage but meaning peradventure inwardly to keep a commemoration of those dead men whose names are there remembered.

Michaelmas term

St. Faith [6 Oct.]	St. Martin [11 Nov.]
St. Edward [13 Oct.]	Edmund [16 Nov.]
St. Luke [18 Oct.]	Katharine [25 Nov.]
Simon and Jude [28 Oct.]	St. Andrew [30 Nov.]
All Souls' [2 Nov.]	Conception of the Virgin Mary [8 Dec.]

It is to be remembered that the first day following every of these feasts noted in each term the Court of the Arches is kept in Bow Church in the forenoon. And the same first day, in the afternoon, is the admiralty court for civil and seafaring causes kept in Southwark, where justice is ministered and execution done continually according to the same.

The second day following every one of the said feasts, the Court of Audience of Canterbury is kept in the consistory in Paul's in the forenoon. And the self day, in the afternoon, in the same place, is the Prerogative Court of Canterbury holden.

The third day after any such feast, in the forenoon, the Consistory Court of the Bishop of London is kept in Paul's Church in the said consistory, and the same third day, in the afternoon, is the Court of the Delegates, and the Court of the Queen's Highness' Commissioners upon Appeals is likewise kept in the same place on the fourth day.

Hilary term

St. Hilary [13 Jan.]	St. Scolastica [10 Feb.]
St. Wolfstan [19 Jan.]	St. Valentine [14 Feb.]
Conversion of St. Paul [25 Jan.]	Ash Wednesday
St. Blaise [3 Feb.]	St. Matthew [24 Feb.]

St. Chad [2 Mar.]   St. Gregory [12 Mar.]
Perpetua and Felicitas [7 Mar.]   Annunciation of Our Lady [25 Mar.]

Note that the four first days of this term be certain and unchanged. The other are altered after the course of the year, and sometime kept and sometime omitted. For if it so happen that one of those feasts fall on Wednesday, commonly called Ash Wednesday, after the day of St. Blaise (so that the same law day after Ash Wednesday cannot be kept because the law day of the other feast doth light on the same), then the second law day after Ash Wednesday shall be kept and the other omitted. And if the law day after Ash Wednesday be the next day after the feast of St. Blaise, then shall all and every court days be observed in order, as they may be kept conveniently. And mark that although Ash Wednesday be put the seventh in order, yet it hath no certain place but is changed as the course of Easter causeth it.

Easter Term

The fifteenth day after Easter   Invention of the Cross [3 May]
St. Alphege [19 Apr.]   Gordian [10 May]
St. Mark [25 Apr.]   St. Dunstan [19 May]
 Ascension Day.

In this term the first sitting is always kept the Monday, being the fifteenth day after Easter, and so forth after the feasts here noted which next follow by course of the year after Easter, and the like space being kept between other feasts.

The rest of the law days are kept to the third of the Ascension, which is the last day of this term. And if it happen that the feast of the Ascension of Our Lord do come before any of the feasts aforesaid, then they are omitted for that year. And likewise if any of those days come before the fifteenth of Easter, those days are omitted also.

Trinity term

Trinity Sunday   St. John [24 June]
Corpus Christi   St. Paul [30 June]
Boniface, bishop [5 June]   Translation Thomas [7 July]
St. Barnaby [11 June]   St. Swithin [15 July]
St. Botolph [17 June]   St. Margaret [20 July]
 St. Ann [26 July].

Here note also that the law days of this term are altered by means of Whitsuntide, and the first sitting is kept always on the first law day after the feast of the Holy Trinity, and the second session is kept the first law day after the idolatrous and papistical feast day called Corpus Christi, except Corpus Christi Day fall on some day afore named, which chanceth sometime and then the fitter day is kept. And after the second session account four days or thereabout and then look which is the next feast day, and the first law day after the said feast shall be the third session. The other law days follow in order, but so many of them are kept as for the time of the year shall be thought meet.

It is also generally to be observed that every day is called a law day that is not Sunday or holy day, and that if, the feast day being known of any court day in any term, the first or second day following be Sunday, then the court day is kept the day after the said holy day or feast.

CHAPTER X

Of Provision Made for the Poor

THERE is no commonwealth at this day in Europe wherein there is not great store of poor people, and those necessarily to be relieved by the wealthier sort, which otherwise would starve and come to utter confusion. With us the poor is commonly divided into three sorts, so that some are poor by impotency, as the fatherless child, the aged, blind, and lame, and the diseased person that is judged to be incurable; the second are poor by casualty, as the wounded soldier, the decayed householder, and the sick person visited with grievous and painful diseases; the third consisteth of thriftless poor, as the rioter that hath consumed all, the vagabond that will abide nowhere but runneth up and down from place to place (as it were seeking work and finding none), and finally, the rogue and strumpet, which are not possible to be divided in sunder but run to and fro over all the realm, chiefly keeping the champaign soils in summer to avoid the scorching

heat, and the woodland grounds in winter to eschew the blustering winds.[1]

For the first two sorts, that is to say, the poor by impotency
and the poor by casualty, which are the true poor indeed and for
whom the Word doth bind us to make some daily provision,
there is order taken throughout every parish in the realm that
weekly collection shall be made for their help and sustentation, to
the end they should not scatter abroad and, by begging here
and there, annoy both town and country. Authority also is given
unto the justices in every county and great penalties appointed
for such as make default, to see that the intent of the statute in
this behalf be truly executed, according to the purpose and meaning of the same, so that these two sorts are sufficiently provided
for, and such as can live within the limits of their allowance (as
each one will do that is godly and well disposed) may well forbear to roam and range about. But if they refuse to be supported
by this benefit of the law and will rather endeavor, by going to
and fro, to maintain their idle trades, then are they adjudged to be
parcel of the third sort and so, instead of courteous refreshing
at home, are often corrected with sharp execution and whip of
justice abroad.[2]

Many there are which, notwithstanding the rigor of the laws
provided in that behalf, yield rather with this liberty (as they
call it) to be daily under the fear and terror of the whip than, by
abiding where they were born or bred, to be provided for by the
devotion of the parishes. I found not long since a note of these
latter sort, the effect whereof ensueth. Idle beggars are such either
through other men's occasion or through their own default. By
other men's occasion (as one way for example) when some
covetous man, such I mean as have the cast [trick], or right vein,
daily to make beggars enough whereby to pester the land, espying a further commodity in their commons, holds, and tenures,
doth find such means as thereby to wipe many out of their

---

[1] Harrison's classification of the poor follows exactly the one submitted
to Edward VI just before his death by a committee headed by Bishop
Ridley and Sir Richard Dobs, Lord Mayor of London, as reported in
Grafton's *Chronicle* (1568, pp. 1321–1322).

[2] A summary of the provisions of 14 Eliz., c. 5 (1572), "An act for the
punishment of vagabonds and for the relief of the poor and impotent."

occupyings and turn the same unto his private gains.[3] Hereupon
it followeth that, although the wise and better minded do either
forsake the realm for altogether and seek to live in other countries, as France, Germany, Barbary, India, Moscovia, and very
Calicut, complaining of no room to be left for them at home,
[and] do so behave themselves that they are worthily to be accounted among the second sort, yet the greater part, commonly
having nothing to stay upon, are willful and thereupon do either
prove idle beggars or else continue stark thieves till the gallows
do eat them up, which is a lamentable case.

Certes in some men's judgments these things are but trifles
and not worthy the regarding. Some also do grudge at the great
increase of people in these days, thinking a necessary brood of
cattle far better than a superfluous augmentation of mankind. But
I can liken such men best of all unto the Pope and the devil, who
practice the hindrance of the furniture of the number of the
elect to their uttermost, to the end the authority of the one upon
earth, the deferring of the locking up of the other in everlasting
chains, and the great gains of the first may continue and endure
the longer. But if it should come to pass that any foreign invasion
should be made—which the Lord God forbid for His mercy's
sake!—then should these men find that a wall of men is far better
than stacks of corn and bags of money and complain of the
want when it is too late to seek remedy.[4] The like occasion
caused the Romans to devise their law *agraria*, but the rich, not
liking of it, and the covetous, utterly condemning it as rigorous
and unprofitable, never ceased to practice disturbance till it was
quite abolished.[5] But to proceed with my purpose.

Such as are idle beggars through their own default are of two
sorts and continue their estates either by casual or mere voluntary means;[6] those that are such by casual means are in the

---

[3] "A thing often seen. At whose hands shall the blood of these men be
required?"—*H*.

[4] This paragraph was added in 1587, when talk of a Spanish invasion was
abroad.

[5] Various agrarian laws, such as those of the Gracchi, Tiberius and
Gaius (133 and 123–122 B.C.), limited the holdings of wealthy landowners
and proposed to distribute the excess to poorer citizens.

[6] *Continue their estate by casual . . . means:* that is, use their disabilities,
which were originally accidental (casual), as an excuse to continue begging;
they are to be distinguished from those who feign such disabilities (use
"voluntary means").

beginning justly to be referred either to the first or second sort of poor afore mentioned, but, degenerating into the thriftless sort, they do what they can to continue their misery and with such impediments as they have to stray and wander about, as creatures abhorring all labor and every honest exercise. Certes I call these casual means, not in respect of the original of their poverty but of the continuance of the same, from whence they will not be delivered, such is their own ungracious lewdness and froward disposition. The voluntary means proceed from outward causes, as by making of corrosives and applying the same to the more fleshy parts of their bodies, and also laying of ratsbane, spearwort, crowfoot,[7] and suchlike unto their whole members, thereby to raise pitiful and odious sores and move the hearts of the goers by such places where they lie to yearn at their misery and thereupon bestow large almesse [alms] upon them. How artificially they beg, what forcible speech, and how they select and choose out words of vehemency, whereby they do in manner conjure or adjure the goer-by to pity their cases, I pass over to remember, as judging the name of God and Christ to be more conversant in the mouths of none and yet the presence of the Heavenly Majesty further off from no men than from this ungracious company. Which maketh me to think that punishment is far meeter for them than liberality or almesse, and sith Christ willeth us chiefly to have a regard to Himself and His poor members.

Unto this nest is another sort to be referred, more sturdy than the rest, which, having sound and perfect limbs, do yet notwithstanding sometime counterfeit the possession of all sorts of diseases. Divers times in their apparel also they will be like servingmen or laborers; oftentimes they can play the mariners and seek for ships which they never lost. But in fine they are all thieves and caterpillars in the commonwealth and by the Word of God not permitted to eat, sith they do but lick the sweat from the true laborers' brows and bereave the godly poor of that which is due unto them to maintain their excess, consuming the charity of well-disposed people bestowed upon them after a most wicked and detestable manner.

It is not yet full threescore years since this trade began, but

---

[7] *Ratsbane:* arsenic; *spearwort* and *crowfoot:* herbs of the genus *Ranunculus.*

how it hath prospered since that time it is easy to judge, for they are now supposed, of one sex and another, to amount unto above 10,000 persons, as I have heard reported. Moreover, in counterfeiting the Egyptian rogues, they have devised a language among themselves which they name "canting" but other, "peddlers' French," a speech compact thirty years since of English and a great number of odd words of their own devising, without all order or reason; and yet such is it as none but themselves are able to understand. The first deviser thereof was hanged by the neck, a just reward no doubt for his deserts and a common end to all of that profession. A gentleman also of late hath taken great pains to search out the secret practices of this ungracious rabble.[8] And among other things he setteth down and describeth three-and-twenty sorts of them, whose names it shall not be amiss to remember, whereby each one may take occasion to read and know, as also by his industry, what wicked people they are and what villainy remaineth in them.

The several disorders and degrees amongst our idle vagabonds

1. Rufflers [thieving beggars, apprentice uprightmen]
2. Uprightmen [leaders of robber bands]
3. Hookers or anglers [thieves who steal through open windows with hooks]
4. Rogues [rank-and-file vagabonds]
5. Wild rogues [those born of rogues]
6. Priggers of prancers [horse thieves]
7. Palliards [male and female beggars, traveling in pairs]
8. Fraters [sham proctors, pretending to beg for hospitals, etc.]
9. Abrams [feigned lunatics]
10. Fresh-water mariners or whipjacks [beggars pretending shipwreck] [9]
11. Dummerers [sham deaf-mutes]
12. Drunken tinkers [thieves using the trade as a cover]

[8] "Thomas Harman."—*H*. All of Harrison's details about beggars' cant are drawn from Harman's *Caveat or Warning for Common Cursitors* (1566, ed. Frederick J. Furnivall, EETS, Ex. Ser., IX, 1869, 17–91). In Harman the "several degrees" of vagabonds provide the chapter headings.

[9] Harrison unaccountably omits Harman's "counterfeit cranks," beggars feigning epilepsy.

13. Swadders or peddlers [thieves pretending to be peddlers]
14. Jarkmen [forgers of licenses] or patricoes [hedge priests].

Of womenkind

1. Demanders for glimmer or fire [female beggars pretending loss from fire]
2. Bawdy baskets [female peddlers]
3. Morts [prostitutes and thieves]
4. Autem [married] morts
5. Walking [unmarried] morts
6. Doxies [prostitutes who begin with uprightmen]
7. Dells [young girls, incipient doxies]
8. Kinchin morts [female beggar children]
9. Kinchin coes [male beggar children].

The punishment that is ordained for this kind of people is very sharp, and yet it cannot restrain them from their gadding; wherefore the end must needs be martial law,[10] to be exercised upon them as upon thieves, robbers, despisers of all laws, and enemies to the commonwealth and welfare of the land. What notable robberies, pilferies, murders, rapes, and stealings of young children, burning, breaking, and disfiguring their limbs to make them pitiful in the sight of the people I need not to rehearse; but for their idle roguing about the country the law ordaineth this manner of correction:[11] the rogue being apprehended, committed to prison, and tried in the next assizes (whether they be of jail delivery or sessions of the peace), if he happen to be convicted for a vagabond, either by inquest of office or the testimony of two honest and credible witnesses upon their oaths, he is then immediately adjudged to be grievously whipped and burned through the gristle of the right ear with an hot iron of the compass of an inch about, as a manifestation of his wicked life and due punishment received for the same. And this judgment is to be executed upon him except some honest person worth £5 in the Queen's books in goods or 20s. in lands, or some rich householder to be allowed by the justices, will be bound in recognizance to retain him in his service for one whole year. If

[10] *Martial law:* apparently for "law of the marshal," the officer responsible for the custody of prisoners.
[11] The remainder of the chapter, except for the digression on the indiscriminate appetite of bears, is drawn from 14 Eliz., c. 5.

he be taken the second time and proved to have forsaken his said service, he shall then be whipped again, bored likewise through the other ear, and set to service; from whence if he depart before a year be expired and happen afterward to be attached again, he is condemned to suffer pains of death as a felon (except before excepted) without benefit of clergy or sanctuary, as by the statute doth appear. Among rogues and idle persons, finally, we find to be comprised all proctors that go up and down with counterfeit licenses, cozeners, and such as gad about the country using unlawful games, practicers of physiognomy and palmistry, tellers of fortunes, fencers, players,[12] minstrels, jugglers, peddlers, tinkers, pretensed scholars, shipmen, prisoners gathering for fees, and others, so oft as they be taken without sufficient license. From among which company our bearwards are not excepted, and just cause; for I have read that they have either voluntarily or for want of power to master their savage beasts been occasion of the death and devoration of many children in sundry countries by which they have passed, whose parents never knew what was become of them. And for that cause there is and have been many sharp laws made for bearwards in Germany, whereof you may read in other.[13] But to our rogues. Each one also that harboreth or aideth them with meat or money is taxed and compelled to fine with the Queen's Majesty for every time that he doth so succor them, as it shall please the justices of peace to assign, so that the taxation exceed not 20*s.*, as I have been informed. And thus much of the poor and such provision as is appointed for them within the realm of England.

[12] The statute specifies "common players in interludes." Harrison's own opinion of the Elizabethan actor was not high. Furnivall quotes a 1572 entry in Harrison's Chronology: "Plays are banished for a time out of London, lest the resort unto them should engender a plague, or rather disperse it being already begun. Would to God these common plays were exiled for altogether as seminaries of impiety, and their theaters pulled down as no better than houses of bawdry. It is an evident token of a wicked time when players wax so rich that they can build such houses. As much I wish also to our common bearbaitings, used on the Sabbath days" (ed. of Harrison, I, liv–lv).

[13] Harrison's source here is *Historia de gentibus septentrionalibus,* XVIII, xxvii (Rome, 1555, and many later editions in epitome), by Olaus Magnus (1490–1558), Archbishop of Upsala.

CHAPTER XI

Of Sundry Kinds of Punishments Appointed for Malefactors

IN CASES of felony, manslaughter, robbery, murder, rape, piracy, and such capital crimes as are not reputed for treason or hurt of the state, our sentence pronounced upon the offender is to hang till he be dead. For of other punishments used in other countries we have no knowledge or use, and yet so few grievous crimes committed with us as elsewhere in the world. To use torment, also, or question by pain and torture in these common cases, with us is greatly abhorred, sith we are found alway to be such as despise death and yet abhor to be tormented, choosing rather frankly to open our minds than to yield our bodies unto such servile halings and tearings as are used in other countries. And this is one cause wherefore our condemned persons do go so cheerfully to their deaths, for our nation is free, stout, haughty, prodigal of life and blood, as Sir Thomas Smith saith (*lib.* 2, *cap.* 25 [24], *De republica*),[1] and therefore cannot in any wise digest to be used as villeins and slaves, in suffering continually beating, servitude, and servile torments. No, our jailers are guilty of felony by an old law of the land if they torment any prisoner committed to their custody, for the revealing of his complices.

The greatest and most grievous punishment used in England for such as offend against the state is drawing from the prison to the place of execution upon an hurdle or sled, where they are hanged till they be half dead and then taken down and quartered alive; after that, their members and bowels are cut from their bodies and thrown into a fire provided near-hand and within their own sight, even for the same purpose. Sometimes, if the trespass be not the more heinous, they are suffered to hang till they be quite dead. And whensoever any of the nobility are convicted of high treason by their peers, that is to say, equals

---

[1] The entire paragraph, added in 1587, is drawn from Smith. See p. 94, n. 1.

(for an inquest of yeomen passeth not upon them, but only of the lords of the Parliament), this manner of their death is converted into the loss of their heads only, notwithstanding that the sentence do run after the former order. In trial of cases concerning treason, felony, or any other grievous crime not confessed, the party accused doth yield, if he be a nobleman, to be tried by an inquest (as I have said) of his peers; if a gentleman, by gentlemen; and an inferior, by God and by the country, to wit, the yeomanry (for combat or battle is not greatly in use), and being condemned of felony, manslaughter, etc., he is eftsoons hanged by the neck till he be dead and then cut down and buried. But if he be convicted of willful murder done either upon pretended malice or in any notable robbery, he is either hanged alive in chains near the place where the fact was committed or else, upon compassion taken, first strangled with a rope, and so continueth till his bones consume to nothing. We have use neither of the wheel nor of the bar as in other countries; but when willful manslaughter is perpetrated, beside hanging, the offender hath his right hand commonly stricken off before or near unto the place where the act was done, after which he is led forth to the place of execution and there put to death according to the law.

The word "felon" is derived of the Saxon words "fell" and "one," that is to say, an evil and wicked one, a one of untamable nature and lewdness not to be suffered for fear of evil example and the corruption of others. In like sort in the word "felony" are many grievous crimes contained,[2] as breach of prison (*an.* 1 of Edward II); disfigurers of the prince's liege people (*an.* 5 of Henry IV); hunting by night with painted faces and visors (*an.* 1 of Henry VII); rape, or stealing of women and maidens (*an.* 3 of Henry VII); conspiracy against the person of the prince (*an.* 3 of Henry VII); embezzling of goods committed by the master to the servant above the value of 40*s.* (*an.* 17 of Henry VIII); carrying of horse or mares into Scotland (*an.* 23 of Henry VIII); sodomy and buggery (*an.* 25 of Henry VIII); stealing of hawks' eggs (*an.* 31 of Henry VIII); conjuring, sorcery, witch-

---

[2] Harrison takes the following list of crimes and pertinent acts from the entry under "Felony" in the collection of statutes edited by William Rastell and printed by Tottel in 1574, or from some similar edition.

craft, and digging up of crosses (*an.* 33 of Henry VIII); proph-
esying upon arms, cognizances, names, and badges (*an.* 33 of
Henry VIII); casting of slanderous bills (*an.* 37, Henry VIII);
willful killing by poison (*an.* 1 of Edward VI); departure of a
soldier from the field (*an.* 2 of Edward VI); diminution of coin,
all offenses within case of praemunire,[3] embezzling of records,
goods taken from dead men by their servants, stealing of whatsoever cattle, robbing by the highway, upon the sea, or of dwelling
houses, letting-out of ponds, cutting of purses, stealing of deer
by night, counterfeiters of coin, evidences, charters, and writings,
and divers other needless to be remembered.

If a woman poison her husband, she is burned alive; if the servant kill his master, he is to be executed for petty treason; he
that poisoneth a man is to be boiled to death in water or lead,
although the party die not of the practice; in cases of murder
all the accessories are to suffer pains of death accordingly. Per-
jury is punished by the pillory, burning in the forehead with the
letter *P*, the rewalting [overthrowing] of the trees growing upon
the grounds of the offenders, and loss of all his movables. Many
trespasses also are punished by the cutting of one or both ears
from the head of the offender, as the utterance of seditious words
against the magistrates, fray-makers, petty robbers, etc. Rogues
are burned through the ears; carriers of sheep out of the land, by
the loss of their hands; such as kill by poison are either boiled or
scalded to death in lead or seething water. Heretics are burned
quick; harlots and their mates, by carting, ducking, and doing of
open penance in sheets, in churches and marketsteads, are often
put to rebuke. Howbeit, as this is counted with some either as
no punishment at all to speak of or but smally regarded of the
offenders, so I would wish adultery and fornication to have some
sharper law. For what great smart is it to be turned out of an
hot sheet into a cold or after a little washing in the water to be
let loose again unto their former trades? Howbeit, the dragging
of some of them over the Thames between Lambeth and Westminster at the tail of a boat is a punishment that most terrifieth
them which are condemned thereto; but this is inflicted upon

[3] *Praemunire:* originally a writ to prosecute a person accused of maintaining
the supremacy of papal jurisdiction in England, later extended to any offense
incurring the penalty of forfeiture of goods and imprisonment.

them by none other than the Knight Marshal, and that within the compass of his jurisdiction and limits only.[4] Canute was the first that gave authority to the clergy to punish whoredom, who at that time found fault with the former laws as being too severe in this behalf. For before the time of the said Canute the adulterer forfeited all his goods to the King and his body to be at his pleasure; and the adulteress was to lose her eyes or nose, or both if the case were more than common; whereby it appeareth of what estimation marriage was amongst them, sith the breakers of that holy estate were so grievously rewarded. But afterward the clergy dealt more favorably with them, shooting rather at the punishments of such priests and clerks as were married than the reformation of adultery and fornication, wherein you shall find no example that any severity was showed, except upon such laymen as had defiled their nuns. As in theft, therefore, so in adultery and whoredom, I would wish the parties trespassant to be made bond or slaves unto those that received the injury, to sell and give where they listed, or to be condemned to the galleys; for that punishment would prove more bitter to them than half an hour's hanging or than standing in a sheet, though the weather be never so cold.

Manslaughter in time past was punished by the purse, wherein the quantity or quality of the punishment was rated after the state and calling of the party killed, so that one was valued sometime at 1,200, another at 600 or 200 shillings. And by a statute made under Henry the First, a citizen of London at 100, whereof elsewhere I have spoken more at large. Such as kill themselves are buried in the field with a stake driven through their bodies.

Witches are hanged or sometimes burned; but thieves are hanged (as I said before), generally on the gibbet or gallows, saving in Halifax, where they are beheaded after a strange manner and whereof I find this report. There is and hath been of ancient time a law, or rather a custom, at Halifax, that whosoever doth commit any felony and is taken with the same or confess the fact upon examination, if it be valued by four constables to amount to the sum of 13½ d., he is forthwith beheaded upon one of the next market days (which fall usually upon the Tues-

---

[4] *Knight Marshal:* the judicial officer of the royal court, whose jurisdiction extended to offenses within the court or its verge.

days, Thursdays, and Saturdays) or else upon the same day that he is so convicted, if market be then holden. The engine wherewith the execution is done is a square block of wood of the length of four foot and an half, which doth ride up and down in a slot, rabbet, or regal [groove] between two pieces of timber that are framed and set upright, of five yards in height. In the nether end of the sliding block is an ax, keyed, or fastened with an iron into the wood, which, being drawn up to the top of the frame, is there fastened by a wooden pin (with a notch made into the same after the manner of a Samson's post),[5] unto the midst of which pin also there is a long rope fastened that cometh down among the people, so that when the offender hath made his confession and hath laid his neck over the nethermost block, every man there present doth either take hold of the rope or putteth forth his arm so near to the same as he can get, in token that he is willing to see true justice executed, and, pulling out the pin in this manner, the head block wherein the ax is fastened doth fall down with such a violence that if the neck of the transgressor were so big as that of a bull it should be cut in sunder at a stroke and roll from the body by an huge distance. If it be so that the offender be apprehended for [theft of] an ox, oxen, sheep, kine, horse, or any such cattle, the self beast or other of the same kind shall have the end of the rope tied somewhere unto them, so that they, being driven, do draw out the pin, whereby the offender is executed. Thus much of Halifax law, which I set down only to show the custom of that country in this behalf.[6]

Rogues and vagabonds are often stocked and whipped; scolds are ducked upon cucking stools in the water. Such felons as stand mute and speak not at their arraignment are pressed to death by huge weights laid upon a board that lieth over their breast and a sharp stone under their backs, and these commonly hold their peace, thereby to save their goods unto their wives and children, which, if they were condemned, should be confiscated to the prince. Thieves that are saved by their books and

[5] *Samson's post:* a kind of mousetrap, which falls over the victim when a supporting notched stick is removed.
[6] The notorious gibbet law of Halifax was one of the last survivals of the Old English law of infangthief. Harrison, of course, is more interested in the guillotine than in the legal implications of the summary process.

clergy [7] for the first offense, if they have stolen nothing else but oxen, sheep, money, or suchlike, which be no open robberies as by the highway side, or assailing of any man's house in the night without putting him in fear of his life or breaking up of his walls or doors, are burned in the left hand upon the brawn of the thumb with an hot iron, so that if they be apprehended again that mark bewrayeth them to have been arraigned of felony before, whereby they are sure at that time to have no mercy. I do not read that this custom of saving by the book is used anywhere else than in England; neither do I find (after much diligent inquiry) what Saxon prince ordained that law. Howbeit, this I generally gather thereof, that it was devised to train the inhabiters of this land to the love of learning, which before contemned letters and all good knowledge, as men only giving themselves to husbandry and the wars; the like whereof I read to have been amongst the Goths and Vandals, who for a time would not suffer even their princes to be learned for weakening of their courages, nor any learned men to remain in the council house, but by open proclamation would command them to avoid whensoever anything touching the state of the land was to be consulted upon. Pirates and robbers by sea are condemned in the court of the admiralty and hanged on the shore at low watermark, where they are left till three tides have overwashed them. Finally, such as having walls and banks near unto the sea and do suffer the same to decay (after convenient admonition), whereby the water entereth and drowneth up the country, are by a certain ancient custom apprehended, condemned, and staked in the breach, where they remain forever as parcel of the foundation of the new wall that is to be made upon them, as I have heard reported.

And thus much in part of the administration of justice used in our country, wherein notwithstanding that we do not often hear of horrible, merciless, and willful murders (such, I mean, as are not seldom seen in the countries of the main), yet now and then some manslaughter and bloody robberies are perpetrated and committed contrary to the laws, which be severely punished and in such wise as I before reported. Certes there is no greater mischief done in England than by robberies, the first by young shifting gentlemen, which oftentimes do bear more port than

---

[7] *Books and clergy:* originally the clergy's right of appeal from temporal to ecclesiastical jurisdiction, later extended to anyone who could read as an exemption from the sentence for certain first offenses.

they are able to maintain. Secondly, by servingmen, whose wages cannot suffice so much as to find them breeches; wherefore they are now and then constrained either to keep highways and break into the wealthy men's houses with the first sort or else to walk up and down in gentlemen's and rich farmers' pastures, there to see and view which horses feed best, whereby they many times get something, although with hard adventure; it hath been known by their confession at the gallows that some one such chapman hath had forty, fifty, or sixty stolen horses at pasture here and there abroad in the country at a time, which they have sold at fairs and markets far off, they themselves in the mean season being taken about home for honest yeomen and very wealthy drovers till their dealings have been bewrayed. It is not long since one of this company was apprehended, who was before-time reputed for a very honest and wealthy townsman; he uttered also more horses than any of his trade, because he sold a reasonable pennyworth and was a fair-spoken man. It was his custom likewise to say, if any man hucked hard with him about the price of a gelding, "So God help me, gentleman or sir, either he did cost me so much or else, by Jesus, I stole him." Which talk was plain enough, and yet such was his estimation that each believed the first part of his tale and made no account of the latter, which was the truer indeed.

Our third annoyers of the commonwealth are rogues, which do very great mischief in all places where they be come. For whereas the rich only suffer injury by the first two, these spare neither rich nor poor, but whether it be great gain or small, all is fish that cometh to net with them; and yet I say, both they and the rest are trussed up apace. For there is not one year commonly wherein three hundred or four hundred of them are not devoured and eaten up by the gallows in one place and other. It appeareth by Cardan (who writeth it upon the report of the Bishop of Lexovia) in the geniture of King Edward the Sixth, how Henry the Eighth, executing his laws very severely against such idle persons, I mean, great thieves, petty thieves, and rogues, did hang up threescore-and-twelve thousand of them in his time.[8]

---

[8] *Cardan:* Girolamo Cardano (1501–1576), Italian mathematician, physician, and astrologer. In his horoscope (geniture) of Edward VI, Cardan cites the Bishop of Lisieux as his authority for the statement that Henry VIII executed 72,000 thieves in the last two years of his reign (*Liber duodecim geniturarum* in *Opera*, Lyons, 1663, V, 508). The figure is clearly inflated.

He seemed for a while greatly to have terrified the rest, but since his death the number of them is so increased, yea, although we have had no wars, which are a great occasion of their breed (for it is the custom of the more idle sort, having once served or but seen the other side of the sea under color of service, to shake hand with labor forever, thinking it a disgrace for himself to return unto his former trade), that except some better order be taken or the laws already made be better executed, such as dwell in uplandish [inland, remote] towns and little villages shall live but in small safety and rest.

For the better apprehension also of thieves and man-killers there is an old law in England very well provided, whereby it is ordered that if he that is robbed or any man complain and give warning of slaughter or murder committed, the constable of the village whereunto he cometh and crieth for succor is to raise the parish about him and to search woods, groves, and all suspected houses and places where the trespasser may be or is supposed to lurk; and not finding him there, he is to give warning unto the next constable, and so one constable, after search made, to advertise another from parish to parish till they come to the same where the offender is harbored and found. It is also provided that if any parish in this business do not her duty but suffereth the thief (for the avoiding of trouble sake), in carrying him to the jail if he should be apprehended or other letting of their work, to escape, the same parish is not only to make fine to the King but also the same, with the whole hundred wherein it standeth, to repay the party robbed his damages and leave his estate harmless.[9] Certes this is a good law; howbeit, I have known by mine own experience felons, being taken, to have escaped out of the stocks, being rescued by other for want of watch and guard; that thieves have been let pass because the covetous and greedy parishioners would neither take the pains nor be at the charge to carry them to prison, if it were far off; that when hue and cry have been made even to the faces of some constables, they have said, "God restore your loss! I have other business at this time." And by such means the meaning of many a good law is left unexecuted, malefactors emboldened, and many a poor man turned out of that which he hath sweat and taken great

[9] This account of hue and cry is based largely on Smith, II, xx.

pains for toward the maintenance of himself and his poor children and family.

CHAPTER XII

Of the Manner of Building
and Furniture of Our Houses

THE greatest part of our building in the cities and good towns of England consisteth only of timber, for as yet few of the houses of the commonalty (except here and there in the West Country towns) are made of stone, although they may (in my opinion) in divers other places be builded so good cheap of the one as of the other. In old time the houses of the Britons were slightly set up with a few posts and many raddles,[1] with stable and all offices under one roof, the like whereof almost is to be seen in the fenny countries and northern parts unto this day, where for lack of wood they are enforced to continue this ancient manner of building. It is not in vain, therefore, in speaking of building, to make a distinction between the plain and woody soils; for as in these our houses are commonly strong and well-timbered—so that in many places there are not above four, six, or nine inches between stud and stud—so in the open and champaign countries they are enforced for want of stuff to use no studs at all but only frank posts, rasens, beams, prick posts, groundsels, summers (or dormants), transoms, and such principals, with here and there a girding,[2] whereunto they fasten their splints or raddles, and then cast it all over with thick clay to keep out the wind, which otherwise would annoy them. Certes this rude kind of building made the Spaniards in Queen Mary's days to wonder, but chiefly when they saw what large diet was used in many of

[1] *Raddles:* the network of flexible sticks or branches woven between posts to support clay or plaster.
[2] *Frank posts:* apparently angle posts; *prick posts:* secondary, side posts; *groundsels* and *rasens:* horizontal timbers at the base and top of the posts; *summers* or *dormants:* horizontal bearing timbers; *transoms:* crosspieces, especially those spanning an opening; *girding:* girder, joist.

these so homely cottages; insomuch that one of no small reputation amongst them said after this manner, "These English," quoth he, "have their houses made of sticks and dirt, but they fare commonly so well as the king." Whereby it appeareth that he liked better of our good fare in such coarse cabins than of their own thin diet in their princelike habitations and palaces. In like sort, as every country house is thus appareled on the outside, so is it inwardly divided into sundry rooms above and beneath; and where plenty of wood is, they cover them with tiles [shingles], otherwise with straw, sedge, or reed, except some quarry of slate be near-hand, from whence they have for their money so much as may suffice them.

The clay wherewith our houses are impaneled is either white, red, or blue; and of these the first doth participate very much with the nature of our chalk, the second is called loam,[3] but the third eftsoons changeth color so soon as it is wrought, notwithstanding that it look blue when it is thrown out of the pit. Of chalk also we have our excellent asbestos or white lime made in most places, wherewith, being quenched [slaked], we strike [smooth] over our clay works and stone walls in cities, good towns, rich farmers' and gentlemen's houses; otherwise, instead of chalk (where it wanteth, for it is so scant that in some places it is sold by the pound), they are compelled to burn a certain kind of red stone as in Wales, and elsewhere other stones and shells of oysters and like fish found upon the seacoast, which being converted into lime doth naturally (as the other) abhor and eschew water, whereby it is dissolved, and nevertheless desire oil, wherewith it is easily mixed, as I have seen by experience. Within their doors also such as are of ability do oft make their floors and parget[4] of fine alabaster burned, which they call plaster of Paris, whereof in some places we have great plenty and that very profitable against the rage of fire.

In plastering likewise of our fairest houses over our heads, we use to lay first a lain [layer] or two of white mortar tempered with hair upon laths, which are nailed one by another (or sometimes upon reed or wickers, more dangerous for fire, and made fast here and there with sap-laths,[5] for falling down), and finally

---

[3] *Loam:* clay mixed with water, sand, dung, straw, etc., used in plastering.
[4] *Floors:* ceilings; *parget:* plastered walls.
[5] *Sap-laths:* flexible laths of sapwood.

cover all with the aforesaid plaster, which beside the delectable whiteness of the stuff itself is laid on so even and smoothly as nothing in my judgment can be done with more exactness. The walls of our houses on the inner sides in like sort be either hanged with tapestry, arras work, or painted cloths, wherein either divers histories, or herbs, beasts, knots, and suchlike are stained, or else they are ceiled [paneled] with oak of our own or wainscot brought hither out of the East [Baltic] countries, whereby the rooms are not a little commended, made warm, and much more close than otherwise they would be. As for stoves, we have not hitherto used them greatly, yet do they now begin to be made in divers houses of the gentry and wealthy citizens, who build them not to work and feed in, as in Germany and elsewhere, but now and then to sweat in, as occasion and need shall require it.

This also hath been common in England, contrary to the customs of all other nations and yet to be seen (for example, in most streets of London), that many of our greatest houses have outwardly been very simple and plain to sight, which inwardly have been able to receive a duke with his whole train and lodge them at their ease. Hereby moreover it is come to pass that the fronts of our streets have not been so uniform and orderly builded as those of foreign cities, where (to say truth) the utterside of their mansions and dwellings have oft more cost bestowed upon them than all the rest of the house, which are often very simple and uneasy within, as experience doth confirm. Of old time our country houses instead of glass did use much lattice, and that made either of wicker or fine rifts [strips] of oak in checkerwise. I read also that some of the better sort in and before the times of the Saxons (who notwithstanding used some glass also since the time of Benedict Biscop, the monk that brought the feat of glazing first into this land)[6] did make panels of horn instead of glass and fix them in wooden calms [frames]. But as horn in windows is now quite laid down in every place, so our lattices are also grown into less use, because glass is come to be so plentiful and within a very little so good cheap, if not better than the other.

---

[6] *Benedict Biscop* (?628–690): founder of the monasteries at Wearmouth and Jarrow. According to Bede (*Lives of the Holy Abbots*) he imported from Gaul glassmakers, who taught the English their craft.

I find obscure mention of the specular stone [7] also to have been found and applied to this use in England, but in such doubtful sort as I dare not affirm it for certain. Nevertheless, certain it is that antiquity used it before glass was known, under the name of selenites. And how glass was first found I care not greatly to remember [if I do remember] even at this present, although it be directly beside my purposed matter. In Syria Phoenices, which bordereth upon Jewry [Judea], and near to the foot of Mount Carmel there is a moor or marsh, whereout riseth a brook called sometime Belus, and falleth into the sea near to Ptolemais [Acre]. This river was fondly ascribed unto Baal and also honored under that name by the infidels, long time before there was any king in Israel. It came to pass also as a certain merchant [8] sailed that way, loaden with *nitrum* [sodium carbonate], the passengers went to land for to repose themselves and to take in some store of fresh water into their vessel. Being also on the shore, they kindled a fire and made provision for their dinner, but because they wanted trivets or stones whereon to set their kettles on, ran by chance into the ship and brought great pieces of *nitrum* with them, which served their turn for that present. To be short, the said substance being hot and beginning to melt, it mixed by chance with the gravel that lay under it and so brought forth that shining substance which now is called glass; [9] and [this happened] about the time of Semiramis. When the company saw this, they made no small account of their success and forthwith began to practice the like in other mixtures, whereby great variety of the said stuff did also ensue. Certes for the time this history may well be true, for I read of glass in Job, [10] but for the rest I refer me to the common opinion conceived by writers. Now to turn again to our windows.

Heretofore also the houses of our princes and noblemen were often glazed with beryl (an example whereof is yet to be seen in Sudley Castle) [11] and in divers other places with fine crystal, but this especially in the time of the Romans, whereof also some

---

[7] *Specular stone:* a semitransparent substance, perhaps mica or crystalline gypsum (selenites).

[8] *Merchant:* merchantman, trading ship.

[9] This account of the origin of glass is translated from Pliny, *Natural History*, XXXVI, lxv.

[10] "Gold and glass cannot equal it" (28:17).

[11] Leland, *Itinerary* (ed. Smith, II, 56).

fragments have been taken up in old ruins. But now these are not in use, so that only the clearest glass is most esteemed; for we have diverse sorts, some brought out of Burgundy, some out of Normandy, much out of Flanders, beside that which is made in England, which would be so good as the best if we were diligent and careful to bestow more cost upon it, and yet as it is each one that may will have it for his building. Moreover the mansion houses [dwellings] of our country towns and villages (which in champaign ground stand all together by streets and joining one to another but in woodland soils dispersed here and there, each one upon the several grounds of their owners) are builded in such sort generally as that they have neither dairy, stable, nor brewhouse annexed unto them under the same roof (as in many places beyond the sea and some of the north parts of our country) but all separate from the first and one of them from another. And yet for all this they are not so far distant in sunder but that the goodman lying in his bed may lightly hear what is done in each of them with ease and call quickly unto his meinie [household] if any danger should attach [seize] him.

The ancient manors and houses of our gentlemen are yet, and for the most part, of strong timber, in framing whereof our carpenters have been and are worthily preferred before those of like science among all other nations. Howbeit, such as be lately builded are commonly either of brick or hard stone or both, their rooms large and comely, and houses of office further distant from their lodgings. Those of the nobility are likewise wrought with brick and hard stone, as provision may best be made, but so magnificent and stately as the basest house of a baron doth often match in our days with some honors of princes in old time. So that if ever curious building did flourish in England, it is in these our years, wherein our workmen excel and are in manner comparable in skill with old Vitruvius, Leon Battista, and Serlio.[12] Nevertheless, their estimation, more than their greedy and servile covetousness, joined with a lingering humor, causeth them often to be rejected and strangers preferred to greater bargains, who

---

[12] *Marcus Vitruvius Pollio:* military engineer with Julius Caesar in Africa; *Leon Battista Alberti* (1404-1472): Italian humanist, painter, musician, and architect; *Sebastian Serlio* (1473-1554): Italian painter and architect, designer of part of Fontainebleau. All three wrote treatises on architecture which were influential in the Renaissance.

are more reasonable in their takings and less wasters of time by a great deal than our own.

The furniture of our houses also exceedeth and is grown in manner even to passing delicacy; and herein I do not speak of the nobility and gentry only but likewise of the lowest sort in most places of our South Country that have anything at all to take to. Certes in noblemen's houses it is not rare to see abundance of arras, rich hangings of tapestry, silver vessel, and so much other plate as may furnish sundry cupboards, to the sum oftentimes of £1,000 or £2,000 at the least, whereby the value of this and the rest of their stuff doth grow to be almost inestimable. Likewise in the houses of knights, gentlemen, merchantmen, and some other wealthy citizens, it is not geason [uncommon] to behold generally their great provision of tapestry, Turkey work,[13] pewter, brass, fine linen, and thereto costly cupboards of plate, worth £500 or £600 or £1,000, to be deemed by estimation. But as herein all these sorts do far exceed their elders and predecessors, and in neatness and curiosity the merchant all other, so in time past the costly furniture stayed there, whereas now it is descended yet lower, even unto the inferior artificers and many farmers, who, by virtue of their old and not of their new leases, have for the most part learned also to garnish their cupboards with plate, their joint beds[14] with tapestry and silk hangings, and their tables with carpets and fine napery, whereby the wealth of our country (God be praised therefor and give us grace to employ it well) doth infinitely appear. Neither do I speak this in reproach of any man, God is my judge, but to show that I do rejoice rather to see how God hath blessed us with His good gifts; and whilst I behold how that, in a time wherein all things are grown to most excessive prices and what commodity soever is to be had is daily plucked from the commonalty by such as look into every trade, we do yet find the means to obtain and achieve such furniture as heretofore hath been unpossible.

There are old men yet dwelling in the village where I remain which have noted three things to be marvelously altered in England within their sound remembrance, and other three things too-

---

[13] *Turkey work:* Turkish tapestry, or imitations of it.

[14] *Joint beds:* beds made by joiners, more ornamental than carpenters' work.

too much increased. One is the multitude of chimneys lately erected, whereas in their young days there were not above two or three, if so many, in most uplandish towns of the realm (the religious houses and manor places of their lords always excepted, and peradventure some great personages), but each one made his fire against a reredos [back of an open hearth] in the hall, where he dined and dressed his meat.

The second is the great (although not general) amendment of lodging, for (said they) our fathers, yea, and we ourselves also, have lien full oft upon straw pallets, on rough mats covered only with a sheet, under coverlets made of dagswain or hap-harlots [15] (I use their own terms), and a good round log under their heads instead of a bolster or pillow. If it were so that our fathers or the goodman of the house had within seven years after his marriage purchased a mattress or flock-bed,[16] and thereto a sack of chaff to rest his head upon, he thought himself to be as well lodged as the lord of the town, that peradventure lay seldom in a bed of down or whole feathers, so well were they contented and with such base kind of furniture, which also is not very much amended as yet in some parts of Bedfordshire and elsewhere further off from our southern parts. Pillows (said they) were thought meet only for women in childbed. As for servants, if they had any sheet above them it was well, for seldom had they any under their bodies to keep them from the pricking straws that ran oft through the canvas of the pallet and rased their hardened hides.

The third thing they tell of is the exchange of vessel, as of treen [wooden] platters into pewter, and wooden spoons into silver or tin. For so common were all sorts of treen stuff in old time that a man should hardly find four pieces of pewter (of which one was peradventure a salt) in a good farmer's house, and yet for all this frugality (if it may so be justly called) they were scarce able to live and pay their rents at their days without selling of a cow or an horse or more, although they paid but £4 at the uttermost by the year.[17] Such also was their poverty that if some one odd farmer or husbandman had been at the alehouse, a thing greatly used in those days, amongst six or seven of his

---

[15] *Dagswain* and *hap-harlots:* coverlets of coarse, shaggy material.
[16] *Flock-bed:* a mattress stuffed with coarse tufts of wool or cotton.
[17] "This was in the time of general idleness."—*H.*

neighbors, and there in a bravery to show what store he had did cast down his purse, and therein a noble or 6s. in silver, unto them (for few such men then cared for gold, because it was not so ready payment, and they were oft enforced to give a penny for the exchange of an angel), it was very likely that all the rest could not lay down so much against it; whereas in my time, although peradventure £4 of old rent be improved to £40, £50, or £100, yet will the farmer, as another palm or date tree,[18] think his gains very small toward the end of his term if he have not six or seven years' rent lying by him, therewith to purchase a new lease, beside a fair garnish of pewter on his cupboard, with so much more in odd vessel going about the house, three or four feather beds, so many coverlets and carpets of tapestry, a silver salt, a bowl for wine (if not an whole nest), and a dozen of spoons to furnish up the suit [set]. This also he taketh to be his own clear, for what stock of money soever he gathereth and layeth up in all his years, it is often seen that the landlord will take such order with him for the same when he reneweth his lease, which is commonly eight or six years before the old be expired (sith it is now grown almost to a custom that if he come not to his lord so long before, another shall step in for a reversion and so defeat him outright), that it shall never trouble him more than the hair of his beard when the barber hath washed and shaven it from his chin.

And as they commend these, so (beside the decay of house-keeping [hospitality] whereby the poor have been relieved) they speak also of three things that are grown to be very grievous unto them, to wit: the enhancing of rents lately mentioned; the daily oppression of copyholders, whose lords seek to bring their poor tenants almost into plain servitude and misery, daily devising new means and seeking up all the old how to cut them shorter and shorter, doubling, trebling, and now and then seven times increasing their fines, driving them also for every trifle to lose and forfeit their tenures (by whom the greatest part of the realm doth stand and is maintained), to the end they may fleece them yet more, which is a lamentable hearing. The third thing

---

[18] In reference to the proverb, "The heavier the weight the palm tree bears, the taller it grows." See Morris Palmer Tilley, *A Dictionary of the Proverbs in England in the Sixteenth and Seventeenth Centuries* (Ann Arbor, 1950), P37.

they talk of is usury, a trade brought in by the Jews, now perfectly practiced almost by every Christian and so commonly that he is accounted but for a fool that doth lend his money for nothing.[19] In time past it was *sors pro sorte*, that is, the principal only for the principal; but now, beside that which is above the principal, properly called *usura*, we challenge *fenus* [interest], that is, commodity of soil and fruits of the earth, if not the ground itself. In time past also one of the hundred was much; from thence it rose unto two, called in Latin *usura, ex sextante;* three, to wit, *ex quadrante;* then to four, to wit, *ex triente;* then to five, which is *ex quincunce;* then to six, called *ex semisse,* etc., as the account of the *assis* ariseth, and coming at the last unto *usura ex asse,* it amounteth to twelve in the hundred, and therefore the Latins call it *centesima,* for that in the hundred month it doubleth the principal; [20] but more of this elsewhere. See Cicero against Verres, Demosthenes against Aphobus, and Athenaeus (*lib.* 13, *in fine*); [21] and when thou hast read them well, help, I pray thee, in lawful manner to hang up such as take *centum pro cento,*[22] for they are no better worthy, as I do judge in conscience.

Forget not also such landlords as use to value their leases at a secret estimation given of the wealth and credit of the taker, whereby they seem (as it were) to eat them up and deal with bondmen; so that if the lessee be thought to be worth £100, he shall pay no less for his new term or else another to enter with hard and doubtful covenants. I am sorry to report it, much more grieved to understand of the practice, but most sorrowful of all to understand that men of great port and countenance are so far from suffering their farmers to have any gain at all that

[19] The statute 13 Eliz., c. 8 (1571) gave semilegal status to interest rates up to 10 per cent.

[20] Latin terms for interest were based on the highest permissible amount in the late republic, a rate of 12 per cent a year, called *usura ex asse* or *centesima; usura ex sextante* was ⅙ of that rate, *ex quadrante* ¼, *ex triente* ⅓, *ex quincunce* 5⁄12, and *ex semisse* ½.

[21] Cicero accuses Verres of appropriating public money to his own use and lending it at 24 per cent interest (*Verrine Orations,* II, iii, 165); in his first oration against Aphobus, Demosthenes cites 12 per cent as the normal interest on a well-secured loan (ix) and 18 per cent as the standard return on a dowry (xvii). Athenaeus quotes the diatribe of Lysias against Aeschines, who had defaulted on a loan (*Deipnosophists,* XIII, 611–612). The references are borrowed from Budé, *De asse* (Lyons, 1551, pp. 110–113).

[22] "By the year."—*H.* That is, 100 per cent annual interest.

they themselves become graziers, butchers, tanners, sheepmasters, woodmen, and *denique quid non* [finally what not?], thereby to enrich themselves and bring all the wealth of the country into their own hands, leaving the commonalty weak or as an idol with broken or feeble arms, which may in a time of peace have a plausible show but when necessity shall enforce have an heavy and bitter sequel.

CHAPTER XIII

Of Cities and Towns in England

As IN old time we read that there were eight-and-twenty flamens and archflamens in the south part of this isle [1] and so many great cities under their jurisdiction, so in these our days there is but one or two fewer [2] and each of them also under the ecclesiastical regiment of some one bishop or archbishop, who in spiritual cases have the charge and oversight of the same. So many cities, therefore, are there in England and Wales as there be bishoprics and archbishoprics. For notwithstanding that Lichfield and Coventry, and Bath and Wells do seem to extend the aforesaid number unto nine-and-twenty, [3] yet neither of these couples are to be accounted but as one entire city and see of the bishop, sith one bishopric can have relation but unto one see and the said see be situate but in one place, after which the bishop doth take his name.

It appeareth by our old and ancient histories that the cities of this southerly portion have been of exceeding greatness and beauty, whereof some were builded in the time of the Samoth-

---

[1] *Flamens:* supposedly the pagan British equivalent of bishops. The detail, often repeated in the chronicles, derives ultimately from Geoffrey of Monmouth, who specifies twenty-eight flamens and three archflamens (IV, xix).

[2] "Six-and-twenty cities in England."—*H.*

[3] Harrison's apparent discrepancy concerning the number of cities (twenty-six or twenty-seven, not counting Coventry and Wells?) may result from the ambiguous status of Westminster, which was the seat of a bishopric, 1540–1547.

eans,[4] and of which not a few in these our times are quite decayed and the places where they stood worn out of all remembrance. Such also for the most part as yet remain are marvelously altered, insomuch that whereas at the first they were large and ample, now are they come either unto a very few houses or appear not to be much greater in comparison than poor and simple villages. Antoninus, the most diligent writer of the thoroughfares of Britain,[5] noteth among other these ancient towns following: as Sitomagus, which he placeth in the way from Norwich, as Leland supposeth [6] (wherein they went by Colchester), to London; Noviomagus, that lieth between Carlisle and Canterbury, within ten miles east of London; and likewise Neomagus and Niomagus, which take their names of their first founder, Magus, the son of Samothes and second King of the Celts that reigned in this island; [7] and not *a profunditate* only, as Bodin affirmeth out of Pliny, as if all the towns that ended in *-magus* should stand in holes and low grounds,[8] which is to be disproved in divers cities in the main as also here with us. Of these moreover Sir Thomas Elyot supposeth Neomagus to have stood somewhere about Chester, and George Lily, in his book of the names of ancient places, judgeth Niomagus to be the very same that we do now call Buckingham,[9] and lieth far from the shore. And as these and sundry other now perished took their denomination of this prince, so there are divers causes which move me to conjecture that

[4] *Samotheans:* the dynasty founded by Samothes: see p. 163, n. 1.

[5] The Antonine Itinerary is an extant register of roads, stations, and distances in the Roman Empire, apparently dating from the time of Antoninus Caracalla (211–217), with later additions. Harrison printed the routes in Britain as an appendix to his *Description:* see p. 406.

[6] In the prose gloss to his collection of Latin poems on topographical and antiquarian themes, *Genethliacon* (1543), under "Iceni," Leland identifies the Venta Icinorum of the Antonine Itinerary as Norwich.

[7] John Bale attributes the founding of these cities to the mythical Magus (*Scriptorum illustrium* [1557–1559], p. 2).

[8] *Jean Bodin* (1530–1596): French political philosopher. In his *Method for the Easy Comprehension of History* (Paris, 1566; trans. Beatrice Reynolds, New York, 1945, p. 355) he cites Pliny's derivation of Bodincomagum (Turin) as the "deep town."

[9] *Sir Thomas Elyot* (?1490–1546): humanist and diplomat; his Latin-English dictionary, which contains the reference, was first published in 1538. *George Lily* (d. 1559): antiquarian and cleric, chaplain to Cardinal Pole; his *Nova et antiqua locorum nomina in Anglia* was printed in Paul Jovius, *Descriptio Britanniae* (Venice, 1548). But Harrison borrows both references from Bale, p. 2.

Salisbury doth rather take the first name of Sarron,[10] the son of the said Magus, than of Caesar, Caradoc, or Severus (as some of our writers do imagine),[11] or else at the leastwise of Salisburge [Salzburg] of the main, from whence some Saxons came to inhabit in this land. And for this latter, not unlikely, sith before the coming of the Saxons the King of the Suessiones had a great part of this island in subjection, as Caesar saith; and in another place that such of Belgia as stale over hither from the main builded and called divers cities after the names of the same from whence they came, I mean such as stood upon the coast, as he himself doth witness.[12] But sith conjectures are no verities, and mine opinion is but one man's judgment, I will not stand now upon the proof of this matter, lest I should seem to take great pains in adding new conjectures unto old, in such wise to detain the heads of my readers about these trifles that otherwise peradventure would be far better occupied in matters of more importance. To proceed, therefore.

As, soon after the first inhabitation of this island, our cities began no doubt to be builded and increased, so they ceased not to multiply from time to time till the land was thoroughly furnished with her convenient numbers, whereof some at this present with their ancient names do still remain in knowledge, though divers be doubted of and many more perished by continuance of time and violence of the enemy. I doubt not also but the least of these were comparable to the greatest of those which stand in our time; for sith that in those days the most part of the island was reserved unto pasture, the towns and villages either were not at all (but all sorts of people dwelled in the cities indifferently,[13] an image of which estate may yet be seen in Spain) or at the leastwise stood not so thick as they did afterward in the time of the Romans, but chiefly after the coming of the Saxons and after them the Normans, when every lord builded a church near unto

---

[10] "Sarronium, Sarron's burg."—*H.* Sarisbury is a frequent form of the name in the chronicles.

[11] *Caradoc:* the Welsh form of Caractacus, British chieftain who led the resistance to the Roman invasion of 48–51; *Lucius Septimius Severus* (146–211): Roman emperor who spent the last three years of his life fighting in Britain. "Caer Caradoc," "Severia," and "Caesaris Burgum" are sometimes identified with Salisbury.

[12] *Gallic War*, II, iv, and V, xii.

[13] "Greater cities in times past when husbandmen also were citizens."—*H.*

his own mansion house and thereto imparted the greatest portion of his lands unto sundry tenants, to hold the same of him by copy of court roll, which rolls were then kept in some especial place indifferently appointed by them and their lord so that the one could have no resort unto them without the other, by which means the number of towns and villages was not a little increased. If any man be desirous to know the names of those ancient cities that stood in the time of the Romans, he shall have them here at hand in such wise as I have gathered them out of our writers, observing even their manner of writing of them so near as to me is possible, without alteration of any corruption crept up into the same.[14]

1. London, otherwise called Trenovanton; Cair Lud; Londinum, or Longidinium; Augusta, of the legion [15] Augusta that sojourned there when the Romans ruled here.

2. York,[16] otherwise called Cairbranke; Urovicum or Yurewiic; Eorwiic or Eoforwiic; Yeworwiic; Eboracum; Victoria, of the legion Victrix that lay there sometime.

3. Canterbury: Durorverno, *alias* Durarvenno; Dorobernia; Cantwarbirie.

4. Colchester: Cair Colon; Cair Colden; Cair Colkin, of Coilus; [17] Cair Colun, of the river that runneth thereby; Colonia, of the colony planted there by the Romans; Coloncester; Camulodunum.[18]

5. Lincoln: Cair Lud Coit, of the woods that stood about it; Cair Loichoit, by corruption; Lindum; Lindocollinum.

6. Warwick (had sometime nine parish churches): Cair Guttelin; Cair Line, or Cair Leon; Cair Gwair; Cair Umber; Cair Gwaerton.

---

[14] Accordingly I have made no attempt to regularize the spellings in this catalogue. Harrison's principal sources seem to be the Antonine Itinerary and the list of cities at the beginning of Henry of Huntingdon's *Chronicle*.

[15] "A legion contained sixty centuries, thirty manipuli, three cohorts."—*H*. *Manipuli:* maniples, subdivisions of a legion numbering either 60 or 120 men.

[16] "Leovitius placeth York in Scotland (*De eclipsibus*)."—*H*. Cyprianus von Leowitz, or Leovitius (d. 1574), was a Bohemian astrologer; the reference is to his *Eclipsium omnium* (Augsburg, 1556, sig. R2v), where *Eboracum Scotiae* appears in a list of cities.

[17] That is, of merry old King Cole, who is associated with Colchester in Geoffrey (V, vi).

[18] "Pliny (*lib*. II, *cap*. lxxv), Tacitus [*Annals*, XII, xxxii and XIV, xxxi-xxxii], Ptolemy [*Geography*, II, iii]."—*H*.

7. Chester-upon-Usk (was a famous university in the time of Arthur): Cair legion, Carlheon, Cairlium, Legecester, Civitas legionum.

8. Carlisle: Cair Lueill, Cair Leill, Lugibalia, Cair Doill.

9. St. Albans: Cair Maricipit; Cair Municip; Verolamium; Verlamcester; Cair Wattelin, of the street whereon it stood.[19]

10. Winchester: Cair Gwent, Cair Gwin, Cair Wine, Venta Simenorum.

11. Cirencester: Cair Churne, Cair Kyrne, Cair Kery, Cair Cery, Cirnecester, Churnecester.

12. Silchester: Cair Segent,[20] Selecester.

13. Bath: Cair Badon, Thermae, Aquae solis.

14. Shaftesbury: Cair Paladour, Septonia.

15. Worcester: Wigornia, Cair Gworangon, Brangonia, Cair Frangon, Woorkecester.

16. Chichester: Cair Key, or Kair Kis; Cair Chic.

17. Bristol: Cair Oder nant Badon, Oder, Cair Bren, Venta Belgarum, Brightstow.

18. Rochester: Durobrevis, corruptly Durobrovis, Dubobrus, Durobrius; Rofcester; Roffa.

19. Portchester: Cair Peris, Cair Poreis.

20. Carmarthen: Cair Maridunum, Cair Merdine, Maridunum, Cair Marlin, Cair Fridhin.

21. Gloucester: Cair Clowy, Cair Glow, Claudiocestria.

22. Leicester: Cair Beir; Cair Leir; Cair Lirion; Wirall, *teste* Matth. West. 895.[21]

23. Cambridge: Grantabric, Cair Graunt.

24. * Cair Urnach, peradventure Burgh Castle.

25. * Cair Cucurat.

26. * Cair Draiton, now a slender village.

27. * Cair Celennon.

28. * Cair Megwaid.

As for Cair Dorme (another whereof I read likewise), it stood

---

[19] The old Roman Watling Street.

[20] "Cair Segent stood upon the Thames, not far from Reading."—*H.* So Henry of Huntingdon (ed. Thomas Arnold, Rolls Ser., LXXIV, 1879, 7).

[21] Matthew Westminster, under 895, misinterprets the *Anglo-Saxon Chronicle* in identifying Chester with the peninsula of Wirral.

somewhere upon the Nene in Huntingdonshire, but now unknown sith it was twice razed to the ground, first by the Saxons, then by the Danes, so that the ruins thereof are in these days not extant to be seen.[22] And in like sort I am ignorant where most of them stood that are noted with the star. I find in like sort mention of a noble city called Alcluid, over and beside these afore mentioned, sometime builded by Ebracus of Britain, as the fame goeth, and finally destroyed by the Danes about the year of grace 870. It stood upon the banks of the River Cluda [Clyde], to wit, between it and the blank on the north and the Lound Lake on the west,[23] and was sometime march between the Britons and the Picts and likewise the Picts and the Scots; nevertheless, the castle (as I hear) doth yet remain and hath been since well repaired by the Scots and called Dombrittain or Dunbritton [Dumbarton], so that it is not an hard matter by these few words to find where Alcluid stood. I could here, if leisure served and haste of the printer not require dispatch, deliver the ancient names of sundry other towns, of which Stafford in time past was called Stadtford and therefore (as I guess) builded, or the name altered, by the Saxons; Kinebanton now [is called] Kimbolton. But if any man be desirous to see more of them, let him resort to Hoveden in the *Life of Henry the Second* and there he shall be further satisfied of his desire in this behalf.[24]

It should seem, when these ancient cities flourished, that the same town which we now call St. Albans did most of all excel, but chiefly in the Romans' time,[25] and was not only nothing inferior to London itself but rather preferred before it because it was newer and made a *municipium* of the Romans, whereas the other was old and ruinous and inhabited only by the Britons, as the most part of the island was also in those days. Good notice

[22] Henry of Huntingdon (p. 7).

[23] *The blank:* the haste of the printer mentioned below seems to have prevented Harrison from ascertaining the correct name, Loch Lomond, in this 1587 addition; *Lound Lake:* Loch Long. The passage is Harrison's answer to Higden (*Polychronicon*, I, xlviii), who seeks to identify Alcluid with Chester or Aldburgh in Yorkshire.

[24] *Hoveden:* Roger of Hoveden (d. ?1201), clerk to Henry II and chronicler. The second part of his work begins with the accession of Henry II. But there is little in Hoveden about these ancient names, and the reference may be an error for Henry of Huntingdon.

[25] "When Alban was martyred, Asclepiodotus was legate in Britain."—*H.* In Bede, Asclepiodotus is titled captain of the Praetorian bands (I, vi).

hereof also is to be taken by Matthew Paris [26] and others before him, out of whose writings I have thought good to note a few things whereby the majesty of this ancient city may appear unto posterity and the former estate of Verlamcester not lie altogether (as it hath done hitherto) raked up [buried] in forgetfulness through the negligence of such as might have deserved better of their successors by leaving the description thereof in a book by itself, sith many particulars thereof were written to their hands that now are lost and perished. Tacitus in the fourteenth book of his history maketh mention of it, showing that in the rebellion of the Britons the Romans there were miserably distressed: *Eadem clades,* saith he, *municipio Verolamio fuit.*[27] And hereupon Nennius in his catalogue of cities calleth it "Cair municip," as I before have noted. Ptolemy speaking of it doth place it among the Catyeuchlanes, but Antoninus maketh it one-and-twenty Italian miles from London, placing Sullomaca nine mile from thence, whereby it is evident that Sullomaca stood near to Barnet, if it were not the very same. Of the old compass of the walls of Verulamium there is now small knowledge to be had by the ruins, but of the beauty of the city itself you shall partly understand by that which followeth at hand, after I have told you for your better intelligence what *municipium Romanorum* is; for there is great difference between that and *colonia Romanorum,* sith *colonia alio traducitur a civitate Roma,* but *municipes aliunde in civitatem veniunt, suisque juribus et legibus vivunt;*[28] moreover their soil is not changed into the nature of the Roman, but they

[26] *Matthew Paris* (d. 1259): monk of St. Albans and chronicler. Most of Harrison's details in the following passages concerning the excavations of Ealdred and Eadmer are freely embroidered from Matthew Paris' account in his *Vitae abbatum S. Albani* (ed., as absorbed into Thomas Walsingham's *Gesta abbatum,* by H. T. Riley, Rolls Ser., XXVIII, Pt. IV, Vol. I, 1867, pp. 24–28). Harrison actually found all of the relevant passages in Leland (*Collectanea,* 1715, III, 164–167).

[27] "The same calamity befell the *municipium* of Verulamium," that is, like London it was sacked by the rebellious Britons led by Boadicea (*Annals,* XIV, xxxiii). Harrison borrowed the references here to Tacitus, Nennius, and Ptolemy from Leland's prose commentary on his topographical poem, *Cygnea cantio* (1545), under "Verulamium."

[28] "A *colonia* is the transferring to another place of citizens of Rome," but "the members of a *municipium* achieve citizenship in another fashion, and live under their own statutes and laws." Harrison's definitions derive from the compendium *Dies geniales* (IV, x) of Alexander ab Alexandro (d. 1523), Neapolitan jurist and humanist.

live in the steadfast friendship and protection of the Romans, as did sometime the Caerites, who were the first people which ever obtained that privilege. The British Verulamians, therefore, having for their noble service in the wars deserved great commendations at the hands of the Romans, they gave unto them the whole freedom of Romans, whereby they were made *municipes* and became more free in truth than their colonies could be. To conclude, therefore, *municipium* is a city enfranchised and endued with Roman privileges, without any alteration of her former inhabitants or privileges, whereas a colony is a company sent from Rome into any other region or province to possess either a city newly builded or to replenish the same, from whence her former citizens have been expelled and driven out. Now to proceed.

In the time of King Edgar it fell out that one Ealdred was abbot there, who being desirous to enlarge that house, it came into his mind to search about in the ruins of Verulamium (which now was overthrown by the fury of the Saxons and Danes) to see if he might there come by any curious pieces of work wherewith to garnish his building taken in hand. To be short, he had no sooner begun to dig among the rubbish but he found an exceeding number of pillars, pieces of antique work, thresholds, doorframes, and sundry other pieces of fine masonry for windows and suchlike, very convenient for his purpose. Of these also some were of porphyrite stone, some of diverse kinds of marble, touch,[29] and alabaster, beside many curious devices of hard metal; in finding whereof he thought himself an happy man and his success to be greatly guided by St. Alban. Besides these also he found sundry pillars of brass and sockets of latten [brass], alabaster, and touch, all which he laid aside by great heaps, determining in the end (I say) to lay the foundation of a new abbey; but God so prevented his determination that death took him away before his building was begun. After him succeeded one Eadmer, who followed the doings of Ealdred to the uttermost and therefore not only perused what he had left with great diligence but also caused his pioneers [diggers] to search yet further within the old walls of Verulamium, where they not only found infinite other pieces of excellent workmanship but came at the last to certain vaults under the ground, in which stood

[29] *Touch:* touchstone, black marble or basalt.

divers idols and not a few altars, very superstitiously and religiously adorned as the pagans left them, belike in time of necessity. These images were of sundry metals and some of pure gold; their altars likewise were richly covered, all which ornaments Eadmer took away and not only converted them to other use in his building but also destroyed an innumerable sort of other idols, whose estimation consisted in their forms, and substances could do no service. He took up also sundry curious pots, jugs, and cruses [jars] of stone and wood most artificially wrought and carved, and that in such quantity, besides infinite store of fine household stuff, as if the whole furniture of the city had been brought thither of purpose to be hidden in those vaults. In proceeding further he took up divers pots of gold, silver, brass, glass, and earth, whereof some were filled with the ashes and bones of the gentiles, the mouths being turned downwards (the like of which, but of finer earth, were found in great numbers also of late in a well at Little Massingham in Norfolk, of six or eight gallons apiece, about the year 1578, and also in the time of Henry the Eighth), and not a few with the coins of the old Britons and Roman emperors. All which vessels the said abbot brake into pieces, and, melting the metal, he reserved it in like sort for the garnishing of his church.

He found likewise in a stone wall two old books, whereof one contained the rites of the gentiles about the sacrifices of their gods, the other (as they now say) the martyrdom of St. Alban,[30] both of them written in old British letters, which, either because no man then living could read them or for that they were not worth the keeping, were both consumed to ashes, saving that a few notes were first taken out of this latter concerning the death of their Alban. Thus much have I thought good to note of the former beauty of Verulamium, whereof infinite other tokens have been found since that time, and divers within the memory of man of passing workmanship, the like whereof hath nowheres else been seen in any ruins within the compass of this isle, either for cost or quantity of stuff.

Furthermore, whereas many are not afraid to say that the Thames came sometimes by this city, indeed it is nothing so; but that the Verlume (afterward called Ver and the Mure) did and doth so still (whatsoever Gildas talketh hereof, whose books may

[30] "This soundeth like a lie."—*H.*

be corrupted in that behalf),[31] there is yet evident proof to be confirmed by experience. For albeit that the river be now grown to be very small by reason of the ground about it, which is higher than it was in old time, yet it keepeth in manner the old course and runneth between the old city that was and the new town that is standing on Holmehurst Crag, as I beheld of late.[32] Those places also which now are meadow beneath the abbey were sometimes a great lake, mere, or pool, through which the said river ran and (as I read) with a very swift and violent course, whereas at this present it is very slow and of no such depth as of ancient times it hath been. But hear what mine author saith further of the same. As those aforesaid workmen digged in these ruins, they happened oftentimes upon limpet shells, pieces of rusty anchors, and keels of great vessels;[33] whereupon some by and by gathered that either the Thames or some arm of the sea did beat upon that town, not understanding that these things might as well happen in great lakes and meres, whereof there was one adjoining to the north side of the city, which lay then (as some men think) unwalled, but that also is false. For being there upon occasion this summer past, I saw some remnant of the old walls standing in that place, which appeared to have been very substantially builded; the ruins likewise of a greater part of them are to be seen running along by the old chapel hard by in manner of a bank. Whereby it is evident that the new town standeth clean without the limits of the old, and that the bridge whereof the history of St. Alban speaketh was at the nether end of Holywell Street or thereabout, for so the view of the place doth enforce me to conjecture. This mere (which the Latin copy of the description of Britain, written of late by Humphrey Llwyd, our countryman, calleth corruptly *stagnum enaximum* for *stagnum maximum*)[34] at the first belonged to the king, and thereby

[31] Gildas tells of St. Alban's miracle of opening a dry path through the Thames (chap. viii), but the identification of the river seems to be a later addition to the text. Harrison is again citing Leland's commentary in the *Cygnea cantio.*

[32] Harrison added the passages concerning his own observations at St. Albans to the 1587 edition.

[33] Matthew Paris (pp. 24–25).

[34] *Humphrey Llwyd* (1527–1568): Welsh physician and antiquarian; the reference is to his *Commentarioli Britannicae descriptionis fragmentum* (Cologne, 1572, fol. 20v), translated into English by Thomas Twyne as *The Breviary of Britain* (1573).

Offa in his time did reap no small commodity. It continued also until the time of Aelfric, the seventh abbot of that house, who bought it outright of the King then living and by excessive charges drained it so narrowly that within a while he left it dry (saving that he reserved a channel for the river to have her usual course, which he held up with high banks), because there was always contention between the monks and the King's servants, which fished on that water unto the King's behoof.[35]

In these days, therefore, remaineth no manner mention of this pool but only in one street, which yet is called Fishpool Street, whereof this may suffice for the resolution of such men as seek rather to yield to an inconvenience than that their Gildas should seem to mistake this river.

Having thus digressed to give some remembrance of the old estate of Verulamium, it is now time to return again unto my former purpose. Certes I would gladly set down, with the names and number of the cities, all the towns and villages in England and Wales, with their true longitudes and latitudes, but as yet I cannot come by them in such order as I would; howbeit, the tale of our cities is soon found by the bishoprics, sith every see hath such prerogative given unto it as to bear the name of a city and to use *regale jus*[36] within her own limits. Which privilege also is granted to sundry ancient towns in England, especially northward, where more plenty of them is to be found by a great deal than in the South. The names therefore of our cities are these:

London	Worcester	Chester
York	Gloucester	Chichester
Canterbury	Hereford	Oxford
Winchester	Salisbury	Peterborough
Carlisle	Exeter	Llandaff
Durham	Bath	St. David's
Ely	Lichfield	Bangor
Norwich	Bristol	St. Asaph.
Lincoln	Rochester	

Whose particular plots and models with their descriptions shall ensue, if it may be brought to pass that the cutters can make dis-

[35] Matthew Paris (pp. 23–24).
[36] *Regale jus: jura regalia*, royal prerogatives.

patch of them before this chronology be published.[37] Of towns and villages likewise thus much will I say, that there were greater store in old time (I mean within three or four hundred year past) than at this present. And this I note out of divers records, charters, and donations (made in times past unto sundry religious houses, as Glastonbury, Abingdon, Ramsey, Ely, and suchlike), and whereof in these days I find not so much as the ruins. Leland in sundry places complaineth likewise of the decay of parishes in great cities and towns, missing in some six or eight or twelve churches and more, of all which he giveth particular notice. For albeit that the Saxons builded many towns and villages, and the Normans well more at their first coming, yet since the first two hundred years after the latter conquest they have gone so fast again to decay that the ancient number of them is very much abated. Ranulf, the monk of Chester,[38] telleth of general survey made in the fourth, sixteenth, and nineteenth of the reign of William Conqueror, surnamed "the Bastard," wherein it was found that (notwithstanding the Danes had overthrown a great many) there were to the number of 52,000 towns, 45,002 parish churches, and 75,000 knights' fees,[39] whereof the clergy held 28,015. He addeth moreover that there were divers other builded since that time, within the space of an hundred years after the coming of the Bastard, as it were in lieu or recompense of those that William Rufus pulled down for the erection of his New Forest. For by an old book which I have, and sometime written as it seemeth by an undersheriff of Nottingham, I find even in the time of Edward the Fourth 45,120 parish churches and but 60,216 knights' fees, whereof the clergy held as before 28,015, or at the least 28,000, for so small is the difference which he doth seem to use. Howbeit, if the assertions of such as write in our time concerning this matter either are or ought to be of any credit in this behalf, you shall not find above 17,000 towns and

[37] The engravers seem not to have met the deadline in 1577. If these city maps survive, they have not been identified. In Holinshed's *History of England* (1577, after p. 1868) a two-page prospect of Edinburgh, with military embellishments, is used to illustrate the siege of the castle in 1573.

[38] *Ranulf:* presumably Ranulf Higden (d. 1364), monk of St. Werburg's in Chester, although I cannot find the passage Harrison cites in his *Polychronicon.*

[39] *Knight's fee:* in the feudal system, the amount of land which entailed on the holder the services of one armed knight to the sovereign; a fief.

villages, and 9,210 [40] in the whole, which is little more than a fourth part of the aforesaid number, if it be thoroughly scanned.

Certes this misfortune hath not only happened unto our isle and nation but unto most of the famous countries of the world heretofore, and all by the greedy desire of such as would live alone and only to themselves. And hereof we may take example in Candy, of old time called Creta, which (as Homer writeth) was called *Hecatompolis* because it contained an hundred cities, but now it is so unfurnished that it may hardly be called *Tripolis*. Diodorus Siculus saith that Egypt had once 18,000 cities, which so decayed in process of time that when Ptolemy Lagus reigned there were not above 3,000; but in our days, both in all Asia and Egypt, this lesser number shall not very readily be found.[41] In time past in Lincoln (as the fame goeth) there have been two-and-fifty parish churches, and good record appeareth for eight-and-thirty; but now if there be four-and-twenty, it is all.[42] This inconvenience hath grown altogether to the church by appropriations made unto monasteries and religious houses, a terrible canker and enemy to religion.

But to leave this lamentable discourse of so notable and grievous an inconvenience, growing (as I said) by encroaching and joining of house to house and laying land to land, whereby the inhabitants of many places of our country are devoured and eaten up and their houses either altogether pulled down or suffered to decay by little and little, although sometime a poor man peradventure doth dwell in one of them, who, not being able to repair it, suffereth it to fall down and thereto thinketh himself very friendly dealt withal if he may have an acre of ground assigned unto him whereon to keep a cow or wherein to set cabbages, radishes, parsnips, carrots, melons, pompions [pumpkins], or suchlike stuff, by which he and his poor household liveth as by their principal food, sith they can do no better. And as for wheaten bread, they eat it when they can reach unto the price of it, contenting themselves in the meantime with bread made of oats or barley: a poor estate, God wot! Howbeit, what care our

---

[40] The phrase "and 9,210" (for "or 9,210"?) was added in 1587 as an alternate figure. Saxton's atlas (see n. 47) gives a total of 9,725, counting Wales.

[41] Harrison borrowed these classical references from Bodin's *Method* (trans. Reynolds, p. 318).

[42] Leland, *Itinerary* (ed. Smith, I, 30).

great encroachers? But in divers places where rich men dwelled sometime in good tenements, there be now no houses at all but hopyards and sheds for poles or peradventure gardens, as we may see in Castle Hedingham [43] and divers other places. But to proceed.

It is so that, our soil being divided into champaign ground and woodland, the houses of the first lie uniformly builded in every town together, with streets and lanes, whereas in the woodland countries (except here and there in great market towns) they stand scattered abroad, each one dwelling in the midst of his own occupying. And as in many and most great market towns there are commonly three hundred or four hundred families or mansions and two thousand communicants, or peradventure more, so in the other, whether they be woodland or champaign, we find not often above forty, fifty, or threescore households and two or three hundred communicants, whereof the greatest part nevertheless are very poor folks, oftentimes without all manner of occupying, sith the ground of the parish is gotten up into a few men's hands, yea, sometimes into the tenure of one, two, or three, whereby the rest are compelled either to be hired servants unto the other or else to beg their bread in misery from door to door.

There are some (saith Leland) which are not so favorable when they have gotten such lands as to let the houses remain upon them to the use of the poor; but they will compound with the lord of the soil to pull them down for altogether, saying that if they did let them stand, they should but toll [attract] beggars to the town, thereby to surcharge the rest of the parish and lay more burden upon them. But alas! these pitiful men see not that they themselves hereby do lay the greatest log upon their neighbors' necks. For sith the prince doth commonly lose nothing of his duties accustomable to be paid, the rest of the parishioners that remain must answer and bear them out, for they plead more charge other ways, saying, "I am charged already with a light horse; [44] I am to answer in this sort and after that manner." And it is not yet altogether out of knowledge that where the king had £7 13s.

---

[43] *Castle Hedingham:* in Essex, the family seat of the Earls of Oxford.

[44] *"Charged . . . with a light horse":* according to the statute of 4&5 Philip and Mary, c. 2, anyone with an estate valued at 100 marks was required to furnish a "light horse with furniture of harness and weapon"; see p. 31.

at a task [tax levy] gathered of fifty wealthy householders of a parish in England, now, a gentleman having three parts of the town in his own hands, four households do bear all the aforesaid payment, or else Leland is deceived in his *Commentaries* (*lib.* 13), lately come to my hands,[45] which thing he especially noted in his travel over this isle. A common plague and enormity, both in the heart of the land and likewise upon the coasts.

Certes a great number complain of the increase of poverty, laying the cause upon God as though He were in fault for sending such increase of people or want of wars that should consume them, affirming that the land was never so full, etc., but few men do see the very root from whence it doth proceed. Yet the Romans found it out when they flourished and therefore prescribed limits to every man's tenure and occupying. Homer commendeth Achilles for overthrowing of five-and-twenty cities, but in mine opinion Ganges is much better preferred by Suidas for building of threescore in Inde, where he did plant himself. I could (if need required) set down in this place the number of religious houses and monasteries, with the names of their founders, that have been in this island, but sith it is a thing of small importance I pass it over as impertinent to my purpose. Yet herein I will commend sundry of the monastical votaries, especially monks, for that they were authors of many goodly boroughs and endwares [46] near unto their dwellings, although otherwise they pretended to be men separated from the world. But alas! their covetous minds one way in enlarging their revenues, and carnal intent another, appeared herein too-too much. For being bold from time to time to visit their tenants, they wrought oft great wickedness and made those endwares little better than brothel houses, especially where nunneries were far off or else no safe access unto them. But what do I spend my time in the rehearsal of these filthinesses? Would to God the memory of them might perish with the malefactors!

My purpose was also at the end of this chapter to have set

---

[45] Harrison originally borrowed the MS of Leland's *Commentaries*, or *Itinerary*, from John Stow in 1576 (see p. 4, n. 5). Stow's surviving transcript includes only ten books, however. The above passage, added in 1587, indicates that other volumes, probably dealing with the eastern counties, were extant but had already been separated from the body of Leland's work. No one besides Harrison is known to have seen the missing Bk. XIII.

[46] *Endwares:* apparently hamlets or suburbs.

down a table of the parish churches and market towns throughout all England and Wales, but sith I cannot perform the same as
I would I am forced to give over my purpose; yet by these few
that ensue you shall easily see what order I would have used
according to the shires if I might have brought it to pass.

Shires	*Market towns*	*Parishes*
Middlesex	3	73
London, within the walls and without		120
Surrey	6	140
Sussex	18	312
Kent	17	398
Cambridge	4	163
Bedford	9	13 [for 113?]
Huntingdon	5	78
Rutland	2	47
Berkshire	11	150
Northampton	10	326
Buckingham	11	196
Oxford	10	216
Southampton	18	248
Dorset	19	279
Norfolk	26	625
Suffolk	25	575
Essex	18	415 [47]

[47] The 1577 edition adds: "And these I had of a friend of mine, by whose
travail and his master's excessive charges I doubt not but my countrymen ere
long shall see all England set forth in several shires, after the same manner
that Ortelius hath dealt with other countries of the main, to the great benefit
of our nation and everlasting fame of the aforesaid parties." The references
are explained by a passage in *The Description of Britain*, where Harrison
notes that the Darent River in Kent "riseth at Tandridge or thereabouts,
as I have been informed by Christopher Saxton's card [map] late made of
the same, and the like (I hope) he will do in all the several shires of England, at the infinite charges of Sir Thomas Seckford, Knight and Master of
the Requests, whose zeal unto his country herein I cannot but remember,
and so much the rather for that he meaneth to imitate Ortelius and somewhat
beside this hath holpen me in the names of the towns by which these rivers
for the Kentish part do run. Would to God his plots were once finished for
the rest!" (1587, p. 51; see also p. 107). Sir Thomas Seckford (d. 1588), a
Suffolk gentleman of wealth and antiquarian interests, about 1573 commissioned Christopher Saxton, a young Yorkshireman, to survey and map all
the English counties. The English part of the atlas was apparently ready in
1577, probably to coincide with the appearance of Holinshed's *Chronicles;*

CHAPTER XIV

Of Castles and Holds

It hath been of long time a question in controversy and not yet determined whether holds and castles near cities or anywhere in the heart of commonwealths are more profitable or hurtful for the benefit of the country. Nevertheless, it seemeth by our own experience that we here in England suppose them altogether unneedful. This also is apparent by the testimony of sundry writers, that they have been the ruin of many a noble city. Of Old Salisbury I speak not; of Antwerp I say nothing more than of sundry other,[1] whereof some also in my time never cease to encroach upon the liberties of the cities adjoining, thereby to hinder them what and wherein they may. For my part I never read of any castle that did good unto the city abutting thereon, but only the capitol of Rome and yet but once good unto the same, in respect of the nine times whereby it brought it into danger of

---

the maps of the Welsh counties and the title page were printed in 1579. Harrison, in dedicating his *Description of Scotland* to Seckford, again acknowledged his debt to Saxton's maps: "Having by your singular courtesy received great help in my description of the rivers and streams of Britain, and by conference of my travail with the platforms of those few shires of England which are by your infinite charges already finished (as the rest shall be in time, by God's help, for the inestimable benefit of such as inhabit this island)" (1587, p. 3). The table in the text is probably a clue to the maps with which Harrison was familiar; all were engraved by 1576. In some instances he seems to have taken his figures on market towns and parishes directly from the cartouches on the individual maps. In other cases no such figures appear and Harrison must have received his information directly from Saxton. There are, however, a number of discrepancies between Harrison's figures and those given by Saxton in the complete table which precedes the atlas. Oddly, Harrison made no attempt to expand his list or even to correct the obvious error in 1587, but he did cancel the reference to Saxton.

[1] In *The Description of Britain* (1587, p. 57) Harrison gives a detailed account of how "the soldiers of the castle and canons of Old Sarum fell at odds, insomuch that after often brawls they fell at last to sad blows," the result being the decay of that town and the removal of the bishopric to New Salisbury. The reference to Antwerp concerns the "Spanish fury," the massacre of the town in 1576 by the Spanish garrison of the castle.

utter ruin and confusion. Aristotle utterly denieth that any castle at all can be profitable to a commonwealth well governed. Timotheus [Timoleon] of Corinth affirmeth that a castle in a commonwealth is but a breeder of tyrants. Pyrrhus, King of Epirus, being received also on a time into Athens, among other courtesies showed unto him they led him also into their castle of Pallas, who at his departure gave them great thanks for the friendly entertainment but with this item, that they should let so few kings come into the same as they might, "lest," saith he, "they teach you to repent too late of your great gentleness." Caietanus, in his *Commonwealth* hath, finally, no liking of them, as appeareth in his eighth book of that most excellent treatise.[2] But what have I to deal whether they be profitable or not, sith my purpose is rather to show what plenty we have of them, which I will perform so far as shall be needful?

There have been in times past great store of castles and places of defense within the realm of England, of which some were builded by the Britons, many by the Romans, Saxons, and Danes, but most of all by the barons of the realm in and about the time of King Stephen, who licensed each of them to build so many as them listed upon their own demesnes, hoping thereby that they would have employed their use to his advantage and commodity.[3] But finally, when he saw that they were rather fortified against himself in the end than used in his defense, he repented all too late of his inconsiderate dealing, sith now there was no remedy but by force for to subdue them. After his decease King Henry the Second came no sooner to the crown but he called to mind the inconvenience which his predecessor had suffered and he himself might in time sustain by those fortifications. Therefore one of the first things he did was an attempt to raze and deface the most part of these holds. Certes he thought it better to hazard the meeting of the enemy now and then in the plain field than to live in perpetual fear of those houses and the rebellion of his lords upon every light occasion conceived, who then were full so strong as he if not more strong; and that made them the readier to withstand and gainsay many of those

[2] *Caietanus:* Francesco Patrizi (1413-1494), Italian humanist, Bishop of Gaeta. Harrison derives all his classical references here from Patrizi's *Moral Method of Civil Policy,* trans. Richard Robinson (1576), fol. 72r-v.

[3] "Henry the Third also raised divers."—*H.*

proceedings which he and his successors from time to time intended. Hereupon, therefore, he caused more than eleven hundred of their said castles to be razed and overthrown, whereby the power of his nobility was not a little restrained. Since that time also not a few of those which remained have decayed, partly by the commandment of Henry the Third and partly of themselves, or by conversion of them into the dwelling houses of noblemen, their martial fronts being removed, so that at this present there are very few or no castles at all maintained within England, saving only upon the coasts and marches of the country, for the better keeping back of the foreign enemy whensoever he shall attempt to enter and annoy us.

The most provident prince that ever reigned in this land for the fortification thereof against all outward enemies was the late prince of famous memory, King Henry the Eighth, who, beside that he repaired most of such as were already standing, builded sundry out of the ground. For having shaken off the more than servile yoke of popish tyranny and espying that the Emperor was offended for his divorce from Queen Catherine, his aunt, and thereto understanding that the French king had coupled the Dolphin, his son, with the Pope's niece and married his daughter to the King of Scots (whereby he had cause more justly to suspect than safely to trust any one of them all, as Lambarde saith),[4] he determined to stand upon his own defense; and therefore, with no small speed and like charge, he builded sundry blockhouses, castles, and platforms upon divers frontiers of his realm, but chiefly the east and southeast parts of England, whereby (no doubt) he did very much qualify the conceived grudges of his adversaries and utterly put off their hasty purpose of invasion. But would to God he had cast his eye toward Harwich and the coasts of Norfolk and Suffolk, where nothing as yet is done! albeit there be none so fit and likely places for the enemy to enter upon as in those parts, where at a full sea they may touch upon the shore and come to land without re-

---

[4] All of the sentence through "of his realm" is closely paraphrased from Lambarde's *Perambulation of Kent* (1576), p. 117. *The Emperor:* Charles V; *the French king:* Francis I, who married his son Henry to Catherine de' Medici, niece of Pope Clement VII, and his daughter Madeleine to James V of Scotland.

sistance.[5] And thus much briefly for my purpose at this present. For I need not to make any long discourse of castles, sith it is not the nature of a good Englishman to regard to be caged up as in a coop and hedged in with stone walls but rather to meet with his enemy in the plain field at handstrokes, where he may traverse his ground, choose his plot, and use the benefit of sunshine, wind, and weather to his best advantage and commodity. Isocrates also saith that towers, walls, bulwarks, soldiers, and plenty of armor are not the best keepers of kingdoms, but friends, love of subjects, and obedience unto martial discipline, which they want that show themselves either cruel or covetous toward their people.[6]

As for those tales that go of Beeston Castle, how it shall save all England on a day, and likewise the brag of a rebellious baron in old time named Hugh Bigod, that said in contempt of King Henry the Third and about the fiftieth year of his reign,

> If I were in my castle of Bungay,
> Upon the water of Waveney,
> I would not set a button by the King of Cockney,[7]

I repute them but as toys; the first mere vain, the second fondly uttered (if any such thing were said), as many other words are and have been spoken of like holds (as Wallingford, etc.), but now grown out of memory and with small loss not heard of among the common sort. Certes the castle of Bungay was overthrown by the aforesaid prince the same year that he overthrew the walls and castle of Leicester, also the castles of Thirsk and [Kirkby] Malzeard appertaining to Roger Mowbray, and that of

[5] "In these days the coast of Norfolk is the weakest, as may yet appear by Weybourne Hope and other places of the same."—*H.* The sentence in the text was added in 1587.

[6] Apparently based on *Areopagiticus,* 142, *Helen,* 214–215, and similar passages, but the citation is borrowed from Patrizi, *De regno et regis institutione,* II, i (Paris, 1582, fol. 511r).

[7] *King of Cockney:* there was a Master of the Revels of this name at Lincoln's Inn, hence the phrase may mean "mock king," or perhaps "Cockney" is simply equivalent to London. Harrison seems to have confused Hugh Bigod (d. 1177), 1st Earl of Norfolk, a very rebellious baron under Henry II, with his great-grandsons, Roger (d. 1270), 4th Earl, and Hugh (d. 1266), Chief Justiciar under Henry III.

Framlingham, belonging likewise to Hugh Bigod, whereof in the chronology following you may read at large.[8]

I might here in like sort take occasion to speak of sundry strong places where camps of men have lien and of which we have great plenty here in England in the plain fields, but I pass over to talk of any such needless discourses. This nevertheless concerning two of them is not to be omitted, to wit, that the one near unto Cambridge, now Gogmagog's Hill, was called Windlebury beforetime, as I read of late in an old pamphlet.[9] And to say the truth, I have often heard them named Winterbury Hills, which difference may easily grow by corruption of the former word; the place likewise is very large and strong. The second is to be seen in the edge of Shropshire, about two miles from Clun, between two rivers, the Clun or Colonus, and the Tewie, otherwise named Themis [Teme], whereunto there is no access but at one place. The Welshmen call it Caer Caradoc, and they are of the opinion that Caractacus, King of the Silures, was overcome there by Ostorius, at such time as he fled to Cartismandua, Queen of the Brigantes, for succor, who betrayed him to the Romans as you may see in Tacitus.[10]

CHAPTER XV

Of Palaces Belonging to the Prince

IT LIETH not in me to set down exactly the number and names of the palaces belonging to the prince nor to make any description of Her Grace's court, sith my calling is and hath been such as that I have scarcely presumed to peep in at her gates; much less, then, have I adventured to search out and know the estate of those houses and what magnificent behavior is to be seen within them.

[8] Holinshed under 1176 recounts the razing of these castles by Henry II.

[9] "The Wandles in time past were called Windles."—*H*. Wandlebury is the usual name for this ancient hill fort, but it appears in the *Historia Eliensis* as "Wyndilbyry." See *Victoria History of the County of Cambridge*, II (London, 1948), 39–41.

[10] *Annals*, XII, xxxiii–xxxvi, but all of Harrison's details about this site in Shropshire come from Humphrey Llwyd, *Breviary of Britain*, trans. Twyne, fols. 33v–34r.

Yet thus much will I say generally of all the houses and honors pertaining to Her Majesty, that they are builded either of square stone or brick or else of both. And thereunto, although their capacity and hugeness be not so monstrous as the like of divers foreign princes are to be seen in the main and newfound nations of the world, yet are they so curious, neat, and commodious as any of them, both for conveyance of offices and lodgings and excellency of situation, which is not the least thing to be considered of in building. Those that were builded before the time of King Henry the Eighth retain to these days the show and image of the ancient kind of workmanship used in this land, but such as he erected after his own device (for he was nothing inferior in this trade to Hadrian the Emperor and Justinian the Lawgiver) do represent another manner of pattern, which, as they are supposed to excel all the rest that he found standing in this realm, so they are and shall be a perpetual precedent unto those that do come after to follow in their works and buildings of importance. Certes masonry did never better flourish in England than in his time. And albeit that in these days there be many goodly houses erected in the sundry quarters of this island, yet they are rather curious to the eye like paper work than substantial for continuance, whereas such as he did set up excel in both and therefore may justly be preferred far above all the rest.

The names of those which come now to my remembrance and are as yet reserved to Her Majesty's only use at pleasure are these, for of such as are given away I speak not, neither of those that are utterly decayed, as Baynard's Castle in London, builded in the days of the Conqueror by a nobleman called William Baynard, whose wife Inga [Juga] builded the Priory of Little Dunmow [1] in the days of Henry the First, neither of the Tower Royal there also, etc., sith I see no cause wherefore I should remember them and many of the like, of whose very ruins I have no certain knowledge. Of such, I say therefore, as I erst mentioned, we have first of all Whitehall at the west end of London (which is taken for the most large and principal of all the rest), [which] was first a lodging of the archbishops of York, then pulled down, begun by Cardinal Wolsey, and finally enlarged and finished by King Henry the Eighth. By east of this standeth

---

[1] *Little Dunmow:* in Essex, near Harrison's Radwinter.

Durham Place, sometime belonging to the bishops of Durham but converted also by King Henry the Eighth into a palace royal and lodging for the prince. Of Somerset Place I speak not, yet if the first beginner thereof (I mean the Lord Edward, the learned and godly Duke of Somerset)[2] had lived, I doubt not but it should have been well finished and brought to a sumptuous end, but as untimely death took him from that house and from us all, so it proved the stay of such proceeding as was intended about it. Whereby it cometh to pass that it standeth as he left it. Neither will I remember the Tower of London, which is rather an armory and house of munition and thereunto a place for the safekeeping of offenders than a palace royal for a king or queen to sojourn in. Yet in times past I find that Belline held his abode there, and thereunto extended the site of his palace in such wise that it stretched over the Broken Wharf and came further into the city, insomuch that it approached near to Belline's Gate,[3] and as it is thought some of the ruins of his house are yet extant, howbeit patched up and made warehouses in that tract of ground in our times. St. James's, sometime a nunnery, was builded also by the same prince. Her Grace hath also Oatlands, Ashridge, Hatfield, Havering, Enfield, Eltham, Langley, Richmond (builded by Henry the Fifth), Hampton Court (begun sometime by Cardinal Wolsey and finished by her father), and thereunto Woodstock, erected by King Henry the First, in which the Queen's Majesty delighteth greatly to sojourn, notwithstanding that in time past it was the place of a parcel of her captivity, when it pleased God to try her by affliction and calamity.

For strength Windlesor, or Windsor, is supposed to be the chief, a castle builded in time past by King Arthur, or before him by Arviragus[4] as it is thought, and repaired by Edward the Third, who erected also a notable college there. After him divers of his successors have bestowed exceeding charges upon the same, which notwithstanding are far surmounted by the Queen's Majesty now living, who hath appointed huge sums of money to be employed upon the ornature and alteration of the mold according to the form of building used in our days, which is

---

[2] *Duke of Somerset:* Protector under Edward VI, beheaded in 1552.

[3] *Belline's Gate:* Billingsgate, built according to Geoffrey of Monmouth (III, x) by the legendary Belline, son of Dunwallo Molmutius.

[4] *Arviragus:* mythical King of England, son of Cymbeline.

more for pleasure than for either profit or safeguard. Suc
hath been the estimation of this place that divers kings have not
only been interred there but also made it the chief house of
assembly and creation of the knights of the honorable Order of
the Garter, than the which there is nothing in this land more
magnificent and stately.

Greenwich was first builded by Humphrey, Duke of Gloucester, upon the Thames-side four miles east from London, in
the time of Henry the Sixth, and called Pleasance. Afterwards it
was greatly enlarged by King Edward the Fourth, garnished by
King Henry the Seventh, and finally made perfect by King
Henry the Eighth, the only phoenix [paragon] of his time for
fine and curious masonry.

Not far from this is Dartford and not much distant also from
the south side of the said stream, sometime a nunnery builded
by Edward the Third but now a very commodious palace, whereunto it was also converted by King Henry the Eighth. Eltham
(as I take it) was builded by King Henry the Third if not before.
There are beside these, moreover, divers other. But what shall I
need to take upon me to repeat all and tell what houses the
Queen's Majesty hath? sith all is hers, and when it pleaseth her
in the summer season to recreate herself abroad and view the
estate of the country and hear the complaints of her poor commons injured by her unjust officers or their substitutes, every
nobleman's house is her palace, where she continueth during
pleasure and till she return again to some of her own, in which
she remaineth so long as pleaseth her.

The court of England, which necessarily is holden always
where the prince lieth, is in these days one of the most renowned
and magnificent courts that are to be found in Europe. For
whether you regard the rich and infinite furniture of household,
order of officers, or the entertainment of such strangers as daily
resort unto the same, you shall not find many equal thereunto,
much less one excelling it in any manner of wise. I might here
(if I would or had sufficient disposition of matter conceived of
the same) make a large discourse of such honorable ports, of such
grave councilors and noble personages as give their daily attendance upon the Queen's Majesty there. I could in like sort set
forth a singular commendation of the virtuous beauty or beautiful virtues of such ladies and gentlewomen as wait upon her

person, between whose amiable countenances and costliness of attire there seemeth to be such a daily conflict and contention as that it is very difficult for me to guess whether of the twain shall bear away the pre-eminence. This further is not to be omitted, to the singular commendation of both sorts and sexes of our courtiers here in England, that there are very few of them which have not the use and skill of sundry speeches, beside an excellent vein of writing beforetime not regarded.[5] Would to God the rest of their lives and conversations were correspondent to these gifts! For as our common courtiers (for the most part) are the best learned and endued with excellent gifts, so are many of them the worst men when they come abroad that any man shall either hear or read of.[6] Truly it is a rare thing with us now to hear of a courtier which hath but his own language. And to say how many gentlewomen and ladies there are that, beside sound knowledge of the Greek and Latin tongues, are thereto no less skillful in the Spanish, Italian, and French, or in some one of them, it resteth not in me, sith I am persuaded that, as the noblemen and gentlemen do surmount in this behalf, so these come very little or nothing at all behind them for their parts, which industry God continue and accomplish that which otherwise is wanting!

Beside these things I could in like sort set down the ways and means whereby our ancient ladies of the court do shun and avoid idleness, some of them exercising their fingers with the needle, other in caulwork [ornamental netting], divers in spinning of silk, some in continual reading either of the Holy Scriptures or histories of our own or foreign nations about us, and divers in writing volumes of their own or translating of other men's into our English and Latin tongue, whilst the youngest sort in the meantime apply their lutes, citterns, prick song,[7] and all kind of music, which they use only for recreation sake when they have leisure and are free from attendance upon the Queen's Majesty or such as they belong unto. How many of the eldest sort also are skillful in surgery and distillation of waters,[8] beside

---

[5] "English courtiers the best learned and the worst livers."—*H.*

[6] These two sentences, together with other phrases that modify Harrison's ingenuous praise of the Elizabethan court, were added in 1587.

[7] *Cittern:* a guitar-like instrument; *prick song:* descant, music in parts.

[8] *Distillation of waters:* preparation of medicinal drinks.

sundry other artificial practices pertaining to the ornature and commendations of their bodies, I might (if I listed to deal further in this behalf) easily declare, but I pass over such manner of dealing lest I should seem to glaver [flatter] and curry favor with some of them. Nevertheless, this I will generally say of them all, that as each of them are cunning in something whereby they keep themselves occupied in the court, so there is in manner none of them but when they be at home can help to supply the ordinary want of the kitchen with a number of delicate dishes of their own devising, wherein the Portingale is their chief counselor, as some of them are most commonly with the clerk of the kitchen, who useth (by a trick taken up of late) to give in a brief rehearsal of such and so many dishes as are to come in at every course throughout the whole service in the dinner or supperwhile, which bill [menu] some do call a memorial, other a billet, but some a fillet, because such are commonly hanged on the file and kept by the lady or gentlewoman unto some other purpose. But whither am I digressed?

I might finally describe the large allowances in [household] offices and yearly liveries, and thereunto the great plenty of gold and silver plate, the several pieces whereof are commonly so great and massy and the quantity thereof so abundantly serving all the household that (as I suppose) Cinyras, Croesus, and Crassus [9] had not the like furniture; nay, if Midas were now living and once again put to his choice, I think he could ask no more or rather not half so much as is there to be seen and used. But I pass over to make such needless discourses, resolving myself that even in this also, as in all the rest, the exceeding mercy and loving-kindness of God doth wonderfully appear towards us, in that He hath so largely endued us with these His so ample benefits.

In some great princes' courts beyond the seas—and which even for that cause are likened unto hell by divers learned writers that have spent a great part of their time in them, as Henry Cornelius Agrippa, one (for example) who in his epistle *Ad aulicum quendam*, saith thus:

An non in inferno es amice, qui es in aula, ubi daemonum habitatio est, qui illic suis artibus humana licet effigie regnant, atque ubi scelerum

[9] *Cinyras, Croesus, Crassus:* proverbial models of immense wealth.

schola est, et animarum jactura ingens, ac quicquid uspiam est perfidiae ac doli, quicquid crudelitatis et inclementiae, quicquid effraenatae superbiae, et rapacis avariciae, quicquid obscenae libidinis, faedissimae impudicitiae, quicquid nefandae impietatis, et morum pessimorum, totum illic acervatur cumulatissime, ubi stupra, raptus, incestus, adulteria, principum et nobilium ludi sunt, ubi fastus et tumor, ira, livor, faedaque cupido cum sociis suis imperavit, ubi criminum omnium procellae virtutumque omnium inenarrabile naufragium, etc.[10]

—in such great princes' courts (I say) it is a world to see what lewd behavior is used among divers of those that resort unto the same, and what whoredom, swearing, ribaldry, atheism, dicing, carding, carousing, drunkenness, gluttony, quarreling, and such-like inconveniences do daily take hold, and sometimes even among those in whose estates the like behavior is least convenient (whereby their talk is verified which say that everything increaseth and groweth in the courts of princes saving virtue, which in such places doth languish and daily fade away), all which enormities are either utterly expelled out of the court of England or else so qualified by the diligent endeavor of the chief officers of Her Grace's household that seldom are any of these things apparently seen there without due reprehension and such severe correction as belongeth to those trespasses. Finally, to avoid idleness and prevent sundry transgressions, otherwise likely to be committed and done, such order is taken that every office hath either a Bible or the books of the *Acts and Monuments of the Church of England* [11] or both, beside some histories and chronicles lying therein for the exercise of such as come into

---

[10] "Or are you not in hell, my friend, who are at court, which is the home of devils, who by their arts reign there, even though they do so in human form, and where there is a school of vices and a vast loss of souls, and in which whatever is treacherous and deceitful, whatever cruel and merciless, whatever uncontrollably proud and graspingly avaricious, whatever lewdly wanton, filthily immodest, whatever heinously impious and most viciously immoral, all are there concentrated in fullest abundance, where debaucheries, rape, incest, adultery are the pastimes of princes and nobles, where arrogance and pride, rage, envy, and foul greed with their companion vices have gained the sway, where the storms of all crimes and the indescribable shipwreck of all virtues, etc." *Henry Cornelius Agrippa von Nettesheim* (1486–1535): German physician and scholar with a legendary reputation as a magician. The language of this letter "To a certain courtier" is close to that of the attack on "royal economy" in Agrippa's *De incertitudine et vanitate scientiarum et artium* (Antwerp, 1531), chap. lxviii.

[11] That is, John Foxe's famous *Book of Martyrs*, of which there were English editions in 1563, 1570, and 1576; see p. 416.

the same, whereby the stranger that entereth into the court of England upon the sudden shall rather imagine himself to come into some public school of the universities, where many give ear to one that readeth, than into a prince's palace, if you confer the same with those of other nations. Would to God all honorable personages would take example of Her Grace's godly dealing in this behalf and show their conformity unto these her so good beginnings! which if they would, then should many grievous offenses (wherewith God is highly displeased) be cut off and restrained, which now do reign exceedingly in most noble and gentlemen's houses, whereof they see no pattern within Her Grace's gates.

I might speak here of the great trains and troops of servingmen also, which attend upon the nobility of England in their several liveries and with differences of cognizances on their sleeves whereby it is known to whom they appertain. I could also set down what a goodly sight it is to see them muster in the court, which being filled with them doth yield the contemplation of a noble variety unto the beholder, much like to the show of the peacock's tail in the full beauty or of some meadow garnished with infinite kinds and diversity of pleasant flowers. But I pass over the rehearsal hereof to other men, who more delight in vain amplification than I and seek to be more curious in these points than I profess to be.

The discipline of firm peace also that is maintained within a certain compass of the prince's palace is such as is nothing inferior to that we see daily practiced in the best-governed holds and fortresses. And such is the severe punishment of those that strike within the limits prohibited that, without all hope of mercy, benefit of clergy, or sanctuary, they are sure to lose their right hands at a stroke, and that in very solemn manner, the form whereof I will set down and then make an end of this chapter to deal with other matters.[12]

At such time, therefore, as the party transgressing is convicted by a sufficient inquest impaneled for the same purpose, and the time come of the execution of the sentence, the sergeant of the king's woodyard provideth a square block, which he bringeth to some appointed place, and therewithal a great beetle

[12] Harrison here and in the following paragraph summarizes the provisions of the statute 33 Henry VIII, c. 12.

[mallet], staple, and cords wherewith to fasten the hand of the offender unto the said block until the whole circumstance of his execution be performed. The yeoman of the scullery likewise, for the time being, doth provide a great fire of coals hard by the block, wherein the searing irons are to be made ready, against the chief surgeon to the prince, or his deputy, shall occupy the same. Upon him also doth the sergeant or chief farrier attend with those irons, whose office is to deliver them to the said surgeon when he shall be ready by searing to use the same. The groom of the salary [13] for the time being, or his deputy, is furthermore appointed to be ready with vinegar and cold water, and not to depart from the place until the arm of the offender be bound up and fully dressed. And as these things are thus provided, so the sergeant-surgeon is bound from time to time to be ready to execute his charge and sear the stump, when the hand is taken from it. The sergeant of the cellar is at hand also with a cup of red wine, and likewise the chief officer of the pantry with manchet bread to give unto the said party after the execution done and the stump seared, as the sergeant of the ewery is with cloths wherein to wind and wrap up the arm, the yeoman of the poultry with a cock to lay unto it, the yeoman of the chandlery with seared cloths, and finally, the master cook, or his deputy, with a sharp dressing knife, which he delivereth at the place of execution to the sergeant of the larder, who doth hold it upright in his hand until the execution be performed by the public officer appointed thereunto. And this is the manner of punishment ordained for those that strike within the prince's palace or limits of the same. Which should first have been executed on Sir Edmund Knyvet in the year 1541. But when he had made great suit to save his right hand for the further service of the King in his wars and willingly yielded to forgo his left, in the end the King pardoned him of both, to no small benefit of the offender and publication of the bountiful nature that remained in the prince.[14]

The like privilege almost is given to churches and churchyards, although in manner of punishment great difference do appear. For he that brawleth or quarreleth in either of them is by and by

---

[13] *Salary:* the statute reads "salcery," that is, saucery, the household department charged with preparing sauces.

[14] *Sir Edmund Knyvet* (d. 1546): sergeant-porter to the King; he was convicted of striking a retainer of the Earl of Surrey.

suspended *ab ingressu ecclesiae* [from entering the church] until he be absolved, as he is also that striketh with the fist or layeth violent hands upon any whomsoever. But if he happen to smite with staff, dagger, or any manner of weapon, and the same be sufficiently found by the verdict of twelve men at his arraignment, beside excommunication he is sure to lose one of his ears, without all hope of release. But if he be such a one as hath been twice condemned and executed, whereby he hath now none ears, then is he marked with an hot iron upon the cheek, and by the letter *F*, which is seared deep into his flesh; he is from thenceforth noted as a common barrator [quarreler] and fray-maker and thereunto remaineth excommunicate till by repentance he deserve to be absolved.[15] To strike a clerk, also (that is to say, a minister), is plain excommunication, and the offender not to be absolved but by the prince or his especial commission. Such also is the general estate of the excommunicate in every respect that he can yield no testimony in any matter so long as he so standeth. No bargain or sale that he maketh is available in law, neither any of his acts whatsoever pleadable, whereby he liveth as an outlaw and a man altogether out of the prince's protection, although it be not lawful to kill him nor any man otherwise outlawed without the danger of felony.

CHAPTER XVI

Of Armor and Munition

How well or how strongly our country hath been furnished in times past with armor and artillery, it lieth not in me as of myself to make rehearsal. Yet that it lacked both in the late time of Queen Mary, not only the experience of mine elders but also the talk of certain Spaniards not yet forgotten did leave some manifest notice. Upon the first I need not stand, for few will deny it.

---

[15] A summary of 5&6 Edward VI, c. 4. According to the statute, by the letter *F* the offenders "may be known and taken for fray-makers and fighters."

For the second, I have heard that when one of the greatest peers of Spain espied our nakedness in this behalf and did solemnly utter in no obscure place that "it should be an easy matter in short time to conquer England, because it wanted armor," his words were then not so rashly uttered as they were politicly noted. For albeit that for the present time their efficacy was dissembled and semblance made as though he spake but merrily, yet at the very entrance of this our gracious Queen unto the possession of the crown, they were so providently called to remembrance and such speedy reformation sought of all hands for the redress of this inconvenience that our country was sooner furnished with armor and munition from divers parts of the main (beside great plenty that was forged here at home) than our enemies could get understanding of any such provision to be made. By this policy also was the no small hope conceived by Spaniards utterly cut off, who, of open friends being now become our secret enemies and thereto watching a time wherein to achieve some heavy exploit against us and our country, did thereupon change their purposes, whereby England obtained rest that otherwise might have been sure of sharp and cruel wars. Thus a Spanish word uttered by one man at one time overthrew or at the leastwise hindered sundry privy practices of many at another.

In times past the chief force of England consisted in their longbows. But now we have in manner generally given over that kind of artillery and for longbows indeed do practice to shoot compass [1] for our pastime, which kind of shooting can never yield any smart stroke nor beat down our enemies as our countrymen were wont to do at every time of need. Certes the Frenchmen and rutters,[2] deriding our new archery in respect of their corselets, will not let in open skirmish, if any leisure serve, to turn up their tails and cry, "Shoot, English!" and all because our strong shooting is decayed and laid in bed. But if some of our Englishmen now lived that served King Edward the Third in his wars with France, the breech of such a varlet should have been nailed to his bum with one arrow and another feathered in his bowels before he should have turned about to see who shot the first. But as our shooting is thus in manner utterly decayed among

[1] *To shoot compass:* to send an arrow in a high trajectory.
[2] *Rutters:* horsemen or troopers, especially those from Germany.

us one way, so our countrymen wax skillful in sundry other points, as in shooting in small pieces, the caliver,[3] and handling of the pike, in the several uses whereof they are become very expert.

Our armor differeth not from that of other nations and therefore consisteth of corselets, Almain rivets,[4] shirts of mail, jacks quilted and covered over with leather, fustian, or canvas, over thick plates of iron that are sewed in the same, and of which there is no town or village that hath not her convenient furniture. The said armor and munition likewise is kept in one several place of every town appointed by the consent of the whole parish, where it is always ready to be had and worn within an hour's warning. Sometime also it is occupied when it pleaseth the magistrate either to view the able men and take note of the well-keeping of the same, or finally to see those that are enrolled to exercise each one his several weapon, at the charge of the townsmen of each parish, according to his appointment. Certes there is almost no village so poor in England (be it never so small) that hath not sufficient furniture in a readiness to set forth three or four soldiers, as one archer, one gunner, one pike, and a billman at the least.[5] No, there is not so much wanting as their very liveries and caps, which are least to be accounted of if any haste required; so that if this good order may continue, it shall be unpossible for the sudden enemy to find us unprovided. As for able men for service, thanked be God, we are not without good store, for by the musters taken [in] 1574 and 1575 our number amounted to 1,172,674, and yet were they not so narrowly taken but that a third part of this like multitude was left unbilled and uncalled. What store of munition and armor the Queen's Majesty hath in her storehouses, it lieth not in me to yield account, sith I suppose the same to be infinite. And whereas it was commonly said after the loss of Calais that England should never recover the store of ordnance there left and lost, that same is at this time proved false, sith even some of the same persons do now confess that this land was never better furnished with these things in any king's days that reigned since the Conquest.

---

[3] *Caliver:* a light harquebus or musket.

[4] *Almain rivets:* light armor made of overlapping plates sliding on rivets.

[5] *Pike, bill:* both were long staffs with pointed steel heads; a bill also had a hook-shaped blade.

The names of our greatest ordnance are commonly these:

Robinet, whose weight is 200 pounds, and it hath 1¼ inches within the mouth.

Falconet weigheth 500 pounds, and his wideness is 2 inches within the mouth.

Falcon hath 800 pounds and 2½ inches within the mouth.

Minion poiseth 1,100 pounds and hath 3¼ inches within the mouth.

Saker hath 1,500 pounds and is 3½ inches wide in the mouth.

Demiculverin weigheth 3,000 pounds and hath 4½ inches within the mouth.

Culverin hath 4,000 pounds and 5½ inches within the mouth.

Demicannon, 6,000 pounds and 6½ inches within the mouth.

Cannon, 7,000 pounds and 8 inches within the mouth.

E.-cannon,[6] 8,000 pounds and 7 inches within the mouth.

Basilisk, 9,000 pounds, 8¾ inches within the mouth.

By which proportions also it is easy to come by the weight of every shot, how many scores it doth flee at point-blank,[7] how much powder is to be had to the same, and finally, how many inches in height each bullet ought to carry:[8]

The names of the greatest ordnance	Weight of the shot	Scores of carriage	Pounds of powder	Height of bullet
Robinet	1 *li.* [lb.]	0	½	1
Falconet	2 *li.*	14	2	1¾
Falcon	2½	16	2½	2¼
Minion	4½	17	4½	3
Saker	5	18	5	3¼
Demiculverin	9	20	9	4
Culverin	18	25	18	5¼
Demicannon	30	38	28	6¼
Cannon	60	20	44	7¾
E.-cannon	42	20	20	6¾
Basilisk	60	21	60	8¼ [9]

[6] *E.-cannon*: Eliza-cannon, better known as the cannon-royal.

[7] *How many scores it doth flee*: the range, measured in scores of paces, the gunners' pace being five feet; *at point-blank*: aimed horizontally.

[8] *Inches in height*: the diameter of the shot.

[9] I have not attempted to correct Harrison's figures, although there are clearly some misprints in the table, particularly with regard to the Eliza-cannon.

I might here take just occasion to speak of the prince's armories. But what shall it need, sith the whole realm is her armory and therefore her furniture infinite? The Turk had one gun made by one Urban, a Dane, the caster of his ordnance, which could not be drawn to the siege of Constantinople but by seventy yokes of oxen and two thousand men; he had two other there also whose shot poised above two talents [10] in weight, made by the same Urban. But to proceed. As for the armories of some of the nobility (whereof I also have seen a part), they are so well furnished that within some one baron's custody I have seen threescore or a hundred corselets at once, beside calivers, handguns, bows, sheaves of arrows, pikes, bills, poleaxes, flasks, touchboxes, targets, etc.,[11] the very sight whereof appalled my courage. What would the wearing of some of them do then (trow you) if I should be enforced to use one of them in the field? But thanked be God, our peaceable days are such as no man hath any great cause to occupy them at all but only taketh good leisure to have them in a readiness, and therefore both high and low in England,

Cymbala pro galeis pro scutis tympana pulsant.[12]

I would write here also of our manner of going to the wars, but what hath the long black gown to do with glistering armor? What sound acquaintance can there be betwixt Mars and the Muses? Or how should a man write anything to the purpose of that wherewith he is nothing acquainted? This nevertheless will I add of things at home, that seldom shall you see any of my countrymen above eighteen or twenty years old to go without a dagger at the least at his back or by his side, although they be aged burgesses or magistrates of any city, who in appearance are most exempt from brabbling and contention. Our nobility wear commonly swords or rapiers with their daggers, as doth every common servingman also that followeth his lord and master. Some desperate cutters we have in like sort which carry two daggers or two rapiers in a sheath always about them, wherewith in every drunken fray they are known to work much mischief; their swords and daggers also are of a great length and longer than the

---

[10] *Talent:* a Greek measure of weight, probably about fifty-six lbs. here.

[11] *Poleaxes:* short-handled battle-axes; *flasks:* containers for gunpowder; *touchboxes:* boxes for priming powder or tinder; *targets:* light shields.

[12] "Strike cymbals rather than helmets, drums rather than shields" (Ovid, *Fasti,* IV, 213).

like used in any other country, whereby each one pretendeth to have the more advantage of his enemy. But as many orders have been taken for the intolerable length of these weapons, so I see as yet small redress, but where the cause thereof doth rest, in sooth for my part I wot not.

I might here speak of the excessive staves which divers that travel by the way do carry upon their shoulders, whereof some are twelve or thirteen foot long, beside the pike of twelve inches, but, as they are commonly suspected of honest men to be thieves and robbers or at the leastwise scarce true men which bear them, so by reason of this and the like suspicious weapons the honest traveler is now enforced to ride with a case of dags [pistols] at his saddlebow or with some pretty short snapper [handgun], whereby he may deal with them further off in his own defense before he come within the danger of these weapons. Finally, no man traveleth by the way without his sword or some such weapon with us except the minister, who commonly weareth none at all unless it be a dagger or hanger [short sword] at his side. Seldom also are they or any other wayfaring men robbed without the consent of the chamberlain, tapster, or hostler where they bait [13] and lie, who, feeling at their alighting whether their capcases or budgets [14] be of any weight or not by taking them down from their saddles, or otherwise see their store in drawing of their purses, do by and by give intimation to some one or other attendant daily in the yard or house or dwelling hard by upon such matches whether the prey be worth the following or no. If it be for their turn, then the gentleman peradventure is asked which way he traveleth and whether it please him to have another guest to bear him company at supper, who rideth the same way in the morning that he doth, or not. And thus, if he admit him or be glad of his acquaintance, the cheat is half wrought. And often it is seen that the new guest shall be robbed with the old, only to color out the matter and keep him from suspicion. Sometimes when they know which way the passenger traveleth they will either go before and lie in wait for him or else come galloping apace after, whereby they will be sure, if he ride not the stronger, to be fingering with his purse. And these

[13] *Bait:* to stop at an inn, especially to feed horses.
[14] *Capcases:* traveling bags; *budgets:* pouches or wallets.

are some of the policies of such shrews or close, booted [15] gentlemen as lie in wait for fat booties by the highways, and which are
most commonly practiced in the winter season about the feast
of Christmas, when servingmen and unthrifty gentlemen want
money to play at the dice and cards, lewdly spending in such
wise whatsoever they have wickedly gotten till some of them,
sharply set upon their chevisances, be trussed up in a Tyburn
tippet,[16] which happeneth unto them commonly before they come
to middle age. Whereby it appeareth that some sort of youth will
oft have his swing [fling], although it be in a halter.

I might also entreat of our old manner of warfare used in and
before the time of Caesar, whenas the chief brunt of our fight
was in *essedis*, or wagons; [17] but this I also pass over, noting nevertheless out of Propertius that our said wagons were gorgeous
and gaily painted, which he setteth down in these four verses
ensuing (*Arethusae ad Lycotam, lib. 4, eleg. 3*):

> *Te modo viderunt iteratos Bactra per ortus,*
> *Te modo munito Sericus hostis equo,*
> *Hibernique Getae, pictoque Brittannia curru,*
> *Ustus et Eoa discolor Indus aqua.*[18]

CHAPTER XVII

Of the Navy of England

THERE is nothing that hath brought me into more admiration of
the power and force of antiquity than their diligence and care
had of their navies; wherein, whether I consider their speedy
building or great number of ships which some one kingdom or
region possessed at one instant, it giveth me still occasion either

---

[15] *Shrews:* rascals; *close:* secretive; *booted:* ready to ride. "Close-booted" is
an alternative reading, but the sense is obscure.
[16] *Chevisances:* trickery, frauds; *Tyburn tippet:* slang for the hangman's
rope, from the place of execution at London.
[17] *Gallic War*, IV, xxxiii.
[18] "Now Bactra has seen you revisit the East, now the Serican foe with
armored steed, and the wintry Getae and Britain with her painted chariots,
and the Indian with burnt complexion beside the Eastern Sea," (ll. 7-10).

to suspect the history or to think that in our times we come very far behind them. For what a thing is it to have a ship grow-ing on the stub [stump] and sailing on the sea within the space of five-and-fifty days? And yet such a navy was to be seen in the first war of Carthage, led thither by Duilius the Roman. In the wars also against Hiero 220 tall ships bare leaf and sail within five-and-forty days. In the second war of Carthage the navy that went with Scipio was felled in the wood and seen to sail on the sea fully furnished in six weeks, which unto them that are ignorant of things doth seem to be false and unpossible.[1] In like manner, for multitude, we find in Polybius that at one skirmish on the sea the Romans lost seven hundred vessels, which bare each of them five rows of oars on a side, and the Carthaginians five hundred.[2] And albeit the forms and apparel of these vessels were not altogether correspondent to our ships and galleys made in these days, yet the capacity of most of them did not only match but far exceed them; so that if one of their biremes only contained so much in burden as a ship of ours of six hundred ton, what shall we think of those which had seven rows of oars walking on a side?

But lest I should seem to speak more of these foreign things than the course of the history doth permit without license to digress, give me leave (I beseech thee, gentle reader) to wade yet a little further in the report of these ancient forms and kinds of vessels. For albeit that the discourse hereof maketh little to the description of our present navy in England, yet shall the re-port thereof not be unprofitable and unpleasant to such as shall read among the writings of their capacities and molds. It shall not be amiss, therefore, to begin at the navy of Xerxes, of which each mean vessel (as appeareth by Herodotus) was able to receive 230 soldiers, and some of them three hundred.[3] These were called triremes and were indeed galleys that had three rows of oars on every side; for the word *navis* is indifferently applied so well to the galley as ship, as to the conversant in histories is easy to be found. In old time also they had galleys of 4 rows, 5 rows, 6, 7, 8, 9, 12, yea, 15 rows of oars on a side; judge you then of what

---

[1] All three examples are drawn from Pliny, *Natural History*, XVI, lxxiv.
[2] *Histories*, I, 63.
[3] *History*, VII, 184. But all the classical references in this paragraph are borrowed from Budé, *De asse* (Lyons, 1551, pp. 643–645).

quantity those vessels were. Pliny (*lib.* 7) noteth one Damastes to be the first maker of the galleys with 2 rows called biremes; Thucydides referreth the triremes to Aminocles of Corinth; the quadriremes were devised by Aristotle of Carthage, the quinquiremes by Mnesigiton of Salamis, the galley of 6 rows by Xenagoras of Syracuse; from this to the tenth Mnesigiton brought up; Alexander the Great caused one to be made of 12, Ptolemy Soter of 15, Demetrius, the son of Antigonus, of 30, Ptolemy Philadelphus of 40, Ptolemy Tryphon of 50; [4] all which above four were none other (in mine opinion) than unwieldy carts and more serving for pleasure and to gaze upon than any use in the wars for which they should be devised. But of all other I note one of 40 rows which Ptolemy Philopator builded, containing 280 cubits in length and 48 cubits in breadth; it held also 4,000 oars [oarsmen], 400 mariners, and 3,000 soldiers, so that in the said vessel were 7,400 persons, a report incredible if truth and good testimony did not confirm the same.[5] I must needs confess, therefore, that the ancient vessels far exceeded ours for capacity; nevertheless, if you regard the form and the assurance from peril of the sea and therewithal the strength and nimbleness of such as are made in our time, you shall easily find that ours are of more value than theirs; for as the greatest vessel is not always the safest, so that of most huge capacity is not always the aptest to shift and brook the seas, as might be seen by the "Great Henry," [6] the hugest vessel that ever England framed in our times. Neither were the ships of old like unto ours in mold and manner of building above the water (for of low galleys in our seas we make small account) nor so full of ease within, sith time hath engendered more skill in the wrights and brought all things to more perfection than they had in the beginning. And now to come unto our purpose at the first intended.

The navy of England may be divided into three sorts, of which the one serveth for the wars, the other for burden, and the third for fishermen which get their living by fishing on the sea. How many of the first order are maintained within the realm it passeth my cunning to express, yet sith it may be parted into

---

[4] Pliny, VII, lvi. Harrison has the details somewhat garbled.
[5] Athenaeus, *The Deipnosophists*, V, 203–204.
[6] The "Henry Grace à Dieu," launched in 1514, burned accidentally in 1553. At 1,000 tons the ship had a reputation for clumsiness.

the Navy Royal and common fleet, I think good to speak of those that belong unto the prince, and so much the rather for that their number is certain and well known to very many. Certes there is no prince in Europe that hath a more beautiful or gallant sort of ships than the Queen's Majesty of England at this present, and those generally are of such exceeding force that two of them, being well appointed and furnished as they ought, will not let to encounter with three or four of those of other countries, and either bouge them [stave them in] or put them to flight if they may not bring them home.

Neither are the molds of any foreign barks so conveniently made to brook so well one sea as another, lying upon the shore in any part of the Continent, as those of England. And therefore the common report that strangers make of our ships amongst themselves is daily confirmed to be true, which is that for strength, assurance, nimbleness, and swiftness of sailing there are no vessels in the world to be compared with ours. And all these are committed to the regiment and safe custody of the admiral, who is so called (as some imagine) of the Greek word *almiras*, a captain on the sea, for so saith Zonaras (in "Basilio Macedone" and "Basilio Porphyriogenito"),[7] though other fetch it from *ad mare*, the Latin words, another sort from *amyras*, the Saracen magistrate, or from some French derivation; but these things are not for this place, and therefore I pass them over. The Queen's Highness hath at this present (which is the four-and-twentieth of her reign)[8] already made and furnished to the number of four- or five-and-twenty great ships, which lie for the most part in Gillingham Road, beside three galleys, of whose particular names and furnitures (so far forth as I can come by them) it shall not be amiss to make report at this time.

The names of so many ships belonging to Her Majesty as
I could come by at this present:

"The Bonadventure"	"Foresight"
"Elizabeth Jonas" [9]	"Swift Suit" ["Swiftsure"]

[7] *Zonaras:* Byzantine historian of the twelfth century; his *Annals* cover the period from the Creation to 1118.

[8] That is, 1582. A number of such dated passages occur to suggest that Harrison worked on the revised edition over a period of years.

[9] The 1577 edition adds: "a name devised by Her Grace in remembrance of her own deliverance from the fury of her enemies, from which in one respect she was no less miraculously preserved than was the prophet Jonas from the belly of the whale."

"White Bear"

"Philip and Mary" [10]

"Triumph"

"Bull"

"Tiger" [11]

"Antelope"

"Hope"

"Lion"

"Victory"

"Mary Rose"

"Aid"

"Handmaid"

"Dreadnought"

"Swallow"

"Jennet"

"Bark of Boulogne" [12]

"Achates"

"Falcon"

"George"

"Revenge"

It is said that, as kings and princes have in the young days of the world and long since framed themselves to erect every year a city in some one place or other of their kingdoms (and no small wonder that Sardanapalus should begin and finish two, to wit, Anchiale and Tarsus in one day),[13] so Her Grace doth yearly build one ship or other to the better defense of her frontiers from the enemy. But as of this report I have no assured certainty, so it shall suffice to have said so much of these things; yet this I think worthy further to be added, that if they should all be driven to service at one instant (which God forbid), she should have a power by sea of about nine or ten thousand men, which were a notable company, beside the supply of other vessels appertaining to her subjects to furnish up her voyage.

Beside these Her Grace hath other in hand also, of whom hereafter, as their turns do come about, I will not let to leave some further remembrance. She hath likewise three notable galleys, the "Speedwell," the "Tryright," and the "Black Galley," with the sight whereof and rest of the Navy Royal it is incredible to say how greatly Her Grace is delighted, and not without great cause (I say), sith by their means her coasts are kept in quiet and sundry foreign enemies put back, which otherwise would invade us. The number of those that serve for burden, with the other whereof I have made mention already and whose use is daily seen as occasion serveth in time of the wars, is to me utterly unknown. Yet if the report of one record be anything at all to be credited, there are 135 ships that exceed 500 ton;

[10] Renamed the "Nonpareil" in time for the Armada.

[11] The 1577 edition adds: "so called of her exceeding nimbleness in sailing and swiftness of course."

[12] The same list, together with the three galleys mentioned later, is given by Lambarde, *Perambulation of Kent* (1576), pp. 276-277. The last four names were added in 1587.   [13] Strabo, *Geography*, XIV, v, 9.

topmen under 100 and above 40, 656; hoys, 100; but of hulks, ketches, fisherboats, and crayers [14] it lieth not in me to deliver the just account, sith they are hardly to come by. Of these also there are some of the Queen's Majesty's subjects that have two or three, some, four or six, and (as I heard of late) one man, whose name I suppress for modesty's sake, hath been known not long since to have had sixteen or seventeen, and employed them wholly to the wafting in and out of our merchants, whereby he hath reaped no small commodity and gain.

I might take occasion to tell of the notable and difficult voyages made into strange countries by Englishmen and of their daily success there, but as these things are nothing incident to my purpose, so I surcease to speak of them. Only this will I add, to the end all men shall understand somewhat of the great masses of treasure daily employed upon our navy, how there are few of those ships of the first and second sort that, being appareled and made ready to sail, are not worth £ 1,000, or 3,000 ducats at the least, if they should presently be sold. What shall we think then of the greater, but especially of the Navy Royal, of which some one vessel is worth two of the other, as the shipwrights have often told me? It is possible that some covetous person hearing this report will either not credit it at all or suppose money so employed to be nothing profitable to the Queen's coffers, as a good husband said once when he heard there should be provision made for armor, wishing the Queen's money to be rather laid out to some speedier return of gain unto Her Grace, "because the realm," saith he, "is in case good enough," and so peradventure he thought. But if as by store of armor for the defense of the country he had likewise understanded that the good keeping of the sea is the safeguard of our land, he would have altered his censure and soon given over his judgment.

For in times past, when our nation made small account of navigation, how soon did the Romans, then the Saxons, and last of all the Danes invade this island, whose cruelty in the end enforced our countrymen, as it were even against their wills, to provide for ships from other places and build at home of their own, whereby their enemies were oftentimes distressed. But

---

[14] *Topmen:* ships having tops on their masts; *hoys:* flat-bottomed, bargelike vessels; *hulks:* large merchant ships; *ketches:* smaller two-masted vessels; *crayers:* small trading vessels.

most of all were the Normans therein to be commended. For in a short process of time after the conquest of this island and good consideration had for the well-keeping of the same, they supposed nothing more commodious for the defense of the country than the maintenance of a strong navy, which they speedily provided, maintained, and thereby reaped in the end their wished security, wherewith before their times this island was never acquainted. Before the coming of the Romans I do not read that we had any ships at all, except a few made of wicker and covered with buffle [buffalo, ox] hides, like unto the which there are some to be seen at this present in Scotland (as I hear), although there be a little (I wot not well what) difference between them. Of the same, also, Solinus speaketh, so far as I remember; nevertheless, it may be gathered by his words how the upper parts of them above the water only were framed of the said wickers and that the Britons did use to fast all the whiles they went to the sea in them, but whether it were done for policy or superstition as yet I do not read.[15]

In the beginning of the Saxons' regiment we had some ships also, but as their number and mold was little and nothing to the purpose, so Egbert was the first prince that ever thoroughly began to know this necessity of a navy and use the service thereof in the defense of his country. After him, also, other princes, as Alfred, Edgar, Ethelred, etc., endeavored more and more to store themselves at the full with ships of all quantities, but chiefly Edgar, for he provided a navy of 1,600, *alias* 3,600 sail, which he divided into four parts and sent them to abide upon four sundry coasts of the land to keep the same from pirates. Next unto him (and worthy to be remembered) is Ethelred, who made a law that every man holding 310 hidelands should find a ship furnished to serve him in the wars.[16] Howbeit, and as I said before, when all their navy was at the greatest it was not comparable for force and sure building to that which afterward

[15] *Gaius Julius Solinus* (fl. A.D. 200): author of *Collectanea rerum memorabilium*, a geographical summary based largely on Pliny. As translated by Arthur Golding (1587, sig. P2v) the passage reads: "They sail in keels of wicker done over with neat's leather. How long soever their passage continueth, the passengers abstain from meat." Hector Boece mentions the currachs of the Scottish Highlanders, "made of osiers and covered with bullhides" (*Des. Scot.*, trans. Harrison, 1587, p. 22).

[16] These details about the Anglo-Saxon navies derive from Florence of Worcester's *Chronicle*, under 833, 975, and 1008.

the Normans provided, neither that of the Normans anything like to the same that is to be seen now in these our days.

For the journeys also of our ships you shall understand that a well-builded vessel will run or sail commonly 300 leagues or 900 miles in a week, or peradventure some will go 2,200 leagues in 6½ weeks. And surely if their lading be ready against they come thither, there be of them that will be here, at the West Indies, and home again in twelve or thirteen weeks from Colchester, although the said Indies be 800 leagues from the cape or point of Cornwall, as I have been informed. This also I understand by report of some travelers, that if any of our vessels happen to make a voyage to Hispaniola, or New Spain, called in time past Quinquezia [Quisquica] and Haiti, and lieth between the north tropic and the equator, after they have once touched at the Canaries (which are eight days' sailing or 250 leagues from Sanlúcar de Barrameda in Spain), they will be there in thirty or forty days and home again in Cornwall in other eight weeks, which is a goodly matter, beside the safety and quietness in the passage. But more of this elsewhere.

CHAPTER XVIII

Of Fairs and Markets

THERE are (as I take it) few great towns in England that have not their weekly markets, one or more granted from the prince, in which all manner of provision for household is to be bought and sold for ease and benefit of the country round about. Whereby, as it cometh to pass that no buyer shall make any great journey in the purveyance of his necessities, so no occupier shall have occasion to travel far off with his commodities, except it be to seek for the highest prices, which commonly are near unto great cities, where round and speediest utterance is always to be had. And as these have been in times past erected for the benefit of the realm, so are they in many places too-too much abused, for the relief and ease of the buyer is not so much intended in them as the benefit of the seller. Neither are the magistrates for the most part (as men loath to displease their neighbors for their one year's dignity) so careful in their offices as of right and duty they should be. For in most of these markets neither assizes of bread [1] nor orders for goodness and sweetness of grain and other commodities that are brought thither to be sold are any whit looked unto but each one suffered to sell or set up what and how himself listeth, and this is one evident cause of dearth and scarcity in time of great abundance.

I could (if I would) exemplify in many, but I will touch no one particularly, sith it is rare to see in any country town (as I said) the assize of bread well kept according to the statute. And yet if any country baker happen to come in among them on the market day with bread of better quantity, they find fault by and by with one thing or another in his stuff; whereby the honest poor man, whom the law of nations do commend for that he endeavoreth to live by any lawful means, is driven away and no more to come there upon some round penalty by virtue of their privileges. Howbeit, though they are so nice in the proportion of their bread, yet in lieu of the same there is such heady ale and beer in most of them as for the mightiness thereof among such as seek it out is commonly called huffcap, the maddog, father-whoreson, angels'-food, dragons'-milk, go-by-the-wall, stride-wide, and lift-leg, etc. And this is more to be noted, that when one of late fell by God's providence into a troubled conscience, after he had considered well of his rechless life and dangerous estate, another, thinking belike to change his color and not his mind, carried him straightway to the strongest ale as to the next physician. It is incredible to say how our maltbugs lug [suck] at this liquor, even as pigs should lie in a row lugging at their dam's teats till they lie still again and be not able to wag. Neither did Romulus and Remus suck their she-wolf, or shepherd's wife, Lupa, with such eager and sharp devotion as these men hale at huffcap till they be red as cocks and little wiser than their combs. But how am I fallen from the market into the alehouse? In returning, therefore, unto my purpose, I find that in corn great abuse is daily suffered, to the great prejudice of the town and country, especially the poor artificer and householder

---

[1] *Assizes of bread:* the statutory regulation of the weight, price, and ingredients of bread.

which tilleth no land but, laboring all the week to buy a bushel or two of grain on the market day, can there have none for his money, because bodgers, loders,[2] and common carriers of corn do not only buy up all but give above the price to be served of great quantities. Shall I go any further? Well, I will say yet a little more and somewhat by mine own experience.

At Michaelmas-time poor men must make money of their grain that they may pay their rents. So long, then, as the poor man hath to sell, rich men will bring out none but rather buy up that which the poor bring, under pretense of seed corn or alteration of grain, although they bring none of their own, because one wheat often sowen without change of seed will soon decay and be converted into darnel. For this cause, therefore, they must needs buy in the markets, though they be twenty miles off, and where they be not known, promising there, if they happen to be espied (which, God wot, is very seldom) to send so much to their next market, to be performed I wot not when.

If this shift serve not (neither doth the fox use always one track for fear of a snare), they will compound with someone of the town where the market is holden, who for a pot of huffcap or merry-go-down will not let to buy it for them, and that in his own name. Or else they wage one poor man or other to become a bodger and thereto get him a license upon some forged surmise; which being done, they will feed him with money to buy for them till he hath filled their lofts, and then if he can do any good for himself, so it is; if not, they will give him somewhat for his pains at this time and reserve him for another year. How many of the like providers stumble upon blind creeks at the seacoast,[3] I wot not well, but that some have so done and yet do under other men's wings the case is too-too plain. But who dare find fault with them when they have once a license? Yea, though it be but to serve a mean gentleman's house with corn, who hath cast up all his tillage because he boasteth how he can buy his grain in the market better cheap than he can sow his land, as the rich grazier often doth also upon the like device because grazing requireth a smaller household and less attendance and charge.

---

[2] *Bodgers:* badgers, itinerant dealers in grain, who buy in the market to sell again; *loders:* laders, those who freight ships, but perhaps here simply synonymous with carriers. Both terms occur in the statute 5 Eliz., c. 12, which required their licensing.

[3] That is, smuggle grain out of the country.

If any man come to buy a bushel or two for his expenses unto the market cross, answer is made, "Forsooth, here was one even now that bade me money for it, and I hope he will have it." And to say the truth, these bodgers are fair chapmen, for there are no more words with them but, "Let me see it, what shall I give you? Knit it up, I will have it, go carry it to such a chamber, and if you bring in twenty seam more in the weekday to such an inn or solar [4] where I lay my corn, I will have it and give you [——] pence or more in every bushel for six weeks' day of payment than another will." Thus the bodgers bear away all, so that the poor artificer and laborer cannot make his provision in the markets, sith they will hardly nowadays sell by the bushel nor break their measure; and so much the rather for that the buyer will look (as they say) for so much overmeasure in a bushel as the bodger will do in a quarter. Nay, the poor man cannot oft get any of the farmer at home, because he provideth altogether to serve the bodger or hath an hope, grounded upon a greedy and insatiable desire of gain, that the sale will be better in the market, so that he must give twopence or a groat more in a bushel at his house than the last market craved or else go without it and sleep with an hungry belly. Of the common carriage of corn over unto the parts beyond the seas I speak not; or at the leastwise, if I should, I could not touch it alone but needs must join other provision withal, whereby not only our friends abroad but also many of our adversaries and countrymen, the papists, are abundantly relieved (as the report goeth); but sith I see it not, I will not so trust mine ears as to write it for a truth. But to return to our markets again.

By this time the poor occupier hath all sold his crop for need of money, being ready peradventure to buy again ere long. And now is the whole sale of corn in the great occupiers' hands, who hitherto have threshed little or none of their own but bought up of other men so much as they could come by. Henceforth also they begin to sell, not by the quarter or load at the first, for marring the market, but by the bushel or two, or an horseload at the most, thereby to be seen to keep the cross, either for a show or to make men eager to buy, and so as they may have it for money, not to regard what they pay. And thus corn waxeth dear, but it

[4] *Seam:* a horseload, about eight bushels; *solar:* a loft or garret used as a granary.

will be dearer the next market day. It is possible also that they mislike the price in the beginning for the whole year ensuing, as men
supposing that corn will be little worth for this and of better
price in the next year. For they have certain superstitious observations whereby they will give a guess at the sale of corn for
the year following. And our countrymen do use commonly for
barley, where I dwell, to judge after the price at Baldock upon
St. Matthew's Day [September 21] and for wheat as it is sold in
seedtime. They take in like sort experiment by sight of the first
flocks of cranes that flee southward in winter, the age of the
moon in the beginning of January, and such other apish toys,
as by laying twelve corns upon the hot hearth for the twelve
months, etc., whereby they show themselves to be scant good
Christians; but what care they so they may come by money?

Hereupon also will they thresh out three parts of the old corn
toward the latter end of the summer when new cometh apace to
hand, and cast the same in the fourth unthreshed, where it shall
lie until the next spring or peradventure till it must and putrefy.
Certes it is not dainty [rare] to see musty corn in many of our
great markets of England, which these great occupiers bring
forth when they can keep it no longer. But as they are enforced
oftentimes upon this one occasion somewhat to abate the price,
so a plague is not seldom engendered thereby among the poorer
sort that of necessity must buy the same, whereby many thousands of all degrees are consumed, of whose deaths (in mine
opinion) these farmers are not unguilty. But to proceed. If they
lay not up their grain or wheat in this manner, they have yet
another policy whereby they will seem to have but small store
left in their barns; for they will gird their sheaves by the band
and stack it up of new in less room, to the end it may not only
seem less in quantity but also give place to the corn that is yet
to come into the barn or growing in the field. If there happen
to be such plenty in the market on any market day that they
cannot sell at their own price, then will they set it up in some
friend's house against another or the third day and not bring it
forth till they like of the sale. If they sell any at home, beside
harder measure it shall be dearer to the poor man that buyeth
it by twopence or a groat in a bushel than they may sell it in the
market. But as these things are worthy redress, so I wish that
God would once open their eyes that deal thus to see their own

errors; for as yet some of them little care how many poor men suffer extremity, so that they may fill their purses and carry away the gain.

It is a world, also, to see how most places of the realm are pestered with purveyors, who take up eggs, butter, cheese, pigs, capons, hens, chickens, hogs, bacon, etc., in one market under pretense of their commissions and suffer their wives to sell the same in another or to poulterers of London. If these chapmen be absent but two or three market days, then we may perfectly see these wares to be more reasonably sold and thereunto the crosses sufficiently furnished of all things. In like sort, since the number of buttermen have so much increased and since they travel in such wise that they come to men's houses for their butter faster than they can make it, it is almost incredible to see how the price of butter is augmented; whereas, when the owners were enforced to bring it to the market towns and fewer of these butter buyers were stirring, our butter was scarcely worth 18*d.* the gallon that now is worth 3*s.* 4*d.* and perhaps 5*s.* Whereby also I gather that the maintenance of a superfluous number of dealers in most trades, tillage always excepted, is one of the greatest causes why the prices of things become excessive, for one of them do commonly use to outbid another. And whilst our country commodities are commonly bought and sold at our private houses, I never look to see this enormity redressed or the markets well furnished.

I could say more, but this is even enough and more peradventure than I shall be well thanked for; yet true it is, though some think it no trespass. This, moreover, is to be lamented, that one general measure is not in use throughout all England, but every market town hath in manner a several bushel, and the lesser it be the more sellers it draweth to resort unto the same. Such also is the covetousness of many clerks of the market that, in taking view of measures, they will alway so provide that one and the same bushel shall be either too big or too little at their next coming, and yet not depart without a fee at the first; so that, what by their mending at one time and impairing the same at another, the country is greatly charged and few just measures to be had in any stead. It is oft found likewise that divers unconscionable dealers have one measure to sell by and another to buy withal; the like is also in weights and yet all sealed and branded.

Wherefore it were very good that these two were reduced unto one standard, that is, one bushel, one pound, one quarter, one hundred, one tale,[5] one number; so should things in time fall into better order and fewer causes of contention be moved in this land.[6] Of the complaint of such poor tenants as pay rent-corn unto their landlords I speak not, who are often dealt withal very hardly. For beside that in the measuring of ten quarters for the most part they lose one through the iniquity of the bushel (such is the greediness of the appointed receivers thereof), fault is found also with the goodness and cleanness of the grain. Whereby some piece of money must needs pass unto their purses to stop their mouths withal, or else my lord will not like of the corn, "Thou art worthy to lose thy lease, etc." Or if it be cheaper in the market than the rate allowed for it is in their rents, then must they pay money and no corn, which is no small extremity. And thereby we may see how each one of us endeavoreth to fleece and eat up another.

Another thing there is in our markets worthy to be looked unto and that is the recarriage of grain from the same into lofts and solars, of which before I gave some intimation; wherefore if it were ordered that every seller should make his market by an hour, or else the bailie [bailiff] or clerk of the said market to make sale thereof according to his discretion, without liberty to the farmer to set up their corn in houses and chambers, I am persuaded that the prices of our grain would soon be abated. Again, if it were enacted that each one should keep his next market with his grain and not to run six, eight, ten, fourteen, or twenty miles from home to sell his corn where he doth find the highest price, and thereby leaveth his neighbors unfurnished, I do not think but that our markets would be far better served than at this present they are. Finally, if men's barns might be indifferently viewed immediately after harvest, and a note gathered by an estimate and kept by some appointed and trusty person for that purpose, we should have much more plenty of corn in our town crosses than as yet is commonly seen, because each one hideth and hoardeth what he may, upon purpose either

[5] *Tale:* the number included in a quantity.
[6] The 1577 edition added: "But more of this hereafter in the next book, where I have inserted a little treatise which I sometimes collected of our weights and measures, and their comparison with those of the ancient Greeks and Romans." Harrison's treatise comprised chapters xxii–xxv of Book III in the 1577 edition. They were dropped in 1587. See p. 453, n. 1.

that it will be dearer or that he shall have some privy vein by bodgers, who do accustomably so deal that the sea doth load away no small part thereof into other countries and our enemies, to the great hindrance of our commonwealth at home, and more likely yet to be except some remedy be found. But what do I talk of these things or desire the suppression of bodgers, being a minister? Certes I may speak of them right well, as feeling the harm in that I am a buyer; nevertheless, I speak generally in each of them.

To conclude, therefore, in our markets all things are to be sold necessary for man's use; and there is our provision made commonly for all the week ensuing. Therefore, as there are no great towns without one weekly market at the least, so there are very few of them that have not one or two fairs or more within the compass of the year assigned unto them by the prince. And albeit that some of them are not much better than Louse Fair [7] or the common kirkmesses [8] beyond the sea, yet there are divers not inferior to the greatest marts in Europe, as Sturbridge Fair near to Cambridge, Bristol Fair, Bartholomew Fair at London, Lynn Mart, Cold Fair at Newport Pond [9] for cattle, and divers other, all which, or at leastwise the greatest part of them (to the end I may with the more ease to the reader and less travail to myself fulfill my task in their recital), I have set down according to the names of the months wherein they are holden at the end of this book, where you shall find them at large as I borrowed the same from J. Stow and the reports of others.[10]

CHAPTER XIX

Of Parks and Warrens

IN EVERY shire of England there is great plenty of parks, whereof some here and there, to wit, wellnear to the number of two hundred, for her daily provision of that flesh appertain to the

---

[7] *Louse Fair:* later Rag Fair in London.
[8] *Kirkmesses:* kermises, in Germany and the I v Countries annual fairs.
[9] *Newport Pond:* now Newport, near H ..rison's Radwinter. In *The Description of Britain* (1587, p. 36) the fair is spelled Cole; John Norden calls it Colt Fair. [10] See pp. 392–397.

prince, the rest to such of the nobility and gentlemen as have their lands and patrimonies lying in or near unto the same. I would gladly have set down the just number of these enclosures to be found in every county, but, sith I cannot so do, it shall suffice to say that in Kent and Essex only are to the number of an hundred, and twenty in the bishopric of Durham, wherein great plenty of fallow deer is cherished and kept. As for warrens of conies, I judge them almost innumerable and daily like to increase, by reason that the black skins of those beasts are thought to countervail [match] the prices of their naked carcasses, and this is the only cause why the gray are less esteemed. Near unto London their quickest merchandise is of the young rabbits, wherefore the older conies are brought from further off, where there is no such speedy utterance of rabbits and sucklings in their season nor so great loss by their skins, sith they are suffered to grow up to their full greatness with their owners.

Our parks are generally enclosed with strong pale[1] made of oak, of which kind of wood there is great store cherished in the woodland countries from time to time in each of them, only for the maintenance of the said defense and safekeeping of the fallow deer from ranging about the country. Howbeit, in times past divers have been fenced in with stone walls (especially in the times of the Romans, who first brought fallow deer into this land, as some conjecture), albeit those enclosures were overthrown again by the Saxons and Danes, as Caversham, Tonmer, and Woodstock, beside other in the West Country and one also at Bolton. Among other things also to be seen in that town, there is one of the fairest clocks in Europe.[2] Where no wood is, they are also enclosed with piles of slate; and thereto it is doubted of many whether our buck or doe are to be reckoned in wild or tame beasts or not. Pliny deemeth them to be wild; Martial is also of the same opinion where he saith, *Imbelles damae quid nisi praeda sumus?*[3] And so in time past the like controversy was about bees, which the lawyers call *feras* (tit., "*De acquirendo rerum dominio,*" *et lib.* 2, *instit.*)[4] But Pliny, attempting to decide

---

[1] *Pale:* paling, a fence of stakes driven into the ground.

[2] Leland, *Itinerary* (ed. Smith, V, 140).

[3] "What are we, unwarlike deer, but prey?" (*Epigrams*, XIII, xciv); Pliny classes *damae*, fallow deer, as wild in his *Natural History*, VIII, lxxix.

[4] *Feras:* wild; Bracton, *De legibus et consuetudinibus Angliae*, at the beginning of Bk. II, "Of Acquiring Dominion over Things."

the quarrel, calleth them *medias inter feras et placidas aves.*[5] But whither am I so suddenly digressed?

In returning, therefore, unto our parks, I find also the circuit of these enclosures in like manner contain oftentimes a walk of four or five miles, and sometimes more or less. Whereby it is to be seen what store of ground is employed upon that vain commodity, which bringeth no manner of gain or profit to the owner, sith they commonly give away their flesh, never taking penny for the same, except the ordinary fee and parts of the deer given unto the keeper by a custom, who, beside 3*s.* 4*d.* or 5*s.* in money, hath the skin, head, umbles [numbles, entrails], chine, and shoulders, whereby he that hath the warrant for an whole buck hath in the end little more than half, which in my judgment is scarcely equal dealing; for venison in England is neither bought nor sold as in other countries but maintained only for the pleasure of the owner and his friends. Albeit I heard of late of one ancient lady which maketh a great gain by selling yearly her husband's venison to the cooks (as another of no less name will not stick to ride to the market to see her butter sold), but not performed without infinite scoffs and mocks, even of the poorest peasants of the country, who think them as odious matters in ladies and women of such countenance to sell their venison and their butter as for an earl to feel his oxen, sheep, and lambs, whether they be ready for the butcher or not, or to sell his wool unto the clothier or to keep a tanhouse or deal with suchlike affairs as belong not to men of honor but rather to farmers or graziers; for which such, if there be any, may well be noted (and not unjustly) to degenerate from true nobility and betake themselves to husbandry.

And even the same enormity took place sometime among the Romans and entered so far as into the very senate, of whom some one had two or three ships going upon the sea, pretending provision for their houses but in truth following the trades of merchandise, till a law was made which did inhibit and restrain them. Livy also telleth of another law which passed likewise against the senators by Claudius, the tribune, and help only of C. Flaminius, that no senator or he that had been father to any senator should possess any ship or vessel above the capacity of three hundred amphoras,[6] which was supposed sufficient for the

[5] "In the middle between wild and tame winged species" (VIII, lxxxii).
[6] *Amphoras:* wine jars; liquid measures of about six gals. This was the Lex Claudia of 218 B.C. (Livy, XXI, lxiii).

carriage and recarriage of such necessities as should appertain unto his house, sith further trading with merchandises and commodities doth declare but a base and covetous mind, not altogether void of envy that any man should live but he, or that if any gain were to be had he only would have it himself, which is a wonderful dealing and must needs prove in time the confusion of that country wherein such enormities are exercised.

Where in times past many large and wealthy occupiers were dwelling within the compass of some one park, and thereby great plenty of corn and cattle seen and to be had among them, beside a more copious procreation of human issue, whereby the realm was always better furnished with able men to serve the prince in his affairs, now there is almost nothing kept but a sort of wild and savage beasts, cherished for pleasure and delight; and yet some owners, still desirous to enlarge those grounds as either for the breed and feeding of cattle, do not let daily to take in more, not sparing the very commons whereupon many townships now and then do live, affirming that we have already too great store of people in England and that youth by marrying too soon do nothing profit the country but fill it full of beggars, to the hurt and utter undoing (they say) of the commonwealth.

Certes if it be not one curse of the Lord to have our country converted in such sort, from the furniture of mankind into the walks and shrouds [shelters] of wild beasts, I know not what is any.[7] How many families also these great and small games (for so most keepers call them) have eaten up and are likely hereafter to devour, some men may conjecture but many more lament, sith there is no hope of restraint to be looked for in this behalf because the corruption is so general. But if a man may presently give a guess at the universality of this evil by contemplation of the circumstance, he shall say at the last that the twentieth part of the realm is employed upon deer and conies already, which seemeth very much if it be duly [8] considered of.

King Henry the Eighth, one of the noblest princes that ever reigned in this land, lamented oft that he was constrained to hire foreign aid, for want of competent store of soldiers here at home,

---

[7] "The decay of the people is the destruction of a kingdom."—*H*. The 1577 edition adds to the note: "Neither is any man born to possess the earth alone."

[8] So in 1577; the 1587 edition reads "be not," apparently in error.

perceiving (as it is indeed) that such supplies are oftentimes more hurtful than profitable unto those that entertain them, as may chiefly be seen in Valens, the Emperor, our Vortigern,[9] and no small number of others. He would oft marvel in private talk how that, when seven or eight princes ruled here at once, one of them could lead thirty or forty thousand men to the field against another, or two of them a hundred thousand against the third, and those taken out only of their own dominions. But as he found the want, so he saw not the cause of this decay, which grew beside this occasion now mentioned; also by laying house to house and land to land, whereby many men's occupyings were converted into one and the breed of people not a little thereby diminished. The avarice of landlords, by increasing of rents and fines, also did so weary the people that they were ready to rebel with him that would arise, supposing a short end in the wars to be better than a long and miserable life in peace.

Privileges and faculties [licenses for monopolies] also are another great cause of the ruin of a commonwealth and diminution of mankind; for whereas law and nature doth permit all men to live in their best manner and whatsoever trade they be exercised in, there cometh some privilege or other in the way which cutteth them off from this or that trade, whereby they must needs shift soil and seek unto other countries. By these, also, the greatest commodities are brought into the hands of few, who embase, corrupt, and yet raise the prices of things at their own pleasures. Example of this last I can give also in books, which (after the first impression of any one book) are for the most part very negligently handled; whereas if another might print it so well as the first,[10] then would men strive which of them should do it best; and so it falleth out in all other trades.

It is an easy matter to prove that England was never less furnished with people than at this present; for if the old records of every manor be sought and search made to find what tenements are fallen either down or into the lord's hands, or brought and

---

[9] *Valens:* Eastern Roman Emperor in 364–378, who permitted the Goths to settle south of the Danube in Roman territory; *Vortigern:* King of the Britons ca. 450, who employed the Saxons under Hengist and Horsa against the Scots and Picts and allowed them to settle in England.

[10] By the rules of the Stationers' Company the entry in their Registers of a book by a printer or publisher gave him sole rights in the printing of that work.

united together by other men, it will soon appear that in some one manor seventeen, eighteen, or twenty houses are shrunk. I know what I say by mine own experience, notwithstanding that some one cottage be here and there erected of late, which is to little purpose. Of cities and towns either utterly decayed or more than a quarter or half diminished, though some one be a little increased here and there, of towns pulled down for sheepwalks and no more but the lordship's now standing in them, beside those that William Rufus pulled down in his time, I could say somewhat, but then I should swerve yet further from my purpose, whereunto I now return.

We had no parks left in England at the coming of the Normans, who added this calamity also to the servitude of our nation, making men of the best sort furthermore to become keepers of their game, whilst they lived in the meantime upon the spoil of their revenues and daily overthrew towns, villages, and an infinite sort of families for the maintenance of their venery [hunting]. Neither was any park supposed in these times to be stately enough that contained not at the least eight or ten hidelands, that is, so many hundred acres or families (or, as they have been always called in some places of the realm, carucates or cartwares),[11] of which one was sufficient in old time to maintain an honest yeoman.

King John, traveling on a time northwards, to wit, 1209, to war upon the King of Scots because he had married his daughter to the Earl of Boulogne without his consent, in his return overthrew a great number of parks and warrens, of which some belonged to his barons but the greatest part to the abbots and prelates of the clergy. For hearing (as he traveled) by complaint of the country how these enclosures were the chief decay of men and of tillage in the land, he sware with an oath that he would not suffer wild beasts to feed upon the fat of his soil and see the people perish, for want of ability to procure and buy them food, that should defend the realm. Howbeit, this act of his was so ill taken by the religious and their adherents that they inverted his intent herein

---

[11] "In Lincolnshire the word hide or hideland was never in use in old time as in other places, but for hide they used the word carucate or cartware or team, and these were of no less compass than an hideland" (*Des. Brit.*, 1587, p. 30). Harrison gives as his source *The Chronicle of Hugh Candidus* (ed. W. T. Mellows, p. 72).

to another end, affirming most slanderously how he did it rather of purpose to spoil the corn and grass of the commons and Catholics that held against him of both estates, and by so doing to impoverish and bring the north part of the realm to destruction, because they refused to go with him into Scotland. If the said prince were alive in these days, wherein Andrew Boorde saith there are more parks in England than in all Europe (over which he traveled in his own person),[12] and saw how much ground they consume, I think he would either double his oaths or lay the most of them open, that tillage might be better looked unto. But this I hope shall not need in time, for the owners of a great sort of them begin now to smell out that such parcels might be employed to their more gain, and therefore some of them do grow to be disparked.

Next of all we have the frank chase, which taketh something both of park and forest, and is given either by the King's grant or prescription. Certes it differeth not much from a park; nay, it is in manner the selfsame thing that a park is, saving that a park is environed with pale, wall, or suchlike, the chase alway open and nothing at all enclosed, as we see in Enfield and Malvern Chases. And as it is the cause of the seizure of the franchise of a park not to keep the same enclosed, so it is the like in a chase if at any time it be imparked. It is trespass and against the law also for any man to have or make a chase, park, or free warren without good warranty of the King by his charter or perfect title of prescription; for it is not lawful for any subject either to carnilate, that is, build stone houses, embattle, have the wreck of the sea, or keep the assize of bread, ale, or wine, or set up furels, tumbrel, thew,[13] or pillory, or enclose any ground to the aforesaid purposes within his own soil, without his warrant and grant.

The beasts of the chase were commonly the buck, the roe, the fox, and the marten. But those of venery in old time were the

---

[12] *Dietary of Health* (ed. Frederick J. Furnivall, EETS, Ex. Ser., X, 1870, 274), but the reference is borrowed from John Stow, *Summary of English Chronicles* (1570), fol. 4r.

[13] *Carnilate:* actually to crenelate, furnish with battlements, a synonym for embattle; *wreck of the sea:* whatever is cast ashore; *furels:* the word seems unique to Harrison, perhaps related to furca or forches, meaning gallows; *tumbrel, thew:* instruments of punishment, both of which have been identified with the cucking stool, a chair in which the offender was fastened and either exposed to public ridicule or ducked.

hart, the hare, the boar, and the wolf; but as this held not in the time of Canute, so instead of the wolf the bear is now crept in, which is a beast commonly hunted in the East [Baltic] countries and fed upon as excellent venison, although with us I know not any that feed thereon or care for it at all. Certes it should seem that forests and frank chases have always been had and religiously preserved in this island for the solace of the prince and recreation of his nobility; howbeit, I read not that ever they were enclosed more than at this present, or otherwise fenced than by usual notes of limitation, whereby their bounds were remembered from time to time, for the better preservation of such venery and vert [14] of all sorts as were nourished in the same. Neither are any of the ancient laws prescribed for their maintenance before the days of Canute now to be had, sith time hath so dealt with them that they are perished and lost. Canute, therefore, seeing the daily spoil that was made almost in all places of his game, did at the last make sundry sanctions and decrees, whereby from thenceforth the red and fallow deer were better looked to throughout his whole dominions.

We have in these days divers forests in England and Wales, of which some belong to the King and some to his subjects, as Waltham Forest, Windsor, Pickering, Feckenham, Delamere, Gillingham, Kingswood, Wenleysdale, Clun, Rath, Bradon, Wire, Chartley, Leicester, Lee, Rockingham, Selwood, New Forest, Wychwood, Hatfield, Savernake, Westbury, Blackmore, Peak, Dean, Penrice, and many other now clean out of my remembrance, and which, although they are far greater in circuit than many parks and warrens, yet are they in this our time less devourers of the people than these latter, sith beside much tillage many towns are found in each of them, whereas in parks and warrens we have nothing else than either the keeper's and warrener's lodge, or at least the manor place of the chief lord and owner of the soil.

I find also by good record that all Essex hath in time past wholly been forest ground, except one cantred or hundred; but how long it is since it lost the said denomination, in good sooth, I do not read. This nevertheless remaineth yet in memory, that the town of Walden in Essex, standing in the limits of the aforesaid county, doth take her name thereof. For in the Celtic tongue,

---

[14] *Vert:* green vegetation serving as cover for deer.

wherewith the Saxon or Scythian speech doth not a little participate, huge woods and forests were called *wealds;* and likewise their
druids were named *walie* or *waldie*[15] because they frequented the
woods and there made sacrifice among the oaks and thickets. So
that if my conjecture in this behalf be anything at all, the aforesaid town taketh denomination of *weald* and *end,* as if I should say,
"The end of the woody soil"; for being once out of that parish,
the champaign is at hand. Or it may be that it is so called of
weald and *dene,* for I have read it written in old evidences
"Waldaene," with a diphthong. And to say truth, *dene* is the old
Saxon word for a vale or low bottom, as *dune* or *don* is for an hill
or hilly soil.[16] Certes if it be so, then Walden taketh her name of
the woody vale in which it sometime stood. But the first derivation liketh me better; and the highest part of the town is called
also Chipping Walden of the Saxon word *ʒipping,* which signifieth "leaning" or "hanging"[17] and may very well be applied
thereunto, sith the whole town hangeth as it were upon the sides
of two hills, whereof the lesser runneth quite through the midst
of the same. I might here for further confirmation of these things
bring in mention of the Weald of Kent, but this may suffice for
the use of the word *weald,* which now differeth much from
wold. For as that signifieth a woody soil, so this betokeneth a soil
without wood or plain champaign country without any store of
trees, as may be seen in Cotswold, Porkewold, etc.[18]

Beside this I could say more of our forests and the aforesaid
enclosures also, and therein to prove by the book of forest law
that the whole county of Lancashire hath likewise been forest
heretofore. Also how William the Bastard made a law that whosoever did take any wild beast within the King's forest should lose
an ear, as Henry the First did punish them either by life or limb,
which ordinance was confirmed by Henry the Second and his
peers at Woodstock,[19] whereupon great trouble ensued under

---

[15] Jean Bodin, *Method for the Easy Comprehension of History* (trans.
Reynolds, p. 346).

[16] *Dene:* OE *denu,* dean; *dune* or *don:* OE *dún,* down.

[17] "ʒipping, of going up to any place."—*H.* Actually "chipping" is a
variant of "cheaping," a market.

[18] The distinction between *weald* and *wold,* and the names Cotswold and
Porkewold (?) are borrowed from Humphrey Llwyd, *The Breviary of
Britain,* trans. Twyne, fols. 15v-16r.

[19] The Assize of the Forest of 1184.

King John and Henry the Third, as appeareth by the chronicles; but it shall suffice to have said so much as is set down already.

Howbeit, that I may restore one antiquity to light which hath hitherto lien as it were raked up in the embers of oblivion, I will give out those laws that Canute made for his forest, whereby many things shall be disclosed concerning the same (whereof peradventure some lawyers have no knowledge), and divers other notes gathered touching the ancient estate of the realm not to be found in other. But before I deal with the great charter (which, as you may perceive, is in many places unperfect by reason of corruption and want also of congruity, crept in by length of time, not by me to be restored), I will note another brief law which he made in the first year of his reign at Winchester, afterward inserted into these his later constitutions (canon 32 [30]) and beginning thus in his own Saxon tongue: *Ic will that elc one, etc.*, "I will and grant that each one shall be worthy of such venery as he by hunting can take either in the plains or in the woods, within his own fee or dominion; but each man shall abstain from my venery in every place, where I will that my beasts shall have firm peace and quietness, upon pain to forfeit so much as a man may forfeit." [20] Hitherto the statute made by the aforesaid Canute, which was afterward confirmed by King Edward, surnamed "the Confessor," and ratified by the Bastard in the fourth year of his reign. Now followeth the great charter itself, in such rude order and Latin as I find it word for word, and which I would gladly have turned into English if it might have sounded to any benefit of the unskillful and unlearned.

[Harrison here provides the first printing of the dubiously authentic forest laws of Canute. They run to thirty-four "canons," treating in detail the administration of the forests and penal statutes against unlawful hunting and forestry. Furnivall's edition includes an English translation from John Manwood, *Brief Collection of the Laws of the Forest*, 1592. Harrison's chapter ends:]

And these are the constitutions of Canute concerning the forest, very barbarously translated by those that took the same in hand.

---

[20] This law appears as Article 77 of Canute's code, as printed by Lambarde, *Archaiŏnomia* (1568), sig. Ll2v.

Howbeit, as I find it, so I set it down without any alteration of my copy in any jot or tittle.

CHAPTER XX

Of Gardens and Orchards

AFTER such time as Calais was won from the French, and that our countrymen had learned to trade into divers countries (whereby they grew rich), they began to wax idle also and thereupon not only left off their former painfulness and frugality but in like sort gave themselves to live in excess and vanity, whereby many goodly commodities failed and in short time were not to be had amongst us. Such strangers also as dwelled here with us, perceiving our sluggishness and espying that this idleness of ours might redound to their great profit, forthwith employed their endeavors to bring in the supply of such things as we lacked continually from foreign countries, which yet more augmented our idleness. For having all things at reasonable prices, as we supposed, by such means from them, we thought it mere madness to spend either time or cost about the same here at home. And thus we became enemies to our own welfare, as men that in those days reposed our felicity in following the wars, wherewith we were often exercised both at home and other places.

Besides this, the natural desire that mankind hath to esteem of things far-sought, because they be rare and costly, and the irksome contempt of things near-hand, for that they are common and plentiful, hath borne no small sway also in this behalf amongst us. For hereby we have neglected our own good gifts of God growing here at home, as vile and of no valure, and had every trifle and toy in admiration that is brought hither from far countries, ascribing I wot not what great forces and solemn estimation unto them, until they also have waxen old; after which they have been so little regarded, if not more despised amongst us than our own. Examples hereof I could set down many and in many things, but sith my purpose is to deal at this time with gardens and orchards, it shall suffice that I touch them only and show our inconstancy in the same, so far as shall seem and be convenient for my turn.

I comprehend, therefore, under the word "garden" all such grounds as are wrought with the spade by man's hand, for so the case requireth. Of wine I have written already elsewhere sufficiently,[1] which commodity (as I have learned further since the penning of that book) hath been very plentiful in this island, not only in the time of the Romans but also since the Conquest, as I have seen by record; yet at this present have we none at all or else very little to speak of growing in this island, which I impute not unto the soil but the negligence of my countrymen.

Such herbs, fruits, and roots also as grow yearly out of the ground of seed have been very plentiful in this land, in the time of the first Edward and after his days; but in process of time they grew also to be neglected, so that from Henry the Fourth till the latter end of Henry the Seventh and beginning of Henry the Eighth there was little or no use of them in England, but they remained either unknown or supposed as food more meet for hogs and savage beasts to feed upon than mankind. Whereas in my time their use is not only resumed among the poor commons —I mean of melons, pompions, gourds, cucumbers, radishes, skirrets, parsnips, carrots, cabbages, navews,[2] turnips, and all kinds of salad herbs—but also fed upon as dainty dishes at the tables of delicate merchants, gentlemen, and the nobility, who make their provision yearly for new seeds out of strange countries, from whence they have them abundantly. Neither do they now stay with such of these fruits as are wholesome in their kinds, but adventure further upon such as are very dangerous and hurtful, as the verangenes,[3] mushrooms, etc., as if Nature had ordained all for the belly or that all things were to be eaten, for whose mischievous operation the Lord in some measure hath given and provided a remedy.

Hops in time past were plentiful in this land; afterwards also their maintenance did cease, and now, being revived, where are any better to be found? Where any greater commodity to be raised by them? Only poles are accounted to be their greatest charge. But sith men have learned of late to sow ashen keys in

---

[1] See pp. 435–437.

[2] *Pompions:* pumpkins; *skirrets:* a species of water parsnip cultivated for its tubers; *navews:* rape or cole.

[3] *Verangenes:* brinjals, the fruit of the eggplant.

ashyards [4] by themselves, that inconvenience in short time will be redressed. Madder hath grown abundantly in this island, but of long time neglected and now a little revived, and offereth itself to prove no small benefit unto our country, as many other things else which are now fetched from us, as we beforetime, when we gave ourselves to idleness, were glad to have them [from] other.

If you look into our gardens annexed to our houses, how wonderfully is their beauty increased, not only with flowers, which Columella calleth *terrena sydera*, saying,

Pingit et in varios terrestria sydera flores,[5]

and variety of curious and costly workmanship, but also with rare and medicinable herbs sought up in the land within these forty years; so that in comparison of this present the ancient gardens were but dunghills and laystows to such as did possess them. How art also helpeth nature in the daily coloring, doubling, and enlarging the proportion of our flowers, it is incredible to report; for so curious and cunning are our gardeners now in these days that they presume to do in manner what they list with Nature, and moderate her course in things as if they were her superiors.

It is a world also to see how many strange herbs, plants, and annual fruits are daily brought unto us from the Indies, Americans, Taprobane [Ceylon], Canary Isles, and all parts of the world; the which, albeit that in respect of the constitutions of our bodies they do not grow for us, because that God hath bestowed sufficient commodities upon every country for her own necessity, yet for delectation sake unto the eye and their odoriferous savors unto the nose they are to be cherished and God to be glorified also in them, because they are His good gifts and created to do man help and service. There is not almost one nobleman, gentleman, or merchant that hath not great store of these flowers, which now also do begin to wax so well acquainted with our soils that we may almost account of them as parcel of our own commodities.

They have no less regard in like sort to cherish medicinable

---

[4] *Ashen keys:* the winged seeds of the ash tree; *ashyards:* for hopyards?

[5] "He paints in varied flowers, which are earthly stars" (*De re rustica,* X, 96).

herbs fetched out of other regions nearer hand, insomuch that I have seen in some one garden to the number of three hundred or four hundred of them if not more, of the half of whose names within forty years past we had no manner knowledge. But herein I find some cause of just complaint, for that we extol their uses so far that we fall into contempt of our own, which are in truth more beneficial and apt for us than such as grow elsewhere, sith (as I said before) every region hath abundantly within her own limits whatsoever is needful and most convenient for them that dwell therein. How do men extol the use of tobacco in my time, whereas in truth (whether the cause be in the repugnancy of our constitution unto the operation thereof or that the ground doth alter her force, I cannot tell) it is not found of so great efficacy as they write.[6] And beside this our common germander or thistle bennet is found and known to be so wholesome and of so great power in medicine as any other herb, if they be used accordingly. I could exemplify after the like manner in sundry other, as the sarsaparilla, mechoacan,[7] etc., but I forbear so to do because I covet to be brief.

And truly the estimation and credit that we yield and give unto compound medicines made with foreign drugs is one great cause wherefore the full knowledge and use of our own simples [8] hath been so long raked up in the embers. And as this may be verified so to be one sound conclusion, for the greater number of simples that go unto any compound medicine, the greater confusion is found therein because the qualities and operations of very few of the particulars are thoroughly known. And even so our continual desire of strange drugs, whereby the physician and apothecary only hath the benefit, is no small cause that the use of our simples here at home doth go to loss and that we tread those herbs under our feet whose forces, if we knew and could apply them to our necessities, we would honor and have in reverence as

[6] Furnivall prints the following entry from Harrison's Chronology under 1573: "In these days the taking in of the smoke of the Indian herb called tobacco by an instrument formed like a little ladle, whereby it passeth from the mouth into the head and stomach, is greatly taken up and used in England against rheums and some other diseases engendered in the lungs and inward parts, and not without effect" (I, lv). These two references are among the earliest mentions of tobacco in English.

[7] The medicinal roots of both plants had recently been introduced from the New World.

[8] *Simples:* medicines composed of one herb or plant.

to their case behooveth. Alas, what have we to do with such Arabian and Grecian stuff as is daily brought from those parties [regions] which lie in another clime? And therefore the bodies of such as dwell there are of another constitution than ours are here at home. Certes they grow not for us but for the Arabians and Grecians. And albeit that they may by skill be applied unto our benefit, yet to be more skillful in them than in our own is folly; and to use foreign wares when our own may serve the turn is more folly; but to despise our own and magnify above measure the use of them that are sought and brought from far is most folly of all, for it savoreth of ignorance or at the leastwise of negligence, and therefore worthy of reproach.

Among the Indians, who have the most present cures for every disease of their own nation, there is small regard of compound medicines and less of foreign drugs, because they neither know them nor can use them but work wonders even with their own simples. With them also the difference of the clime doth show her full effect. For whereas they will heal one another in short time with application of one simple, etc., if a Spaniard or Englishman stand in need of their help, they are driven to have a longer space in their cures and now and then also to use some addition of two or three simples at the most, whose forces unto them are thoroughly known, because their exercise is only in their own, as men that never sought or heard what virtue was in those that came from other countries. And even so did Marcus Cato, the learned Roman, endeavor to deal in his cures of sundry diseases, wherein he not only used such simples as were to be had in his own country but also examined and learned the forces of each of them, wherewith he dealt so diligently that in all his lifetime he could attain to the exact knowledge but of a few and thereto wrote of those most learnedly, as would easily be seen if those his books were extant. For the space also of six hundred years the colewort only was a medicine in Rome for all diseases, so that his virtues were thoroughly known in those parts.[9]

In Pliny's time the like affection to foreign drugs did rage among the Romans, whereby their own did grow in contempt. Crying out therefore of this extreme folly (*lib.* 22, *cap.* 24), he speaketh after this manner: *Non placent remedia tam longe*

[9] Pliny, XX, xxxiii, who quotes extensively from Cato's extant discussion of the medicinal virtues of colewort or cabbage (*De re rustica*, clvi–clvii).

nascentia, non enim nobis gignuntur, immo ne illis quidem, alioquin non venderent; si placet etiam superstitionis gratia emantur, quoniam supplicamus, etc. Salutem quidem sine his posse constare, vel ob id probabimus, ut tanto magis sui tandem pudeat.[10]

For my part I doubt not, if the use of outlandish [foreign] drugs had not blinded our physicians of England in times past, but that the virtues of our simples here at home would have been far better known and so well unto us as those of India are to the practitioners of those parts, and thereunto be found more profitable for us than the foreign either are or may be. This also will I add, that even those which are most common by reason of their plenty and most vile because of their abundance are not without some universal and especial efficacy, if it were known, for our benefit, sith God in nature hath so disposed His creatures that the most needful are the most plentiful and serving for such general diseases as our constitution most commonly is affected withal. Great thanks, therefore, be given unto the physicians of our age and country, who not only endeavor to search out the use of such simples as our soil doth yield and bring forth but also to procure such as grow elsewhere, upon purpose so to acquaint them with our clime that they in time, through some alteration received from the nature of the earth, may likewise turn to our benefit and commodity and be used as our own.

The chief workman, or as I may call him, the founder of this device, is Carolus Clusius,[11] the noble herbarist, whose industry hath wonderfully stirred them up unto this good act. For albeit that Matthiolus, Rembert, L'Obel,[12] and other have traveled very far in this behalf, yet none hath come near to Clusius, much less gone further in the finding and true descriptions of such herbs as of late are brought to light. I doubt not but if this man were in

---

[10] "Medicinal herbs that come from such a distance are not satisfactory; they certainly are not produced for us, nor even for the natives, who then would not sell them. Let them be bought, if desired, for the sake of religious rites, since we worship [with frankincense and costmary]. But I shall prove that health can last without them, so that at last it may be so much the more ashamed of itself [for seeking such luxuries]" (XXII, lvi).

[11] *Carolus Clusius:* Charles de l'Écluse (1526-1609), French physician and botanist, whose *Rariorum plantarum historia* was published at Antwerp in 1557.

[12] *Matthiolus:* Pietro Andrea Mattioli (1500-1577); *Rembert:* Rembert Dodoens (1518-1585); *L'Obel:* Matthias de l'Obel (1538-1616). All three were physicians and botanists who wrote notable herbals.

England but one seven-years, he would reveal a number of herbs growing with us whereof neither our physicians nor apothecaries as yet have any knowledge. And even like thanks be given unto our nobility, gentlemen, and others for their continual nutriture and cherishing of such homeborn and foreign simples in their gardens; for hereby they shall not only be had at hand and preserved, but also their forms made more familiar to be discerned and their forces better known than hitherto they have been.

And even as it fareth with our gardens, so doth it with our orchards, which were never furnished with so good fruit nor with such variety as at this present. For beside that we have most delicate apples, plums, pears, walnuts, filberts, etc., and those of sundry sorts, planted within forty years past, in comparison of which most of the old trees are nothing worth, so have we no less store of strange fruit, as apricots, almonds, peaches, figs, corn trees [13] in noblemen's orchards. I have seen capers, oranges, and lemons, and heard of wild olives growing here, beside other strange trees brought from far whose names I know not. So that England for these commodities was never better furnished, neither any nation under their clime more plentifully endued with these and other blessings from the most high God, who grant us grace withal to use the same to His honor and glory and not as instruments and provocations unto further excess and vanity, wherewith His displeasure may be kindled, lest these His benefits do turn unto thorns and briars unto us for our annoyance and punishment, which He hath bestowed upon us for our consolation and comfort.

We have in like sort such workmen as are not only excellent in grafting the natural fruits but also in their artificial mixtures, whereby one tree bringeth forth sundry fruits and one and the same fruit of diverse colors and tastes, dallying as it were with Nature and her course, as if her whole trade were perfectly known unto them; of hard fruits they will make tender, of sour sweet, of sweet yet more delicate, bereaving also some of their kernels, other of their cores, and finally enduing them with the savor of musk, amber, or sweet spices at their pleasures. Divers also have written at large of these several practices, and some of them how to convert the kernels of peaches into almonds, of small fruit to make far greater, and to remove or add superfluous

---

[13] *Corn trees:* cornel trees, the cornelian cherry.

or necessary moisture to the trees, with other things belonging to their preservation, and with no less diligence than our physicians do commonly show upon our own diseased bodies, which to me doth seem right strange.

And even so do our gardeners with their herbs, whereby they are strengthened against noisome blasts and preserved from putrefaction and hindrance; whereby some such as were annual are now made perpetual, being yearly taken up and either reserved in the house or, having the ross [filth] pulled from their roots, laid again into the earth, where they remain in safety. What choice they make also in their waters, and wherewith some of them do now and then keep them moist, it is a world to see; insomuch that the apothecaries' shops may seem to be needful also to our gardens and orchards, and that in sundry wise; nay, the kitchen itself is so far from being able to be missed among them that even the very dishwater is not without some use amongst our finest plants. Whereby and sundry other circumstances not here to be remembered I am persuaded that albeit the gardens of the Hesperides were in times past so greatly accounted of because of their delicacy, yet if it were possible to have such an equal judge as by certain knowledge of both were able to pronounce upon them, I doubt not but he would give the prize unto the gardens of our days and generally over all Europe, in comparison of those times wherein the old exceeded.

Pliny and other speak of a rose that had threescore leaves growing upon one button,[14] but if I should tell of one which bare a triple number unto that proportion, I know I shall not be believed and no great matter though I were not; howbeit, such a one was to be seen in Antwerp, 1585, as I have heard, and I know who might have had a slip or stallon [15] thereof, if he would have ventured £10 upon the growth of the same, which should have been but a tickle [risky] hazard and therefore better undone, as I did always imagine.

For mine own part, good reader, let me boast a little of my garden, which is but small and the whole area thereof little above three hundred foot of ground, and yet, such hath been my good luck in purchase of the variety of simples that, notwithstanding my small ability, there are very near three hundred of

[14] Pliny actually mentions the *centifolia*, a hundred-petaled rose (XXI, x).
[15] *Stallon:* apparently for stolon, a shoot.

one sort and other contained therein, no one of them being common or usually to be had. If therefore my little plot, void of all cost in keeping, be so well furnished, what shall we think of those of Hampton Court, Nonsuch, Theobalds, Cobham Garden,[16] and sundry other appertaining to divers citizens of London, whom I could particularly name if I should not seem to offend them by such my demeanor and dealing?

CHAPTER XXI

Of Waters Generally

THERE is no one commodity in England whereof I can make less report than of our waters. For albeit our soil abound with water in all places and that in the most ample manner, yet can I not find by some experience that almost any one of our rivers hath such odd and rare qualities as divers of the main are said to be endued withal. Vitruvius writeth of a well in Paphlagonia whose water seemeth as it were mixed with wine, and addeth thereto that divers become drunk by superfluous taking of the same. The like force is found *in amne Licesio*, a river of Thrace, upon whose banks a man shall hardly miss to find some traveler or other sleeping for drunkenness by drinking of that liquor. Near also unto Ephesus are certain wells which taste like sharp vinegar and therefore are much esteemed of by such as are sick and evil at ease in those parts. At Hierapolis is a spring of such force (as Strabo saith) that the water thereof mixed with certain herbs of choice doth color wool with such a gloss that the dye thereof contendeth with scarlet, murrey, and purple, and oft overcometh the same. The Cydnus in Tarsus of Cilicia is of such virtue that whoso batheth himself therein shall find great ease of the gout that runneth over all his joints. In one of the Fortunate Isles (saith Pomponius, the cosmographer) are two springs, one of the which bringeth immoderate laughter to him that drinketh thereof, the other sadness and restraint of that effect, whereby the last is

---

[16] *Nonsuch:* the royal palace near Cheam in Surrey; *Theobalds:* Burghley's manor in Hertfordshire; *Cobham:* the seat of Harrison's patron in Kent.

taken to be a sovereign medicine against the other, to the great admiration of such as have beholden it. At Susa in Persia there is a spring which maketh him that drinketh down any of the water to cast all his teeth; but if he only wash his mouth withal, it maketh them fast and his mouth to be very healthful. So there is a river among the Gadarenes, whereof if a beast drink he forthwith casteth hoof, hair, and horns, if he have any. Also a lake in Assyria, near unto the which there is a kind of gluey matter to be found, which holdeth such birds as by hap do light thereon so fast as birdlime, by means whereof very many do perish and are taken that light upon the same; howbeit, if any portion hereof happen to be set on fire by casualty or otherwise, it will never be quenched but by casting on of dust, as Caietanus doth report.[1] Another at Halicarnassus, called Salmacis, which is noted to make such men effeminate as drink of the water of the same. Certes it may be (saith Strabo) that the water and air of a region may qualify the courage of some men, but none can make them effeminate nor any other thing, because of such corruption in them, sooner than superfluous wealth and inconstancy of living and behavior, which is a bane unto all natures (*lib.* 4).[2] All which, with many other not now coming to memory, as the Lethe, Styx, Phlegethon, Cocytus, etc., have strange and incredible reports made of them by the new and ancient writers, the like whereof are not to be found in England, which I impute wholly to the blessing of God, who hath ordained nothing amongst us in this our temperate region but that which is good, wholesome, and most commodious for our nation.

We have therefore no hurtful waters amongst us, but all wholesome and profitable for the benefit of the people. Nevertheless, as none of them is to be found without her fish, so we know by experience that divers turn ash, some other elm and oaken stakes or poles, that lie or are thrown into them, into hard stone in long continuance of time, which is the strangest thing that I can learn at this present whereupon to rest for a certainty. Yet I read of divers wells whereunto our old writers ascribe either wonderful

[1] *Caietanus:* Francesco Patrizi. This entire list of miraculous waters (with the exception of the Gadarene river, based on Strabo, XVI, ii) is closely paraphrased from Patrizi's *Moral Method of Civil Policy,* trans. Robinson, fol. 69r–v.

[2] *Geography,* XIV, ii.

virtues or rare courses, as of one upon the shore, beyond the which the sea floweth every day twice a large mile and more, and yet is the surge of that water always seven foot from the salt sea, whereby it should seem that the head of the spring is movable. But alas, I do not easily believe it, more than that which is written of the Lilingwan Lake in Wales, which is near to the Severn and receiveth the flowing sea into her channel as it were a gulf and yet is never full; but, when the sea goeth away by reason of the ebb, it casteth up the water with such violence that her banks are overflown and drowned, which is an absurd report. They add also that if all the people of the country stood near to the same with their faces toward the lake in such manner that the dashing of the water might touch and wet their clothes, they should have no power to go from thence but mauger their resistance be drawn into that gulf and perish; whereas if they turned their backs unto the same, they should suffer no such inconvenience, though they stood never so near.[3]

Many other suchlike toys I could set down of other wells and waters of our country. But why should I write that for other men to read whereto I give no credit myself, more than to the report which Johannes du Choul doth make in his description of Pilate's Lake, *In Monte Pilati in Gallia,* or Boccaccio of the Scaphagiolo in the Apennine Hills,[4] or Felix Malleolus of Pilate's Lake *in Monte Fracto* (whereof Jacobus de Voragine, Bishop of Genoa, and Joachimus Vadianus, *In Pompon. Melam,* do also make mention),[5] sith I take them but for fables and far unworthy that any good man should stain his paper with such frivolous matters as are reported of them, being devised at the first by Satan, the father of lies, for the holding of the ignorant and credulous in their superstitions and errors. Such also is the tale

[3] This account of Lilingwan, or Linligwan, Lake is translated from Geoffrey of Monmouth, IX, vii.

[4] According to Boccaccio ("*De lacubus*" in *De montibus, sylvis, fontibus,* Venice, 1473), a pebble thrown into this tarn (It., *Scaffaiolo*) caused violent storms in the vicinity.

[5] *Johannes (Jean) du Choul:* French naturalist, whose *Descriptio Montis Fracti sive Montis Pilati in Helvetia* was printed at Lyons in 1555; *Felix Malleolus,* or Haemmerlein (1389–1460): Swiss theologian; *Jacobus de Voragine* (?1230–?1298): Italian chronicler and hagiographer, Archbishop of Genoa, author of *The Golden Legend; Joachimus Vadianus,* or von Watt (1484–1551): Swiss scholar, who published in 1518 a commentary on the geography of Pomponius Mela. These legends concern the illusions associated with the tarn in which Pilate, as a suicide, was fabled to have been buried.

that goeth of Winifred's Well,[6] and nothing inferior to that of Mercury near to Port Caperia [Porta Capena] in Rome, wherein such as went by would dip branches of bay and sprinkle the same upon themselves and so many as stood about them, calling upon Mercury and craving pardon for their sins, as if that ceremony had been of force unto forgiveness and remission of their trespasses.[7] And so it appeareth partly by Cicero, who (being a man neither thinking well of their own gods nor liking of the augurs) doth write in his first *De legibus* (except my memory fail me), *Aspersione aquae labem tolli corpoream, et castimoniam corporis praestari,*[8] which maketh me to think further that they thought it equal with our late holy water, wherewith it may be compared.

I might further also (if I would) make relation of divers wells which have wrought many miracles in time of superstition, as St. Botolph's Well in Hadstock, St. German's Well at Faulk-bourne,[9] Holywell at St. Albans and London, and sundry other in other places; but as their virtues are now found out to be but baits to draw men and women unto them, either for gain unto the places where they were or satisfaction of the lewd disposition of such as hunted after other game, so it shall suffice to have touched them far off. Only this will I add, that we have no hurtful waters, no, not unto our sheep, though it please Cardan to avouch otherwise;[10] for our waters are not the causes but the signs of their infections when they drink, as I elsewhere have noted in the chapter of cattle; as also that we have a spring near Saffron Walden, and not far from the house of the Lord Audley, which is of such force that it looseth the body of him that drinketh thereof in very gentle manner and beside that is very delectable and pleasant to be taken, as I have found by experience. I hear also of two wells near London, of which the one is very excellent water, the other will bear no soap, and yet so situate that the one is hard by the other.[11] And thus much of waters.

---

[6] *Winifred's Well:* at Holywell in Flintshire, noted for miraculous cures.

[7] Ovid, *Fasti, V,* 673–692.

[8] "By sprinkling of water bodily sin is removed and purity of the body maintained" (based on *De legibus,* II, x, 24).

[9] *Hadstock, Faulkbourne:* towns in Essex. Harrison seems to be remembering local legends.   [10] See p. 310.

[11] Harrison mentions these same wells in *The Description of Britain* (1587, p. 130), placing them at "Landien," apparently in Wales (Llan Dinam in Montgomeryshire?).

CHAPTER XXII

Of Woods and Marshes

IT SHOULD seem by ancient records and the testimony of sundry authors that the whole countries of Loegria and Cambria, now England and Wales, have sometimes been very well replenished with great woods and groves, although at this time the said commodity be not a little decayed in both, and in such wise that a man shall oft ride ten or twenty miles in each of them and find very little or rather none at all, except it be near unto towns, gentlemen's houses, and villages, where the inhabitants have planted a few elms, oaks, hazels, or ashes about their dwellings for their defense from the rough winds and keeping of the stormy weather from annoyance of the same.

This scarcity at the first grew (as it is thought) either by the industry of man, for maintenance of tillage (as we understand the like to be done of late by the Spaniards in the West Indies, where they fired whole woods of very great compass, thereby to come by ground whereon to sow their grains), or else through the covetousness of such as, in preferring of pasture for their sheep and greater cattle, do make small account of firebote [firewood] and timber, or, finally, by the cruelty of the enemies, whereof we have sundry examples declared in our histories. Howbeit, where the rocks and quarry grounds are I take the sward [1] of the earth to be so thin that no tree of any greatness, other than shrubs and bushes, is able to grow or prosper long therein, for want of sufficient moisture wherewith to feed them with fresh humor, or at the leastwise of mold, to shroud, stay upright, and cherish the same in the blustering winter's weather till they may grow unto any greatness and spread or yield their roots downright [vertically down] into the soil about them; and this either is or may be one other cause wherefore some places are naturally void of wood. But to proceed.

[1] *Sward:* the upper layer of ground.

Although I must needs confess that there is good store of great wood or timber here and there even now in some places of England, yet in our days it is far unlike to that plenty which our ancestors have seen heretofore, when stately building was less in use. For albeit that there were then greater number of messuages [2] and mansions almost in every place, yet were their frames so slight and slender that one mean dwelling house in our time is able to countervail very many of them, if you consider the present charge with the plenty of timber that we bestow upon them. In times past men were contented to dwell in houses builded of sallow, willow, plum tree, hardbeam,[3] and elm, so that the use of oak was in manner dedicated wholly unto churches, religious houses, princes' palaces, noblemen's lodgings, and navigation, but now all these are rejected and nothing but oak any whit regarded.

And yet see the change, for when our houses were builded of willow, then had we oaken men; but now that our houses are come to be made of oak, our men are not only become willow but a great many, through Persian delicacy crept in among us, altogether of straw, which is a sore alteration.[4] In those the courage of the owner was a sufficient defense to keep the house in safety, but now the assurance of the timber, double doors, locks, and bolts must defend the man from robbing. Now have we many chimneys, and yet our tenderlings complain of rheums, catarrhs, and poses [colds]. Then had we none but reredoses, and our heads did never ache. For as the smoke in those days was supposed to be a sufficient hardening for the timber of the house, so it was reputed a far better medicine to keep the goodman and his family from the quack [hoarseness] or pose, wherewith as then very few were oft acquainted.

Of the curiousness of these piles I speak not, sith our workmen are grown generally to such an excellency of device in the frames now made that they far pass the finest of the old. And such is their husbandry in dealing with their timber that the same stuff which in time past was rejected as crooked, unprofitable, and to no use but the fire doth now come in the fronts

---

[2] *Messuages:* dwelling houses with their outbuildings and the land they occupy.

[3] *Sallow:* a species of willow; *hardbeam:* hornbeam.

[4] "Desire of much wealth and ease abateth manhood and overthroweth a manly courage."—*H.*

and best part of the work. Whereby the common saying is likewise in these days verified in our mansion houses which erst was said only of the timber for ships, that "no oak can grow so crooked but it falleth out to some use," and that necessary in the navy.

It is a world to see, moreover, how divers men, being bent to building and having a delectable vein in spending of their goods by that trade, do daily imagine new devices of their own to guide their workmen withal, and those more curious and excellent always than the former. In the proceeding also of their works, how they set up, how they pull down, how they enlarge, how they restrain, how they add to, how they take from, whereby their heads are never idle, their purses never shut, nor their books of account never made perfect.

Destruunt, aedificant, mutant quadrata rotundis,[5]

saith the poet. So that if a man should well consider of all the odd crotchets in such a builder's brain, he would think his head to have even enough of those affairs only and therefore judge that he should not well be able to deal in any other. But such commonly are our workmasters that they have, beside this vein aforementioned, either great charge of merchandises, little less business in the commonwealth, or, finally, no small dealings otherwise incident unto them, whereby gain ariseth and some trouble oft among withal. Which causeth me to wonder not a little how they can play the parts so well of so many sundry men, whereas divers other, of greater forecast in appearance, can seldom shift well or thrive in any one of them. But to our purpose.

We have many woods, forests, and parks, which cherish trees abundantly, although in the woodland countries there is almost no hedge that hath not some store of the greatest sort, beside infinite numbers of hedgerows, groves, and springs that are maintained of purpose for the building and provision of such owners as do possess the same. Howbeit, as every soil doth not bear all kinds of wood, so there is not any wood, park, hedgerow, grove, or forest that is not mixed with divers, as oak, ash, hazel, hawthorn, birch, beech, hardbeam, hull, sorfe, quicken, asp,[6] poplars, wild

---

[5] "They tear down, they build up, they change the square to round" (based on Horace, *Epistles*, I, i, 100).

[6] *Hull:* holly; *sorfe:* sorb; *quicken:* mountain ash; *asp:* aspen.

cherry, and suchlike, whereof oak hath always the pre-eminence, as most meet for building and the navy, whereunto it is reserved. This tree bringeth forth also a profitable kind of mast, whereby such as dwell near unto the aforesaid places do cherish and bring up innumerable herds of swine. In time of plenty of this mast our red and fallow deer will not let to participate thereof with our hogs, more than our neat; yea, our common poultry also, if they may come unto them. But as this abundance doth prove very pernicious unto the first, so the eggs which these latter do bring forth (beside blackness in color and bitterness of taste) [7] have not seldom been found to breed divers diseases unto such persons as have eaten of the same.

I might add in like sort the profit ensuing by the bark of this wood, whereof our tanners have great use in dressing of leather and which they buy yearly in May by the fathom,[8] as I have oft seen, but it shall not need at this time to enter into any such discourse; only this I wish, that our sole and upper leathering may have their due time and not be hasted on by extraordinary sleights, as with ash bark, etc. Whereby, as I grant that it seemeth outwardly to be very thick and well done, so if you respect the sadness [solidity] thereof, it doth prove in the end to be very hollow and not able to hold out water. Nevertheless, we have good laws for redress of this enormity, but it cometh to pass in these as in the execution of most penal statutes. For the gains to be gotten by the same being given to one or two hungry and unthrifty persons, they make a show of great reformation at the first and for a little while, till they find that following of suit in law against the offenders is somewhat too chargeable [costly] and tedious. This, therefore, perceived, they give over the law and fall to the admission of gifts and rewards to wink at things past, and when they have once gone over their ground with this kind of tillage, then do they tender licenses and offer large dispensations unto him that shall ask the same, thereby to do what him listeth in his trade for an yearly pension, whereby the briber now groweth to some certain revenues and the tanner to so great liberty that his leather is much worse than before. But is not this a mock-

---

[7] "The like have I seen where hens do feed upon the tender blades of garlic."—*H.*

[8] *Fathom:* here probably a bale measuring six feet on a side.

ery of our laws and manifest illusion of the good subject, whom they thus pill and poll [plunder]? [9]

Of all oak growing in England, the park oak is the softest and far more spalt and brickle [10] than the hedge oak. And of all in Essex, that growing in Bardfield Park is the finest for joiners' craft, for oftentimes have I seen of their works made of that oak so fine and fair as most of the wainscot that is brought hither out of Dansk [Denmark], for our wainscot is not made in England. Yet divers have assayed to deal with our oaks to that end, but not with so good success as they have hoped, because the ab [11] or juice will not so soon be removed and clean drawn out, which some attribute to want of time in the salt water. Nevertheless, in building, so well the hedge as the park oak go all one way, and never so much hath been spent in a hundred years before as is in ten year of our time; for every man almost is a builder, and he that hath bought any small parcel of ground, be it never so little, will not be quiet till he have pulled down the old house (if any were there standing) and set up a new after his own device. But whereunto will this curiosity come?

Of elm we have great store in every highway and elsewhere, yet have I not seen thereof any together in woods or forests but where they have been first planted and then suffered to spread at their own wills. Yet have I known great woods of beech and hazel in many places, especially in Berkshire, Oxfordshire, and Buckinghamshire, where they are greatly cherished and converted to sundry uses by such as dwell about them. Of all the elms that ever I saw, those in the south side of Dovercourt in Essex near Harwich are the most notable, for they grow (I mean) in crooked manner that they are almost apt for nothing else but navy timber, great ordnance, and beetles [mallets]; and such thereto is their natural quality that, being used in the said behalf, they continue longer and more long than any the like trees

[9] The statute 5 Eliz., c. 8 prescribed in hopeful detail the proper method of tanning, currying, and cutting leather. Outside London the examination of leather for the maintenance of proper standards was entrusted to "two, three, or more persons, of the most honest and skillful men," yearly appointed by the "mayors, bailiffs, and other head officers." Their power, however, extended only to seizing the questionable goods and instituting proceedings against the offenders.

[10] *Spalt:* liable to split; *brickle:* brittle.

[11] *Ab:* the word seems unique to Harrison and is probably a misprint for "sap."

in whatsoever parcel else of this land, without cuphar, shaking,[12] or cleaving, as I find.

Ash cometh up everywhere of itself and with every kind of wood. And as we have very great plenty and no less use of these in our husbandry, so are we not without the plane, the yew, the sorfe, the chestnut, the line,[13] the black cherry, and suchlike. And although that we enjoy them not in so great plenty now in most places as in times past, or the other [trees] afore remembered, yet have we sufficient of them all for our necessary turns and uses, especially of yew, as may be seen betwixt Rotherham and Sheffield, and some steads of Kent also, as I have been informed.

The fir, frankincense,[14] and pine we do not altogether want, especially the fir, whereof we have some store in Chatley Moor in Derbyshire, Shropshire, Amounderness, and a moss near Manchester, not far from Leicester's house, although that in time past not only all Lancashire but a great part of the coast between Chester and the Solve [Solway] were well stored.[15] As for the frankincense and pine, they have been planted only in colleges and cloisters by the clergy and religious heretofore. Wherefore (in mine opinion) we may rather say that we want them altogether, for except they grew naturally and not by force, I see no cause why they should be accounted for parcel of our commodities. We have also the asp, whereof our fletchers make their arrows. The several kinds of poplars of our turners have great use for bowls, trays, troughs, dishes, etc. Also the alder, whose bark is not unprofitable to dye black withal and therefore much used by our country wives in coloring their knit hosen.

I might here take occasion to speak of the great sales yearly made of wood, whereby an infinite quantity hath been destroyed within these few years, but I give over to travail in this behalf. Howbeit, thus much I dare affirm, that if woods go so fast to decay in the next hundred year of grace as they have done and are like to do in this, sometimes for increase of sheepwalks and some maintenance of prodigality and pomp (for I have known a well-

---

[12] *Cuphar:* cracking; *shaking:* splitting.

[13] *Line:* lind, the lime, or linden.

[14] *Frankincense:* a species of pine.

[15] These details derive from Leland, *Itinerary* (ed. Smith, IV, 5, 10, and V, 6, 16, 42). Leland's "Chatley Moor in Derbyshire" (V, 42) seems to be an error for Chat Moss in Lancashire; the *Itinerary* mentions Tabley in Cheshire, "Mr. Leicester's place; hereabout in a moss is fir wood" (IV, 5).

burnished gentleman that hath borne threescore at once in one pair of galligaskins to show his strength and bravery),[16] it is to be feared that the fenny bote, [such as] broom, turf, gale, heath, furze, brakes, whins, ling, dies, hassocks, flags,[17] straw, sedge, reed, rush, and also sea coal will be good merchandise even in the city of London, whereunto some of them even now have gotten ready passage and taken up their inns in the greatest merchants' parlors. A man would think that our laws were able enough to make sufficient provision for the redress of this error and enormity likely to ensue.[18] But such is the nature of our countrymen that, as many laws are made, so they will keep none; or, if they be urged to make answer, they will rather seek some crooked construction of them to the increase of their private gain than yield themselves to be guided by the same for a common wealth and profit to their country. So that in the end, whatsoever the law saith, we will have our wills, whereby the wholesome ordinances of the prince are contemned, the travail of the nobility and councilors as it were derided, the commonwealth impoverished, and a few only enriched by this perverse dealing. Thus many thousand persons do suffer hindrance by this their lewd behavior. Hereby the wholesome laws of the prince are oft defrauded and the good-meaning magistrate in consultation about the commonwealth utterly neglected.

I would wish that I might live no longer than to see four things in this land reformed, that is: the want of discipline in the church; the covetous dealing of most of our merchants in the preferment of the commodities of other countries and hindrance of their own; the holding of fairs and markets upon the Sunday to be

[16] "This gentleman caught such an heat with this sore load that he was fain to go to Rome for physic, yet it could not save his life, but he must needs die homewards."—*H. Well-burnished:* from the verb "to burnish," to grow portly or increase in breadth, in reference to the width of his galligaskins, or breeches.

[17] *Fenny bote:* combustible material from the fens; bote is properly the right of a tenant to take timber for repairs, firing, etc., but Harrison, having in mind the term "firebote" (see p. 275), seems to understand it as any material suitable for fuel. *Brakes:* either bracken or clumps of brushwood; *whins:* lumps of furze or gorse; *ling:* heather; *dies:* perhaps for deas, the dea-nettle or dead nettle; *hassocks:* thick tufts of coarse grass; *flags:* reeds or rushes.

[18] The statute 35 Henry VIII, c. 17 (revived and made perpetual by 13 Eliz., c. 25), dealing with the conservation of woods, included the provision that none over two acres was to be converted into tillage or pasture.

abolished and referred to the Wednesdays; and that every man in whatsoever part of the champaign soil [who] enjoyeth forty acres of land and upwards, after that rate, either by free deed, copyhold, or fee farm, might plant one acre of wood or sow the same with oak mast, hazel, beech, and sufficient provision be made that it may be cherished and kept. But I fear me that I should then live too long, and so long that I should either be weary of the world or the world of me, and yet they are not such things but they may easily be brought to pass.

Certes every small occasion in my time is enough to cut down a great wood, and every trifle sufficeth to lay infinite acres of corn ground unto pasture. As for the taking down of houses, a small fine will bear out a great many. Would to God we might once take example of the Romans, who in restraint of superfluous grazing made an exact limitation how many head of cattle each estate might keep and what numbers of acres should suffice for that and other purposes.[19] Neither was wood ever better cherished or mansion houses maintained than by their laws and statutes. Such also was their care in the maintenance of navigation that it was a great part of the charge of their consuls yearly to view and look unto the hills whereon great timber did grow, lest their unnecessary faults[20] for the satisfaction of the private owner and his covetous mind might prove a prejudice unto the commonwealth, in the hindrance of sufficient stuff for the furniture of their navy. Certes the like hereof is yet observed in Venice. Read also, I pray you, what Suetonius writeth of the consulship of Bibulus and Caesar.[21] As for the wood that Ancus Marcius dedicated toward the maintenance of the common navy,[22] I pass it over as having elsewhere remembered it unto another end. But what do I mean to speak of these, sith my purpose is only to talk of our own woods? Well, take this then for a final conclusion in

[19] The Lex Licinia of 375 B.C. limited individual holdings of the public land to 500 jugera and private herds grazing on that land to 100 large and 500 smaller animals.

[20] *Faults:* probably for "falls," fellings of timber.

[21] When Julius Caesar and Bibulus were chosen consuls, they were assigned the provinces of least importance (described by Suetonius as "woods and pastures"), with the intent of braking Caesar's growing power (*Lives of the Caesars,* I, xix). Harrison seems to have misunderstood the passage.

[22] *Ancus Marcius:* fourth King of Rome (642–617 B.C.); the notion of his dedicating a wood to the navy seems to be based on a misreading of Livy, I, xxxiii.

woods, that beside some countries are already driven to sell their wood by the pound, which is an heavy report, within these forty years we shall have little great timber growing above forty years old; for it is commonly seen that those young staddles which we leave standing at one-and-twenty years' fall are usually at the next sale cut down without any danger of the statute,[23] and serve for firebote if it please the owner to burn them.

Marshes and fenny bogs we have many in England, though not now so many as some of the old Roman writers do specify, but more in Wales, if you have respect unto the several quantities of the countries. Howbeit, as they are very profitable in the summer half of the year, so are a number of them, which lie low and near to great rivers, to small commodity in the winter part, as common experience doth teach. Yet this I find of many moors, that in times past they have been harder ground and sundry of them well replenished with great woods that now are void of bushes. And for example hereof we may see the trial (beside the roots that are daily found in the deeps of Monmouth, where turf is digged, also in Wales [around] Abergavenny and [in] Merioneth) in sundry parts of Lancashire, where great store of fir hath grown in times past, as I said, and the people go unto this day into their fens and marshes with long spits, which they dash here and there up to the very cronge [handle] into the ground. In which practice (a thing commonly done in winter), if they happen to smite upon any fir trees which lie there at their whole lengths, or other blocks, they note the place, and about harvest time, when the ground is at the driest, they come again and get them up and, afterward carrying them home, apply them to their uses. The like do they in Shropshire with the like, which hath been felled in old time within seven miles of Salop. Some of them foolishly suppose the same to have lien there since Noah's flood, and other, more fond than the rest, imagine them to grow even in the places where they find them, without all consideration that in times past the most part, if not all Loegria and Cambria, was generally replenished with wood, which, being felled or overthrown upon sundry occasions, was left lying

---

[23] *Staddles:* young trees left to reforest the area. The statute 35 Henry VIII, c. 17 specified that in woods felled at twenty-four years or under, twelve "standels or storers" in every acre were to be left standing and not felled until they were ten inches square, three feet from the ground.

in some places still on the ground and in process of time became to be quite overgrown with earth and molds, which molds, wanting their due sadness, are now turned into moory plots. Whereby it cometh to pass also that great plenty of water cometh between the new loose sward and the old hard earth that, being drawn away by ditching and drains (a thing soon done, if our countrymen were painful in that behalf), might soon leave a dry soil to the great lucre and advantage of the owner.

We find in our histories that Lincoln was sometime builded by Lud, brother to Cassibelan, who called it Caer Ludcoit of the great store of woods that environed the same;[24] but now the commodity is utterly decayed there, so that if Lud were alive again, he would not call it his city in the wood but rather his town in the plains, for the wood (as I hear) is wasted altogether about the same. The hills called The Peak were in like sort named Mennith and Orcoit, that is, the woody hills and forests. But how much wood is now to be seen in those places, let him that hath been there testify if he list; for I hear of no such store there as hath been in time past by those that travel that way. And thus much of woods and marshes, and so far as I can deal with the same.

CHAPTER XXIII

Of Baths and Hot Wells

As ALMIGHTY God hath in most plentiful manner bestowed infinite and those very notable benefits upon this isle of Britain, whereby it is not a little enriched, so in hot and natural baths (whereof we have divers in sundry places) it manifestly appeareth that He hath not forgotten England. There are sundry baths, therefore, to be found in this realm, of which the first is called St. Vincent's, the second Holywell,[1] both being places (in my

---

[24] Ranulf Higden, *Polychronicon* (ed. C. Babington, Rolls Ser., XLI, Vol. II, 1869, 63). *Coit:* modern Welsh *coed*, woods.

[1] St. Vincent's Rocks near Bristol and Winifred's Well at Holywell in Flintshire.

opinion) more obscure than the other two and yet not seldom sought unto by such as stand in need. For albeit the fame of their forces be not so generally spread, yet in some cases they are thought to be nothing inferior to the other, as divers have often affirmed by their own experience and trial.

The third place wherein hot baths are to be found is near unto Buxton, a town in Derbyshire, situate in the high Peak, not passing sixteen miles from Manchester or Market Chesterford and twenty from Derby, where about eight or nine several wells are to be seen, of which three are counted to be most excellent; but of all, the greatest is the hottest, void of corruption, and compared (as Jones saith) with those of Somersetshire [at Bath], so cold, indeed, as a quart of boiling water would be made if five quarts of running water were added thereunto; whereas on the other side, those of Bath likened unto these have such heat appropriated unto them as a gallon of hot water hath when a quart of cold is mixed with the same. Hereupon the effect of this bath worketh more temperately and pleasantly (as he writeth) than the other. And albeit that it maketh not so great speed in cure of such as resort unto it for help, yet it dealeth more effectually and commodiously than those in Somersetshire and infer[reth, occasions] withal less grievous accidents in the restraining of natural issues, strengthening the affeebled members, assisting the lively forces, dispersing annoyous oppilations, and qualifying of sundry griefs, as his experience hath oft confirmed. The like virtues have the other two but not in such measure, and therefore their operation is not so speedily perceived. [2]

The fourth place where baths are is King's Newnham and within certain miles of Coventry, the water whereof (as it is thought) proceedeth from some rock of alum, and this I understand by divers glovers which have been there and also by mine own experience, that it hath a taste much like to alum liquor and yet nothing unpleasant nor unsavory in the drinking. There are three wells in all, but the chiefest and best of them riseth out of an hill and runneth toward the south, and from thence infinite

[2] The entire paragraph is paraphrased from *The Benefit of the Ancient Baths of Buxton* (1572), fols. 1v–2r, by John Jones, a physician who had practiced at both Buxton and Bath. Market Chesterford is Harrison's misreading of Jones's Market Chesterfield, i.e., Chesterfield in Derbyshire.

plenty of water without any notable diminution of the spring is daily carried into sundry parties of the realm and drunk by such as have need to occupy the same. Of the other two, one is reserved for such as be comely personages and void of loathsome diseases; the other is left common for tag and rag, but cleansed daily as the other is, whereby it becometh the wholesomer. Many diseases also are cured in the same, as the palsy, dimness of sight, dullness of hearing, but especially the colic and the stone, old sores and green wounds; so that I suppose there was never any compound medicine of greater and more speedy force in these behalfs than the use of this simple liquor is to such as do frequent it.

The said water hath a natural property also following it which is rare, for if a leaf or stick of ash, oak, etc., do fall into the same, within a short space such store of fine sand (coming no doubt out of the earth with the water) will congeal and gather about it that, the form being reserved and the inner part not lightly altered, it will seem to become an hard stone and much like unto that which is engendered in the kidneys of a man, as I have seen by experience. At the first entrance it is very cold, but after a season it warmeth the goer-in, casting him into an indifferent heat. And this is furthermore remembered of it, that no man hath yet sustained any manner of impeachment through the coldness of the same. The virtue thereof was found, 1579, about Whitsuntide, by a man who had wounded himself and, coming by the same water, thought only to wash the blood from his hand therewith and so to go home and seek for help by surgery; finally, finding the pain well assuaged and the wound fair cleansed, he departed, and, misliking his usual medicines, he eftsoons came again, and so often indeed unto the said water till his hand was healed outright without any other practice. By this means also he became a counselor to other being hurt or in pain, that they should try the virtue of this spring, who, finding ease also, gave out such commendation of the said water that now at this present their fame is fully equal and the resort unto them nothing inferior to that of the old baths. Beside this the cures of such diseases as their forces do extend unto is much more speedy than we may have at the other, and this is one commodity also not smally to be considered of.

The fifth place of baths or medicinable wells is at an hamlet called Newton,[3] a little from St. Neots, or (as we pronounce it) St. Needs, which is ten or twelve miles from Cambridge, where two springs are known to be, of which the one is very sweet and fresh, the other brackish and salt; this is good for scabs and lepery [4] (as it is said), the other for dimness of sight. Very many also do make their repair unto them for sundry diseases, some returning whole and some nothing at all amended because their cure is without the reach and working of those waters. Never went people so fast from the church, either unto a fair or market, as they go to these wells and those near Rugby, both places being discovered in this 1579 of grace. I hear of another well to be found also about Ratcliff near London, even at the same season. But sith rumors are now spread almost of every spring, and vain tales fly about in manner of every water, I surcease to speak at all of any other till further experience do try whether they be medicinable or not; and yet I doubt not but most of these already mentioned have heretofore been known and remembered also, though confusedly, by the writers of old time, and yet in process of time either neglected or forgotten, by means of sundry troubles and turmoils made in this realm by Danes and other outward enemies, whereby their manifold benefit hath wonderfully been missed.

The last place of our baths is a city in Somersetshire, which taketh his name of the hot waters there to be seen and used. At the first it was called Caer Bladud, and not Caer Bledune, as some would have it, for that is the old name of the ancient castle at Malmesbury, which the Saxons named Yngleburne; [5] Ptolemy afterward called it *Thermae*, other *Aquae solis*,[6] or Scamannia or Acmancester, but now it hight [is called] generally Bath in English, and under that name it is likely to continue. The city of itself is a very ancient thing no doubt, as may yet appear by divers notable antiquities engraved in stone to be seen in the walls thereof, and first of all between the south gate and the west, and betwixt the west gate and the north.

The first is the antique head of a man, made all flat, with great locks of hair, much like to the coin that I have seen of Antius

---

[3] *Newton:* probably in error for (Hail) Weston.
[4] *Scabs:* skin diseases; *lepery:* leprosy.
[5] Leland, *Itinerary* (ed. Smith, I, 131).
[6] *Aquae solis:* or *Aquae sulis,* the name given Bath in the Antonine Itinerary.

the Roman. The second, between the south and the north gate, is an image as I take it of Hercules, for he held in each hand a serpent, and so doth this. Thirdly, there standeth a man on foot with a sword in his one hand and a buckler stretched out in the other. There is also a branch that lieth folded and wreathed into circles, like to the wreath of Alcimedon.[7] There are moreover two naked images, whereof the one embraceth the other, beside sundry antique heads with ruffled hair, a greyhound running, and at his tail certain Roman letters, but so defaced that no man living can read them at this present. There is moreover the image of Laocoön environed with two serpents and another inscription; and all these between the south and the west gates, as I have said before.

Now between the west and north gate are two inscriptions, of which some words are evident to be read, the residue are clean defaced. There is also the image of a naked man, and a stone in like sort which hath *cupidines et labruscas intercurrentes* [cupids and vines intertwined], and a table having at each hand an image vined and finely flourished both above and beneath. Finally (saving that I saw afterward the image of a naked man grasping a serpent in each hand), there was an inscription of a tomb or burial, wherein these words did plainly appear, *vixit annos xxx* [lived 30 years], but so diffusedly written that letters stood for whole words and two or three letters combined into one. Certes I will not say whether these were set into the places where they now stand by the gentiles or brought thither from other ruins of the town itself and placed afterward in those walls, in their necessary reparations.

But howsoever the matter standeth, this is to be gathered by our histories, that Bladud first builded that city there and peradventure might also kindle the sulphurous veins, of purpose to burn continually there in the honor of Minerva,[8] by which occasion the springs thereabout did in process of time become hot and not unprofitable for sundry kinds of diseases. Indeed the later pagans dreamed that Minerva was the chief goddess and governess of these waters, because of the nearness of her temple unto

---

[7] *Wreath of Alcimedon:* Virgil, *Eclogues*, III, 36–46. The phrase is Harrison's, but otherwise this paragraph and the next are borrowed almost verbatim from Leland (I, 140–141).

[8] Geoffrey of Monmouth, II, x.

the same. Solinus addeth furthermore how that in her said temple the fire which was continually kept did never consume into dead sparkles, but, so soon as the embers thereof were cold, they congealed into clots of hard stone;[9] all which I take to be nothing else than the effect of the aforesaid fire, of the sulphurous vein kindled in the earth from whence the waters do come. That these baths or waters are derived from such, the marcasites, which the Grecians call *pyritis, per antonomasiam* [10] (for, being smit with the iron, it yieldeth more sparks than any flint or chalcedony and therefore seemeth to deserve the name above the rest), and besides these other, stones mixed with some copper and daily found upon the mountains thereabouts will bear sufficient witness, though I would write the contrary. Doctor Turner also, the father of English physic and an excellent divine, supposeth that these springs do draw their forces from sulphur; or if there be any other thing mingled withal, he guesseth that it should be saltpeter, because he found an obscure likelihood of the same even in the Cross Bath. But that they participate with any alum at all, he could never till his dying day be induced to believe.[11]

I might here (if I thought it necessary) entreat of the notable situation of the city,[12] which standeth in a pleasant bottom, environed on every side with great hills, out of the which come so many springs of pure water by sundry ways unto the city and in such abundance as that every house is served with the same by pipes of lead, the said metal being the more plenteous and less of value unto them because it is not had far off from those quarters. It should not be amiss also to speak of the four gates, number of parish churches, bridges, religious houses dissolved, and their founders if place did serve therefor; but, forsomuch as my purpose is not to deal in this behalf, I will omit the mention of these things and go in hand with the baths themselves, whereof in the title of this chapter I protested to entreat.

---

[9] *Collectanea rerum memorabilium,* chap. xxxiv.

[10] "The pyrites is found almost in every vein of metal in great plenty, diversities, and color, and sometimes mixed with that metal of whose excrements it consisteth."—H. *Pyritis per antonomasiam:* that is, pyrites, another name for marcasite, based on the Greek root, *pyr,* fire.

[11] William Turner, *A Book of the Bath of Bath,* published at the end of his *Herbal* (1568), sigs. *2v-*3r.

[12] Here Harrison resumes his borrowing from Leland (I, 140-143), which continues through the next five paragraphs.

There are two springs of water (as Leland saith) in the west-southwest part of the town, whereof the biggest is called the Cross Bath of a certain cross that was erected sometime in the midst thereof. This bath is much frequented by such as are diseased with lepery, pocks, scabs, and great aches, yet of itself it is very temperate and pleasant, having eleven or twelve arches of stone in the sides thereof for men to stand under when rain doth aught annoy them.

The Common Bath, or as some call it, the Hot Bath, is two hundred foot or thereabout from the Cross Bath, less in compass within the wall than the other, and with only seven arches wrought out of the main enclosure. It is worthily called the Hot Bath, for at the first coming into it men think that it would scald their flesh and loose it from the bone; but after a season and that the bodies of the comers thereto be warmed thoroughly in the same, it is more tolerable and easy to be borne. Both these baths be in the middle of a little street and join to St. Thomas' Hospital,[13] so that it may be thought that Reginald, Bishop of Bath, made his house near unto these common baths only to succor such poor people as should resort unto them.

The King's Bath is very fair and large, standing almost in the middle of the town, at the west end of the cathedral church. It is compassed about with a very high stone wall, and the brims thereof are mured round about, wherein be two-and-thirty arches for men and women to stand in separately, who, being of the gentry for the most part, do resort thither indifferently but not in such lascivious sort as unto other baths and hothouses of the main, whereof some write more a great deal than modesty should reveal and honesty perform.[14] There went a sluice out of this bath which served in times past the priory with water, which was derived out of it unto two places and commonly used for baths, but now I do not think that they remain in usage.

As for the color of the water of all the baths, it is most like to a deep blue, and reeketh much after the manner of a seething pot, commonly yielding somewhat a sulphurous taste and very unpleasant savor. The water also that runneth from the two small

[13] Leland says, correctly, St. John's Hospital.
[14] "Hothouses [bathhouses] in some countries little better than brothels."— *H*. The latter part of the sentence in the text is Harrison's addition to Leland.

baths goeth by a dike into the Avon by west and beneath the bridge; but the same that goeth from the King's Bath turneth a mill and after goeth into Avon above Bath Bridge, where it loseth both force and taste and is like unto the rest. In all the three baths a man may evidently see how the water bubbleth up from the springs.[15] This is also to be noted, that at certain times all entrances into them is utterly prohibited, that is to say, at high noon and midnight; for at those two seasons and a while before and after they boil very fervently and become so hot that no man is able to endure their heat, or any while sustain their force and vehement working. They purge themselves furthermore from all such filth as the diseased do leave in each of them, wherefore we do forbear the rash entrance into them at that time; and so much the rather for that we would not, by contraction of any new diseases, depart more grievously affected than we came unto the city, which is indeed a thing that each one should regard. For these causes, therefore, they are commonly shut up from half an hour after ten of the clock in the forenoon to half an hour after one in the afternoon and likewise at midnight, at which times the keeper of them resorteth to his charge, openeth the gates, and leaveth (or should leave) free passage unto such as come unto them. Hitherto Leland.

What cost of late hath been bestowed upon these baths by divers of the nobility, gentry, commonalty, and clergy it lieth not in me to declare; yet, as I hear, they are not only very much repaired and garnished with sundry curious pieces of workmanship, partly touching their commendation and partly for the ease and benefit of such as resort unto them, but also better ordered, cleanlier kept, and more friendly provision made for such poverty as daily repaireth thither. But notwithstanding all this, such is the general estate of things in Bath that the rich men may spend while they will and the poor beg whilst they list for their maintenance and diet so long as they remain there; and yet I deny not but that there is very good order in that city for all degrees. But where shall a man find any equal regard of poor and rich, though God doth give these His good gifts freely and unto both alike?

I would here entreat further of the customs used in these baths, what number of physicians daily attend upon those waters,

[15] The borrowing from Leland ends here.

for no man (especially such as be able to entertain them) doth enter into these baths before he consult with the physician, also what diet is to be observed, what particular diseases are healed there, and to what end the comers thither do drink ofttimes of that medicinable liquor, but then I should exceed the limits of a description. Wherefore I pass it over to others, hoping that some man ere long will vouchsafe to perform that at large which the famous clerk, Doctor Turner, hath briefly yet happily begun touching the effects and working of the same. For hitherto I do not know of many that have travailed in the natures of those baths of our country with any great commendation, much less of any that hath revealed them at the full for the benefit of our nation or commodity of strangers that resort unto the same.

CHAPTER XXIV

Of Antiquities Found

HAVING taken some occasion to speak here and there in this treatise of antiquities, it shall not be amiss to deal yet more in this chapter with some of them apart and by themselves, whereby the secure authority of the Romans over this island may in some cases more manifestly appear. For such was their possession of this island on this side of the Tyne that they held not one or two or a few places only under their subjection but all the whole country from east to west, from the Tyne to the British Sea, so that there was no region void of their governance; notwithstanding that until the death of Lucius and extinction of his issue they did permit the successors of Lud and Cymbeline to reign and rule amongst them, though under a certain tribute, as elsewhere I have declared.

The chief cause that urgeth me to speak of antiquities is the pains that I have taken to gather great numbers of them together, intending (if ever my Chronology shall happen to come abroad) to set down the lively portraitures of every emperor engraven in the same; also the faces of Pompey, Crassus, the seven kings of the Romans, Cicero, and divers other, which I have provided ready for the purpose, beside the monuments and lively images of sundry philosophers and kings of this island since the time of Edward the Confessor. Whereof, although presently I want a few, yet I do not doubt but to obtain them all if friendship, at the leastwise procured for money, shall be able to prevail. But as it hath done hitherto, so the charges to be employed upon these brazen or copper images will hereafter put by the impression of that treatise, whereby it may come to pass that long travail shall soon prove to be spent in vain and much cost come to very small success. Whereof yet I force not greatly, sith by this means I have reaped some commodity unto myself by searching of the histories, which often minister store of examples ready to be used in my function, as occasion shall move me.[1] But to proceed with my purpose.

Before the coming of the Romans there was a kind of copper money current here in Britain, as Caesar confesseth in the fifth book of his *Commentaries*, but I find not of what manner it was. Hereto he addeth a report of certain rings of a proportionate weight, which they used in his time instead likewise of money.[2] But as hitherto it hath not been my luck (I say) to have the certain view of any of these, so after the coming of the Romans they enforced us to abandon our own and receive such imperial moneys or coins as for the payment of their legions was daily brought over unto them. What coins the Romans had it is easy to be known, and from time to time much of it is found in many places of this island, as well of gold and silver as of copper, brass, and other metal much like steel, almost of every emperor. So that I account it no rare thing to have of the Roman coin, albeit that it still represent an image of our captivity and may be a good admonition for us to take heed how we yield ourselves to the regiment of strangers.

Of the store of these moneys found upon the Kentish coast I have already made mention in the description of Richborough and chapter of isles adjacent unto the British Albion,[3] and there

[1] Presumably as *exempla* in sermons.
[2] *Gallic War*, V, xii.
[3] "Ethelbert, the first Christian King of Kent, did hold his palace in this town, and yet none of his coin hath hitherto been found there as is daily that of the Romans, whereof many pieces of silver and gold so well as of brass, copper, and other metal have often been showed unto me" (*Des. Brit.*, 1587, p. 30).

showed also how simple fishermen have had plenty of them, and that the conies in making proffers and holes to breed in have scraped them out of the ground in very great abundance.[4] In speaking also of St. Albans in the chapter of towns and villages, I have not omitted to tell what plenty of these coins have been gathered there, wherefore I shall not need here to repeat the same again. Howbeit, this is certain, that the most part of all these antiquities to be found within the land and distant from the shore are to be gotten either in the ruins of ancient cities and towns decayed or in enclosed burrows [shelters], where their legions accustomed sometime to winter, as by experience is daily confirmed.

What store hath been seen of them in the city of London, which they called *Augusta,* of the legion that sojourned there, and likewise in York, named also *Victrix* of the legion *Victoria,* or *Altera Roma* [Other Rome] (because of the beauty and fine building of the same), I myself can partly witness, that have seen and often had of them, if better testimony were wanting. The like I may affirm of Colchester, where those of Claudius, Hadrian, Trajan, Vespasian, and other are oftentimes plowed up or found by other means; also of Canterbury, Andredeschester (now decayed), Rochester, then called Durobrevum, Winchester, and divers other beyond the Thames, which for brevity sake I do pass over in silence. Only the chief of all and where most are found indeed is near unto Caerleon and Caergwent [Caerwent] in South Wales, about Kenchester (three miles above Hereford), Aldborough, Ancaster, Bramdon,[5] Dodington (where a spur and piece of a chain of gold were found in King Henry the Eighth his days, besides much of the said Roman coin), Binchester, Camalet [Queen's Camel, Somersetshire], Lacock-upon-Avon, and Lincoln, Dorchester, Warwick, and Chester, where they are often had in very great abundance.

It seemeth that Ancaster hath been a great thing, for many square and colored pavements, vaults, and arches are yet found and often laid open by such as dig and plow in the fields about the same. And amongst these one Uresby, or Roseby, a plow-

[4] Leland, *Itinerary* (ed. Smith, IV, 64). *Proffers:* essays, attempts (to burrow).
[5] *Bramdon:* perhaps Barham in Kent, which Leland spells "Barehamdoune" (IV, 41).

man, did ear [plow] up not long since a stone like a trough, covered with another stone, wherein was great foison [plenty] of the aforesaid coins. The like also was seen not yet forty years agone about Grantham. But in King Henry the Eighth his days an husbandman had far better luck at Harlaxton, two miles from the aforesaid place, where he found not only great plenty of this coin but also an huge brass pot, and therein a large helmet of pure gold, richly fretted with pearl and set with all kind of costly stones; he took up also chains much like unto beads of silver, all which, as being (if a man might guess any certainty by their beauty) not likely to be long hidden, he presented to Queen Catherine, then lying at Peterborough, and therewithal a few ancient rolls of parchment written long agone, though so defaced with moldiness and rotten for age that no man could well hold them in his hand without falling into pieces, much less read them by reason of their blindness.[6] In the beginning of the same King's days also, at Killey [Kyloe?] a man found as he eared an arming girdle, harnessed with pure gold, and a great massy pommel, with a cross hilt for a sword of the same metal, beside studs and harness for spurs and the huge long spurs of like stuff, whereof one Doctor Ruthall got a part into his hands.[7]

The burrows, or buries, whereof I spake before were certain plots of ground wherein the Roman soldiers did use to lie when they kept in the open fields as chosen places, from whence they might have easy access unto their adversaries if any outrage were wrought or rebellion moved against them. And as these were the usual abodes for those able legions that served daily in the wars, so had they other certain habitations for the old and forworn

[6] Most of Harrison's details about the discovery of Roman antiquities are freely embroidered around notes in Leland's *Itinerary*. As an example of Harrison's genius for expansion I quote all of the relevant passages in Leland: "In the south end of it [Ancaster] be oftentimes found in plowing great square stones of old buildings and Roman coins of brass and silver. In the west end of it, where now meadows be, are found in ditching great vaults. . . . An old man of Ancaster told me that by Ureby, or Roseby [the hamlet of Rauceby], a plowman took up a stone and found another stone under it, wherein was a square hole having Roman coin in it. He told me also that a plowman took up in the fields of Harlaxton, a two miles from Grantham, a stone, under the which was a pot of brass and an helmet of gold, set with stones in it, the which was presented to Catherine, Princess Dowager. There were beads of silver in the pot and writings corrupted" (I, 27–28).

[7] Leland (V, 55). *Thomas Ruthall*: Bishop of Durham (1509–1523).

[exhausted] soldiers, whereby divers cities grew in time to be replenished with Roman colonies, as Caerleon, Colchester, Chester, and such other, of which Colchester bare the name of *Colonia* long time and wherein A. Plautius builded a temple unto the Goddess of Victory (after the departure of Claudius), which Tacitus calleth *aram sempiternae dominationis*,[8] a perpetual monument of that our British servitude.

But to return unto our burrows, they were generally walled about with stone walls and so large in compass that some did contain thirty, forty, threescore, or eighty acres of ground within their limits; they had also divers gates or ports unto each of them, and of these not a few remain to be seen in our time, as one, for example, not far from Great Chesterford in Essex, near to the limits of Cambridgeshire, which I have often viewed and wherein the compass of the very wall with the places where the gates stood is easy to be discerned; the like also is to be seen at a place within two miles south of Burton, called the Burrow Hills.[9] In these therefore and suchlike, and likewise at Evolsburg,[10] now St. Neots, or St. Needs, and sundry other places, especially upon the shore and coasts of Kent, as Dover, Rye, Romney, Lydd, etc., is much of their coin also to be found, and some pieces or other are daily taken up, which they call burrow-pence, dwarfs'-money, hags'-pence, fairy-groats, Jews'-money, and by other foolish names not worthy to be remembered.

At the coming of the Saxons the Britons used these holds as rescues for their cattle in the day and night, when their enemies were abroad; the like also did the Saxons against the Danes, by which occasions (and now and then by carrying of their stones to help forward other buildings near at hand) many of them were thrown down and defaced which otherwise might have continued for a longer time, and so Your Honor would say if you should happen to peruse the thickness and manner of building of those said walls and burrows. It is not long since a silver saucer of very ancient making was found near to Saffron Walden in the open field among the Sturbury Hills [11] and eared up by a plow, but of such massy greatness that it weighed better than twenty

---

[8] Based on *Annals*, XIV, xxxi.
[9] Leland (IV, 19). *Burton:* Burton Lazars in Leicestershire.
[10] *Evolsburg:* Enolsbury, Eynesbury.
[11] "Sturbury a place where an army hath lien."—*H.*

ounces, as I have heard reported. But if I should stand in these things until I had said all that might be spoken of them, both by experience and testimony of Leland in his *Commentaries of Britain* and the report of divers yet living, I might make a greater chapter than would be either convenient or profitable to the reader; wherefore so much only shall serve the turn for this time as I have said already of antiquities found within our island, especially of coin, whereof I purposed chiefly to entreat.

CHAPTER XXV

Of the Coins of England

THE Saxon coin before the Conquest is in manner utterly unknown to me; howbeit, if my conjecture be anything, I suppose that 1s. of silver in those days did counterpeise [1] our common ounce, though afterward it came to pass that it arose to 20d. and so continued until the time of King Henry the Eighth, who first brought it to 3s. 4d. and afterward our silver coin unto brass and copper moneys, by reason of those inestimable charges which divers ways oppressed him. And as I gather such obscure notice of the shilling, which is called in Latin *solidus*, so I read more manifestly of another which is the forty-eighth part of a pound and this also current among the Saxons of our isle, so well in gold as in silver, at such time as 240 of their pennies made up a just pound, 5d. went to the shilling, and 4s. to the ounce. But to proceed with my purpose. After the death of King Henry, Edward, his son, began to restore the aforesaid coin again unto fine silver; so Queen Mary, his successor, did continue his good purpose, notwithstanding that in her time the Spanish money was very common in England by reason of her marriage with Philip, King of Spain.

After her decease, the Lady Elizabeth, her sister and now our most gracious Queen, sovereign, and princess, did finish the matter wholly, utterly abolishing the use of copper and brazen coin; and, converting the same into guns and great ordnance, she

---

[1] *Counterpeise:* counterpoise, equal in value.

restored sundry coins of fine silver, as pieces of ¾ d., of 1d., of
1½ d., pieces of 2d., of 3d., of 4d. (called the groat), of 6d.
(usually named the teston), and shilling of 12d., whereon she
hath imprinted her own image and emphatical superscription.[2]

Our gold is either old or new. The old is that which hath remained since the time of King Edward the Third or been coined
by such other princes as have reigned since his decease, without
any abasing or diminution of the fineness of that metal. Thereof
also we have yet remaining the ryal, the George noble, the Henry
ryal, the salute, the angel, and their smaller pieces, as halves or
quarters, though these in my time are not so common to be seen.
I have also beheld the sovereign of 20s. and the piece of 30s.;
I have heard likewise of pieces of 40s., £3, £5, and £10. But sith
there were few of them coined and those only at the commandment of kings, yearly to bestow where Their Majesties thought
good in lieu of New Year's gifts and rewards, it is not requisite
that I should remember them here amongst our current moneys.

The new gold is taken for such as began to be coined in the
latter days of King Henry the Eighth, at which time the fineness
of the metal began to be very much allayed and is not likely to
be restored for aught that I can see; and yet is it such as hath
been coined since by his successors, princes of this realm, in
value and goodness equal and not inferior to the coin and current
gold of other nations, where each one doth covet chiefly to
gather up our old finer gold, so that the angels, ryals, and nobles
are more plentifully seen in France, Italy, and Flanders than they
be by a great deal within the realm of England, if you regard
the payments which they daily make in those kinds of our coin.
Our [gold] pieces now current are of 10s., 5s., and 2s. 6d. only,
and those of sundry stamps and names, as half sovereigns (equal
in weight with our current shilling, whereby that gold is valued
at ten times so much silver), quarters of sovereigns (otherwise
called crowns), and half crowns, likewise angels,[3] half angels,
and quarters of angels; or if there be any other, in good sooth
I know them not, as one scarcely acquainted with any silver at
all, much less then (God it wot) with any store of gold.

The first current shilling, or silver pieces of 12d., stamped
within memory were coined by King Henry the Eighth in the

[2] "Elizabetha D[ei] G[racia] Ang[lie] Fra[ncie] et   Hib[ernie] Regina."
[3] Under Elizabeth the angel was valued at 10s.

twentieth year of his reign, and those of 5s. and of 2s. 6d. and
the half-shilling by King Edward the Sixth, but the odd pieces
above remembered under the groat by our high and mighty
princess, Queen Elizabeth, the name of the groat, penny, twopence, halfpenny, and farthing, in old time the greatest silver
moneys if you respect their denominations only, being more
ancient than that I can well discuss of the time of their beginnings. Yet thus much I read, that King Edward the First in the
eighth year of his reign did first coin the penny and smallest
pieces of silver roundwise, which before were square and wont
to bear a double cross with a crest, in such sort that the penny
might easily be broken either into halves or quarters; by which
shift only the people came by small moneys, as halfpence and
farthings, that otherwise were not stamped nor coined of set
purpose.

Of foreign [gold] coins we have all the ducats, the single,
double, and the double double, the crusadoes with the long cross
and the short, the portague, a piece very solemnly kept of divers [4]
and yet ofttimes abased with washing or absolutely counter-
feited, and finally, the French and Flemish crowns, only current among us so long as they hold weight. But of silver coins,
as the sols [sous] tournois, whereof ten make a shilling, as the
franc doth two shillings, and three francs the French crown,
etc., we have none at all; yet are the dalders [dollars, taler] and
such oftentimes brought over but nevertheless exchanged as bul-
lion according to their fineness and weight and afterward converted into coin by such as have authority.

In old time we had sundry mints in England and those commonly kept in abbeys and religious houses before the Conquest,
where true dealing was commonly supposed most of all to dwell,
as at Ramsey, St. Edmundsbury [Bury St. Edmunds], Canterbury, Glastonbury, Peterborough, and suchlike, sundry exem-
plificates [copies] of the grants whereof are yet to be seen in
writing, especially that of Peterborough under the confirmation
of Pope Eugenius; whereunto it appeareth further by a charter
of King Edgar (which I have) that they either held it or had
another in Stamford.[5] But after the Normans had once gotten

---

[4] The portague, a Portuguese gold coin ranging in value from £3 5s. to
£4 10s., was often kept as a keepsake or heirloom.
[5] *The Chronicle of Hugh Candidus* (ed. W. T. Mellows, 1949, pp. 110, 35).

the kingdom into their fingers, they trusted themselves best with the oversight of their mints and therefore erected divers of their own, although they afterward permitted some for small pieces of silver unto sundry of the houses aforesaid. In my time divers mints are suppressed, as Southwark, Bristol, etc., and all coinage is brought into one place, that is to say, the Tower of London, where it is continually holden and perused but not without great gain to such as deal withal.

There is also coinage of tin holden yearly at two several times, that is to say, Midsummer and Michaelmas, in the West Country, which at the first hearing I supposed to have been of money of the said metal and granted by privilege from some prince unto the towns of Helston, Truro, and Lostwithiel.[6] Howbeit, upon further examination of the matter, I find it to be nothing so but an office only erected for the prince, wherein he is allowed the ordinary customs of that metal, and such blocks of tin as have passed the hands of his officers are marked with an especial stamp, whereby it is known that the custom due for the same hath ordinarily been answered.

It should seem (and in my opinion is very likely to be true) that while the Romans reigned here, Kingston-upon-Thames (sometime a right noble city and place where the Saxon kings were usually crowned) was the chief place of their coinage for this province. For in earing [plowing] of the ground about that town in times past and now of late (besides the curious foundation of many goodly buildings that have been ripped up by plows, and divers coins of brass, silver, and gold with Roman letters in painted pots found there), in the days of Cardinal Wolsey one such huge pot was discovered, full as it were of new silver lately coined, another with plates of silver ready to be coined, and the third with chains of silver and such broken stuff ready (as it should appear) to be melted into coinage,[7] whereof let this suffice to countenance out my conjecture.

Of coins current before the coming of the Romans, I have elsewhere declared that there were none at all in Britain, but as the islanders of Scylira, the old Romans, Armenians, Scythians, Sericans, Sarmatians, Indians, and Essences did barter ware for ware, so the Britons used brass or rings of iron, brought unto a

[6] Leland, *Itinerary* (ed. Smith, I, 193, 198, 205).
[7] Leland (IV, 85).

certain proportion, instead of money, as the Lacedaemonians and Byzantines also did, and the Achivi (as Homer writeth), who had (saith he) rough pieces of brass and iron instead of coin, wherewith they purchased their wines.[8]

[8] *Iliad*, VII, 472–473; *Achivi:* Achaeans, Greeks.

BOOK III

The Description of England [continued]

CHAPTER I

Of Cattle Kept for Profit

THERE is no kind of tame cattle usually to be seen in these parts of the world whereof we have not some and that great store in England, as horses, oxen, sheep, goats, swine, and far surmounting the like in other countries, as may be proved with ease. For where are oxen commonly more large of bone, horses more decent and pleasant in pace, kine more commodious for the pale [suitable for enclosures], sheep more profitable for wool, swine more wholesome of flesh, and goats more gainful to their keepers than here with us in England?

But to speak of them peculiarly, I suppose that our kine are so abundant in yield of milk, whereof we make our butter and cheese, as the like anywhere else, and so apt for the plow in divers places as either our horses or oxen. And albeit they now and then twin, yet herein they seem to come short of that commodity which is looked for in other countries, to wit, in that they bring forth most commonly but one calf at once. The gains also gotten by a cow (all charges borne) hath been valued at 20s. yearly, but now, as land is enhanced, this proportion of gain is much abated, and likely to decay more and more if ground arise to be yet dearer, which God forbid if it be His will and pleasure. I heard of late of a cow in Warwickshire belonging to Thomas Bruer of Studley, which in six years had sixteen calves, that is, four at once in three calvings and twice twins, which unto many may seem a thing incredible.

In like manner our oxen are such as the like are not to be found in any country of Europe, both for greatness of body and sweetness of flesh, or else would not the Roman writers have preferred them before those of Liguria.[1] In most places our graziers are

[1] In *The Description of Britain* (1587, p. 36) Harrison specifies Columella (*De re rustica*, III, viii, 3), but the Mevania whose cattle the Roman writer praises is modern Bevagna in Umbria, not, as Harrison assumes, Anglesey.

now grown to be so cunning that if they do but see an ox or bullock and come to the feeling of him, they will give a guess at his weight and how many score or stone of flesh and tallow he beareth, how the butcher may live by the sale, and what he may have for the skin and tallow, which is a point of skill not commonly practiced heretofore. Some such graziers also are reported to ride with velvet coats and chains of gold about them, and in their absence their wives will not let to supply those turns with no less skill than their husbands, which is an hard work for the poor butcher, sith he through this means can seldom be rich or wealthy by his trade. In like sort the flesh of our oxen and kine is sold both by hand and by weight as the buyer will; but in young ware rather by weight, especially for the steer and heifer, sith the finer beef is the lightest, whereas the flesh of bulls and old kine, etc., is of sadder [denser] substance and therefore much heavier as it lieth in the scale.

Their horns also are known to be more fair and large in England than in any other places, except those which are to be seen among the Paeones,[2] which quantity, albeit that it be given to our breed generally by nature, yet it is now and then helped also by art. For when they be very young many graziers will oftentimes anoint their budding horns or tender tips with honey, which mollifieth the natural hardness of that substance and thereby maketh them to grow unto a notable greatness. Certes it is not strange in England to see oxen whose horns have the length of a yard or three foot between the tips, and they themselves thereto so tall as the height of a man of mean and indifferent stature is scarce equal unto them. Nevertheless, it is much to be lamented that our general breed of cattle is not better looked unto, for the greatest occupiers wean least store, because they can buy them (as they say) far better cheap than to raise and bring them up. In my time a cow hath risen from four nobles to four marks[3] by this means, which notwithstanding were no great price if they did yearly bring forth more than one calf apiece, as I hear they do in other countries.

Our horses moreover are high and although not commonly of such huge greatness as in other places of the main, yet if you respect the easiness of their pace it is hard to say where their

---

[2] "Athenaeus, *lib.* 10, *cap.* 8 [XI, 476]."—*H.*
[3] That is, from £1 6s. 8d. to £2 13s. 4d.

like are to be had. Our land doth yield no asses, and therefore we want the generation also of mules and somers [pack mules]; and therefore the most part of our carriage is made by these [horses], which remaining stoned are either reserved for the cart or appointed to bear such burdens as are convenient for them. Our cart or plow horses (for we use them indifferently) are commonly so strong that five or six of them (at the most) will draw three thousandweight of the greatest tale [4] with ease for a long journey, although it be not a load of common usage, which consisteth only of two thousand, or fifty foot of timber, forty bushels of white salt or six-and-thirty of bay [salt], or five quarters of wheat, [as] experience daily teacheth and I have elsewhere remembered. Such as are kept also for burden will carry four hundredweight commonly, without any hurt or hindrance. This furthermore is to be noted, that our princes and the nobility have their carriage commonly made by carts, whereby it cometh to pass that when the Queen's Majesty doth remove from any one place to another, there are usually four hundred cartwares [teams], which amount to the sum of 2,400 horses, appointed out of the countries adjoining, whereby her carriage is conveyed safely unto the appointed place. Hereby also the ancient use of somers and sumpter [pack] horses is in manner utterly relinquished, which causeth the trains of our princes in their progresses to show far less than those of the kings of other nations.

Such as serve for the saddle are commonly gelded and now grown to be very dear among us, especially if they be well colored, justly limbed, and have thereto an easy ambling pace. For our countrymen, seeking their ease in every corner where it is to be had, delight very much in these qualities but chiefly in their excellent paces, which besides that it is in manner peculiar unto horses of our soil and not hurtful to the rider or owner sitting on their backs, it is moreover very pleasant and delectable in his ears, in that the noise of their well-proportioned pace doth yield comfortable sound as he traveleth by the way.

Yet is there no greater deceit used anywhere than among our horsekeepers, horsecorsers [horse dealers], and hostlers, for such is the subtle knavery of a great sort of them (without exception of any of them, be it spoken, which deal for private gain) that

[4] *Of the greatest tale:* that is, reckoning the hundredweight at 112 pounds; see p. 457.

an honest-meaning man shall have very good luck among them if he be not deceived by some false trick or other. There are certain notable markets wherein great plenty of horses and colts is bought and sold, and whereunto such as have need resort yearly to buy and make their necessary provision of them, as Ripon, Newport Pond, Woolpit, Harborough, and divers other. But as most drovers are very diligent to bring great store of these unto those places, so many of them are too-too lewd [wicked] in abusing such as buy them. For they have a custom to make them look fair to the eye, when they come within two days' journey of the market to drive them till they sweat and for the space of eight or twelve hours, which being done they turn them all over the backs into some water, where they stand for a season, and then go forward with them to the place appointed, where they make sale of their infected ware and such as by this means do fall into many diseases and maladies.

Of such outlandish horses as are daily brought over unto us I speak not, as the jennet of Spain, the courser of Naples, the hobby of Ireland, the Flemish roil, and Scottish nag, because that further speech of them cometh not within the compass of this treatise, and for whose breed and maintenance (especially of the greatest sort) King Henry the Eighth erected a noble studdery and for a time had very good success with them, till the officers, waxing weary, procured a mixed brood of bastard races, whereby his good purpose came to little effect. Sir Nicholas Arnold of late hath bred the best horses in England and written of the manner of their production; [5] would to God his compass of ground were like to that of Pella in Syria, wherein the king of that nation had usually a studdery of thirty thousand mares and three hundred stallions, as Strabo doth remember (*lib.* 16 [ii, 10]). But to leave this, let us see what may be said of sheep.

Our sheep are very excellent, sith for sweetness of flesh they pass all other. And so much are our wools to be preferred before those of Milesia [Miletus] and other places that if Jason had known the value of them that are bred and to be had in Britain, he would never have gone to Colchis to look for any there. For as Dionysius Alexandrinus saith in his *De situ orbis*, it may by

---

[5] *Sir Nicholas Arnold* (?1507–1581): M.P. for Gloucestershire, lord justice in Ireland; no trace remains of his writings on horse breeding.

spinning be made comparable to the spider's web.[6] What fools, then, are our countrymen, in that they seek to bereave themselves of this commodity by practicing daily how to transfer the same to other nations, in carrying over their rams and ewes to breed and increase among them? The first example hereof was given under Edward the Fourth, who, not understanding the bottom of the suit of sundry traitorous merchants that sought a present gain with the perpetual hindrance of their country, licensed them to carry over certain numbers of them into Spain, who, having license but for a few, shipped very many,[7] a thing commonly practiced in other commodities also, whereby the prince and her land are not seldom times defrauded. But such is our nature and so blind are we indeed that we see no inconvenience before we feel it, and for a present gain we regard not what damage may ensue to our posterity. Hereto some other man would add also the desire that we have to benefit other countries and to impeach our own. And it is so sure as God liveth that every trifle which cometh from beyond the sea, though it be not worth 3*d.*, is more esteemed than a continual commodity at home with us which far exceedeth that value.

In time past the use of this commodity [wool] consisted (for the most part) in cloth and worsteds; but now by means of strangers succored here from domestical persecution,[8] the same hath been employed unto sundry other uses, as mockadoes, baize, velures, grograines,[9] etc., whereby the makers have reaped no small commodity. It is furthermore to be noted, for the Low Countries of Belgia know it, and daily experience (notwithstand-

---

[6] *Dionysius Alexandrinus:* the name given Dionysius Periegetes (fl. A.D. 300) by Thomas Twyne, who translated his geographical poem as *The Survey of the World, or Situation of the Earth* (1572), sig. C5r.

[7] "King Edward concluded an amity and league with Henry, King of Castile, and John, King of Aragon, at the concluding whereof he granted license for certain Cotswold sheep to be transported into the country of Spain (as people report), which have there so multiplied and increased that it hath turned the commodity of England much to the Spanish profit" (Holinshed, *History of England*, 1587, under 1466).

[8] Including apparently Harrison's wife, "Marion Isebrand, daughter to William Isebrand and Anne, his wife, sometime of Anderne [Andres] near unto Guînes in Picardy" (Harrison's will, Furnivall, IV, 222–224).

[9] *Mockadoes:* wool cloths; *velures:* velvets; *grograines:* grograms, coarse fabrics of silk and mohair.

ing the sharpness of our laws to the contrary)[10] doth yet confirm it, that although our rams and wethers do go thither from us never so well headed according to their kind, yet after they have remained there a while they cast there their heads, and from thenceforth they remain polled, without any horns at all.

Certes this kind of cattle is more cherished in England than standeth well with the commodity of the commons or prosperity of divers towns, whereof some are wholly converted to their feeding; yet such a profitable sweetness is found in their fleece, such necessity in their flesh, and so great a benefit in the manuring of barren soil with their dung and piss that their superfluous numbers are the better borne withal. And there is never an husbandman (for now I speak not of our great sheepmasters, of whom some one man hath twenty thousand) but hath more or less of this cattle feeding on his fallows and short grounds, which yield the finer fleece, as Virgil (following Varro) well espied (*Georg.* 3) where he saith:

> *Si tibi lanicium curae, primum aspera sylva,*
> *Lappaeque tribulique absint, fuge pabula laeta.*[11]

Nevertheless, the sheep of our country are often troubled with the rot (as are our swine with the measles, though never so generally), and many men are now and then great losers by the same; but after the calamity is over, if they can recover and keep their new stocks sound for seven years together, the former loss will easily be recompensed with double commodity. Cardan writeth that our waters are hurtful to our sheep;[12] howbeit, this is but his conjecture, for we know that our sheep are infected by going to the water, and take the same as a sure and certain token that a rot hath gotten hold of them, their livers and lights being already distempered through excessive heat, which enforceth them the rather to seek unto the water. Certes there is no parcel of the main wherein a man shall generally find more fine and wholesome water than in England, and therefore it is

[10] According to the statute 8 Eliz., c. 3, the penalties for exporting sheep, as a first offense, were forfeiture of all possessions, a year's imprisonment, and severance of the left hand, which was to be nailed up in a market place. For a second offense the punishment was death.

[11] "If wool is your care, first remove the prickly growth of burs and thorns; avoid rich fodder" (ll. 384–385).

[12] *De subtilitate rerum* (Nuremberg, 1550, p. 227).

impossible that our sheep should decay by tasting of the same. Wherefore the hindrance by rot is rather to be ascribed to the unseasonableness and moisture of the weather in summer, also their licking in of mildews, gossamer, rowty fogs,[13] and rank grass, full of superfluous juice; but specially (I say) to overmoist weather, whereby the continual rain piercing into their hollow fells soaketh forthwith into their flesh, which bringeth them to their banes [deaths]. Being also infected, their first show of sickness is their desire to drink, so that our waters are not unto them *causa aegritudinis* but *signum morbi*,[14] whatsoever Cardan do maintain to the contrary.

There are (and peradventure no small babes) which are grown to be so good husbands that they can make account of every ten kine to be clearly worth £20 in common and indifferent years, if the milk of five sheep be daily added to the same. But as I wot not how true this surmise is, because it is no part of my trade, so I am sure hereof, that some housewives can and do add daily a less proportion of ewes' milk unto the cheese of so many kine, whereby their cheese doth the longer abide moist and eateth more brickle [crisp] and mellow than otherwise it would.

Goats we have plenty and of sundry colors in the west parts of England, especially in and towards Wales and amongst the rocky hills, by whom the owners do reap no small advantage; some also are cherished elsewhere in divers steads for the benefit of such as are diseased with sundry maladies, unto whom (as I hear) their milk, cheese, and bodies of their young kids are judged very profitable and therefore inquired for of many far and near. Certes I find among the writers that the milk of a goat is next in estimation to that of the woman, for that it helpeth the stomach, removeth oppilations and stoppings of the liver, and looseth the belly. Some place also next unto it the milk of the ewe, and thirdly that of the cow. But hereof I can show no reason; only this I know, that ewes' milk is fulsome [cloying], sweet, and such in taste as, except such as are used unto it, no man will gladly yield to live and feed withal.

As for swine, there is no place that hath greater store nor more wholesome in eating than are these here in England, which nevertheless do never any good till they come to the table. Of these

---

[13] *Rowty fogs:* the coarse, rank, second growth of grass.
[14] "Not the cause of sickness but an indication of disease."

some we eat green for pork and other dried up into bacon to have it of more continuance. Lard we make some, though very little, because it is chargeable; neither have we such use thereof as is to be seen in France and other countries, sith we do either bake our meat with sweet suet of beef or mutton and baste all our meat with sweet or salt butter, or suffer the fattest to baste itself by leisure. In champaign countries they are kept by herds and an hogherd appointed to attend and wait upon them, who commonly gathereth them together by his noise and cry and leadeth them forth to feed abroad in the fields. In some places also women do scour and wet their clothes with their dung, as other do with hemlocks and nettles, but such is the savor of the clothes touched withal that I cannot abide to wear them on my body, more than such as are scoured with the refuse soap, than the which (in mine opinion) there is none more unkindly savor.

Of our tame boars we make brawn, which is a kind of meat not usually known to strangers (as I take it), otherwise would not the swart rutters [German cavalry] and French cooks at the loss of Calais (where they found great store of this provision almost in every house) have attempted with ridiculous success to roast, bake, broil, and fry the same for their masters till they were better informed. I have heard moreover how a nobleman of England not long since did send over an hogshead of brawn ready-soused to a Catholic gentleman of France, who, supposing it to be fish, reserved it till Lent, at which time he did eat thereof with very great frugality. Thereto he so well liked of the provision itself that he wrote over very earnestly and with offer of great recompense for more of the same fish against the year ensuing; whereas if he had known it to have been flesh, he would not have touched it (I dare say) for a thousand crowns without the Pope's dispensation. A friend of mine also, dwelling sometime in Spain, having certain Jews at his table, did set brawn before them, whereof they did eat very earnestly, supposing it to be a kind of fish not common in those parties, but when the goodman of the house brought in the head in pastime among them to show what they had eaten, they rose from the table, hied them home in haste, each of them procuring himself to vomit, some by oil and some by other means, till (as they supposed) they had cleansed their stomachs of that prohibited food.

With us it is accounted a great piece of service at the table from November until February be ended, but chiefly in the Christmastime. With the same also we begin our dinners each day after other, and because it is somewhat hard of digestion a draught of malvesey [malvasia, malmsey], bastard, or muscatel is usually drunk after it, where either of them are conveniently to be had; otherwise the meaner sort content themselves with their own drink [beer], which at that season is generally very strong, and stronger indeed than in all the year beside. It is made commonly of the fore part of a tame boar, set up for the purpose by the space of a whole year or two, especially in gentlemen's houses (for the husbandmen and farmers never frank [15] them for their own use above three or four months, or half a year at the most), in which time he is dieted with oats and peason [peas], and lodged on the bare planks of an uneasy cote till his fat be hardened sufficiently for their purpose; afterward he is killed, scalded, and cut out, and then of his former parts is our brawn made; the rest is nothing so fat, and therefore it beareth the name of souse only and is commonly reserved for the servingman and hind [farm hand], except it please the owner to have any part thereof baked, which are then handled of custom after this manner. The hinder parts being cut off, they are first drawn with lard and then sodden [boiled]; being sodden, they are soused in claret wine and vinegar a certain space and afterward baked in pasties and eaten of many instead of the wild boar, and truly it is very good meat; the pestles [hams] may be hanged up a while to dry before they be drawn with lard, if you will, and thereby prove the better.

But hereof enough, and therefore to come again unto our brawn. The neck pieces, being cut off round, are called collars of brawn, the shoulders are named shields; only the ribs retain the former denomination, so that these aforesaid pieces deserve the name of brawn; the bowels of the beast are commonly cast away because of their rankness, and so were likewise his stones till a foolish fantasy got hold of late amongst some delicate dames, who have now found the means to dress them also with great cost for a dainty dish and bring them to the board as a service among other of like sort, though not without note of their desire to the provocation of fleshly lust, which by this their

---

[15] *Frank:* fatten in a sty.

fond curiosity is not a little revealed. When the boar is thus cut out, each piece is wrapped up, either with bulrushes, osier peels, tape, inkle, or suchlike, and then sodden in a lead [pot] or caldron together till they be so tender that a man may thrust a bruised rush or soft straw clean through the fat, which being done they take it up and lay it abroad to cool; afterward, putting it into close vessels, they pour either good small ale or beer mingled with verjuice and salt thereto till it be covered, and so let it lie (now and then altering and changing the sousing drink lest it should wax sour) till occasion serve to spend it out of the way. Some use to make brawn of great barrow hogs and seethe them and souse the whole as they do that of the boar; and in my judgment it is the better of both and more easy of digestion. But of brawn thus much, and so much may seem sufficient.

CHAPTER II

Of Wild and Tame Fowls

ORDER requireth that I speak somewhat of the fowls also of England, which I may easily divide into the wild and tame; but alas, such is my small skill in fowls that to say the truth I can neither recite their numbers nor well distinguish one kind of them from another. Yet this I have by general knowledge, that there is no nation under the sun which hath already in the [seasonable] time of the year more plenty of wild fowl than we, for so many kinds as our island doth bring forth, and much more would have if those of the higher soil might be spared but one year or two from the greedy engines [nets] of covetous fowlers, which set only for the pot and purse. Certes this enormity bred great trouble in King John's days, insomuch that, going in progress about the tenth of his reign, he found little or no game wherewith to solace himself or exercise his falcons. Wherefore, being at Bristol in the Christmas ensuing, he restrained all manner of hawking or taking of wild fowl throughout England for a season, whereby the land within few years was thoroughly replenished again. But what stand I upon this impertinent discourse?

Of such therefore as are bred in our land, we have the crane, the bittern, the wild and tame swan, the bustard, the heron, curlew, snite [snipe], wild goose, wind or dotterel, brant, lark, plover of both sorts, lapwing, teal, widgeon, mallard, sheldrake, shoveler, pewit, sea mew, barnacle, quail (who only with man are subject to the falling sickness), the knot, the oliet or olive [oyster catcher], the dunbird, woodcock, partridge, and pheasant, besides divers other whose names to me are utterly unknown, and much more the taste of their flesh, wherewith I was never acquainted. But as these serve not at all seasons, so in their several turns there is no plenty of them wanting whereby the tables of the nobility and gentry should seem at any time furnished.

But of all these the production of none is more marvelous, in my mind, than that of the barnacle, whose place of generation we have sought ofttimes so far as the Orcades [Orkney Islands], whereas peradventure we might have found the same nearer home, and not only upon the coasts of Ireland but even in our own rivers. If I should say how either these or some such other fowl not much unlike unto them have bred of late times (for their place of generation is not perpetual but as opportunity serveth and the circumstances do minister occasion) in the Thames mouth, I do not think that many will believe me; yet such a thing hath there been seen, where a kind of fowl had his beginning upon a short, tender shrub standing near unto the shore, from whence when their time came they fell down, either into the salt water and lived or upon the dry land and perished, as Péna, the French herbarian, hath also noted in the very end of his herbal.[1] What I for mine own part have seen here by experience, I have already so touched in the chapter of islands that it should be but time spent in vain to repeat it here again. Look therefore in the description of Man, or Manaw [Mona], for more of these barnacles, as also in the eleventh chapter of *The Description of Scotland*, and I do not doubt but you shall in some respect be satisfied in the generation of these fowls.[2] As for

[1] Pierre Péna and Matthias de l'Obel, *Stirpium adversaria nova* (1570), p. [458].
[2] "For my part I have been very desirous to understand the uttermost of the breeding of barnacles and questioned with divers persons about the same. I have read also whatsoever is written by foreign authors touching the

egrets, paupers,[3] and suchlike, they are daily brought unto us from beyond the sea, as if all the fowl of our country could not suffice to satisfy our delicate appetites.

Our tame fowl are such (for the most part) as are common both to us and to other countries, as cocks, hens, geese, ducks, peacocks of Inde, pigeons (now an hurtful fowl by reason of

---

generation of that fowl and sought out some places where I have been assured to see great numbers of them, but in vain. Wherefore I utterly despaired to obtain my purpose till this present year of grace, 1584, and month of May, wherein, going to the court at Greenwich from London by boat, I saw sundry ships lying in the Thames, newly come home either from Barbary or the Canary Isles (for I do not well remember now from which of these places), on whose sides I perceived an infinite sort of shells to hang so thick as could be, one by another. Drawing near also I took off ten or twelve of the greatest of them, and afterward having opened them I saw the proportion of a fowl in one of them more perfectly than in all the rest, saving that the head was not yet formed because the fresh water had killed them all (as I take it) and thereby hindered their perfection. Certainly the feathers of the tail hung out of the shell at least two inches, the wings (almost perfect, touching form) were guarded with two shells or shields proportioned like the self wings, and likewise the breastbone had her coverture also of like shelly substance, and altogether resembling the figure which L'Obel and Péna do give forth in their description of this fowl; so that I am now fully persuaded that it is either the barnacle that is engendered after one manner in these shells or some other seafowl to us as yet unknown. For by the feathers appearing and form so apparent it cannot be denied but that some bird or other must proceed of this substance, which by falling from the sides of the ships in long voyages may come to some perfection" (*Des. Brit.*, 1587, p. 38).

"Now it is come to hand that I entreat of those geese which are engendered by the sea, whose procreation hath hitherto been thought to have been made upon trees. But the opinion is false, and yet sith their generation is strange indeed, I have not a little travailed and with no small diligence endeavored to search out the truth hereof, whereby I learn that their engendrure is rather to be referred to the sea than anything else, if my conjecture be aught; for although that they are in sundry wise producted, yet I find the same to be performed continually in the sea and not elsewhere, as shall appear hereafter. All trees cast into that element in process of time become worm-eaten, and in the holes thereof are the said worms to be found, though very little and small (in comparison to that they be afterward) to be perceived at the first. In the beginning these worms do show their heads and feet, and last of all their plumes and wings. Finally, when they are come to the just measure and quantity of geese, they fly in the air as other fowls do" (*Des. Scot.*, 1587, p. 17).

One of the most persistent myths of unnatural history was this association of the marine barnacle with the barnacle goose, a winter visitor to England whose Arctic breeding grounds were unknown.

[3] *Paupers:* popelers, spoonbills.

their multitudes and number of houses daily erected for their increase, which the bowers [husbandmen] of the country call in scorn almshouses and dens of thieves and suchlike), whereof there is great plenty in every farmer's yard. They are kept there also to be sold either for ready money in the open markets or else to be spent at home in good company amongst their neighbors without reprehension or fines. Neither are we so miserable in England (a thing only granted unto us by the especial grace of God and liberty of our princes) as to dine or sup with a quarter of a hen, or to make so great a repast with a cockscomb as they do in some other countries; but if occasion serve, the whole carcasses of many capons, hens, pigeons, and suchlike do oft go to wrack, beside beef, mutton, veal, and lamb, all which at every feast are taken for necessary dishes amongst the commonalty of England.

The gelding of cocks, whereby capons are made, is an ancient practice brought in of old time by the Romans when they dwelt here in this land; but the gelding of turkeys or Indish peacocks is a newer device and certainly not used amiss, sith the rankness of that bird is very much abated thereby and the strong taste of the flesh in sundry wise amended. If I should say that ganders grow also to be gelded, I suppose that some will laugh me to scorn, neither have I tasted at any time of such a fowl so served, yet have I heard it more than once to be used in the country, where their geese are driven to the field like herds of cattle by a gooseherd, a toy also no less to be marveled at than the other. For as it is rare to hear of a gelded gander, so is it strange to me to see or hear of geese to be led to the field like sheep; yet so it is, and their gooseherd carrieth a rattle of paper or parchment with him when he goeth about in the morning to gather his goslings together, the noise whereof cometh no sooner to their ears than they fall to gaggling and hasten to go with him. If it happen that the gates be not yet open or that none of the house be stirring, it is ridiculous to see how they will peep under the doors and never leave creaking [cackling] and gaggling till they be let out unto him to overtake their fellows. With us where I dwell they are not kept in this sort nor in many other places, neither are they kept so much for their bodies as their feathers. Some hold furthermore an opinion that in overrank soils their dung doth so qualify the battableness [fertility] of the soil that their cattle is thereby kept from the garget and sundry other diseases, although some of them come to their ends now and then by licking up of their feathers. I might here make mention of other fowls producted by the industry of man, as between the pheasant cock and dunghill hen, or between the pheasant and the ringdove, the peacock and the turkey hen, the partridge and the pigeon, but sith I have no more knowledge of these than what I have gotten by mine ear, I will not meddle with them. Yet Cardan, speaking of the second sort, doth affirm it to be a fowl of excellent beauty.[4]

I would likewise entreat of other fowls, which we repute unclean, as ravens, crows, pies, choughs, rooks, kites, jays, ringtails, starlings, woodspikes, woodnaws,[5] ravens, etc., but sith they abound in all countries, though peradventure most of all in England (by reason of our negligence), I shall not need to spend any time in the rehearsal of them. Neither are our crows and choughs cherished of purpose to catch up the worms that breed in our soils (as Polydore supposeth),[6] sith there are no uplandish towns but have (or should have) nets of their own in store to catch them withal. Sundry acts of Parliament are likewise made for their utter destruction, as also the spoil of other ravenous fowls hurtful to poultry, conies, lambs, and kids, whose valuation of reward to him that killeth them is after the head, a device brought from the Goths, who had the like ordinance for the destruction of their white crows, and tale [count] made by the beck [beak], which killed both lambs and pigs. The like order is taken with us for our vermins, as with them also for the rootage out of their wild beasts, saving that they spared their greatest bears, especially the white, whose skins are by custom and privilege reserved to cover those planchers [planks] whereupon their priests do stand at Mass, lest he should take some unkind cold in such a long piece of work; and happy is the man that may provide them for him, for he shall have pardon enough for that so religious an act to last if he will till doomsday do approach, and many thousands after.[7] Nothing therefore can be more unlikely to be true than

---

[4] *De rerum varietate*, VII, xxxvi.

[5] *Ringtails:* females of the hen harrier; *woodspikes:* woodspecks, woodpeckers; *woodnaws:* perhaps a local name for a species of woodpecker (woodgnaws?).

[6] *English History,* I (ed. Sir Henry Ellis, Camden Soc., XXXVI, 1846, 23).

[7] These details about the Goths, but not the bias, come from Olaus Magnus, *Historia de gentibus septentrionalibus,* IV, xv and XVI, i.

that these noisome creatures are nourished amongst us to devour our worms, which do not abound much more in England than elsewhere in other countries of the main.

It may be that some look for a discourse also of our other fowls in this place at my hand, as nightingales, thrushes, blackbirds, mavises, ruddocks, redstarts or dunnocks, larks, tivits, kingfishers, buntings, turtles white or gray, linnets, bullfinches, goldfinches, washtails, cherry-crackers, yellowhammers, felfars,[8] etc., but I should then spend more time upon them than is convenient. Neither will I speak of our costly and curious aviaries daily made for the better hearing of their melody and observation of their natures; but I cease also to go any further in these things, having (as I think) said enough already of these that I have named.

CHAPTER III

Of Fish Usually Taken upon Our Coasts

I HAVE in my description of waters, as occasion hath served, entreated of the names of some of the several fishes which are commonly to be found in our rivers. Nevertheless, as every water hath a sundry mixture and therefore is not stored with every kind, so there is almost no house, even of the meanest bowers, which have not one or mo ponds or holes, made for reservation of water, unstored with some of them, as with tench, carp, bream, roach, dace, eels, or suchlike as will live and breed together.

Certes it is not possible for me to deliver the names of all such kinds of fishes as our rivers are found to bear; yet lest I should seem injurious to the reader in not delivering so many of them as have been brought to my knowledge, I will not let to set them down as they do come to mind. Besides the salmons, therefore, which are not to be taken from the midst [middle] of September to the midst of November, and are very plentiful in our greatest

---

[8] *Dunnocks:* hedge sparrows; *tivits:* tewits, lapwings; *washtails:* pied wagtails; *cherry-crackers:* hawfinches; *felfars:* fieldfares.

rivers, as their young store [stock] are not to be touched from mid-April unto Midsummer, we have the trout, barbel, grail, pout, chevin, pike, gudgeon, smelt, perch, menan, shrimps, crevises,[1] lampreys, and suchlike, whose preservation is provided for by very sharp laws, not only in our rivers but also in plashes [pools] or lakes and ponds,[2] which otherwise would bring small profit to the owners and do much harm by continual maintenance of idle persons, who would spend their whole times upon their banks, not coveting to labor with their hands nor follow any good trade.

Of all these there are none more prejudicial to their neighbors that dwell in the same water than the pike and eel, which commonly devour such fish or fry and spawn as they may get and come by. Nevertheless, the pike is friend unto the tench, as to his leech [physician] and surgeon. For when the fishmonger hath opened his side and laid out his rivet [liver] and fat unto the buyer for the better utterance of his ware, and cannot make him away at that present, he layeth the same again into the proper place and, sewing up the wound, he restoreth him to the pond where tenches are, who never cease to suck and lick his grieved place till they have restored him to health and made him ready to come again to the stall, when his turn shall come about. I might here make report how the pike, carp, and some other of our river fishes are sold by inches of clean fish, from the eyes or gills to the crotch of the tails, but it is needless; also how the pike, as he ageth, receiveth diverse names, as from a fry to a gilthead, from a gilthead to a pod, from a pod to a jack, from a jack to a pickerel, from a pickerel to a pike, and last of all to a luce; also that a salmon is the first year a graveling and commonly so big as an herring, the second a salmon peal, the third a pug, and the fourth a salmon, but this is in like sort unnecessary.

I might finally tell you how that in fenny rivers' sides, if you cut a turf and lay it with the grass downwards upon the earth in such sort as the water may touch it as it passeth by, you shall have a brood of eels, it would seem a wonder; and yet it is

---

[1] *Grail*: perhaps for grayling; *chevin*: chub; *menan*: minnow; *crevises*: crayfish.

[2] The statute 5 Eliz., c. 21 established three months' imprisonment (and seven years' parole) as the penalty for any person who "shall wrongfully fish in any of the said ponds, pools, moats, etc."

believed with no less assurance of some than that an horsehair laid in a pail full of the like water will in short time stir and become a living creature. But sith the certainty of these things is rather proved by few than the certainty of them known unto many, I let it pass at this time. Nevertheless, this is generally observed in the maintenance of fry, so well in rivers as in ponds, that in the time of spawn we use to throw in faggots made of willow and sallow, and now and then of bushes for want of the other, whereby such spawn as falleth into the same is preserved and kept from the pike, perch, eel, and other fish, of which the carp also will feed upon his own and thereby hinder the store and increase of proper kind. Some use in every fifth or seventh year to lay their great ponds dry for all the summertime, to the end they may gather grass and a thin sward [sod] for the fish to feed upon, and afterwards store them with breeders, after the water be let of new again into them; finally, when they have spawned, they draw out the breeders, leaving not above four or six behind even in the greatest ponds, by means whereof the rest do prosper the better, and this observation is most used in carp and bream; as for perch (a delicate fish) it prospereth everywhere, I mean, so well in ponds as rivers and also in moats and pits, as I do know by experience, though their bottoms be but clay. More would I write of our fresh fish if any more were needful; wherefore I will now turn over unto such of the salt water as are taken upon our coasts.

As our fowls, therefore, have their seasons, so likewise have all our sorts of sea fish, whereby it cometh to pass that none, or at the leastwise very few of them, are to be had at all times. Nevertheless, the seas that environ our coasts are of all other most plentiful; for as by reason of their depth they are a great succor, so our low shores minister great plenty of food unto the fish that come thereto, no place being void or barren either through want of food for them or the falls of filthy rivers, which naturally annoy them. In December, therefore, and January we commonly abound in herring and red fish, as rochet[3] and gurnard. In February and March we feed on plaice, trouts, turbot, mussels, etc. In April and May with mackerel and cockles. In June and July with conger. In August and September with haddock and herring, and the two months ensuing with the same, as also thornback and

[3] *Rochet:* the red gurnard.

ray of all sorts, all which are the most usual and wherewith our common sort are best of all refreshed.

For mine own part I am greatly acquainted neither with the seasons nor yet with the fish itself, and therefore if I should take upon me to describe or speak of either of them absolutely, I should enterprise more than I am able to perform and go in hand with a greater matter than I can well bring about. It shall suffice therefore to declare what sorts of fishes I have most often seen, to the end I may not altogether pass over this chapter without the rehearsal of something, although the whole sum of that which I have to say be nothing indeed, if the performance of a full discourse hereof be anything hardly required.

Of fishes, therefore, as I find five sorts, the flat, the round, the long, the legged, and shelled, so the flat are divided into the smooth, scaled, and tailed. Of the first are the plaice, the butt, the turbot, birt,[4] fluke or sea flounder, dory, dab, etc. Of the second, the soles, etc. Of the third, our chaits, maidens, kingstons, flathe,[5] and thornback, whereof the greater be for the most part either dried and carried into other countries, or sodden, soused, and eaten here at home, whilst the lesser be fried or buttered soon after they be taken, as provision not to be kept long for fear of putrefaction. Under the round kinds are commonly comprehended lumps, an ugly fish to sight and yet very delicate in eating if it be kindly dressed, the whiting (an old waiter or servitor in the court),[6] the rochet, sea bream, pirle,[7] hake, sea trout, gurnard, haddock, cod, herring, pilchard, sprat, and suchlike. And these are they whereof I have best knowledge and be commonly to be had in their times upon our coasts. Under this kind also are all the great fish contained, as the seal, the dolphin, the porpoise, the thirlepoole,[8] whale, and whatsoever is round of body, be it never so great and huge. Of the long sort are congers, eels, garfish, and such other of that form. Finally, of the legged kind we have not many, neither have I seen any more of this

---

[4] *Birt:* apparently another name for turbot.

[5] *Chaits:* apparently skates; *maidens:* maids, the young skates; *kingstons:* angelfish; *flathe:* ray or skate.

[6] In reference to the proverbial use of the term "whitings" for flatterers.

[7] *Pirle:* perhaps for "pearl," a local name for brill, but in that case it should be classified as a flatfish.   [8] *Thirlepoole:* a species of whale.

sort than the *polypus*,[9] called in English the lobster, crayfish or crevise, and the crab. As for the little crayfishes, they are not taken in the sea but plentifully in our fresh rivers, in banks and under stones, where they keep themselves in most secret manner and oft by likeness of color with the stones among which they lie deceive even the skillful takers of them, except they use great diligence. Carolus Stephanus, in his *Maison rustique*,[10] doubted whether these lobsters be fish or not and in the end concludeth them to grow of the purgation of the water, as doth the frog, and these also not to be eaten, for that they be strong and very hard of digestion. But hereof let other determine further.

I might here speak of sundry other fishes now and then taken also upon our coasts, but sith my mind is only to touch either all such as are usually gotten, or so many of them only as I can well rehearse upon certain knowledge, I think it good at this time to forbear the further entreaty of them. As touching the shelly sort, we have plenty of oysters, whose valure in old time for their sweetness was not unknown in Rome (although Mucianus, as Pliny noteth, *lib*. 32, *cap*. 6 [xxi], prefer the Cyzicene before them), and these we have in like manner of diverse quantities, and no less variety also of our mussels and cockles. We have in like sort no small store of great whelks, scallops, and periwinkles, and each of them brought far into the land from the seacoast in their several seasons. And albeit our oysters are generally forborne in the four hot months of the year, that is to say, May, June, July, and August, which are void of the letter R, yet in some places they be continually eaten, where they be kept in pits, as I have known by experience. And thus much of our sea fish, as a man in manner utterly unacquainted with their diversity of kinds; yet so much have I yielded to do, hoping hereafter to say somewhat more and more orderly of them, if it shall please God that I may live and have leisure once again to peruse this treatise and so make up a perfect piece of work of that which, as you now see, is very slenderly attempted and begun.

[9] *Polypus:* properly the octopus or cuttlefish.
[10] *Carolus Stephanus:* Charles Estienne (?1504–1564), French printer, physician, and scholar; the cited passage occurs in his collection of tracts on husbandry, *L'Agriculture et maison rustique*, IV, xiii (Lyons, 1583, fol. 284v).

CHAPTER IV

Of Savage Beasts and Vermins

It is none of the least blessings wherewith God hath endued this island that it is void of noisome beasts, as lions, bears, tigers, pards [leopards], wolves, and suchlike, by means whereof our countrymen may travel in safety and our herds and flocks remain for the most part abroad in the field without any herdman or keeper.

This is chiefly spoken of the south and southwest parts of the island. For whereas we that dwell on this side of the Tweed may safely boast of our security in this behalf, yet cannot the Scots do the like in every point within their kingdom, sith they have grievous [dangerous] wolves and cruel foxes, beside some other of like disposition continually conversant among them, to the general hindrance of their husbandmen and no small damage unto the inhabiters of those quarters. The happy and fortunate want of these beasts in England is universally ascribed to the politic government of King Edgar, who, to the intent the whole country might once be cleansed and clearly rid of them, charged the conquered Welshmen (who were then pestered with these ravenous creatures above measure) to pay him a yearly tribute of wolves' skins to be gathered within the land. He appointed them thereto a certain number of three hundred, with free liberty for their prince to hunt and pursue them over all quarters of the realm, as our chronicles do report. Some there be which write how Ludwall, prince of Wales, paid yearly to King Edgar this tribute of three hundred wolves, whose carcasses, being brought into Loegria, were buried at Wolfpit in Cambridgeshire, and that by means thereof within the compass and term of four years none of those noisome creatures were left to be heard of within Wales and England. Since this time, also, we read not that any wolf hath been seen here that hath been bred within the bounds and limits of our country; howbeit, there have been divers brought over from beyond the seas for greediness of gain and to make money only by the gazing and gaping of our people upon them, who covet oft to see them, being strange beasts in their eyes and seldom known, as I have said, in England.[1]

Lions we have had very many in the north parts of Scotland, and those with mains of no less force than they of Mauretania were sometimes reported to be; but how and when they were destroyed, as yet I do not read. They had in like sort no less plenty of wild and cruel bulls, which the princes and their nobility in the frugal time of the land did hunt and follow for the trial of their manhood and by pursuit either on horseback or foot in armor, notwithstanding that many times they were dangerously assailed by them. But both these savage creatures are now not heard of, or at the leastwise the latter scarcely known in the south parts. Howbeit, this I gather by their being here, that our island was not cut from the main by the great deluge or flood of Noah, but long after, otherwise the generation of those and other like creatures could not have extended into our islands. For that any man would of set purpose replenish the country with them for his pleasure and pastime in hunting I can in no wise believe.

Of foxes we have some, but no great store, and also badgers in our sandy and light grounds, where woods, furzes, broom, and plenty of shrubs are to shroud them in when they be from their burrows, and thereto warrens of conies at hand to feed upon at will. Otherwise in clay, which we call the cledgy mold, we seldom hear of any because the moisture and toughness of the soil is such as will not suffer them to draw[2] and make their burrows deep. Certes if I may freely say what I think, I suppose that these two kinds (I mean foxes and badgers) are rather preserved by gentlemen to hunt and have pastime withal at their own pleasures than otherwise suffered to live as not able to be destroyed because of their great numbers. For such is the scantity of them here in England in comparison of the plenty that is to be seen in other countries, and so earnestly are the inhabitants bent to root them out that, except it had been to bear thus with the recreations of their superiors in this behalf, it

---

[1] Harrison borrows this account of Edgar and Ludwall almost verbatim from Abraham Fleming, *Of English Dogs* (1576), pp. 23–24; see p. 339, n. 2. The local legend associated with Wolfpit is Harrison's addition.

[2] *To draw*: to extend, elongate (their burrows).

could not otherwise have been chosen but that they should have been utterly destroyed by many years agone.

I might here entreat largely of other vermin, as the polecat, the miniver, the weasel, stoat, fulmart [foumart], squirrel, fitchew, and suchlike, which Cardan includeth under the word *mustela*,[3] also of the otter and likewise of the beaver, whose hinder feet and tail only are supposed to be fish. Certes the tail of this beast is like unto a thin whetstone, as the body unto a monstrous rat; the beast also itself is of such force in the teeth that it will gnaw an hole through a thick plank or shear through a double billet in a night; it loveth also the stillest rivers, and it is given to them by nature to go by flocks unto the woods at hand, where they gather sticks wherewith to build their nests, wherein their bodies lie dry above the water, although they so provide most commonly that their tails may hang within the same. It is also reported that their said tails are a delicate dish and their stones of such medicinable force that (as Vertomannus saith) four men smelling unto them each after other did bleed at the nose through their attractive force, proceeding from a vehement savor wherewith they are endued; there is greatest plenty of them in Persia, chiefly about Balascham, from whence they and their dried cods are brought into all quarters of the world, though not without some forgery by such as provide them.[4] And of all these here remembered, as the first sorts are plentiful in every wood and hedgerow, so these latter, especially the otter (for to say the truth, we have not many beavers, but only in the Teivi in Wales),[5] is not wanting or to seek in many but most streams and rivers of this isle; but it shall suffice in this sort to have named them, as I do finally the marten, a beast of the chase, although for number I worthily doubt whether that of our beavers or martens may be thought to be the less.

Other pernicious beasts we have not, except you repute the great plenty of red and fallow deer, whose colors are oft garled [speckled] white and black, all white, or all black, and store of

---

[3] *De subtilitate rerum* (Nuremberg, 1550, p. 232).

[4] *Vertomannus:* Ludovico Varthema, Italian traveler of the early sixteenth century; the passage occurs in his *Itinerary in the Near East*, III, iv (trans. Richard Eden, 1576), but Harrison actually cites at second hand from Cardan (*De subtilitate*, p. 233).

[5] Giraldus Cambrensis, *Itinerarium Cambriae*, II, iii (ed. James F. Dimock, *Opera*, Rolls Ser., XXI, Vol. VI, 1868, 114–115).

conies amongst the hurtful sort. Which, although that of themselves they are not offensive at all, yet their great numbers are thought to be very prejudicial and therefore justly reproved of many, as are in like sort our huge flocks of sheep, whereon the greatest part of our soil is employed almost in every place and yet our mutton, wool, and fells never the better cheap. The young males which our fallow deer do bring forth are commonly named according to their several ages: for the first year it is a fawn, the second a puckot [pricket], the third a sorrel, the fourth a sore, the fifth a buck of the first head, not bearing the name of a buck till he be five years old, and from henceforth his age is commonly known by his head or horns. Howbeit, this notice of his years is not so certain but that the best woodman may now and then be deceived in that account, for in some grounds a buck of the first head will be so well headed as another in a high rowty [coarse] soil will be in the fourth. It is also much to be marveled at that, whereas they do yearly mew [shed] and cast their horns, yet in fighting they never break off where they do grife [6] or mew. Furthermore, in examining the condition of our red deer, I find that the young male is called in the first year a calf, in the second a brocket, the third a spay [spade], the fourth a stagon [staggard] or stag, the fifth a great stag, the sixth an hart, and so forth unto his death. And with him in degree of venery are accounted the hare, boar, and wolf.

The fallow deer, as bucks and does, are nourished in parks, and conies in warrens and burrows. As for hares, they run at their own adventure, except some gentleman or other (for his pleasure) do make an enclosure for them. Of these, also, the stag is accounted for the most noble game, the fallow deer is the next, then the roe, whereof we have indifferent store, and last of all the hare, not the least in estimation because the hunting of that seely [defenseless] beast is mother to all the terms, blasts, and artificial devices that hunters do use. All which (notwithstanding our custom) are pastimes more meet for ladies and gentlewomen to exercise, whatsoever Franciscus Patricius saith to the contrary in his *Institution of a Prince*,[7] than for men of courage to follow,

---

[6] *Grife:* graff, graft.

[7] Francesco Patrizi defends deer hunting as a princely sport in his *De regno et regis institutione*, III, vii (Paris, 1582, fol. 123r–v). The following details about Alexander and lion and boar hunting derive from the same source, II, i, and III, vi (fols. 47r, 119v–121v).

whose hunting should practice their arms in tasting of their manhood and dealing with such beasts as eftsoons will turn again
and offer them the hardest [danger] rather than their horses'
feet, which many times may carry them with dishonor from the
field.

Surely this noble kind of hunting only did great princes frequent in times past, as it may yet appear by the histories of their
times, especially of Alexander, who at vacant times hunted the
tiger, the pard, the boar, and the bear, but most willingly lions,
because of the honorable estimation of that beast, insomuch that
at one time he caused an odd or chosen lion (for force and
beauty) to be let forth unto him hand to hand, with whom he had
much busyness, albeit that in the end he overthrew and killed the
beast. Hereunto, beside that which we read of the usual hunting
of the princes and kings of Scotland of the wild bull, wolf, etc.,
[we have] the example of King Henry the First of England, who,
disdaining (as he termed them) to follow or pursue cowards,
cherished of set purpose sundry kinds of wild beasts, as bears,
libards [leopards], ounces, lions, at Woodstock and one or two
other places in England, which he walled about with hard stone,
an. 1120, and where he would often fight with some one of them
hand to hand when they did turn again and make any reise
[attack] upon him; but chiefly he loved to hunt the lion and the
boar, which are both very dangerous exercises, especially that
with the lion, except some policy be found wherewith to trouble
his eyesight in any manner of wise. For though the boar be
fierce and hath learned by nature to harden his flesh and skin
against the trees, to sharpen his teeth, and defile himself with
earth, thereby to prohibit the entrance of the weapons, yet is the
sport somewhat more easy, especially where two stand so near
together that the one (if need be) may help and be a succor to
the other. Neither would he cease for all this to follow his pastime,
either on horseback or on foot as occasion served, much like the
younger Cyrus. I have read of wild boars and bulls to have been
about Blackley near Manchester,[8] whither the said prince would
now and then resort also for his solace in that behalf, as also to
come by those excellent falcons then bred thereabouts; but now
they are gone, especially the bulls, as I have said already.

---

[8] Leland, *Itinerary* (ed. Smith, V, 43).

King Henry the Fifth in his beginning thought it a mere scoffery to pursue any fallow deer with hounds or greyhounds, but supposed himself always to have done a sufficient act when he had tired them by his own travel on foot and so killed them with his hands in the upshot of that exercise and end of his recreation. Certes herein he resembled Polymnestor Milesius, of whom it is written how he ran so swiftly that he would and did very often overtake hares for his pleasure, which I can hardly believe; and therefore much less that one Ladas did run so lightly and swiftly after like game that as he passed over the sand he left not so much as the prints of his feet behind him.[9] And thus did very many in like sort with the hart (as I do read), but this I think was very long agone, when men were far higher and swifter than they are now, and yet I deny not but rather grant willingly that the hunting of the red deer is a right princely pastime.

In divers foreign countries they cause their red and fallow deer to draw the plow, as we do our oxen and horses. In some places, also, they milk their hinds as we do here our kine and goats. And the experience of this latter is noted by Giraldus Cambrensis to have been seen and used in Wales, where he did eat cheese made of hinds' milk at such time as Baldwin, Archbishop of Canterbury, preached the crusade there, when they were both lodged in a gentleman's house, whose wife of purpose kept a dairy of the same.[10] As for the plowing with ures [11] (which I suppose to be unlikely, because they are in mine opinion untamable) and elks, a thing commonly used in the East [Baltic] countries, here is no place to speak of it, since we want these kind of beasts, neither is it my purpose to entreat at large of other things than are to be seen in England. Wherefore I will omit to say any more of wild and savage beasts at this time, thinking myself to have spoken already sufficiently of this matter, if not too much, in the judgment of the curious.

[9] Solinus, *Collectanea rerum memorabilium,* chap. v.
[10] *Itinerarium Cambriae,* II, xi (ed. Dimock, p. 141).
[11] *Ures:* aurochs, an extinct species of wild ox.

CHAPTER V

Of Hawks and Ravenous Fowls

I CANNOT make (as yet) any just report how many sorts of hawks are bred within this realm. Howbeit, which of those that are usually had among us are disclosed within this land, I think it more easy and less difficult to set down. First of all, therefore, that we have the eagle common experience doth evidently confirm, and divers of our rocks whereon they breed, if speech did serve, could well declare the same. But the most excellent aerie of all is not much from Chester, at a castle called Dinas Bran, sometime builded by Brennus, as our writers do remember. Certes this castle is no great thing but yet a pile sometime very strong and inaccessible for enemies, though now all ruinous as many other are. It standeth upon an hard rock, in the side whereof an eagle breedeth every year. This also is notable in the overthrow of her nest (a thing oft attempted), that he which goeth thither must be sure of two large baskets and so provide to be let down thereto that he may sit in the one and be covered with the other, for otherwise the eagle would kill him and tear the flesh from his bones with her sharp talons, though his apparel were never so good.[1] The common people call this fowl an erne, but as I am ignorant whether the word eagle and erne do show any difference of sex, I mean between the male and female, so we have great store of them. And near to the places where they breed the commons complain of great harm to be done by them in their fields, for they are able to bear a young lamb or kid unto their nests, therewith to feed their young and come again for more. I was once of the opinion that there was a diversity of kind between the eagle and the erne, till I perceived that our nation used the word erne in most places for the eagle.

We have also the lanner and the lanneret, the tercel and the goshawk, the musket and the sparhawk, the jack and the hobby, and finally some (though very few) marlions.[2] And these are all

---

[1] Leland, *Itinerary* (ed. Smith, III, 90).

[2] *Musket:* male sparrow hawk; *jack:* male hawk; *marlions:* merlins.

the hawks that I do hear as yet to be bred within this island. Howbeit, as these are not wanting with us, so are they not very plentiful, wherefore such as delight in hawking do make their chief purveyance and provision for the same out of Dansk, Germany, and the East [Baltic] countries, from whence we have them in great abundance and at excessive prices, whereas at home and where they be bred they are sold for almost right naught, and usually brought to the markets as chickens, pullets, and pigeons are with us, and there bought up to be eaten (as we do the aforesaid fowls) almost of every man. It is said that the sparhawk preyeth not upon the fowl in the morning that she taketh over even but, as loath to have double benefit by one seely [trifling] fowl, doth let it go to make some shift for itself. But hereof as I stand in some doubt, so this I find among the writers worthy the noting, that the sparhawk is enemy to young children, as is also the ape; but of the peacock she is marvelously afraid and so appalled that all courage and stomach for a time is taken from her upon the sight thereof.[3] But to proceed with the rest.

Of other ravenous birds we have also very great plenty, as the buzzard, the kite, the ringtail, dun-kite,[4] and such as often annoy our country dames by spoiling of their young breeds of chickens, ducks, and goslings, whereunto our very ravens and crows have learned also the way; and so much are our ravens given to this kind of spoil that some idle and curious heads of set purpose have manned, reclaimed,[5] and used them instead of hawks, when other could not be had. Some do imagine that the raven should be the vulture, and I was almost persuaded in times past to believe the same, but finding of late a description of the vulture which better agreeth with the form of a second kind of eagle, I freely surcease to be longer of that opinion; for as it hath after a sort the shape, color, and quantity of an eagle, so are the legs and feet more hairy and rough, their sides under their wings better covered with thick down (wherewith also their gorge [throat] or a part of their breast under their throats is armed, and not with feathers) than are the like parts of the eagle, and unto which portraiture

[3] All these details about sparhawks come from Olaus Magnus, *Historia de gentibus septentrionalibus*, XIX, i–ii.

[4] *Ringtail:* female of the hen harrier; *dun-kite:* the marsh harrier.

[5] *Manned, reclaimed:* both are technical hawking terms. "To man" is to accustom a hawk to the presence of men; "to reclaim" is to call a hawk back to the wrist.

there is no member of the raven (who is also very black of color) that can have any resemblance; we have none of them in England to my knowledge; if we have, they go generally under the name of eagle or erne. Neither have we the *pygargus,* or gripe,[6] wherefore I have no occasion to entreat further. I have seen the carrion crows so cunning also by their own industry of late that they have used to soar over great rivers (as the Thames, for example) and suddenly coming down have caught a small fish in their feet and gone away withal without wetting of their wings. And even at this present the aforesaid river is not without some of them, a thing (in my opinion) not a little to be wondered at.

We have also ospreys, which breed with us in parks and woods, whereby the keepers of the same do reap in breeding time no small commodity; for, so soon almost as the young are hatched, they tie them to the butt ends or ground ends of sundry trees,[7] where the old ones, finding them, do never cease to bring fish unto them, which the keepers take and eat from them, and commonly is such as is well fed or not of the worst sort.[8] It hath not been my hap hitherto to see any of these fowls and partly through mine own negligence, but I hear that it hath one foot like an hawk to catch hold withal and another resembling a goose wherewith to swim;[9] but whether it be so or not so, I refer the further search and trial thereof unto some other. This nevertheless is certain, that both alive and dead, yea, even her very oil is a deadly terror to such fish as come within the wind of it. There is no cause wherefore I should describe the cormorant amongst hawks, of which some be black and many pied, chiefly about the Isle of Ely, where they are taken for the night raven, except I should call him a water hawk. But sith such dealing is not convenient, let us now see what may be said of our venomous worms and how many kinds we have of them within our realm and country.

---

[6] *Pygargus:* properly, the osprey or sea eagle; *gripe:* vulture.

[7] Olaus Magnus, XIX, iv, describing the custom in Scandinavia. Harrison misreads, perhaps willfully, the Latin: the falconers do not tie the young birds to the butt ends of trees; rather, they tie up the butt ends of the birds (*anos pullorum ligaculo stringunt*) to limit their ingestion.

[8] *Well fed or not of the worst sort:* for *nec putridas, sed recentes,* not rotten but freshly taken.

[9] Olaus Magnus, XIX, iii.

CHAPTER VI

Of Venomous Beasts

IF I should go about to make any long discourse of venomous beasts or worms [snakes] bred in England, I should attempt more than occasion itself would readily offer, sith we have very few worms but no beasts at all that are thought by their natural qualities to be either venomous or hurtful. First of all, therefore, we have the adder (in our old Saxon tongue called an *aetter*),[1] which some men do, not rashly, take to be the viper. Certes if it be so, then is it not the viper author of the death of her parents, as some histories affirm,[2] and thereto Encelius, a late writer (in his *De re metallica, lib.* 3, *cap.* 38),[3] where he maketh mention of a she-adder which he saw in Sala, whose womb (as he saith) was eaten out after a like fashion, her young ones lying by her in the sunshine as if they had been earthworms. Nevertheless, as he nameth them *viperas*, so he calleth the male *echis* and the female *echidna*, concluding in the end that *echis* is the same serpent which his countrymen to this day call *ein Atter*, as I have also noted before out of a Saxon dictionary. For my part, I am persuaded that the slaughter of their parents is either not true at all, or not always (although I doubt not but that Nature hath right well provided to inhibit their superfluous increase by some means or other), and so much the rather am I led hereunto for that I gather by Nicander that of all venomous worms the viper only bringeth out her young alive and therefore is called in Latin *vipera quasi vivipara*;[4] but of her own death he doth not (to my

---

[1] *Aetter:* properly venom, *naedra* being the OE term for viper.

[2] "Galen, *De theriaca ad Pisonem* [ix]; Pliny, *lib.* 10, *cap.* 62 [lxxxii]."—*H.* All of the classical references in this paragraph are borrowed from the commentary on Dioscorides by Pietro Andrea Mattioli, II, xvi.

[3] *Encelius:* Christoph Entzelt (1517–1583), German historian and Lutheran minister; his *De re metallica* appeared in editions of 1551 and 1557 at Frankfort.

[4] That is, the etymology of viper is "viviparous," producing living young. *Nicander:* a Greek poet, apparently of the second century B.C.; the cited passage is in his *Theriaca*, ll. 133–136.

remembrance) say anything. It is testified also by other in other words and to the like sense, that *echis id est vipera sola ex serpentibus non ova sed animalia parit.*[5] And it may well be, for I remember that I have read in Philostratus (*De vita Apollonii*) how he saw a viper licking her young.[6] I did see an adder once myself that lay (as I thought) sleeping on a molehill, out of whose mouth came eleven young adders of twelve or thirteen inches in length apiece, which played to and fro in the grass one with another, till some of them espied me. So soon, therefore, as they saw my face, they ran again into the mouth of their dam, whom I killed and then found each of them shrouded in a distinct cell or pannicle[7] in her belly, much like unto a soft white jelly, which maketh me to be of the opinion that our adder is the viper indeed.[8]

The color of their skin is for the most part like rusty iron or iron gray; but such as be very old resemble a ruddy blue, and as once in the year, to wit, in April or about the beginning of May, they cast their old skins (whereby as it is thought their age reneweth), so their stinging bringeth death, without present remedy be at hand, the wounded never ceasing to swell neither the venom to work till the skin of the one break and the other ascend upward to the heart, where it finisheth the natural effect, except the juice of dragons (in Latin called *Dracunculus minor*)[9] be speedily ministered and drunk in strong ale, or else some other medicine taken of like force, that may countervail and overcome the venom of the same. The length of them is most commonly two foot and somewhat more, but seldom doth it extend unto two foot six inches except it be in some rare and monstrous one, whereas our snakes are much longer and seen sometimes to surmount a yard or three foot, although their poison be nothing so grievous and deadly as the others. Our adders lie in winter under stones, as Aristotle also saith of the viper (*lib.* 8, *cap.* 15),[10] and in holes of the earth, rotten stubs of trees, and amongst the dead leaves, but in the heat of the summer they

[5] "The *echis* or viper alone among snakes bears living young rather than eggs"; apparently derived from Aristotle, *Historia animalium*, III, i.

[6] *Life of Apollonius of Tyana*, II, xiv.

[7] *Pannicle*: properly a membrane but here apparently used for "sac."

[8] "See Aristotle, [*Historia*] *animalium, lib. 5, cap. ultimo* [xxxiv] and Theophrastus [*Enquiry into Plants*], *lib.* 7, *cap.* 13 [xiv]."—H.

[9] *Dragons*: dragonwort, *Dracunculus vulgaris.*

[10] *Historia animalium.*

come abroad and lie either round on heaps or at length upon some hillock or elsewhere in the grass. They are found only in our woodland countries and highest grounds, where sometimes (though seldom) a speckled stone called *echites*, in Dutch *ein Atterstein*, is gotten out of their dried carcasses, which divers report to be good against their poison.[11] As for our snakes, which in Latin are properly named *angues*, they commonly are seen in moors, fens, loamy walls, and low bottoms.

And as we have great store of toads where adders commonly are found, so do frogs abound where snakes do keep their residence. We have also the slowworm, which is black and grayish of color and somewhat shorter than an adder. I was at the killing once of one of them and thereby perceived that she was not so called of any want of nimble motion but rather of the contrary. Nevertheless, we have a blindworm to be found under logs in woods and timber that hath lien long in a place, which some also do call (and upon better ground) by the name of slowworms, and they are known easily by their more or less variety of striped colors, drawn longways from their heads, their whole bodies little exceeding a foot in length, and yet is their venom deadly.

This also is not to be omitted, that now and then in our fenny countries other kinds of serpents are found of greater quantity than either our adder or our snake; but as these are not ordinary and oft to be seen, so I mean not to entreat of them among our common annoyances. Neither have we the scorpion, a plague of God sent not long since into Italy, and whose poison (as Apollodorus saith) is white,[12] neither the tarantula or Neapolitan spider, whose poison bringeth death except music be at hand. Wherefore I suppose our country to be the more happy (I mean, in part), for that it is void of these two grievous annoyances wherewith other nations are plagued.

We have also efts, both of the land and water, and likewise the noisome swifts [lizards], whereof to say any more it should be but loss of time, sith they are well known and no region to my knowledge found to be void of many of them. As for flies (sith it shall not be amiss a little to touch them also) we have none

---

[11] "Solinus, *cap.* 40 [xlix]; Pliny, *lib.* 37, *cap.* 11 [lxxii]."—*H*. The references are borrowed from Entzelt, III, xxxviii, who calls the *echites* "*ein Naterstein*."

[12] Pliny, XI, xxx.

that can do hurt or hindrance naturally unto any, for whether they be cut-waisted or whole-bodied, they are void of poison and all venomous inclination. The cut- or girt-waisted (for so I English the word *insecta*) are the hornets, wasps, bees, and suchlike, whereof we have great store and of which an opinion is conceived that the first do breed of the corruption of dead horses, the second of pears and apples corrupted, and the last of kine and oxen, which may be true, especially the first and latter in some parts of the beast and not their whole substances, as also in the second, sith we have never wasps but when our fruit beginneth to wax ripe. Indeed Virgil and others speak of a generation of bees by killing or smothering of a bruised bullock or calf, and laying his bowels or his flesh wrapped up in his hide in a close house for a certain season,[13] but how true it is hitherto I have not tried. Yet sure I am of this, that no one living creature corrupteth without the production of another, as we may see by ourselves, whose flesh doth alter into lice, and also in sheep for excessive numbers of flesh flies if they be suffered to lie unburied or uneaten by the dogs and swine, who often and happily prevent such needless generations.

As concerning bees, I think it good to remember that whereas some ancient writers affirm it to be a commodity wanting in our island, it is now found to be nothing so. In old time, peradventure, we had none indeed, but in my days there is such plenty of them in manner everywhere that in some uplandish towns there are one hundred or two hundred hives of them, although the said hives are not so huge as those of the East Country but far less, as not able to contain above one bushel of corn or five pecks at the most. Pliny (a man that of set purpose delighteth to write of wonders), speaking of honey, noteth that in the north regions the hives in his time were of such quantity that some one comb contained eight foot in length,[14] and yet (as it should seem) he speaketh not of the greatest. For in Podolia, which is now subject to the King of Poland, their hives are so great and combs so abundant that huge boars [bears] overturning and falling into them are drowned in the honey before they can recover and find the means to come out.[15]

---

[13] *Georgics*, IV, 295–314.
[14] *Natural History*, XI, xiv.
[15] Olaus Magnus, *Historia de gentibus septentrionalibus*, XXII, iv.

Our honey also is taken and reputed to be the best, because it is harder, better wrought, and cleanlier vesseled up than that which cometh from beyond the sea, where they stamp and strain their combs, bees, and young blowings [eggs, larvae] altogether into the stuff, as I have been informed. In use also of medicine our physicians and apothecaries eschew the foreign, especially that of Spain and Pontus, by reason of a venomous quality naturally planted in the same, as some write, and choose the homemade, not only by reason of our soil, which hath no less plenty of wild thyme growing therein than in Sicilia and about Athens, and maketh the best stuff, as also for that it breedeth (being gotten in harvest time) less choler, and which is oftentimes (as I have seen by experience) so white as sugar and corned as if it were salt. Our hives are made commonly of rye straw and waddled [wattled] about with bramble quarters, but some make the same of wicker and cast [plaster] them over with clay. We cherish none in trees but set our hives somewhere on the warmest side of the house, providing that they may stand dry and without danger both of the mouse and moth. This furthermore is to be noted, that whereas in vessels of oil that which is nearest the top is counted the finest, and of wine, that in the midst, so of honey the best, which is heaviest and moistest, is always next the bottom and evermore casteth and driveth his dregs upward toward the very top, contrary to the nature of other liquid substances, whose grounds and lees do generally settle downwards. And thus much as by the way of our bees and English honey.

As for the whole-bodied, as the cantharides and such venomous creatures of the same kind to be abundantly found in other countries, we hear not of them, yet have we beetles, horseflies, turd-bugs or dors [dorbeetles] (called in Latin *scarabei*), the locust or the grasshopper (which to me do seem to be one thing, as I will anon declare), and suchlike, whereof let other entreat that make an exercise in catching of flies but a far greater sport in offering them to spiders. As did Domitian sometime and another prince yet living, who delighted so much to see the jolly combats betwixt a stout fly and an old spider that divers men have had great rewards given them for their painful provision of flies made only for this purpose. Some parasites, also, in the time of the aforesaid Emperor (when they were disposed to laugh at his folly and yet would seem in appearance to gratify his fantastical head with some show of dutiful demeanor), could devise to set their lord on work by letting a flesh fly privily into his chamber, which he forthwith would eagerly have hunted (all other business set apart) and never ceased till he had caught her into his fingers; whereupon arose the proverb, *ne musca quidem*, uttered first by Vibius Priscus, who being asked whether anybody was with Domitian, answered, *Ne musca quidem*, whereby he noted his folly.[16] There are some coxcombs here and there in England, learning it abroad as men transregionate, which make account also of this pastime as of a notable matter, telling what a fight is seen between them if either of them be lusty and courageous in his kind. One also hath made a book of the spider and the fly, wherein he dealeth so profoundly and beyond all measure of skill that neither he himself that made it, neither anyone that readeth it, can reach unto the meaning thereof.[17] But if those jolly fellows, instead of the straw that they thrust into the fly's tail (a great injury no doubt to such a noble champion), would bestow the cost to set a foolscap upon their own heads, then might they with more security and less reprehension behold these notable battles.

Now as concerning the locust, I am led by divers of my country, who (as they say) were either in Germany, Italy, or Pannonia, 1542, when those nations were greatly annoyed with that kind of fly, and affirm very constantly that they saw none other creature than the grasshopper during the time of that annoyance, which was said to come to them from the Meotides.[18] In most of our translations, also, of the Bible the word *locusta* is Englished "a grasshopper," and thereunto (Leviticus 11) it is reputed among the clean food, otherwise John the Baptist would never have lived with them in the wilderness. In Barbary, Numidia, and sundry other places of Africa, as they have been, so are they eaten to this day powdered in barrels, and therefore the people of those parts are called *Acridophagi;* nevertheless, they shorten the life of the

---

[16] *Ne musca quidem:* not even a fly; Suetonius (*Lives of the Caesars*, VIII, "Domitian," iii), attributes the remark to Vibius Crispus.

[17] John Heywood's poem *The Spider and the Fly* (1556). Heywood's Roman Catholic sympathies are as likely to have been the source of Harrison's antipathy as the obscurity of the allegory. The passage is the only reference in *The Description* to contemporary English literature.

[18] *Meotides:* from Maeotis Palus, the ancient name for the Sea of Azov.

eaters by the production at the last of an irksome and filthy disease.[19] In India they are three foot long, in Ethiopia much shorter, but in England seldom above an inch. As for the cricket called in Latin *cicada*, he hath some likelihood [likeness] but not very great with the grasshopper, and therefore he is not to be brought in as an umpire in this case. Finally Matthiolus [20] and so many as describe the locust do set down none other form than that of our grasshopper, which maketh me so much the more to rest upon my former imagination, which is that the locust and grasshopper are one.

CHAPTER VII

Of Our English Dogs and Their Qualities

THERE is no country that may (as I take it) compare with ours in number, excellency, and diversity of dogs. And therefore, if Polycrates of Samos were now alive, he would not send to Epirus for such merchandise but to his further cost provide them out of Britain, as an ornament to his country and piece of husbandry for his commonwealth, which he furnished of set purpose with Molossian and Laconian dogs, as he did the same also with sheep out of Attica and Miletus, goats from Scyros and Naxos, swine out of Sicilia, and artificers out of other places.[1] Howbeit, the learned Dr. Caius in his Latin treatise unto Gesner, *De canibus Anglicis*,[2] bringeth them all into three sorts: that is, the gentle kind serving for game; the homely kind apt for sundry uses; and the currish kind meet for many toys. For my part I can say no more of them than he hath done already. Wherefore I will here

---

[19] "See Diodorus Siculus [III, xxix]."—*H.*

[20] *Matthiolus:* Mattioli in his commentary on Dioscorides, II, xlvi, which is also the source for Harrison's information about the plague of 1542.

[1] Athenaeus, *The Deipnosophists*, XII, 540.

[2] John Caius' brief treatise (1570) was originally written for Conrad von Gesner (1516–1565), the Swiss naturalist. Harrison follows, however, not Caius' Latin but a free translation by Abraham Fleming, *Of English Dogs* (1576). Except for some of the scholarly citations and the personal anecdotes, the language of this chapter is largely Fleming's.

set down only a sum of that which he hath written of their names and natures, with the addition of an example or two now lately had in experience, whereby the courages of our mastiffs shall yet more largely appear.

As for those of other countries, I have not to deal with them, neither care I to report out of Pliny that dogs were sometime killed in sacrifice and sometime their whelps eaten as a delicate dish (*lib.* 29, *cap.* 4 [xiv]). Wherefore if any man be disposed to read of them, let him resort to Pliny (*lib.* 8, *cap.* 40 [lxi]), who (among other wonders) telleth of an army of two hundred dogs, which fetched a king of the Garamantes out of captivity, mauger the resistance of his adversaries; also to Cardan (*lib.* 10, "*De animalibus*"), Aristotle, etc., who write marvels of them, but none further from credit than Cardan, who is not afraid to compare some of them for greatness with oxen and some also for smallness unto the little field mouse.[3] Neither do I find any far writer of great antiquity that maketh mention of our dogs, Strabo excepted, who saith that the Gauls did sometime buy up all our mastiffs to serve in the forewards [vanguard] of their battles, wherein they resembled the Colophonians [and] Castabalenses of Calicut and Phoenicia, of whom Pliny also speaketh,[4] but they had them not from us.

The first sort, therefore, he divideth either into such as rouse the beast and continue the chase, or springeth the bird and bewrayeth her flight by pursuit. And as these are commonly called spaniels, so the other are named hounds, whereof he maketh eight sorts,[5] of which the foremost excelleth in perfect smelling, the second in quick espying, the third in swiftness and quickness, the fourth in smelling and nimbleness, etc., and the last in subtlety and deceitfulness. These (saith Strabo) are most apt for game and called *sagaces* by a general name, not only because of their

[3] *De subtilitate rerum*, Bk. X, "*De perfectis animalibus*" (Nuremberg, 1550, p. 229).

[4] Strabo, IV, v, 2, which is also the source for the citation in the next paragraph; Pliny (VIII, lxi) is not responsible for the odd misidentifications of these cities.

[5] Fleming actually makes two separate classifications of hounds, five types according to their prime faculties, as in the remainder of this sentence (the "etc." is Harrison's gratuitous addition), and eight types according to the named breeds, as later in the paragraph. Harrison's telescoping of the two divisions makes for confusion.

skill in hunting, but also for that they know their own and the names of their fellows most exactly. For if the hunter see any one to follow skillfully and with likelihood of good success, he biddeth the rest to hark and follow such a dog, and they eftsoons obey so soon as they hear his name. The first kind of these are also commonly called harriers, whose game is the fox, the hare, the wolf (if we had any), hart, buck, badger, otter, polecat, lobster [stoat], weasel, cony, etc.; the second hight [is named] a terrier, and it hunteth the badger and gray [6] only; the third a bloodhound, whose office is to follow the fierce and now and then to pursue a thief or beast by his dry foot [scent]; the fourth hight a gaze-hound, who hunteth by the eye; the fifth a greyhound, cherished for his strength, swiftness, and stature, commended by Grattius in his *De venatione* and not unremembered by Hercules Stroza in a like treatise, but above all other those of Britain, where he saith:

et magna spectandi mole Britanni;[7]

also by Nemesianus, *libro Cynegeticon,* where he saith:

Divisa Britannia mittit
Veloces nostrique orbis venatibus aptos,[8]

of which sort also some be smooth, of sundry colors, and some shake-haired;[9] the sixth a limer, that excelleth in smelling and swift running; the seventh a tumbler; and the eighth a thief, whose offices (I mean of the latter two) incline only to deceit,[10] wherein they are oft so skillful that few men would think so mischievous a wit to remain in such silly creatures.

Having made this enumeration of dogs which are apt for the chase and hunting, he cometh next to such as serve the falcons in their times, whereof he maketh also two sorts: one that findeth his game on the land, another that putteth up [starts]

---

[6] *Gray:* a synonym for badger.

[7] "British [greyhounds] are to be seen in great numbers."

[8] "Island Britain sends us swift ones, suitable for the chase in our country" (ll. 225–226). *Grattius:* Roman poet, contemporary with Ovid; *Hercules Stroza:* Ercole Strozzi (1471–1508), Italian neo-Latin poet; *Nemesianus:* Roman poet of the third century A.D. All three works cited appear in the collection *Venatus et aucupium,* ed. Johann Adam Lonicer (Frankfort, 1582).

[9] *Shake-haired:* shock-haired, having rough, thick hair.

[10] That is, as Fleming explains in detail (pp. 11–12), they employ a number of devious tricks in hunting.

such fowl as keepeth in the water; and of these this is commonly most usual for the net or train, the other for the hawk, as he doth show at large. Of the first he saith that they have no peculiar names assigned to them severally, but each of them is called after the bird which by natural appointment he is allotted to hunt or serve, for which consideration some be named dogs for the pheasant, some for the falcon, and some for the partridge. Howbeit, the common name for all is spaniel (saith he), and thereupon alludeth as if these kinds of dogs had been brought hither out of Spain. In like sort we have of water spaniels in their kind.

The third sort of dogs of the gentle kind is the spaniel gentle, or comforter, or (as the common term is) the fisting hound, and those are called *melitei* of the island Malta, from whence they were brought hither. These are little and pretty, proper and fine, and sought out far and near to satisfy the nice delicacy of dainty dames and wanton women's wills, instruments of folly to play and dally withal in trifling away the treasure of time, to withdraw their minds from more commendable exercises, and to content their corrupt concupiscences with vain disport, a silly poor shift to shun their irksome idleness. These sybaritical puppies, the smaller they be (and thereto if they have an hole in the fore parts of their heads), the better they are accepted, the more pleasure also they provoke, as meet playfellows for mincing mistresses to bear in their bosoms, to keep company withal in their chambers, to succor with sleep in bed and nourish with meat at board, to lie in their laps and lick their lips as they lie (like young Dianas) in their wagons and coaches. And good reason it should be so, for coarseness with fineness hath no fellowship, but featness [prettiness] with neatness hath neighborhood enough. That plausible proverb therefore, verified sometime upon a tyrant, namely that he loved his sow better than his son, may well be applied to some of this kind of people, who delight more in their dogs, that are deprived of all possibility of reason, than they do in children, that are capable of wisdom and judgment.[11] Yea, they oft feed them of the best, where the poor man's child at their doors can hardly come by the worst. But the former abuse peradventure reigneth where there hath been long want of issue, else where barrenness is the best blossom of beauty,

[11] As the ornate style suggests, this passage on lap dogs comes almost verbatim from Fleming, pp. 20–21.

or finally, where poor men's children, for want of their own issue, are not ready to be had. It is thought of some that it is very wholesome for a weak stomach to bear such a dog in the bosom, as it is for him that hath the palsy to feel the daily smell and savor of a fox. But how truly this is affirmed, let the learned judge; only it shall suffice for Dr. Caius to have said thus much of spaniels and dogs of the gentle kind.

Dogs of the homely kind are either shepherds' curs or mastiffs. The first are so common that it needeth me not to speak of them. Their use, also, is so well known in keeping the herd together (either when they graze or go before the shepherd) that it should be but in vain to spend any time about them. Wherefore I will leave this cur unto his own kind and go in hand with the mastiff, tiedog, or bandog, so called because many of them are tied up in chains and strong bonds in the daytime, for doing hurt abroad, which is an huge dog, stubborn, ugly, eager, burdenous of body (and therefore but of little swiftness), terrible and fearful to behold, and oftentimes more fierce and fell than any Arcadian or Corsican cur. Our Englishmen, to the intent that these dogs may be more cruel and fierce, assist nature with some art, use, and custom. For although this kind of dog be capable of courage, violent, valiant, stout, and bold, yet will they increase these their stomachs [bravery] by teaching them to bait the bear, the bull, the lion, and other suchlike cruel and bloody beasts (either brought over or kept up at home for the same purpose), without any collar to defend their throats, and oftentimes thereto they train them up in fighting and wrestling with a man (having for the safeguard of his life either a pikestaff, club, sword, or privy coat)[12] whereby they become the more fierce and cruel unto strangers.

The Caspians made so much account sometime of such great dogs that every able man would nourish sundry of them in his house of set purpose, to the end they should devour their carcasses after their deaths, thinking the dogs' bellies to be the most honorable sepulchers. The common people also followed the same rate, and therefore there were tiedogs kept up by public ordinance to devour them after their deaths, by means whereof these beasts became the more eager and with great difficulty after

[12] *Privy coat:* a coat of mail worn under ordinary dress.

a while restrained from falling upon the living.[13] But whither am I digressed? In returning, therefore, to our own, I say that of mastiffs, some bark only, with fierce and open mouth, but will not bite; some do both bark and bite; but the cruelest do either not bark at all or bite before they bark, and therefore are more to be feared than any of the other. They take also their name of the word "mase" [14] and "thief" (or "master thief" if you will), because they often stound [stun] and put such persons to their shifts in towns and villages, and are the principal causes of their apprehension and taking. The force which is in them surmounteth all belief, and the fast hold which they take with their teeth exceedeth all credit; for three of them against a bear, four against a lion, are sufficient to try masteries with them.

King Henry the Seventh, as the report goeth, commanded all such curs to be hanged, because they durst presume to fight against the lion, who is their king and sovereign. The like he did with an excellent falcon, as some say, because he feared not hand-to-hand to match with an eagle, willing his falconers in his own presence to pluck off his head after he was taken down, saying that it was not meet for any subject to offer such wrong unto his lord and superior, wherein he had a further meaning. But if King Henry the Seventh had lived in our time, what would he have done to one English mastiff which alone and without any help at all pulled down first an huge bear, then a pard, and last of all a lion, each after other, before the French king in one day, when the Lord Buckhurst was ambassador unto him,[15] and whereof if I should write the circumstances, that is, how he took his advantage, being let loose unto them, and finally drave them into such exceeding fear that they were all glad to run away when he was taken from them, I should take much pains and yet reap but small credit; wherefore it shall suffice to have said thus much thereof.

Some of our mastiffs will rage only in the night; some are to be tied up both day and night. Such also as are suffered to go loose about the house and yard are so gentle in the daytime

[13] Derived from Francesco Patrizi, *De regno et regis institutione*, III, vi (Paris, 1582, fol. 116r).

[14] *Mase:* maze, stupefy.

[15] *Lord Buckhurst:* Thomas Sackville (1536–1608), later Lord Treasurer and Earl of Dorset; this diplomatic mission took place in 1571.

that children may ride on their backs and play with them at their pleasures. Divers of them likewise are of such jealousy over their master and whosoever of his household that if a stranger do embrace or touch any of them they will fall fiercely upon them, unto their extreme mischief if their fury be not prevented. Such an one was the dog of Nicomedes, King sometime of Bithynia, who, seeing Consigne, the Queen, to embrace and kiss her husband as they walked together in a garden, did tear her all to pieces, mauger his resistance and the present aid of such as attended on them.[16] Some of them moreover will suffer a stranger to come in and walk about the house or yard where him listeth, without giving over to follow him; but if he put forth his hand to touch anything, then will they fly upon him and kill him if they may. I had one myself once which would not suffer any man to bring in his weapon further than my gate, neither those that were of my house to be touched in his presence. Or if I had beaten any of my children, he would gently have assayed to catch the rod in his teeth and take it out of my hand, or else pluck down their clothes to save them from the stripes, which in my opinion is not unworthy to be noted.

And thus much of our mastiffs, creatures of no less faith and love towards their masters than horses, as may appear even by the confidence that Masinissa reposed in them, insomuch that, mistrusting his household servants, he made him a guard of dogs, which many a time delivered him from their treasons and conspiracies even by their barking and biting; nor of less force than the Molossian race, brought from Epirus into some countries, which the poets feign to have original from the brazen dog that Vulcan made and gave to Jupiter, who also delivered the same to Europa, she to Procris, and Procris to Cephalus, as Julius Pollux noteth (*lib.* 5, *cap.* 5 [39]);[17] neither unequal in carefulness to the mastiff of Alexander Phereus, who by his only courage and attendance kept his master long time from slaughter, till at the last he was removed by policy and the tyrant killed sleeping. The story goeth thus: Thebe, the wife of the said Phereus, and her three brethren conspired the death of her husband, who fearing the dog only, she found the means to allure him from his

[16] Pliny, VIII, lxi.
[17] *Julius Pollux:* a Greek rhetorician of the second century A.D.; the reference is to his *Onomasticon*.

chamber door by fair means unto another house hard by, whilst they should execute their purpose. Nevertheless, when they came to the bed where he lay sleeping, they waxed fainthearted till she did put them in choice either that they should dispatch him at once or else that she herself would wake her husband and give him warning of his enemies, or at the leastwise bring in the dog upon them, which they feared most of all and therefore quickly dispatched him.[18]

The last sort of dogs consisteth of the currish kind meet for many toys, of which the whappet[19] or prick-eared cur is one. Some men call them warners, because they are good for nothing else but to bark and give warning when anybody doth stir or lie in wait about the house in the night season. Certes it is unpossible to describe these curs in any order, because they have no any one kind proper unto themselves but are a confused company mixed of all the rest. The second sort of them are called turnspits, whose office is not unknown to any.[20] And as these are only reserved for this purpose, so in many places our mastiffs (beside the use which tinkers have of them in carrying their heavy budgets) are made to draw water in great wheels out of deep wells, going much like unto those which are framed for our turnspits, as is to be seen at Royston, where this feat is often practiced.

Besides these, also, we have sholts, or curs, daily brought out of Iceland and much made of among us, because of their sauciness and quarreling. Moreover they bite very sore and love candles exceedingly, as do the men and women of their country; but I may say no more of them because they are not bred with us. Yet this will I make report of by the way, for pastime's sake, that when a great man of those parts came of late into one of our ships, which went thither for fish, to see the form and fashion of the same, his wife, appareled in fine sables, abiding on the deck whilst her husband was under the hatches with the mariners, espied a pound or two of candles hanging at the mast, and, being

[18] This story and the preceding one about Masinissa are borrowed from Patrizi, III, vi and II, i (fols. 113r–114v, 50r–v).

[19] *Whappet:* from the verb "to wap," or bark.

[20] "For when any meat is to be roasted, they go into a wheel, which they, turning about with the weight of their bodies, so diligently look to their business that no drudge nor scullion can do the feat more cunningly" (Fleming, pp. 34–35).

loath to stand there idle alone, she fell to and eat them up every one, supposing herself to have been at a jolly banquet and showing very pleasant gesture when her husband came up again unto her.

The last kind of toyish curs are named dancers, and those, being of a mongrel sort also, are taught and exercised to dance in measure at the musical sound of an instrument, as at the just stroke of a drum, sweet accent of the cittern, and pleasant harmony of the harp, showing many tricks by the gesture of their bodies, as: to stand bolt upright, to lie flat upon the ground, to turn round as a ring, holding their tails in their teeth, to saw [21] and beg for meat, to take a man's cap from his head, and sundry such properties, which they learn of their idle roguish masters, whose instruments they are to gather gain, as old apes clothed in motley and colored short-waisted jackets are for the like vagabonds, who seek no better living than that which they may get by fond pastime and idleness.

I might here entreat of other dogs, as of those which are bred between a bitch and a wolf and called *lycisca*, a thing very often seen in France, saith Franciscus Patricius in his *Commonwealth*,[22] as procured of set purpose and learned, as I think, of the Indians, who tie their salt [23] bitches often in woods that they might be lined by tigers;[24] also between a bitch and a fox, or a bear and a mastiff. But as we utterly want the first sort, except they be brought unto us, so it happeneth sometime that the other two are engendered and seen at home amongst us. But of all the rest heretofore remembered in this chapter, there is none more ugly and odious in sight, cruel and fierce in deed, nor untractable in hand than that which is begotten between the bear and the bandog. For whatsoever he catcheth hold of, he taketh it so fast that a man may sooner tear and rend his body in sunder than get open his mouth to separate his chops. Certes he regardeth neither wolf, bear, nor lion, and therefore may well be compared with those two dogs which were sent to Alexander out of India (and procreated, as it is thought, between a mastiff and male tiger, as be those also of Hyrcania) or to them that are bred in Arcadia,

---

[21] *To saw:* to paw the air.
[22] Patrizi, III, vi (fol. 116v).
[23] *Salt:* in heat.
[24] Pliny, VIII, lxi.

where copulation is oft seen between lions and bitches, as the like is in France (as I said) between she-wolves and dogs, whereof let this suffice, sith the further tractation of them doth not concern my purpose, more than the confutation of Cardan's talk (*De subt.*, *lib.* 10), who saith that after many generations dogs do become wolves and contrariwise;[25] which if it were true, then could not England be without many wolves; but nature hath set a difference between them, not only in outward form but also in inward disposition of their bones, wherefore it is unpossible that his assertion can be sound.

CHAPTER VIII

Of Our Saffron and the Dressing Thereof

As THE saffron of England, which Platina reckoneth among spices,[1] is the most excellent of all other (for it giveth place neither to that of Cilicia, whereof Solinus speaketh,[2] neither to any that cometh from Cilicia, where it groweth upon the Mount Taurus, Tmolus, Italy, Aetolia, Sicilia, or Lycia) in sweetness, tincture, and continuance, so of that which is to be had amongst us, the same that grows about Saffron Walden, sometime called Waldenburg, in the edge of Essex, first of all planted there in the time of Edward the Third, and that of Gloucestershire and those westerly parts, which some think to be better than that of Walden, surmounteth all the rest and therefore beareth worthily the higher price, by 6d. or 12d. most commonly in the pound.

The root of the herb that beareth this commodity is round, much like unto an indifferent [medium-sized] chestnut, and yet it is not cloved as the lily, nor flaked as the scallion, but hath a sad [dense] substance *inter bulbosa*, as *Orchis, Hyacinthus orientalis*, and *satyrion*. The color of the rind is not much differing from the innermost shell of a chestnut, although it be not altogether so

---

[25] *De subtilitate* (p. 229).

[1] See n. 21.

[2] *Collectanea rerum memorabilium*, chap. l. The repetition of Cilicia in the sentence occurs through a 1587 addition.

black as the said shell, neither altogether so brickle as is the pill [skin] of an onion. So long as the leaf flourisheth, the root is little and small; but when the grass is withered, the head[3] increaseth and multiplieth, the fillets also or small roots die, so that when the time doth come to take them up, they have no roots at all but so continue until September, that [when] they do grow again; and before the chive be grounded,[4] the smallest heads are also most esteemed, but whether they be great or small, if sheep or neat may come to them on the heap as they lie in the field, they will devour them as if they were hay or stubble; some also will root for them in very eager manner. The leaf, or rather the blade thereof, is long and narrow as grass, which come up always in October after the flowers be gathered and gone, pointed on a little tuft much like unto our sives.[5] Sometimes our cattle will feed upon the same; nevertheless, if it be bitten whilst it is green the head dieth, and therefore our crokers[6] are careful to keep it from such annoyance until it begin to wither, and then also will the cattle soonest taste thereof; for until that time the juice thereof is bitter. In every flower we find commonly three chives and three yellows [stamens], and double the number of leaves. Of twisted flowers I speak not, yet is it found that two flowers grow together, which bring forth five chives, so that always there is an odd chive and odd yellow, though three or four flowers should come out of one root.

The whole herb is named in Greek *crocos*, but of some (as Dioscorides saith) *castor, cynomorphos*, or Hercules'-blood; yet in the Arabian speech (from whence we borrow the name which we give thereunto) I find that it is called *zahafaran*, as Rembert doth bear witness.[7] The cause wherefore it was called *crocus* was this (as the poets feign, specially those from whom Galen hath borrowed the history which he noteth in his ninth book, *De medicamentis secundum loca*, where he writeth after this manner, although I take Crocus to be the first that used this commodity): A certain young gentleman called Crocus went to play

---

[3] *Head:* the root or corm.

[4] *Chive:* the three branches of the stigma; *grounded:* ground, pulverized.

[5] *Sives:* Harrison apparently uses this variant spelling of cives or chives to distinguish the herb from the stigma of saffron.

[6] *Crokers:* cultivators of saffron.

[7] Rembert Dodoens, *A New Herbal*, trans. Henry Lyte (1578), p. 216, including all of these variant names.

at quoits in the field with Mercury, and, being heedless of himself, Mercury's quoit happened by mishap to hit him on the head, whereby he received a wound that ere long killed him altogether, to the great discomfort of his friends. Finally, in the place where he bled, saffron was after found to grow, whereupon the people, seeing the color of the chive as it stood (although I doubt not but it grew there long before), adjudged it to come of the blood of Crocus, and therefore they gave it his name. And thus far Rembert, who with Galen, etc., differ very much from Ovid's *Metamorphoses*, 4, who writeth also thereof.[8] Indeed the chive, while it remaineth whole and unbruised, resembleth a dark red, but, being broken and converted into use, it yieldeth a yellow tincture. But what have we to do with fables?

The heads of saffron are raised [9] in July, either with plow, raising [spade], or tined hook; and, being scoured from their ross or filth and severed from such heads as are engendered of them since the last setting, they are interred again in July and August by ranks or rows, and, being covered with molds, they rest in the earth, where they cast forth little fillets and small roots like unto a scallion until September, in the beginning of which month the ground is pared [10] and all weeds and grass that groweth upon the same removed, to the intent that nothing may annoy the flower whenas his time doth come to rise.

These things being thus ordered in the latter end of the aforesaid month of September, the flower beginneth to appear, of a whitish blue, fesse [pale blue], or sky color, and in the end showing itself in the own kind, it resembleth almost the *leucotion* of Theophrastus,[11] saving that it is longer and hath in the midst thereof three chives, very red and pleasant to behold. These flowers are gathered in the morning before the rising of the sun, which otherwise would cause them to welk or flitter.[12] And the chives being picked from the flowers, these are thrown into the dunghill, the other dried upon little kells [kilns] covered with strained canvases upon a soft fire, whereby, and by the weight that

---

[8] Dodoens, p. 217; this source also includes the references to Galen and Ovid, although Crocus is specified as a "young wench."

[9] That is, the corms are turned up out of the ground.

[10] *Pared:* the turf or vegetation is removed.

[11] "See Rembert."—*H.*

[12] *Welk:* dry up, *flitter:* wither.

is laid upon them, they are dried and pressed into cakes and then bagged up for the benefit of their owners.

In good years we gather fourscore or an hundred pounds of wet saffron of an acre, which being dried doth yield twenty pounds of dry and more. Whereby, and sith the price of saffron is commonly about 20s. in money or not so little, it is easy to see what benefit is reaped by an acre of this commodity towards the charges of the setter, which indeed are great, but yet not so great as he shall be thereby a loser if he be anything diligent. For admit that the triple tillage of an acre doth cost 13s. 4d. before the saffron be set, the clodding [13] 16d., the taking of every load of stones from the same 4d., the raising of every quarter of heads 6d., and so much for cleansing of them, besides the rent of 10s. for every acre, thirty load of dung, which is worth 6d. the load, to be laid on the first year, for the setting 23s. 4d., for the paring 5s., 6d. for the picking of a pound wet, etc.; yea, though he hire it ready set and pay £10 for the same, yet shall he sustain no damage if warm weather and open season do happen at the gathering. This also is to be noted, that every acre asketh twenty quarters of heads, placed in ranks two inches one from another in long beds, which contain eight or ten foot in breadth. And after three years that ground will serve well and without compest [compost] for barley by the space of eighteen or twenty years together, as experience doth confirm. The heads also of every acre at the raising will store an acre and an half of new ground, which is a great advantage, and it will flower eight or ten days together. But the best saffron is gathered at the first, at which time four pounds of wet saffron will go very near to make one of dry; but in the midst [of the flowering period] five pounds of the one will make but one of the other, because the chive waxeth smaller, as six at the last will do no more but yield one of the dried, by reason of the chive which is now very lean and hungry. After twenty years, also, the same ground may be set with saffron again. And in lieu of a conclusion take this for a perpetual rule, that heads coming out of a good ground will prosper best in a lighter soil, and contrariwise, which is one note that our crokers do carefully observe.

The heads are raised every third year about us, to wit, after

[13] *Clodding:* removing of clods, harrowing.

Midsummer [June 24], when the ross cometh dry from the heads; and commonly in the first year after they be set they yield very little increase; yet that which then cometh is counted the finest and greatest chive, and best for medicine, and called saffron *du hort*. The next crop is much greater, but the third exceedeth, and then they raise again about Walden and in Cambridgeshire. In this period of time, also, the heads are said to child, that is, to yield out of some parts of them divers other headlets, whereby it hath been seen that some one head hath been increased (though with his own detriment) to three or four or five or six, which augmentation is the only cause whereby they are sold so good cheap. For to my remembrance I have not known four bushels, or a coomb, of them to be valued much above 2*s.* 8*d.*, except in some odd years that they arise to 8 or 10*s.* the quarter, and that is when overgreat store of winter's water hath rotted the most of them as they stood within the ground, or heat in summer parched and burnt them up.

In Norfolk and Suffolk they raise but once in seven years; but as their saffron is not so fine as that of Cambridgeshire and about Walden, so it will not cake, tinge, nor hold color withal, wherein lieth a great part of the value of this stuff. Some crafty jacks [knaves] use to mix it with scraped brazil or with the flower of *Sonchus* [sow thistle], which cometh somewhat near indeed to the hue of our good saffron (if it be late gathered), but it is soon bewrayed both by the depth of the color and hardness. Such also was the plenty of saffron about twenty years past that some of the townsmen of Walden gave the one-half of the flowers for picking of the other, and sent them ten or twelve miles abroad into the country, whilst the rest, not thankful for the abundance of God's blessing bestowed upon them (as wishing rather more scarcity thereof, because of the keeping up of the price), in most contemptuous manner murmured against Him, saying that He did shit saffron, therewith to choke the market.[14] But as they showed themselves no less than ingrate infidels in this behalf, so the Lord considered their unthankfulness and gave them ever since such scarcity as the greatest murmurers have now the least store; and most of them are either worn out of occupying or remain scarce able to maintain their grounds without the help of

[14] Furnivall (I, liii) prints a similar entry from Harrison's Chronology, dated 1556 (1557?).

other men. Certes it hath generally decayed about Saffron Walden since the said time, until now of late within these two years that men began again to plant and renew the same, because of the great commodity. But to proceed.

When the heads be raised and taken up, they will remain sixteen or twenty days out of the earth, or more; yea, peradventure a full month. Howbeit, they are commonly in the earth again by St.-James's-tide [July 24] or very shortly after. For as if they be taken up before Midsummer or beginning of July, the heads will shrink like a roasted warden,[15] so after August they will wax dry, become unfruitful, and decay. And I know it by experience, in that I have carried some of them to London with me; and notwithstanding that they have remained there unset by the space of forty days and more, yet some of them have brought forth two or three flowers apiece, and some flowers three or five chives, to the great admiration of such as have gathered the same and not been acquainted with their nature and country where they grew. The crokers or saffron-men do use an observation a little before the coming up of the flower, and sometime in the taking up at Midsummertide, by opening of the heads to judge of plenty and scarcity of this commodity to come. For if they see as it were many small hairy veins of saffron to be in the midst of the bulb, they pronounce a fruitful year. And to say truth, at the cleaving of each head a man shall discern the saffron by the color and see whereabouts the chive will issue out of the root. Warm, dark nights, sweet dews, fat grounds (chiefly the chalky), and misty mornings are very good for saffron; but frost and cold do kill and keep back the flower, or else shrink up the chive.

And thus much have I thought good to speak of English saffron, which is hot in the second and dry in the first degree,[16] and most plentiful, as our crokers hold, in that year wherein ewes twin most. But as I can make no warrantise hereof, so I am otherwise sure that there is no more deceit used in any trade than in saffron. For in the making they will grease the papers on the kell with a little candle grease, to make the worst saffron have so good a color as the best; afterwards also they will sprinkle butter thereon to make the weight better. But both these are bewrayed either by a quantity thereof holden over the fire in a silver spoon

---

[15] *Warden:* a variety of pear.
[16] Dodoens, p. 217.

or by the softness thereof between the forefinger and the thumb; or thirdly, by the color thereof in age, for, if you lay it by far worse saffron of other countries, the color will bewray the forgery by the swartness of the chive, which otherwise would excel it, and thereunto, being sound, remain crisp, brickle, and dry; and finally, if it be holden near the face, will strike a certain biting heat upon the skin and eyes,[17] whereby it is adjudged good and merchant ware indeed among the skillful crokers.

Now if it please you to hear of any of the virtues thereof, I will note these ensuing at the request of one who required me to touch a few of them with whatsoever brevity I listed. Therefore our saffron (beside the manifold use that it hath in the kitchen and pastry, also in our cakes at bride-ales and thanksgivings of women)[18] is very profitably mingled with those medicines which we take for the diseases of the breast, of the lungs, of the liver, and of the bladder; it is good also for the stomach, if you take it in meat, for it comforteth the same and maketh good digestion; being sodden [steeped] also in wine, it not only keepeth a man from drunkenness but encourageth also unto procreation of issue. If you drink it in sweet wine, it enlargeth the breath and is good for those that are troubled with the phthisic and shortness of the wind; mingled with the milk of a woman and laid upon the eyes it stayeth such humors as descend into the same and taketh away the red weals and pearls [cataracts] that oft grow about them; it killeth moths if it be sewed in paper bags very thin and laid up in presses [cupboards] amongst tapestry or apparel; also it is very profitably laid unto all inflammations, painful aposthumes [abcesses], and the shingles; and doth no small ease unto deafness if it be mingled with such medicines as are beneficial unto the ears; it is of great use also in ripening of botches [boils] and all swellings proceeding of raw humors. Or if it shall please you to drink the root thereof with malvesey [malmsey], it will marvelously provoke urine, dissolve and expel gravel, and yield no small ease to them that make their water by dropmeals [drops].[19] Finally, three drams thereof taken

---

[17] The second and fourth of these tests are given by Pliny, XXI, xvii.

[18] *Thanksgivings of women:* churchings; see p. 131, n. 16.

[19] The list of remedies to this point, except for that concerning the usefulness of saffron against moths, added in 1587, is taken from Dodoens, p. 217. The verbal similarities are sufficiently close to raise the suspicion that Harrison had seen the translation in MS.

at once, which is about the weight of 1*s.* 9½*d.*, is deadly poison, as Dioscorides doth affirm,[20] and drunk in wine (saith Platina, *lib.* 3, *cap.* 13, *De honesta voluptate*)[21] doth haste on drunkenness, which is very true. And I have known some that by eating only of bread more than of custom strained with saffron have become like drunken men, and yet otherwise well known to be but competent drinkers. For further confirmation of this also, if a man do but open and ransack a bag of one hundred- or two hundredweight, as merchants do when they buy it of the crokers, it will strike such an air into their heads which deal withal that for a time they shall be giddy and sick (I mean for two or three hours' space), their noses and eyes in like sort will yield such plenty of rheumatic water that they shall be the better for it long after, especially their eyesight, which is wonderfully clarified by this means; howbeit, some merchants, not liking of this physic, muffle themselves as women do when they ride and put on spectacles set in leather, which doth in some measure (but not for altogether) put by the force thereof.

There groweth some saffron in many places of Almain [Germany] and also about Vienna in Austria, which latter is taken for the best that springeth in those quarters. Instead of this some do use the *Carthamus* [safflower], called amongst us bastard saffron, but neither is this of any value, nor the other in any wise comparable unto ours. Whereof let this suffice, as of a commodity brought into this island in the time of Edward the Third and not commonly planted till Richard the Second did reign. It would grow very well (as I take it) about the Chiltern Hills and in all the Vale of the White Horse, so well as in Walden and Cambridgeshire, if they were careful of it. I hear of some also to be cherished already in Gloucestershire and certain other places westward. But of the fineness and tincture of the chive I hear not as yet of any trial.

Would to God that my countrymen had been heretofore (or were now) more careful of this commodity! Then would it no doubt have proved more beneficial to our island than our cloth or wool. But alas! so idle are we and heretofore so much given to

[20] *De materia medica*, I, 25.

[21] *Platina:* Bartholomaeus Sacchi de Platina (1421–1481), Italian historian of the Popes; his treatise on hygiene, *De obsoniis ac honesta voluptate,* was first published in Rome ca. 1473 and frequently reprinted.

ease, by reason of the smallness of our rents, that few men regard to search out which are their best commodities. But if landlords hold on to raise the rents of their farms as they begin, they will enforce their tenants to look better unto their gains and scratch out their rent from under every clod that may be turned aside. The greatest mart for saffron is at Aquila in Abruzzi, where they have an especial weight for the same of ten pounds less in the hundred than that of Florence and Lucca, but how it agreeth with ours it shall appear hereafter.[22]

CHAPTER IX

Of Quarries of Stone for Building

QUARRIES with us are pits or mines, out of which we dig our stone to build withal, and of these, as we have great plenty in England, so are they of divers sorts and those very profitable for sundry necessary uses. In times past the use of stone was in manner dedicated to the building of churches, religious houses, princely palaces, bishops' manors, and holds only; but now that scrupulous observation is altogether infringed and building with stone so commonly taken up that amongst noblemen and gentlemen the timber frames are supposed to be not much better than paper work, of little continuance, and least continuance of all. It far passeth my cunning to set down how many sorts of stone for building are to be found in England, but much further to call each of them by their proper names. Howbeit, such is the curiosity of our countrymen that, notwithstanding Almighty God hath so blessed our realm in most plentiful manner with such and so many quarries apt and meet for piles of longest continuance, yet we, as loathsome of this abundance or not liking of the plenty, do commonly leave these natural gifts to mold and cinder in the ground and take up an artificial brick, in burning whereof a great part of the wood of this land is daily consumed and spent, to the no small decay of that commodity and hindrance of the poor, that perish oft for cold.

[22] Presumably in Harrison's treatise on weights and measures; see p. 453, n. 1.

Our elders have from time to time, following our natural vice in misliking of our own commodities at home and desiring those of other countries abroad, most esteemed the Caen stone that is brought hither out of Normandy; and many even in these our days, following the same vein, do covet in their works almost to use none other. Howbeit, experience on the one side and our skillful masons on the other (whose judgment is nothing inferior to those of other countries) do affirm that in the north and south parts of England and certain other places there are some quarries which for hardness and beauty are equal to the outlandish [foreign] grit. This may also be confirmed by the King's Chapel at Cambridge, the greatest part of the square stone whereof was brought thither out of the North. Some commend the vein of white freestone, slate, and mere stone which is between Pentewan and the Black Head in Cornwall for very fine stuff.[1] Other do speak much of the quarries at Hamdon, nine miles from Melbury,[2] and paving stone of Purbeck. For toph stone [tufa] not a few allow of the quarry that is at Dursley, divers mislike not of the veins of hard stone that are at Oxford and Burford.[3] One praiseth the freestone at Manchester and Prestbury in Gloucestershire; another the quarries of the like in Richmond.[4] The third liketh well of the hard stone in Clee Hill in Shropshire; the fourth of that of Trowbridge, Weldon, and Terrington.[5] Whereby it appeareth that we have quarries enow and good enough in England, sufficient for us to build withal, if the peevish contempt of our own commodities, and delectations to enrich other countries, did not catch such foolish hold upon us. It is also verified (as any other way) that all nations have rather need of England than England of any other. And this I think may suffice for the substance of our works.

Now if you have regard to their ornature, how many mines of sundry kinds of coarse and fine marble are there to be had in England? But chiefly one in Staffordshire, another near to The

[1] Leland, *Itinerary* (ed. Smith, I, 202); *mere stone:* a misreading of Leland's "more stone [moorstone]," a variety of granite found in Cornwall.

[2] "Mr. Strangeways now alate began to build richly at his common dwelling house in Melbury Park [Dorset], and caused 3,000 load of freestone to be fetched from Hamdon quarry [Somerset] nine miles off" (Leland, IV, 73).

[3] Leland (V, 96; at Burford in Oxfordshire, V, 74).

[4] Leland (IV, 6, 134, 32).

[5] Leland (V, 189; I, 136, 11, 65).

Peak, the third at Vaudey [Abbey], the fourth at Snodhill (longing to the Lord Chandos), the fifth at Egglestone, which is of black marble spotted with gray or white spots, the sixth not far from Durham.[6] Of white marble also we have store, and so fair as the Marpesian of Paros Isle. But what mean I to go about to recite all, or the most excellent? sith these which I have named already are not altogether of the best, nor scarcely of any value in comparison of those whose places of growth are utterly unknown unto me, and whereof the black marble spotted with green is none of the vilest sort, as may appear by parcel of the pavement of the lower part of the choir of Paul's in London, and also in Westminster [Abbey], where some pieces thereof are yet to be seen and marked, if any will look for them.

If marble will not serve, then have we the finest alabaster that may elsewhere be had, as about St. David's of Wales; also near to Beaumanor, which is about four or five miles from Leicester, and taken to be the best, although there are divers other quarries hereof beyond the Trent, as in Yorkshire, etc.,[7] and fully so good as that, whose names at this time are out of my remembrance. What should I talk of the plaster of Axholme (for of that which they dig out of the earth in sundry places of Lincoln- and Derbyshires, wherewith they blanch their houses instead of lime, I speak not); certes it is a fine kind of alabaster. But sith it is sold commonly but after 12*d.* the load, we judge it to be but vile and coarse. For my part, I cannot skill of stone, yet in my opinion it is not without great use for plaster of Paris, and such is the mine of it that the stones thereof lie in flakes one upon another like planks or tables, and under the same is an exceeding hard stone very profitable for building, as hath oftentimes been proved.[8] This is also to be marked further of our plaster white and gray, that not contented with the same, as God by the quarry doth send and yield it forth, we have now devised to cast it in molds for windows and pillars of what form and fashion we list, even as alabaster itself; and with such stuff sundry houses in Yorkshire are furnished of late. But of what continuance this

[6] Leland seems not to mention the quarries in Staffordshire and Derbyshire; the other references occur at I, 23; V, 176; IV, 29; V, 129.

[7] Leland mentions only the alabaster of Beaumanor (I, 20).

[8] Most of these details concerning Axholme alabaster or gypsum come from Leland (I, 38).

device is like to prove, the time to come shall easily bewray. In the meantime Sir Ralph Burcher,[9] knight, hath put the device in practice and affirmeth that six men in six months shall travail in that trade to see greater profit to the owner than twelve men in six years could before this trick was invented.

If neither alabaster nor marble doth suffice, we have the touchstone, called in Latin *Lydius lapis* [Lydian stone], shining as glass, either to match in sockets with our pillars of alabaster or contrariwise; or if it please the workman to join pillars of alabaster or touch with sockets of brass, pewter, or copper, we want not also these metals. So that I think no nation can have more excellent and greater diversity of stuff for building than we may have in England, if ourselves could so like of it. But such, alas, is our nature that not our own but other men's do most of all delight us; and for desire of novelty we oft exchange our finest cloth, corn, tin, and wools for halfpenny cockhorses for children, dogs of wax or of cheese, twopenny tabors, leaden swords, painted feathers, gewgaws for fools, dogtricks for dizzards,[10] hawkshoods, and suchlike trumpery, whereby we reap just mockage and reproach in other countries.

I might remember here our pits for millstones that are to be had in divers places of our country, as in Anglesey, Kent, also at Queen Hope of blue grit,[11] of no less value than the Cologne, yea, than the French stones, our grindstones for hardware men. Our whetstones are no less laudable than those of Crete and Lacedaemonia, albeit we use no oil with them, as they did in those parties, but only water, as the Italians and Naxians do with theirs; whereas they that grow in Cilicia must have both oil and water laid upon them or else they make no edge.[12] These also are divided either into the hard grit, as the common that shoemakers use, or the soft grit called hones, to be had among the barbers, and those either black or white, and the rub [whetstone] or brickle stone, which husbandmen do occupy in the whetting of their scythes.

In like manner slate of sundry colors is everywhere in manner

<hr>

[9] Sir Ralph Bourchier of Benningborough, Yorkshire?
[10] *Dogtricks for dizzards:* trifling tricks for fools.
[11] The millstones of Anglesey and Queen Hope (Hope in Flintshire) are mentioned by Leland (III, 134, 73).
[12] Pliny, XXXVI, xlvii.

to be had, as is the flint and chalk, the shalder [13] and the pebble. Howbeit, for all this we must fetch them still from far, as did the Hull men their stones out of Iceland, wherewith they paved their town for want of the like in England, or as Sir Thomas Gresham did when he bought the stones in Flanders wherewith he paved the Bourse.[14] But as he will answer peradventure that he bargained for the whole mold and substance of his workmanship in Flanders, so the Hullanders or Hull men will say how that stock-fish is light loading, and therefore they did ballast their vessels with these Iceland stones to keep them from turning over in their so tedious a voyage.[15]

And thus much briefly of our quarries of stone for building, wherein oftentimes the workmen have found strange things enclosed, I mean lively creatures shut up in the hard stones and living there without respiration or breathing, as frogs, toads, etc., whereof you shall read more in the Chronology following; also in Caius Langius, William of Newburgh, Agricola, Cornelius of Amsterdam, Bellogius (*De aquatilibus*), Albert the Great (*lib.* 19 [I], *cap.* 9, *De rebus metallicis*), and Goropius (in "*Niloscopio*," p. 237), etc.[16] Sometime also they find precious stones (though seldom) and some of them perfectly squared by nature, and much like unto the diamond found of late in a quarry of marble at Naples, which was so perfectly pointed as if all the workmen in the world had consulted about the performance of that workmanship.

I know that these reports unto some will seem incredible, and therefore I stand the longer upon them; nevertheless, omitting to speak particularly of such things as happen amongst us and rather seeking to confirm the same by the like in other countries, I will

---

[13] *Shalder*: apparently a flake or splinter of stone, but in this sense the word seems unique to Harrison.

[14] *Sir Thomas Gresham* (?1519–1579): merchant, banker, and diplomat, who completed his Royal Exchange in 1568.

[15] Leland (I, 50).

[16] *William of Newburgh* (?1136–1198): English monastic chronicler; *Georg Agricola* (1494–1555): German physician and naturalist, the reference being to his *De natura fossilium; Bellogius:* Pierre Belon (?1517–1564), French naturalist; *Albert the Great* (?1206–1280): German philosopher and theologian; *Goropius:* Jean Becan (1518–1572), Flemish antiquary, the citation (further explained in the next paragraph) being to Bk. III of his *Origines Antwerpianae* (Antwerp, 1569). I cannot positively identify either Caius Langius or Cornelius of Amsterdam.

deliver a few more examples, whereby the truth hereof shall so much the better appear. For in the midst of a stone not long since found at Chios, upon the breaking up thereof there was seen *caput Panisci* [17] enclosed therein, very perfectly formed, as the beholders do remember. How come the grains of gold to be so fast enclosed in the stones that are and have been found in the Spanish Baetis? But this is most marvelous, that a most delectable and sweet oil, comparable to the finest balm or oil of spike [18] in smell, was found naturally included in a stone, which could not otherwise be broken but with a smith's hammer. Goropius doth tell of a perch perfectly formed to be found in Britain, but as then committed into hard stone upon the top of a crag. Aristotle and Theophrastus speak of fishes digged out of the earth far from the sea in Greece, which Seneca also confirmeth, but with addition that they are perilous to be eaten. In Pope Martin's time a serpent was found fast enclosed in a rock, as the kernel is within the nut, so that no air could come to it, and in my time another in a coffin of stone at Avignon, wherein a man had been buried, which so filled the room and lay so close from air that all men wondered how it was possible for the same to live and continue so long time there. Finally, I myself have seen stones opened and within them the substances of corrupted worms like unto adders (but far shorter), whose crests and wrinkles of body appeared also therein, as if they had been engraved in the stones by art and industry of man. Wherefore to affirm that as well living creatures as precious stones, gold, etc., are now and then found in our quarries shall not hereafter be a thing so incredible as many talking philosophers, void of all experience, do affirm and willfully maintain against such as hold the contrary.

CHAPTER X

Of Sundry Minerals

WITH how great benefits this island of ours hath been endued from the beginning, I hope there is no godly man but will readily

---

[17] *Caput Panisci:* a head of the little Pan.　　　[18] *Spike:* spick, lavender.

confess and yield unto the Lord God His due honor for the same. For we are blessed every way, and there is no temporal commodity necessary to be had or craved by any nation at God's hand that He hath not in most abundant manner bestowed upon us Englishmen, if we could see to use it and be thankful for the same. But alas (as I said in the chapter precedent), we love to enrich them that care not for us but for our great commodities, and one trifling toy not worth the carriage, coming (as the proverb saith) in three ships from beyond the sea, is more worth with us than a right good jewel easy to be had at home. They have also the cast [ruse] to teach us to neglect our own things, for if they see that we begin to make any account of our commodities (if it be so that they have also the like in their own countries), they will suddenly abase the same to so low a price that, our gain not being worthy our travail, and the same commodity with less cost ready to be had at home from other countries (though but for a while), it causeth us to give over our endeavors and, as it were, by and by to forget the matter whereabout we went before, to obtain them at their hands. And this is the only cause wherefore our commodities are oft so little esteemed of. Some of them can say without any teacher that they will buy the case [skin] of a fox of an Englishman for a groat and make him afterward give 12*d*. for the tail. Would to God we might once wax wiser and each one endeavor that the commonwealth of England may flourish again in her old rate, and that our commodities may be fully wrought at home (as cloth, if you will for an example) and not carried out to be shorn and dressed abroad, while our clothworkers here do starve and beg their bread and for lack of daily practice utterly neglect to be skillful in this science! But to my purpose.

We have in England great plenty of quicksilver, antimony, sulphur, black lead, and orpiment red and yellow. We have also the finest alum (wherein the diligence of one of the greatest favorers of the commonwealth of England of a subject hath been of late egregiously abused and even almost with barbarous incivility),[1] and of no less force against fire, if it were used in our

---

[1] "The Lord Mountjoy."—*H*. James Blount (1533–1581), sixth Lord Mountjoy, owned the royal patent to make alum and went heavily into debt attempting to bring the process to perfection.

parietings,[2] than that of Lipara, which only was in use sometime amongst the Asians and Romans, and whereof Sulla had such trial that when he meant to have burned a tower of wood erected by Archelaus, the lieutenant of Mithridates, he could by no means set it on fire in a long time because it was washed over with alum, as were also the gates of the Temple of Jerusalem with like effect, and perceived when Titus commanded fire to be put unto the same.[3]

Beside this we have also the natural cinnabar or vermilion, the sulphurous glebe [earth] called bitumen,[4] in old time used for mortar and yet burned in lamps where oil is scant and geason [scarce], the chrysocolla, copperas,[5] and mineral stone, whereof petroleum is made, and that which is most strange, the mineral pearl,[6] which as they are for greatness and color most excellent of all other, so are they digged out of the mainland and in sundry places far distant from the shore. Certes the western part of the land hath in times past greatly abounded with these and many other rare and excellent commodities, but now they are washed away by the violence of the sea, which hath devoured the greatest part of Cornwall and Devonshire on either side; and it doth appear yet by good record that, whereas now there is a great distance between the Scilly Isles and point of the Land's End, there was of late years to speak of scarcely a brook or drain of one fathom water between them, if so much, as by those evidences appeareth and are yet to be seen in the hands of the lord and chief owner of those isles. But to proceed.

Of coal mines we have such plenty in the north and western parts of our island as may suffice for all the realm of England, and so must they do hereafter indeed, if wood be not better cherished than it is at this present. And to say the truth, notwithstanding that very many of them are carried into other countries of the main, yet their greatest trade beginneth now to grow from the forge into the kitchen and hall, as may appear already in most cities and towns that lie about the coast, where they have

[2] *Parietings:* pargeting, plastering.
[3] *Archelaus:* Greek general, twice defeated by Sulla in 86 B.C. Jerusalem was razed by Titus in A.D. 70.
[4] *Bitumen:* mineral pitch, or asphalt.
[5] *Chrysocolla:* either borax or malachite; *copperas:* sulphates of copper, iron, and zinc.
[6] *Mineral pearl:* probably perlite, a form of obsidian.

but little other fuel, except it be turf and hassock. I marvel not a little that there is no trade of these [coals] into Sussex and Southamptonshire, for want whereof the smiths do work their iron with charcoal. I think that far carriage be the only cause, which is but a slender excuse to enforce us to carry them unto the main from hence.

Beside our coal mines we have pits in like sort of white plaster, and of fat and white (and other-colored) marl, wherewith in many places the inhabiters do compest their soil, and which doth benefit their land in ample manner for many years to come. We have saltpeter for our ordnance and salt soda for our glass, and thereto in one place a kind of earth (in Surrey, as I ween, hard by Cuddington, and sometime in the tenure of one Croxton of London) which is so fine to make molds for goldsmiths and casters of metal that a load of it was worth 5s. thirty years agone; none such again, they say, in England.[7] But whether there be or not, let us not be unthankful to God for these and other His benefits bestowed upon us, whereby He showeth Himself a loving and merciful father unto us, which contrariwise return unto Him, in lieu of humility and obedience, nothing but wickedness, avarice, mere contempt of His will, pride, excess, atheism, and no less than Jewish ingratitude.

CHAPTER XI

Of Metals To Be Had in Our Land

ALL metals receive their beginning of quicksilver and sulphur, which are as mother and father to them. And such is the purpose of Nature in their generations that she tendeth always to the procreation of gold; nevertheless, she seldom reacheth unto that her end because of the unequal mixture and proportion of these two in the substance engendered, whereby impediment and corruption is induced, which as it is more or less doth show itself in the metal that is produced. First of all, therefore, the substance

[7] Leland, *Itinerary* (ed. Smith, IV, 121), who identifies the owner as "Crompton" and the value as "two crowns" or 10s. a load.

of sulphur and quicksilver, being mixed in due proportion, after long and temperate decoction in the bowels of the earth, orderly engrossed [1] and fixed, becometh gold, which Encelius [2] doth call the sun and right heir of Nature; but if it swerve but a little (saith he) in the commixtion and other circumstances, then doth it product silver, the daughter, not so noble a child as gold, her brother, which among metal is worthily called the chief. Contrariwise, the substances of the aforesaid parents mixed without proportion and less digested and fixed in the entrails of the earth, whereby the radical moisture becometh combustible and not of force to endure heat and hammer, doth either turn into tin, lead, copper, or iron, which were the first metals known in time past unto antiquity, although that in these days there are divers other, whereof neither they nor our alchemists had ever any knowledge.

Of these, therefore, which are reputed among the third sort, we here in England have our parts, and, as I call them to mind, so will I entreat of them and with such brevity as may serve the turn, and yet not altogether omit to say somewhat of gold and silver also, because I find by good experience how it was not said of old time without great reason that all countries have need of Britain and Britain itself of none. For truly if a man regard such necessities as nature only requireth, there is no nation under the sun that can say so much as ours, sith we do want none that are convenient for us. Wherefore if it be a benefit to have any gold at all, we are not void of some, neither likewise of silver, whatsoever Cicero affirmeth to the contrary (*lib.* 4, *Ad Atticum, epi.* 16 [17]), in whose time they were not found: *Britannici belli exitus,* saith he, *expectatur, constat enim aditus insulae esse munitos mirificis molibus: etiam illud jam cognitum est, neque argenti scrupulum esse ullum in illa insula, neque ullam spem praedae nisi ex mancipiis, ex quibus nullos puto te litteris aut musicis eruditos expectare.* [3] And albeit that we have no such abundance of these (as some other countries do yield), yet have

[1] *Engrossed: inspissata,* condensed.

[2] *Encelius:* Christoph Entzelt, from whose *De re metallica* (Frankfort, 1557), pp. 2–3, this entire paragraph is freely translated.

[3] "The outcome of the war in Britain is awaited anxiously, for it is well known that the approach to the island is defended by extraordinary masses of rock; and also it has been learned that there is not a scrap of silver in that island nor any hope of booty, except from slaves, among whom I don't imagine you can anticipate any with literary or musical accomplishments."

my rich countrymen store enough of both in their purses, where in time past they were wont to have least, because the garnishing of our churches, tabernacles, images, shrines, and apparel of the priests consumed the greatest part, as experience hath confirmed.

Of late my countrymen have found out I wot not what voyage into the West Indies, from whence they have brought some gold, whereby our country is enriched; but of all that ever adventured into those parts, none have sped better than Sir Francis Drake, whose success, 1582, hath far passed even his own expectation.[4] One John Frobisher in like manner, attempting to seek out a shorter cut by the northerly regions into the peaceable sea and kingdom of Cathay, happened, 1577, upon certain islands by the way, wherein great plenty of much gold appeared, and so much that some letted not to give out for certainty that Solomon had his gold from thence wherewith he builded the Temple. This golden show made him so desirous also of like success that he left off his former voyage and returned home to bring news of such things as he had seen. But when after another voyage it was found to be but dross, he gave over both the enterprises and now keepeth home without any desire at all to seek into far countries.[5] In truth, such was the plenty of ore there seen and to be had that if it had holden perfect might have furnished all the world with abundance of that metal; the journey also was short and performed in four or five months, which was a notable encouragement. But to proceed.

Tin and lead, metals which Strabo noteth in his time to be carried unto Marsilis [Marseilles] from hence, as Diodorus also confirmeth,[6] are very plentiful with us, the one in Cornwall, Devonshire, and elsewhere in the North, the other in Derbyshire, Weardale, and sundry places of this island, whereby my countrymen do reap no small commodity, but especially our pewterers, who in time past employed the use of pewter only upon dishes, pots, and a few other trifles for service here at home, whereas now they are grown unto such exquisite cunning that they can in

[4] From both his West Indian expedition of 1572–1573 and his circumnavigation in 1577–1580 Drake returned laden with piratical plunder.

[5] Sir Martin Frobisher (?1535–1594) was distracted from his expeditions in search of the Northwest Passage (1576–1578) by the discovery on Baffin Island of pyrites, or fool's gold.

[6] Strabo, III, ii, 9, and Diodorus Siculus, V, xxxviii, 4, neither of whom mentions lead.

manner imitate by infusion any form or fashion of cup, dish, salt, bowl, or goblet which is made by goldsmith's craft, though they be never so curious, exquisite, and artificially forged. Such furniture of household of this metal as we commonly call by the name of vessel is sold usually by the garnish, which doth contain twelve platters, twelve dishes, twelve saucers, and those are either of silver fashion, or else with broad or narrow brims, and bought by the pound, which is now valued at 6*d*. or 7*d*., or peradventure at 8*d*. Of porringers, pots, and other like I speak not, albeit that in the making of all these things there is such exquisite diligence used, I mean for the mixture of the metal and true making of this commodity (by reason of sharp laws provided in that behalf), as the like is not to be found in any other trade. I have been also informed that it consisteth of a composition which hath thirty pounds of kettle brass to a thousand pounds of tin, whereunto they add three or four pounds of tinglass [bismuth]; but as too much of this doth make the stuff brickle, so the more the brass be, the better is the pewter and more profitable unto him that doth buy and purchase the same. But to proceed.

In some places beyond the sea a garnish of good flat English pewter of an ordinary making (I say flat because dishes and platters in my time begin to be made deep like basins and are indeed more convenient both for sauce, broth, and keeping the meat warm) is esteemed almost so precious as the like number of vessels that are made of fine silver, and in manner no less desired amongst the great estates, whose workmen are nothing so skillful in that trade as ours, neither their metal so good nor plenty so great as we have here in England. The Romans made excellent looking glasses of our English tin; howbeit, our workmen were not then so exquisite in that feat as the Brundusians, wherefore the wrought metal was carried over unto them by way of merchandise, and very highly were those glasses esteemed of till silver came generally in place, which in the end brought the tin into such contempt that in manner every dishwasher refused to look in other than silver glasses for the attiring of her head. Howbeit, the making of silver glasses had been in use before Britain was known unto the Romans, for I read that one Praxiteles devised them in the young time of Pompey, which was before the coming of Caesar into this island.[7]

[7] Pliny, XXXIII, xlv, who names the inventor Pasiteles.

There were mines of lead sometimes also in Wales, which endured so long till the people had consumed all their wood by melting of the same (as they did also at Comeristwith, six miles from Stradfleur)[8] and I suppose that in Pliny's time the abundance of lead (whereof he speaketh) was to be found in those parts (in the 17th [Chap. xlix] of his 34th book); also he affirmeth that it lay in the very sward of the earth, and daily gotten in such plenty that the Romans made a restraint of the carriage thereof to Rome, limiting how much should yearly be wrought and transported over the sea.

And here by the way it is worthy to be noted of a crow which a miner of tin, dwelling near Comeristwith (as Leland saith),[9] had made so tame that it would daily fly and follow him to his work and other places, wheresoever he happened to travel. This laborer, working on a time in the bottom or valley where the first mine was known to be, did lay his purse and girdle by him, as men commonly do that address themselves to apply their business earnestly and he himself also had used from time to time before. The crow likewise was very busy flittering about him and so much molested him that he waxed angry with the bird and in his fury threatened to wring off his neck if he might once get him into his hands; to be short, in the end the crow hastily caught up his girdle and purse and made away withal so fast as her wings could carry her. Hereupon the poor man, falling into great agony (for he feared to lose peradventure all his money), threw down his mattock at adventure and ran after the bird, cursing and menacing that he should lose his life if ever he got him again; but as it fell out, the crow was the means whereby his life was saved, for he had not been long out of the mine ere it fell down and killed all his fellows. If I should take upon me to discourse and search out the cause of the thus dealing of this bird at large, I should peradventure set myself further into the briars than well find which way to come out again, yet am I persuaded that the crow was God's instrument herein, whereby the life of this poor laborer was preserved. It was done also in another order than that which I read of another tame crow kept

[8] Leland, *Itinerary* (ed. Smith, III, 123). *Comeristwith:* Cwmystwyth in Cardiganshire; *Stradfleur:* Strata Florida, or Caron Uwch Clawdd.

[9] *Itinerary* (III, 124). Harrison embroiders freely on Leland's terse mention of the incident.

up by a shoemaker of Dutchland [Germany] in his shop or stove, who, seeing the same to sit upon the perch among his shoon [shoes] very heavily and drowsy, said unto the bird, "What aileth my jack, why art thou sad and pensive?" The crow, hearing his master speak after this sort unto him, answered (or else the devil within him) out of the Psalter, *Cogitavi dies antiquos et [annos] aeternos in mente habui.*[10] But whither am I digressed, from lead unto crows and from crows unto devils? Certes it is now high time to return unto our metals and resume the tractation of such things as I had erst in hand.

Iron is found in many places, as in Sussex, Kent, Weardale, Mendip, Walsall, as also in Shropshire, but chiefly in the woods betwixt Belvos and Willocke, or Wicberie,[11] near Manchester, and elsewhere in Wales. Of which mines divers do bring forth so fine and good stuff as any that cometh from beyond the sea, beside the infinite gains to the owners, if we would so accept it or bestow a little more cost in the refining of it. It is also of such toughness that it yieldeth to the making of clarichord [clavichord] wire in some places of the realm. Nevertheless, it was better cheap with us when strangers only brought it hither, for it is our quality when we get any commodity to use it with extremity towards our own nation, after we have once found the means to shut out foreigners from the bringing in of the like. It breedeth in like manner great expense and waste of wood, as doth the making of our pots and table vessel of glass, wherein is much loss sith it is so quickly broken, and yet (as I think) easy to be made tougher if our alchemists could once find the true birth or production of the red man,[12] whose mixture would induce a metallical toughness unto it, whereby it should abide the hammer.[13]

Copper is lately not found but rather restored again to light. For I have read of copper to have been heretofore gotten in our island; howbeit, as strangers have most commonly the governance of our mines, so they hitherto make small gains of this in hand in the north parts, for (as I am informed) the profit doth very

[10] "Psal. 76."—*H.* "I have considered the days of old, I have had in mind the years of ancient times" (77:5).
[11] Leland (V, 18). *Belvos:* Buildwas in Shropshire; *Willocke, or Wicberie:* a misreading of Leland's "Wenloke [Wenlock]."
[12] *Red man:* an alchemical term, perhaps red sulphide of mercury.
[13] See p. 128.

hardly countervail the charges, whereat wise men do not a little marvel, considering the abundance which that mine doth seem to offer and as it were at hand. Leland, our countryman, noteth sundry great likelihoods of natural copper mines to be eastwards, as between Dodman and Tywardreath in the sea cliffs,[14] beside other places, whereof divers are noted here and there in sundry places of this book already, and therefore it shall be but in vain to repeat them here again; as for that which is gotten out of the marcasite,[15] I speak not of it sith it is not incident to my purpose. In Dorsetshire also a copper mine lately found is brought to good perfection.

As for our steel, it is not so good for edge tools as that of Cologne, and yet the one is often sold for the other and like tale [count] used in both, that is to say, thirty gads to the sheaf and twelve sheaves to the burden.[16] Our alchemy [17] is artificial and thereof our spoons and some salts are commonly made and preferred before our pewter with some, albeit in truth it be much subject to corruption, putrefaction, more heavy and foul to handle than our pewter; yet some ignorant persons affirm it to be a metal more natural, and the very same which Encelius calleth *plumbum cinereum*, the Germans *Wisemute, Mithan*, and *Counterfey*, adding that where it groweth silver cannot be far off.[18] Nevertheless, it is known to be a mixture of brass, lead, and tin (of which this latter occupieth the one-half), but after another proportion than is used in pewter. But, alas, I am persuaded that neither the old Arabians nor new alchemists of our time did ever hear of it, albeit that the name thereof do seem to come out of their forge. For the common sort indeed do call it alchemy, an unwholesome metal (God wot) and worthy to be banished and driven out of the land.

And thus I conclude with this discourse, as having no more to say of the metals of my country, except I should talk of brass, bell metal, and such as are brought over for merchandise from other countries, and yet I cannot but say that there is some brass found also in England, but so small is the quantity that it is not greatly to be esteemed or accounted of.

---

[14] *Itinerary* (I, 323). *Eastwards:* apparently in error for westwards.
[15] *Marcasite:* apparently copper pyrites.
[16] *Gads:* bars of steel; *sheaf:* a bundle of steel; *burden:* a load of 120 pounds.
[17] *Alchemy:* a metal, manufactured to imitate gold.
[18] Entzelt, pp. 60–61.

CHAPTER XII

Of Precious Stones

THE old writers remember few other stones of estimation to be found in this island than that which we call jet and they in Latin *gagates*, whereunto furthermore they ascribe sundry properties as usually practiced here in times past, whereof none of our writers do make any mention at all. Howbeit, whatsoever it hath pleased a number of strangers (upon false surmise) to write of the usages of this our country about the trial of the virginity of our maidens by drinking the powder hereof against the time of their bestowing in marriage,[1] certain it is that even to this day there is some plenty to be had of this commodity in Derbyshire and about Berwick, whereof rings, salts, small cups, and sundry trifling toys are made, although that in many men's opinions nothing so fine as that which is brought over by merchants daily from the main. But as these men are drowned with the common error conceived of our nation, so I am sure that in discerning the price and value of things no man now living can go beyond the judgment of the old Romans, who preferred the jet of Britain before the like stones bred about Lucca and all other countries wheresoever. Marbodus Gallus also, writing of the same among other of estimation, saith thus:

> *Nascitur in Lycia lapis et prope gemma Gagates,*
> *Sed genus eximium saecunda Britannia mittit;*
> *Lucidus et niger est, levis et levissimus idem,*
> *Vicinas paleas trahit attritu calefactus,*
> *Ardet aqua lotus, restinguitur unctus olivo.*[2]

---

[1] "Laon[icus] Chalcondyles."—*H.* Chalcondyles was a Byzantine writer whose history covers the period 1298–1463.

[2] "This precious stone originates in Lycia near Gagas, but the other Britain sends an excellent kind, shiny, black, light, and also very smooth; when warmed by rubbing, it attracts nearby chaff; bathed in water it ignites; anointed with oil it is extinguished." *Marbodus Gallus:* Marbode (1035–1123), Bishop of Rennes; the quoted passage comes from his famous *Liber de gemmis* (printed in *Patrologia Latina*, ed. J.-P. Migne, CLXXI, col. 1751).

The German writers confound it with amber as if it were a kind thereof, but as I regard not their judgment in this point, so I read that it taketh name of Gagas, a city and river in Cilicia, where it groweth in plentiful manner, as Dioscorides saith.[3] Nicander (in *Theriaca*) calleth it *engangin* and *gangitin*, of the plenty thereof that is found in the place aforesaid, which he calleth Ganges, and where they have great use of it in driving away of serpents by the only perfume thereof. Charles, the fourth emperor of that name, glazed the church withal that standeth at the fall of Tanger,[4] but I cannot imagine what light should enter thereby. The writers also divide this stone into five kinds, of which the one is in color like unto lion-tawny, another straked [streaked] with white veins, the third with yellow lines, the fourth is garled [speckled] with divers colors, among which some are like drops of blood (but those come out of Inde), and the fifth shining black as any raven's feather.

Moreover, as jet was one of the first stones of this isle whereof any foreign account was made, so our pearls also did match with it in renown, insomuch that the only desire of them caused Caesar to adventure hither, after he had seen the quantities and heard of our plenty of them while he abode in France,[5] and whereof he made a tabard which he offered up in Rome to Venus, where it hung long after as a rich and notable oblation and testimony of the riches of our country.[6] Certes they are to be found in these our days and thereto of divers colors, in no less numbers than ever they were in old time. Yet are they not now so much desired, because of their smallness and also for other causes, but especially sith church work, as copes, vestments, albs, tunicles, altar cloths, canopies, and such trash are worthily abolished, upon which our countrymen superstitiously bestowed no small quantities of them. For I think there were few churches or religious houses, besides bishops' miters, books, and other pontifical vestures, but were either thoroughly fretted or notably garnished

---

[3] *De materia medica*, V, 146, but this entire paragraph is drawn from Christoph Entzelt, *De re metallica* (1557), pp. 183–185.

[4] *Fall:* the discharge of a river. Charles IV, Roman Emperor (1355–1378), rebuilt the church of St. Stephen in Tangermünde, a town (of which Entzelt was pastor) standing at the juncture of the Tanger and Elbe Rivers.

[5] Suetonius, *Lives of the Caesars*, I, xlvii.

[6] Pliny, IX, lvii.

with huge numbers of them. Marbodus likewise, speaking of pearls, commendeth them after this manner:

Gignit et insignes antiqua Britannia baccas, etc.[7]

Marcellinus [8] also (*lib.* 23, *in ipso fine*) speaketh of our pearls and their generation, but he preferreth greatly those of Persia before them, which to me doth seem unequally done. But as the British jet or orient pearl were in old time esteemed above those of other countries, so time hath since the conquest of the Romans revealed many other, insomuch that at this season there are found in England the aetites (in English called the ernestone, but for "erne" some pronounce "eagle") and the hematite or bloodstone, and these very pure and excellent; also the chalcedony, the porphyrite, the crystal, and those other which we call calaminares and speculares,[9] besides a kind of diamond or adamant which, although it be very fair to sight, is yet much softer (as most are that are found and bred toward the north) than those that are brought hither out of other countries. We have also upon our coast the white coral, nothing inferior to that which is found beyond the sea in the Elbe, near to the fall of Tanger, or to the red and black, whereof Dioscorides entreateth (*lib.* 5, *cap.* 8 [139]).[10] We have in like sort sundry other stones daily found in cliffs and rocks (beside the loadstone, which is oftentimes taken up out of our mines of iron), whereof such as find them have either no knowledge at all or else do make but small account, being seduced by outlandish [foreign] lapidaries, whereof the most part discourage us from the searching and seeking out of our own commodities, to the end that they may have the more free utterance of their natural and artificial wares, whereby they get great gains amongst such as have no skill.

I have heard that the best trial of a stone is to lay it on the nail of the thumb and so to go abroad into the clear light, where if the color hold in all places alike, the stone is thought to be natural and good; but if it alter, especially toward the nail, then is it not sound but rather to be taken for an artificial piece of practice. If

[7] "Ancient Britain produces remarkable pearls" (*Liber de gemmis*, col. 1766).

[8] *Marcellinus:* Ammianus Marcellinus (fl. ca. 360–390), Roman historian.

[9] *Calaminares:* calamine, zinc carbonate; *speculares:* specular, a species of mica or selenite.

[10] Entzelt, pp. 160, 163.

this be true, it is an experiment worthy the noting. Cardan also hath it in his *De subtilitate*; [11] if not, I have read more lies than this, as one for example out of Cato, who saith that a cup of ivy will hold no wine at all. [12] I have made some vessels of the same wood which refuse no kind of liquor, and therefore I suppose that there is no such *antipathia* between wine and our ivy as some of our reading philosophers (without all manner of practice) will seem to infer amongst us, and yet I deny not but the ivy of Greece or Italy may have such a property; but why should not the ivy then of France somewhat participate withal in the like effect, which groweth in an hotter soil than ours is? For as Battista Porta saith, it holdeth not also in the French ivy, [13] wherefore I cannot believe that it hath any such quality at all as Cato ascribeth unto it.

What should I say more of stones? Truly I cannot tell, sith I have said what I may already and peradventure more than I think necessary, and that causeth me to pass over those that are now and then taken out of our oysters, toads, mussels, snails, and adders, and likewise such as are found upon sundry hills in Gloucestershire, which have naturally such sundry proportions, forms, and colors in them as pass all human possibility to imitate, be the workman never so skillful and cunning; [14] also those that are found in the heads of our perches and carps, much desired of such as have the stone and yet of themselves are no stones but rather shells or gristles, which in time consume to nothing.

This yet will I add, that if those which are found in mussels (for I am utterly ignorant of the generation of pearls) be good pearl indeed, I have at sundry times gathered more than an ounce of them, of which divers have holes already entered by nature, some of them not much inferior to great peason in quantity and thereto of sundry colors, as it happeneth amongst such as are brought from the easterly coast to Saffron Walden in Lent, when for want of flesh stale stinking fish and welked [dried-up] mussels are thought to be good meat; for other fish is too dear amongst us, when law doth bind us to use it. See more for the

---

[11] "*Lib. 7.*"—H. "*De lapidibus*" (Nuremberg, 1550, pp. 193–194).
[12] *De agricultura*, cxi.
[13] *Battista Porta:* Giovanni Battista della Porta (1535–1615), Italian playwright and physicist; Harrison's citation comes from his *Magiae naturalis*, XVIII, iv.   [14] Leland, *Itinerary* (ed. Smith, III, 101).

generation of pearls in *The Description of Scotland,* for there you shall be further informed out of Boece in that behalf.[15] They are called orient because of the clearness, which resembleth the color of the clear air before the rising of the sun. They are also sought for in the latter end of August, a little before which time the sweetness of the dew is most convenient for that kind of fish which doth engender and conceive them, whose form is flat and much like unto a limpet. The further north also that they be found, the brighter is their color and their substances of better valure, as lapidaries do give out.

CHAPTER XIII

Of Salt Made in England

THERE are in England certain wells where salt is made, whereof Leland hath written abundantly in his *Commentaries of Britain* and whose words only I will set down in English as he wrote them, because he seemeth to have had diligent consideration of the same, without adding anything of mine own to him, except it be where necessity doth enforce me for the mere aid of the reader in the understanding of his mind.[1]

Directing therefore his journey from Worcester in his peregrination and laborious travel over England, he saith thus: from Worcester I rode to the Wich by enclosed soil, having meetly [moderately] good corn ground, sufficient wood, and good pasture, about a six-miles off. Wich standeth somewhat in a valley or low ground, betwixt two small hills on the left ripe (for so he

[15] "There are of another sort which are longer and greater than either of these [mussels and cockles], called horse mussels, to be had in Dee and Don, and in these are the pearls engendered. . . . These early in the morning, in the gentle, clear, and calm air, lift up their upper shells and mouths a little above the water, and there receive of the fine and pleasant breath or dew of heaven, and afterwards, according to the measure and quantity of this vital force received, they first conceive, then swell, and finally product the pearl" (*Des. Scot.,* 1587, p. 15).

[1] As Harrison indicates, the following account of the salt springs at Droitwich in Worcestershire is taken almost verbatim from the *Itinerary* (ed. Smith, II, 92–94).

calleth the bank of every brook throughout all his English treatises) of a pretty river, which not far beneath the Wich is called Salope [Salwarpe] Brook. The beauty of the town in manner standeth in one street, yet be there many lanes in the town besides. There is also a mean church in the main street, and once in the week an indifferent round market. The town of itself is somewhat foul and dirty when any rain falleth, by reason of much carriage through the streets, which are very ill paved or rather not paved at all. The great advancement also hereof is by making of salt. And though the commodity thereof be singular great, yet the burgesses be poor generally, because gentlemen have for the most part gotten the great gain of it into their hands, whilst the poor burgesses yield unto all the labor.[2]

There are at this present time three hundred salters [3] and three salt springs in the town of Wich, whereof the principal is within a buttshot [bowshot] of the right ripe (or bank) of the river that there cometh down, and this spring is double so profitable in yielding of salt liquor as both the other. Some say (or rather fable) that this salt spring did fail in the time of Richard de la Wyche, Bishop of Chichester, and that afterwards by his intercession it was restored to the profit of the old course (such is the superstition of the people); in remembrance whereof, or peradventure for the zeal which the Wichmen and salters did bear unto Richard de la Wyche, their countryman, they used of late times on his day (which cometh once in the year) to hang this salt spring or well about with tapestry and to have sundry games, drinkings, and foolish revels at it. But to proceed.

There be a great number of salt cotes [4] about this well, wherein the salt water is sodden in leads [boiled in caldrons] and brought to the perfection of pure white salt. The other two salt springs be on the left side of the river, a pretty way lower than the first and (as I found) at the very end of the town. At these also be divers furnaces to make salt, but the profit and plenty of these two are nothing comparable to the gain that riseth by the greatest. I asked of a salter how many furnaces they had at all the three

---

[2] "A common plague in all things of any great commodity, for one beateth the bush but another catcheth the birds, as we may see in batfowling."—*H.*

[3] This number of salters is attributed by Leland not to Droitwich but to Nantwich in Cheshire (IV, 4).

[4] *Salt cotes:* buildings or places where salt is extracted by boiling.

springs, and he numbered them to eighteen score, that is 360, saying how every one of them paid yearly 6s. 8d. to the King. The truth is that of old they had liberties given unto them for 300 furnaces or more, and thereupon they give a fee farm (or *vectigal*)[5] of £100 yearly. Certes the pension is as it was, but the number of furnaces is now increased to 400. There was of late search made for another salt spring thereabouts, by the means of one Newport, a gentleman dwelling at the Wich, and the place where it was appeareth, as doth also the wood and timber which was set about it to keep up the earth from falling into the same. But this pit was not since occupied, whether it were for lack of plenty of the salt spring or for letting or hindering of the profit of the other three. Methink [6] that if wood and sale of salt would serve, they might dig and find more salt springs about the Wich than three, but there is somewhat else in the wind. For I heard that of late years a salt spring was found in another quarter of Worcestershire, but it grew to be without any use, sith the Wichmen have such a privilege that they alone in those quarters shall have the making of salt.[7]

The pits be so set about with gutters that the salt water is easily turned to every man's house, and at Nantwich very many troughs go over the river for the commodity of such as dwell on the other side of the same. They seethe also their salt water in furnaces of lead and lade out the salt, some in cases of wicker through which the water draineth and the salt remaineth. There be also two or three, but very little, salt springs at Dertwich [8] in a low bottom, where salt is sometime made. Of late, also, a mile from Combermere Abbey, a piece of an hill did sink, and in the same pit rose a spring of salt water, where the abbot began to make salt, but the men of the city compounded with the abbot and covent [convent] that there should be none made there, whereby the pit was suffered to go to loss. And although it yielded salt water still of itself, yet it was spoiled at the last and filled up with filth.

[5] *Vectigal:* the rent paid for lease of public lands in Rome.
[6] *Methink:* "men think" in Leland.
[7] "Privileges do sometimes harm."—*H.*
[8] *Dertwich:* a hamlet near Malpas in Cheshire, according to Leland. Harrison interpolates into Leland's account of Droitwich this entire paragraph drawn from the description in the *Itinerary* of Nantwich (IV, 4).

The Wichmen use the commodity of their salt springs in drawing and decocting the water of them only by six months in the year, that is, from Midsummer to Christmas, as (I guess) to maintain the price of salt or for saving of wood, which I think to be their principal reason. For making of salt is a great and notable destruction of wood and shall be greater hereafter, except some provision be made for the better increase of firing. The lack of wood also is already perceived in places near the Wich, for whereas they used to buy and take their wood near unto their occupyings, those wonted springs [sources] are now decayed and they be enforced to seek their wood so far as Worcester Town and all the parts about Bromsgrove, Alvechurch, and Alcester. I asked a salter how much wood he supposed yearly to be spent at these furnaces, and he answered that by estimation there was consumed about six thousand load, and it was round pole wood for the most, which is easy to be cleft and handsomely riven in pieces. The people that are about the furnaces are very ill colored, and the just rate of every furnace is to make four loads of salt yearly, and to every load goeth five or six quarters,[9] as they make their accounts. If the furnacemen make more in one furnace than four loads, it is (as it is said) employed to their own avail.

And thus much hath Leland left in memory of our white salt, who in another book not now in my hands hath touched the making also of bay salt in some part of our country. But sith that book is delivered again to the owner,[10] the tractation of bay salt cannot be framed in any order, because my memory will not serve to show the true manner and the place. It shall suffice therefore to have given such notice of it, to the end the reader may know that as well the bay as white are wrought and made in England, and more white also upon the west coast toward Scotland, in Essex, and elsewhere; out of the salt water, between Wyre and Cockermouth, which commonly is of like price with our wheat. Finally, having thus intermeddled our artificial salt with our minerals, let us give over and go in hand with such metals as are growing here in England.[11]

[9] *Quarters:* of eight bushels.

[10] Presumably John Stow (see p. 4, n. 5); the passage in Leland (IV, 10) concerns the saltmaking "between Wyre and Cockermouth" referred to below.

[11] In the 1577 edition the present chapter xi followed.

CHAPTER XIV

Of Our Account of Time and Her Parts

As *libra* is *as* or *assis* to the Romans for their weight,[1] and the foot is standard measure, so in our account of the parts of time we take the day, consisting of four-and-twenty hours, to be the greatest of the least and least of the greatest whereby we keep our reckoning; for of the hour (to say the truth) the most ancient Romans, Greeks, nor Hebrews had [not] any use, sith they reckoned by watches, and whereof also Censorinus (*cap.* 19) showeth a reason wherefore they were neglected.[2] For my part I do not see any great difference used in the observation of time and her parts between our own and any other foreign nation, wherefore I shall not need to stand long on this matter. Howbeit, to the end our exact order herein shall appear unto all men, I will set down some short rehearsal thereof and that in so brief manner as unto me is possible. As for our astronomical practices, I mean not to meddle with them, sith their course is uniformly observed overall.

Our common order therefore is to begin at the minute, which containeth one-sixtieth part of an hour, as at the smallest part of time known unto the people, notwithstanding that in most places they descend no lower than the half-quarter or quarter of the hour, and from whence they proceed unto the hour, to wit, the four-and-twentieth part of that which we call the common and natural day, which doth begin at midnight and is observed continually by clocks, dials, and astronomical instruments of all sorts. The artificial variety of which kind of ware is so great here in England as no place else (in mine opinion) can be comparable therein to this isle. I will not speak of the cost bestowed upon them in pearl and stone, neither of the valure of metal

[1] That is, the pound (*libra*) is the standard unit.
[2] *Censorinus:* author, in A.D. 238, of an astrological and chronological treatise, *De die natali.* Harrison is apparently referring to Censorinus' remark that the division of the day into hours was not observed in Rome until the invention of the sundial (chap. xxiii).

whereof they have been made, as gold, silver, etc., and almost no abbey or religious house without some of them. This only shall suffice to note here (as by the way), that as antiquity hath delighted in these things, so in our time pomp and excess spendeth all, and nothing is regarded [except] that [which] bringeth in no bread.

Of unequal or temporal hours [3] or days our nation hath no regard, and therefore to show their quantities, differences, and divisions into the greater and the lesser—whereof the latter containeth one unequal hour or the rising of half a sign, the other of a whole sign, which is in two hours' space, whereof Mark seemeth to speak (*cap.* 15 c 25),[4] as the rest of the Evangelists (yea, and he also, *ibid.*, vers. 33)[5] do of the other (Matthew, 27 e 45, Luke, 23 e 44, John, 19 b 14)—it should be but in vain. In like sort, whereas the elder Egyptians, Italians, Bohemians, later Athenians, and Jews begin their day at the sunset overnight,[6] the Persians, Babylonians, Grecians, and Noribergians at the sunrising (each of them accounting their days and nights by unequal hours), also the elder Athenians, Arabians, Dutchmen, Umbers [Umbri], Etrurians, and astronomers at high noon and so reckon from noon to noon, we, after Hipparchus [7] and the later Egyptians, or to speak more properly, imitating the Roman manner used in the church there of long time, choose the very point of midnight, from whence we account twelve equal hours unto midday ensuing and other twelve again unto the aforesaid point, according to these verses:

> *Mane diem Graeca gens incipit astra sequentes*
> *In medio lucis Judaeis vespere, sancta*
> *Inchoat ecclesia media sua tempora nocte.*[8]

And this is our general order for the natural day.

Of the artificial we make so far account as that we reckon it day when the sun is up and night when the sun leaveth our

[3] *Unequal hours:* planetary hours, one-twelfth of the period from sunrise to sunset.   [4] "And it was the third hour, and they crucified him."

[5] "And when the sixth hour was come, there was darkness over the whole land until the ninth hour." The following citations are to the parallel passages in the other Gospels.   [6] *Overnight:* on the preceding evening.

[7] *Hipparchus* (fl. 161–126 B.C.): the greatest of the Greek astronomers.

[8] "The Greek people, following the stars, begin their day in the morning, the Jews solemnly at twilight in the evening; the church commences her days in the middle of the night." But the Latin is unclear.

horizon. Otherwise also we divide it into two parts, that is to say, forenoon and afternoon, not regarding the ruddy, shining, burning, and warming seasons (of three unequal hours apiece, which others seem to divide into springtime, summer, autumn, and winter in like curious manner), and whereof I read these verses:

> *Solis equi lucis dicuntur quatuor horae,*
> *Haec rubet, haec splendet, haec calet, illa tepet.*[9]

Indeed our physicians have another partition of the day, as men of no less learning no doubt than the best of foreign countries, if we could so conceive of them. And herein they concur also with those of other nations, who for distinction in regiment of our humors divide the artificial day and night in such wise as these verses do import, and are indeed a general rule which each of them doth follow:

> *Tres lucis primas, noctis tres sanguinis imas,*
> *Vis cholerae medias lucis sex vendicat horas.*
> *Datque melam primas noctis, tres lucis et imas,*
> *Centrales ponas sex noctis phlegmatis horas.*[10]

Or thus, as Tannstetter hath given them forth in his prelections: [11]

> *A nona noctis donec sit tertia lucis,*
> *Est dominus sanguis, sex inde sequentibus horis*
> *Est dominans cholera, dum lucis nona sit hora*
> *Post niger humid inest donec sit tertia noctis,*
> *Posthaec phlegma venit, donec sit nona quietis.*

In English thus, in effect:

> Three hours ere sun do rise, and so many after, blood;
> From nine to three at afternoon, hot choler bears the sway;
> Even so to nine at night, swart choler hath to rule,
> As phlegm from thence to three at morn; six hours each one I say.

[9] "The course of the sun through the day is said to have four periods: the first is ruddy, the next shines, the next burns, the last is warm."
[10] "The sanguine temperament claims the first three hours of the day and the last three of the night, the choleric the six middle hours of the day; give the melancholic the first three of the night and the last three of the day; you may assign the middle six hours of the night to the phlegmatic."
[11] *Tannstetter:* Georg Tannstetter Collimitius (1482–1535), Bavarian mathematician and astrologer, lecturer at the University of Vienna; *prelections:* lectures, a reference to his *Artificium de applicatione astrologie ad medicinam* (Strasbourg, 1531), fol. 11v.

In like sort for the night we have none other parts than the twilight, dark-night, midnight, and cock's crowing, whereas the Latins divide the same into seven parts, as *vesper* (or *vesperugo* as Plautus calleth it, as Virgil useth the word *hesper*),[12] the evening, which is immediately after the setting of the sun; *crepusculum*, the twilight (which some call *prima fax*, because men begin then to light candles), when it is between day and night, light and darkness, or properly neither day nor night; *concubium*, the still of the night, when each one is laid to rest; *intempestum*, the dull or dead of the night, which is midnight, when men be in their first or dead sleep; *gallicinium*, the cock's crowing; *conticinium*, when the cocks have left crowing; *matutinum*, the breach of the day; and *diluculum sive aurora*, the ruddy, orange, golden, or shining color seen immediately before the rising of the sun, and is opposite to the evening, as *matutinum* is to the twilight.

Other there are which do reckon by watches, dividing the night after sunsetting into four equal parts. Of which the first beginneth at evening, called the first watch, and continueth by three unequal hours, and so forth until the end of the ninth hour, whereat the fourth watch entereth, which is called the morning watch because it concurreth partly with the dark night and partly with the morning and breach of the day before the rising of the sun.

As for the original of the word hour, it is very ancient but yet not so old as that of the watch, whereof we shall read abundantly in the Scriptures, which was devised first among soldiers for their better safeguard and change of watchmen in their camps; the like whereof is almost used among our seafaring men, which they call "clearing of the glass,"[13] and performed from time to time with great heed and some solemnity. Hereunto the word *hora* among the Grecians signified so well the four quarters of the year as the four-and-twentieth part of the day, and limits of any form. But what stand I upon these things to let my purpose stay? To proceed therefore.

Of natural days is the week compacted, which consisteth of seven of them, the Friday being commonly called among the

---

[12] Plautus, *Amphitruo*, l. 275; Virgil, *Eclogues*, X, 77. This entire paragraph is derived from Censorinus, chap. xxiv.

[13] *Glass*: hourglass.

vulgar sort either king or worling,[14] because it is either the fairest or foulest of the seven, albeit that I cannot guess of any reason why they should so imagine. The first of these entereth with Monday, whereby it cometh to pass that we rest upon the Sunday which is the seventh in number, as Almighty God hath commanded in His Word. The Jews begin their week upon our Saturday at the setting of the sun, and the Turks in these days with the Saturday, whereby it cometh to pass that as the Jews make our last day the first of their week, so the Turks make the Jewish Sabbath the beginning of their *hebdoma*, because Mahomet, their prophet (as they say), was born and dead upon the Friday, and so he was indeed except their Alcoran deceive them. The Jews do reckon their days by their distance from their Sabbath, so that the first day of their week is the first day of the Sabbath and so forth unto the sixth. The Latins and Egyptians accounted their days after the seven planets, choosing the same for the denominator of the day that entereth his regiment with the first unequal hour of the same after the sun be risen. Howbeit, as this order is not wholly retained with us, so the use of the same is not yet altogether abolished, as may appear by our Sunday, Monday, and Saturday.

The rest were changed by the Saxons, who in remembrance of Theut, sometime their prince, called the second day of the week Theutsdach, the third Woden, Othin, Othon, or Edon, or Wodensdach. Also of Thor they named the fourth day Thorsdach, and of Frea, wife to Woden, the fifth was called Freadach. Albeit there are (and not amiss as I think) that suppose them to mean by Thor, Jupiter, by Woden, Mercury, by Frea (or Frigga, as Saxo calleth her), Venus, and finally, by Theut, Mars, which if it be so then it is an easy matter to find out the German Mars, Venus, Mercury, and Jupiter, whereof you may read more hereafter in my Chronology. The truth is that Frea, albeit that Saxo giveth her scant a good report, for that she loved one of her husband's men better than himself,[15] had seven sons by Woden: the first, father to Wecca, of whom descended those that were afterwards kings of Kent; Fethelgeta was the second, and of him came the kings of Mercia; Balday the third, father to the kings of

---

[14] *Worling:* warling, something despised.
[15] *Saxo:* Saxo Grammaticus (?1150–?1206), Danish historian and poet; the cited passage occurs in his *Danish History*, I, xxv.

the West Saxons; Beldagius the fourth, parent to the kings of Bernicia or Northumberland; Weogodach the fifth, author of the kings of Deira; Caser the sixth, race [root] of the East Angle race; and Nascad, original burgeon [bud] of the kings of Essex. As for the kings of Sussex, although they were of the same people, yet were they not of the same strain, as our old monuments do express. But to proceed.

As certain of our days suffered this alteration by the Saxons, so in our churches we retained for a long time the number of days or of feries [16] from the Sabbath after the manner of the Jews, I mean until the service after the Roman use was abolished, which custom was first received (as some think) by Pope Sylvester, though other say by Constantine, albeit another sort do affirm that Sylvester caused the Sunday only to be called the Lord's Day and dealt not with the rest.

In like manner, of weeks our months are made, which are so called of the moon, each one containing eight-and-twenty days or four weeks, without any further curiosity. For we reckon not our time by the year of the moon, as the Jews, Grecians, or Romans did at the first, or as the Turks, Arabians, and Persians do now, neither any parcel thereof by the said planet, as in some part of the West Indies, where they have neither week, month, nor year, but only a general account of hundreds and thousands of moons.[17] Wherefore if we say or write a month, it is to be expounded of eight-and-twenty days or four weeks only, and not of her usual period of nine-and-twenty days and one-and-thirty minutes. Or (if you take it at large) for a month of the common calendar, which nevertheless in pleas and suits is nothing at all allowed of, sith the moon maketh her full revolution in eight-and-twenty days or four weeks, that is, unto the place where she left the sun, notwithstanding that he be now gone and at her return not to be found very often in that sign wherein she before had left him. Plutarch writeth of divers barbarous nations which reckoned a more or less number of these months for whole years, and that of these some accounted but three, as the Arcadians did four, the Acarnanians six, and the Egyptians

[16] *Feries:* ferias, weekdays.
[17] *"Trivetbus in Antartico."*—H. A garbled reference to André Thevet (1502–1590), French traveler, whose work on America was translated by T. Hacket as *The New Found World, or Antarctic* (1568, fol. 61r).

but one for a whole year, which causeth them to make such a large account of their antiquity and original.[18] But forsomuch as we are not troubled with any such disorder, it shall suffice that I have generally said of months and their quantities at this time. Now a word or two of the ancient Roman calendar.[19]

In old time each month of the Roman calendar was reckoned after the course of the moon, and their entrances were uncertain, as were also the changes of that planet, whereby it came to pass that the day of the change was the first of the month, howsoever it fell out. But after Julius Caesar had once corrected the same, the several beginnings of every one of them did not only remain fixed, but also the old order in the division of their parts continued still unaltered, so that the month is yet divided as before into calends, ides, and nones, albeit that in my days the use of the same be but small and their order retained only in our calendars for the better understanding of such times as the historiographers and old authors do remember. The reckoning also of each of these goeth (as you see) after a preposterous order, whereby the Romans did rather note how many days were to the next change from the precedent than contrariwise, as by perusal of the same you shall more easily perceive.

The days also of the change of the month of the moon are called *calendae*, which in time of paganism were consecrated to Juno and sacrifice made to that goddess on the same. On these days also and on the ides and nones they would not marry. Likewise the morrow after each of them were called *dies atri*, black days, as were also divers other, and those either by reason of some notable overthrow or mishap that befell unto the Romans upon those days or in respect of some superstitious imagination conceived of evil success likely to fall out upon the same. Of some they were called *dies Aegyptiaci*. Whereby it appeareth that this peevish estimation of these days came from that nation. And as we do note our holy and festival days with red letters in our calendars, so did the Romans their principal feasts and circle of the moon either in red or golden letters, and their victories in white in their public or consulary tables. This also is more to be added, that if any good success happened afterward

---

[18] *Life of Numa*, xviii, 4.
[19] The following account is largely derived from Macrobius, *Saturnalia*, I, xii–xvi.

upon such day as was already black in their calendar, they would solemnly enter it in white letters by rasing out of the black, whereby the black day was turned into white and wherein they not a little rejoiced.

The word *calendae* (in Greek *neomenia*) is derived of *calo*, to call; for upon the first day of every month the priest used to call the people of the city and country together in Calabra, for so the place was called where they met, and show them by a custom how many days were from the said calends to the nones and what feasts were to be celebrated between that and the next change. Their order is retrograde because that, after the month was half expired or the moon past the full, they reckoned by the days to come until the next change, as seventeen days, sixteen days, fourteen days, etc., as the Greeks did in the later decade only, for they had no use of calends. The very day therefore of the change is called *calendae*, dedicated to Juno, who thereof was also called *Calendaris*. At the first also the fasts or feast days were known by none other means unto the people but by the denunciation [proclamation] of the priests (as I said) upon this day, till Flavius Scriba [20] caused them to be written and published in their common calendars, contrary to the will and meaning of the senate, for the ease and benefit of the people, as he pretended.

The nones commonly are not above four or six in every month, and so long as the nones lasted, so long did the markets continue, and therefore they were called *nonae quasi nundinae*.[21] In them also were neither holy days more than is at this present (except the day of the Purification of Our Lady) nor sacrifice offered to the gods, but each one applied his business and kept his market, reckoning the first day after the calends or change to be the fourth or sixth day before the fair ended. Some think that they were called *nonae* of the word *non, quia in iisdem dii non coluntur* [22] (for as Ovid saith, *Nonarum tutela deo caret*),[23] or for that the nones were always on the ninth day before the ides; other because *Nundina dea* was honored the ninth day before the ides, albeit I suppose rather that *Nundina dea* (a goddess far younger

---

[20] *Flavius Scriba:* Gnaeus Flavius, curule aedile in 303 B.C.
[21] *Nundinae:* market day.
[22] "No, because on them no gods are worshiped."
[23] "The nones lack a tutelary god" (*Fasti*, I, 57).

than the name of *nonae*) took her name of the nones, whereon it was a custom among the Romans *lustrare infantes ac nomina maribus imponere*,[24] as they did with their maidchildren upon the eighth; but howsoever this be, sure it is that they were the mart days of every month, wherein the people bought, sold, exchanged, or bartered, and did nothing else.

The ides are so named of the Etruscan word *iduare*, to divide, and before that Caesar altered the calendar, they divided the month commonly by the midst. But afterward, when he had added certain days thereto, thereby to make it agree to the year of the sun (which he intruded about the end of every month, because he would not alter the celebration of their usual feasts, whereof the chief were holden always upon the day of the ides), then came they short of the midst, sometime by two or three days. In these, therefore (which always are eight), the merchants had leisure to pack up and convey their merchandise, to pay their creditors, and make merry with their friends.

After the ides do the calends follow, but in a decreasing order (as I noted), as the moon doth in light when she is past the full. But herein lieth all the mystery, if you can say so many days before the next change or new moon as the number there expressed doth betoken, as for sixteen calends so many days before the next conjunction, etc. (as is above remembered). Of these calends, I mean touching their number in every month, I find these verses ensuing:

> *Janus et Augustus denas novemque December,*
> *Junius, Aprilis, September, et ipse November*
> *Ter senas retinent, Februs bis octo calendas,*
> *Julius, October, Mars, Maius [s]eptadecemque.*

In English thus:

> December, Jan., and August month full nineteen calends have,
> Septemb, April, Novemb, and June twice nine they do desire,
> Sixteen foul February hath, no more can he well crave,
> October, May, and July hot, but seventeen do require.[25]

---

[24] "To purify babies and christen the males."

[25] The English mnemonic verse is clearly homemade. Harrison polished it somewhat in 1587, but March remained lost.

In like manner do the nones and ides:

> *Sex Maius nonas, October, Julius, et Mars,*
> *Quatuor at reliqui, dabit idus quilibet octo.*

To July, March, October, May, six nones I hight,
The rest but four, and as for ides they keep still eight.

Again, touching the number of days in every month:

> *Junius, Aprilis, Septemque, Novemque, tricenos,*
> *Unum plus reliqui, Februs tenet octo vicenos,*
> *At si bissextus fuerit superadditur unus.*

> Thirty days hath November,
>   April, June, and September,
> Twenty-and-eight hath February alone,
>   and all the rest thirty-and-one,
>   but in the leap you must add one.

Our year is counted after the course of the sun, and although the church hath some use of that of the moon for observation of certain movable feasts, yet it is reducible to that of the sun, which in our civil dealings is chiefly had in use. Herein only I find a scruple, that the beginning thereof is not uniform and certain, for most of our records bear date the twenty-fifth of March and our calendars the first of January, so that with us Christ is born before He be conceived. Our sundry officers also have sundry entrances into their charges of custom, which breedeth great confusion, whereas if all these might be referred to one original (and that to be the first of January), I do not think but that there would be more certainty and less trouble for our historiographers, notaries, and other officers in their account of the year.

In old time the Athenians began their year with the change of the moon that fell nearest to the entrance of the sun into the Crab, the Latins at the winter solstice or his going into the Goat, the Jews in civil case at the later equinoctial and in ecclesiastical with the first. They of Calicut begin their year somewhere in September but upon no day certain, sith they first consult with their wizards, who pronounce one day or other thereof to be most happy (as the year goeth about), and therewith they make their entrance, as Osorius doth remember, who addeth that upon the eleventh calends of September they have solemn plays, much like to the idol-games, and that they write in leaves of tree with a pencil instead of paper, which is not found among them.[26] Some of the old Grecians began their year also in September, but sith we seek herein but for the custom of our country only, it shall be enough to affirm that we make our account from the calends or first of January, and from the midst of the night which is *limes* [boundary] between that and the last of December, whereof this may suffice.

I might speak of the cynic year also in this place (for the ease of our English readers), sometime in use amongst the Egyptians, which containeth 1,460 common years, whose beginning is always reckoned from the rising of the Lesser Dog. The first use thereof entered the self year wherein the Olympiads were restored. And forsomuch as this nation hath no use of intercalation, at the end of every 1,460 years they added an whole year of intercalation, because there are 365 leap years in the period, so that 1,460 Julian years do contain 1,461 after the Egyptians' account, whereby their common year is found to be less than ours. Furthermore, whereas our intercalation for the leap year is somewhat too much by certain minutes, which in 115 years amount unto about an whole day, if one intercalation in so many were omitted our calendar would be the more perfect; and I would wish that the same year wherein the said intercalation, truly found out, should be overpassed might be observed and called *annus magnus Elizabethae*, in perpetual remembrance of our noble and sovereign princess now reigning amongst us.

I might here say somewhat also of the prime and her alteration, which is risen higher by five days in our common calendar than it was placed by Julius Caesar;[27] and in seven thousand years some write would grow to an error of an whole, if the world should last so long. But forsomuch as in some calendars of ours it is reduced again to the day of every [lunar] change, it shall suffice to say no more thereof. The Pope also hath made a general correction of the calendar, wherein he hath reduced it to the

---

[26] *Osorius:* Jeronimo Osorio da Fonseca (1506–1580), Portuguese scholar, Bishop of Silves; the reference is to Bk. II of his *History of King Emmanuel* (first printed at Lisbon, 1571).

[27] *Prime:* the golden number, used to determine the phases of the moon in any given solar year. Since it was based on the Metonic lunar cycle of nineteen years, which produces an error of one day every 308 years, by the sixteenth century new moons were occurring four or five days earlier than the golden numbers indicated.

same that it was or should have been at the Council of Nice.[28] Howbeit, as he hath abolished the use of the golden number, so hath he continued the epact,[29] applying it unto such general use as doth now serve both the turns, whose reformation had also ere this time been admitted into England if it had not proceeded from him, against whom and all whose ordinances we have so faithfully sworn and set our hands.

Certes the next omission is to be performed, if all princes would agree thereto, in the leap year that shall be about the year of grace 1668,[30] if it shall please God that the world may last so long, and then may our calendar also stand without any alteration as it doth already. By this also it appeareth how the defect of our calendar may be supplied from the Creation, wherein the first equinoctial is seen higher toward the beginning of March than Caesar's calendar now extant doth yield unto by seven days.[31] For as in Caesar's time the true equinoctial was pointed out to happen (as Stadius [32] also noteth) either upon or about the sixteenth or seventeenth of March, albeit the manifest appearance thereof was not found until the five-and-twentieth of that month in their dials or by eyesight, so at the beginning of the world the said entrance of the sun into the Ram must needs fall out to be about the twentieth or one-and-twentieth of April as the calendar now standeth, if I fail not in my numbers.[33]

[28] In 1582 Pope Gregory XIII restored the vernal equinox to March 21, where it had been at the time of the Nicene Council, by dropping ten days from the calendar. To prevent a recurrence of the slippage he directed that henceforth three intercalations should be suppressed in every four hundred years.

[29] *Epact:* a number representing the age of the moon at the beginning of the calendar year.

[30] That is, the omission of the usual intercalated day in leap year. According to the Gregorian reformation, the suppression would occur in 1700, which was the date Harrison specified in 1577.

[31] That is, in Harrison's time the vernal equinox was occurring on March 11.

[32] *Joannes Stadius* (1527–1579): Flemish mathematician, author of a commentary on L. A. Florus.

[33] Harrison's argument here is based on the tradition that Creation occurred at the vernal equinox, when the sun was entering the sign of Aries (the Ram). Since the equinox came on March 11 in the 1580's, and on March 25 in Caesar's time, it had moved back fourteen days in approximately 1,600 years. Harrison actually assumed the Creation took place about 4,000 B.C.; in the intervening 5,600 years the equinox would have regressed forty-nine days, giving a date around April 29 for the Creation. Harrison's mathematics are not impeccable.

Above the year we have no more parts of time that carry any several names with them, except you will affirm the word age to be one, which is taken for a hundred years and signifieth in English so much as *seculum* or *aevum* doth in Latin; neither is it needful to remember that some of my countrymen do reckon their times not by years but by summers and winters, which is very common among us. Wherefore, to shut up this chapter withal, you shall have a table of the names of the days of the week after the old Saxon and Scottish manner, which I have borrowed from amongst our ancient writers as I have perused their volumes.[34]

The present names

Monday	Friday
Tuesday	Saturday
Wednesday	Sunday, or the
Thursday	Lord's Day

The old Saxon names

Monendeg	Frigesdeg
Tuesdeg	Saterdeg
Wodnesdeg	Sunnandeg
Thunresdeg	

The Scottish usage

Diu Luna	Diu Friach
Diu Mart	Diu Satur
Diu Yath	Diu Seroll
Diu Ethamon	

CHAPTER XV

Of Our Principal Fairs and Markets

I HAVE heretofore said sufficiently of our fairs in the chapter of fairs and markets, and now to perform my promise there made I

[34] Harrison found these names in Leland (*Collectanea*, 1715, III, 99), whose source was the marginalia in a MS of Bede's *De temporibus* (apparently identical with St. John's College, Oxford, MS 17). Leland actually gives the Saxon names Tithesdae and Thodnesdeg for Harrison's Tuesdeg and Wodnesdeg, and the Scottish Diu Triach for Diu Friach.

set down here so many of our fairs as I have found out by mine own observation and help of others in this behalf.[1] Certes it is impossible for me to come by all, sith there is almost no town in England but hath one or more such marts holden yearly in the same, although some of them (I must needs confess) be scarce comparable to Louse Fair, and little else bought or sold in them more than good drink, pies, and some peddlery trash; wherefore it were no loss if divers of them were abolished. Neither do I see whereunto this number of paltry fairs tendeth so much as to the corruption of youth, who (all other business set apart) must needs repair unto them, whereby they often spend not only the week-days but also the Lord's Sabbath in great vanity and riot. But such hath been the iniquity of ancient times. God grant therefore that, ignorance being now abolished and a further insight into things grown into the minds of magistrates, these old errors may be considered of and so far reformed as that thereby neither God may be dishonored nor the commonwealth of our country anything diminished.

In the meantime, take this table here ensuing instead of a calendar of the greatest, sith that I cannot or at the leastwise care not to come by the names of the less, whose knowledge cannot be so profitable to them that be far off as they are oft prejudicial to such as dwell near-hand to the places where they be holden and kept, by pilferers that resort unto the same.

Fairs in January

The 6th day, being Twelfth-day, at Salisbury; the 25th, being St. Paul's Day, at Bristol, at Gravesend, at Churchingford, at Northallerton in Yorkshire, where is kept a fair every Wednesday from Christmas until June.

Fairs in February

The 1st day at Bromley [Kent]. The 2nd at [King's] Lynn, at Bath, at Maidstone, at Bicklesworth [Biggleswade, Beds.], at Budworth. The 14th at Faversham. On Ash Wednesday at Lich-

---

[1] Such tables of fairs are commonplace in almanacs of the time, but Harrison's direct source was the list appended to John Stow's *Summary of English Chronicles* (1575); see p. 253. In 1587 Harrison added a number of fairs (which I here asterisk), seemingly from his own experience. I have preserved Harrison's spellings only when they are significantly different from the modern forms, or when I cannot identify the towns.

field, at Tamworth, at Royston, at Exeter, at Abingdon, at Chichester. The 24th at Henley-on-Thames, at Tewkesbury.

Fairs in March

On the 12th day at Stamford, Sappesford,* and at Sudbury. The 13th day at Wye, at The Mount [St. Michael's Mount], and at Bodmin in Cornwall. The 5th Sunday in Lent at Grantham, at Salisbury. On Monday before Our Lady Day [25th] in Lent at Wisbech, at Kendal, Denbigh in Wales. On Palm Sunday Even at Pomfret [Pontefract]. On Palm Sunday at Worcester. The 20th day at Durham. On Our Lady Day in Lent at Northampton, at Maldon, at Great Chart, at Newcastle [upon Tyne]. And all the Lady Days at Huntingdon. And at Saffron Walden * on Midlent Sunday.

Fairs in April

The 5th day at Wallingford. The 7th at Derby. The 9th at Bicklesworth [Biggleswade], at Belinsworth. On Monday after at Evesham in Worcestershire. On Tuesday in Easter Week at Northfleet, at Rochford, at Hitchin. The 3rd Sunday after Easter at Louth. The 22nd at Stabford [Stockport, Ches.]. On St. George's Day [23rd] at Charing, at Ipswich, at Tamworth, at Ampthill, at Hinninham [Castle Hedingham, Essex], at Guildford, at St. Pomb's in Cornwall. On St. Mark's Day [25th] at Derby, at Dunmow in Essex. The 26th at Tenterden in Kent.

Fairs in May

On May Day at Ripon, at Penryn in Cornwall, at Oswestry in Wales, at Laxfield in Suffolk, at Stow-the-Old [Stow-on-the-Wold], at Reading, at Leicester, at Chelmsford, at Maidstone, at Brickhill, at Blackburn, at Congleton, at Stokeney land * [Stoke by Nayland, Suff.]. The 3rd at Bromyard, at Henningham, at Elstow, Waltham Holy Cross,* and Hedingham Castle.* [2] The 7th at Beverley, at Newton [in Makerfield, Lancs.], at Oxford. On Ascension Day at Newcastle [upon Tyne], at Yarm, at Brimechame [Birmingham], at St. Ede's [St. Neots], at Bishop's Stortford, at Wicham [Wigan], at Middlewich, at Stopford [Stockport], at Chapel-en-le-Frith. On Whitsun Even at Skipton

---

[2] *Hedingham Castle*: the 1587 addition duplicates "Henningham," which also refers to Castle Hedingham in Essex.

in Craven. On Whitsunday at Richel [Ryhill], at Gribby, and every Wednesday fortnight at Kingston-on-Thames, at Ratesdale [Rochdale], at Kirkby Stephen in Westmorland. On Monday in Whitsun Week at Darrington, at Exeter, at Bradford, at Reigate, at Burton [in Lonsdale, Yorks.], at Salford, at Whitchurch [Hants.], at Cockermouth, at Appleby, at Bicklesworth [Biggleswade], at Stoke by Clare.* On Tuesday in Whitsun Week at Lewes, at Rochford, at Canterbury, at Ormskirk, at Penrith, at Long Melford.* On Wednesday in Whitsun Week at Sandbach, at Royston.* On Trinity Sunday at Kendal and at Rowell [Rothwell]. On Thursday after Trinity Sunday at Prescot, at Stapford [Stockport], at St. Anne's, at Newbury, at Coventry, at St. Ede's [St. Neots], at Bishop's Stortford, at Ross. The 9th [3] at Rochester, at Dunstable. The 27th day at Lenham. The 29th at Cranbrook. On Monday in Rogation Week at Reach,* and Sunday after Ascension Day at Thaxted.*

Fairs in June

The 9th day at Maidstone. The 11th at Wokingham, at Newborough [Anglesey], at Bardfield,* at Macclesfield, and Holt. The 17th at Hadstock.* The 23rd at Shrewsbury, at St. Albans. The 24th day at Horsham [Sussex], at Bedale, at Strackstock, at St. Anne's, at Wakefield, at Colchester, at Reading, at Bedford, at Barnwell beside Cambridge, at Wolverhampton, at Cranbrook, at Gloucester, at Lincoln, at Peterborough, at Windsor, at Harlestone, at Lancaster, at West Chester, at Halifax, at Ashbourne. The 27th at Folkestone. The 28th at Headcorn, at St. Pomb's. The 29th at Woodhurst, at Marlborough, at Halesworth, at Wolverhampton, at Petersfield, at Leominster, at Sudbury, at Gargrainge, at Bromley.

Fairs in July

The 2nd at Congleton, at Ashton-under-Lyne. The Sunday after the 3rd of July at Royston.* The 11th at Partney and at Lydd. The 15th at Pinchbeck. The 17th at Winchcomb. The 20th at Uxbridge, at Catesby, at Bolton. The 22nd at Marlborough, at Winchester, at Colchester, at Tetbury, at Cooling,* at Yealdon * [Ickleton, Cambs.], at Bridgnorth, at Clitheroe, at

---

[3] In error for "19th."

Northwich in Cheshire, at Keswick, at Battlefield, at Bicklesworth [Biggleswade]. The 25th at Bristol, at Dover, at Chilham, at Derby, at Ipswich, at Northampton, at Dudley in Staffordshire, at St. James's beside London, at Reading, at Erith in the Isle,* at Walden,* at Thremhall,*[4] at Baldock,* at Louth, at Malmesbury, at Bromley [Kent], at Chichester, at Liverpool, at Altergam [Altrincham], at Ravenglass in the North. The 26th at Tiptree.* The 27th at Canterbury, at Horsham, at Richmond in the North, at Warrington, at Chapel-en-le-Frith.

Fairs in August

The 1st day at Exeter, at Faversham, at Dunstable, at St. Ede's [St. Neots], at Bedford, at Northam Church [Northchurch, Herts.], at Wisbech, at York, at Romney, at Newton [in Maker-field, Lancs.], at Yeland [Elland, Yorks.] The 4th at Linton* The 10th at Waltham [Holy Cross], at Thaxted,* at Blackmore [Essex], at Hungerford, at Bedford, at Stroud, at Farnham, at St. Lawrence by Bodmin, at Walton [Waltham St. Lawrence, Berks.], at Croyley [Crowland, Lincs.], at Settle, at New Brentford. The 15th at Cambridge,* at Dunmow, at Carlisle, at Preston in Andall [Amounderness], at Wakefield on the two Lady Days, and upon the Sunday after the 15th day of August at Haverhill.* On Bartholomew Day [24th] at London, at Beggar's Bush beside Rye, at Tewkesbury, at Sudbury, at Rye, at Nantwich, at Pagets, at Bromley,[5] at Northwich, at Northallerton, at Dover. On the Sunday after Bartholomew Day at Sandwich [Sandbach, Ches.]. The 27th [at Nantwich][6] and at Ashford.

Fairs in September

The 1st day at St. Giles at the Bush [Herts.]. The 8th day at Woolpit,* at Wakefield, at Sturbridge, in Southwark at London, at Snide [Snaith], at Reculver, at Guisborough both the Lady Days, at Partney. The three Lady Days at Blackburn, at Gisburn in Yorkshire, at Halton, at Uttoxeter. On Holy-Rood Day [14th] at Richmond in Yorkshire, at Ripon a horsefair, at Penhale, at

---

[4] *Thremhall:* a former Augustinian priory and manor in Stansted Mountfichet, Essex.

[5] *At Pagets, at Bromley:* probably for "at Bagots, near Abbots Bromley, Staffs."

[6] The missing fair is supplied from Stow.

Bersley [Barnsley, Yorks.], at Waltham Abbey, at Wotton-under-Edge, at Smalding, at Chesterfield, at Denbigh in Wales. On St. Matthew's Day [21st] at Marlborough, at Bedford, at Croydon, at Hedon in Holderness, at St. Edmundsbury [Bury St. Edmunds], at Malton, at St. Ives [Hunts.], at Shrewsbury, at Lenham, at Witnall, at Sittingbourne, at Braintree, at Baldock,* at [St.] Catherine's Hill beside Guildford, at Dover, at Eastry. The 29th day, being Michaelmas Day, at Canterbury, at Malton * a noble horsefair, at Lancaster, at Blackburn, at West Chester, at Cockermouth, at Ashbourne, at Hadleigh, at Malden an horse-fair,⁷ at Weyhill, at Newbury, and at Leicester.

Fairs in October

The 4th day at Mitchell [St. Michael's, Corn.]. The 6th day at St. Faith's beside Norwich, at Maidstone. The 8th at [Market] Harborough, at Hereford, at Bishop's Stortford. On St. Edward's Day [13th] at Royston, at Gravesend, at Windsor, at Marshfield. The 9th day at Colchester. On St. Luke's Even [17th] at Ely, at Wrickle [Writtle, Essex], at Upavon, at Thirsk, at Bridgnorth, at Standon, at Charing, at Burton-on-Trent, at Charlton, at Wigan, at [St.] Frideswide's in Oxford, at Tideswell, at Middlewich, at Holt in Wales. The 21st day at Saffron Walden, at Newmarket, at Hertford, at Cirencester, at Stokesley. The 23rd at Preston, at Bicklesworth [Biggleswade], at Rochdale, at Whitchurch [Salop.]. The 28th at Newmarket * and Hertford.* On All Saints' Even at Wakefield and at Ruthin.

Fairs in November

The 2nd at Bletchingley, at Kingston, at Macclesfield, at Epping.* The 6th day at Newport Pond [Essex], at Stanley[-Leonard, Glos.], at Tregony, at Salford, at Lesford, and Wetshod Fair at Hertford.* The 10th at Lenton. The 11th at Marlborough, at Dover. The 13th at St. Edmundsbury [Bury St. Edmunds], at Guildford. The 17th day at Low [Harlow, Essex], at Hythe. The 19th at Horsham. On St. Edmund's Day [20th] at Hythe, at Ingatestone. The 23rd day at Sandwich. On St. Andrew's Day [30th] at Collingbourne, at Rochester, at Petersfield, at Maiden-

---

⁷ Perhaps a reference to Maldon in Essex, but more likely to the famous horsefair held from St. Matthew's Day to Michaelmas at Malton in Yorkshire, duplicated by Harrison's 1587 addition earlier in the sentence.

head, at Bewdley, at Warrington in Lancashire, at Bedford [Bradford] in Yorkshire, at Oswestry in Wales, and at Paul's Belcham * [Belchamp St. Paul, Essex].

Fairs in December

On the 5th day at Pluckley. On the 6th at Cased,* at Hedingham,* [8] at Spalding, at Exeter, at Sevenoaks, at Arundel, and at Northwich in Cheshire. The 7th day at Sandhurst. The 8th day, being the Conception of Our Lady, at Clitheroe in Lancashire, at Malpas in Cheshire. The 29th at Canterbury and at Salisbury.

CHAPTER XVI

Of Our Inns and Thoroughfares

THOSE towns that we call thoroughfares [1] have great and sumptuous inns builded in them for the receiving of such travelers and strangers as pass to and fro. The manner of harboring wherein is not like to that of some other countries, in which the host or goodman of the house doth challenge a lordly authority over his guests, but clean otherwise, sith every man may use his inn as his own house in England, and have for his money how great or little variety of victuals and what other service himself shall think expedient to call for. Our inns are also very well furnished with napery, bedding, and tapestry, especially with napery; for beside the linen used at the tables, which is commonly washed daily, is such and so much as belongeth unto the estate and calling of the guest. Each comer is sure to lie in clean sheets, wherein no man hath been lodged since they came from the laundress or out of the water wherein they were last washed. If the traveler have an horse his bed doth cost him nothing, but if he go on foot he is sure to pay a penny for the same; but whether he be horseman or footman, if his chamber be once appointed he may carry the key with him, as of his own house, so long as he lodgeth there. If he lose aught whilst he abideth in the inn, the host is bound by a

---

[8] *At Cased, at Hedingham:* apparently a misprint for Castle Hedingham.
[1] *Thoroughfares:* towns through which there is much passage of travelers.

general custom to restore the damage, so that there is no greater security anywhere for travelers than in the greatest inns of England.

Their horses in like sort are walked, dressed, and looked unto by certain hostlers or hired servants, appointed at the charges of the goodman of the house, who in hope of extraordinary reward will deal very diligently after outward appearance in this their function and calling. Herein, nevertheless, are many of them blameworthy, in that they do not only deceive the beast oftentimes of his allowance by sundry means, except their owners look well to them, but also make such packs with slipper merchants[2] which hunt after prey (for what place is sure from evil and wicked persons?) that many an honest man is spoiled of his goods as he traveleth to and fro, in which feat also the counsel of the tapsters, or drawers of drink, and chamberlains is not seldom behind or wanting. Certes I believe not that chapman or traveler in England is robbed by the way without the knowledge of some of them; for when he cometh into the inn and alighteth from his horse, the hostler forthwith is very busy to take down his budget or capcase[3] in the yard from his saddlebow, which he peiseth [weighs] slyly in his hand to feel the weight thereof; or if he miss of this pitch,[4] when the guest hath taken up his chamber the chamberlain that looketh to the making of the beds will be sure to remove it from the place where the owner hath set it, as if it were to set it more conveniently somewhere else, whereby he getteth an inkling whether it be money or other short wares, and thereof giveth warning to such odd guests as haunt the house and are of his confederacy, to the utter undoing of many an honest yeoman as he journeyeth by the way. The tapster in like sort for his part doth mark his behavior and what plenty of money he draweth when he payeth the shot, to the like end, so that it shall be an hard matter to escape all their subtle practices. Some think it a gay matter to commit their budgets at their coming to the goodman of the house, but thereby they oft bewray themselves. For albeit their money be safe for the time that it is in his hands (for you shall not hear that a man is robbed in his inn), yet after their departure the host can make no war-

---

[2] *Slipper merchants:* deceitful rogues.
[3] *Capcase:* a small traveling bag.
[4] *Pitch:* a net set for catching fish.

rantise of the same, sith his protection extendeth no further than the gate of his own house, and there cannot be a surer token unto such as pry and watch for those booties than to see any guest deliver his capcase in such manner.

In all our inns we have plenty of ale, beer, and sundry kinds of wine, and such is the capacity of some of them that they are able to lodge two hundred or three hundred persons and their horses at ease, and thereto with a very short warning make such provision for their diet as to him that is unacquainted withal may seem to be incredible. Howbeit, of all in England there are no worse inns than in London, and yet many are there far better than the best that I have heard of in any foreign country, if all circumstances be duly considered. But to leave this and go in hand with my purpose. I will here set down a table of the best thoroughfares and towns of greatest travel of England, in some of which there are twelve or sixteen such inns at the least, as I before did speak of. And it is a world to see how each owner of them contendeth with other for goodness of entertainment of their guests, as about fineness and change of linen, furniture of bedding, beauty of rooms, service at the table, costliness of plate, strength of drink, variety of wines, or well using of horses. Finally, there is not so much omitted among them as the gorgeousness of their very signs at their doors, wherein some do consume £30 or £40, a mere vanity in mine opinion, but so vain will they needs be, and that not only to give some outward token of the innkeeper's wealth but also to procure good guests to the frequenting of their houses in hope there to be well used. Lo, here the table now at hand, for more of our inns I shall not need to speak.[5]

The way from Walsingham to London

From Walsingham to Pickenham	12 miles
From Pickenham to Brandon Ferry	10 miles
From Brandon Ferry to Newmarket	10 miles
From Newmarket to Babraham	10 miles
From Babraham to Barkway	20 miles
From Barkway to Puckeridge	7 miles

[5] The first nine of these itineraries are borrowed from John Stow's *Summary of English Chronicles* (1575). The routes from Dover to Cambridge, Canterbury to Oxford, and London to Cambridge seem to be based largely on Harrison's own travels.

From Puckeridge to Ware	5 miles
From Ware to Waltham	8 miles
From Waltham to London	12 miles

The way from Berwick to York, and so to London

From Berwick to Belford	12 miles
From Belford to Alnwick	12 miles
From Alnwick to Morpeth	12 miles
From Morpeth to Newcastle	12 miles
From Newcastle to Durham	12 miles
From Durham to Darlington	13 miles
From Darlington to Northallerton	14 miles
From Northallerton to Topcliffe	7 miles
From Topcliffe to York	16 miles
From York to Tadcaster	8 miles
From Tadcaster to Wentbridge	12 miles
From Wentbridge to Doncaster	8 miles
From Doncaster to Tuxford	18 miles
From Tuxford to Newark	10 miles
From Newark to Grantham	10 miles
From Grantham to Stamford	16 miles
From Stamford to Stilton	12 miles
From Stilton to Huntingdon	9 miles
From Huntingdon to Royston	15 miles
From Royston to Ware	12 miles
From Ware to Waltham	8 miles
From Waltham to London	12 miles

The way from Caernarvon to Chester, and so to London

From Caernarvon to Conway	24 miles
From Conway to Denbigh	12 miles
From Denbigh to Flint	12 miles
From Flint to Chester	10 miles
From Chester to Wich [Nantwich]	14 miles
From Wich to Stone	15 miles
From Stone to Lichfield	16 miles
From Lichfield to Coleshill	12 miles
From Coleshill to Coventry	8 miles

And so from Coventry to London as hereafter followeth.

The way from Cockermouth to Lancaster, and so to London

From Cockermouth to Keswick	6 miles
From Keswick to Grocener [Grasmere]	8 miles
From Grocener to Kendal	14 miles

From Kendal to Burton	7 miles
From Burton to Lancaster	8 miles
From Lancaster to Preston	20 miles
From Preston to Wigan	14 miles
From Wigan to Warrington	20 miles
From Warrington to Newcastle	20 miles
From Newcastle to Lichfield	20 miles
From Lichfield to Coventry	20 miles
From Coventry to Daventry	14 miles
From Daventry to Towcester	10 miles
From Towcester to Stony Stratford	6 miles
From Stony Stratford to Brickhill	7 miles
From Brickhill to Dunstable	7 miles
From Dunstable to St. Albans	10 miles
From St. Albans to Barnet	10 miles
From Barnet to London	10 miles

The way from Yarmouth to Colchester, and so to London

From Yarmouth to Beccles	8 miles
From Beccles to Blythburgh	7 miles
From Blythburgh to Snape Bridge	8 miles
From Snape Bridge to Woodbridge	8 miles
From Woodbridge to Ipswich	5 miles
From Ipswich to Colchester	12 miles
From Colchester to Easterford [Kelvedon]	8 miles
From Easterford to Chelmsford	10 miles
From Chelmsford to Brentwood	10 miles
From Brentwood to London	15 miles

The way from Dover to London

From Dover to Canterbury	12 miles
From Canterbury to Sittingbourne	12 miles
From Sittingbourne to Rochester	8 miles
From Rochester to Gravesend	5 miles
From Gravesend to Dartford	6 miles
From Dartford to London	12 miles

The way from St. Buryan in Cornwall to London

From St. Buryan to The Mount	20 miles
From The Mount to Truro	12 miles
From St. Truro to Bodmin	20 miles
From Bodmin to Launceston	20 miles
From Launceston to Okehampton	15 miles
From Okehampton to Crockernwell	10 miles

From Crockernwell to Exeter	10 miles
From Exeter to Honiton	12 miles
From Honiton to Chard	10 miles
From Chard to Crewkerne	7 miles
From Crewkerne to Sherborne	10 miles
From Sherborne to Shaftesbury	10 miles
From Shaftesbury to Salisbury	18 miles
From Salisbury to Andover	15 miles
From Andover to Basingstoke	18 miles
From Basingstoke to Hartford [Bridge]	8 miles
From Hartford to Bagshot	8 miles
From Bagshot to Staines	8 miles
From Staines to London	15 miles

The way from Bristol to London

From Bristol to Marshfield	10 miles
From Marshfield to Chippenham	10 miles
From Chippenham to Marlborough	15 miles
From Marlborough to Hungerford	8 miles
From Hungerford to Newbury	7 miles
From Newbury to Reading	15 miles
From Reading to Maidenhead	10 miles
From Maidenhead to Colnbrook	7 miles
From Colnbrook to London	15 miles

The way from St. David's to London

From St. David's to Axford [6]	20 miles
From Axford to Carmarthen	10 miles
From Carmarthen to Newton [7]	10 miles
From Newton to Lanbury [Llandovery]	10 miles
From Lanbury to Brecon	16 miles
From Brecon to Hay[-on-Wye]	10 miles
From Hay to Hereford	14 miles
From Hereford to Ross[-on-Wye]	9 miles
From Ross to Gloucester	12 miles
From Gloucester to Cirencester	15 miles
From Cirencester to Faringdon	16 miles
From Faringdon to Abingdon	7 miles
From Abingdon to Dorchester	7 miles
From Dorchester to Henley	12 miles

---

[6] *Axford:* for Arford, Haverfordwest. The first two distances are reversed.

[7] *Newton:* New-town, Dynevor Castle near Llandilo.

From Henley to Maidenhead	7 miles
From Maidenhead to Colnbrook	7 miles
From Colnbrook to London	15 miles

Of thoroughfares, from Dover to Cambridge

From Dover to Canterbury	12 miles
From Canterbury to Rochester	20 miles
From Rochester to Gravesend	5 miles
From Gravesend over the Thames to Horndon	4 miles
From Horndon to Chelmsford	12 miles
From Chelmsford to Dunmow	10 miles
From Dunmow to Thaxted	5 miles
From Thaxted to Radwinter [8]	3 miles
From Radwinter to Linton	5 miles
From Linton to Babraham	3 miles
From Babraham to Cambridge	4 miles

From Canterbury to Oxford

From Canterbury to London	43 miles
From London to Uxbridge or Colnbrook	15 miles
From Uxbridge to Beaconsfield	7 miles
From Beaconsfield to East Wycombe	5 miles
From Wycombe to Stokenchurch	5 miles
From Stokenchurch to Tetsworth	5 miles
From Tetsworth to Wheatley	6 miles
From Wheatley to Oxford	4 miles

From London to Cambridge

From London to Edmonton	6 miles
From Edmonton to Waltham	6 miles
From Waltham to Hoddesdon	5 miles
From Hoddesdon to Ware	3 miles
From Ware to Pulcherchurch [Puckeridge]	5 miles
From Pulcherchurch to Barkway	7 miles
From Barkway to Fowlmere	6 miles
From Fowlmere to Cambridge	6 miles
Or thus better way:	
From London to Hoddesdon	17 miles
From Hoddesdon to Hadham	7 miles
From Hadham to Saffron Walden	12 miles
From Saffron Walden to Cambridge	10 miles

[8] The main road actually passed through Saffron Walden, five miles west of Radwinter. Harrison is misrouting travelers through his own parish.

Of certain ways in Scotland, out of
Reginald Wolfe his annotations [9]

From Berwick to Edinburgh

From Berwick to Chirnside	10 miles
From Chirnside to Coldingham	3 miles
From Coldingham to Pinkerton	6 miles
From Pinkerton to Dunbar	6 miles
From Dunbar to Linton	6 miles
From Linton to Haddington	6 miles
From Haddington to Seton	4 miles
From Seton to Aberlady or Musselburgh	8 miles
From thence to Edinburgh	8 miles

From Edinburgh to Berwick another way

From Edinburgh to Dalkeith	5 miles
From Dalkeith to Newbattle and Lauder	5 miles
From Lauder to Ursildon [Earlston]	6 miles
From Ursildon to Dryburgh	5 miles
From Dryburgh to Cariton [10]	6 miles
From Cariton to Berwick	14 miles

From Edinburgh to Dunbrittain [Dumbarton] westward

From Edinburgh to Kirkliston	6 miles
From Kirkliston to Linlithgow	6 miles
From Linlithgow to Falkirk over Forth	6 miles
From thence to Stirling upon Forth	6 miles
From Stirling to Dunbrittain	24 miles

From Stirling to Kinghorn eastward

From Stirling to Doune in Menteith	3 miles
From Doune to Cambuskenneth	3 miles
From Cambuskenneth to Alwie [Alloa] upon Forth	4 miles
From Alwie to Culross in Fife	10 miles
From Culross to Dunfermline	2 miles
From Dunfermline to Everkennin [Inverkeithing]	2 miles

---

[9] *Reginald Wolfe:* the London printer who originally planned the work which came to be known under Holinshed's name. He died in 1573, before Harrison had been enlisted as a contributor, but Harrison makes clear that he had known Wolfe (see p. 416), and he had access to the materials Wolfe had assembled for his project: in *The Description of Britain* he mentions a map "which I had sometime of Reginald Wolfe" and Wolfe's "great card, not yet finished nor likely to be published" (1587, pp. 33, 39).

[10] *Cariton:* Kelso? Carham?

| From Everkennin to Aberdour on Forth | 3 miles |
| From Aberdour to Kinghorn upon Forth | 3 miles |

From Kinghorn to Taymouth

From Kinghorn to Dysart in Fife	3 miles
From Dysart to Cupar	8 miles
From Cupar to St. Andrews	14 miles
From St. Andrews to the Taymouth	6 miles

From Taymouth to Stockford

From Taymouth to Balmerino Abbey	4 miles
From thence to Lindores Abbey	4 miles
From Lindores to St. John's Town [Perth]	12 miles
From St. John's to Scone	5 miles
From thence to Abernethy, where the Earn runneth into the Tay	15 miles
From Abernethy to Dundee [11]	15 miles
From Dundee to Arbroath and Muros [Montrose]	24 miles
From Muros to Aberdeen	20 miles
From Aberdeen to the water of Doney [12]	20 miles
From thence to the river of Spey	30 miles
From thence to Stockford in Ross, and so to the Ness of Haben, a famous point on the west side [13]	30 miles

From Carlisle to Whithorn westward

From Carlisle over the ferry against Redkirk	4 miles
From thence to Dumfries	20 miles
From Dumfries to the ferry of Cree	40 miles
From thence to Wigtown	3 miles
From thence to Whithorn	12 miles

Hitherto of the common ways of England and Scotland, whereunto I will adjoin the old thoroughfares ascribed to Antoninus, to the end that by their conference the diligent reader may have further consideration of the same than my leisure will permit me. In setting forth also thereof I have noted such diver-

[11] This itinerary seems garbled; the route should run from Lindores to Abernethy to St. John's Town to Scone to Dundee.

[12] That is, following the River Don?

[13] *Stockford:* John Leslie's *History of Scotland*, trans. Father James Dalrymple in 1596 (ed. E. G. Cody, Scottish Text Soc., I, 1888, 42), mentions "a famous ford in the River of Forn [now Beauly] called the Stockford of the Ross." *Ness of Haben:* unidentified.

sity of reading as hath happened in the sight of such written and printed copies as I have seen in my time. Notwithstanding, I must confess the same to be much corrupted in the rehearsal of the miles.[14]

[14] Harrison concludes his *Description of England* with his version of the Antonine Itinerary (see p. 205, n. 5), which is here omitted.

BOOK I

The Description of Britain [excerpts]

The Description of Britain

TABLE OF CONTENTS [1]

[1] The table of contents for *The Description of Britain* provides a quick summary of the topics Harrison treated. The figures in brackets indicate the number of columns to which the chapters ran in the 1587 edition. Asterisked chapters are those here reprinted in whole or in part.

CHAPTER VI

Of the Languages Spoken in This Island

WHAT language came first with Samothes and afterward with Albion and the giants of his company [1] it is hard for me to determine, sith nothing of sound credit remaineth in writing which may resolve us in the truth hereof. Yet of so much are we certain, that the speech of the ancient Britons and of the Celts had great affinity one with another, so that they were either all one or at leastwise such as either nation with small help of interpreters might understand other and readily discern what the speaker meant. Some are of the opinion that the Celts spake Greek and how the British tongue resembled the same which was spoken in Grecia before Homer did reform it; but I see that these men do speak without authority, and therefore I reject them, for if the Celts which were properly called Gauls did speak Greek, why did Caesar in his letters sent to Rome use that language because that if they should be intercepted they might not understand them, or why did he not understand the Gauls, he being so skillful in the language, without an interpreter? [2] Yet I deny not but that the Celtish and British speeches might have great affinity one with another, and the British above all other with the Greek, for both do appear by certain words, as first in *tri* for three, *march* for an horse, and *trimarchia*, whereof Pausanias speaketh, for both. [3] Athenaeus also writeth of Bathanasius, a captain of the Gauls, [4] whose name is mere British, compounded

---

[1] See pp. 162–163.
[2] *Gallic War*, V, xlviii; I, xix. The entire sentence is borrowed from Bodin, *Method for the Easy Comprehension of History* (trans. Reynolds, p. 352).
[3] *Description of Greece*, X, xix, 11. *Trimarchia:* a division of Gallic cavalry. The citations and etymologies to the end of the paragraph come from Humphrey Llwyd, *The Breviary of Britain*, trans. Twyne, fols. 54v–55v.
[4] *Deipnosophists*, VI, 234.

of *bath* and *ynad*, and signifieth "a noble or comely judge." And whereas he saith that the relics of the Gauls took up their first dwelling about Ister [the Danube] and afterward divided themselves in such wise that they which went and dwelled in Hungary were called Scordisci, and the other, that inhabited within the dominion of Tyrol, Brenni [Breuni], whose seat was on the Mount Brenner, parcel of the Alps, what else signifieth the word *yscaredich* in British, from whence the word "Scordisci" cometh, but "to be divided"?

Hereby, then, and sundry other the like testimonies, I gather that the British and the Celtish speeches had great affinity one with another, as I said, which Caesar (speaking of the similitude or likeness of religion in both nations) doth also aver, and Tacitus (*in vita Agricolae*) in like sort plainly affirmeth,[5] or else it must needs be that the Gauls which invaded Italy and Greece were mere Britons, of whose likeness of speech with the Greek tongue I need not make any trial, sith no man (I hope) will readily deny it. Appianus, talking of the Brenni, calleth them Cymbres, and by this I gather also that the Celts and the Britons were indifferently called Cimbri in their own language, or else that the Britons were the right Cimbri, who unto this day do not refuse to be called by that name.

Bodin, writing of the means by which the original of every kingdom and nation is to be had and discerned, setteth down three ways whereby the knowledge thereof is to be found: one is (saith he) the infallible testimony of the sound writers, the other the description and site of the region, the third the relics of the ancient speech remaining in the same.[6] Which latter, if it be of any force, then I must conclude that the speech of the Britons and Celts was sometime either all one or very like one to another, or else it must follow that the Britons overflowed the Continent under the name of Cimbres, being peradventure associate in this voyage or mixed by invasion with the Danes and Norwegians, who are called Cimbri and Cymmerii, as most writers do remember. This also is evident (as Plutarch likewise confesseth *in vita Marii*), that no man knew from whence the Cimbres came in his days,[7] and therefore I believe that they came out of Britain, for all the main was well known unto them, I mean even to the

[5] *Gallic War*, V, xiii; *Agricola*, xi.
[6] *Method* (p. 336).   [7] Llwyd, fol. 51v.

uttermost part of the North, as may appear furthermore by the slaves which were daily brought from thence unto them, whom of their countries they called Davi for Daci, Getae for Goths, etc., for of their conquests I need not make rehearsal, sith they are commonly known and remembered by the writers, both of the Greeks and Latins.

The British tongue called Camberaec [Cymraeg] doth yet remain in that part of the island which is now called Wales, whither the Britons were driven after the Saxons had made a full conquest of the other which we now call England, although the pristinate integrity thereof be not a little diminished by mixture of the Latin and Saxon speeches withal. Howbeit, many poesies and writings (in making whereof that nation hath evermore delighted) are yet extant in my time whereby some difference between the ancient and present language may easily be discerned, notwithstanding that among all these there is nothing to be found which can set down any sound and full testimony of their own original, in remembrance whereof their bards and cunning [learned] men have been most slack and negligent. Giraldus in praising the Britons affirmeth that there is not one word in all their language that is not either Greek or Latin.[8] Which being rightly understanded and conferred with the likeness that was in old time between the Celts' and the British tongues will not a little help those that think the old Celtish to have some savor of the Greek. But howsoever that matter standeth, after the British speech came once over into this island, sure it is that it could never be extinguished, for all the attempts that the Romans, Saxons, Normans, and Englishmen could make against that nation in any manner of wise.

Pedigrees and genealogies, also, the Welsh Britons have plenty in their own tongue, insomuch that many of them can readily derive the same either from Brut or some of his band even unto Aeneas and other of the Trojans, and so forth unto Noah without any manner of stop.[9] But as I know not what credit is to be given unto them in this behalf, although I must needs confess that their ancient bards were very diligent in their collection and had also public allowance or salary for the same, so I dare not absolutely impugn their assertions, sith that in times past all nations (learn-

[8] Giraldus Cambrensis, *Descriptio Cambriae*, I, xv (ed. Dimock, *Opera*, VI, 194).   [9] *Descriptio Cambriae*, I, iii (pp. 167–168).

ing it no doubt of the Hebrews) did very solemnly preserve the catalogues of their descents, thereby either to show themselves of ancient and noble race or else to be descended from some one of the gods. But,

> *Stemmata quid faciunt? quid prodest Pontice longo*
> *Sanguine censeri? aut quid avorum ducere turmas? etc.*[10]

Next unto the British speech the Latin tongue was brought in by the Romans and in manner generally planted through the whole region, as the French was after by the Normans. Of this tongue [Latin] I will not say much, because there are few which be not skillful in the same. Howbeit, as the speech itself is easy and delectable, so hath it perverted the names of the ancient rivers, regions, and cities of Britain in such wise that in these our days their old British denominations are quite grown out of memory and yet those of the new Latin left as most uncertain. This remaineth also unto my time, borrowed from the Romans, that all our deeds, evidences, charters, and writings of record are set down in the Latin tongue, though now very barbarous, and thereunto the copies and court rolls and processes of courts and leets registered in the same.

The third language apparently known is the Scythian [German], or High Dutch, induced at the first by the Saxons (which the Britons call Saysonaec [Sassenach], as they do the speakers Sayson),[11] an hard and rough kind of speech, God wot, when our nation was brought first into acquaintance withal, but now changed with us into a far more fine and easy kind of utterance, and so polished and helped with new and milder words that it is to be avouched how there is no one speech under the sun spoken in our time that hath or can have more variety of words, copy [copiousness] of phrases, or figures and flowers of eloquence than hath our English tongue, although some have affirmed us rather to bark as dogs than talk like men, because the most of our words (as they do indeed) incline unto one syllable. This also is to be noted as a testimony remaining still of our language derived from the Saxons, that the general name for the most part of every skillful artificer in his trade endeth in "-here" with us,

---

[10] "Of what use are pedigrees? What good is it, Ponticus, to be valued for ancient blood? Or to display a host of ancestors?" (based on Juvenal, VIII, 1–2).   [11] Llwyd, fol. 13r.

albeit the *h* be left out and "-er" only inserted,[12] as "scrivenhere," "writehere," "shiphere," etc., for scrivener, writer, and shipper, etc., beside many other relics of that speech never to be abolished.

After the Saxon tongue came the Norman, or French, language over into our country, and therein were our laws written for a long time. Our children also were by an especial decree taught first to speak the same, and thereunto enforced to learn their constructions in the French whensoever they were set to the grammar school. In like sort, few bishops, abbots, or other clergymen were admitted unto any ecclesiastical function here among us but such as came out of religious houses from beyond the seas, to the end they should not use the English tongue in their sermons to the people. In the court also it grew into such contempt that most men thought it no small dishonor to speak any English there. Which bravery took his hold at the last likewise in the country with every plowman, that even the very carters began to wax weary of their mother tongue and labored to speak French, which as then was counted no small token of gentility. And no marvel, for every French rascal when he came once hither was taken for a gentleman only because he was proud and could use his own language, and all this (I say) to exile the English and British speeches quite out of the country.

But in vain, for in the time of King Edward the First, to wit, toward the latter end of his reign, the French itself ceased to be spoken generally, but most of all and by law in the midst of Edward the Third, and then began the English to recover and grow in more estimation than before, notwithstanding that among our artificers the most part of their implements, tools, and words of art retain still their French denominations even to these our days, as the language itself is used likewise in sundry courts, books of record, and matters of law, whereof here is no place to make any particular rehearsal. Afterward, also, by diligent travail of Geoffrey Chaucer and John Gower in the time of Richard the Second, and after them of John Scogan and John Lydgate, monk of Bury,[13] our said tongue was brought to an excellent pass, notwithstanding that it never came unto the type of perfection

[12] The Anglo-Saxon suffix is properly "-ere."
[13] *John Gower* (?1325–1408) and *John Lydgate* (?1370–?1451): English poets; *John Scogan*: apparently in error for Henry Scogan (?1361–1407), friend and disciple of Chaucer.

until the time of Queen Elizabeth, wherein John Jewel, Bishop of Sarum, John Foxe,[14] and sundry learned and excellent writers have fully accomplished the ornature of the same, to their great praise and immortal commendation, although not a few other do greatly seek to stain the same by fond affectation of foreign and strange words, presuming that to be the best English which is most corrupted with external [foreign] terms of eloquence and sound of many syllables.

But as this excellency of the English tongue is found in one, and the south, part of this island, so in Wales the greatest number (as I said) retain still their own ancient language, that of the north part of the said country being less corrupted than the other, and therefore reputed for the better in their own estimation and judgment.[15] This also is proper to us Englishmen, that sith ours is a mean language and neither too rough nor too smooth in utterance, we may with much facility learn any other language, beside Hebrew, Greek, and Latin, and speak it naturally as if we were homeborn in those countries; and yet on the other side it falleth out, I wot not by what other means, that few foreign nations can rightly pronounce ours without some, and that great, note of imperfection, especially the Frenchmen, who also seldom write anything that savoreth of English truly. It is a pastime to read how Natalis Comes in like manner, speaking of our affairs, doth clip the names of our English lords.[16] But this of all the rest doth breed most admiration with me, that if any stranger do hit upon some likely pronunciation of our tongue, yet in age he swerveth so much from the same that he is worse therein than ever he was, and thereto peradventure halteth not a little also in his own, as I have seen by experience in Reginald Wolfe [17] and other, whereof I have justly marveled.

The Cornish and Devonshire men, whose country the Britons call Cernyw, have a speech in like sort of their own, and such as hath indeed more affinity with the Armorican [Breton] tongue

---

[14] *John Jewel* (1522–1571): Bishop of Salisbury, apologist for the English church; *John Foxe* (1516–1587): author of the *Acts and Monuments*, or *Book of Martyrs*. Harrison's principle of selection here seems extraliterary.

[15] *Descriptio Cambriae*, I, vi (p. 177).

[16] *Natalis Comes*: Natale Conti (?1520–?1580), Italian humanist; his *Universae historiae sui temporis* was published at Venice in 1581. *Clip*: clepe, name.

[17] *Reginald Wolfe* (d. 1573): a Dutchman who became a successful London printer; see p. 404, n. 9.

than I can well discuss of. Yet in mine opinion they are both but a corrupted kind of British, albeit so far degenerating in these days from the old that if either of them do meet with a Welshman they are not able at the first to understand one another, except here and there in some odd words, without the help of interpreters. And no marvel (in mine opinion) that the British of Cornwall is thus corrupted, sith the Welsh tongue that is spoken in the north and south part of Wales doth differ so much in itself as the English used in Scotland doth from that which is spoken among us here in this side of the island, as I have said already.

The Scottish English hath been much broader and less pleasant in utterance than ours, because that nation hath not till of late endeavored to bring the same to any perfect order, and yet it was such in manner as Englishmen themselves did speak for the most part beyond the Trent, whither any great amendment of our language had not as then extended itself. Howbeit, in our time the Scottish language endeavoreth to come near if not altogether to match our tongue in fineness of phrase and copy of words. And this may in part appear by an history of the Apocrypha translated into Scottish verse by Hudson, dedicated to the King of that country and containing six books, except my memory do fail me.[18]

Thus we see how that under the dominion of the King of England and in the south parts of the realm we have three several tongues, that is to say, English, British, and Cornish, and even so many are in Scotland, if you account the English speech for one, notwithstanding that for breadth and quantity of the region, I mean only of the soil of the main island, it be somewhat less to see to than the other. For in the north part of the region, where the wild Scots, otherwise called the redshanks or rough-footed Scots[19] (because they go barefooted and clad in mantles over their saffron shirts after the Irish manner) do inhabit, they speak good Irish, which they call *Gachtlet*, as they say of one Gathelus,[20] whereby they show their original to have in times past been

[18] Thomas Hudson, *The History of Judith in the Form of a Poem* (Edinburgh, 1584), translated from the French of Du Bartas.

[19] *Redshanks:* a Scottish highlander, so called because his legs were red from exposure; *rough-footed:* wearing shoes of undressed leather.

[20] *Gathelus:* a legendary Greek who settled first in Egypt (where he fought under Moses and married the Pharaoh's daughter, Scota), then Portugal, and finally in Spain. His descendants led some of the Scots to Ireland and later to Scotland.

fetched out of Ireland, as I noted also in the chapter precedent, and whereunto Vincent (*cap.* "*De insulis oceani*") doth yield his assent, saying that Ireland was in time past called Scotia: *Scotia, eadem,* saith he, *et Hibernia, proxima Britanniae insula, spatio terrarum angustior, sed situ foecundior; Scotia autem a Scotorum gentibus traditur appellata, etc.*[21] Out of the fourteenth book of Isidore, entitled *Originum,* where he also addeth that it is called Hibernia because it bendeth toward Iberia.[22] But I find elsewhere that it is so called by certain Spaniards which came to seek and plant their inhabitation in the same, whereof in my Chronology I have spoken more at large.

In the Isles of the Orcades, or Orkney as we now call them, and such coasts of Britain as do abut upon the same, the Gottish [Gothic] or Danish speech is altogether in use, and also in Shetland, by reason (as I take it) that the princes of Norway held those islands so long under their subjection, albeit they were otherwise reputed as rather to belong to Ireland, because that the very soil of them is enemy to poison, as some write, although for my part I had never any sound experience of the truth hereof. And thus much have I thought good to speak of our old speeches and those five languages now usually spoken within the limits of our island.

CHAPTER XI

The Description of the Thames and Such Rivers as Fall into the Same

. . . HAVING in this manner briefly touched this noble river [1] and such brooks as fall into the same, I will now add a particular

[21] "Scotia, or Hibernia, the island nearest to Britain, is smaller in area but more fertile; Scotia is said to be so called of the Scottish race"; from the *Speculum naturale* of Vincent of Beauvais (?1190–?1264), French encyclopedist.

[22] Isidore, Bishop of Seville (d. 636), *Etymologiarum, sive Originum,* XIV, 6.

[1] *This noble river:* the Thames. The following excerpt is Harrison's digression from his purely topographical description of the Thames.

description of each of these last by themselves, whereby their courses also shall be severally described to the satisfaction of the studious. But ere I take the same in hand, I will insert a word or two of the commodities of the said river, which I will perform with so much brevity as is possible, hereby also finding out his whole tract and course from the head to the fall thereof into the sea. It appeareth evidently that the length thereof is at the least one hundred and eighty miles, if it be measured by the journeys of the land. And as it is in course the longest of the three famous rivers of this isle, so it is nothing inferior unto them in abundance of all kind of fish, whereof it is hard to say which of the three have either most plenty or greatest variety, if the circumstances be duly weighed. What some other write of the rivers of their countries it skilleth [matters] not, neither will I (as divers do) invent strange things of this noble stream, therewith to nobilitate and make it more honorable; but this will I in plain terms affirm, that it neither swalloweth up bastards of the Celtish brood, or casteth up the right-begotten that are thrown in, without hurt into their mother's lap, as Politian fableth of the Rhine (*Epistolarum, lib.* 8, *epi.* 6),[2] nor yieldeth clots of gold as the Tagus doth, but an infinite plenty of excellent, sweet, and pleasant fish, wherewith such as inhabit near unto her banks are fed and fully nourished.

What should I speak of the fat and sweet salmons daily taken in this stream, and that in such plenty (after the time of the smelt be past) as no river in Europe is able to exceed it? What store also of barbels, trouts, chevins [chub], perches, smelts, breams, roaches, daces, gudgeons, flounders, shrimps, etc., are commonly to be had therein I refer me to them that know by experience better than I, by reason of their daily trade of fishing in the same. And albeit it seemeth from time to time to be as it were defrauded in sundry wise of these her large commodities by the insatiable avarice of the fishermen, yet this famous river complaineth commonly of no want, but the more it loseth at one time, the more it yieldeth at another. Only in carps it seemeth to be scant, sith it is not long since that kind of fish was brought over into England, and but of late to speak of into this stream, by the violent rage of sundry landfloods that brake open the

[2] *Politian:* Angelo Poliziano (1454–1494), Italian humanist and neo-Latin poet.

heads and dams of divers gentlemen's ponds, by which means it became somewhat partaker also of this said commodity, whereof erst it had no portion that I could ever hear. Oh, that this river might be spared but even one year from nets, etc.! But alas, then should many a poor man be undone. In the meantime it is lamentable to see how it is and hath been choked of late with sands and shelves, through the penning and wresting of the course of the water for commodity's sake. But as this is an inconvenience easily remedied, if good order were taken for the redress thereof, so now the fine or prise [3] set upon the ballast sometime freely given to the merchants by patent, even unto the land's end (*jusques au poinct*), will be another cause of harm unto this noble stream, and all through an advantage taken at the want of an *i* in the word *ponct*, which grew through an error committed by an English notary unskillful in the French tongue, wherein that patent was granted.[4]

Furthermore, the said river floweth and filleth all his channels twice in the day and night, that is, in every twelve hours once; and this ebbing and flowing holdeth on for the space of seventy miles within the mainland, the stream or tide being always highest at London when the moon doth exactly touch the northeast and south or west points of the heavens, of which one is visible, the other under the earth and not subject to our sight. These tides also differ in their times, each one coming later than other by so many minutes as pass ere the revolution and natural course of the heavens do reduce and bring about the said planet unto those her former places, whereby the common difference between one tide and another is found to consist of twenty-four minutes, which wanteth but twelve of an whole hour in four-and-twenty, as experience doth confirm. In like sort we see by daily trial that each tide is not of equal height and greatness, for at the full and change of the moon we have the greatest floods, and such is their ordinary course that as they diminish from their changes and fulls unto the first and last quarters, so afterwards they increase again until they come to the full and change. Sometimes also they rise so high (if the wind be at the north or northeast, which bringeth in the water with more vehemency, because the tide which filleth

---

[3] *Fine:* boundary, limit; *prise:* the legal right to take something. ˙

[4] That is, the limit intended in the patent, "to the end of land" (*au point*), was erroneously written as "to the bridge" (*au pont*).

the channel cometh from Scotlandward) that the Thames over-floweth her banks near unto London, which happeneth espe-cially in the fulls and changes of January and February, wherein the lower grounds are of custom soonest drowned. This order of flowing in like sort is perpetual, so that when the moon is upon the southwest and north of points, then is the water by London at the highest; neither do the tides alter, except some rough winds out of the west or southwest do keep back and check the stream in his entrance, as the east and northeast do hasten the coming in thereof, or else some other extraordinary occasion put by the ordinary course of the northern seas, which fill the said river by their natural return and flowing. And that both these do happen eft among,[5] I refer me to such as have not seldom ob-served it, as also the sensible chopping in of three or four tides in one natural day, whereof the unskillful [ignorant] do descant many things.

But howsoever these small matters do fall out and how often soever this course of the stream doth happen to be disturbed, yet at two several times of the age of the moon the waters re-turn to their natural course and limits of time exactly. Polydore saith that this river is seldom increased or rather never over-floweth her banks by landfloods,[6] but he is herein very much deceived, as it shall be more apparently seen hereafter. For the more that this river is put by of her right course, the more the water must of necessity swell with the white waters which run down from the land, because the passage cannot be so swift and ready in the winding as in the straight course. These landfloods also do greatly strain the fineness of the stream, insomuch that after a great landflood you shall take haddocks with your hands beneath the bridge as they float aloft upon the water, whose eyes are so blinded with the thickness of that element that they can-not see where to become and make shift to save themselves before death take hold of them. Otherwise the water of itself is very clear and in comparison next unto that of the sea, which is most subtle and pure of all other, as that of great rivers is most excel-lent in comparison of smaller brooks, although Aristotle will

[5] *Eft:* moreover; *among:* from time to time. But the words are probably a misprint for "oft among," a phrase Harrison uses elsewhere (p. 277), ap-parently to mean no more than "often."

[6] Polydore Vergil, *English History* (Camden Soc., XXXVI, 20).

have the salt water to be most gross because a ship will bear a greater burden on the sea than on the fresh water and an egg sink in this that swimmeth on the other.[7] But he may easily be answered by the quantity of room and abundance of waters in the sea, whereby it becometh of more force to sustain such vessels as are committed to the same, and whereunto the greatest rivers (God wot) are nothing comparable. I would here make mention of sundry bridges placed over this noble stream, of which that of London is most chiefly to be commended, for it is in manner a continual street, well replenished with large and stately houses on both sides and situate upon twenty arches, whereof each one is made of excellent free squared stone, every of them being three-score foot in height and full twenty in distance one from another, as I have often viewed.[8]

In like manner I could entreat of the infinite number of swans daily to be seen upon this river, the two thousand wherries and small boats, whereby three thousand poor watermen are maintained[9] through the carriage and recarriage of such persons as pass or repass from time to time upon the same, beside those huge tide boats, tilt boats,[10] and barges which either carry passengers or bring necessary provision from all quarters of Oxfordshire, Berkshire, Buckinghamshire, Bedfordshire, Hertfordshire, Middlesex, Essex, Surrey, and Kent unto the city of London. But forsomuch as these things are to be repeated again in the particular description of London annexed to his card,[11] I surcease at this time to speak any more of them here, as not lingering but hasting to perform my promise made even now, not yet forgotten, and in performance whereof I think it best to resume the description of this noble river again into my hands, and in adding whatsoever is before omitted, to deliver a full and perfect demonstration of his course. . . .

---

[7] *Meteorologica*, II, iii, 359.

[8] Yet the description of London Bridge is actually based on Stow's (at the beginning of his *Summary of English Chronicles*, 1575), who in turn borrowed it from Polydore Vergil (p. 3). Polydore, however, specifies twenty piers rather than arches.

[9] "Whose gains come in most plentifully in the termtime."—*H.*

[10] *Tide boats:* boats which travel with the tide; *tilt boats:* boats having a tilt or awning.

[11] See p. 215, n. 37.

CHAPTER XVI

Of Such Falls of Waters as Join with
the Sea between Humber and the Thames

. . . THERE is a pretty water that beginneth near unto Gwinbach, or Wimbish, Church in Essex,[1] a town of old and yet belonging to the Fitzwalters, taking name of *gwin*, which is beautiful or fair, and *bache*, that signifieth a wood, and not without cause, sith not only the hills on each side of the said rillet but all the whole parish hath sometime abounded in woods; but now in manner they are utterly decayed, as the like commodity is everywhere, not only through excessive building for pleasure more than profit, which is contrary to the ancient end of building, but also for more increase of pasture and commodity to the lords of the soil through their sales of that emolument, whereby the poor tenants are enforced to buy their fuel and yet have their rents in triple manner enhanced. This said brook runneth directly from thence unto Radwinter, now a parcel of Your Lordship's possessions in those parts, descended from the Chamberlains, who were some-time chief owners of the same. By the way also it is increased with sundry pretty springs, of which Pantwell is the chief (whereof some think the whole brook to be named Pant) and which (to say the truth) hath many a leasing [lie] fathered on the same. Certes by the report of common fame it hath been a pretty water and of such quantity that boats have come in time past from Beeleigh Abbey beside Maldon unto the moors in Rad-winter for corn. I have heard also that an anchor was found there near to a red willow, when the watercourses by act of Parliament were surveyed and reformed throughout England, which maketh not a little with the aforesaid relation.

But this is strangest of all, that a lord sometime of Wimbish (surnamed "The Great Eater" because he would break his fast

[1] This concluding passage from Harrison's comprehensive catalogue of English streams is included here as one part of his topographical survey that depends on his own travels and experience, although some of the details are clearly drawn from Saxton's map of Essex.

with a whole calf and find no bones therein, as the fable goeth), falling at contention with the Lord John of Radwinter, could work him none other injury but by stopping up the head of Pantwell to put by the use of a mill which stood by the church of Radwinter and was served by that brook abundantly. Certes I know the place where the mill stood, and some posts thereof do yet remain. But see the malice of mankind, whereby one becometh a wolf unto the other in their mischievous moods. For when the lord saw his mill to be so spoiled, he in revenge of his loss brake the neck of his adversary, when he was going to horseback, as the constant report affirmeth. For the lord of Radwinter, holding a parcel of his manor of Radwinter Hall of the Fitzwalters, his son was to hold his stirrup at certain times when he should demand the same. Showing himself therefore pressed on a time to do his said service, as the Fitzwalter was ready to lift his leg over the saddle, he by putting back his foot gave him such a thrust that he fell backward and brake his neck, whereupon ensued great trouble, till the matter was taken up by public authority and that servile office converted into a pound of pepper, which is truly paid to this day.

But to leave these impertinent discourses and return again to the springs whereby our Pant, or Gwin, is increased. There is likewise another in a pasture belonging to the Grange, now in possession of William Bird, Esquire, who holdeth the same in the right of his wife, but in time past belonging to Tilty Abbey. The third cometh out of the yard of one of Your Lordship's manors there, called Radwinter Hall. The fourth from John Cockswet's house, named the Rotherwell, which, running under Rothers Bridge, meeteth with the Gwin, or Pant, on the northwest end of Ferrant's Mead, southeast of Radwinter Church, whereof I have the charge by Your Honor's favorable preferment.

I might take occasion to speak of another rill which falleth into the Rother from Bendyshe Hall, but because it is for the most part dry in summer I pass it over. Yet I will not omit to speak also of the manor, which was the chief lordship sometime of a parish or hamlet called Bendyshes, now worn out of knowledge and united partly to Radwinter and partly to Ashdon. It belonged first to the Bendyshes, gentlemen of a very ancient house yet extant, of which one laying the said manor to mortgage to the monks of Faversham, at such time as King Edward the Third went to the siege of Calais, thereby to furnish himself the better toward the service of his prince, it came to pass that he stayed longer beyond the sea than he supposed. Whereupon he came before his day to confer with his creditors, who, commending his care to come out of debt, willed him in friendly manner not to suspect any hard dealing on their behalfs, considering his business in service of the King was of itself cause sufficient to excuse his delay of payment upon the day assigned. Hereupon he went over again unto the siege of Calais. But when the day came the monks for all this made seizure of the manor and held it continually without any further recompense, mauger all the friendship that the aforesaid Bendyshe could make. The said gentleman also took this cozening part in such choler that he wrote a note yet to be seen among his evidences, whereby he admonisheth his posterity to beware how they trust either knave monk or knave friar, as one of the name and descended from him by lineal descent hath more than once informed me. Now to resume our springs that meet and join with our Pant.

The next is named Froshwell [Freshwell]. And of this spring doth the whole hundred bear the name, and after this confluence the river itself whereunto it falleth (from by north), so far as I remember. Certes all these, saving the first and second, are within Your Lordship's town aforesaid. The stream, therefore, running from hence (and now, as I said, called Froshwell, of *frosc*, which signifieth a frog) hasteth immediately unto Old [Great] Sampford, then through New [Little] Sampford Park, and afterward with full stream (receiving by the way the Finch Brook that cometh through Finchingfield) to Shalford, Bocking, Stisted, Paswiic [Pattiswick], and so to Blackwater, where the name of Froshwell ceaseth, the water being from henceforth (as I hear) commonly called Blackwater until it come to Maldon, where it falleth into the salt arm of the sea that beateth upon the town, and which of some (except I be deceived) is called also Pant; and so much the rather I make this conjecture for that Ithancester stood somewhere upon the banks thereof and in the hundred of Dansey [Dengie], whose ruins (as they say) also are swallowed up by the said stream,[2] which cannot be verified in our

[2] *Ithancester:* a Roman town at Bradwell-on-Sea, on the south bank of the Blackwater.

river that runneth from Pantwell, which at the mouth and fall into the great current exceedeth not (to my conjecture) above one hundred foot. But to return to our Pant, alias the Gwin. From Blackwater it goeth to Coggeshall, Easterford [Kelvedon], Braxted, and Wickham [Bishops], where it meeteth with the Barus [Brain], and so going together as one they descend to Heybridge and finally into the salt water above Maldon and at hand, as is aforesaid. As for the Barus, it riseth in a stately park of Essex called Bardfield, belonging to Sir Thomas Wroth whilst he lived, who hath it to him and his heirs males forever from the Crown.[3] Being risen, it hasteth directly to Old [Great] Saling, Braintree, crossing a rillet by the way coming from Rayne, Black Notley, White Notley, Faulkbourne, Witham, and falleth into the Blackwater beneath Braxted on the south.

Beside this, the said Pant, or Gwin, receiveth the Chelm, or Chelmer, which ariseth also in Wimbish aforesaid, where it hath two heads, of which the one is not far from Broadoaks (where Master Thomas Wiseman, Esquire, dwelleth), the other nigh unto a farm called Highams in the same parish, and joining ere long in one channel they hie them toward Thaxted under Proud's Bridge, meeting in the way with a rill coming from Boyton End, whereby it is somewhat increased. Being past Thaxted it goeth by Tilty and soon after receiveth one rill which riseth on the north side of Lindsell and falleth into the Chelmer by northeast at Tilty aforesaid, and another coming from southwest,[4] rising southeast from Lindsell, at Much [Great] Easton. From thence then holding on still with the course, it goeth to Canfield the More [Great Canfield], Dunmow, Little Dunmow, Felstead, Leighs, both Walthams, Springfield, and so to Chelmsford. Here upon the south side I find the issue of a water that riseth five miles (or thereabouts) south and by west of the said town, from whence it goeth to Mountnessing, Buttsbury (there receiving a rill from by west), to Ingatestone, Margaretting, Widford Bridge, Writtle Bridge, and so to Chelmsford (crossing also the second water that descendeth from Roxford [Roxwell] southwest of Writtle by the way), whereof let this suffice.

From hence the Chelmer goeth directly toward Maldon by

---

[3] *Sir Thomas Wroth* (1516-1573): Tudor statesman who was granted the manor of Bardfield in 1550.

[4] *Southwest:* in error for northeast.

Baddow, Ulting, Woodham Walter, Beeleigh, and so to Blackwater northwest of Maldon, receiving nevertheless ere it come fully thither a beck also that goeth from Leighs Park to Little Leighs, Great Leighs, Hatfield Peverel, Ulting, and so into Blackwater (whereof I spake before), as Maldon Stream doth a rill from by south over against St. Osyth [5] and also another by Bradwell. After which the said stream, growing also to be very great, passeth by the Tolleshunts, Tollesbury, and so forth into the main sea near unto Mersea, between which fall and the place where Salute [Salcott] Water entereth into the land, Plautius abode the coming of Claudius sometime into Britain, when he, being hardly beset, did send unto him for aid and speedy succor, who also, being come, did not only rescue his legate but in like manner won Colchester and put it to the spoil, if it be Camulodunum.[6]

The Burne [Burnham, Crouch] riseth somewhere about Runwell and thence goeth to Hull Bridge, South Fambridge, Kirkeshot [Creeksea] Ferry, and so to Foulness. And as this is the short course of that river, so it brancheth and the south arm thereof receiveth a water coming from Hawkwell to Great Stambridge, and beneath Paglesham doth meet by south with the said arm and so finish up his course, as we do our voyage also about the coast of England.

Thus have I finished the description of such rivers and streams as fall into the ocean according to my purpose, although not in so precise an order and manner of handling as I might if information promised had been accordingly performed, or others would if they had taken the like in hand. But this will I say of that which is here done, that from the Solway by west, which parteth England and Scotland on that side, to the Tweed, which separateth the said kingdoms on the east, if you go backward, contrary to the course of my description, you shall find it so exact as, beside a very few by-rivers, you shall not need to use any further advice for the finding and falls of the aforesaid streams. For such hath been my help of Master Seckford's cards [7] and conference with other men about these that I dare pronounce them to be perfect and exact. Furthermore this I have also to

[5] *St. Osyth:* for Osea Island in the Blackwater estuary.
[6] Dio Cassius, *Roman History*, LX, xxi, but the sack of Colchester occurred later, under the governorship of Suetonius Paulinus.   [7] See pp. 219–220, n. 47.

remember, that in the courses of our streams I regard not so much to name the very town or church as the limits of the parish. And therefore, if I say it goeth by such a town, I think my duty discharged if I hit upon any part or parcel of the parish. This also hath not a little troubled me, I mean the evil writing of the names of many towns and villages, of which I have noted some one man in the description of a river to write one town two or three manner of ways, whereby I was enforced to choose one (at adventure most commonly) that seemed the likeliest to be sound in mine opinion and judgment.

Finally, whereas I minded to set down an especial chapter of ports and creeks lying on each coast of the English part of this isle, and had provided the same in such wise as I judged most convenient, it came to pass that the greater part of my labor was taken from me by stealth, and therefore, as discouraged to meddle with that argument, I would have given over to set down anything therefor at all, and so much the rather for that I see it may prove a spur unto further mischief as things come to pass in these days. Nevertheless, because a little thereof is passed in the beginning of the book, I will set down that parcel thereof which remaineth, leaving the supply of the rest either to myself hereafter (if I may come by it) or to some other that can better perform the same.[8]

CHAPTER XVIII

Of the Air, Soil, and Commodities of This Island

THE air (for the most part) throughout the island is such as, by reason in manner of continual clouds, is reputed to be gross and

---

[8] The following chapter, in which Harrison again complains of "being too-too much abused by some that have bereft me of my notes in this behalf," lists briefly only the ports on the eastern and southeastern coasts, concluding, "So many shires only are left unto me at this time, wherefore of force I must abruptly leave off to deal any further with the rest, whose knowledge I am right sure would have been profitable, and for the which I hoped to have reaped great thanks at the hands of such seafaring men as should have had use hereof."

nothing so pleasant as that is of the main. Howbeit, as they which affirm these things have only respect to the impediment or hindrance of the sunbeams by the interposition of the clouds and oft engrossed air, so experience teacheth us that it is no less pure, wholesome, and commodious than is that of other countries, and (as Caesar himself hereto addeth) much more temperate in summer than that of the Gauls, from whom he adventured hither.[1] Neither is there anything found in the air of our region that is not usually seen amongst other nations lying beyond the seas. Wherefore we must needs confess that the situation of our island (for benefit of the heavens) is nothing inferior to that of any country of the main, wheresoever it lie under the open firmament. And this Plutarch knew full well, who affirmeth a part of the Elysian Fields to be found in Britain and the isles that are situate about it in the ocean.[2]

The soil of Britain is such as, by the testimonies and reports both of the old and new writers and experience also of such as now inhabit the same, is very fruitful and such indeed as bringeth forth many commodities whereof other countries have need, and yet itself (if fond niceness were abolished) needless of those that are daily brought from other places. Nevertheless, it is more inclined to feeding and grazing than profitable for tillage and bearing of corn, by reason whereof the country is wonderfully replenished with neat and all kind of cattle, and such store is there also of the same in every place that the fourth part of the land is scarcely manured [cultivated] for the provision and maintenance of grain. Certes this fruitfulness was not unknown unto the Britons long before Caesar's time, which was the cause wherefore our predecessors living in those days in manner neglected tillage and lived by feeding and grazing only. The graziers themselves also then dwelled in movable villages by companies, whose custom was to divide the ground amongst them and each one not to depart from the place where his lot lay (a thing much like to the Irish creaght)[3] till by eating up of the country about him he was enforced to remove further and seek for better pasture. And this was the British custom (as I learn) at first.

[1] *Gallic War*, V, xii.
[2] *Life of Sertorius*, viii, although the "Atlantic islands" of the passage are dubiously British.
[3] *Creaght:* a nomadic herd of cattle.

It hath been commonly reported that the ground of Wales is neither so fruitful as that of England, neither the soil of Scotland so bountiful as that of Wales, which is true for corn and for the most part; otherwise, there is so good ground in some parts of Wales as is in England, albeit the best of Scotland be scarcely comparable to the mean of either of both. Howbeit, as the bounty of the Scottish doth fail in some respect, so doth it surmount in other, God and Nature having not appointed all countries to yield forth like commodities.

But where our ground is not so good as we would wish, we have (if need be) sufficient help to cherish our ground withal and to make it more fruitful. For beside the compest that is carried out of the husbandmen's yards, ditches, ponds, dovehouses, or cities and great towns, we have with us a kind of white marl, which is of so great force that if it be cast over a piece of land but once in threescore years it shall not need of any further compesting. Hereof also doth Pliny speak (*lib.* 17, *cap.* 6, 7, 8 [iv]), where he affirmeth that our marl endureth upon the earth by the space of fourscore years, insomuch that it is laid upon the same but once in a man's life, whereby the owner shall not need to travail twice in procuring to commend [4] and better his soil. He calleth it *marga*, and, making diverse kinds thereof, he finally commendeth ours and that of France above all other, which lieth sometime a hundred foot deep, and far better than the scattering of chalk upon the same, as the Hedui [Aedui] and Pictones did in his time or as some of our days also do practice; albeit divers do like better to cast on lime, but it will not so long endure, as I have heard reported.

There are also in this island great plenty of fresh rivers and streams, as you have heard already, and these thoroughly fraught with all kinds of delicate fish accustomed to be found in rivers. The whole isle likewise is very full of hills, of which some (though not very many) are of exceeding height, and divers extending themselves very far from the beginning, as we may see by Shooter's Hill, which, rising east of London and not far from the Thames, runneth along the south side of the island westward until it come to Cornwall. Like unto these also are the Crowdon Hills, which, though under diverse names (as also the other),

---

[4] *Commend:* apparently a coinage, from "mend," with an intensive prefix.

from The Peak do run into the borders of Scotland. What should I speak of the Cheviot Hills, which reach twenty miles in length? [5] of the Black Mountains in Wales, which go from [blank] to [blank] miles at the least in length? [6] of the Clee Hills in Shropshire, which come within four miles of Ludlow and are divided from some part of Worcester by the Teme? [7] of the Grames [Grampians] in Scotland, and of our Chiltern, which are eighteen miles at the least from one end of them, which reach from Henley in Oxfordshire to Dunstable in Bedfordshire, and are very well replenished with wood and corn? [8] notwithstanding that the most part yield a sweet short grass, profitable for sheep. Wherein, albeit they of Scotland do somewhat come behind us, yet their outward defect is inwardly recompensed not only with plenty of quarries (and those of sundry kinds of marble, hard stone, and fine alabaster) but also rich mines of metal, as shall be showed hereafter.

In this island likewise the winds are commonly more strong and fierce than in any other places of the main, which Cardan also espied,[9] and that is often seen upon the naked hills not guarded with trees to bear and keep it off. That grievous inconvenience also enforceth our nobility, gentry, and commonalty to build their houses in the valleys, leaving the high grounds unto their corn and cattle, lest the cold and stormy blasts of winter should breed them greater annoyance; whereas in other regions each one desireth to set his house aloft on the hill, not only to be seen afar off and cast forth his beams of stately and curious workmanship into every quarter of the country, but also (in hot habitations) for coldness' sake of the air, sith the heat is never so vehement on the hilltop as in the valley, because the reverberation of the sunbeams either reacheth not so far as the highest or else becometh not so strong as when it is reflected upon the lower soil.

[5] Leland, *Itinerary* (ed. Smith, V, 67).

[6] Harrison left the distances blank. In Leland (III, 104) the passage reads, "Among all the mountains of that shire [Brecknock] Black Mountain is most famous, for he stretcheth, as I have learned, his roots on one side within a four or five miles of Monmouth and on the other side as near to Carmarthen."

[7] Leland (V, 189).

[8] Leland (V, 7).

[9] *Problemata naturalium*, I, 18.

But to leave our buildings unto the purposed place (which notwithstanding have very much increased, I mean, for curiosity and cost, in England, Wales, and Scotland within these few years) and to return to the soil again. Certainly it is even now in these our days grown to be much more fruitful than it hath been in times past. The cause is for that our countrymen are grown to be more painful, skillful, and careful through recompense of gain than heretofore they have been, insomuch that my *synchroni*, or timefellows [contemporaries], can reap at this present great commodity in a little room; whereas of late years a great compass hath yielded but small profit, and this only through the idle and negligent occupation of such as daily manured and had the same in occupying. I might set down examples of these things out of all the parts of this island, that is to say, many of England, more out of Scotland, but most of all out of Wales, in which two last rehearsed very little other food and livelihood was wont to be looked for (beside flesh) more than the soil of itself and the cow gave; the people in the meantime living idly, dissolutely, and by picking [robbing] and stealing one from another. All which vices are now (for the most part) relinquished, so that each nation manureth her own, with triple commodity to that it was beforetime.

The pasture of this island is according to the nature and bounty of the soil, whereby in most places it is plentiful, very fine, battable [fertile], and such as either fatteth our cattle with speed or yieldeth great abundance of milk and cream, whereof the yellowest butter and finest cheese are made. But where the blue clay aboundeth (which hardly drinketh up the winter's water in long season), there the grass is speary, rough, and very apt for bushes, by which occasion it cometh nothing so profitable unto the owner as the other.

The best pasture ground of all England is in Wales, and of all the pasture in Wales that of Cardigan is the chief. I speak of the same which is to be found in the mountains there, where the hundredth part of the grass growing is not eaten but suffered to rot on the ground, whereby the soil becometh matted and divers bogs and quick-moors made withal in long continuance, because all the cattle in the country are not able to eat it down.[10] If it be

---

[10] Leland (III, 123). *Quick-moors:* so Leland, for quickmires, quagmires.

to be accounted good soil on which a man may lay a wand overnight and on the morrow find it hidden and overgrown with
grass, it is not hard to find plenty thereof in many places of this
land. Nevertheless, such is the fruitfulness of the aforesaid county
that it far surmounteth this proportion, whereby it may be compared for battableness with Italy, which in my time is called the
paradise of the world, although by reason of the wickedness of
such as dwell therein it may be called the sink and drain of hell;
so that whereas they were wont to say of us that our land is good
but our people evil, they did but only speak it, whereas we know
by experience that the soil of Italy is a noble soil but the dwellers
therein far off from any virtue or goodness.

Our meadows are either bottoms (whereof we have great store
and those very large, because our soil is hilly) or else such as we
call land meads [11] and borrowed from the best and fattest pastur-
ages. The first of them are yearly and often overflown by the
rising of such streams as pass through the same or violent falls of
land waters [12] that descend from the hills about them. The other
are seldom or never overflown, and that is the cause wherefore
their grass is shorter than that of the bottoms, and yet is it far
more fine, wholesome, and battable [fattening], sith the hay of
our low meadows is not only full of sandy cinder, which breedeth sundry diseases in our cattle, but also more rowty, foggy, [13]
and full of flags, and therefore not so profitable for stover [feed]
and forage as the higher meads be. The difference furthermore
in their commodities is great, for whereas in our land meadows
we have not often above one good load of hay or peradventure
a little more in an acre of ground (I use the word *carrucata* or
carruca, which is a wainload and, as I remember, used by Pliny,
lib. 33, *cap.* 11 [xlix]), in low meadows we have sometimes three
but commonly two or upward, as experience hath oft confirmed.

Of such as are twice mowed I speak not, sith their later math
[mowing] is not so wholesome for cattle as the first, although
in the mouth more pleasant for the time, for thereby they become
oftentimes to be rotten or to increase so fast in blood that the
garget and other diseases do consume many of them before the

[11] *Land meads:* tracts of meadow land.
[12] *Land waters:* waters flowing through or over land, such as springs and
runoff.
[13] *Rowty:* rank; *foggy:* coarse.

owners can seek out any remedy, by phlebotomy or otherwise. Some superstitious fools suppose that they which die of the garget are ridden with the nightmare,[14] and therefore they hang up stones which naturally have holes in them and must be found unlooked for, as if such a stone were an apt cockshot [15] for the devil to run through and solace himself withal, whilst the cattle go scot-free and are not molested by him. But if I should set down but half the toys that superstition hath brought into our husbandmen's heads in this and other behalfs, it would ask a greater volume than is convenient for such a purpose, wherefore it shall suffice to have said thus much of these things.

The yield of our corn ground is also much after this rate following. Throughout the land (if you please to make an estimate thereof by the acre) in mean and indifferent years, wherein each acre of rye or wheat, well tilled and dressed, will yield commonly sixteen or twenty bushels, an acre of barley six-and-thirty bushels, of oats and suchlike four or five quarters, which proportion is notwithstanding oft abated toward the North, as it is oftentimes surmounted in the South. Of mixed corn, as peason and beans sown together, tares and oats (which they call bullimong), rye and wheat (named maslin), here is no place to speak, yet their yield is nevertheless much after this proportion, as I have often marked. And yet is not this, our great foison [rich harvest], comparable to that of hotter countries of the main. But of all that ever I read, the increase which Eldad Danius writeth of in his *De imperio Judaeorum in Aethiopia* surmounteth, where he saith that in the field near to the Sabbatic River, called in old time Goshen, the ground is so fertile that every grain of barley growing doth yield an hundred kernels at the least unto the owner.[16]

Of late years, also, we have found and taken up a great trade in planting of hops, whereof our moory hitherto and unprofitable grounds do yield such plenty and increase that there are few

[14] *Nightmare:* a female monster, fabled to press upon and suffocate people and animals at night.

[15] *Cockshot:* cockshy, a target.

[16] *Eldad Danius:* Eldad Ben Mahli, the Danite, Jewish traveler and philologist of the ninth century A.D., to whom was attributed the account of the Ten Tribes from which Harrison is citing (published in a Latin translation at Paris, 1563, chap. v). *Sabbatic:* the Sabbation, or Sambation, a legendary river which, according to Eldad, protected the Lost Tribes.

farmers or occupiers in the country which have not gardens and hops growing of their own, and those far better than do come from Flanders unto us. Certes the corruptions used by the Flemings and forgery daily practiced in this kind of ware gave us occasion to plant them here at home, so that now we may spare and send many over unto them. And this I know by experience, that some one man, by conversion of his moory grounds into hopyards, whereof before he had no commodity, doth raise yearly by so little as twelve acres in compass two hundred marks, all charges borne toward the maintenance of his family. Which industry God continue! though some secret friends of Flemings let not to exclaim against this commodity as a spoil of wood, by reason of the poles, which nevertheless after three years do also come to the fire and spare their other fuel.

The cattle which we breed are commonly such as for greatness of bone, sweetness of flesh, and other benefits to be reaped by the same give place unto none other, as may appear first by our oxen, whose largeness, height, weight, tallow, hides, and horns are such as none of any other nation do commonly or may easily exceed them. Our sheep likewise, for good taste of flesh, quantity of limbs, fineness of fleece, caused by their hardness of pasturage, and abundance of increase (for in many places they bring forth two or three at an eaning),[17] give no place unto any, more than do our goats, who in like sort do follow the same order, and our deer come not behind. As for our conies, I have seen them so fat in some soils, especially about Meall and Disnege, that the grease of one, being weighed, hath peised very near six or seven ounces. All which benefits we first refer to the grace and goodness of God and next of all unto the bounty of our soil, which He hath endued with so notable and commodious fruitfulness.

But as I mean to entreat of these things more largely hereafter, so will I touch in this place one benefit which our nation wanteth, and that is wine, the fault whereof is not in our soil but the negligence of our countrymen (especially of the south parts), who do not inure the same to this commodity, and which by reason of long discontinuance is now become unapt to bear any grapes almost for pleasure and shadow, much less, then, the plain fields or several vineyards for advantage and commodity. Yet of

[17] *Eaning:* yeaning, bringing forth young.

late time some have assayed to deal for wine, as to Your Lordship also is right well known. But sith that liquor, when it cometh to the drinking, hath been found more hard than that which is brought from beyond the sea, and the cost of planting and keeping thereof so chargeable that they may buy it far better cheap from other countries, they have given over their enterprises, without any consideration that as in all other things so neither the ground itself in the beginning nor success of their travail can answer their expectation at the first, until such time as the soil be brought as it were into acquaintance with this commodity, and that provision may be made for the more easiness of charge to be employed upon the same.

If it be true that where wine doth last and endure well there it will grow no worse, I muse not a little wherefore the planting of vines should be neglected in England. That this liquor might have grown in this island heretofore, first the charter that Probus the Emperor gave equally to us, the Gauls, and Spaniards is one sufficient testimony.[18] And that it did grow here, beside the testimony of Bede (*lib.* 1, *cap.* 1),[19] the old notes of tithes for wine that yet remain in the accounts of some parsons and vicars in Kent and elsewhere, besides the records of sundry suits commenced in divers ecclesiastical courts, both in Kent, Surrey, etc., also the enclosed parcels almost in every abbey yet called the vineyards, may be a notable witness, as also the plot which we now call East Smithfield in London, given by Canute, sometime King of this land, with other soil thereabout unto certain of his knights, with the liberty of a guild, which thereof was called Knighten Guild. The truth is (saith John Stow, our countryman and diligent travailer in the old estate of this my native city) that it is now named Portsoken Ward and given in time past to the religious house within Aldgate. Howbeit, first Otwell, then Archovell, Otto, and finally Geoffrey, Earl of Essex, constables of the Tower of London, withheld that portion from the said house until the reign of King Stephen and thereof made a vineyard to their great commodity and lucre.[20] The Isle of Ely also was in the first times of the Normans called *Le Ile des vignes*. And good

---

[18] *Scriptores historiae Augustae*, "Probus," xviii, 8.

[19] At the beginning of his *Ecclesiastical History* Bede mentions that vines are found in some places in England.

[20] Stow, *The Chronicles of England* (1580), under 1115. See also his *Survey of London* (ed. Kingsford, I, 120-123).

record appeareth that the bishop there had yearly three or four tun at the least given him *nomine decimae*,[21] beside whatsoever oversum of the liquor did accrue to him by leases and other escheats, whereof also I have seen mention. Wherefore our soil is not to be blamed, as though our nights were so exceeding short that in August and September the moon, which is lady of moisture and chief ripener of this liquor, cannot in any wise shine long enough upon the same, a very mere toy and fable right worthy to be suppressed, because experience convinceth [confutes] the upholders thereof, even in the Rhenish wines.

The time hath been also that woad—wherewith our countrymen dyed their faces (as Caesar saith),[22] that they might seem terrible to their enemies in the field, and also women and their daughters-in-law did stain their bodies and go naked in that pickle to the sacrifices of their gods, coveting to resemble therein the Ethiopians, as Pliny saith (*lib. 22, cap.* 1 [ii])—and also madder have been (next unto our tin and wools) the chief commodities and merchandise of this realm. I find also that rape oil hath been made within this land. But now our soil either will not or at the leastwise may not bear either woad or madder; I say not that the ground is not able so to do but that we are negligent, afraid of the pilling [exhausting] of our grounds and careless of our own profit, as men rather willing to buy the same of others than take any pain to plant them here at home. The like I may say of flax, which by law ought to be sown in every country town in England, more or less,[23] but I see no success of that good and wholesome law, sith it is rather contemptuously rejected than otherwise dutifully kept in any place of England.

Some say that our great number of laws do breed a general negligence and contempt of all good order, because we have so many that no subject can live without the transgression of some of them, and that the often alteration of our ordinances doth much harm in this respect, which (after Aristotle) doth seem to carry some reason withal, for, as Cornelius Gallus hath:

Eventus varios res nova semper habet.[24]

[21] *Nomine decimae:* as tithes.   [22] *Gallic War,* V, xiv.
[23] As part of a statute "for the maintenance of the navy" (5 Eliz., c. 5), every owner in certain areas of sixty acres of tillable land was required to plant one acre with flax.
[24] "Eleg. 2."—*H.* "A new lawsuit always produces different results." *Gaius Cornelius Gallus* (?69–26 B.C.): Roman poet and politician.

But very many let not to affirm that the greedy corruption of the promoters on the one side, facility in dispensing with good laws and first breach of the same in the lawmakers and superiors, and private respects [25] of their establishment on the other are the greatest causes why the inferiors regard no good order, being always so ready to offend without any faculty [authority] one way as they are otherwise to presume upon the examples of their betters when any hold is to be taken.[26] But as in these things I have no skill, so I wish that fewer licenses for the private commodity but of a few were granted (not that thereby I deny the maintenance of the prerogative royal, but rather would with all my heart that it might be yet more honorably increased), and that everyone which by feed friendship (or otherwise) doth attempt to procure aught from the prince [27] that may profit but few and prove hurtful to many might be at open assizes and sessions denounced enemy to his country and common wealth of the land.

Glass also hath been made here in great plenty before and in the time of the Romans, and the said stuff also, beside fine scissors, shears, collars of gold and silver for women's necks, cruses and cups of amber, were a parcel of the tribute which Augustus in his days laid upon this island. In like sort he charged the Britons with certain implements and vessels of ivory (as Strabo saith).[28] Whereby it appeareth that in old time our countrymen were far more industrious and painful in the use and application of the benefits of their country than either after the coming of the Saxons or Normans, in which they gave themselves more to idleness and following of the wars.

If it were requisite that I should speak of the sundry kinds of mold, as the cledgy or clay, whereof are diverse sorts (red, blue, black, and white), also the red or white sandy, the loamy, rosilly,[29] gravelly, chalky, or black, I could say that there are so many diverse veins in Britain as elsewhere in any quarter of like quantity in the world. Howbeit, this I must needs confess, that the

---

[25] *Private respects:* discrimination, partiality.

[26] *"Principes longe magis exemplo quam culpa peccare."*—H. "Rulers usually do much more harm by their example than by their sin."

[27] Harrison prudently dropped a 1577 dilation, "the prince (who is not acquainted with the bottom of the estate of common things)."

[28] A misreading of the *Geography* (IV, v, 3), where Strabo mentions a tax on ivory imported into Britain.

[29] *Rosilly:* a soil intermediate between sand and clay.

sandy and cledgy do bear great sway, but the clay most of all, as hath been and yet is always seen and felt through plenty and dearth of corn. For if this latter (I mean the clay) do yield her full increase (which it doth commonly in dry years for wheat), then is there general plenty, whereas if it fail, then have we scarcity, according to the old rude verse set down of England but to be understood of the whole island, as experience doth confirm:

> When the sand doth serve the clay,
> Then may we sing wellaway;
> But when the clay doth serve the sand,
> Then is it merry with England.

I might here entreat of the famous valleys in England, of which one is called the Vale of White Horse, another of Evesham, commonly taken for the granary of Worcestershire, the third of Aylesbury, that goeth by Thame, the roots of Chiltern Hills, to Dunstable, Newport Pagnell, Stony Stratford, Buckingham, Burston Park, etc.[30] Likewise of the fourth of Whitehart or Blackmoor in Dorsetshire. The fifth of Ringdale, or Renidale, corruptly called Ringtail, that lieth (as mine author saith) upon the edge of Essex and Cambridgeshire, and also the Marshwood Vale; but forsomuch as I know not well their several limits, I give over to go any further in their description.

In like sort it should not be amiss to speak of our fens, although our country be not so full of this kind of soil as the parties beyond the seas, to wit, Narbonne, etc., and thereto of other pleasant bottoms, the which are not only endued with excellent rivers and great store of corn and fine fodder for neat and horses in time of the year (whereby they are exceeding beneficial unto their owners), but also of no small compass and quantity in ground. For some of our fens are well known to be either of 10, 12, 16, 20, or 30 miles in length, that of the Girwies yet passing all the rest, which is full 60 (as I have often read).[31] Wherein

---

[30] Leland (II, 110-111).

[31] "The Girwies [Gyrwas], which inhabit in the fens (for *gyr* in the old Saxon speech doth signify deep fens and marshes), and these beginning at Peterborough eastward, extend themselves by the space of threescore miles and more, as Hugh of Peterborough writeth" (*Des. Brit.*, 1587, p. 101; *The Chronicle of Hugh Candidus*, ed. W. T. Mellows, pp. 4-5). The following description of Ely and its privileges comes from the same passage in Hugh's *Chronicle*.

also Ely the famous isle standeth, which is seven miles every way and whereunto there is no access but by three causeys,[32] whose inhabitants in like sort by an old privilege may take wood, sedge, turf, etc., to burn, likewise hay for their cattle and thatch for their houses of custom, and each occupier in his appointed quantity throughout the isle; albeit that covetousness hath now begun somewhat to abridge this large benevolence and commodity, as well in the said isle as most other places of this land.

Finally, I might discourse in like order of the large commons laid out heretofore by the lords of the soils for the benefit of such poor as inhabit within the compass of their manors. But as the true intent of the givers is now in most places defrauded, insomuch that not the poor tenants inhabiting upon the same but their landlords have all the commodity and gain, so the tractation of them belongeth rather to the second book. Wherefore I mean not at this present to deal withal, but reserve the same wholly unto the due place whilst I go forward with the rest, setting down nevertheless by the way a general commendation of the whole island, which I find in an ancient monument,[33] much unto this effect:

> *Illa quidem longe celebris splendore, beata*
> *Glebis, lacte, favis, supereminet insula cunctis,*
> *Quas regit ille Deus, spumanti cuius ab ore*
> *Profluit oceanus, etc.*

and a little after:

> *Testis Lundonia ratibus, Wintonia Baccho,*
> *Herefordia grege, Worcestria, fruge redundans,*
> *Batha lacu, Salabyra feris, Cantuaria pisce,*
> *Eboraca sylvis, Excestria clara metallis,*
> *Norwicum Dacis hybernis, Cestria Gallis,*
> *Cicestrum Norwagenis, Dunelmia praepinguis,*
> *Testis Lincolnia gens infinita decore,*
> *Testis Eli formosa situ, Doncastria visu, etc.*[34]

[32] *Causeys:* causeways, raised ways over the fens.

[33] The "ancient monument" is Henry of Huntingdon, *History of the English* (ed. Arnold, Rolls Ser., LXXIV, 11).

[34] "This famous land, widely renowned for riches, blessed in fields, milk, and honey, exceeding all other islands over which God rules, whose seas flow past its foaming shore. . . . Witness London for ships, Winchester for wine, Hereford for the flock, Worcester abounding in grain, Bath for waters, Salisbury for game, Canterbury for fish, York for woods, Exeter famous for

CHAPTER XIX

*Of the Four Highways Sometime Made in Britain
by the Princes of This Island*

THERE are which, endeavoring to bring all things to their Saxon original, do affirm that this division of ways (whereof we now entreat) should appertain unto such princes of that nation as reigned here since the Romans gave us over, and hereupon they infer that Watling Street was builded by one Wattle from the east unto the west. But how weak their conjectures are in this behalf the antiquity of these streets itself shall easily declare, whereof some parcels, after a sort, are also set down by Antoninus [1] and those that have written of the several journeys from hence to Rome, although peradventure not in so direct an order as they were at the first established. For my part, if it were not that I desire to be short in this behalf, I could with such notes as I have already collected for that purpose make a large confutation of divers of their opinions concerning these passages, and thereby rather ascribe the original of these ways to the Romans than either the British or Saxon princes. But sith I have spent more time in the tractation of the rivers than was allotted unto me, and that I see great cause (notwithstanding my late alleged scruple) wherefore I should hold with our Galfride [2] before any other, I will omit at this time to discourse of these things as I would and say what I may for the better knowledge of their courses, proceeding therein as followeth.

---

metals." The following two lines are clearly corrupt; in the MS printed in the Rolls Series they read, *Norvicium Dacis* [Danis?], *Hibernis Cestria, Gallis/ Cicestrum, Norwageniis Dunelma propinquans:* "Norwich is close to the Danes, Chester to the Irish, Chichester to the French, Durham to the Norwegians." Harrison's version concludes, "Witness Lincoln for its extremely handsome people, witness Ely for its beautiful location, Doncaster [Rochester in Rolls MS] for its appearance."

[1] In the Antonine Itinerary; see p. 205, n. 5.

[2] *Galfride:* Geoffrey of Monmouth, from whom Harrison derives the following account of Dunwallo Molmutius and Belline (II, xvii, and III, v; see pp. 163–164).

First of all I find that Dunwallo, King of Britain, about 483 years before the birth of Our Saviour Jesus Christ, seeing the subjects of his realm to be in sundry wise oppressed by thieves and robbers as they traveled to and fro, and being willing (so much as in him lay) to redress these inconveniences, caused his whole kingdom to be surveyed, and then, commanding four principal ways to be made, which should lead such as traveled into all parts thereof from sea to sea, he gave sundry large privileges unto the same, whereby they became safe and very much frequented. And as he had regard herein to the security of his subjects, so he made sharp laws grounded upon justice for the suppression of such wicked members as did offer violence to any traveler that should be met withal or found within the limits of those passages. How and by what parts of this island these ways were conveyed at the first, it is not so wholly left in memory but that some question is moved among the learned concerning their ancient courses. Howbeit, such is the shadow remaining hitherto of their extensions that, if not at this present perfectly, yet hereafter it is not unpossible but that they may be found out and left certain unto posterity.

It seemeth by Galfride that the said Dunwallo did limit out those ways by doles and marks [boundaries and limits], which being in short time altered by the avarice of such irreligious persons as dwelt near and encroached upon the same (a fault yet justly to be found almost in every place, even in the time of our most gracious and sovereign Lady Elizabeth, wherein the lords of the soils do unite their small occupying only to increase a greater proportion of rent; and therefore they either remove or give license to erect small tenements upon the highways' sides and commons, whereunto in truth they have no right and yet out of them also do raise a new commodity), and question moved for their bounds before Belline, his son, he, to avoid all further controversy that might from thenceforth ensue, caused the same to be paved with hard stone of eighteen foot in breadth, ten foot in depth, and in the bottom thereof huge flint stones also to be pitched, lest the earth in time should swallow up his workmanship and the higher ground overgrow their rising crests. He endued them also with larger privileges than before, protesting that if any man whosoever should presume to infringe his peace and violate the laws of his kingdom in any manner of wise near unto or upon those ways, he should suffer such punishment, without all hope to escape (by friendship or mercy), as by the statutes of this realm lately provided in those cases were due unto the offenders. The names of these four ways are the Fosse, the Guithelin,[3] or Watling, the Erming [Ermine], and the Icknield.

[In the 1577 edition Harrison, deriving his information largely from Leland's *Itinerary*, devoted the remainder of this chapter to tracing the routes of the Roman roads through England. In 1587 he added the following conclusion:]

Now to speak generally of our common highways through the English part of the isle (for of the rest I can say nothing), you shall understand that in the clay or cledgy soil they are often very deep and troublesome in the winter half. Wherefore, by authority of Parliament an order is taken for their yearly amendment,[4] whereby all sorts of the common people do employ their travail for six days in summer upon the same. And albeit that the intent of the statute is very profitable for the reparations of the decayed places, yet the rich do so cancel their portions and the poor so loiter in their labors that of all the six scarcely two good days' works are well performed and accomplished in a parish on these so necessary affairs.

Besides this, such as have land lying upon the sides of the ways do utterly neglect to ditch and scour their drains and watercourses, for better avoidance of the winter waters (except[5] it may be set off or cut from the meaning of the statute), whereby the streets do grow to be much more gulled[6] than before and thereby very noisome for such as travel by the same. Sometimes, also, and that very often, these days' works are not employed upon those ways that lead from market to market, but each surveyor amendeth such by-plots[7] and lanes as seem best for his own commodity and more easy passage unto his fields and pastures. And whereas in some places there is such want of stones as thereby the inhabitants are driven to seek them far off in other soils, the owners of the lands wherein those stones are to be had,

---

[3] *Guithelin:* a legendary British king; see p. 166.
[4] Harrison cites below the provisions of 5 Eliz., c. 13 and 18 Eliz., c. 10.
[5] *Except:* leaving out of account. Harrison seems to have in mind the vagueness of 5 Eliz., c. 13, which ordered the ditching to be done "from time to time."
[6] *Gulled:* channeled, rutted.   [7] *By-plots:* outlying tracts of land.

and which hitherto have given money to have them borne away, do now reap no small commodity by raising the same to excessive prices, whereby their neighbors are driven to grievous charges, which is another cause wherefore the meaning of that good law is very much defrauded.[8] Finally, this is another thing likewise to be considered of, that the trees and bushes growing by the streets' sides do not a little keep off the force of the sun in summer for drying up of the lanes. Wherefore, if order were taken that their boughs should continually be kept short and the bushes not suffered to spread so far into the narrow paths, that inconvenience would also be remedied and many a slough prove hard ground that yet is deep and hollow.

Of the daily encroaching of the covetous upon the highways, I speak not. But this I know by experience, that whereas some streets within these five-and-twenty years have been in most places 50 foot broad according to the law, whereby the traveler might either escape the thief or shift the mire or pass by the loaden cart without danger of himself and his horse, now they are brought unto 12 or 20 or 26 at the most, which is another cause also whereby the ways be the worse and many an honest man encumbered in his journey.[9] But what speak I of these things, whereof I do not think to hear a just redress because the error is so common and the benefit thereby so sweet and profitable to many, by such houses and cottages as are raised upon the same?

CHAPTER XX

Of the General Constitution of the Bodies of the Britons

SUCH as are bred in this island are men for the most part of a good complexion, tall of stature, strong in body, white of color,

---

[8] The statutes gave the supervisors the right to appropriate stone necessary for the maintenance of roads.

[9] A further glimpse of the difficulties of travel is provided by Harrison's mention of the "mill above Ramsey Bridge [near Harwich, in southeastern Essex], where I was once almost drowned (by reason of the ruinous bridge which leadeth over the stream, being there very great)" (*Des. Brit.*, 1587, p. 105).

and thereto of great boldness and courage in the wars. As for their general comeliness of person, the testimony of Gregory the Great at such time as he saw English captains [1] sold at Rome shall easily confirm what it is, which yet doth differ in sundry shires and soils, as also their proportion of members, as we may perceive between Herefordshire [2] and Essex men or Cambridgeshire and the Londoners for the one, and Pokington and Sedbury for the other, these latter being distinguished by their noses and heads, which commonly are greater there than in other places of the land.

As concerning the stomachs [bravery] also of our nation in the field, they have always been in sovereign admiration among foreign princes; for such hath been the estimation of our soldiers from time to time, since our isle hath been known unto the Romans, that wheresoever they have served in foreign countries the chief brunts of service have been reserved unto them. Of their conquests and bloody battles won in France, Germany, and Scotland our histories are full, and where they have been overcome, the victorers themselves confessed their victories to have been so dearly bought that they would not gladly covet to overcome often after such difficult manner. In martial prowess there is little or no difference between Englishmen and Scots, for albeit that the Scots have been often and very grievously overcome by the force of our nation, it hath not been for want of manhood on their parts, but through the mercy of God showed on us and His justice upon them, sith they always have begun the quarrels and offered us mere [unmitigated] injury with great despite and cruelty.

Leland, noting somewhat of the constitution of our bodies, saith these words (grounding I think upon Aristotle, who writeth that such as dwell near the North are of more courage and strength of body than skillfulness or wisdom): [3] the Britons are white in color, strong of body, and full of blood, as people inhabiting near the North and far from the equinoctial line, where the soil is not so fruitful and therefore the people not so feeble; whereas contrariwise, such as dwell toward the course of the sun are less of stature, weaker of body, more nice, delicate, fearful

[1] *Captains:* in error for captives? Bede, *Ecclesiastical History*, II, i.
[2] *Herefordshire:* probably in error for Hertfordshire.
[3] *Problems*, XIV, xv-xvi.

by nature, blacker in color, and some so black indeed as any crow or raven. Thus saith he. Howbeit, as those which are bred in sundry places of the main do come behind us in constitution of body, so I grant that in pregnancy of wit, nimbleness of limbs, and politic inventions they generally exceed us, notwithstanding that otherwise these gifts of theirs do often degenerate into mere subtlety, instability, unfaithfulness, and cruelty. Yet Alexander ab Alexandro is of the opinion that the fertilest region doth bring forth the dullest wits, and contrariwise the harder soil the finest heads.[4] But in mine opinion the most fertile soil doth bring forth the proudest nature, as we may see by the Campanians, who (as Cicero also saith) had *Penes eos ipsum domicilium superbiae.*[5] But neither of these opinions do justly take hold of us, yet hath it pleased the writers to say their pleasures of us.

And for that we dwell northward, we are commonly taken by the foreign historiographers to be men of great strength and little policy, much courage and small shift, because of the weak abode of the sun with us, whereby our brains are not made hot and warmed, as Pachymeres noteth (*lib.* 3),[6] affirming further that the people inhabiting in the north parts are white of color, blockish, uncivil, fierce, and warlike, which qualities increase as they come nearer unto the pole; whereas the contrary pole giveth contrary gifts, blackness, wisdom, civility, weakness, and cowardice; thus saith he. But alas, how far from probability, or as if there were not one and the same conclusion to be made of the constitutions of their bodies which dwell under both the poles. For in truth his assertion holdeth only in their persons that inhabit near unto and under the equinoctial.

As for the small tarriance of the sun[7] with us, it is also confuted by the length of our days. Wherefore his reason seemeth better to uphold that of Alexander ab Alexandro afore alleged than to prove that we want wit because our brains are not warmed by the tarriance of the sun. And thus also doth Comines

---

[4] *Dies geniales*, IV, xiii, from which the references in this paragraph to Aristotle and Cicero are also drawn.

[5] "In their land the very seat of pride" (Cicero, *De lege agraria*, II, xxxv, 97).

[6] *George Pachymeres* (1242-?1310): Byzantine historian.

[7] "*Non vi sed virtute, non armis sed ingenio vincuntur Angli.*"—H. "The English are conquered not by force but by valor, not by arms but by skill."

burden us after a sort in his history, and after him Bodin.[8] But thanked be God that all the wit of his countrymen, if it may be called wit, could never compass to do so much in Britain as the strength and courage of our Englishmen (not without great wisdom and forecast) have brought to pass in France. The Gauls in time past contemned the Romans (saith Caesar) because of the smallness of their stature;[9] howbeit, for all their greatness (saith he) and at the first brunt in the wars they show themselves to be but feeble, neither is their courage of any force to stand in great calamities. Certes in accusing our wisdom in this sort he[10] doth (in mine opinion) increase our commendation. For if it be a virtue to deal uprightly, with singleness of mind, sincerely and plainly, without any such suspicious fetches in all our dealings as they commonly practice in their affairs, then are our countrymen to be accounted wise and virtuous. But if it be a vice to color craftiness, subtle practices, doubleness, and hollow behavior with a cloak of policy, amity, and wisdom, then are Comines and his countrymen to be reputed vicious, of whom this proverb hath of old time been used as an earmark of their dissimulation: *Galli ridendo, fidem frangunt, etc.*[11]

How these latter points take hold in Italy I mean not to discuss. How they are daily practiced in many places of the main, and he accounted most wise and politic that can most of all dissemble, here is no place justly to determine (neither would I wish my countrymen to learn any such wisdom), but that a king of France could say, *Qui nescit dissimulare, nescit regnare* (or *vivere*),[12] their own histories are testimonies sufficient. Galen, the noble physician, transferring the forces of our natural humors from the body to the mind, attributeth to the yellow color prudence, to the black constancy, to blood mirth, to phlegm courtesy, which being mixed more or less among themselves do yield an infinite variety.[13] By this means therefore it cometh to pass that he whose

---

[8] *Philippe de Comines* (?1445-?1511): French historian; the reference is to his *Memoirs*, IV, vi; Bodin, *Method for the Easy Comprehension of History* (trans. Reynolds, p. 127).

[9] *Gallic War*, II, xxx.

[10] *He:* Comines, the references to Bodin and Caesar having been added in 1587.

[11] "The Gauls laughingly break faith." Bodin (p. 100) attributes the remark to Vopiscus, one of the *scriptores historiae Augustae.*

[12] "He who does not know how to dissemble does not know how to rule (or live)" (attributed to Louis XI).   [13] Bodin (p. 124).

nature inclineth generally to phlegm cannot but be courteous, which joined with strength of body and sincerity of behavior (qualities universally granted to remain so well in our nation as other inhabitants of the North), I cannot see what may be an hindrance why I should not rather conclude that the Britons do excel such as dwell in the hotter countries than for want of craft and subtleties to come any whit behind them.

It is but vanity also for some to note us (as I have often heard in common table talk) as barbarous because we so little regard the shedding of our blood, and rather tremble not when we see the liquor of life to go from us (I use their own words). Certes if we be barbarous in their eyes because we be rather inflamed than appalled at our wounds, then are those objectors flat cowards in our judgment, sith we think it a great piece of manhood to stand to our tackling until the last drop, as men that may spare much because we have much, whereas they having less are afraid to lose that little which they have, as Frontinus also noteth.[14] As for that which the French write of their own manhood in their histories, I make little account of it, for I am of the opinion that as an Italian writing of his credit, a papist entreating of religion, a Spaniard of his meekness, or a Scot of his manhood is not to be builded on, no more is a Frenchman to be trusted in the report of his own affairs, wherein he doth either dissemble or exceed, which is a foul vice in such as profess to deal uprightly. Neither are we so hard to strangers as Horace would seem to make us,[15] sith we love them so long as they abuse us not and make account of them so far forth as they despise us not. And this is generally to be verified in that they use our privileges and commodities for diet, apparel, and trade of gain in so ample manner as we ourselves enjoy them, which is not lawful for us to do in their countries, where no stranger is suffered to have work if an homeborn be without. But to proceed with our purpose.

With us (although our good men care not to live long but

[14] *Sextus Julius Frontinus* (?30-?104): Roman governor of Britain (74-78). Apparently the reference is to his story of Commius the Atrebatian (*Stratagems*, II, xiii, 11), who tricked Caesar into thinking he had managed an escape, by raising his sails although his ships were stranded on the beach ("stand to our tackling").

[15] *Britannos hospitibus feros:* "the British, fierce to strangers" (*Odes*, III, iv, 33).

to live well) some do live an hundred years, very many unto fourscore; as for threescore, it is taken but for our entrance into age, so that in Britain no man is said to wax old till he draw unto threescore, at which time "God speed you well" cometh in place; as Epaminondas [16] sometime said in mirth, affirming that until thirty years of age, "You are welcome" is the best salutation, and from thence to threescore, "God keep you," but after threescore it is best to say, "God speed you well," for at that time we begin to grow toward our journey's end, whereon many a one have very good leave to go. These two are also noted in us (as things appertaining to the firm constitutions of our bodies), that there hath not been seen in any region so many carcasses of the dead to remain from time to time without corruption as in Britain, and that after death, by slaughter or otherwise, such as remain unburied by four or five days together are easy to be known and discerned by their friends and kindred; whereas Tacitus and other complain of sundry nations, saying that their bodies are *tam fluidae substantiae* [17] that within certain hours the wife shall hardly know her husband, the mother her son, or one friend another after their lives be ended. In like sort the comeliness of our living bodies do continue from middle age (for the most) even to the last gasp, specially in mankind. And albeit that our women, through bearing of children, do after forty begin to wrinkle apace, yet are they not commonly so wretched and hard-favored to look upon in their age as the Frenchwomen and divers of other countries, with whom their men also do much participate, and thereto be so often wayward and peevish that nothing in manner may content them.

I might here add somewhat also of the mean stature generally of our women, whose beauty commonly exceedeth the fairest of those of the main, their comeliness of person and good proportion of limbs most of theirs that come over unto us from beyond the seas. This nevertheless I utterly mislike in the poorer sort of them, for the wealthier do seldom offend herein, that, being of themselves without government, they are so careless in the education of their children (wherein their husbands also are to be blamed), by means whereof very many of them, neither fearing God, neither regarding either manners or obedience, do oftentimes

---

[16] *Epaminondas* (d. 362 B.C.): Theban general and statesman.
[17] *Tam fluidae substantiae:* so soft (or unstable) in substance.

come to confusion, which (if any correction or discipline had been used toward them in youth) might have proved good members of their commonwealth and country by their good service and industry. I could make report likewise of the natural vices and virtues of all those that are born within this island, but as the full tractation hereof craveth a better head than mine to set forth the same, so will I give place to other men that list to take it in hand. Thus much therefore of the constitutions of our bodies, and so much may suffice.

APPENDIX I

Harrison on Weights and Measures
[excerpts]

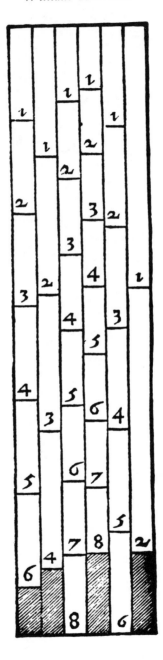

CHAPTER XXII

Of the Manner of Measuring the Length and Breadth of Things after the English Usage [1]

THE first and smallest of our measures is the barleycorn, whereof three, being taken out of the midst of the ear, well dried, and laid endwards one to another, are said to make an inch, which the Latins measure after the breadth of the thumb and therefore of some is called *pollicare*, although the true name thereof be *uncia,* as I have often read. That which they call *digitus,* or the fingerbreadth, is not in use with us, yet is it the sixteenth part of their foot, as the inch is the twelfth of ours. Each palm, or handbreadth, containeth also four of their fingers, as by the figure here ensuing may easily be perceived, which I have set down only to the end that whoso listeth may behold the diversity not only between the Roman measure and ours but also of their own standard, which hath changed oft among them.

Certes it could not well be brought to pass to give out the whole foot, because the quantity of the page would not suffer me so to do, wherefore I have exemplified only in the half, which I hope shall abundantly satisfy each one that is desirous to see and perceive their difference. The first column therefore setteth down the half-foot, after the standard of England. The second seemeth to be a Roman foot, found out of late by Bartholomaeus

[1] In 1577 Harrison concluded Book III with four chapters on weights and measures. All of chapter xxii is here included and those passages of the succeeding three chapters which deal with English weights and measures. This part of *The Description* has not been previously reprinted; the four chapters were dropped in 1587 because Harrison had expanded them for separate publication. His "labors were vain," he explains in a melancholy note added to the MS, since in 1588 "a proclamation of new standard weights came out" (*Eighth Report of the Royal Commission on Historical MSS,* 1881, pp. 639-640). This MS, which was preserved at Londonderry and seen by Furnivall (I, v), has apparently shared the fate of Harrison's Chronology (see p. xviii, n. 3).

Marlianus and set down to be seen in his *Topography of Rome*.[2] Therein also every fingerbreadth containeth two of the old assize, whereby he maketh not sixteen but only eight in the whole, as you may there behold. The third is that which Budé had sometime delivered unto him, who was very curious in searching of the weights and measures of old time, as may yet appear by his excellent treatise *De asse*, wherein his singular skill in this behalf doth evidently appear.[3]

The fourth was found long since by Leonardus de Portis in a garden at Rome belonging to Angelus Colotius.[4] The fifth is the half-foot of Paris, divided by the inch and yet equal to the Roman standard described by Budé. The last showeth the quantity of their palm, whereof their foot hath four, and each palm containeth four fingers, as I have said already. By this tablet also you may see how each standard exceedeth or cometh short of other. Wherefore it shall not need for me to stay any longer upon their differences, which may so well and better be determined by the eye.

Of our measures, therefore, 3 barleycorns do make an inch, 12 inches yield a foot, 3 foot are our yard, 1 yard and 9 inches give an elne [ell]; 7 foot yield a fathom, by the standard, although we use commonly to call the space between the tops of our middle fingers (when our arms be stretched out at length) by that name also; the same likewise being called *passus* sometimes, as the height of a man is *status* and supposed to be all one with the lesser fathom or extension of his arms. But to proceed.

Sixteen foot and an half or 5½ yards do make a pole, in whose area are 272½ of our feet. Four[5] poles in length and one in breadth do yield a rodde, or rode [rood], of ground, which some call a farthingdeal or yardland. Four roddes do give an acre, whose plot hath 43,600 [square feet], or 40 pole in length and thereto 4 in breadth.

The ancient Romans had for their land, as Columella saith (*lib.* 5, *cap.* 1),[6] the fingerbreadth, the foot of 16 fingerbreadths, the pace 5 foot. *Actus* every way had a 120 foot. In Hispania

[2] Joannes Bartholomaeus Marlianus, *Urbis Romae topographia* (Rome, 1544), p. 11.

[3] I cannot identify the edition of Budé's *De asse* from which Harrison drew his scale.

[4] Leonhardus Porcius, *De re pecuniaria antiqua* (Cologne, 1551), p. 160.

[5] *Four:* apparently in error for forty.

[6] *De re rustica;* the entire paragraph is based on Columella.

Baetica it hight [was called] *agnua*, but in Gallia *arepen*. *Jugerum* had 2 *actus* and was so called *tamquam a junctis actibus*,[7] so that it contained one way 240 foot and 120 another, that is, 28,800 foot in the whole plot. *Porca*, 7,200 feet; *versus*, 8,640; *agna*, 14,400. The furlong hath 125 paces or 625 feet. Eight furlongs also made a mile. *Centuria* hath 200 *jugera*, but in old time, only 100, for notwithstanding that the first be doubled, yet it retaineth still the pristinate denomination, as we see in the word "tribe," which was at the first but one part of the three, whereinto the whole people of Rome were severed and divided. But let us return unto our own again.

In like sort for such as travel: 5 foot measured by the said inch make a pace, and 125 paces do yield a furlong. Eight furlongs or 1,000 paces is a mile, and after this geometrical pace are our miles measured, which some notwithstanding do reckon by about 278 turns of a cart's wheels, whose compass is commonly of 18 foot of the standard and height 5½ foot, as I have been informed by wheelwrights in the city.

By the foot also we measure glass and timber and all others our buildings. By the yard, our woolen cloth, tapestry, arras, silks, and laces, but our linen by the elne. Finally, our woods and pastures are laid out by the pole, and thereto our hedging and ditching after the same rate, although the depth of our ditches is measured by the foot and likewise their breadth, as experience daily confirmeth. Besides this we have also another kind of measuring, and that is by the fathom, the use whereof is only seen in the digging of pits, wells, and mines, measuring of ropes, and sounding the depth of the sea, when dread of peril enforceth our mariners to see unto their safeguard. It is furthermore a common opinion amongst us that every 100 acres of ground contain just a mile in compass round about, but as I have not yet examined how truly this is said, so I am most sure that a plot of 400 acres shall not yield a like proportion by the one-half, whensoever you walk about it.

And even thus would I end with this chapter, concerning our manner of measuring before remembered, were it not that I think good to set down what I have gathered of the like measurings as they have been used in other countries, where they also do reckon

---

[7] That is, *jugerum* derives its name from the fact that it joined (*jungere*) two *actus*.

by the grain, making their account much after such manner as followeth: the *digitus,* or fingerbreadth, hath 4 grains laid side to side, the *uncia major* 3 fingers; the palm hath 4 fingers, their *dichas* 2 handbreadths or 8 fingers, their span 3 handbreadths or 12 fingerbreadths; their foot is 16 fingers or 4 handbreadths, their foot and half, in Latin *sesquipes* or *cubitus,* 24 fingerbreadths, the step 2½ foot, the common pace 3 foot, the geometrical 5 foot, the *orgyia* 6 foot, as I gather out of Suidas, the league 3 miles English, the common Dutch mile 4,000 paces, the great Dutch mile 5,000 paces. In like sort the Latins and we do measure our journeys by miles, the Grecians by furlongs, the French and Spanish by leagues, the Egyptians by signs, the Persians by parasangs, of which each one containeth 30 furlongs.

As for the old British mile that includeth 1,500 paces English, it shall not greatly need to make any discourse of it, and so much the less sith it is yet in use and not forgotten among the Welshmen, as Leland hath noted in his *Commentaries of Britain,*[8] wherefore it may suffice to have said thus much of the same, and so of all the rest, being mindful to go forward and make an end of this treatise.

CHAPTER XXIII

Of English Weights and Their Comparison with Others

THE least of our weights is a grain, between which and the ounce we have the half-quarter, the half, and three-quarters of the ounce. In old time these smaller parts were commonly reckoned by pieces of coin and not by quarter and half-quarter as we do now. As by the farthing, or fourth part of a penny, which weighed 8 grains, the halfpenny that peised 16, and penny that counterpeised 32 and was indeed the 32nd[1] part of an ounce, so that for the half-quarter we said 2½*d.,* for the quarter 5*d.,*

---

[8] *Itinerary* (ed. Smith, III, 106, 115, etc.).
[1] In error for 20th.

and half ounce 10*d*., which is now grown out of use and our coin so enhanced that 60 of our pence do hardly make an ounce, and 11 grains suffice with the more to counterpeise a penny. . . .

We have also a weight called the pound, whereof are two sorts, the one taking name of troy, containing 12 ounces (after which our liquid and dry measures are weighed and our plate sold), the other commonly called avoirdupois, whereby our other artificers and chapmen do buy and sell their wares. The first of these containeth 7,680 grains, whereas the other hath 10,240. Each of them also are divided into the half-quarter, quarter, and half-pound, and three-quarters, as we have said before in the description of the ounce. . . .

Hitherto also I have spoken of small weights; now let us see what they be that are of the greater sort, but first of such as are in use in England, reckoning not after troy weight but avoirdupois, whose pound hath 16 ounces, as I have said before. Of great weight therefore we have: the clove weighing 7 pound or half a stone; the half-quartern of 14 pound, in wool a stone, whereof 26 do make a sack; the quartern of 28 pound, in wool a tod; the half-hundred of 56 pound; the hundred of 112 or 1,792 ounces.

And these are usually reckoned next unto the hundredweight, which is the greatest of all that we do commonly use, and of which divers other are commonly made about the sale of our tin, lead, flax, spice, and all kind of merchandise with others, whose quantities and names are utterly unknown unto me. Beef is either sold by the stone of 8 pound or by the score. Cheese by the weigh. And hereof we find two several weights, whereof one containeth 32 cloves, each clove being of 7 pound (although some books have one but of 6), whereby the one weigh hath 224, the other 256 pound, that is, 36 cloves and 4 pound overweight. This is moreover to be noted, that the word hundred is not always used after one sort in weight or tale [count], for, as 5 score are oft taken for an hundred in some respect, as in money and men, so 120 do make but an hundred, as in cattle, etc., after another account. But if you deal by weight, then 112 is always your just number. And as the hundred is the greatest here in England, so the talent was the greatest in Greece and other countries. Howbeit, as our hundreds in tale do differ from our hundreds in weight, so did the talents differ one from another. . . .

CHAPTER XXIV

Of Liquid Measures

HITHERTO have I spoken of weights; now it resteth that I do the like of such liquid measures as are presently used in England and have been of old time amongst the Grecians and Romans. Wherein I will deal so faithfully as I may, to the end this travail of mine may be some help to such as shall come after in conferring foreign with our homemade weights and measures, and for the better understanding of the histories wherein such things are spoken of. The first, therefore, of our English measures is a spoonful, which hath one of our drachmas [drams] and 6 grains; an assay, taste, or sippet, 4 spoonfuls or 4 drachmas and 24 grains; a farthingdeal is a quarter of a pound, pint, or 3 ounces of troy; an muytch [1] 6 ounces or half a pint; a pint 12 ounces, or a pound, or 4 farthingdeals; a quart 24 ounces, 2 pints, or 2 pound troy; a pottle 48 ounces, or 4 pound, or so many pints; a gallon 96 ounces, or 8 pound, or 8 pints; a firkin 8 gallons, or 64 pound, and this in ale, soap, and herring; the kilderkin 16 gallons; the barrel 32 gallons. And these are our mere English liquid measures.

The rest that we have are outlandish [foreign] vessels and such as are brought over unto us with wares from other countries. And yet are we not altogether guided by this rate (the more pity), but in some things several measures are used and received, as for example, the firkin of beer hath 9 gallons, the kilderkin 18 gallons, the barrel 36. As for the hogshead of beer, it is lately come up, and because I see none made of this assize, but only the empty casks of wine reserved to this use, I pass over to say anything thereof. If it were according to the standard for beer, it should contain 72 gallons, which now hath but 64.

But of eels and salmon, the firkin 10½ gallons, the half-barrel 21 gallons, the barrel 42 gallons, the butt 84 gallons. Yet some statutes limit our eel measure in an equality unto that of herrings,

---

[1] *Muytch:* I have not found any other references to this measure, but the "mutchkin" is an old Scottish equivalent to a quarter of a pint.

of which 120 go to the hundred and 10,000 to the last, as they are commonly sold.

Of wine and such vessels thereof as come from beyond the seas we have the rundlet of 18 gallons and a pottle, the barrel, which is rare, of 31 gallons, the hogshead of 63 gallons, the tierce of 84 gallons, the pipe or butt of 126 gallons, the tun of 252. There are also thirds of pipes, or hogsheads, and of barrels, which are likewise called tertians, but of these I say nothing because their division is easy. Such also hath been the care of our magistrates heretofore that these very vessels have had their limitation of weight, insomuch that the firkin should weigh 6 pound 6 ounces, the half-barrel or kilderkin 13 pound, the barrel 26 *li.*, whereof let this suffice.

And these are the quantities and names of most of our liquid measures. . . .

CHAPTER XXV

Of the Dry Measures of England and Their Comparison with Others

As BEFORE we see in the moist, so do all our dry measures fetch their original from the spoonful, etc., until they come at the gallon, beyond the which we have the peck, or farthingdeal of a bushel (for that is our English word for a fourth part) of 2 gallons, half-bushel of 4 gallons; bushel of 8 gallons, or 64 pound troy; strike of 2 bushels, or 128 pound, or 16 gallons; coomb, raser, or curnock of 4 bushels, or 256 pound, or 32 gallons; quarter or seam of 8 bushels, or 512 pound, or 64 gallons; weigh or 6 quarters of 5,702 [3,072] pound, or 384 gallons, as by the rule of proportion is easy to be found.

By these measures also we measure our mustard seed, rape seed, carrot roots, salt, and fruit, notwithstanding that the filling of the bushel be diverse, sith in corn, salt, and seeds we strike [level] with a rule, but in apples and roots we pour them on by heaps. This is furthermore to be considered, that although one wheat or barley be heavier than another, as the soil is wet or dry, barley commonly than oats, rye than barley, wheat than rye, etc., also in liquid wares, oil compared with wine and both with honey, yet the measure framed after the aforesaid weights doth mete them all indifferently, so that the quantity of the standard and not the quality of ware measured is always to be looked on. Indeed it is found by experience that, a like measure of wine, oil, and honey being weighed together, the oil shall be lighter by a ninth part than the wine, and the honey heavier than the wine almost by a third. Certes there is nothing that cometh nearer the weight of wine than the purest water, and yet one wine is heavier than another, as waters also are, of which the most gross is evermore the weightiest. . . .

Furthermore, in turning over such old books as came unto my hands, I find also this note ensuing, in which carat hath four grains, penny eight carats. Every grain of batement a penny in gold, but, after France, Venice, and some other places, they have but six carats in the penny and four grains in the carat, which odds groweth by the difference of weights, for beyond the sea they have twenty-four pence in the ounce, which is four pence more in value than the ounce English, after the old account of pence. By these carats pearls and stones are valued and sold, but not gold, which hath nevertheless the name of carats in his poise, but after another proportion.

APPENDIX II

Corrections to Furnivall

Corrections to Furnivall

SINCE the present edition is not intended to supplant completely the text given by Furnivall, which preserves the original spelling and the changes made between the 1577 and 1587 versions, I include the following substantive corrections to Furnivall's edition. Some of Furnivall's readings simply reproduce the uncorrected states of certain pages. Asterisked items are printer's errors occurring in 1587. The citations are to part, page, and line numbers in Furnivall's edition.

I,	25, 17	*troublesome] treble sum
	25, 29	ease] case
	26, 23	oversight friendship] oversight & friendship
	29, 25	dates] daies
	48, 10	nephue?] nephue
	51, 10	same] fame
	53, 2	*afore] a fire
	61, 23	Percians] Mercians
	65, 33	*fame] same
	67, 19	abbat at] abbat of
	74, 21	willest] wiliest
	74, 36	*scholers] scholes
	77, 37	banting] hanting
	80, 1	dates] daies
	97, 8-9	*wapentaxes] wapentakes
	113, 9	repare] restore
	129, 24	*defendants] descendants
	149, 24	Lire] Tire
	177, 26	upon] on
	201, 5	to betweene] to go betweene
	233, 22	open champaine] open and champaine
	250, 31	Dumbritton] Dunbritton
	251, 7	those] these

	252, 8	*veviunt*] *veniunt*
	255, 2	Holmechirst] Holmehirst
	256, 23	*Regaleius*] *Regale ius*
	265, 18	eare] eie
	281, 29	1¼] 1¾
	284, 26	nothing] noting
	284, 34	*Eva*] *Eoa*
	297, 26	off] oft
	340, 13	*ash, barke] ash barke
	341, 7	*without] with our
	351, 10	wealth] wreath
II,	7, 21	*laetae*] *laeta*
	25, 31	doo; finailie] doo finallie
	40, 26	Narus] Naxus
	40, 28	*Anglicus*] *Anglicis*
	42, 15	*Bratius] Gratius
	64, 16	Narians] Naxians
	96, 11	*epta*] *septa*
	96, 13	*June] Jan
	98, 30	*writer] write
	107, 26	as lodgeth] as he lodgeth
III,	127, 1	aire, and soyle] aire, soyle
	127, 10	off] oft
	128, 10	it fond] if fond
	130, 10	Leme? of the Crames] Teme? of the Grames
	134, 12	*imperie*] *imperio*
	136, 21	Kent, elsewhere] Kent, & elsewhere
	140, 13	Kingtaile] Ringtaile
	141, 24	*Lundoniaratibus*] *Lundonia ratibus*
	141, 25	*frugeredundans*] *fruge redundans*
	150, 13	captives] captains
	153, 4	in all their] in their
	153, 25	courtesie: and which] courtesie: which
	154, 13	that an] that as an

Index

West Indies, 117, 129, 246, 265, 275, 366, 384

West Saxons, 44, 46, 47, 48, 167; Ks. of, 383-384; *see also* Alfred, Cenwalh, Ceolric, Cynegils, Edward the Elder, Egbert, Ine

Westbury, Wilts., 160

Westbury Forest, Hants., 260

Westminster, Matthew, *Flores Historiarum* cited, 57n., 63, 208; H.'s source, 47n., 48n., 51n., 60n., 63n.

Westminster, 157, 189; Abbey, 171, 358, *and* Henry VII's Chapel, 69; Hall, 91n., 167, 170, 176; School, xxviii, 76; see of, 63, 204n.

Westmorland, 61, 87, 160

Wetshod Fair, Herts., 396

Weybourne Hope, Norfolk, 223n.

Weyhill, Hants., 396

Weymouth, Dorset, 156

Wharton, Lord, 122

wheat, 135, 250, 434, 439; in beer, 137-138; in bread, 133-135

Wheatley, Oxon., 403

Whitchurch, Hants., 394

Whitchurch, Salop, 396

White, John, Bp. of Winchester (1556-1559), 32-33

White, Sir Thomas (1492-1567), London merchant, 78

White Hall, Oxon., 79

White Horse Vale, Berks., 355, 439

Whitehall Palace, Westminster, 225

Whitehart Vale, Dorset, 439

Whithorn, Wigtownshire, 405

Whithorn, *called Ad Candidam Casam*, see of, 63, 64

Wiccies, 48

Wich, *see* Droitwich *and* Nantwich

Wickham Bishops, Essex, 426

Widford Bridge, Essex, 426

Wigan, Lancs., 157, 393, 396, 401

Wight, Isle of, xvi, xix, 46

Wigtown, Wigtownshire, 405

Wilfrid, St., Abp. of York (669-678, 686-691), 56, 59

William, Archdeacon of Durham (d. 1249), 78

William, Archdeacon of Salisbury (ca. 1278), 65

William, Bp. of London (1051-1075), 13

William of Malmesbury, *Gesta regum Anglorum,* cited, 63

William of Newburgh, chronicler, cited, 360

William Rufus, K. of England (1087-1100), 16-17, 61, 215, 258

William the Conqueror, *called* The Bastard, 44, 113, 261, 262

William the Lion, K. of Scotland (1165-1214), 22, 258

Willoughby, Lord, 122

Wilton, Lord Grey of, 122

Wilton, Wilts., 14, 160

Wilton, *see* Wiltshire

Wiltshire, *or* Wilton, 46, 87, 88, 160

Wimbish, *or* Gwinbach, Essex, 28n., 30n., 423, 426

Wimund, Bp. of Man (?1109-?1140), 62

Winchcomb, Glos., 394

Winchelsea, Robert de, *called* Reginald, Abp. of Canterbury, 49

Winchelsea, Sussex, 161

Winchester, Marquis of, 122

Winchester, *or* Winton, Hants., 42n., 159, 167, 214, 262, 294, 394, 440; ancient names, 208; School, 76

Winchester, see of, 45-46, 47, 48; Bps. of, 46, 109, 123; *see also* Beaufort, Henry; Ethelwold; Foxe, Richard; Frithustan; Gardiner, Stephen; Heddi; Ponet, John; Stratford, John de; Waynflete, William; White, John; Wolsey, Thomas; Wykeham, William of

Windlebury, *or* Wandlebury, Hills, Cambs., 224

windows, 197, 198-199; stained, 35-36

Windrush River, Oxon. *and* Glos., 88

Windsor, Lord, 122

Windsor, Berks., 154, 394, 396; Castle, 105, 226-227; St. George's Chapel, 40-41n., 107-111; Forest, 260; School, 76

wines, 128, 132, 139, 144, 313, 354, 399, 459, 460; list of, 130; no domestic, 130, 264, 435-437

Wingfield, Sir Anthony (d. 1552), statesman, 107

Wini, Bp. of London (666-?675), 56

Winifred's Well, Holywell, Flintshire, 274, 284n.

A CATALOG OF SELECTED
DOVER BOOKS
IN ALL FIELDS OF INTEREST

A CATALOG OF SELECTED DOVER
BOOKS IN ALL FIELDS OF INTEREST

CONCERNING THE SPIRITUAL IN ART, Wassily Kandinsky. Pioneering work by father of abstract art. Thoughts on color theory, nature of art. Analysis of earlier masters. 12 illustrations. 80pp. of text. 5⅜ × 8½.   23411-8 Pa. $3.95

ANIMALS: 1,419 Copyright-Free Illustrations of Mammals, Birds, Fish, Insects, etc., Jim Harter (ed.). Clear wood engravings present, in extremely lifelike poses, over 1,000 species of animals. One of the most extensive pictorial sourcebooks of its kind. Captions. Index. 284pp. 9 × 12.   23766-4 Pa. $12.95

CELTIC ART: The Methods of Construction, George Bain. Simple geometric techniques for making Celtic interlacements, spirals, Kells-type initials, animals, humans, etc. Over 500 illustrations. 160pp. 9 × 12. (USO)   22923-8 Pa. $9.95

AN ATLAS OF ANATOMY FOR ARTISTS, Fritz Schider. Most thorough reference work on art anatomy in the world. Hundreds of illustrations, including selections from works by Vesalius, Leonardo, Goya, Ingres, Michelangelo, others. 593 illustrations. 192pp. 7⅛ × 10¼.   20241-0 Pa. $9.95

CELTIC HAND STROKE-BY-STROKE (Irish Half-Uncial from "The Book of Kells"): An Arthur Baker Calligraphy Manual, Arthur Baker. Complete guide to creating each letter of the alphabet in distinctive Celtic manner. Covers hand position, strokes, pens, inks, paper, more. Illustrated. 48pp. 8¼ × 11.
    24336-2 Pa. $3.95

EASY ORIGAMI, John Montroll. Charming collection of 32 projects (hat, cup, pelican, piano, swan, many more) specially designed for the novice origami hobbyist. Clearly illustrated easy-to-follow instructions insure that even beginning papercrafters will achieve successful results. 48pp. 8¼ × 11.   27298-2 Pa. $2.95

THE COMPLETE BOOK OF BIRDHOUSE CONSTRUCTION FOR WOOD-WORKERS, Scott D. Campbell. Detailed instructions, illustrations, tables. Also data on bird habitat and instinct patterns. Bibliography. 3 tables. 63 illustrations in 15 figures. 48pp. 5¼ × 8½.   24407-5 Pa. $1.95

BLOOMINGDALE'S ILLUSTRATED 1886 CATALOG: Fashions, Dry Goods and Housewares, Bloomingdale Brothers. Famed merchants' extremely rare catalog depicting about 1,700 products: clothing, housewares, firearms, dry goods, jewelry, more. Invaluable for dating, identifying vintage items. Also, copyright-free graphics for artists, designers. Co-published with Henry Ford Museum & Green-field Village. 160pp. 8¼ × 11.   25780-0 Pa. $9.95

HISTORIC COSTUME IN PICTURES, Braun & Schneider. Over 1,450 costumed figures in clearly detailed engravings—from dawn of civilization to end of 19th century. Captions. Many folk costumes. 256pp. 8⅜ × 11¾.   23150-X Pa. $11.95

STICKLEY CRAFTSMAN FURNITURE CATALOGS, Gustav Stickley and L. & J. G. Stickley. Beautiful, functional furniture in two authentic catalogs from 1910. 594 illustrations, including 277 photos, show settles, rockers, armchairs, reclining chairs, bookcases, desks, tables. 183pp. 6½ × 9¼. 23838-5 Pa. $9.95

AMERICAN LOCOMOTIVES IN HISTORIC PHOTOGRAPHS: 1858 to 1949, Ron Ziel (ed.). A rare collection of 126 meticulously detailed official photographs, called "builder portraits," of American locomotives that majestically chronicle the rise of steam locomotive power in America. Introduction. Detailed captions. xi + 129pp. 9 × 12. 27393-8 Pa. $12.95

AMERICA'S LIGHTHOUSES: An Illustrated History, Francis Ross Holland, Jr. Delightfully written, profusely illustrated fact-filled survey of over 200 American lighthouses since 1716. History, anecdotes, technological advances, more. 240pp. 8 × 10¾. 25576-X Pa. $11.95

TOWARDS A NEW ARCHITECTURE, Le Corbusier. Pioneering manifesto by founder of "International School." Technical and aesthetic theories, views of industry, economics, relation of form to function, "mass-production split" and much more. Profusely illustrated. 320pp. 6⅛ × 9¼. (USO) 25023-7 Pa. $9.95

HOW THE OTHER HALF LIVES, Jacob Riis. Famous journalistic record, exposing poverty and degradation of New York slums around 1900, by major social reformer. 100 striking and influential photographs. 233pp. 10 × 7⅞. 22012-5 Pa $10.95

FRUIT KEY AND TWIG KEY TO TREES AND SHRUBS, William M. Harlow. One of the handiest and most widely used identification aids. Fruit key covers 120 deciduous and evergreen species; twig key 160 deciduous species. Easily used. Over 300 photographs. 126pp. 5⅜ × 8½. 20511-8 Pa. $3.95

COMMON BIRD SONGS, Dr. Donald J. Borror. Songs of 60 most common U.S. birds: robins, sparrows, cardinals, bluejays, finches, more—arranged in order of increasing complexity. Up to 9 variations of songs of each species. Cassette and manual 99911-4 $8.95

ORCHIDS AS HOUSE PLANTS, Rebecca Tyson Northen. Grow cattleyas and many other kinds of orchids—in a window, in a case, or under artificial light. 63 illustrations. 148pp. 5⅜ × 8½. 23261-1 Pa. $4.95

MONSTER MAZES, Dave Phillips. Masterful mazes at four levels of difficulty. Avoid deadly perils and evil creatures to find magical treasures. Solutions for all 32 exciting illustrated puzzles. 48pp. 8¼ × 11. 26005-4 Pa. $2.95

MOZART'S DON GIOVANNI (DOVER OPERA LIBRETTO SERIES), Wolfgang Amadeus Mozart. Introduced and translated by Ellen H. Bleiler. Standard Italian libretto, with complete English translation. Convenient and thoroughly portable—an ideal companion for reading along with a recording or the performance itself. Introduction. List of characters. Plot summary. 121pp. 5¼ × 8½. 24944-1 Pa. $2.95

TECHNICAL MANUAL AND DICTIONARY OF CLASSICAL BALLET, Gail Grant. Defines, explains, comments on steps, movements, poses and concepts. 15-page pictorial section. Basic book for student, viewer. 127pp. 5⅜ × 8½. 21843-0 Pa. $4.95

BRASS INSTRUMENTS: Their History and Development, Anthony Baines. Authoritative, updated survey of the evolution of trumpets, trombones, bugles, cornets, French horns, tubas and other brass wind instruments. Over 140 illustrations and 48 music examples. Corrected and updated by author. New preface. Bibliography. 320pp. 5⅜ × 8½. 27574-4 Pa. $9.95

HOLLYWOOD GLAMOR PORTRAITS, John Kobal (ed.). 145 photos from 1926–49. Harlow, Gable, Bogart, Bacall; 94 stars in all. Full background on photographers, technical aspects. 160pp. 8⅜ × 11¼. 23352-9 Pa. $11.95

MAX AND MORITZ, Wilhelm Busch. Great humor classic in both German and English. Also 10 other works: "Cat and Mouse," "Plisch and Plumm," etc. 216pp. 5⅜ × 8½. 20181-3 Pa. $5.95

THE RAVEN AND OTHER FAVORITE POEMS, Edgar Allan Poe. Over 40 of the author's most memorable poems: "The Bells," "Ulalume," "Israfel," "To Helen," "The Conqueror Worm," "Eldorado," "Annabel Lee," many more. Alphabetic lists of titles and first lines. 64pp. 5³⁄₁₆ × 8¼. 26685-0 Pa. $1.00

SEVEN SCIENCE FICTION NOVELS, H. G. Wells. The standard collection of the great novels. Complete, unabridged. First Men in the Moon, Island of Dr. Moreau, War of the Worlds, Food of the Gods, Invisible Man, Time Machine, In the Days of the Comet. Total of 1,015pp. 5⅜ × 8½. (USO) 20264-X Clothbd. $29.95

AMULETS AND SUPERSTITIONS, E. A. Wallis Budge. Comprehensive discourse on origin, powers of amulets in many ancient cultures: Arab, Persian, Babylonian, Assyrian, Egyptian, Gnostic, Hebrew, Phoenician, Syriac, etc. Covers cross, swastika, crucifix, seals, rings, stones, etc. 584pp. 5⅜ × 8½. 23573-4 Pa. $12.95

RUSSIAN STORIES/PYCCKNE PACCKA3bl: A Dual-Language Book, edited by Gleb Struve. Twelve tales by such masters as Chekhov, Tolstoy, Dostoevsky, Pushkin, others. Excellent word-for-word English translations on facing pages, plus teaching and study aids, Russian/English vocabulary, biographical/critical introductions, more. 416pp. 5⅜ × 8½. 26244-8 Pa. $8.95

PHILADELPHIA THEN AND NOW: 60 Sites Photographed in the Past and Present, Kenneth Finkel and Susan Oyama. Rare photographs of City Hall, Logan Square, Independence Hall, Betsy Ross House, other landmarks juxtaposed with contemporary views. Captures changing face of historic city. Introduction. Captions. 128pp. 8¼ × 11. 25790-8 Pa. $9.95

AIA ARCHITECTURAL GUIDE TO NASSAU AND SUFFOLK COUNTIES, LONG ISLAND, The American Institute of Architects, Long Island Chapter, and the Society for the Preservation of Long Island Antiquities. Comprehensive, well-researched and generously illustrated volume brings to life over three centuries of Long Island's great architectural heritage. More than 240 photographs with authoritative, extensively detailed captions. 176pp. 8¼ × 11. 26946-9 Pa. $14.95

NORTH AMERICAN INDIAN LIFE: Customs and Traditions of 23 Tribes, Elsie Clews Parsons (ed.). 27 fictionalized essays by noted anthropologists examine religion, customs, government, additional facets of life among the Winnebago, Crow, Zuni, Eskimo, other tribes. 480pp. 6⅛ × 9¼. 27377-6 Pa. $10.95

FRANK LLOYD WRIGHT'S HOLLYHOCK HOUSE, Donald Hoffmann. Lavishly illustrated, carefully documented study of one of Wright's most controversial residential designs. Over 120 photographs, floor plans, elevations, etc. Detailed perceptive text by noted Wright scholar. Index. 128pp. 9¼ × 10¾.
27133-1 Pa. $11.95

THE MALE AND FEMALE FIGURE IN MOTION: 60 Classic Photographic Sequences, Eadweard Muybridge. 60 true-action photographs of men and women walking, running, climbing, bending, turning, etc., reproduced from rare 19th-century masterpiece. vi + 121pp. 9 × 12. 24745-7 Pa. $10.95

1001 QUESTIONS ANSWERED ABOUT THE SEASHORE, N. J. Berrill and Jacquelyn Berrill. Queries answered about dolphins, sea snails, sponges, starfish, fishes, shore birds, many others. Covers appearance, breeding, growth, feeding, much more. 305pp. 5¼ × 8¼. 23366-9 Pa. $7.95

GUIDE TO OWL WATCHING IN NORTH AMERICA, Donald S. Heintzelman. Superb guide offers complete data and descriptions of 19 species: barn owl, screech owl, snowy owl, many more. Expert coverage of owl-watching equipment, conservation, migrations and invasions, etc. Guide to observing sites. 84 illustrations. xiii + 193pp. 5⅜ × 8½. 27344-X Pa. $8.95

MEDICINAL AND OTHER USES OF NORTH AMERICAN PLANTS: A Historical Survey with Special Reference to the Eastern Indian Tribes, Charlotte Erichsen-Brown. Chronological historical citations document 500 years of usage of plants, trees, shrubs native to eastern Canada, northeastern U.S. Also complete identifying information. 343 illustrations. 544pp. 6½ × 9¼. 25951-X Pa. $12.95

STORYBOOK MAZES, Dave Phillips. 23 stories and mazes on two-page spreads: Wizard of Oz, Treasure Island, Robin Hood, etc. Solutions. 64pp. 8¼ × 11.
23628-5 Pa. $2.95

NEGRO FOLK MUSIC, U.S.A., Harold Courlander. Noted folklorist's scholarly yet readable analysis of rich and varied musical tradition. Includes authentic versions of over 40 folk songs. Valuable bibliography and discography. xi + 324pp. 5⅜ × 8½. 27350-4 Pa. $7.95

MOVIE-STAR PORTRAITS OF THE FORTIES, John Kobal (ed.). 163 glamor, studio photos of 106 stars of the 1940s: Rita Hayworth, Ava Gardner, Marlon Brando, Clark Gable, many more. 176pp. 8⅜ × 11¼. 23546-7 Pa. $11.95

BENCHLEY LOST AND FOUND, Robert Benchley. Finest humor from early 30s, about pet peeves, child psychologists, post office and others. Mostly unavailable elsewhere. 73 illustrations by Peter Arno and others. 183pp. 5⅜ × 8½.
22410-4 Pa. $5.95

YEKL and THE IMPORTED BRIDEGROOM AND OTHER STORIES OF YIDDISH NEW YORK, Abraham Cahan. Film Hester Street based on Yekl (1896). Novel, other stories among first about Jewish immigrants on N.Y.'s East Side. 240pp. 5⅜ × 8½. 22427-9 Pa. $6.95

SELECTED POEMS, Walt Whitman. Generous sampling from *Leaves of Grass*. Twenty-four poems include "I Hear America Singing," "Song of the Open Road," "I Sing the Body Electric," "When Lilacs Last in the Dooryard Bloom'd," "O Captain! My Captain!"—all reprinted from an authoritative edition. Lists of titles and first lines. 128pp. 5$\frac{3}{16}$ × 8¼. 26878-0 Pa. $1.00

THE BEST TALES OF HOFFMANN, E. T. A. Hoffmann. 10 of Hoffmann's most important stories: "Nutcracker and the King of Mice," "The Golden Flowerpot," etc. 458pp. 5⅜ × 8½. 21793-0 Pa. $8.95

FROM FETISH TO GOD IN ANCIENT EGYPT, E. A. Wallis Budge. Rich detailed survey of Egyptian conception of "God" and gods, magic, cult of animals, Osiris, more. Also, superb English translations of hymns and legends. 240 illustrations. 545pp. 5⅜ × 8½. 25803-3 Pa. $11.95

FRENCH STORIES/CONTES FRANÇAIS: A Dual-Language Book, Wallace Fowlie. Ten stories by French masters, Voltaire to Camus: "Micromegas" by Voltaire; "The Atheist's Mass" by Balzac; "Minuet" by de Maupassant; "The Guest" by Camus, six more. Excellent English translations on facing pages. Also French-English vocabulary list, exercises, more. 352pp. 5⅜ × 8½. 26443-2 Pa. $8.95

CHICAGO AT THE TURN OF THE CENTURY IN PHOTOGRAPHS: 122 Historic Views from the Collections of the Chicago Historical Society, Larry A. Viskochil. Rare large-format prints offer detailed views of City Hall, State Street, the Loop, Hull House, Union Station, many other landmarks, circa 1904–1913. Introduction. Captions. Maps. 144pp. 9⅜ × 12¼. 24656-6 Pa. $12.95

OLD BROOKLYN IN EARLY PHOTOGRAPHS, 1865–1929, William Lee Younger. Luna Park, Gravesend race track, construction of Grand Army Plaza, moving of Hotel Brighton, etc. 157 previously unpublished photographs. 165pp. 8⅞ × 11¾. 23587-4 Pa. $13.95

THE MYTHS OF THE NORTH AMERICAN INDIANS, Lewis Spence. Rich anthology of the myths and legends of the Algonquins, Iroquois, Pawnees and Sioux, prefaced by an extensive historical and ethnological commentary. 36 illustrations. 480pp. 5⅜ × 8½. 25967-6 Pa. $8.95

AN ENCYCLOPEDIA OF BATTLES: Accounts of Over 1,560 Battles from 1479 B.C. to the Present, David Eggenberger. Essential details of every major battle in recorded history from the first battle of Megiddo in 1479 B.C. to Grenada in 1984. List of Battle Maps. New Appendix covering the years 1967–1984. Index. 99 illustrations. 544pp. 6½ × 9¼. 24913-1 Pa. $14.95

SAILING ALONE AROUND THE WORLD, Captain Joshua Slocum. First man to sail around the world, alone, in small boat. One of great feats of seamanship told in delightful manner. 67 illustrations. 294pp. 5⅜ × 8½. 20326-3 Pa. $5.95

ANARCHISM AND OTHER ESSAYS, Emma Goldman. Powerful, penetrating, prophetic essays on direct action, role of minorities, prison reform, puritan hypocrisy, violence, etc. 271pp. 5⅜ × 8½. 22484-8 Pa. $5.95

MYTHS OF THE HINDUS AND BUDDHISTS, Ananda K. Coomaraswamy and Sister Nivedita. Great stories of the epics; deeds of Krishna, Shiva, taken from puranas, Vedas, folk tales; etc. 32 illustrations. 400pp. 5⅜ × 8½. 21759-0 Pa. $9.95

BEYOND PSYCHOLOGY, Otto Rank. Fear of death, desire of immortality, nature of sexuality, social organization, creativity, according to Rankian system. 291pp. 5⅜ × 8½. 20485-5 Pa. $8.95

A THEOLOGICO-POLITICAL TREATISE, Benedict Spinoza. Also contains unfinished Political Treatise. Great classic on religious liberty, theory of government on common consent. R. Elwes translation. Total of 421pp. 5⅜ × 8½. 20249-6 Pa. $8.95

MY BONDAGE AND MY FREEDOM, Frederick Douglass. Born a slave, Douglass became outspoken force in antislavery movement. The best of Douglass' autobiographies. Graphic description of slave life. 464pp. 5⅜ × 8½.   22457-0 Pa. **$8.95**

FOLLOWING THE EQUATOR: A Journey Around the World, Mark Twain. Fascinating humorous account of 1897 voyage to Hawaii, Australia, India, New Zealand, etc. Ironic, bemused reports on peoples, customs, climate, flora and fauna, politics, much more. 197 illustrations. 720pp. 5⅜ × 8½.   26113-1 Pa. **$15.95**

THE PEOPLE CALLED SHAKERS, Edward D. Andrews. Definitive study of Shakers: origins, beliefs, practices, dances, social organization, furniture and crafts, etc. 33 illustrations. 351pp. 5⅜ × 8½.   21081-2 Pa. **$8.95**

THE MYTHS OF GREECE AND ROME, H. A. Guerber. A classic of mythology, generously illustrated, long prized for its simple, graphic, accurate retelling of the principal myths of Greece and Rome, and for its commentary on their origins and significance. With 64 illustrations by Michelangelo, Raphael, Titian, Rubens, Canova, Bernini and others. 480pp. 5⅜ × 8½.   27584-1 Pa. **$9.95**

PSYCHOLOGY OF MUSIC, Carl E. Seashore. Classic work discusses music as a medium from psychological viewpoint. Clear treatment of physical acoustics, auditory apparatus, sound perception, development of musical skills, nature of musical feeling, host of other topics. 88 figures. 408pp. 5⅜ × 8½. 21851-1 Pa. **$9.95**

THE PHILOSOPHY OF HISTORY, Georg W. Hegel. Great classic of Western thought develops concept that history is not chance but rational process, the evolution of freedom. 457pp. 5⅜ × 8½.   20112-0 Pa. **$9.95**

THE BOOK OF TEA, Kakuzo Okakura. Minor classic of the Orient: entertaining, charming explanation, interpretation of traditional Japanese culture in terms of tea ceremony. 94pp. 5⅜ × 8½.   20070-1 Pa. **$3.95**

LIFE IN ANCIENT EGYPT, Adolf Erman. Fullest, most thorough, detailed older account with much not in more recent books, domestic life, religion, magic, medicine, commerce, much more. Many illustrations reproduce tomb paintings, carvings, hieroglyphs, etc. 597pp. 5⅜ × 8½.   22632-8 Pa. **$10.95**

SUNDIALS, Their Theory and Construction, Albert Waugh. Far and away the best, most thorough coverage of ideas, mathematics concerned, types, construction, adjusting anywhere. Simple, nontechnical treatment allows even children to build several of these dials. Over 100 illustrations. 230pp. 5⅜ × 8½.   22947-5 Pa. **$7.95**

DYNAMICS OF FLUIDS IN POROUS MEDIA, Jacob Bear. For advanced students of ground water hydrology, soil mechanics and physics, drainage and irrigation engineering, and more. 335 illustrations. Exercises, with answers. 784pp. 6⅛ × 9¼.   65675-6 Pa. **$19.95**

SONGS OF EXPERIENCE: Facsimile Reproduction with 26 Plates in Full Color, William Blake. 26 full-color plates from a rare 1826 edition. Includes "The Tyger," "London," "Holy Thursday," and other poems. Printed text of poems. 48pp. 5¼ × 7.
24636-1 Pa. **$4.95**

OLD-TIME VIGNETTES IN FULL COLOR, Carol Belanger Grafton (ed.). Over 390 charming, often sentimental illustrations, selected from archives of Victorian graphics—pretty women posing, children playing, food, flowers, kittens and puppies, smiling cherubs, birds and butterflies, much more. All copyright-free. 48pp. 9¼ × 12¼.   27269-9 Pa. **$5.95**

PERSPECTIVE FOR ARTISTS, Rex Vicat Cole. Depth, perspective of sky and sea, shadows, much more, not usually covered. 391 diagrams, 81 reproductions of drawings and paintings. 279pp. 5⅜ × 8½. 22487-2 Pa. $6.95

DRAWING THE LIVING FIGURE, Joseph Sheppard. Innovative approach to artistic anatomy focuses on specifics of surface anatomy, rather than muscles and bones. Over 170 drawings of live models in front, back and side views, and in widely varying poses. Accompanying diagrams. 177 illustrations. Introduction. Index. 144pp. 8⅜ × 11¼. 26723-7 Pa. $8.95

GOTHIC AND OLD ENGLISH ALPHABETS: 100 Complete Fonts, Dan X. Solo. Add power, elegance to posters, signs, other graphics with 100 stunning copyright-free alphabets: Blackstone, Dolbey, Germania, 97 more—including many lower-case, numerals, punctuation marks. 104pp. 8⅛ × 11. 24695-7 Pa. $8.95

HOW TO DO BEADWORK, Mary White. Fundamental book on craft from simple projects to five-bead chains and woven works. 106 illustrations. 142pp. 5⅜ × 8. 20697-1 Pa. $4.95

THE BOOK OF WOOD CARVING, Charles Marshall Sayers. Finest book for beginners discusses fundamentals and offers 34 designs. "Absolutely first rate . . . well thought out and well executed."—E. J. Tangerman. 118pp. 7¾ × 10⅝. 23654-4 Pa. $5.95

ILLUSTRATED CATALOG OF CIVIL WAR MILITARY GOODS: Union Army Weapons, Insignia, Uniform Accessories, and Other Equipment, Schuyler, Hartley, and Graham. Rare, profusely illustrated 1846 catalog includes Union Army uniform and dress regulations, arms and ammunition, coats, insignia, flags, swords, rifles, etc. 226 illustrations. 160pp. 9 × 12. 24939-5 Pa. $10.95

WOMEN'S FASHIONS OF THE EARLY 1900s: An Unabridged Republication of "New York Fashions, 1909," National Cloak & Suit Co. Rare catalog of mail-order fashions documents women's and children's clothing styles shortly after the turn of the century. Captions offer full descriptions, prices. Invaluable resource for fashion, costume historians. Approximately 725 illustrations. 128pp. 8⅜ × 11¼. 27276-1 Pa. $11.95

THE 1912 AND 1915 GUSTAV STICKLEY FURNITURE CATALOGS, Gustav Stickley. With over 200 detailed illustrations and descriptions, these two catalogs are essential reading and reference materials and identification guides for Stickley furniture. Captions cite materials, dimensions and prices. 112pp. 6½ × 9¼. 26676-1 Pa. $9.95

EARLY AMERICAN LOCOMOTIVES, John H. White, Jr. Finest locomotive engravings from early 19th century: historical (1804–74), main-line (after 1870), special, foreign, etc. 147 plates. 142pp. 11⅜ × 8¼. 22772-3 Pa. $10.95

THE TALL SHIPS OF TODAY IN PHOTOGRAPHS, Frank O. Braynard. Lavishly illustrated tribute to nearly 100 majestic contemporary sailing vessels: Amerigo Vespucci, Clearwater, Constitution, Eagle, Mayflower, Sea Cloud, Victory, many more. Authoritative captions provide statistics, background on each ship. 190 black-and-white photographs and illustrations. Introduction. 128pp. 8⅞ × 11¾. 27163-3 Pa. $13.95

EARLY NINETEENTH-CENTURY CRAFTS AND TRADES, Peter Stockham (ed.). Extremely rare 1807 volume describes to youngsters the crafts and trades of the day: brickmaker, weaver, dressmaker, bookbinder, ropemaker, saddler, many more. Quaint prose, charming illustrations for each craft. 20 black-and-white line illustrations. 192pp. 4⅝ × 6. 27293-1 Pa. $4.95

VICTORIAN FASHIONS AND COSTUMES FROM HARPER'S BAZAR, 1867–1898, Stella Blum (ed.). Day costumes, evening wear, sports clothes, shoes, hats, other accessories in over 1,000 detailed engravings. 320pp. 9⅜ × 12¼.
22990-4 Pa. $13.95

GUSTAV STICKLEY, THE CRAFTSMAN, Mary Ann Smith. Superb study surveys broad scope of Stickley's achievement, especially in architecture. Design philosophy, rise and fall of the Craftsman empire, descriptions and floor plans for many Craftsman houses, more. 86 black-and-white halftones. 31 line illustrations. Introduction. 208pp. 6½ × 9¼. 27210-9 Pa. $9.95

THE LONG ISLAND RAIL ROAD IN EARLY PHOTOGRAPHS, Ron Ziel. Over 220 rare photos, informative text document origin (1844) and development of rail service on Long Island. Vintage views of early trains, locomotives, stations, passengers, crews, much more. Captions. 8⅞ × 11¾. 26301-0 Pa. $13.95

THE BOOK OF OLD SHIPS: From Egyptian Galleys to Clipper Ships, Henry B. Culver. Superb, authoritative history of sailing vessels, with 80 magnificent line illustrations. Galley, bark, caravel, longship, whaler, many more. Detailed, informative text on each vessel by noted naval historian. Introduction. 256pp. 5⅜ × 8½. 27332-6 Pa. $6.95

TEN BOOKS ON ARCHITECTURE, Vitruvius. The most important book ever written on architecture. Early Roman aesthetics, technology, classical orders, site selection, all other aspects. Morgan translation. 331pp. 5⅜ × 8½. 20645-9 Pa. $8.95

THE HUMAN FIGURE IN MOTION, Eadweard Muybridge. More than 4,500 stopped-action photos, in action series, showing undraped men, women, children jumping, lying down, throwing, sitting, wrestling, carrying, etc. 390pp. 7⅞ × 10⅝.
20204-6 Clothbd. $24.95

TREES OF THE EASTERN AND CENTRAL UNITED STATES AND CANADA, William M. Harlow. Best one-volume guide to 140 trees. Full descriptions, woodlore, range, etc. Over 600 illustrations. Handy size. 288pp. 4½ × 6⅜.
20395-6 Pa. $5.95

SONGS OF WESTERN BIRDS, Dr. Donald J. Borror. Complete song and call repertoire of 60 western species, including flycatchers, juncoes, cactus wrens, many more—includes fully illustrated booklet. Cassette and manual 99913-0 $8.95

GROWING AND USING HERBS AND SPICES, Milo Miloradovich. Versatile handbook provides all the information needed for cultivation and use of all the herbs and spices available in North America. 4 illustrations. Index. Glossary. 236pp. 5⅜ × 8½. 25058-X Pa. $6.95

BIG BOOK OF MAZES AND LABYRINTHS, Walter Shepherd. 50 mazes and labyrinths in all—classical, solid, ripple, and more—in one great volume. Perfect inexpensive puzzler for clever youngsters. Full solutions. 112pp. 8⅛ × 11.
22951-3 Pa. $4.95

PIANO TUNING, J. Cree Fischer. Clearest, best book for beginner, amateur. Simple repairs, raising dropped notes, tuning by easy method of flattened fifths. No previous skills needed. 4 illustrations. 201pp. 5⅜ × 8½. 23267-0 Pa. $5.95

A SOURCE BOOK IN THEATRICAL HISTORY, A. M. Nagler. Contemporary observers on acting, directing, make-up, costuming, stage props, machinery, scene design, from Ancient Greece to Chekhov. 611pp. 5⅜ × 8½. 20515-0 Pa. $11.95

THE COMPLETE NONSENSE OF EDWARD LEAR, Edward Lear. All nonsense limericks, zany alphabets, Owl and Pussycat, songs, nonsense botany, etc., illustrated by Lear. Total of 320pp. 5⅜ × 8½. (USO) 20167-8 Pa. $6.95

VICTORIAN PARLOUR POETRY: An Annotated Anthology, Michael R. Turner. 117 gems by Longfellow, Tennyson, Browning, many lesser-known poets. "The Village Blacksmith," "Curfew Must Not Ring Tonight," "Only a Baby Small," dozens more, often difficult to find elsewhere. Index of poets, titles, first lines. xxiii + 325pp. 5⅜ × 8¼. 27044-0 Pa. $8.95

DUBLINERS, James Joyce. Fifteen stories offer vivid, tightly focused observations of the lives of Dublin's poorer classes. At least one, "The Dead," is considered a masterpiece. Reprinted complete and unabridged from standard edition. 160pp. 5³⁄₁₆ × 8¼. 26870-5 Pa. $1.00

THE HAUNTED MONASTERY and THE CHINESE MAZE MURDERS, Robert van Gulik. Two full novels by van Gulik, set in 7th-century China, continue adventures of Judge Dee and his companions. An evil Taoist monastery, seemingly supernatural events; overgrown topiary maze hides strange crimes. 27 illustrations. 328pp. 5⅜ × 8½. 23502-5 Pa. $7.95

THE BOOK OF THE SACRED MAGIC OF ABRAMELIN THE MAGE, translated by S. MacGregor Mathers. Medieval manuscript of ceremonial magic. Basic document in Aleister Crowley, Golden Dawn groups. 268pp. 5⅜ × 8½. 23211-5 Pa. $8.95

NEW RUSSIAN-ENGLISH AND ENGLISH-RUSSIAN DICTIONARY, M. A. O'Brien. This is a remarkably handy Russian dictionary, containing a surprising amount of information, including over 70,000 entries. 366pp. 4½ × 6⅛. 20208-9 Pa. $9.95

HISTORIC HOMES OF THE AMERICAN PRESIDENTS, Second, Revised Edition, Irvin Haas. A traveler's guide to American Presidential homes, most open to the public, depicting and describing homes occupied by every American President from George Washington to George Bush. With visiting hours, admission charges, travel routes. 175 photographs. Index. 160pp. 8¼ × 11. 26751-2 Pa. $10.95

NEW YORK IN THE FORTIES, Andreas Feininger. 162 brilliant photographs by the well-known photographer, formerly with *Life* magazine. Commuters, shoppers, Times Square at night, much else from city at its peak. Captions by John von Hartz. 181pp. 9¼ × 10¾. 23585-8 Pa. $12.95

INDIAN SIGN LANGUAGE, William Tomkins. Over 525 signs developed by Sioux and other tribes. Written instructions and diagrams. Also 290 pictographs. 111pp. 6⅛ × 9¼. 22029-X Pa. $3.50

CATALOG OF DOVER BOOKS

THE INFLUENCE OF SEA POWER UPON HISTORY, 1660–1783, A. T. Mahan. Influential classic of naval history and tactics still used as text in war colleges. First paperback edition. 4 maps. 24 battle plans. 640pp. 5⅜ × 8½.
25509-3 Pa. $12.95

THE STORY OF THE TITANIC AS TOLD BY ITS SURVIVORS, Jack Winocour (ed.). What it was really like. Panic, despair, shocking inefficiency, and a little heroism. More thrilling than any fictional account. 26 illustrations. 320pp. 5⅜ × 8½.
20610-6 Pa. $8.95

FAIRY AND FOLK TALES OF THE IRISH PEASANTRY, William Butler Yeats (ed.). Treasury of 64 tales from the twilight world of Celtic myth and legend: "The Soul Cages," "The Kildare Pooka," "King O'Toole and his Goose," many more. Introduction and Notes by W. B. Yeats. 352pp. 5⅜ × 8½.
26941-8 Pa. $8.95

BUDDHIST MAHAYANA TEXTS, E. B. Cowell and Others (eds.). Superb, accurate translations of basic documents in Mahayana Buddhism, highly important in history of religions. The Buddha-karita of Asvaghosha, Larger Sukhavativyuha, more. 448pp. 5⅜ × 8½. ,
25552-2 Pa. $9.95

ONE TWO THREE . . . INFINITY: Facts and Speculations of Science, George Gamow. Great physicist's fascinating, readable overview of contemporary science: number theory, relativity, fourth dimension, entropy, genes, atomic structure, much more. 128 illustrations. Index. 352pp. 5⅜ × 8½.
25664-2 Pa. $8.95

ENGINEERING IN HISTORY, Richard Shelton Kirby, et al. Broad, nontechnical survey of history's major technological advances: birth of Greek science, industrial revolution, electricity and applied science, 20th-century automation, much more. 181 illustrations. ". . . excellent . . ."—Isis. Bibliography. vii + 530pp. 5⅜ × 8¼.
26412-2 Pa. $14.95